Gender

Articulated

Gender

Articulated

_____

Language and the

Socially Constructed Self

KIRA HALL and **MARY BUCHOLTZ**

Editors

Routledge
New York and London

Published in 1995 by

Routledge
29 West 35th Street
New York, New York 10001

Published in Great Britain in 1995 by

Routledge
11 New Fetter Lane
London EC4P 4EE

Copyright © 1995 by Routledge

Printed in the United States of America
Design: Jack Donner

Library of Congress Cataloging-in-Publication Data

Gender articulated : language and the socially constructed self / [edited] by Kira Hall and
    Mary Bucholtz
            p.   cm.
        Includes bibliographical references.
        ISBN 0-415-91398-5 (hb).   ISBN 0-415-91399-3 (pbk.)
        1. Language and languages—Sex differences. 2. Sexism in language.
    3. Women—Language. I. Hall, Kira, 1962 – . II. Bucholtz, Mary, 1966 – .
        P.120.S48G47   1995
        306.4'4'082—dc20   95–16959
                                                                          CIP

For Robin Tolmach Lakoff

Dux femina facti

— *Aeneid* 1.364

Contents

Acknowledgments

We would like to thank the many people who helped us make this book a reality. The enthusiasm of the participants of the Second Berkeley Women and Language Conference inspired us to develop the volume from selected conference papers. The conference itself could not have taken place without the committed efforts of Birch Moonwomon, a founder of the Berkeley Women and Language Group and an organizer, along with us, of the second conference. We are also grateful to the faculty, staff, and students of the Department of Linguistics at the University of California at Berkeley for their support and assistance during the editing process, especially Collin Baker, Anita Liang, and Laurel Sutton, as well as Caitlin Hines of San Francisco State University. Special thanks go to Christine Cipriani, Bill Germano, and Jonathan Korzen at Routledge; to Betty Seaver, our copy editor; and to Anna Livia and Jon McCammond for their patience, understanding, and insightful suggestions at every stage of this project.

The contributors must be recognized for their heroic efforts under a tight deadline and for their exceptional research, which is the lifeblood of this volume and the future of the field of language and gender.

   In addition, we gratefully acknowledge the invaluable support of
Leanne Hinton, not only during the editing process but throughout our
graduate careers. Finally, we would like to thank Robin Tolmach Lakoff for
commenting on the introductory essay and for providing us both with a
rigorous and wide-ranging training in feminist issues in linguistics. We do
not presume to speak for Robin in the discussion that follows but instead
offer our own understanding of her scholarship. In gratitude for her guidance, we dedicate this volume to her.

Introduction

Twenty Years after *Language and Woman's Place*

Mary Bucholtz and Kira Hall

In reflecting on the position of *Gender Articulated* in the current context of language and gender research, we have found it useful to return to the field's foundational text, Robin Lakoff's *Language and Woman's Place* (1975). This is both a timely undertaking, coinciding as it does with the twentieth anniversary of the publication of the book, and a necessary one, for no other study of women's language has been as influential and as controversial as Lakoff's volume. At the time of its publication, *Language and Woman's Place* was met with widespread criticism, yet it launched a far-reaching program of research on language and gender whose effects we still feel today. In light of this apparent paradox and in recognition of the book's continuing influence, the need for a reassessment is evident.[1]

It is not our primary goal in this essay to review and refute the criticisms that have been made of *Language and Woman's Place*; we have very little interest in reviving what is by now a rather tiresome and familiar debate. Instead, we wish to rescue the text for contemporary use by reading it from perspectives that differ from those of earlier reviewers. Previous commentators approached Lakoff's work from a restricted perspective, concentrating as they did on the extent to which the book lived up to the epistemological commitments of their particular fields. By contrast, we examine the book within its own disciplinary context and consider the reception of the work among lay readers outside academia. The necessity of distinguishing academic and general audiences has been brought to light by the recent controversy generated by the publication in 1990 of *You Just Don't Understand*, written by Lakoff's student Deborah Tannen. This popular best-seller on language and gender has been subjected to the same sorts of criticism as *Language and Woman's Place*; the renewal of the debate points up the importance of engaging with such influential texts and understanding them on their own terms, and on the terms of a nonacademic readership.

In looking afresh at *Language and Woman's Place*, we are especially interested in locating the seeds of contemporary research. The significance of the work as a research program has been widely acknowledged, even by its critics (e.g., Thorne 1976), and the ongoing success of its project is manifest in the many links we are able to trace between Lakoff's early work and the essays in the present volume. Clearly, not all these points of convergence are due to direct influence, but Lakoff's book set the terms for research as few others have done.[2] In the following discussion, we note the most salient associations between Lakoff's work and the studies in this book, but many more could have been invoked.

Putting the Text into Context

The historical context of *Language and Woman's Place* has often been misunderstood, even in its own time, and its methods and goals have therefore been challenged in ways that fail to recognize the text's theoretical framework. The book emerged from the intellectual climate that produced the theory of generative semantics, a paradigm that challenged transformational-generative grammar (Chomsky's autonomous model of language) in favor of a more contextually enriched analysis (Lakoff 1989). The struggle for generative semantics consolidated the subfield of pragmatics as part of linguistics and laid the groundwork for other contextual approaches such as cognitive linguistics. This mini-revolution has been said to have been led by the "Four Horsemen of the Apocalypse"—George Lakoff, James McCawley, Paul Postal, and John Robert Ross—but insufficient attention has been paid to the lone horsewoman, Robin Lakoff, who, in addition to her other accomplishments, succeeded in a brief eighty-three pages in bringing feminist analysis into linguistic scholarship, thereby ushering in an exciting program of research that spans linguistics, anthropology, sociology, psychology, and other fields.

That *Language and Woman's Place* represents a position that is consonant with generative semantics has generally been overlooked in surveys of the theory. Randy Allen Harris (1993) lists the book in his bibliography but does not discuss it, except to allude to Lakoff's theoretical shift (which is not as dramatic as he seems to believe) from generative semantics to ordinary-language philosophy and issues of power in language. Frederick Newmeyer's (1986a) more biased account of the rise of generative semantics does not even include Lakoff's work on gender in its bibliography, and his popular history of linguistics (1986b) portrays Lakoff's research in this area as ill conceived.[3]

The book's connection to generative semantics has also been missed by scholars of language and gender. Lakoff's achievement is the more remarkable because she puts forth her vision of a feminist linguistics from a position not in the new subdiscipline of sociolinguistics, which had already begun to advance its empirical methodology within linguistics, but from the very core of the field, within the theoretical mainstream. Thus Lakoff's methods are wholly consistent with her disciplinary commitments at the time: introspection and native-speaker intuition were the central methodology of linguistic investigation (as, indeed, they continue to be); empiricism, then as now, had not taken its place in the toolchest of mainstream linguistics.[4]

It is significant, then, that nearly all of Lakoff's critics were outside her disciplinary milieu; most of the early critiques were by scholars in the empirically oriented social sciences (anthropology, psychology, sociology, speech communication). One of the less antagonistic reviews comes from philosophy (Moulton 1976), which, the author notes, shares Lakoff's introspective methodology. Even one of the very few reviews to be published in a linguistics journal berates Lakoff for using the methodology of linguistics for a "sociolinguistic investigation" (Timm 1976:245), although Lakoff does not pretend that her enterprise is sociolinguistic; it is surely not accidental that the reviewer was herself a sociolinguist.

The lengths to which such partisanship may go is typified by the comments of literary critic Elaine Showalter (1975). Showalter urges feminist scholars to consider the role of women's language in literature, but rejects the contributions that *Language and Woman's Place* might make to this endeavor; she dismisses the text as "embarrassingly self-indulgent" (450). Ironically, however, in her pursuit of a literary "women's language," Showalter embraces work by Erica Jong and other writers that has had a similarly unsympathetic reception. She says of these authors, "In looking at the new poetry, some of which is ragged and angry, we need first of all, as Rich says, to honor the risk, and second to understand it" (452). Yet for Showalter such generosity of spirit does not extend beyond the literary realm, and she makes no attempt to understand the anger—and the utility—of Lakoff's own feminist project. (Indeed, Showalter's goal is called into question altogether by the work of Anna Livia in this volume, who subverts any essentialist understanding of women's literary language in her analysis of butch and femme speech in lesbian fiction.)

Lakoff's willingness to examine multiple linguistic levels in her study has likewise met with reproach from critics (e.g., Timm 1976) yet this same method has come to be recognized as a valuable strategy for locating the full context of interaction, and in this volume it is used with considerable success by Jenny Cook-Gumperz and Michèle Foster, among others. The fixation on hegemonically positivistic methodologies has been relaxed in feminist scholarship generally since the days when these critiques were first issued; the present collection represents a wide variety of methods that take us beyond the scientized discourse that has been advocated in the past.

The test of Lakoff's methods must after all be in the results that they produce, and the range and accuracy of her hypotheses preclude the wholesale dismissal of the text. The work lays out a program of research that has been successfully pursued by many scholars; for this reason one contemporary review completely misses the mark in its prediction that the book would fail to inspire further research (Walum 1977). More telling is another reviewer's comment that "by stimulating others to empirically investigate much of its conjecture, this book has put itself out of date" (Hoffman 1980:314). Although the reviewer speculates that this turn of events was unintentional and perhaps undesirable, such an outcome speaks volumes about the success of Lakoff's agenda, for to have transformed the field is a remarkable and desirable achievement for a programmatic text only five years after its publication.

With respect to theory, Lakoff has been criticized for advocating too strongly the "dominance" position within language and gender, which views gender-based differences in language use as the result of power differences between women and men. This theory still has important explanatory force, as illustrated in these pages by Elinor Ochs and Carolyn Taylor; Susan Herring, Deborah Johnson, and Tamra DiBenedetto; and Norma Mendoza-Denton. Commentators have nevertheless lamented Lakoff's supposed pessimism and her suggestion that women might find it necessary to speak as men do in order to gain male respect. Bonnie McElhinny's chapter reports a similar situation among female police officers; the adoption of "male" speech practices is one survival strategy of this group of women. Lakoff's opponents (e.g., Kramer, Thorne, & Henley 1978), by contrast, often embrace a cultural feminism that valorizes "feminine" features of speech, making a virtue of necessity. But it seems dubious that cultural feminists would have celebrated the use of "women's language" for economic gain among female phone-sex workers, as reported by Kira Hall. At the time she wrote the book, of course, Lakoff herself had little reason to argue for women's agency and autonomy: in 1975 few of her discipline's practitioners were women. In her own contribution to this volume, Lakoff shows that power relations are not static but dynamic, emerging in dialectical struggle between women and those who control hegemonic discourse; a similar point is made by Cathryn Houghton.

Yet it is precisely this insistence on unpleasant realities that makes Lakoff's book overtly political. Lakoff writes from a feminist stance, and names sexism as the primary target of her investigation; Laurel Sutton's chapter in this volume is written in a similar spirit. Lakoff, as the first and perhaps most eloquent writer to raise the specter of male power in discussions of women's language, faced overwhelming criticism from anxious male colleagues. In light of this personal risk, it is the more remarkable that what distinguishes Lakoff's book from most later writings in language and gender research is its author's willingness to look for answers and offer recommendations. The book is a manifesto both for scholars concerned with women's language and for all individuals who seek to remedy social inequalities between women and men. Its call to action, we appreciatively note, is met by an answering call in the chapter by Tara Goldstein.

Such efforts to move from scholarship to political struggle are what give the text, and the field of language and gender, its enduring relevance both within the academy and outside it. In addition to the profound effect it has had in social science research, *Language and Woman's Place* has been perhaps the single most influential text in introducing language and gender issues to lay audiences. The uses to which it has been put by nonacademic readers may trouble feminist scholars, yet we cannot ignore the reverberations of Lakoff's work in the popular culture. The first step in understanding this phenomenon is to recognize the crucial distinction between linguistic ideologies and actual practices.

Language and Lakoff's Place in the Popular Imagination

The distinction between ideologies of language and actual linguistic practice continues to be neglected by many researchers. The proliferation of psychological and sociolinguistic studies that have been formulated to test the empirical validity of Lakoff's identification of "women's language" (e.g., Cameron, McAlinden, & O'Leary 1988; Crosby & Nyquist 1977; Dubois & Crouch 1975; O'Barr & Atkins 1980) is one telling example of this oversight. Yet Lakoff states quite clearly in her introduction that she is interested not in the quantitative realization of linguistic variables but in the cultural expectations that have come to influence their use. That there is something very real about her assertions may be seen in the fact that so many consumers of American popular psychology have embraced her text as part of the "self-help" genre. Although the linguistic reality Lakoff depicts is rooted in cultural ideologies, it is nevertheless a reality, particularly because it continues to be accepted by diverse groups of speakers as a valid representation of their own discursive experiences. In this volume Mary Talbot shows the power of these features in advertisements aimed at teenage girls. Likewise, the current popularity of Tannen's *You Just Don't Understand* speaks to the persistence of the popular ideology of gendered language, for Tannen incorporates many of the features identified by Lakoff fifteen years earlier into her own discussion of women's speech strategies.

Despite the fact that Lakoff's and Tannen's theoretical explanations of the relationship between gender and discourse are not congruent, with Lakoff locating gender differences in hierarchical power structures and Tannen in divergent paths of language socialization, their findings have been embraced by a number of disparate communities. Besides the many avid readers of communication-oriented self-help books (e.g., Butler [1981] 1992; Elgin 1993; Glass 1993; Stone & Bachner [1977] 1994), there are a number of groups whose interest in Lakoff's and Tannen's research could not have been easily predicted by the authors. These groups are as dissimilar as African American journalists in an East Coast workshop on communication, transsexual communication specialists who write for the California-based transgender journals *Cross-talk* and *Transsexual News Telegraph*, Roman Catholic organizers of "marriage encounter" weekends in Alabama, female phone-sex employees in San Francisco and New York City, and speech therapists hired by Hollywood to train male actors to take on female roles in gender-bending films.

Framed in postmodern terms, then, Lakoff appears to have successfully identified the precise hegemonic notions of gender-appropriate language use that Susan Gal in this volume urges contemporary researchers to uncover. The cultural expectations that Lakoff locates through her intuitions and observations reflect the ideologically dominant socialization process of middle-class European American women, the influence of which extends far beyond this subculture (Barrett forthcoming a, b).

Glass's (1993) popular self-help manual, which she directs primarily to heterosexual couples with communication problems, serves as evidence for the existence of these hegemonic expectations. Glass, a speech pathologist in private practice in Beverly Hills, takes ideologies of gendered language use to the extreme in her itemization of precisely 105 communication characteristics that distinguish women from men, among them features of speech, voice, facial expression, and body language. Although the empirically oriented scholar would shudder at such lists, Glass's assertions apparently make sense to many consumers of mainstream American culture, if a book's sales are any indication of its cultural intelligibility. That these traits are truisms among mainstream European Americans suggests the prevalence of a dichotomous model of "women's speech" and "men's speech."

Ironically, Glass's decision to study gendered language can be traced back to her counseling interactions in the mid-1970s with a male-to-female transsexual whose vocal and speech characteristics she had been asked to diagnose. With Lakoff's *Language and Woman's Place*, the only available book on the subject, as her guide, Glass was able to teach her new client how to "sound and act like a woman" (1993:17). Her dabbling in linguistic gender-bending did not end there, however; she was later asked to teach Dustin Hoffman to sound like a woman for the movie *Tootsie*, in which, Glass reports, "Dustin portrayed a woman so brilliantly that he won an Academy Award for his performance" (18). Glass also boasts of her linguistic success with actors like Conrad Bain, star of the television situation comedy *Diff'rent Strokes*, whom she taught not only "how to sound female but how to sound like a Dutch female—accent and all" (20), and with Bain's female costar Dana Plato, whom she taught to speak and behave like a Dutch boy.

Despite all the dichotomous essentialism of Glass's itemized list, the goal of her book is covertly postmodern. She implies that gendered speaking styles exist independently of the speaker, illustrating that they can be manipulated for communicative effect at home and in the workplace. Her book clearly belongs to the popular genre that Deborah Cameron (1995, forthcoming) has called "verbal hygiene," a discourse that promotes certain linguistic practices over others for pragmatic, aesthetic, or even moral reasons. Ironically, however, when verbal hygienists like Glass encourage their readers to improve their communicative skills through the appropriation of other ways of speaking, they parallel postmodern musings on the discursive construction of gender identity and the related assertion that speakers can assume multiple subject positions (Davies & Harré 1990; Davies 1989, 1990). Glass's simple assertion that speakers can learn and appropriate "women's language" or "men's language" for better communicative success (or, in this instance, for happier heterosexual relationships) suggests that language use is not indexically derived from the sex of the er but rather is constructed from a vast array of ideological discursive ɔings. An especially powerful example of how linguistic ideologies be undermined through women's appropriation of men's language is presented by Shigeko Okamoto in this volume.

Folk-linguistic discussions of this kind should therefore be considered more seriously by analysts of language and gender, for they reveal dominant cultural expectations of gender-appropriate behavior. Gender expectations in turn underlie the actual practices in which speakers engage, as Penelope Eckert and Sally McConnell-Ginet demonstrate in the chapter that concludes this volume. Because the speakers of every community invoke dominant language ideologies together with their own local ideologies and practices in order to establish positions of power, the language analyst must become aware of these belief systems before embarking on the study of discursive identity. Any analysis of gender and power, then, should first isolate the external language conventions that influence the community under study, and then ascertain the more local conventions that may or may not override those of the dominant symbolic system. Although external expectations can be found in the public discourses that surround and influence the subordinated community, local values can be found in speakers' own attitudes about their linguistic choices; in their chapters for this volume Mary Bucholtz, María Dolores Gonzales Velásquez, and Birch Moonwomon all make this point from somewhat different perspectives. Once these sets of conventions have been isolated, the researcher can go on to examine how speakers enact, challenge, and subvert them in their everyday interactions. The process of locating ideologies and their uses is, in one way or another, the overriding project of the present collection of essays; and it would not have been possible without the groundwork that Robin Lakoff laid for us in 1975.

From Woman's Place to Women's Places

In recent years, several promising new frameworks for the analysis of language and gender have emerged in linguistics and related fields. These new approaches share a concern with the complexity of actually occurring interactions, and therefore favor ethnographic and discourse-based methodologies over the traditional linguistic methods of native-speaker intuitions and carefully controlled experimental research. Such awareness of the importance of context in the analysis of social interaction has given rise to new ways of understanding gender as a factor in language use: recent theoretical work in language and gender emphasizes that social categories are negotiated rather than fixed, and that the process of negotiation occurs primarily through linguistic practices whose meanings are themselves shifting and variable.

In our organization of this collection of essays, we trace three general analytical stances in the new feminist scholarship on language: the investigation of how cultural paradigms of gender relations are perpetuated through language; the study of women's innovative use of language to subvert this dominant belief system; and the examination of how women construct social identities and communities that are not determined in advance by gender ideologies. Each of the three parts of *Gender Articulated* treats one of these theoretical perspectives; the possibilities offered by each framework are explored from diverse vantage points by the authors in each section. Part 1, "Mechanisms of Hegemony and Control," comprises articles that consider language as a force maintaining gender ideology. Part 2, "Agency through Appropriation," explores how women challenge hegemonic linguistic practices by creatively reinterpreting them for their own uses. Part 3, "Contingent Practices and Emergent Selves," shows how women's construction of and participation in communities of linguistic practice offer new visions of gender and identity as constantly shifting categories. By organizing the volume into these sections, we hope to give shape to the many strands of gender-based language research, both by tracing the history of the discipline and by presenting new analytical directions within each framework.

Mechanisms of Hegemony and Control

The first section of the volume begins with Robin Tolmach Lakoff's examination of some of the means by which women are silenced in contemporary American culture. Lakoff argues against accounts of gender differences in language use that maintain that women and men belong to different cultures. She favors instead a model that incorporates male power as an explanatory factor. In support of her argument, Lakoff locates four strategies of silencing in men's interaction with women, two of which, interruptions and control of the discourse topic, have been much studied by scholars of language and gender and are compatible with a cultural explanation. However, Lakoff uncovers two additional strategies, nonresponse and the control of discursive meaning, that have been largely overlooked by previous researchers. She demonstrates that the cultural view cannot account for these strategies, because their effect, especially in the public arena, is to render women not only silent but invisible. Yet Lakoff finds evidence in contemporary public discourse that women have begun to resist being silenced and to undertake the construction of their own discursive meanings. She illustrates this cultural shift by examining media representations of a number of public figures who symbolize larger social patterns of gender and power—Anita Hill, Hillary Rodham Clinton, Lorena Bobbitt, Tonya Harding, and Nicole Brown Simpson. The inordinate amount of media attention given to these individuals, Lakoff suggests, points to a large-scale change in gender relations that authorizes women's own interpretations of cultural meaning.

Lakoff's work emphasizes the gendered aspects of the metadiscursive level of linguistic meaning, that is, how discourse events are interpreted by female and male participants, media commentators, and members of the general public. Norma Mendoza-Denton's study of the Clarence Thomas confirmation hearings conducted by the U.S. Senate provides an in-depth analysis of how the metadiscursive level can be shaped by the discourse itself, and specifically how race and gender can be represented through speakers' interactional practices. By examining the details of the senators' interaction with Clarence Thomas and Anita Hill during the hearing, Mendoza-Denton demonstrates that the two speakers received very different treatments that in turn influenced the outcome of the hearings. She found that whereas senators surrounded Thomas's turns at talk with respectful silence, they granted Hill only brief silences between her responses and their subsequent questions. Moreover, the senators asked Thomas more yes/no questions, thereby avoiding any inclusion of potentially incriminating details; but they asked Hill questions containing embedded presuppositions that challenged her narrative. Senators also bombarded Hill, but not Thomas, with rapid-fire questions, abruptly changing topics with each one as though interrogating her. These tactics, in conjunction with Thomas's deployment of a weighty "judge style" of speech, as well as his use of dramatic African American discourse strategies like testifying, sermonizing, and signifying, garnered approval for Thomas from both European American and African American audiences. Such strategies were not available to Hill because she needed to resist the stereotypically aggressive and emotional behavior associated with her as an African American woman. Mendoza-Denton's research thus makes explicit the gender- and race-based implications of silence and differential access to speech in the public arena.

Mendoza-Denton demonstrates that time-honored democratic institutions and practices may in fact engender asymmetrical power relations between women and men, both through collective male collaboration and through the strategies of individual men. Susan Herring, Deborah Johnson, and Tamra DiBenedetto discover the same patterns in their examination of the new realm of computer-network discourse, which has been widely touted as a site of democratic exchange. Their results indicate that such a descriptor is overly optimistic. Studying the interaction on two electronic discussion lists, one in an academic discipline in which feminism has had a strong influence and one in which it is largely absent, they found that men consistently dominated interaction on both lists. The authors' topic-based analysis yields further insights: during discussions of issues related to feminism, women's contributions to the list briefly increased, and as a result, some men perceived themselves as being "silenced," and threatened to withdraw from the list. Other strategies that men used to shift the power balance in their own favor include ignoring women's contributions, offering humorous and patronizing responses, and co-opting women's topics. Such research indicates that male domination is still a potent force. But women in the study were able to draw upon counterstrategies that may serve as new methods of empowerment for female users of computer-mediated communication.

Whereas Herring, Johnson, and DiBenedetto, like Mendoza-Denton, consider the gendered component of public talk, Elinor Ochs and Carolyn Taylor show that male authority to evaluate women's narratives is constructed in private discourse as well. In their research in Southern California on middle-class European American families, they found that traditional gender roles are a strong predictor of how power dynamics are played out in everyday narratives. Most of the dinner-table narratives, Ochs and Taylor report, are introduced by mothers and are about themselves or their children. Such narratives are directed to fathers, who evaluate the actions of the protagonist. This evaluative role emerges from the ideology that Ochs and Taylor call "Father knows best." They note that the workings of power in this process are not one-dimensional; children are subject to the control of both the mother and the father. But the power of fathers is more pervasive, for fathers frequently "problematize" the narratives introduced by mothers, turning them into forums for criticism. Even though mothers often strive to regain control of individual narratives by "counter-problematizing" the fathers' critical comments, fathers continue to be reinstantiated as arbiters of the events laid before them. The social relations seen in these data make clear that traditional arrangements of gender often thought to be obsolete are still very much with us and are constantly renewed through everyday narrative practice.

Ochs and Taylor show that women may collude in practices that deprive them of power and autonomy in order to fulfill the role of "mother." Likewise, in her analysis of a feature article on lipstick in a magazine marketed to teenage girls, Mary Talbot demonstrates that the construction of femininity itself is a practice in which institutions and individual women work together, often to women's detriment. Noting that femininity is produced through women's work on their bodies (e.g., through clothing and makeup), Talbot finds that norms of femininity are reinforced by the mass media in order to encourage the consumption of commodities. Over time, women's magazines have increasingly performed this function because of their dependence on advertising, and as magazines have become more dependent on such funding, their texts have assumed a more personalized and friendly tone. In her data, Talbot isolates a variety of devices—such as pronouns, expressive vocabulary and punctuation, and the attribution of shared beliefs—that are used to construct a community between the editorial voice and the reader. Although the pleasure that women and girls may derive from the work of femininity should not be dismissed, Talbot concludes, what is deserving of criticism is the covert exploitation of women's desires and uncertainties for financial profit.

The ideological underpinnings of superficially helpful and supportive discourse is further evidenced by Cathryn Houghton's ethnographic study of a therapy group for poverty-level Latina teenagers. Houghton reports that counselors "discipline" the language of the girls and force them into conformity with the ideology of the mental health industry, in the guise of socializing them into a better way of life through menial work. During group therapy, therapists monitor and correct what they perceive as inappropriate language use such as "talking out of turn," "side talk," and "mothering." Even within the authoritarian environment of the mental institution, however, power can be subverted. Many girls resist the imposition of therapeutic authority by exploiting the language rules of the therapy group to level challenges at counselors or by engaging in an oppositional discourse genre, "girl talk." Far from passively accepting the dominant system of beliefs and values, such patients are actively involved in constructing and deconstructing social relations. But those girls who accept the framework of therapy, gaining "health" in the terms of the therapeutic establishment, thereby internalize a system of social control that sustains existing power relations and the capitalist economy.

Agency through Appropriation

In their fine-grained analysis of controlling forces within language, the chapters in Part 1 address the linguistic strategies through which women challenge existing power relations. Part 2 treats this issue in greater detail, examining ways in which women as producers of language resist and subvert hegemonic notions of gender. The chapters in this section present women as agents who may defy or embrace gendered expectations of language behavior for their own purposes.

Susan Gal's overview of anthropological research on language, gender, and power encourages linguists to study the categories of "women's speech," "men's speech," and "powerful speech" not as indexically derived from the identity of speakers but as culturally constructed within different social groups. Emphasizing the recent work of feminists and cultural analysts like Micaela diLeonardo, Joan Scott, and Janice Radway, Gal proposes a new way of analyzing gender in language use, one that serves as a theoretical challenge to earlier studies that have defined gender relations in terms of static oppositions. By taking a second look at Carol Edelsky's study of gendered ways of speaking in mixed-sex faculty meetings at an American college and Lila Abu-Lughod's discussion of the subversive nature of oral lyric poetry performed by Bedouin women and youths, Gal argues that cultural constructions of language behavior are not merely ideas that differentiate the genders with respect to interaction; they are themselves sources of power that are enacted and contested in talk. In both of these practices, female speakers locate a contradiction in dominant conceptions of language behavior and attempt to subvert ideological structures through rival practices. Female participants in the university setting undermine the hierarchical form of meetings through their introduction of a collaborative discourse practice; female poets among the Bedouin subvert dominant linguistic ideologies of autonomy, personal strength, and sexual modesty by performing expressions of dependency, emotional vulnerability, and romantic longing.

The chapters that follow Gal's in this section demonstrate how hegemonic notions of language behavior, as differently valued cultural creations, are variously appropriated, reworked, and rejected both in the projection of self and in the establishment of relationships. An unusual example of such negotiations is discussed in Kira Hall's study of workers in the telephone-sex industry, who exaggerate popular expectations of feminine speech over the telephone in order to create a certain body fiction. Hall demonstrates how the practices of the workers call into question traditional assumptions about language, gender, and power, for by using the features of a stereotypically feminine and powerless speech style, the women (and men) in the industry gain economic power. Moreover, the workers themselves reject the notion that this arrangement is exploitative; in fact, they view themselves as feminists who are empowered by their linguistic manipulation of men's desires. In taking seriously women's experience of themselves as social agents, Hall's study forces a reanalysis of the reductive dichotomy between "powerful" and "powerless" speech that informs much of the research on language and gender.

Bonnie McElhinny, in an interesting contrast to Hall's work, discusses how women working as police officers in the Pittsburgh police department have learned to project a masculine gender identity in their interactions with the public. She analyzes two conversational interactions—one involving a female police officer taking a report from a victim of domestic assault and the other involving a male police officer performing a similar task—in order to show how the women working in this predominantly male occupation have appropriated a "subordinate" middle-class masculinity in their own nonprojection of emotion. She approaches her data from a postmodern and ethnomethodological perspective that takes into account the fluidity of identity performance in interaction. The chapters by both Hall and McElhinny indicate the need for a more flexible definition of gender and its effects on language use, one that accords speakers more agency to develop a speaking style based upon their occupational choices, personal histories, sexuality, and lifestyles. Both authors incorporate Gal's theoretical interest in linguistic resistance and reinterpretation, and in their ethnographic studies of two very different kinds of work environments, they suggest that such negotiations should become a central focus of language and gender research.

Stereotypically feminine and masculine language may be appropriated not only in real life but in fictional contexts as well. Anna Livia's examination of lesbian authors' uses of gendered speech to represent butch and femme characters demonstrates that in the realm of fiction, as in life, appropriation has multiple meanings. Livia finds that butch speech, as represented by authors, does not conform to the reality of masculine speech style but to the cultural stereotype of such language. Furthermore, a hypermasculine butch speech style was present only in the work of European American authors that Livia examined; African American authors used a more egalitarian style for their butch characters. Livia demonstrates that the origin of butch speech style in fiction lies in gangster films, westerns, and Raymond Chandler's detective fiction. Authors implement the style in two ways: as a sincere representation of butch interactional style, and as a parody of the style that challenges simplistic equations of the butch with masculinity or maleness.

Like Livia's research, Laurel Sutton's study of California college students' use of slang terms for women reminds us that even strongly gendered language may be multivalent. Taking as her starting point several early studies of derogatory labels for women, Sutton finds that women have undertaken an innovative use of such terms. Highly derogatory words like *bitch* and *ho* (whore) may be used not only as insult terms by women or men but also as terms of solidarity among close female friends. Appropriation of this kind has limits, however: although these two negative terms may take on positive meanings, other terms that are more sexually explicit in form cannot be used in the same way. Sutton demonstrates that the bulk of slang words for women are of the second, more strongly negative type. Most slang terms for women in her corpus are negative, and most deal with physical appearance and sexual promiscuity; by contrast, far fewer terms for men are negative, and those that are do not have the same focus upon the body and sexuality. Yet despite this ongoing gender imbalance in insult terms, the possibility of a community of women's assigning positive meanings to such terms points to a creative subversion of the gender expectations that insult terms are designed to enforce.

Shigeko Okamoto's chapter also explores the strategic use of negatively valued language by young women. She argues that speech that contains features marked as male or masculine cannot be mapped simplistically onto a "masculine identity," but may be used creatively by speakers. Examining the discursive styles of young Japanese women, Okamoto points out a generational shift among Japanese students from Tokyo, whose speech contrasts with that used by older married women in its employment of forms traditionally thought of as masculine, less polite, and coarse. Her findings challenge the conservative nature of much previous research on Japanese women's speech, which has tended to further dichotomous notions of gender in its characterization of Japanese female speakers as polite, powerless, and linguistically rigid. Okamoto instead suggests that Japanese women's language is variable and innovative: the female students in her study employ masculine speech forms with their peers both to signal independence from hegemonic expectations of gender and to establish solidarity with one another, jointly constructing an unmarried-student identity.

Contingent Practices and Emergent Selves

Underlying the studies that make up Part 2 is the understanding that through acts of resistance and innovation women shape the contours of their social identities. The chapters in Part 3 further interrogate the notion of a fixed self. They demonstrate that language is a crucial resource for identity construction while cautioning that it has no privileged status in this process. Rather, language is connected to an entire network of practices, knowledges, and subject positions.

Michèle Foster's chapter on the use of language by African American women shows the fluidity of social identity as manifested in language. She finds that the African American women whose speech she examined invoked an identity of Blackness in interaction with other African American speakers by drawing upon shared linguistic practices. In a classroom in which Foster conducted ethnographic research, the effect of this stylistic shift by the instructor was to enhance students' motivation and understanding. At the same time, by taking on multiple roles in the classroom, the instructor was able to reach a variety of students and to demonstrate the importance of being proficient in both the Black and the non-Black speech communities. In a second study in which interviews were conducted with African American teachers, Foster noticed that once interviewees had established a social relationship with the researcher, they began to code-switch from Standard English to African American Vernacular English, primarily in order to express affective meanings in a display of solidarity. Significantly, given claims that women's speech is closer to the standard than men's and that teachers are prescriptive in their language attitudes, Foster reports that female teachers in interviews tended to code-switch into the vernacular more than males did, and that the women's linguistic practices indicated positive attitudes toward African American Vernacular English. Her findings suggest that the subject positions that African American women occupy are more complex than sociolinguists have previously supposed.

Whereas Foster explores the multiple social identities available to members of a single ethnic group, Mary Bucholtz's article on "passing" demonstrates that for individuals whose ethnicity is ambiguous, the notion of identity is even more malleable. Drawing upon recent feminist examinations of ethnic identity and mixed cultural heritage, Bucholtz describes how some American women and girls in certain social contexts may be taken for members of an ethnicity other than their own. At times the decision to cross ethnic boundaries may be conscious; women who do not conform in appearance to their community's expectations may temporarily assume a new ethnic identity, thereby negotiating the restrictions of gender ideology within their own community or the racism of the dominant society. Bucholtz also finds that outsiders frequently impose ethnic categories on individuals of ambiguous background. Rather than accept these readily available ethnicities, individuals assert ethnic identities of their own choosing. Although passing has been described primarily as an issue of boundary crossing in the physical presentation of the self, Bucholtz argues that it is in fact a representation that is shaped largely through linguistic practices. Bucholtz's study shows that essentialist approaches to ethnic identity and community membership obscure the creative work women do to shape their lives.

Foster's and Bucholtz's work demonstrates how important it is to do research that rejects a priori analysis and generalization, and looks closely at speakers' practices and beliefs. This point is also made by Tara Goldstein in her study of female immigrant factory workers in Canada. Many researchers of English as a Second Language assume that non-native adult speakers are motivated to learn English because they see it as a way of advancing their careers. Goldstein finds that for Portuguese women in the Canadian factory in which she conducted her research, Portuguese, not English, is the language associated with success on the job. As assembly-line workers, the women must rely on the friendship and assistance of other workers in order to perform their tasks effectively, and friendship within the production department of the factory is constructed through use of the Portuguese language. Just as solidarity emerges from local linguistic practice, so too is power locally produced through language. "Talking bad" is a gossip activity that imposes language-based sanctions upon workers who fail to fulfill their social obligation to assist other members of the assembly-line community. Thus Portuguese is simultaneously a tool of community and of social control, obviating the need for English. Moreover, the workers do not aspire to higher-paying jobs where English skills are essential, for as women they do not have access to the same opportunities to develop this linguistic resource as do their male counterparts. These facts, notes Goldstein, do not argue against teaching English to immigrant workers but, rather, show that effective ESL instruction must be grounded in a recognition of the gendered nature of such workers' lives, especially the risk of sexual harassment.

Goldstein shows us that the workings of power can sometimes be ironic, in that a position that seems subordinate to outsiders is embraced as powerful by the women within the factory community. Likewise, Jenny Cook-Gumperz takes up an issue first raised by Simone de Beauvoir and expanded upon by Nancy Chodorow: Why do girls aspire to womanhood when it is culturally marked by inferior social status? These theorists conclude that to young girls, the mother is a powerful figure to be emulated, a point that Cook-Gumperz illustrates in her study of the play practices of preschool girls. She shows how girls explore the mother role in a complex speech event called the narrative game, in which children use language to construct an imagined world and sequential events within it. In the partic-ular game studied by Cook-Gumperz, two three-year-old girls pretend to be the mothers of their baby dolls. By manipulating the multiple discourse levels of the game—narration, in-character speech, and real-world speech—the girls display their understanding of the gendered social practice of mothering. This position is ambiguous: on the one hand, the children use powerful language in their role as mothers, but on the other hand, this power is contingent upon their enacting the subordinate role of women. Hence, in creating a gendered self through play the children draw upon the roots of women's secondary status even as they explore its consequences for power within the family unit.

The family is also the focus of María Dolores Gonzales Velásquez's research on three generations of women in Córdova, New Mexico. Gonzales Velásquez locates three linguistic codes in use in this community: Spanish, English, and code-switching. Incorporating Bea Medicine's notion of "cultural brokers," she illustrates how Chicanas' choice of each of these codes in intragroup situations is motivated by solidarity and in-group identity. Gonzales Velásquez's research differs sharply from the majority of previous studies on the use of prestige varieties by minority cultures, which tend to account for code-switching with reference to the speaker's linguistic insecurities and low social position. It also challenges long-standing assumptions about women's use of the most prestigious language variety in their community. Gonzales Velásquez shows how women in Córdova—as possessors of a broad linguistic repertoire—function as cultural intermediaries between their native speech community and the English-speaking community.

Gonzales Velásquez, like Foster and Bucholtz, explores speech at the boundaries between communities. Birch Moonwomon explores the issue of language at the boundaries from a somewhat different perspective; she considers the conjunction of social and linguistic notions of discourse in a graffiti interchange about a case of interracial rape. Such a research site brings together the tension between social and linguistic discourses; between social discourses themselves; and between public and private language use. The exchange upon which Moonwomon focuses takes the form of a text by multiple authors that developed over the course of several months on the wall of a women's bathroom stall on a university campus. The discussion revolves around an alleged gang rape of a female student by four members of the school's football team; the woman who made the accusation was Chinese American and the male students were African American. Hence sexist violence and racist blame are the central topics of the text. Moonwomon reconstructs the development of the discourse and interprets its conventions, finding markers both of solidarity and of power. Her analysis of these rich data thus shows in fine detail how linguistic discourses foster and reflect larger societal discourses or belief systems.

This observation, that linguistic practice and social practice are in a reciprocal relationship, is the central premise of the theoretical framework laid out by Penelope Eckert and Sally McConnell-Ginet in the chapter that concludes the volume. The authors demonstrate that language use at many levels contributes to wider social meanings. Drawing upon Eckert's ethnographic study of a Michigan high school, the authors show that the semantics of group labels, as well as linguistic details at the phonetic level, may have considerable social significance for their users by forging dividing lines between social categories. Eckert and McConnell-Ginet detail the social and linguistic meanings of the two main types of students in the school: "jocks," or those oriented toward corporate values, and "burnouts," or those oriented toward local values. Differences in values and social practices correlate with differences in language use; the burnouts lead the community in an innovation in the vowel system. But because girls and boys have differential access to the practices that mark their identities, girls more than boys turn to language as a place for expressing affiliation. Hence the most innovative speakers are the "burned-out" burnout girls. In analyzing the linguistic data and the social identities that they index, Eckert and McConnell-Ginet illustrate that gender cannot be separated from social class. Their work neatly encapsulates the major themes of the volume: it shows how the hegemonic construction of gender is imposed upon girls' lives; it illustrates female speakers' innovative use of language for their own purposes; and it vividly demonstrates the central role of community values, meanings, and practices in any analysis of language and gender.

Conclusion

The chapters in this volume represent the state of the art in language and gender research. But their scholarly contribution is made fully visible only by considering them in light of the work of the preeminent "old mistress" of the art, Robin Lakoff.[5] *Language and Woman's Place* was and continues to be a highly subversive text. At the time of its publication, it simultaneously threatened the boundaries of linguistics and the assumptions of male linguists. And it has relevance for readers still, both in academia and in the culture at large. We therefore cannot agree with Rita Hoffman (1980) that we should lay the text aside as obsolete; instead, we urge scholars of language and gender to study it for what it suggests about where the field has been and where it is going. We can only hope that the present volume will have the same salutary destabilizing effect, as we usher in the third decade of language and gender research.

Notes

1. Although much of the material in *Language and Woman's Place* was first published as a journal article (Lakoff 1973), we focus on the book-length study both because it includes new material and because its accessibility has made it the more widely discussed publication.

2. We must also acknowledge the important pioneering role of Barrie Thorne and Nancy Henley's (1975) *Language and Sex: Difference and Dominance*, which was published in the same year as *Language and Woman's Place*.

3. In both books Newmeyer takes the opportunity to argue against Lakoff's feminist credentials, based on her comment that women in linguistics disproportionately prefer to "escape into relevance" in fields such as sociolinguistics rather than pursue formal theory (Lakoff 1974:23). Newmeyer's rhetoric can only be called self-serving: "While she did not state whether mathematics and the sciences should also abandon formalism as a step toward sexual equality, she did, astonishingly, explicitly leave open the possibility that the 'indisposition toward formalism among women' might be inherent!" (1986a:134 n.7). Yet in assuming the stance of flabbergasted feminist, Newmeyer fails to recognize that Lakoff's observation is compatible with radical feminist discussions of the period, in which gender differences were posited as biological.

4. Likewise, Lakoff's theoretical assumptions in *Language and Woman's Place* emerge from the intellectual climate in which she worked. Virginia Valian's ([1977] 1981) accusation that Lakoff conflates the fundamental linguistic division between competence (knowledge of language structure) and performance (language use) is untenable, not only because it is unlikely that a linguist trained in the Chomskyan tradition could for a moment forget such a distinction but because the project of generative semantics was in large part to call that very distinction into question.

5. By labeling Lakoff an *old mistress,* we intend not insult but a subversion of English semantics: as Lakoff (1975) herself has observed, *old mistress* is not the equivalent of *old master,* although logically it should be.

References

Barrett, Rusty (forthcoming a). "She is *not* white woman": The appropriation of (white) women's language by African American drag queens. In Mary Bucholtz, Anita Liang, Laurel Sutton, and Caitlin Hines (eds.), *Cultural performances: Proceedings of the Third Berkeley Women and Language Conference.* Berkeley: Berkeley Women and Language Group.

———— (forthcoming b). The homo-genius community. In Anna Livia and Kira Hall (eds.), *Queerly phrased: Language, gender, and sexuality.* New York: Oxford University Press.

Butler, Pamela E. ([1981] 1992). *Self-assertion for women.* San Francisco: Harper-Collins.

Cameron, Deborah (1995). *Verbal hygiene.* London: Routledge.

———— (forthcoming). The language-gender interface: Challenging co-optation. In

Victoria Bergvall, Janet Bing, and Alice Freed (eds.), *Language and gender research: Theory and method.* London: Longman.

Cameron, Deborah, Fiona McAlinden, and Kathy O'Leary (1988). Lakoff in context: The social and linguistic functions of tag questions. In Jennifer Coates and Deborah Cameron (eds.), *Women in their speech communities.* London: Longman. 74–93.

Crosby, Faye, and Linda Nyquist (1977). The female register: An empirical study of Lakoff's hypotheses. *Language in Society* 6: 313–22.

Davies, Bronwyn (1989). *Frogs and snails and feminist tales: Preschool children and gender.* Sydney: Allen and Unwin.

—— (1990). The problem of desire. *Social Problems* 37(4): 501–16.

Davies, Bronwyn, and Rom Harré (1990). Positioning: The discursive production of selves. *Journal for the Theory of Social Behaviour* 20(1): 43–63.

Dubois, Betty, and Isabel Crouch (1975). The question of tag questions in women's speech: They don't really use more of them, do they? *Language in Society* 4: 289–94.

Elgin, Suzette Hadin (1993). *Genderspeak: Men, women, and the gentle art of verbal self-defense.* New York: Wiley.

Glass, Lillian (1993). *He says, she says: Closing the communication gap between the sexes.* New York: Perigree Books.

Harris, Randy Allen (1993). *The linguistics wars.* New York: Oxford University Press.

Hoffman, Rita M. (1980). Language and sex textbooks: A review. *Women's Studies International Quarterly* 3: 313–17.

Kramer, Cheris, Barrie Thorne, and Nancy Henley (1978). Perspectives on language and communication. (Review essay.) *Signs* 3(3): 638–51.

Lakoff, Robin (1973). Language and woman's place. *Language in Society* 2: 45–80.

—— (1974). Pluralism in linguistics. *Berkeley Studies in Syntax and Semantics* 1: 1–36.

—— (1975). *Language and woman's place.* New York: Harper & Row.

—— (1989). The way we were; or, The real actual truth about generative semantics: A memoir. *Journal of Pragmatics* 13: 939–88.

Moulton, Janice (1976). Philosophy. (Review essay.) *Signs* 2(2): 422–33.

Newmeyer, Frederick J. (1986a). *Linguistic theory in America.* 2d ed. San Diego: Academic Press.

—— (1986b). *The politics of linguistics.* Chicago: University of Chicago Press.

O'Barr, William M., and Bowman K. Atkins (1980). "Women's language" or "powerless language"? In Sally McConnell-Ginet, Ruth Borker, and Nelly Furman (eds.), *Women and language in literature and society.* New York: Praeger. 93–110.

Showalter, Elaine (1975). Literary criticism. (Review essay.) *Signs* 1(2): 435–60.

Stone, Janet, and Jane Bachner ([1977] 1994). *Speaking up: A book for every woman who talks.* New York: Carroll and Graf.

Tannen, Deborah (1990). *You just don't understand: Women and men in conversation*. New York: Morrow.

Thorne, Barrie (1976). Review of *Language and Woman's Place*. *Signs* 1(3): 744–46.

Thorne, Barrie, and Nancy Henley (eds.) (1975). *Language and sex: Difference and dominance*. Rowley, MA: Newbury House.

Timm, Lenora (1976). Review of *Language and Woman's Place*. *Lingua* 39: 244–52.

Valian, Virginia ([1977] 1981). Linguistics and feminism. In Mary Vetterling-Braggin (ed.), *Sexist language: A modern philosophical analysis*. Totowa, NJ: Littlefield, Adams. 68–80.

Walum, Laurel Richardson (1977). Review of Mary Ritchie Key's *Male/Female Language*, Robin Lakoff's *Language and Woman's Place*, and Barrie Thorne and Nancy Henley's *Language and Sex: Difference and Dominance*. *Sex Roles* 3(5): 499–501.

Part One

Mechanisms of Hegemony

and Control

I

Cries and Whispers

The Shattering of the Silence

Robin Tolmach Lakoff

Feminists have devoted a great deal of attention over the past quarter century to speech and its effect on gender and power relations.[1] Less consideration has been given to its complement, the absence of speech, or silence, and that much more recently.[2] This lack of attention to the meanings and functions of silence in gender relations is not really surprising. It is easier to perceive what is *there* as meaningful, as opposed to discerning meaning in the absence of a phenomenon. What is explicit and apparent responds to analysis more readily than what must be inferred. So it is not surprising that there exists within linguistics, to my knowledge, only a single collection of papers on silence (Tannen & Saville-Troike 1985). Silence is popularly equated with the absence of content, although we also recognize, if subliminally, the uses of silence in power relations. Adults demand answers of children, superiors of subordinates. The powerless cannot choose to be silent, any more than they can choose to speak, or choose the meaning of their speech.

To my knowledge, the earliest explicit discussion of the communicative functions of silence is that of the psychoanalyst Robert Fliess (1949). Traditional analysts use their own silence as a means of forcing patients to speak, because silence is heavily dispreferred in all Western cultures as a violation of what Harvey Sacks, Emanuel Schegloff, and Gail Jefferson

(1974) refer to as the "basic rule" of conversation: one party at a time, no more and no less. As is true in nonlinguistic contexts as well, power implies the right to violate rules unilaterally. So the analyst's silence is perceived as "normal," part of the process, but the analysand's is interpretable in any of several ways.[3] Fliess suggests an "oral" or hungry silence, representing a desire to take in warmth and love from the other; an "anal" or retentive silence, the refusal to give anything to the hearer; and (of course) a "phallic" silence, an attempt to maintain power and control. We may smile at the reductionistic clarity of this trichotomy, but what is useful in the discussion is the recognition that (like any form of communication) silence is ambiguous; its meaning is discernible only through an understanding of the context in which it occurs.

Silence in discourse can be interpreted from both semantic and pragmatic perspectives. The former, a nonpolitical stance, looks at the absence of speech in terms of its contribution to the meaning participants in a discourse construct for it. The work of conversation analysts on "attributable silences" (gaps, lapses, and pauses) is essentially a semantic account of silence. A pragmatic perspective views nonspeech as the result of the process of "silencing," interactively organized and functional as well as meaningful. The ability of one party in a discourse to prevent another from fully participating ("silencing") arises out of the disparate powers and roles of each, and contributes to the further imbalancing of those roles. The pragmatic perspective does not imply that *all* attributable silences are necessarily political in intention or effect, but it does require that the analyst consider that possibility.

Pragmatic silencing can be broadly divided into two subcategories based on discourse genre: private (or conversational) versus public (or persuasive). Private discourse is normally dyadic, informal, and without explicit intended function beyond the socializing capacity of the conversation itself. Hence any commentary on how it is proceeding (including complaints about interruptions or silences) is generally considered inappropriate.

Public discourse includes all kinds of talk in public settings (e.g., courtrooms, workplaces, political arenas, and media settings) from reciprocal dyads to speeches intended for mass audiences. Unlike private discourse, it is consequential—that is, it is expected to have effects beyond that of mere socialization—and it uses some version of formal style or elaborated code, with the consequent absence of any assumption of mutual trust. The superficial forms of silencing that occur in the private arena may also occur in public settings, but although the form may be identical, the function and consequences are often more serious for the silenced person, and more permanent, in public.

Types of Silencing

Interruption and Topic Control

Because most linguistic attention to discourse has tended to focus on private dyadic conversation, it is not surprising that silencing studies have also been centered there. Two forms of conversational silencing have received a good deal of attention: interruption and topic control (cf. Zimmerman & West 1975; West & Zimmerman 1983; Leet-Pellegrini 1980). Deborah James and Sandra Clarke (1993) have provided a valuable review and critique of many of the interruption studies. They find that the majority of studies of conversational interruption do not corroborate the asserted tendency of men to interrupt women. They note several problems in prior studies. Because traditional conversation analysts eschew statements of function or intention, it becomes impossible for them to distinguish among types of violations of the "one party at a time" or "no gap, no overlap" rule where more than one speaker occupies the floor. Only some types have political (that is, power-related) consequences. One that does not, for instance, is the "cooperative overlap" discussed by Tannen (1981), in which one speaker begins speaking over the end of the previous participant's turn, behavior that is technically interruptive but done in the interest of solidarity rather than control. Additionally, some attempts to take over the floor through interrupting are successful, others not. James and Clarke argue that researchers have been less careful than is desirable in the classification and analysis of conversational interruption. It should be noted that James and Clarke do not disclaim the existence of men's aggressive interruption of women. They merely suggest that the field's currently predominant research paradigm makes corroboration of such assertions very difficult or impossible.

Like interruption, topic choice as a control mechanism presents research problems of interpretation (cf. Leet-Pellegrini 1980), but in the case of topic choice it is even more severe because ethnomethodology frowns on interpretive approaches, and it is impossible to determine topic development meaningfully without recourse to semantic analysis. Scholars recognize intuitively that interruption in conversation is encouraged by, and encourages, power imbalance. But it is much harder to define the behaviors referred to broadly as "interruptions," to isolate them and to measure and analyze them so as to demonstrate the reality behind the intuitions.

Nonresponse

Control is often more subtly achieved by a third technique, silencing by silence, or nonresponse. Like other forms of silencing, it is most effective when employed by the more powerful against the less powerful; in the other direction, it tends to have no real effect or can be countermanded. Nonresponse is often observed at business meetings, when a female executive makes a suggestion to which her male colleagues do not respond even minimally.[4] Nonresponse is not infrequent in classrooms: even when a female student raises her hand and is recognized, her comment often receives no response, especially if the instructor is male.[5] In both types, the same suggestion or comment is often recycled by a male participant a few minutes later, to approbation and serious consideration by the others present.[6]

Annoying and discouraging as interruption is, at least someone who is interrupted knows that she exists and has been noticed. Nonresponse is by contrast annihilating; it signifies that the speaker does not exist, that her utterance *did not happen at all*. It is the lineal descendant of the Victorian tactic of "cutting": the deliberate failure to acknowledge acquaintance with another person (by withholding verbal salutations, eye contact, or hat-tipping, upon meeting in public, for instance) as a way of signifying serious disapproval of really bad behavior, and thus cutting the recipient out of society, in effect dehumanizing her or him.[7]

These three methods of discourse control (interruption, topic control, and nonresponse) are all explicit and thus directly observable by participants, including their targets. The first two differ from the third in being active, but their shared explicitness means that victims of all three can learn to recognize them and take countermeasures (although the passive and silent nature of nonresponse makes that somewhat more difficult).

The Two-Cultures Theory

Because most analysis of gender-linked inequities in access to discourse has been based on private, dyadic conversation, some theorists have suggested that any differences that are observed can be attributed not to any power imbalance between the sexes but to cultural differences between them that create different communicative strategies (cf. Maltz & Borker 1982). In this perspective, males' greater access to conversational participation is explained not by their illegitimate use of their greater power but by the (accidental) coincidence between male styles of discourse and successful floor-gaining strategies. Culture-based theories of conversational imbalance can account for observed interruption and topic-control patterns (if indeed these do exist), but they cannot account for the prevalence of nonresponse, because that is a passive rather than an active strategy, representing not so much a style as a metacomment on the prior speaker's utterance. Still less does it account for the unequal valuation of contributions (ignoring the woman's but valuing the man's), especially in public discourse, the functions and forms of which are predicated on the *formal* connections among participants—that is, the absence of personal relationship—and yet contributions formed according to characteristically feminine patterns are typically judged dismissively on purely stylistic grounds, as indicative of their speakers' lesser rationality or seriousness. What the two-cultures approach defines as the male strategy is implicitly taken as the *right* way to talk in public, and this fact is itself demonstrative of the need for a power-imbalance model alongside a culturally based one.

Interpretive Control

Interruption, topic control, and nonresponse are obvious ways of keeping potential participants from contributing to private or public discourse. But the same result can be accomplished even more subtly and thoroughly by maintaining power over the making of meaning: interpretive control. Women may be permitted to speak, may even receive response to their speech, but it will be up to men (typically, men of the politically dominant group) to determine what both their own and women's communications are to mean. The control of meaning includes the right to name oneself and others; the right to assess one's own behavior and that of others; the right to decide what form or style of language is "good" or "right" or "appropriate"; and the right to determine what a speaker means to say.

Interpretive control is covert and potent, both psychologically and politically. It is often hard to recognize because it can be done silently by those who already have cultural hegemony. It is not blatantly violative, like interruption, or obviously inconsiderate, like nonresponse. Indeed, it is so deeply rooted in our cultural expectations that it becomes hard to notice at all, like those optical illusions in which figure and background blend. Interpretation of the less powerful by the more powerful has been taken for granted in this and many other cultures for so long that it requires special awareness to notice it and novel responses to deal with it.

Silence is analogous to invisibility. Western feminists are apt to pity and scorn women of ancient or non-Western groups whose cultures require them to be literally or symbolically invisible in public. Thus in ancient Athens women of the upper classes were not supposed to appear in public at all (literal public invisibility); in fundamentalist Muslim societies, women must be veiled in public (symbolic public invisibility). We pride ourselves on our liberation from those humiliating constraints. We tend not to realize how recent and partial our liberation really is.

Until the end of the nineteenth century in this and other Western countries, *public woman* was synonymous with *prostitute*, and women who went out in public unescorted, especially at night, were fair game to be treated as prostitutes. (Even today *mujer pública* is a euphemism for 'prostitute' in Spain.) Even after literal invisibility ceased, symbolic forms persisted into the 1960s. In the 1950s, when I was growing up, no proper woman appeared in public without a hat, which typically had a veil attached. True, the veil was short, ending around the bridge of the nose, and flimsy; it might be called metasymbolic. If purdah truly conceals but only symbolically renders the wearer invisible (she is, after all, a perceptible object on the street), the mid-twentieth-century American veil symbolized a more serious veiling. Women were told that the veil made them mysteriously alluring—an interesting idea to be sure (invisibility makes a woman more attractive), but undoubtedly not the full truth.

In the same way, during the early twentieth century women went from literally having no public voice (no vote, no entrée into the professions, and so on) to having no symbolic public voice, that is, no interpretive control. As long as that was the case, conservative elements in society had little to fear. The suffrage was no threat as long as women could elect only men or male-identified women (with very rare exceptions); had no way to pressure officeholders to represent their interests; could not participate as full members of institutions (except under very special circumstances, and with great insecurity); could not propose policy, governmental or institutional, and be taken seriously by those empowered to make changes.

Women in Public Discourse

But things are changing. Over the past several years women have begun to achieve true public desilencing, the appropriation of interpretive control. Those who have traditionally held control unilaterally are (quite properly) alarmed at the signs of change. Many of the stories to which the media have devoted immense amounts of attention since 1991 reflect this struggle. In each case, total victory has not been achieved, but the very fact that the issue of interpretive control (not, of course, explicitly under that name) has been raised so often and so visibly means that such control can never again be presupposed as normal. Things can never go back to the way they were. We have the conservatives to thank for this reorientation, and I think we should be properly grateful.

Evidence for this suggestion comes from a series of recent events, each of which, in one way or another, to various degrees, with more or less success, has increased women's interpretive control over public discourse, their ability to determine the meaning of events in which they are involved. The cases I will discuss are, in order of occurrence:

1. The Clarence Thomas confirmation hearings and their sequelae (fall 1991 and after);
2. The role of Hillary Rodham Clinton as presidential candidate's wife and first lady (1992 and after);
3. The Bobbitt affair (fall and winter 1993);
4. The Nancy Kerrigan–Tonya Harding interaction (winter 1993);
5. The O. J. Simpson murder case (summer 1994 and after).

In addition there have been within this two-and-a-half-year period many discussions in the media on related issues, touching explicitly or otherwise on the anxieties stirred up within the culture by these events and others. The writings of neoconservatives like Norman Podhoretz, Camille Paglia, Neil Gilbert, and Katie Roiphe, to be discussed below, are significant contributions to our understanding of these changes.

The list above may seem tendentious because it mixes the holy with the profane, or at least the serious with the trivial. I don't mean to give all of them equal political weight, much less take all the protagonists equally seriously as conscious, theoretically significant world-changers. What unites them is the media frenzy every one of them has occasioned. I further suggest that, in each case, this media attention is disproportionate to the apparent importance of the event.

In cases (3) and (4), this fact is immediately obvious, but I suggest it is true, in a somewhat different way, even of (1), (2), and (5). Certainly, the confirmation hearings of a nominee for a Supreme Court vacancy are deserving of media attention, especially when they are controversial. But even so, the Anita Hill–Clarence Thomas contretemps attracted extraordinary interest. We might compare them with the Robert Bork confirmation hearings of a few years earlier, equally important, equally controversial, and also televised. It is certainly true that the Bork hearings were hotly discussed while they were going on, and remain in the public's attention, to some degree, even today. But they did not engender anything like the passion, the rancor, the multilayered analyses from all sides, and the continuing reinterpretations that characterize Hill-Thomas, nor did they have significant effects on important subsequent elections, like Hill-Thomas. Likewise, other first ladies have received media attention, but (with the possible exception of Eleanor Roosevelt, and for many of the same reasons), Hillary Rodham Clinton has become a public fixation to a much greater degree than any of her predecessors. So in all five cases, the amount and kind of attention received seems disproportionate and inappropriate to the actual historical importance of the event—unless implicit factors are considered.

That is to say that all five cases pass the Undue Attention Test: in each, more is going on than overtly meets the eye. Media critics often grumble that in cases like these "too much attention" is being paid to matters that are of prurient but ephemeral interest, at the expense of really important concerns (Bosnia, North Korea, Rwanda, and so on). The American public, they say, has been seduced by the media and has become unable to distinguish the significant from the trivial. I argue, rather, that the American public has it right, and the media merely echo the public's intuitions. When Undue Attention is apparently being given to an event, it will always be because that event is *covertly* about something of deep and lasting significance in the culture. These cases have forced a deep, uncomfortable, and persistent reexamination of the identities and possibilities of women and men within the United States.

Let us examine from this perspective each of the cases listed above. Each of the first four seems to have a countercase or dark side that further illustrates its real meaning for us.

Anita Hill and Clarence Thomas (and Paula Corbin Jones–Bill Clinton, the "Dark Side")

Superficially Hill-Thomas was about sexual harassment in the workplace, and whether such activity, if proven, makes its perpetrator unfit for high government office. The discourse was also, however, self-referential: (1) Does a woman have the right to contribute directly to public discourse in a way that reflects badly on male behavior? That is, does a woman have a right to make public meaning, to which we all as a culture must subscribe? (2) What kinds of actions do the words *sexual harassment* refer to? Do they even have semantic reference? (3) Whose definition of public behavior, a woman's or a man's, is authoritative? (4) How do we, the public, view a woman attempting to play this redefining role? Finally, Hill-Thomas had its ultimate and continuing searing effect on public discourse because it showed women how the representatives they elected (with their hard-won franchise) remained unresponsive to their needs, and worse than unresponsive: how they used the ancient techniques of scapegoating and stereotyping to legitimize "business as usual" (cf. Mendoza-Denton, this volume). It is true that, in the immediate situation, Hill did not succeed: Thomas was confirmed. But over the long term, the election of six (later seven) female senators, the embarrassment of Robert Packwood, and the public hearings on the Tailhook incident (even granting the unsatisfactory resolution of the last) are a few indications that Hill's action changed the nature of public discourse and the role women may play in it.

The full significance of Hill's testimony took over a year to surface (cf. McAneny 1992). Although in initial polls women as well as men reported that they did not believe Hill, a year later the statistics for women were reversed, as they realized that the treatment Hill received from the committee was eerily familiar. That, finally, was what Hill-Thomas was about; it is not what Jones-Clinton is about (if the latter is about anything at all). The Paula Corbin Jones harassment case against Bill Clinton has been heavily publicized by conservatives as equivalent to Hill's against Thomas, with the corollary assertion that liberal feminists are hypocritical because they paid more attention to the first than the second. But (leaving aside motive, plausibility, and other relevant differences between the protagonists in each case) Jones's case has been altogether different from Hill's; to the degree that it is possible, Jones has been listened to and treated with respect. Anita Hill made that possible for her—and for the conservatives who created her.

Hillary Rodham Clinton (and Jacqueline Kennedy Onassis, the "Dark Side")

The fracas over Hillary Rodham Clinton is first of all about the right of a woman to name herself, literally and figuratively. To silence is to expropriate a quintessentially human property: the ability to name and define self and environment.

Silencing by taking upon oneself the exclusive right to give names starts as early as Genesis, in which Adam's distinction from all the other creatures (including Eve) is exemplified by the fact that he gets to name them: that is, bring them under his control. To be denied the ability to name oneself or one's context is to be deprived of self-knowledge, and of full consciousness.

A chilling example is to be found in that favorite Shakespearean comedy, *The Taming of the Shrew*. In it we find a horrifying description and enactment of what the mid-twentieth century was to condemn as "brainwashing," when done by Asian communists to American men. But when Petruchio does it to Katharina, it's "taming," the means by which comedic reconciliation is achieved.

The game begins with their first encounter (act 2, scene 1). In about a hundred lines, Petruchio makes it clear that he has the right and the ability to define and name Katharina. In the first twelve lines, he addresses or refers to her as *Kate* eleven times.

Petruchio.	Good morrow, Kate—for that's thy name, I hear.
Katharina.	Well have you heard, but something hard of hearing.
	They call me Katharine that do talk of me.
Petruchio.	You lie, in faith; for you are call'd plain Kate,
	And bonny Kate, and sometimes Kate the curst;
	But Kate, the prettiest Kate in Christendom,
	Kate of Kate Hall, my super-dainty Kate,

For dainties are all Kates, and therefore, Kate,
Take this of me, Kate of my consolation;
Hearing thy mildness praised in every town,
Thy virtues spoke of, and thy beauty sounded,
Yet not so deeply as to thee belongs,
Myself am moved to woo thee for my wife.

Not only does Petruchio implicitly appropriate to himself the right to choose Katharina's name, but the name he chooses is a diminutive (so he forces upon her a relation of intimacy, underscored by his shift halfway through from *you* to *thou*). Of course, this is shocking, but that was then, and we are more evolved today; it can't happen here, or now.

Well, something rather similar can, and does. It isn't just that women's actual *names* are being appropriated (though that certainly happens), but the right to name what is most relevant to our interests is being eroded, in the arguments of the New Right as exemplified by Neil Gilbert and Norman Podhoretz and their pet "feminists," Camille Paglia (1990) and Katie Roiphe (1993).

At issue is who gets to define important points of language:[8] What is feminism, what is good sex, what is rape? The writings revolve around definitions, whether implicitly or explicitly. Even blatant floutings of the rules of logic—in violation of the male ethos—are justified for the cause. For example: Neil Gilbert, a professor of social welfare at the University of California at Berkeley, is interested in appropriating the right to determine what constitutes rape—that is, wresting it from the hands of the "radical feminists" whose definitions "do not square with human attitudes and experiences" (1991:59). A purportedly scientific examination of statistics that charges the feminists with the abandonment of scholarly objectivity in favor of a political agenda, the article is highly tendentious, urging the redefinition of rape. Most surprising for a social scientist, Gilbert assumes a perspective sharply at variance with current cognitive theory in insisting on a pure prototype definition of rape (cf. Rosch 1973) as involving a stranger, violence, a weapon, and so on. But it is emblematic of human cognitive ability to move from prototype to fuzzy cases. This Gilbert cannot do—at least not here. And yet he identifies *his* understanding as consonant with "*human* attitudes and emotions," which in turn are opposed to those of "radical feminists," who are by this definition removed from membership in humanity, and thus stripped of the capacity to make definitions.

Or take Camille Paglia (1990), who (in the sexual persona of a feminist) excoriates "feminists" as sex-haters because they have the temerity to criticize certain aspects of male sexual expression. Like Gilbert's, her argument hangs on a serious logical error: in her case, the exclusion of the middle. The implication is that either you believe (like Freud—for Paglia an epitome of modern science) that all sex is fun sex and good sex (as even Freud did not), or you are a fuddy-duddy killjoy. And even those of us who are comfortable with being bitches quiver at being called old-fashioned or not sexy.

Hillary Rodham Clinton has been the focus of the same kind of hysteria, from the same circles. She has been subject to media and public attention, often in the form of gross insults, to a degree unsurpassed by any other first lady except Eleanor Roosevelt. It is interesting that in both cases, many of the insults have a sexual coloration. In the case of Roosevelt, they involved imputations of lesbianism; with Rodham Clinton, the insults take the form of jokes involving the performance of cunnilingus. This should not be surprising: A favorite way of discrediting women who attempt to have public influence is by sexualizing their activity and thereby rendering them both safe (because they are then seen as servicing men rather than threatening them) and unworthy of being taken seriously (because they are bad women). Additionally, Rodham Clinton has been the subject of interminable critique, back-and-forth shifts in opinion based on very little.

Perhaps the most surprising amount of negative attention that has been lavished on Rodham Clinton has concerned her original decision, when she married, to retain her birth name.[9] It was widely suggested that Bill Clinton's loss of the Arkansas gubernatorial election in 1980 was the result of that decision.

> For her use of the name Rodham, she had been viewed in some circles in Arkansas as alien, and even subversive. One friend recalled standing next to her at a reception at the Rose firm in the late seventies, and seeing a man approach her, jab angrily at the nametag pinned to her blouse, and fairly spit out, "That's not your name!" (Bruck 1994:64)

This is, or should be, an astonishing tale. What's in a name, after all? How can a personal choice be "alien" or "subversive"? What goaded the stranger at the reception to such a state of anger that he was able to transgress normal social boundaries? On reflection, however, it all makes perfect sense. In choosing her name, Rodham Clinton was explicitly co-opting the right to name herself—to choose her own identity; it was not the name per se that was profoundly threatening; it was her insistence on herself as autonomous. She was assuming an active role in making her meaning, establishing her identity, and (in Arkansas in 1980) that was, indeed, "subversive."

Over the past year, as stories about Whitewater and Rodham Clinton's dealings in commodities futures have come to light, there have been repeated media suggestions that the end of her "honeymoon" is at hand, that her prior favorable press is over. What is odd about these assessments is that the "honeymoon" itself was of very short duration, and often ambivalent (there was always carping about her hairbands and stockings). She enjoyed a brief respite upon the presentation of her health-care proposal, but when that, too, was reevaluated, its problems in Congress were laid on Rodham Clinton's head.

From the beginning of her husband's candidacy, Rodham Clinton has continually taken an active part in redefining her persona and the role of the first lady. She experiments with her appearance: changing eyeglasses for contacts early on; lightening and straightening her hair; changing her hairstyle; altering her style of dress. One might criticize this constant remaking as wasting time or even pandering. But I think that, like most of Rodham Clinton's carefully considered actions, it communicates more than is superficially apparent. In making changes, she retains control of her appearance. She is not at the mercy of others' eyes or the camera's lens; she constructs herself as she prefers to be seen.

What is most significant is that Rodham Clinton has shifted the role of the first lady from passive object of voyeurism to active speaker and maker of meaning. She is not so much a photo opportunity as a policy maker. Her position and authority are such that when she speaks she must be heard and responded to as a genuine participant rather than condescended to or ignored. It is still a continuing struggle. After her highly professional presentation of the health-care proposal to Congress, one midwestern senator rose and delivered a lethal compliment: "Your competence just shines out!" Imagine that statement addressed to a man, and it becomes clear that problems still exist in the area of equal perception under law.

All the foregoing suggest another reason for the continuing media problems of both Clintons. They are widely perceived as having exchanged gender stereotypes. The culture feels most comfortable when women are the ones who are warm, interactively responsive, and humanly intuitive. Men, on the other hand, are supposed to be concerned with external business, with pure logic, with strategy. But the Clintons do the opposite. Bill appears to be the one who is warm and charismatic—but a tad fuzzy (his White House is rumored to be in a state of chaos); Hillary, on the other hand, is cool and distant but organized and thorough, her eye ever on the future and the strategy needed to create it. The first couple are (we feel) supposed to be just like us, only better. The trouble with the Clintons is that they are not just like us; or rather, that they are just like lots of us, but we aren't quite prepared to confront that realization, and we blame them for forcing it upon us.

Rodham Clinton's restructuring of her role remains shocking and threatening. Attempts continue to be made to relegate her unobtrusively to properly passive first-ladyhood. One way to accomplish this agenda is to re-objectify the target, to make Rodham Clinton back into a manipulable "it," one who is seen and not heard. Another is to reimpose a stereotypical definition of women, judging Rodham Clinton by how well she conforms to those stereotypical feminine expectations. One example is found in a *Newsweek* story whose headline covers two pages: *SAINT OR SINNER?* The subhead goes into more detail: *Hillary: She wasn't all that greedy in Little Rock. But her pose as selfless public servant set her up for a fall* (Clift & Miller 1994:24).

The headline presents Rodham Clinton as one or the other of two polar opposites and human impossibilities. The dichotomy is one to which women have always been assigned: madonna or whore. Because she isn't a saint (or a madonna), she must be a sinner. The dichotomy forces the reader to see her not as a human being but as a symbol—that is, as an interpreted object. Although Bill Clinton is seen as flawed (chaotic, sexually profligate), he is also allowed good qualities: empathy and passion. The article concerns Rodham Clinton's trading in commodities futures, a story given a lot of press for a one-shot deal fifteen years ago. The subhead seems sympathetic: she wasn't "all that greedy." But because the phrase presupposes that she was greedy to *some* extent, and greed is one of the Seven Deadly Sins, Rodham Clinton necessarily forfeits the "saint" categorization. Then there is her "pose," suggesting another sin, hypocrisy. (If she isn't a full-fledged "saint," she must be an all-out "sinner"; ergo, any appearance of virtue at all must be a "pose.") It is not clear what private investment has to do with public servanthood, selfless or not, but the subhead inextricably links the two: if a woman acts in any way for her own profit, she cannot be in any way self-sacrificing. And finally, the moral of the tale: a woman who behaves this way is a "sinner." Of course, we know what happens to sinners: they "fall," and we know where they end up. In thus cloaking their reportage in the figurative language of Christianity (*saint, sinner, fall*), the authors gain for their subliminal message all the cultural and emotional baggage of religion, reminding us in passing of the cause of the original Fall, a "greedy" woman, which in turn reminds us of the ancient justification for woman's proper subordinate role. The hermeneutics of an authoritative system are thrown into competition with Rodham Clinton's efforts at self-definition.

The consequences of Rodham Clinton's restructuring of her role are striking when she is compared to her counterpart, another Democratic first lady. Jacqueline Kennedy Onassis died in the spring of 1994. Richard Nixon died a week or two earlier. The amount of media attention devoted to retrospectives and funerals was approximately identical. Whatever one thinks of Nixon, he was a figure of significance throughout the late twentieth century; the attention was justified. But Onassis's role as a shaper of history or culture was minimal. Why then was she accorded equal attention? And why did that attention take the form it did?

Typically, the answers are overdetermined. For one thing, to those producing the retrospectives as well as to many readers and viewers, Onassis's death represented the end of their youth. Then too, Onassis had been since the death of John F. Kennedy a determinedly private figure. She refused interviews and avoided being photographed. Dead, she could no longer refuse, and our appetites, starved so long, were sated on the glut of publicity suddenly available.

But that cannot explain it all, nor can it explain the attention lavished on certain details. What was stressed above all was her traditional womanliness and first-ladyhood. "She never took a bad picture," in one commentator's words. Again and again her looks were stressed: her poise, fashionableness, photogenicity. The eulogists were at a loss for memorable quotations, or indeed, any quotations at all. Jackie had been a woman seen but not heard—the ideal. When she spoke at all, it was in a whisper. "Her voice was ever soft / Gentle and low, an excellent thing in woman," as Lear says of Cordelia. As a result, Onassis was the diametric opposite of Rodham Clinton, her silence an offer to be interpreted, her person available to be made into someone else's photographic image. A traditional woman, she achieved the image she desired not by actively representing herself as she wished to be but by a hyperalertness to the presence of the interpreting camera. She never took a bad picture because she could and would match the needs of the camera's lens. She was what was reflected in the eye of the beholder.

Lorena Bobbitt (and Aurelia Macias, the "Dark Side")

It would be unsatisfying to write about women's struggle for interpretive control without an examination of the story of Lorena Bobbitt, who cut off her husband's penis as he lay asleep in bed after (allegedly) raping her. Both were tried: he for spousal sexual assault, she for malicious wounding. He was acquitted (almost all the corroborative evidence in support of her allegation was disallowed by the trial court); she was acquitted on grounds of temporary insanity and spent a few weeks undergoing observation at a mental hospital. Conservatives grumbled that Lorena Bobbitt's verdict allowed her to "get off" by means of an "abuse excuse." But it is really the only verdict that could allow the jury to do one of its extralegal jobs: to function as a Greek chorus, a definer and reinforcer of community morals and values. An acquittal would have "sent the message" that Bobbitt's action was both legal and moral, which would have been clearly intolerable to the status quo. A guilty verdict would have implied, at least, that the act was rational, if not legal; that we the people (whom the jury represents) understand even if we do not quite condone. But the verdict of temporary insanity sent the most comforting (and conservative) message: such an act is crazy, without justification. The verdict was widely condemned in the media as giving aid and comfort to feminism, but in fact it does no such thing.

The case as a whole was widely seen by conservatives in particular and men in general as one of vast and terrifying import. Lorena Bobbitt was frequently represented in the writings of pundits like Rush Limbaugh as a "feminist" whose actions were applauded by her sister "feminazis." If, it was suggested, John Wayne Bobbitt should be convicted and/or she acquitted, it would "send a message" to wives everywhere that they could cut off their husbands' penises with impunity. That, it was implied, was what "they" really wanted to do all along: castrate "us." This was a case about whether the feminazis could perform castration on demand.

In fact, there was not a scintilla of evidence that Lorena Bobbitt was sympathetic to feminism (or had even heard of it) prior to her arrest, much less that the act itself was intended by its perpetrator to be in any way symbolic. She cut it off because it irritated her. By so doing she did not "castrate" him; castration is the removal of the testicles, not the penis (pace Freud, who made, and made much of, the same error). That makes the attention given to the act, and its interpretation, all the more mysterious. In a logical universe, the removal by a private citizen of a body part of another private citizen, while deplorable, would merit little attention. So the Bobbitt case passes the Undue Attention Test.

There is a "dark side" here as well. Not long after Lorena Bobbitt perpetrated her deed, another woman, Aurelia Macias, also the victim of sexual assault by her husband, amputated her husband's testicles with cuticle scissors. Despite the similarity of the actions (and the fact that Macias, unlike Bobbitt, literally castrated her husband), the case received very little attention. Why?

A clue to the mystery is provided by the theory espoused by the French psychoanalytic deconstructionist Jacques Lacan, which equates the possession of a phallus with language-using capacity. Woman, in this interpretation, is silent by nature, because she lacks the organ of speech, and (as Lacan's master put it) "anatomy is destiny."

Then John Bobbitt's crime was that he *talked out of turn* and Lorena *silenced* him by removing his *capacity for speech*. I am not asserting that Lorena Bobbitt is a deconstructionist, but we can understand her act as an attempt to achieve speech through silencing the one responsible for her prior silence: another nail in the coffin of unilateral male control of meaning (even as we grant that Bobbitt herself meant no such thing). Then it becomes clear why the act inspired such a violent and passionate reaction. Bobbitt's act can be (and I believe has been) viewed as the concrete instantiation of that which those traditionally empowered to speak fear the most: women's usurpation of the unilateral right to make meaning. Because Aurelia Macias didn't amputate the symbolic organ of speech, her act, which was equally, and literally, emasculating, was not of nearly as much general communicative interest.

Tonya Harding (and Nancy Kerrigan, the "Dark Side")

A couple of months before the 1994 Winter Olympics, ice skater Nancy Kerrigan was struck on the leg with a steel baton. She recovered, but meanwhile the American public was fixated on the event and its aftermath for a solid month. Suspicion for the attack quickly fell on the entourage of a rival, Tonya Harding. Harding's on-again, off-again husband and her bodyguard were charged with hiring the hit man. The only questions that remained were, What did Harding know, and when did she know it?

Universally, the media made sense of the story by creating a meta-mythic structure within which the story of Harding and Kerrigan worked as a morality play. For full dramatic impact, the rivals were dichotomized and thus made symbolic: Kerrigan as the good woman, Harding the bad. Kerrigan's expected victory (she was favored in the Olympics and eventually won the silver medal, while Harding did very poorly) was therefore in the script, as the moral: good women win, bad girls lose. To point the moral, actual differences between the two, however minor, were given disproportionate weight.

Kerrigan was represented as beautiful, pure, and lovable, Harding as ugly, promiscuous, and menacing. Kerrigan was the Ice Princess, Harding the Troll. The families of both were working-class, but Kerrigan's was depicted as Poor But Honest, Harding's as Trash. Kerrigan's parents were monogamous and devoted to their daughter's well-being; the family lovingly supported Kerrigan's mother, who was almost blind. Kerrigan herself was virginal; she was photographed in white satin costumes with minimal decolletage (they tended to plunge virtuously in the back). She had never been married or, as far as anyone knew, anything but virginal. On the ice she was "graceful," her figure "elegant," befitting the only Olympic event for "ladies" rather than women.

Harding was the opposite—badder than bad. Her parents' marital relationships were complicated, though less so than her own. She was currently separated from her marginally criminal husband, but they continued to live together. No one suggested that she was then or had ever been a virgin. Her hobbies included the unladylike sport of bowling, and she liked to fix cars. She drove a *truck*. Her hair, unlike Kerrigan's, had a mind of its own, being stiff and disobedient. She wore too much of the wrong kind of makeup. She wouldn't smile on cue. Her photographs showed her in a blue satin dress seemingly cut away in front clear to the pubis, although on closer inspection one could see that the gap was filled with flesh-colored mesh. That only made it worse—she was what we used to call a "tease." Perhaps worst of all, she was the wrong candidate for the *ladies'* figure-skating title. Her figure was stubby, her skating style "athletic" (curiously for an Olympic event, this is not an unqualified term of praise). True, of the two, only she could do the triple axel, but in context that was not an unequivocal Good Thing.

Under these terms, Kerrigan had to win. That preconception was bad not only for Harding but for the media, which needed to set up suspense to get attention. Harding, with media help, proceeded to restructure the metamyth—that is, to change the metadiscourse and thus alter the meaning of events.

Ingeniously using interviews and photo ops, Harding worked doggedly to change the characters and thereby the metamyth itself, from Ice Princess versus Troll to Self-Made Horatio Alger Heroine versus Bonbon-Eating Lady. Now Harding began to be portrayed as the plucky girl making her way from rags to riches against all odds, who picked up bottles by the road to pay for skating lessons, who sewed her own skating costumes, who overcame maternal discouragement and abuse. Kerrigan, by comparison, had it given to her on a silver platter. Her niceness was recast as passivity, which in this mythic structure was un-American. So Harding had to win—she was the one with "spunk." Her previous negatives turned positive, and public sympathy began to shift. (It has been suggested that women began to root for Harding, while men stayed with Kerrigan, but I have seen no quantitative corroboration of this claim.)

Because ultimately she lost, and behaved badly while doing so, Harding's reconstruction failed. But it is significant that she made the attempt to change the meaning of the discourse and succeeded at least temporarily.

Nicole Brown Simpson

At this writing, about two weeks after the murder of Nicole Simpson and Ronald Goldman, O. J. Simpson is in custody as the only suspect. What is interesting for this discussion is the abrupt shift in the perception of events from O. J.'s "tragedy" to Nicole's. For the first several days after the killing, media discussion focused on him: his status as football star, all-American hero, film and television celebrity; then as possible murderer and fugitive from justice. All that first week attention was focused on *his* state of mind: how he learned of the murder, whether he did it, why he did it (if he did it), what his defense would consist of. On Saturday one female commentator remarked on the lack of attention to the victims. At just about that time, O. J. Simpson's history of wife-beating came into focus.[10]

Since then events have taken an unprecedented turn. The commentary has shifted strongly to Nicole Simpson's point of view and from there to a general female perspective: the prevalence and menace of spousal abuse. The subject has been treated on virtually every news program, talk show, and magazine show, as well as on the radio and in print. Amazingly too, domestic violence is being seen for the first time unambiguously from the battered woman's perspective. In the past, when the media have dealt with the issue, they have tended to try to be, as they put it, "fair," by giving equal time to representatives of men's advocacy groups, who argue (1) that the battery of husbands by wives is as prevalent and serious as the reverse; (2) that women provoke their battery, and are as much at fault as the batterers, if not more; (3) that women who are battered "ask for it" and really like it, and if they didn't they would just leave. Remarkably, with all the attention lavished on the issue over the past couple of weeks, these arguments have scarcely been heard at all—an astonishing reorganization of perspective.

Nicole Simpson herself was of course in no position to be the deliberate creator of the new perspective. But for perhaps the first time, the female victim's viewpoint was not only seen as worthy of prolonged, serious attention, but was further generalized to force the general public to see certain forms of behavior as formerly only women, and feminists at that, had done. The male perspective on wife-beating, crime, and sports heroes assumed a secondary status.

The existence of all these cases and the extraordinary interest focused on all of them say several things. They show the culture at a nodal moment, when it may go forward or back but can never really revert to the pre-Hill situation. Male discourse control has been wrested from the realm of presupposition and "normality," allowing it to be seen as only one possible choice and to be commented upon as an aberration. The passions generated by all these events make perfect sense seen in this light: we are enmeshed in the most serious cultural revolution of all time, and the stakes are very high.

Psychotherapists, particularly those who do what is sometimes called paradoxical therapy, know that forcing symptoms and repressed feelings into consciousness and conscious control changes their meanings: they can no longer function as keepers of conspiratorial silence. In the same way, bringing old patterns of discourse control into the light of day does not by itself make them vanish, but it does mean that they can no longer remain invisible as background and norm. There will be backlash, attempts to take back unilateral meaning, by men and by women who have adjusted a little too well to the nonresponsible status enjoyed by those who do not contribute to the making of meaning. But as the saying goes, once you open a can of worms, the only way to recan them is to use a larger can. The old Chinese curse has fallen upon us: we live in interesting times.

Postscript

As I review this chapter at the end of February 1995 prior to its imminent publication, I feel compelled to take the opportunity to assess my thinking at the time I first submitted the chapter some nine months ago. Over that period of gestation, things have changed, and not necessarily for the better.

I suggested then that the triumphs, however qualified, of Anita Hill, Hillary Rodham Clinton, and some others meant that the age-old techniques of silencing were being effectively shattered, and that they could never be employed again. I still think this is true. What is important is that the formerly presupposed and implicit has been brought to the fore; the unspoken has been made verbally manifest. But (as I also suggested), its accompaniment has been predictable resentment and backlash.

In American politics 1992 was the "Year of the Woman"; 1994 has been dubbed the "Year of the Angry White Male." Conservative Republican candidates succeeded beyond their rosiest predictions, achieving Republican majorities in the House and Senate. Antidiversity legislation of various kinds has passed (Proposition 187, against undocumented aliens) or is being contemplated and given an excellent chance of success (anti-affirmative-action propositions are on the ballot in California and other states as well as at the federal level). As a result, a number of the gains, communicative and otherwise, that seemed at least marginally secured as late as last June are once again in jeopardy.

There is some cold comfort to be taken in the bad news. I believe that the Angry White Male is less angry than frightened—scared of losing the ancient privilege (and perhaps other things that start with the same letter). One reason I think this is that anger tends to dissipate with action (such as voting in an election and achieving success), but fear hangs on until whatever inspired it is gone. Although the White Male gained his electoral objectives, he still seems unconsoled and is perhaps inconsolable. Fear suggests that its object is worth fearing, and will not be readily vanquished.

The potency of these fears helps to account for some of the discouraging words being bandied about in the public discourse. I think we should try to see all of the following as only partly a step backward; it is as much an augury of a brighter future.

The Atticization of Hillary Rodham Clinton

It was of course too much to hope for that Hillary Rodham Clinton's apparent triumph would remain uncontested. Her health-care proposal was defeated, and blame was placed largely on her for presenting a plan that was too complicated to be understood, a sign of her arrogance and incompetence. (There were, of course, plenty of other reasons that the bill was defeated.) I suspect that if her proposal had been stated in a sentence of fewer than twenty-five monosyllabic words, it would have been excoriated just as roundly.

As a result, Rodham Clinton has become a scarce presence in public. She has made virtually no public statements since the debacle last summer— only a brief comment on her husband's State of the Union message. She appears, at least at this writing, to have been relegated to the attic, where crazy and otherwise dangerous ladies must be kept.

Newtonian Mechanics, or the Heartbreak of Trench Mouth

Newt Gingrich, the new Speaker of the House of Representatives, is taking rhetorical aim at everyone who is a non-"normal" "McGovernik"—that is, everyone other than his Angry White Male constituency. In particular he has delivered himself, in his professorial mode, of some explanations of the Way It Is: why women are unsuited for combat.

Women, it seems, don't do well in warfare, because after thirty days in the trenches they develop "infections," as men do not. Medical science has not at this writing provided an explanation of Newt's explanation, which is really rather odd. Why *thirty* days, not three or forty-two? What "infections" might women get that men are immune to? All that I can conclude is that "infection" is a euphemism for the *m*-word (30 days is pretty close, and it's true that men don't experience it) that Newt dare not speak. What is extraordinary is that the Speaker has not been required to explain publicly what he means, if he does.

Simpson: The Dark Side

We left the O. J. Simpson matter just as O. J. himself was being arrested. Extraordinarily, in a culture in which the public attention span seldom exceeds the eight-second sound bite, interest in the matter has not flagged. Now that the trial itself is under way, reports of the day's events in the courtroom occupy a minimum of five minutes on both the local and national evening news programs, and generally even longer segments on the syndicated tabloid shows.

Interestingly for our purposes, the chief prosecutor, Marcia Clark, is a woman. As a prosecuting attorney must be, she is sharp and aggressive (not that the army of defense attorneys are shrinking violets). And predictably as well as annoyingly, attention has focused on Clark *as a woman* rather than a prosecutor. Clark is regularly called a "bitch" by male courtroom observers for doing what her defense opponents do without attracting notice. It has been noted in the press that Judge Lance Ito sometimes reprimands Clark for behavior that he tolerates or even enjoys from the defense's lead attorney, Johnnie Cochran. There have also been discussions and metadiscussions of Clark's appearance: are her skirts too short, is her hair too curly, her red suit too red? There are suspicions that the jury won't like it. All this reminds us of Tannen's (1994) discussion of women's dress as "marked," that is, worthy of comment no matter what. What is most disturbing, of course, about the markedness of female dress is that the attention paid to it deflects interest in what the woman is actually saying or doing. So it functions as another form of silencing.

Reappropriation of the Right to Make Language

Not surprisingly, supporters of the status quo are trying to reclaim the rhetorical moral high ground, and with it the right to decide what words mean and who can use them. One such struggle currently under way revolves around the use of the word *victim.* Who can be one? Who can call who one?

Members of traditionally disempowered groups, on finding themselves having public voices, have tended to describe their experiences as forms of "victimization." This seems, at least for many of these experiences, a perfectly reasonable description. According to the *American Heritage Dictionary*, a "victim" is "one who is harmed or killed by another." That certainly covers such cases as rape, spousal abuse, sexual harassment, and discrimination, in all of which the historically more powerful party uses his historically legitimized greater power (whether physical, psychological, social, or communicative) to enforce that power discrepancy by harming a less powerful person, thereby "sending a message" that the historical discrepancy had better not be questioned or mitigated ... OR ELSE. But the word *victim* has, of course, a negative side to it, casting its referent as helpless and dependent—as we modern women do not wish to see ourselves. That negative sense provides an opening wedge for opponents of equality. Women, it is suggested, must see themselves as *either* fully autonomous, empowered, and in control *or* as pitiful, helpless "victims." Given that choice, even rational and feminist women may quiver. But the choice itself is deceptive.

It's quite possible to be "victimized" under one or more particular circumstances, victimized by the use of a historical power imbalance, and yet fight that victimization, neither helpless nor hapless. As is normally the case with human possibilities, dichotomy creates false simplifications and misdefinitions. We must realize that we—and others in similar circumstances—can be in the position of working against the grain, going against stereotype and suffering the attendant prejudice and ridicule; but we also know that we don't have to accept this ridicule passively like literal "victims," that is, like human sacrifices. To suggest that the only alternatives are utter denial that inequality exists, or total passivity, is of course attractive to those who would reimpose the silence, and there has been no dearth of talk to that effect.

Perhaps the most shocking attempt to stigmatize victimization was in an article by *New Yorker* dance critic Arlene Croce (December 26, 1994/January 2, 1995). In it Croce assails Bill T. Jones, a choreographer whose most recent work includes commentary on his HIV-positive state. Croce announces that she did not attend the performance of that work ("Still/There") and had no intention of so doing, but felt competent to review it scathingly as an example (along for instance with *Schindler's List*) of a regrettable Cult of Victimization.

Curiously, though, as conservatives like Croce decry the tendency of the historically oppressed to claim victim status, they themselves (and particularly the Angry White Males) have been quick to assert their own victimization. *They* are the ones who cannot speak for fear of the "p.c. police." It is *they* who don't get into college and don't get jobs because of affirmative action. An article in the *New York Times* "Week in Review" section of February 26, 1995, "Now Look Who's Taunting. Now Look Who's Suing," by Jane Gross, discusses a recent rash of sexual-discrimination and harassment lawsuits by men against female superiors. What is missing in this article and others like it is any recognition that men's sexual comments to women, and women's to men, however identical they may appear to superficial inspection, in fact have different meaning because of men's greater physical and political power. The men, of course, see themselves as "victims" in these cases, and to my knowledge no conservative critic has reproached them for this perspective.

Another way in which women's recovery of the right to make meaning is being sabotaged is in the insistence of antifeminist groups that they are "victimized" as much by women as vice versa. I have heard several discussions in the media recently in which so-called pro-life activists have asserted that pro-choice demonstrators harass them as much as the reverse (curiously, though, only pro-choice advocates seem to get killed as a result). Similarly, men's rights groups have taken to arguing vociferously (in part a response to the interest aroused by the Simpson case, discussed above) that men are "abused" by their significant others as much as the reverse. Statistics are frequently cited to support this claim.

It seems to prove the old adage: there are lies, damn lies, and statistics. It turns out that these "statistics" of male abuse, hard and numerical as they are, were gathered by dubious means. When men are identified in police reports as abusers (that is, when women have been sufficiently battered for the police to take an interest), they are frequently questioned later and asked the leading question of whether they were also abused by their partner. Given the opportunity, they are often happy to report that in fact they were (although they seldom report serious, or even noticeable, injuries). Usually the "quid" for which the beating or killing was the "quo" turns out to have been speech, or shoving or slapping. Yet these reports are becoming part of the "truth" about spousal abuse that is reported in the media.

So language is not taken back without a fight—not a surprising conclusion.

Conclusion: The New Rhetoric

Scholarship on language and gender, like any vigorously flourishing field, has changed its emphases over the past twenty years, in part because we solved some of our problems or at least came to understand them better, and in part because it is exciting to focus on a new perspective.

Early on, the emphasis was on words themselves, often studied out of context. We were concerned with pronouns and titles, historical and synchronic semantic derogation, disparities between words used to describe female and male activities. The emphasis was useful: the disparities served as a clear and convincing diagnostic, showing that real differences existed in our attitudes toward women and men.

By the late seventies, a good part of our focus had shifted to conversational strategies, interpersonal communication as a battlefield on which sexual power imbalance was created and reinforced through nonparallel use of interruption and topic choice. Again, this focus was valuable in showing that some of our age-old stereotypes ("women talk too much") are incorrect, and that some of our age-old suspicions (women never get to finish a sentence) are correct.

From there, interest now seems to be moving to the broader sphere of public discourse: language in the workplace, language in politics, and how gender informs these. As always, we strive to present a reasonably objective and descriptivist perspective, in keeping with our scholarly identification.

That is very well, yet perhaps it should not be the be-all and end-all of the study of the interface of gender and public discourse. But at the same time, our conversations with one another in formats like this are not totally satisfying. They begin to resemble preaching to the converted. We all agree that women have special problems presenting their case in the current political and rhetorical climate, and we can marshal no end of footnoted references to prove that claim. But measured descriptivity may no longer be sufficient. It may be time to do some work, within the confines of scholarly discourse or not, on converting the yet unconverted. We must develop a new, persuasive rhetoric.

It has often been noted with frustration that the majority of women do not identify themselves as feminists (although many of these women seem to approve of many of the items on the feminist agenda). We cannot create a new public discourse in which women may participate as full equals until a majority of women (at least) are part of the feminist discussion. But we have not yet developed a means to persuade them.

It puzzles me that conservative rhetoric seems increasingly exclusionary and selfish, yet it appears to have great motive power: it grabs the hearer. But liberal (including feminist) rhetoric is ineffectual. It often sounds preachy, long-winded, or scattered. One interpretation is that hearers are deeply selfish and believe the conservative message because that's what they want to hear. Perhaps, but I hope not. We have to try to provide an equally exhilarating alternative.

We have begun, however tentatively, to break the silence of the millennia. The next step is to learn to speak so that our words can have some effect.

Notes

1. This paper incorporates some of the material of Lakoff (1992).
2. Cf. the issue of *Discourse and Society* (2(2), 1991) devoted to the topic of silence.

3. For some discussion of the relationship between power and interpretability in psychoanalysis, see Lakoff (1990), chap. 4.

4. It is useful to distinguish between *minimal response*—e.g., a grunt, *uh-huh*, or even eye contact—and *nonresponse*, in which there is not even the slightest acknowledgment that an utterance has occurred.

5. For discussion of this and other ways in which girls and women are disadvantaged in educational settings, see American Association of University Women (1992).

6. For discussion of the forms and functions of male-to-female nonresponse in electronic discourse, see Susan Herring, Deborah Johnson, and Tamra DiBenedetto (this volume).

7. An illustration of "cutting"—or, rather, the avoidance of it—can be found in this excerpt from *Through the Looking-Glass*, by Lewis Carroll (chap. 9):

    "You look a little shy: let me introduce you to that leg of mutton," said the Red Queen. "Alice—Mutton: Mutton—Alice." The leg of mutton got up in the dish and made a little bow to Alice; and Alice returned the bow, not knowing whether to be frightened or amused.

    "May I give you a slice?" she said, taking up the knife and fork, and looking from one Queen to the other.

    "Certainly not!" the Red Queen said, very decidedly: "it isn't etiquette to cut any one you've been introduced to. Remove the joint!"

8. One can see the whole discussion of political correctness as precisely to that point: whether those who have always had, by virtue of the power society vests in them, the right to make language should maintain that right, or whether it can be explicitly appropriated by those who have not previously enjoyed it as a means to equalizing power.

9. Interestingly, the same decision on the part of Paula Corbin Jones seems to have gone without media notice.

10. The number of euphemisms for this behavior is remarkable: *spousal abuse, wife-battering, spousal assault, domestic violence*. The profusion of avoidant terminology suggests the ambivalence and discomfort with which the culture views this crime (behavior that is unequivocally condemned has less need of euphemistic reference: *murder*, for example, has no euphemisms).

References

American Association of University Women (1992). *How schools shortchange girls: A study of major findings on girls and education.* Washington, DC: American Association of University Women Educational Foundation.

Bruck, Connie (1994). Profile: Hillary the pol. *New Yorker*, May 30: 58–96.

Clift, Eleanor, and Mark Miller (1994). Hillary: Saint or sinner? *Newsweek*, April 11: 24–26.

Fliess, Robert (1949). Silence and verbalization: A supplement to the theory of the analytic rule. *International Journal of Psychoanalysis* 30: 21–30.

Gilbert, Neil (1991). The phantom epidemic of sexual assault. *Public Interest,* spring: 54–65.

Herring, Susan, Deborah A. Johnson, and Tamra DiBenedetto (this volume). "This discussion is going too far!": Male resistance to female participation on the Internet.

James, Deborah, and Sandra Clarke (1993). Women, men, and interruptions: A critical review. In Deborah Tannen (ed.), *Gender and conversational interaction.* New York: Oxford University Press. 231–80.

Lakoff, Robin T. (1990). *Talking power.* New York: Basic Books.

———— (1992). The silencing of women. In Kira Hall, Mary Bucholtz, and Birch Moonwomon (eds.) *Locating power.* Berkeley: Berkeley Women and Language Group. 344–55.

Leet-Pellegrini, Helena M. (1980). Conversational dominance as a function of gender and expertise. In Howard Giles, W. Peter Robinson, and Philip M. Smith (eds.), *Language: Social psychological perspectives.* Oxford: Pergamon Press. 97–104.

McAneny, Leslie (1992). One year later: Anita Hill "more credible" than Clarence Thomas. *Gallup Poll Monthly,* October: 34.

Maltz, Daniel, and Ruth Borker (1982). A cultural approach to male-female miscommunication. In John J. Gumperz (ed.), *Language and social identity.* Cambridge: Cambridge University Press. 196–216.

Mendoza-Denton, Norma (this volume). Pregnant pauses: Silence and authority in the Anita Hill–Clarence Thomas hearings.

Paglia, Camille (1990). *Sexual personae.* New Haven: Yale University Press.

Podhoretz, Norman (1991). Rape in feminist eyes. *Commentary,* October: 29–35.

Roiphe, Katie (1993). *The morning after.* Boston: Little, Brown.

Rosch, Eleanor (1973). Natural categories. *Cognitive Psychology* 4: 328–50.

Sacks, Harvey, Emanuel Schegloff, and Gail Jefferson (1974). A simplest systematics for the organization of turn taking in conversation. *Language* 50(4): 696–735.

Tannen, Deborah (1981). New York Jewish conversational style. *International Journal of the Sociology of Language* 30: 133–49.

———— (1990). *You just don't understand.* New York: Morrow.

———— (1994). *Talking from 9 to 5.* New York: Morrow.

Tannen, Deborah, and Muriel Saville-Troike (eds.) (1985). *Perspectives on silence.* Norwood, NJ: Ablex.

West, Candace, and Don Zimmerman (1983). Small insults: A study of interruptions in cross-sex conversations between unacquainted persons. In Barrie Thorne, Cheris Kramarae, and Nancy Henley (eds.), *Language, gender, and society.* Rowley, MA: Newbury House. 102–17.

Zimmerman, Don, and Candace West (1975). Sex roles, interruptions, and silences in conversations. In Barrie Thorne and Nancy Henley (eds.), *Language and sex: Difference and dominance.* Rowley, MA: Newbury House. 105–12.

2

Pregnant Pauses

Silence and Authority in the Anita Hill–Clarence Thomas Hearings

Norma Mendoza-Denton

> Cross-examination is an adversarial war of words, sequences, and ideas, a war in which the capability to finesse reality through talk represents the ultimate weapon of domination.
>
> —Gregory Matoesian
> *Reproducing Rape*

Few political events in this decade have captured the American public imagination as did the October 1991 confirmation hearings of Supreme Court Justice Clarence Thomas. The hearings brought to the fore a complex of issues of race, gender, sexuality, and power that has profoundly affected the way in which political discourse is now conducted. Before and during the hearings, women voiced a multiplicity of opinions, from indignation to rage to the conviction that the senators "just didn't get it." After the hearings, public action was added to opinion, and in 1992 a record number of female representatives was elected to public office.

In her essay "No Peace in a Sisterly Space," Julianne Malveaux (1992:143) describes feeling "hypnotic rage ... at the Senate Judiciary Committee's treatment of Anita Hill." What exactly did this treatment consist of? Was it made up solely of malicious insinuations and indignities, such as the extended discussion regarding Hill's "proclivities" or the committee's refusal to allow expert testimony on sexual harassment (Jordan 1992)? What was in the hearings that moved the coalition African American Women in Defense of

Ourselves (1992:291) to a public protest first published in the *New York Times* and later in newspapers across the United States: "As women of African descent ... [we] are particularly outraged by the racist and sexist treatment of Professor Anita Hill, an African American woman who was maligned and castigated for daring to speak publicly of her own experience of sexual abuse"? Why did so many women believe, upon watching the hearings, that Hill was being treated unfairly? Certainly, the hearings had a makeshift legal structure, a stopgap arrangement that provided time limits, testimony given and witnesses called on both sides, and preestablished turn-taking procedures. This is not to say that the hearings proceeded according to "the rules" (for there were no rules in the traditional legal sense)[1] but that even given the structure they took, and adding in the insinuation and the overt attempts to discredit testimony, still something more elusive contributed to our perception of the event and its outcome.

Part of the answer to these questions lies not only in *what* was said but in *how* it was said, in the pragmatic level beyond the semantics—a level found not in printed transcripts of the hearings but in the interactive unfolding of the television drama itself. In this chapter, I examine the hearings as a site for the reproduction of power relations, focusing on how microlevel linguistic features worked in subtle, almost hidden ways to construct a discourse that catapulted many of its listeners into a rage. I begin by orienting the discussion toward some of the premises in language and gender research, and proceed by analyzing the pragmatic features that characterize the Hill-Thomas hearings. I conclude by considering some of the consequences of such linguistic patterns, both for the hearings and for the field of language and gender studies.

Language and Gender: Beyond Essentialism

Twenty years ago Candace West and Donald Zimmerman (1975) began the study of what has proved to be an enduring puzzle. In their analysis of conversational interaction in same-sex and mixed-sex dyads, they found a gender difference in a particular linguistic domain: interruptions. After observing that the men in their study interrupted women much more often than they interrupted other men, and more often than women interrupted either women or men, West and Zimmerman attributed the gender imbalance to men's greater likelihood to exert dominance and power in conversations. In another equally influential study, Pamela Fishman (1978) tape-recorded the conversations of couples living together and found that topics of conversation introduced by men were successfully launched 96 percent of the time, and women's topics succeeded only 36 percent of the time. These studies and others set the groundwork for theoretical discussions of conversational variables and strategies in terms of men's exerting dominance and control, and women's either doing the interactional housework,[2] as it were, or exercising resistance.

More recently, however, the easy unitary relationship between a linguistic form and its social meaning has been dismantled and questioned by researchers (Eckert & McConnell-Ginet 1992a, b; Gal, this volume). Any single linguistic feature may carry different and contradictory social meanings across cultures and even within the same culture. Deborah Cameron (1992:55) stresses the importance of recognizing that many linguistic practices cannot be reduced to tautological statements of the following form: "If a woman does more or less of linguistic feature x, it must mean that [the feature] denotes powerlessness because women are powerless in the social discourse." Such an assertion, Cameron argues, is simply the *post-facto* interpretation of data based on what we know about power relationships between the sexes.

Deborah James and Sandra Clarke's (1993) comparison of various researchers' findings in the domain of interruptions reveals that only seldom are results consistent from one study to the next. One conversational analyst may find that men interrupt more than women; a second may find no gender difference; and a third may find that women interrupt more than men. This observation calls for two related responses, both of which are clearly articulated by Penelope Eckert and Sally McConnell-Ginet (this volume). The first is an invitation to look beyond the generalizations that large-scale abstractions such as "female" and "male" force upon us as researchers. If we essentialize all women into one category, we ignore the many axes (African American, Latina, European American, Californian, Jewish) along which particular women structure their identity. The diversity of influences affecting the dynamics of any single conversation necessarily sets up for failure any comparison of these different studies, particularly because each study works with subjects from different ethnic groups, age populations, and geographical backgrounds who have only their gender in common. Second, we should study language behavior within contextualized, situated settings, conducting microlevel analyses alongside large-scale statistical studies. By doing so, we will better understand the different functions and meanings of a particular interruption, as well as the ways in which that interruption might fit into the dynamics of a contextualized interaction. In this chapter I pursue both of these approaches, observing how the Hill-Thomas hearings were conducted in the intersection of language, gender, and African American issues.

The Study

The senators who conducted the Anita Hill–Clarence Thomas hearings displayed a variety of linguistic strategies that provided a framework within which the literal words of the hearings must be interpreted. Through their rapid-fire interrogation style reminiscent of cross-examination, the employment of questions embedded with unwarranted presuppositions, topic shifts, and the avoidance of verbal acknowledgment, the senators placed Hill in a discursive situation very different from that of Thomas. Thomas's discourse setting was characterized by numerous and lengthy expressions of support and sympathy from the senators, questions that were answerable with a simple "Yes, Senator" or "No, Senator," and weighty, respectful silences following his hyperbolic turns of phrase. The strategies were both conscious (as in rapid-fire interrogation and questions with embedded presuppositions) and below the level of consciousness (as in the differing length of silences given after Hill's versus Thomas's statements).[3] I argue that it is not any one of these strategies alone that created a hostile environment for Hill but, instead, the aggregate, along with the sociopolitical context of the accusations, that served to undermine her testimony. The variables that I have chosen to analyze, and that are explained in greater detail below, are gap length, simple yes/no questions versus tag questions, concise answers, changes of topic, and acknowledgments.

Gap Length

Also known as *wait-time* in the legal literature, *gap length* is the natural complement to interruption. If interruption consists of measurable overlap in the speech of two speakers, and if the fact of interruption might say something, *ceteris paribus*, about the relationship of the speakers in question (regardless of how we choose to characterize this relationship), then gap length, or the measurable silence between the speech of two speakers, is equally worthy of study.

I propose that gap length may reflect important power dimensions within a discourse; it may be used in different ways to legitimize, acknowledge, support, or cast doubt on the statements of the previous speaker. A controlled study of gap length should expose otherwise unnoticed interlocutor attitudes toward different speakers, revealing a more subtle microlevel enactment of power relations. For the purposes of this study, I examined the gap instances that followed statements made by Hill or Thomas and preceded senatorial comments or questions, comparing the length of the silences occurring after Hill's statements with those occurring after Thomas's statements.

(a) \<Statement by Hill> \<Gap> \<Statement by senator>
(b) \<Statement by Thomas> \<Gap> \<Statement by senator>

Speech excerpts conforming to the patterns in (a) and (b), above, were chosen for analysis on the basis of their well-formedness within the legal discourse structure. Because this structure is rigid and has established turn-taking procedures, I did not consider gaps caused by confusion over documents or turn-taking, choosing only those gaps that followed one another within continuous streams of exchange. The total sample size was forty-nine gaps for Hill and forty-six gaps for Thomas. After the excerpts were recorded in computerized digital form, a phonetic analysis software package called Xwaves was used to measure the gap lengths given to each subject.

The results of the analysis revealed a statistically significant difference (at $p < 0.05$ on a 1-tailed t-test) between the mean gap length following Hill's statements (1.046 seconds) and the mean gap length following Thomas's statements (1.386 seconds). This difference can be explained only with reference to the power dynamics that characterized the discourse. The senators employed a number of silencing strategies that served to validate Thomas's statements and weaken Hill's. Most notably, they employed longer gaps after many of Thomas's dramatic, indignant statements in order to underscore the import of his words and allow the weight of his responses to "sink in" with the audience, and they employed shorter gaps after many of Hill's statements so as to obscure her answers, firing rapid questions in succession and giving her little time to think. In addition, the senators frequently employed a short gap followed by a change of topic after answers that were problematic for their case, thereby shifting the focus of the discussion.

Simple Yes/No Questions versus Tag Questions

There are two types of yes/no questions in English: *simple yes/no questions* and *tag questions*. Simple yes/no questions, such as the question asked of Thomas in (c), below, generally carry vacuous presuppositions. Tag questions,[4] in contrast, consist of a statement followed by a question, and as such, can be a powerful way of introducing assumptions. In the question asked of Hill in (d), for instance, the tag *did he?* carries a question force that serves to modify the assertoric force of the declarative clause.

(c)   Did you say these things to Professor Hill?
      Presupposition: Either you did say these things to Professor Hill or you didn't.

(d)   In fact, he did not ask you to have sex with him, did he?
      Presupposition: He did not ask you to have sex with him.

In the first example the epistemological status of the claim is not predetermined; in the second, the presupposition introduced by the statement *he did not ask you to have sex with him* is salient. For the purposes of this study, I compared the number of simple yes/no questions and tag questions directed at Hill with the number of those directed at Thomas.

The analysis revealed that Thomas was asked significantly more simple yes/no questions than Hill (53 percent versus 37 percent of the total questions asked); in contrast, Hill encountered more tag questions than Thomas (27 percent versus 17 percent of the total questions asked). The discrepancy between the ways in which Thomas and Hill were asked questions may have ultimately given the impression that Hill struggled with her testimony and that Thomas performed with ease. The proliferation of simple yes/no questions in Thomas's session made for a relatively smooth testimony; the proliferation of tag questions in Hill's session often led to disjointed responses because many of them contained presuppositions with which she disagreed. Consider the following example, an exchange between Arlen Specter (R-Pa.) and Hill:

> Specter: Professor Hill, you testified that you drew an inference that Judge Thomas might want you to look at pornographic films, but you told the FBI specifically that he never asked you to watch the films, *is that correct?*
>
> Hill: He never said, "Let's go to my apartment and watch films or go to my house and watch films." He did say, "You ought to see this material."
>
> Specter: But when you testify that, as I wrote it down, "We ought to look at pornographic movies together," that was an expression of what was on your mind—
>
> Hill: That was the inference that I drew, yes, with his pressing me for social engagements, yes.
>
> Specter: That's something he might have wanted you to do but the fact is flatly, he never asked you to look at pornographic movies with him.
>
> Hill: With him? No, he did not.

The example illustrates the import of a tag question and the presuppositions that it may introduce. In his first turn, Specter introduces the word *inference* to cast doubt on a statement made by Hill. An inference is by definition not a fact, and Specter's suggestion that Hill presents her evidence in such a manner plays into the already existing context of many senators and journalists asserting that Hill had "fantasies"—a term deliberately used by many of the Republican senators to invoke and leave unspoken the possibility that

Hill's accusations were mere sexual fantasies. In the next turn, Hill attempts to rectify her position, clearly stating what Thomas did say and what he did not say, but Specter returns to his previous argument that Hill's inference was a product of her imagination: *But when you testify that, as I wrote it down, "We ought to look at pornographic movies together," that was an expression of what was on your mind*— Especially noticeable is the way in which Hill tries to rectify Specter's assumptions by challenging them or providing further explanation, a phenomenon I discuss below.

Concise Answers

The third variable in my study, related to the second, is whether Hill or Thomas provided concise answers to the two types of yes/no questions. In a classic trial textbook, Thomas Mauet (1988:220) points out that cross-examination is "the art of slowly making mountains out of molehills. Don't make your big points in one question. Lead up to each point with a series of short, precise questions." Gregory Matoesian (1993:172), in his analysis of rape trials, asserts that these short questions are "designed not so much for securing information but for building a series of progressive 'facts,' eliciting the defendant's agreement to those 'facts,' and assembling her answers to formulate ... [an argument]. The cumulative and progressive establishment of these facts operates as a pre-sequence: as a preliminary to some forth-coming or projected action." The following exchange between Orrin Hatch (R-Utah) and Clarence Thomas nicely exemplifies Matoesian's understanding of a "pre-sequence":

Hatch:	Did you ever say to her in words or substance something like: "There is a pubic hair in my coke"?
Thomas:	No, Senator.
Hatch:	Did you ever refer to your private parts in conversation with Professor Hill?
Thomas:	Absolutely not, Senator.
Hatch:	Did you ever brag to Professor Hill about your sexual prowess?
Thomas:	No, Senator.
Hatch:	Did you ever use the term "Long Dong Silver" in conversations with Professor Hill?
Thomas:	No, Senator.
Hatch:	Did you ever have [a] lunch with Professor Hill in which you talked about sex?
Thomas:	Absolutely not.

By *concise* answer, I mean simple confirmation or denial as with Thomas's responses above—answers that lawyers can build on and that may establish a presequence as described by Matoesian. Any answer that involved a rebuttal of the premises of the question was considered *nonconcise*. The results of the analysis revealed that Hill gave fewer concise answers than Thomas ($p < 0.05$, chi-square $= 3.882$). (See Table 2.1.)

Table 2.1. Types of Answers in Response to Yes/No Questions

Responses	Hill	Thomas
Yes/no, concise	4	13
Yes/no, nonconcise	14	12

Only 16 percent of the questions directed toward Hill elicited a short answer; 30 percent of Thomas's questions prompted some kind of simple affirmation or denial. This result can be explained if we consider that the questions directed at Thomas were formulated by the senators (most of whom are lawyers by training) in a radically different way than the questions directed at Hill. Thomas faced an environment favoring an effortless explanation (realized in the data as a concise answer) much more often than Hill did. The questions directed at Hill contained in many cases false presuppositions and incorrect factual assumptions, and this caused her to elaborate on her answers to a further extent than Thomas did. Additionally, because Hill was the person bringing forth the charges, she needed to provide much more detailed explanation in her answers so as to make her position clear, particularly on the first day of the hearings. Thomas, on the other hand, as the accused party, needed to offer nothing but denial. By asking questions of the form *did you or did you not do* x?, the senators facilitated this denial; their questions did not function as information questions but rather as leading questions that had an obvious "correct" answer. Thomas needed merely to answer concisely.

Change of Topic

This variable refers to the changes of topic initiated by the senators after the conclusion of a statement made by Hill or Thomas. A careful record of topic changes can help determine who controls the structure and nature of the information in the discourse setting. Matoesian refers to topic control as "the second face of power—setting the agenda"; he highlights the asymmetrical distribution of resources to organize topics, frame testimony, and present evidence, all of which are primarily in the hands of the prosecutor, or in this case, the senators. Senators were expected to take turns at questioning Hill and Thomas after their prepared statements were presented. They were free to guide the discussion, introduce topics, and present evidence, all of which were performed with great ceremony and with the stated purpose of "getting to the bottom of this," as summarized by Senator Heflin.

In a discourse setting where one of the overt aims is to find out as much as possible about an incident, one would expect to find a continuity of topic such that participants engage the same topic for several clauses. That is to say, interactants will choose something to talk about and continue to talk about it until they are satisfied that it has been covered in depth. Most results in the data confirm the prevalence of topic continuity, save for one: when Hill provided brief answers to yes/no questions, the topic was *always* changed ($p < 0.01$, chi-square = 9.992). (See Table 2.2.)

Table 2.2. Topic Changes in Response to Hill's Short Answers

Responses	Change of Topic	No Change of Topic
Yes/no, concise, Hill	4	0
All others combined	24	67

The senators' tendency to change the topic directly after a question that Hill answered with ease may be analyzed as a discursive strategy: the senators would topic-switch whenever it became clear that there was no further avenue for contradictions or apparent struggle in Hill's testimony. These shifts of topic may have served to discount Hill's testimony in the eyes of the public, particularly because the senators also refused to acknowledge Hill's assertions, as discussed in the following section.

Acknowledgments

I counted as an acknowledgment any response from the senators that legitimated or supported the statements made or positions taken by Hill or Thomas. Thomas's nonconcise answers were followed by an overt acknowledgment of his position 50 percent of the time. Hill, on the other hand, received no acknowledgments but, rather, a change of topic in 46 percent of the follow-up queries by senators.

This was one of the more blatantly biased aspects of the hearing. When combined with greater gap length, the overt acknowledgments and expressions of sympathy for Thomas after his nonconcise statements served to legitimate his claim. Thomas's slow pace and dramatic delivery succeeded in silencing the entire room, and the content of his arguments, replete with racial and sexual accusations toward the senators and the media, often elicited prolonged apologies and expressions of solidarity from many senators. It is in cases like this that we can forge an interpretation of otherwise puzzling differences in gap length; only by contextualizing a silence can we come closer to an understanding of its meaning. Consider the following example, in which Senator Howell Heflin (D-Ala.) is questioning Thomas. Senator Hatch goes so far as to interrupt out of turn in order to provide additional acknowledgment of Thomas's statement:

> Thomas: Senator, there is a big difference between approaching a case subjectively and watching yourself being lynched. There is <u>no comparison whatsoever</u>.
> [gap: 2.36 seconds]
> Heflin: Ah yes [sighs].
> [gap: 1.12 seconds]
> Hatch: I may add that he has personal knowledge of this as well, and personal justification ... for anger.

In this excerpt, the acknowledgment that the senators provided, combined with two very long silences, gave Thomas's well-crafted phrase added weight. In that 2.36-second span the camera had time to zoom out, give a wide-angle view of the Senate Judiciary Committee, and focus back on Heflin who was nodding gravely. Hatch's overt support of Thomas is characteristic of the positive feedback that Thomas received throughout the hearings from senators of both parties—a reception that Hill rarely experienced.

Implications

The interaction of several factors in the formation of each silent gap makes it difficult to determine the exact cause of statistically significant correlations in the data. Depending on context, silence can be seen as powerful (Bauman 1983) or disempowering (Lakoff, this volume). Western Apaches, for example, use silence to confuse European American outsiders (Basso 1979), and European American men may exert dominance in household situations through nonresponse (Fishman 1978). Susan Gal (this volume) makes the observation that in settings of institutional inequity, when one party must self-expose before another (such as in psychotherapeutic contexts), the silent observer holds all the cards.

With regard to deciphering the complexity of the silences in the Thomas confirmation hearings, there are some relevant observations to be made. Generally speaking, speech is always coconstructed so that the silences are not "owned" by any single person. It may well be that Thomas, speaking at a slower overall rate and constructing responses with long internal pauses, contributed to long gaps to some degree. This is not to say, however, that when combined with all the other linguistic characteristics of the hearings, the silences did not contribute to a public perception of Thomas as getting more television airtime and a more sympathetic ear from the senators. Thomas's statements were followed by pregnant pauses and poignant silences so often that the television cameras had time to wander around the room and focus on his wife, Virginia Thomas, nodding thoughtfully, as well as on some senators' furrowed brows and sympathetic expressions. Thomas's experience (and Hill's lack of experience) as a judge may have contributed to the relative ponderousness of his speech style, which might appropriately be referred to as *judge style* in its slow tempo, frequent rhetorical questioning, and repetition of arguments. By adopting features of a speech style perceived to be powerful, Thomas was able to subvert the position in which he was placed.

Yet this explanation alone is too simple for, as Geneva Smitherman (1995) argues, Thomas also adopted elements from the positively valued African American speech styles of *testifyin, sermonizin,* and *signifyin.* Smitherman locates Thomas's rhetorical posture squarely within the African American tradition, offering the following exchange between Thomas and Senator Heflin as an instance of signifyin.

Heflin:	We're trying to get to the bottom of this, and if she is lying, then I think you can help us prove that she was lying.
Thomas:	Senator, I am incapable of proving the negative. It did not occur.
Heflin:	Well, if it did not occur, I think you are in a position, certainly, your ability to testify to in effect to try to eliminate it from people's minds.
Thomas:	Senator, I didn't create it in people's minds. (230)

Smitherman defines *signifyin* as "the verbal art of ceremonial combativeness in which one person puts down, talks about, 'signifies on' someone or on something someone has said, ... a rhetorical modality ... characterized by indirection, humor, exploitation of the unexpected, and quick verbal repartee" (228). In the above excerpt, Thomas employs such repartee to shift the terms of the debate, exploiting unexpected implications (e.g., *I didn't create it in people's minds*) and taking the upper hand by refusing to acknowledge the very premises of Heflin's questions (*Senator, I am incapable of proving the negative. It did not occur*). By employing discourse patterns associated with both African American style and judge style, Thomas was able to appeal to the majority of popular African American opinion; at the same time he was able to retain some elements of a European American style throughout the

hearings, such as grammar and pronunciation, and make his speech acceptable to the larger audience.

In a similar way, Hill's linguistic options were influenced and constrained
by many factors, but these constraints did not work to her advantage.
African American women clearly have access to the discourse styles
outlined above, as Michèle Foster (this volume) illustrates in her study of an
African American instructor who expresses solidarity by manipulating
grammatical structures and employing figurative language, symbolism, and
gestures. Hill, however, was unable to employ these discourse styles. Why?
Because to mainstream American norms, this style is identified primarily as
male and only secondarily, if at all, as African American. Gloria Hull
(1992:96–97), for instance, characterizes Thomas's performance as "an
aggressive offensive ... high male dudgeon at its best," and apologetically
wishes "that Hill had acted less 'feminine' when confronted with the affi-
davit." But if acting like a Black woman and capitalizing on Black speech
styles is seen as masculine and verbally (and implicitly sexually) aggressive,
then the only recourse is to speak like a white woman. Witness the following
remark that appeared in *Newsweek*:

> Charming in speech and manner, backed by parents of incontestable
> respectability, Miss Hill was the very image of maidenly modesty.
> Yet the forthrightness with which she repeated to the Committee
> and to an audience of untold millions of television listeners Judge
> Thomas's dirty jokes in all their tasteless detail would have done
> credit to a truck driver. (Trilling 1994:12)

In front of European American lawmakers and national television, it was
paramount that Hill not appear to fulfill the cultural stereotype of the Black
woman as verbally and sexually aggressive. Equally important was that she
not fulfill wider female stereotypes of emotionality and hysteria. Because
half the hearings were spent on the subject of her personal credibility (read
purity), Hill was left with no choice but to adopt a dispassionate and clinical
speech style. To have testified any less dispassionately, any less clinically,
would have invoked the very stereotypes she was trying to avoid.

You can't win for losing. The dispassionate speech style that Hill adopted
was deemed highly suspicious by the African American community (Jordan
1992; Malveaux 1992; Smitherman 1995) and made her appear, in the eyes of
many Americans, insincere. Hull (1992:288) observes that "having to talk
like a woman—and a black woman—about gross sexual matters ... forced
Anita Hill into an almost 'prim and proper' self-presentation. Even more
importantly, it compelled her to subdue her emotions and behavior and

deaden her affect. Unfortunately, deadening her affect also helped kill her power." Both Hill and Thomas had to frame their arguments in ways that addressed the dominant society's most damaging mirror-image stereotypes of African American sexuality: Jezebel (the sexually promiscuous Black woman) and the Black rapist (the dangerous, oversexualized Black man). These stereotypes are the legacy of slavery, of the control that whites had over Black bodies, depending on them literally to reproduce their capital. Thomas confronted these stereotypes and uttered their name on national television; his famous "high-tech lynching" speech is a direct allusion to wrongful accusations of Black men as sexually dangerous, and in this context is meant as a symbol for racism in general. Hill chose to deflect the Jezebel stereotype that was continually insinuated (especially in the Doggett episode, in which a coworker claimed that Hill had continually sought to go out with him, thereby implying that she was sexually available if not promiscuous) by acting with remarkable seriousness. Both of these strategies are in principle valid ways of dealing with racist preconceptions. But because of the social context in which they were embedded, it was precisely the employment of these strategies that reinforced public notions of Hill as cold and calculating, and Thomas as standing up to fight the oppression of Black people. In one of the most ironic turns of argument, Thomas was able to insinuate that Hill was "a woman scorned" by implying that she was jealous of his preference for women of "lighter complexion."

The reception of Hill's testimony and the questions centering on her credibility have strong implications. The Senate's dogged refusal to legitimate her claims has paradoxically both undermined women's (and especially African American women's) claims to public discourse, and at the same time encouraged many women to come forward with their own allegations. Kimberlé Krenshaw (1992) argues that Hill's status as an African American woman played a central role in both her representation and her reception. Her multiple marginality in the white/feminist and male/antiracist circles that appropriated her story meant that she could not tell her own story because she was continually interpreted in the frameworks, metaphors, and paradigms of the forces around her. One of those metaphors is rape, another is lynching, and during the hearings they were often invoked side by side. Krenshaw eloquently argues that when Hill came forward with her allegation, each side fit her story to its own metaphor: feminism, that of a raped white woman; antiracism, that of a lynched Black man. Marginal in both metaphors, Hill stood by as her story was taken away and she herself was de-ethnicized by white women and desexualized by Black antiracists.

The tendency of the feminist movement to universalize women's experience, Krenshaw argues, was a powerful disservice to Hill, because the rape metaphor at once took on a life of its own and could continue only as long as it was fed, with Hill cast as a suitable victim. For the casting to be successful, she had to be processed through a quasi-rape trial that attempted to determine her purity as measured by her sexual behavior, as well as whether or not she had consented. Until as late as 1978, consent could not be proved in a court of law unless the victim exercised "utmost resistance"—a behavior that still seems to be a standard requirement of the person in the street. But what is utmost resistance? Certainly, failing to report such a hideous crime for so many years is not utmost resistance, or so the senators and much of the public thought. Meanwhile, European American feminists tried to excuse Hill's silence by invoking her career but failed to take into account the historical exploitation of Black women's bodies and the specific reasons that a Black woman might remain silent in the face of harassment. Indeed, Krenshaw (1992:415) argues that "many Black women have been reluctant to reveal experiences of sexual abuse [because] they fear that their stories might be used to reinforce stereotypes of Black men as sexually threatening." To conclude her argument, Krenshaw chronicles the way in which the lynch metaphor rallied the African American community around Thomas. But there is no equivalent metaphor that tells the tale of Black women's sexual abuse. By speaking directly to the Black experience in speech style as well as content, Thomas won the support of many African Americans. This sort of strategy was utterly unavailable to Hill, who was eventually to align with European American feminists, her most vocal and consistent supporters.

Conclusion

Robin Lakoff (this volume), in her discussion of the literal and metaphorical silencing of women, notes that silence has multiple meanings. Likewise, in analyzing the discourse of the Hill-Thomas hearings, I have come to believe that the silences in this discourse are many, complex, and connected. There is the silence of the people who were not allowed to appear or were intimidated from doing so (other women who were allegedly harassed, as well as expert witnesses on harassment); the silences that appeared throughout the hearings as tacit confirmations of the validity of Thomas's assertions; the silence of senators who would not acknowledge Hill's position during the hearings; the silencing of Hill's story by the cacophony of voices seeking to appropriate her; the silencing of Black women's experiences within the larger feminist enterprise; and finally the silence of Hill, whose narrative was constrained by sociopolitical forces that had already decided how she must speak.

Acknowledgments

I would like to thank Penny Eckert, Dale Spender, John Rickford, and Thomas Veatch for their critical comments and encouragement.

Notes

1. Improvised rules made by powerful people legitimated the proceedings despite internal contradictions, giving the impression that there was a precedent for a public forum of that sort, though in reality there were no legal equivalents. Committee members, because they were senators and not judges (and thus their job is to make policy and not to judge people), and in order to discount rules of legal evidence, voiced the mantra "This is not a trial." Ironically, just as in a court of law, Thomas was repeatedly told, "The presumption [of innocence] is with you" (Biden, D-Del.), although this was in direct contradiction to the policy drawn up at, of all places, the Equal Employment Opportunity Commission (EEOC), which "allowed for the charging party to prevail in cases that lacked third-party evidence" (Ross 1992:52–53).

2. This interactional behavior is also known in language and gender studies as *maintenance work*, a term originally coined by Fishman (1978).

3. By *below the level of consciousness* I refer to a process that is relatively automatic and unmonitored. A shorter pause on average after Hill's statements is surely not something the senators consciously set out to accomplish.

4. My analysis of tag questions here differs from that presented in previous language and gender literature, which frequently links the production of tag questions with powerless (i.e., female) speakers. For a critique of the literature and an insightful discussion of the polysemantic nature of tag questions and other linguistic phenomena, see Cameron (1992).

References

African American Women in Defense of Ourselves (1992). In Robert Chrisman and Robert L. Allen (eds.), *Court of appeal: The Black community speaks out on the racial and sexual politics of Clarence Thomas vs. Anita Hill.* New York: Ballantine Books. 291–92.

Basso, Keith (1979). *Portraits of "the Whiteman": Linguistic play and cultural symbols among the Western Apache.* New York: Cambridge University Press.

Bauman, Richard (1983). *Let your words be few: Symbolism of speaking and silence among seventeenth-century Quakers.* New York: Cambridge University Press.

Cameron, Deborah (1992). *Feminism and linguistic theory.* 2d ed. New York: St. Martin's Press.

Eckert, Penelope, and Sally McConnell-Ginet (1992a). Think practically and look locally: Language and gender as community-based practice. *Annual Review of Anthropology* 21: 461–90.

——— (1992b). Communities of practice: Where language, gender, and power all live. In Kira Hall, Mary Bucholtz, and Birch Moonwomon (eds.), *Locating power: Proceedings of the Second Berkeley Women and Language Conference.* Berkeley: Berkeley Women and Language Group. 89–99.

———— (this volume). Constructing meaning, constructing selves: Snapshots of language, gender, and class from Belten High.

Fishman, Pamela (1978). Interaction: The work that women do. *Social Problems* 25: 397–406.

Foster, Michèle (this volume). "Are you with me?": Power and solidarity in the discourse of African American women.

Gal, Susan (this volume). Language, gender, and power: An anthropological review.

Hull, Gloria (1992). Girls will be girls, and boys will ... flex their muscles. In Robert Chrisman and Robert L. Allen (eds.), *Court of appeal: The Black community speaks out on the racial and sexual politics of Clarence Thomas vs. Anita Hill.* New York: Ballantine Books. 96–99.

James, Deborah, and Sandra Clarke (1993). Women, men, and interruptions: A critical review. In Deborah Tannen (ed.), *Gender and conversational interaction.* New York: Oxford University Press. 231–80.

Jordan, June (1992). Can I get a witness? In Robert Chrisman and Robert L. Allen (eds.), *Court of appeal: The Black community speaks out on the racial and sexual politics of Clarence Thomas vs. Anita Hill.* New York: Ballantine Books. 120–24.

Krenshaw, Kimberlé (1992). Whose story is it, anyway?: Feminist and antiracist appropriations of Anita Hill. In Toni Morrison (ed.), *Race-ing justice, en-gendering power: Essays on Anita Hill, Clarence Thomas, and the construction of social reality.* New York: Pantheon Books. 402–36.

Lakoff, Robin Tolmach (this volume). Cries and whispers: The shattering of the silence.

Malveaux, Julianne (1992). No peace in a sisterly place. In Robert Chrisman and Robert L. Allen (eds.), *Court of appeal: The Black community speaks out on the racial and sexual politics of Clarence Thomas vs. Anita Hill.* New York: Ballantine Books. 143–47.

Matoesian, Gregory (1993). *Reproducing rape: Domination through talk in the courtroom.* Chicago: University of Chicago Press.

Mauet, Thomas (1988). *Fundamentals of trial techniques.* Boston: Little, Brown.

Ross, Andrew (1992). The private parts of justice. In Toni Morrison (ed.), *Race-ing justice, en-gendering power: Essays on Anita Hill, Clarence Thomas, and the construction of social reality.* New York: Pantheon Books. 40–60.

Smitherman, Geneva (1995). Testifyin, sermonizin, and signifyin: Anita Hill, Clarence Thomas, and the African American verbal tradition. In Geneva Smitherman (ed.), *African American women speak out on Anita Hill–Clarence Thomas.* Detroit: Wayne State University Press. 224–42.

Trilling, Diana (1994). Sexual separatism: Is this the direction in which we are heading? *Newsweek*, June 6: 12.

Zimmerman, Don, and Candace West (1975). Sex roles, interruptions, and silences in conversation. In Barrie Thorne and Nancy Henley (eds), *Language and sex: Difference and dominance.* Rowley, MA: Newbury House. 105–12.

3

"This Discussion Is Going Too Far!"

Male Resistance to Female Participation on the Internet

Susan Herring, Deborah A. Johnson, and Tamra DiBenedetto

A number of telling critiques have been made of the male dominance of computer culture (Kirkup 1992; Kramarae in press; Linn 1985; Turkle 1984; Wajcman 1991). It is only within the past several years, however, that researchers have started to undertake empirical investigations of gender in computer-mediated communication (CMC), the human-to-human text-based interactions that take place by means of computer networks. Although computer network technology was originally hailed as a poten-tially democratizing influence on human interaction (Hiltz & Turoff [1978] 1993; Kiesler, Siegel, & McGuire 1984), it is already becoming apparent that men dominate computer-mediated interaction much as they dominate face-to-face interaction: by "talking" more, by taking an authoritative stance in public discourse, and by verbally harassing and intimidating women into accommodation or silence (e.g., Herring 1993a; Kramarae & Taylor 1993).

In this chapter, we explore what happens when women in mixed-sex public discussion groups on the Internet resist their muted status and attempt to speak out on a par with men. Two examples are described, both of which occurred in academic discussion groups considered to be models of appropriate discourse by their members. One group is associated with a feminized (and feminist-influenced) academic field, English composition; the other is associated with the field of linguistics, in which feminism has had a very limited influence. In both examples, female members of the groups contributed to a female-introduced topic at a rate equivalent to that of men for a short period of time. Male members reacted in each case by employing a variety of silencing strategies: first they avoided addressing the women's concerns by dismissing them as trivial or by intellectualizing the discussion away from its original focus; then they erupted into anger and accusations when the women persisted in posting messages on the topic; and finally they co-opted and redefined the terms of the discourse as a means of regaining control. In the nonfeminist group, women fell silent in the face of the men's anger and the discussion died. In the feminist-influenced group, women persisted in voicing their concerns despite anger leveled against them, and were successful in claiming the conversational floor for a short period of time. Ultimately, however, the discussion died and the discourse returned to the status quo, with men once again controlling the floor and introducing most of the topics discussed by the group.

These examples reveal some of the mechanisms by which men may attempt to silence female participation when it temporarily challenges male control of the discourse, even in an otherwise collegial academic forum (cf. Lakoff, this volume). They also illustrate the role played by feminism in empowering women to speak up and continue speaking in the face of active discouragement. Yet neither the men's reactions nor the presence or absence of a feminist context alone is sufficient to explain women's overall muteness in these and similar groups. Even when female participants in one group prevailed in gaining temporary control of the discourse, it had no positive effect on their subsequent participation or on the gender dynamics of the group. This larger reality, in which women retreat to the sidelines while men hold forth in displays of verbal dominance, is indicative of a deeply rooted pattern of female muting and male dominance on the Internet. According to this pattern, repeated individual acts of silencing interact with socialization forces and the male gendering of computer technology to create a larger and more oppressive silencing context.

The present essay is, as far as we know, the first to examine what happens when women participate actively in mixed-sex groups on the Internet. In contrast, much of the previous research on gender "on-line" has focused on establishing women's lack of participation in mixed-sex groups and in computer-mediated communication more generally (Herring 1992, 1993a, b; Kramarae & Taylor 1993; Taylor & Kramarae forthcoming; Wylie 1995). An initial effort was necessary to draw people's attention to this lack, in that it flew in the face of the popular belief that computer networks, with their absence of physical cues, would make status invisible, and thus promote increased participation by women and other traditionally under-represented groups (Graddol & Swann 1989). From the very first, however, empirical studies of Internet discourse revealed a different reality. Cynthia Selfe and Paul Meyer (1991) found that men and high-status participants participated more than women and low-status participants on MBU, an informal academic discussion group, even under conditions where partici-pants had the option of remaining anonymous. The finding that men partic-ipate more than women has since been documented for a number of mixed-sex electronic forums (Balka 1993; Herring 1992, 1993a, b, c; Herring, Johnson, & DiBenedetto 1992; Sproull 1992; Sutton 1994). Men dominate in manner of participation as well, including initiation of new topics (Selfe & Meyer 1991) and use of adversarial language (Broadhurst 1993; Herring 1992, 1993a, c, forthcoming a, b, c; Sutton 1994). Adversarial behavior on the Internet typically renders women silent. This silence, as Laurel Sutton (1994: 517) notes, "could be interpreted as the silence of disapproval, the silence of being fed up, [or] the silence women use when something offen-sive or threatening is said."

Unable to carry on the kinds of discussion they value, some women remain on mixed-sex lists as *lurkers*, or noncontributing observers (Broadhurst 1993). Others retreat to women-centered and women-only lists, some of which are unapologetically separatist (Hall forthcoming).[1] In these subcultures on the margins of cyberspace, it is men who may be silenced if they attempt to dominate discussion or undermine the premises of the group. Susan Herring (forthcoming a, b, c) finds that the interactive style in female-predominant forums is generally supportive and cooperative, with a high incidence of politeness behaviors such as thanks and apologies, and a low incidence of hostile exchanges, or *flaming*. In part for this reason, female-predominant groups are sometimes described as "safe" places for women on-line (Balka 1993), in comparison with the Internet at large, where flaming is ubiquitous and sexual harassment, come-ons, and even electronic stalking are not unknown (Balsamo 1993; Lewis 1994; Taylor & Kramarae forthcoming). Women-centered electronic discussion groups have also been praised for the opportunities they provide women to come together at a grassroots level to share information, create community, or organize around a cause (Korenman & Wyatt forthcoming; Smith & Balka 1988). Interest-ingly, while the number of women-only groups on the Internet continues to grow, groups with a men-only policy are virtually nonexistent.

Nevertheless, not all women retreat to the margins, and not all women who remain in the "malestream" are lurkers. Women sometimes resist the dominant terms of Internet discourse by speaking out in mixed-sex groups, and it is to cases such as these that we now turn.

Two Case Studies: Women Speak Out

In the following pages, we describe two unusual but revealing cases in which women spoke out from a female perspective in mixed-sex groups, and the reactions of male participants to this. We begin by providing background about the two lists, MBU and Linguist, in which the incidents occurred; we then summarize the incidents themselves, the first of which concerned the legitimacy of offering a course on "men's literature," and the second of which concerned the sexist connotations of the word *dog* as used in a billboard advertisement. We then analyze the strategies employed by men to silence (or attempt to silence) female participants, and examine the empowerment strategies employed by women to ensure that their meaning was effectively communicated.

The Lists: MBU and Linguist

The groups in which the acts of silencing took place are in one sense unlikely settings for sexist oppression; both are academic discussion lists frequented primarily by established professionals and graduate students, and both are considered models of decorum according to the standards prevalent within their respective fields. The discussions analyzed here both took place when each list had been in existence for more than a year and a half (more than two years for MBU), and thus their norms of interaction were fairly well established.

At the time of the "men's literature" discussion, in November of 1991, MBU (an acronym for *Megabyte University*) was a relatively small electronic mailing list of around two hundred subscribers that had begun in 1989 as a forum for professionals interested in computers and the teaching of English composition. Many of the subscribers knew one another prior to joining the electronic forum (Selfe & Meyer 1991), and at the time of our observations two years later, the group still retained a somewhat cliquish feel. Nevertheless, members characterized it as friendly and welcoming to newcomers. As the list owner wrote in a posting to a new subscriber, "MBU is a guilt-free, no-fault bitnet list. Lurk or blurt, flame or blame, our electronic arms are open."

MBU is unmoderated—that is, any message sent to the group is posted directly to all subscribers—and messages are typically short, informal, and not uncommonly facetious or irreverent in tone. Topics of discussion that stray from the group's focus of computers and writing are usually tolerated without complaint.

In November 1991 women made up 42 percent of the subscribers whose gender could be inferred from their names, and men 58 percent. Perhaps because of the feminized nature of the field of English composition, men on MBU are less given to bald disagreement and more given to attenuated and supportive messages, even among themselves, than men on other mixed-sex academic lists such as Linguist. Most participants consider themselves to be feminists or supportive of feminist goals,[2] and discussion of gender issues on MBU, though not a frequent occurrence, is not unknown. Because of the article on gender and status on MBU published by Selfe and Meyer (the first author being one of the original members of MBU), some male participants are aware of the tendency for men to dominate discussions, and actively encourage more women to participate.

The Linguist list, devoted to discussion of academic issues in linguistics, already had a large subscribership (around two thousand) at the time the *dog* discussion started in July of 1992.[3] The forum was started in January 1991 by a wife-and-husband team of academic linguists who also serve as its moderators. Messages are previewed by the moderators and sorted into batches related by topic before being distributed to subscribers. As a consequence, exchange of messages on Linguist is less spontaneous than on MBU, in that there is typically a delay between the time a message is sent and when it is posted.

The list is more formal in other respects as well. Messages are often long and carefully crafted, in some instances more akin to academic essays (complete with glossed linguistic examples and references) than conversational interaction. The overall tone of the discourse is serious and frequently agonistic. Nevertheless, participants comment that the discourse is "reasoned and polite" compared with other electronic forums, especially those associated with the cognate fields of artificial intelligence and computer science.

Women account for 36 percent of subscribers to Linguist, and men 64 percent. Women participate less than their numerical presence would indicate, however, contributing only 20 percent of public messages and 12 percent of words on average (Herring 1993c). Although the subject of language and gender is a vital field of research with a large body of literature and many (mostly female) specialists, it is virtually never a topic of Linguist discussions; indeed the *dog* exchange analyzed here is quite possibly the only such discussion to be attempted in the history of the list to date. Discussion of topics in related disciplines in which women tend to specialize, such as sociolinguistics (with the exception of dialectology) and discourse analysis, is also rare. Few linguists identify themselves as feminists, and there has never been any public recognition or questioning of why women participate so little on Linguist.

The Discussions: "Men's Literature" and "If Your Date's a Dog"

The discussions examined here were initially selected for analysis because they were the only extended discussions of gender issues that took place during the period we observed each list (six months for MBU; three and a half years for Linguist). Perhaps for this reason, they contain the highest percentage of messages by women of any discussions observed; gender issues, because they speak directly to women's experience as members of the "second sex," constitute one domain in which women can feel qualified to speak as experts. The discussions also initially attracted our interest because they generated uncharacteristic emotion and conflict on each list. It was only later that we realized that in both cases women had been actively silenced by men, and that despite considerable differences in the content and context of each discussion, the means used to do so were similar. To facilitate discussion of these means, the content of each discussion is summarized below.

The MBU discussion began when a tenured male professor, whom we will call Bill Cathcart,[4] posted a message to MBU in which he described a course he was planning to offer the following semester on "men's litera-ture," and requested additional reading suggestions from members of the group.[5] The proposed course as he described it would look at "selected works of modern fiction," including works by Robert Bly, Ernest Hemingway, Norman Mailer, and William Burroughs, from the point of view of the men's movement.

This post generated two types of response, what we might call, follow-ing Edwin Ardener (1975) and Shirley Ardener (1975), a *dominant* and *subdominant* response. The dominant response was that members of the group obligingly began posting reading suggestions for the men's literature course; all but one of these posts were from men. The subdominant response expressed concern about the legitimacy of offering such a course; all but one member who voiced concern were women. (Later in the discus-sion, the gender polarization would become absolute: the woman who posted the reading suggestion joined the anti-men's-literature-course group, and the man, a vocal advocate of feminism throughout, eventually publicly supported the course.) The dissenting women pointed out that most literature courses were already effectively men's literature courses, and expressed concern that once again time and resources would "be devoted in courses and culture at large to men, leaving less space for women's work."

Although this concern was voiced by several women in the group independently, it was initially largely ignored as men continued to post reading suggestions for the course. In frustration, a few women posted messages questioning why their posts were being met with silence, attempting once again to explain the basis for their concerns. Men responded by protesting that women wanted to deny them the opportunity to explore the social construction of their gender. Several, including Cathcart, declared themselves to have been silenced by the women on the list and by the "hegemony" of feminism in the field of English. Women vigorously denied that the field was hegemonically feminist, citing as counterevidence personal experiences of male domination and sexism in their home departments. Meanwhile, other men joined in to support Cathcart, and other women joined in to support the women concerned about the men's literature course. The conflict reached a climax when, after a period of two days in which women's participation rose to equal that of men, three men who had not participated in the discussion previously committed an act unprecedented in the history of the list: they threatened to unsubscribe in protest.

Oddly enough, the threats had the reverse of their intended effect. Most MBU members readily recognized them as a power-play, and the incident shamed a number of men on the list into expressions of contrition. Women finally succeeded in gaining the floor, and the topic of discussion became male hegemony in English departments. The women's success was mixed, however, in that many men dropped out of the discussion, and those who remained avoided responding to individual women by name, thereby diffusing the women's conversational authority. The women's success was also short-lived: when a man produced statistics about participation in the discussion several days later, he easily became the new center of attention. Female participation dropped back down to about 15 percent of the total, where it had been at the outset of the discussion, and remained at that level for the next several months.

In comparison, the discussion on Linguist was shorter and terminated less ambiguously.[6] The episode began when a female graduate student, Roberta Whalen, posted a message about a billboard she had seen in Salt Lake City. The billboard depicted a Corvette, above which was the slogan *If your date's a dog, get a vet.* The car dealer responsible for the billboard had apparently received criticism about it and had printed a letter in the local newspaper in which he denied it was sexist; *dog*, he maintained, could refer to either sex. Whalen suspected rather that *dog* is used to refer mainly to an unattractive woman, and was requesting examples of its usage from Linguist subscribers. Her desire, she stated, was to "present this car dealership with a huge list of examples to defeat his claim of gender-equity and show his billboard to be the woman-demeaning message I think it is."

This post can be interpreted as communicating messages on two levels: a literal text requesting assistance in determining the meaning (as reflected in common usage) of the word *dog*, and an implied subtext that assumes and solicits support for resistance to the sexism of the billboard. This distinction is crucial in understanding the gendered response the post eventually attracted.

Initially there were only two responses posted to Linguist, both from men. The men responded to the text of the question, quoting dictionary definitions of *dog* as 'an unattractive person of either sex.' The first man, a published expert on English usage, agreed, however, with Whalen's intuition that *dog* is used primarily to refer to an unattractive woman, although he modified her subtext by asserting that men as well as women would perceive the billboard as sexist. The second man, whom we will call John Bryant, upheld the dictionary definition as authoritative, denying that any sexism was involved.

There were no further postings on the topic until two months later, when Whalen posted a summary of the results of her query. She had received a number of private responses from Linguist subscribers (including, apparently, many from women), and had also conducted an informal investigation of her own into people's interpretation of the billboard. It seems that with the exception of women in their teens and early twenties, who could use the term to refer to an unattractive person of either sex, most people agreed that *dog* is used to refer primarily to women, and that the billboard could be interpreted only in that sense. Whalen's summary, although presented informally, was thorough, documenting judgments and examples provided by Linguist respondents, the expert opinion of the senior editor at Merriam-Webster (whom Whalen had telephoned), the results of Whalen's informal survey (including a discussion of generational differences in usage), the statistical results of a study of the usage of animal terms (including *dog*) conducted by another respondent, a summary of dictionary entries, and a list of bibliographic references. The summary was also long, about six printed pages—one of the longest messages ever posted on Linguist by a woman, although posts of that length or longer by men are not uncommon.

At this point, conflict ensued. Several men, including Bryant, posted messages to Linguist criticizing Whalen's conclusions and methodology, focusing (in some cases, hyperliterally) on the text and ignoring or denying the legitimacy of the social subtext—that is, the men basically sustained the view that *dog* in the billboard was not demeaning to women. In response, two women posted messages in which they invoked the subtext of societal sexism to maintain firmly that the billboard was indeed demeaning. Other men then responded in anger, protesting that the discussion was "going too far" and accusing the women in the discussion of politically correct censorship and of lacking a sense of humor. Bryant then posted a lengthy summary of the *dog* discussion in which he represented Whalen as methodologically biased, he himself as acting in the spirit of "good empirical research," and the billboard as nonsexist. This message had a ring of finality to it, and there was no further public discussion of the topic.

Mechanisms of Silencing

The end result of both discussions is that women fell silent, even though no satisfactory resolution had been reached in either discussion; indeed, the masculine interpretation ultimately prevailed (the men's literature course was offered as originally planned; concern with the sexist usage of *dog* was delegitimized). Viewed from a broader perspective, the increased participation by women in these examples was only a temporary deviation in the larger pattern according to which women on both lists contribute on the average less than 25 percent. To understand why women do not speak out more in these and similar mixed-sex forums, in this section we evoke broad cultural arrangements involving gender, and then consider in some detail the specific mechanisms of silencing used in these discussions. Our goals in doing this are (1) to identify and name mechanisms we believe are employed widely to deny women significant influence in public discourse, both in computer-mediated discussions and face to face; and (2) to enable readers to recognize these mechanisms more easily by illustrating how they work in actual interaction.

Two broad cultural mechanisms help partially to explain women's limited participation in public discourse. The first is the muted status of women as a subdominant group. In both the men's literature and the *dog* discussions, women spoke out on a topic related to their experience as women—namely, sexism and sex discrimination. It is talk about experiences such as these, which are not shared by the dominant group, that E. Ardener (1975) and S. Ardener (1975) term *subdominant discourses*. The Ardeners observed that the free expression of subdominant discourses may be impeded by the dominant discourse, which lacks categories (such as the necessary feminist context on Linguist) for interpreting and validating such experiences. Women as a subdominant group are consequently at a disadvantage in articulating their own meanings; they are effectively muted by the arrangements of power within the larger culture (S. Ardener 1975:xii), which in turn become encoded in norms of discourse and in language itself (Spender 1980).

The second cultural mechanism that is relevant here is the lesser speaking rights accorded women in the public domain. It is notable that in both discussions men became openly hostile only when female participation equaled and threatened to exceed male participation in amount; in the *dog* discussion, for instance, Whalen accomplished this by posting a single long message. Amount of talk is correlated with influence and status in the public domain—those who speak more are responded to more, credited with the good ideas that emerge from the discussion, and more likely to be elected group leaders (Hiltz & Turoff [1978] 1993; Wallwork 1978). Spender (1979, 1980) observed that women have a lesser entitlement to speak in public than men, such that when their contribution exceeds 30 percent, they are perceived as dominating the discourse. It stands to reason therefore that when women on MBU and Linguist contributed 50 percent or more, they considerably exceeded their entitlement, provoking the uncharacteristically extreme male reactions described above. Needless to say, such reactions make the goal of fifty-fifty participation difficult to attain, but the problem is ultimately deeper: our perception of how much others speak is biased depending on whether they are female or male.

Nevertheless, there always have been and always will be women who resist culturally imposed limitations on their means of expression—women who devise ways to articulate their meanings despite the handicap of having to speak in a "man made language" (Spender 1980), and who risk censure for inappropriately aggressive behavior by violating the unspoken "30 percent rule" in their attempts to speak out publicly on a par with men; the principal female participants in the men's literature and *dog* discussions are of this type. In response, those who wish to preserve male discursive hegemony employ a variety of specific silencing mechanisms to ignore, discredit, or co-opt women's speech as it occurs. In what follows, we describe some of these mechanisms as they were employed by men to silence women, with varying degrees of success, in the men's literature and the *dog* discussions.

Avoidance

When members of a subdominant group say something that members of the dominant group do not wish to address—for example, because it challenges or is otherwise outside their system of meanings—the initial reaction of the dominant group may be to avoid acknowledging what was communicated. They may pretend not to have heard it (*lack of response*), misconstrue it in some way so as to divert attention away from the original message (*diversion*), or dismiss it as unimportant in a patronizing or humorous way (*dismissal*).

The initial reaction to women's attempts to speak publicly as women on the Internet is often lack of response, for example, not acknowledging that a participant or participants have posted messages. Female participants on MBU initially had a hard time getting the men in the group to acknowledge their concerns about the proposed men's literature course. Nearly two weeks of the discussion went by in which men continued to post reading suggestions (what one woman characterized as "the men's lit party"), seemingly unaware of the women's protests. At that point, Pam Smythson, a full professor and one of the more outspoken women on MBU, posted a message about the "silencing" of women in the discussion.[7]

(1) I am fascinated that my thoughtful [...] response on the "men's lit" thread was met with silence [... M]y own fledgling analysis of MBU discourse from last summer suggests that there is a real pattern of male response to males and lack of response to females in *important* topics on MBU (Here I mean socially important). When threads initiated by women die from lack of response that's silencing; when women do not respond on threads initiated by men for reasons to do with fear (and the fear may be fear of verbal or other reprisal, ridicule, whatever) [...]—that's silencing.

Empirical analysis bears out Smythson's observations about patterns of response on MBU. During the first third of the men's literature discussion, messages posted by men received on average slightly more than 100 percent response (that is, there was more than one response for each message posted), compared with an average response rate of only 64 percent for messages posted by women. Moreover, both women and men directed most of their responses to men throughout the discussion: 33 percent of total responses were men to men, 21 percent women to men, 16 percent men to women, and 11 percent women to women (Herring, Johnson, & DiBenedetto 1992).[8] Women on MBU thus had a harder time than men being recognized as conversational participants in the first place.

Once it becomes impossible to ignore the message the subdominant group is trying to express, the dominant group may deploy tactics to divert discussion away from, or otherwise subvert the communicative intent of, the message. Two types of diversion strategies were employed by men in the discussions analyzed here: *narrow* (or literal) *focus*, and *intellectualization* (or abstraction).

When MBU women persisted and ultimately succeeded in capturing the men's attention with their messages, male responses tended to ignore the women's communicative intent, focusing literally on some aspect of the text instead. In one such case, a female professor, Ellen Siegal, had drawn a parallel between men's literature courses and King Claudius in *Hamlet*, suggesting that both capitalized on immoral situations for their own gain. In response to this, a male professor, William Bart, began discussing how Shakespeare is taught and interpreted by students in the classroom. This led a female graduate student, Shelley Maples, to complain:

(2)   it's like ellen and many of us are trying to make some points about why this men's lit issue is going to the core and eating away, and the come back is not dealing with the issue but with the text used to make the example. it's frustrating. are you (in general) listening to what's being communicated?

A narrow focus on the literal text is found in male responses in the Linguist discussion as well. Whereas all of the women in the *dog* discussion responded directly to the subtext of societal sexism in Whalen's posts, the men initially ignored or denied it, choosing to argue about dictionary definitions instead. The effect of this kind of response is to exclude the poster's communicative intent by focusing attention narrowly on some isolated (often more formal or technical) aspect of the topic. A particularly egregious example of this tactic occurred in the *dog* discussion after Whalen posted her lengthy summary message. A man posted a two-screen reply picking apart the statistics cited in one of the studies: Whalen had quoted percentages from her source calculated to a tenth of a decimal point, which he asserted was statistically insignificant, given the number of subjects involved (150); the figure should have been "about 40%" instead of 38.7 percent. The message was authoritative and judgmental in tone ("If we claim to be doing science, we should at least be doing it right"), and despite the author's disclaimer that he agreed with Whalen's conclusions, his response undermined her credibility.[9] The literal-focus tactic avoids addressing the substance of a topic by narrowing it to only those aspects the respondent chooses to recognize, thereby effectively redefining and redirecting what is being talked about.

Intellectualizing, or abstracting away from the topic (often by invoking a theoretical paradigm), is the most space- and time-consuming avoidance tactic employed by men on academic discussion lists. Men who intellectualize tend to post the longest messages and as a result are successful in derailing the topic of discussion sometimes for considerable stretches, especially when other participants respond in the same vein. For example, at one point in the MBU discussion the question arose as to whether people would feel different about a men's literature course if a woman were to teach it. Bart, the man who would later go off on the Shakespeare tangent, reframed this as an epistemological question: "Are there propositions whose truth depends in strict but non-trivial ways upon who says them?" This was picked up by a male graduate student as "truth vs. persuasion" in a message discussing Aristotle's notions of logos and ethos, leading a third man, a writing program administrator, to refine the issue as one of "extrinsic ethos." Bart then abstracted further by introducing formal logic statements: "If we say 'P is false (because X argues P), but P would be true if it were argued by Y,' we must also concede (except in trivial cases) that in making that statement we are not really concerned with the truth of P" (and so on for several paragraphs). The discussion rambles from this point to Einstein, Piaget, Wittgenstein, and the discovery of self, until finally returning to the topic of gender in a virtually incomprehensible post by an associate professor who abbreviates his name as *sal*:

(3)   Now, about feminine as *other* to masculine perceivers. The answer is yes, ALWAYS [...] UNLESS, there is a fundamental change in epistemological patterns described by Hegel, Kojeve, Girard (and Kristeva among many others). How to do that? I'm not convinced that classical rhetoric is the way, although I'm studying it seriously to understand (or read into) sophistic formulations of the epistemological implications of ethos and pathos with reference to being and becoming (Gorgias) and the whole meditation on complicity (Thracymacus of Calcedon?) as articulated by Bataille and Baudrillard.

Posts such as these not only derail the discussion, but can also intimidate others into quiescence by making them feel intellectually inadequate for not being familiar with all the theories and names the authors mention. It is difficult to escape the conclusion that the men here are posturing, staking out the conversational floor through dense and sometimes incoherent bursts of intellectual-sounding noise. In all, this digression generated eighteen messages, all but two of them from men, and twelve (the longest of these messages) from only two men, Bart and sal. Although this was a side thread to the main discussion, for a time it monopolized the floor, making it difficult for others to focus attention on the men's literature topic.

Male participants also intellectualize on Linguist, and evidence of this is found in the *dog* discussion. As mentioned above, the primary means by which men attempted to discredit Whalen's conclusion that the billboard was sexist was by focusing on her methodology, although aside from the criticism about decimal points, no concrete methodological criticisms were actually articulated. What the men appeared to object to was the fact that Whalen had an interpretation (and a feminist ideological stance) before she started her investigation, namely, that the billboard was demeaning to women. Therefore it was assumed that she hadn't conducted her investigation scientifically, independent of the procedures she had actually followed. Bryant takes the criticism to a new level of abstraction, however, when he writes:

(4)   I think this discussion is important for methodological reasons. I am troubled by the persistent methodological ambiguities in innatist or rationalist studies of grammar between the role of the linguist as native speaker, the linguist as trained professional, and the linguist as exemplifier of/ possessor of a copy of/ the universal grammar. Perhaps such attempted unities are underwritten by an innatist linguistics only within a rather narrow context of formal syntactic operations. In practice, however, this anti-empirical, example-driven methodology seems to have pervaded many studies of semantic and sociolinguistic issues.

These comments, like those in the MBU example, are so abstracted from the issues at stake that it is difficult to interpret them meaningfully in the context of the discussion. Who is "the linguist" in the *dog* debate? Is Whalen being accused of using "innatist" methodology? In what sense is "universal grammar"—or grammar at all, for that matter—involved in the *dog* discussion? The fact that passages such as these are vague and difficult to interpret makes them both more devastating as criticism and unassailable as assertions. They also divert attention away from the substance of the sexism claim, which is what the men seemed to be most uncomfortable with, as evidenced by their defensive posturing.

The last two avoidance tactics we will mention are *patronization* and *humor*, used in such a way as to dismiss women's concerns as unworthy of being taken seriously. The first men to acknowledge female criticism of the proposed men's literature course responded in a patronizing manner. One teased, "Why are people (especially you ladies—oh God!—Women) so disturbed by studying the Male?" Another suggested that the women were being "a wee bit paranoid" in imagining that men's lit courses would have any adverse effect on women's literature studies. (The women targeted by this latter characterization firmly rejected it, and the man who offered it later apologized.) Equally dismissive, though in a more academic tone, is Bryant's characterization of Whalen's study as "non-scholarship":

(5)   I can't avoid the impression that the purpose of the *study* reported here is to impose conformity of meaning and expression in order to make an example of the car dealer that posted the billboard. I can certainly understand that—I think this sort of advocacy rather than any sort of scholarship is an important part of the self-understanding of many academics. But surely ambiguity and plurality of meaning need not be sacrificed.

Not only is Whalen engaged in "advocacy" rather than "scholarship," according to this man, but the advocacy has no external, or social, validity; rather, it is a phase she is passing through in a process of self-understanding. This implies that she is young or in any event immature.

Humor was used extensively in the men's literature discussion when it became apparent that women were seriously disagreeing with men on the list. The subject matter of most of the humor was the men's movement. sal signed a post with a spear composed of ASCII characters and the following message:

(6)   Soooo....HHEYYYahHeyaHeyaHeya.......!!!!!
       / □ \   Grunt
       1   Sniff, sniff
       1
       1   ....sal the spear chucker
       1
       1

Later an anonymous message was posted from "Iron John" at a made-up address: john@MYTHOS.BLY.ORG. A sample of this message is given below:

(7)   HO! Listn to Iron John! Hairy, but wily Hacker and culchur guru! Golden Hall not on Sylabus, golden ball in pond! I see Men and Womyn both afrade of Pond, you must dive in, you must Let John Out!!

The "Iron John" post generated a number of responses in a similar vein, including the text of a Zippy the Pinhead cartoon strip about "male bonding." During these exchanges the issue of the legitimacy of the men's literature course was not addressed, and women remained largely silent.

In keeping with the generally serious tone of Linguist, the *dog* discussion contained no direct attempts at humor. However, two men defended the Corvette billboard on the grounds that it was intended to be humorous, implying that the women who thought it was sexist lacked a sense of humor. Humor in both discussions was thus invoked as a means to dismiss and hence avoid addressing the serious issues of hegemony and sexism that women had raised, and only men participated in humorous exchanges, although as one man on MBU reflected, "The last few sallies make me wonder: some of us seem maybe to protest too much . . . Are we afraid of something here?"

Confrontation

Discursive strategies such as those described above are often successful in discouraging women from persisting in attempting to communicate their own meanings. Sometimes, however, women persist despite the obstacles thrown up in their path. When this happened in the men's literature and the *dog* discussions, men retreated to the next line of defense—confronting women with anger and accusations.

Consider what happened in the *dog* discussion. Two men responded critically to Whalen's summary, one focusing on the statistics as described above, and the other, Bryant, accusing Whalen of "doing violence to the data" by suppressing the implications of the billboard that "don't fit her particular political agenda." Bryant focused on one of the dictionary definitions of *dog* as 'a man of low moral character' in order to assert that the billboard was not demeaning to women:

(8) When [people] read the billboard, they might be more likely to conclude that the *dog*, i.e., person of low character, was a male. Right?

To this, two women responded firmly that based on their understanding, such was not the case. Neither of the women's messages was angry or insulting in tone—they were simply firm in disagreeing. One of the responses came from a high-profile female professor of linguistics, Arlene Price:

(9) wrong, as I see it. sure, _dog_ can refer to a male low-life, but i know of NO stereotype that says females will attract males of high moral character if they have a fancy sportscar. in contrast, there is a very well-entrenched stereotype that males will attract good-looking females if they have a fancy sportscar. thus which sense of this polysemous item is selected is not random—context counts.

In response, however, three men, none of whom had previously participated in the *dog* discussion, posted messages accusing the women of censorship in the name of "political correctness," and of lacking a sense of humor. One such response began with alarmed-sounding exclamations:

(10)   This discussion is going a bit too far! The goal of the original post-
       ing was apparently to gather data to pressure the car-dealer into
       taking his sign down because the poster found it offensive. Perhaps
       the next target should be t.v. shows like Miami Vice? Nobody has
       ever produced any evidence that you can change the way people
       think by suppressing the public expression of their thoughts.

Another man concludes with a rhetorical question: "So I wonder: is there humor after PC?" Although none of the men allude in their protests to the amount or nature of women's participation in the discussion, it was only when other women chimed in and supported Whalen's interpretation (push-ing the number of words contributed by women up to that point to an unheard-of 77 percent of the total) that men were moved to protest the "sexism" interpretation in strong (for Linguist) terms.

The correlation between male protests and amount or persistence of female participation might be dismissed as a coincidence were it not for the fact that a similar pattern is evident on MBU. There were two days in a row during which women posted more messages than men in the men's litera-ture discussion. This came about not because men on MBU posted any less, but because women's rate of posting increased, in part because new women had entered the discussion, and in part in response to a call by Smythson for more female participation. This increase in female posting activity was closely followed by two events. First, men began to complain of being silenced by women on the list and in the field of English more generally. Cathcart, the original poster on the men's literature course, articulates this position most eloquently and at greatest length. A portion of one of his posts is reproduced below:

(11)   I've been pretty circumspect about posting anything to the net on
       this issue without thinking it through carefully first, and I suspect
       many of the men have as well. I feel I am operating, both in my
       department and nationally in the field, in a theoretical and critical
       environment that is hegemonically feminist, and that I'd best be
       careful what I say and how I say it. [. . .L]ook what happens when
       we propose to go beyond or away from feminism in any fashion:
       we get bashed, guilt-tripped. [. . .] What's at stake here is, indeed,
       about power relations, but what academic feminists seem not to

> be able to admit is how powerful they indeed are within this dis-
> course community. That is why men have been silent lately, and it's
> silencing just like the silencing women suffer outside the academy.
> [...] I see this, to tell the truth, at this time and place, as bullying.
> Ellen and shelley, you may not feel very powerful outside this net
> or this discourse community, but here on the inside you've come
> very close to shutting all of us men up and down.

In a similar vein, other men commented that they "weigh nearly every
word [they] say [...] with this kind of topic"; that they are "staying silent"
because the likelihood of misinterpretation makes it "not worth talking";
or that they feel there is "a PC build-up of bias" against them. Judging by
some of the messages protesting to this effect, "silencing" for men involves
having to think carefully about what they say before they say it, or possibly
not saying something that they otherwise would have said. No doubt these
men are experiencing in small measure what most women experience as a
way of life; nevertheless, in objective terms the men can hardly be said to be
silent in the discussion, because they contributed 70 percent of the words
overall. Moreover, the post by Cathcart quoted in part above is 1,098 words
long, the longest single message in the entire discussion, and four other
lengthy messages were contributed by men on the same day as well. This
illustrates how subjective the notion of "silence" can be—one feels subjec-
tively silenced anytime one is constrained from speaking to the full extent
of one's assumed entitlement.

The second confrontational event followed a day later: three men threatened to cancel their membership to the group in protest over the "tone" of
the men's literature debate, which they described as "contentious," characterized by "anger," "insults," "vituperation," and "vilification." One of the
men, Jim Johnson, explicitly blames the contentiousness on those who criticized Cathcart's course:

> (12) In the collegial spirit of MBU, Bill asked for suggested readings in a
>   course he wants to offer, and instead of suggestions he's received
>   vilifications. I'll check periodically on Usenet, and when MBU
>   becomes a collegial forum again I'll sign on.

Women are effectively accused of "vilifying" Cathcart and of being "uncol-
legial," despite the fact that the only direct vilification to have occurred was
in messages posted by Cathcart himself, in which he accused two of the
women of "bullying," "bashing," and "guilt-tripping" men on the list.

No doubt this extreme reaction is not exclusively due to the fact that
women's participation rose to exceed that of men for two days in a row—

had women participated as enthusiastically in support of male views, the reaction would likely have been different. It is striking, however, that this was the only time on MBU when women participated as actively, or more actively, than men on a major topic, and it is also the only time (possibly in the history of the list) that anyone has threatened publicly to unsubscribe. Similarly, it is striking that the *dog* discussion on Linguist was one of only two times that women have (started to) participate more than men on any topic, and both times the discussion was cut off prematurely by male protests.

Expression of anger is a powerful intimidation mechanism, especially when used against women, who, in mainstream American culture, are socialized to please others and avoid conflict. Women who speak out are implicitly told: Your behavior is inappropriate and violates standards of what is socially tolerable; if you persist, you may be responsible for driving decent peace-loving people away and (by implication) ultimately destroying the harmony of the group. The effect of this strategy in the Linguist discussion was to silence any further commentary by women.

Yet, anger is a two-edged sword, for in addition to intimidating others, it reveals that one is vulnerable, that something caused one to lose some self-control. In the MBU discussion, male threats to unsubscribe from the list were perceived by the group as a sign of weakness and an admission of guilt in the charges that men were attempting to silence women in the discussion. As one of the regular female participants, Alice Cass, commented:

(13) Sorry if I'm being dense, but I don't see anything in the exchange of messages on men's lit that I could rightly call "vilification." But I think I could accurately call Jim Johnson's farewell address a clear instance of "silencing," figuratively tossing an insult over his shoulder as he slams the door behind him.

Men were also quick to castigate the would-be unsubscribers, perhaps to clear themselves of the onus that immediately fell on that group. A successful writer and high-profile MBU participant, Mitchell James, wrote:

(14) The calls for boycott (pun intended) take on the quality of plain old (GeorgieBoy style, Stormin' igNorin'em) powerplay, and tend to cast a naked light upon the thoughtless and clearly absurd claims that women hold disproportionate (or any substantial) power in this or any other academic discourse.

Another man described the men who boycotted as "sissies," and yet another man in referring to the incident characterized male academics as "gonad heads." Only one of the men who threatened to unsubscribe actually did; another was simply silent; and the third remained an active participant, contritely commenting later, "I can't believe I ever considered leaving."

Suddenly men were virtually tripping over themselves to say the politically correct thing. The man who had threatened to unsubscribe but remained and the other man who actually did unsubscribe both sent messages (the latter from outside the list) assuring the group that their desire to unsubscribe "had nothing to do with the men's movement/women's movement at all"; indeed they appreciated "a lively debate on gender issues" and could "think of few more worthwhile issues than the nature of what we do and who we really are." Men suddenly agreed that "the cultural game is stacked against women. This prejudice [. . .] is so absurd, so stupid, so wasteful that it would be worthy of only laughter and amazement were it also not so evident, so painful, so tragic." Of course, these men themselves "do not consider anybody inherently better or worse at anything simply because they are biologically this, that or the other." One or two men even went so far as to intimate that the men's literature course might be problematic after all.

The women, it seemed, had won the day. Their persistence and, ultimately, the men's going too far in resisting them and embarrassing themselves in the process had finally won them the conversational floor and the right to control the topic, which then became the problem of male hegemony in English departments. Women even began getting more responses to their messages (up from 69 percent to 89 percent), and the rate of response to male messages dropped (from more than 100 percent to 72 percent). In the words of one woman, although it took "a small war on MBU" to raise people's consciousnesses, and although women continue to have problems in being heard generally, she was "heartened by the latest responses."

Co-optation

What happened next on MBU illustrates what is perhaps the most pervasive and subtle silencing mechanism of all: male co-optation of the terms of the discourse. Through the use of this mechanism, men take over and reformulate women's ideas as their own, in the process often putting a spin on them that is consistent with their own goals. The ultimate outcome is that men once again become the authorities and do most of the talking, and women sink back into a muted condition. There are clear examples of co-optation at work in the MBU and the Linguist discussions, both occurring after the expressions of anger directed toward female participants. These examples appear to have the function of reclaiming the terms of the discourse for men after they had lost some ground by being forced to acknowledge women's bid for the discursive floor.

Consider first the men's literature discussion. After the climax of the "war" had passed, women moved on to a new topic, but men spent considerable time commenting on and reconstructing what had happened. The eloquent quotation from James cited above is a good example of this. In this passage, James performs two acts of co-optation: first, he interprets the male threats to unsubscribe as "calls for boycott," thereby defining them as organized, politically motivated acts of resistance, and immaturely motivated ones at that (cf. the pun on *boy*). This proved to be an influential turn of phrase, because the label *boycott* and its associated connotations were taken up by others in describing the actions of the unsubscribers in subsequent messages. Second, in evoking "the thoughtless and clearly absurd claims that women hold disproportionate (or any substantial) power in [...] any [...] academic discourse," and indeed in characterizing the "boycott" as a power play, James rewords assertions that had already been made (in the case of the former, repeatedly) by women in the discussion. However, others then respond to him and credit him rather than the women as the source of the ideas. For example, one man writes:

(15) More disturbing is the claim that feminist politics are now dominant in the humanities. Let me be the first to second Mitchell James' reply to that [quotes James's post]:

Feminist politics are by no stretch of the imagination dominant at my institution—or any other academic institution or organization I know about.

Ironically, this exchange exemplifies a concern expressed by Maples early in the discussion about the men's literature course: "My concern is that once again the questioning process is only being validated because it is articulated by a man's voice, ... while once again, the viability of women's voices are jammed out." The basic strategy here seems to be to keep talking and articulating one's own interpretation of events. It having been determined by the outcome of the "war" that the topic of discussion was feminism, men actively started talking about feminism, sounding in some cases more feminist than the women. After the men had regained control of the discourse in this manner, they moved on to other topics.

Another exercise of co-optation occurred in response to statistics posted later by one of the men about participation in the men's literature discussion. The statistics showed that men had posted the most to the discussion, and moreover that three men—sal, Bart, and Cathcart—had together contributed one-third of all words posted by men. Bart responded by redefining *silencing,* one of the key terms in the debate, such that men can claim to be silenced even when they talk more:

> (16) [I]t doesn't necessarily follow that the one with the most words dominates the conversation or that the one with the least is silenced. I have often not felt silenced in conversations in which I said little or nothing. And I have often felt silenced in conversations in which I did a disproportionate share of the talking. (Don't we all feel silenced when a lecture goes sour, for instance?) Whether I feel silenced or not is not a function of how much I say but of whether I feel that my premises have been fairly addressed.

By redefining silencing to include how one feels "when a lecture goes sour," Bart strips the term of its sociopolitical significance and renders it banal; by reversing the association of amount of talk with power, he discursively creates a universe in which men can do a disproportionate share of the talking and not only do women have no right to feel silenced but the men can declare themselves to be silenced on other grounds. Women emerge in this conceptualization as without recourse, and men with justification for whatever they do. Fortunately, although two or three other men (including sal) supported dismissing the statistics as unimportant, there is no evidence that anyone other than its originator accepted Bart's reversed definition of silencing.

The *dog* discussion also offers an excellent example of co-optation in the final message of the discussion, which was posted by Bryant. To begin with, Bryant includes as the subject header of his post *Summary: *dog* as sexist language,* exploiting the common practice on Linguist for responses to a query to be collected and summarized in a single message. However, this is normally done by the person who posted the query, in this case Whalen. For Bryant to co-opt her position in this way is to speak "for" her, when in fact he had spoken "against" her throughout the discussion. Bryant summarizes the discussion in only three lines, then spends sixty-nine lines reiterating his criticisms of Whalen's position, in which he asserts, "So again, the [. . .] slogan is simply not sexist per se." He goes on to say that "[women in the discussion] seemed to adopt a traditionalist, somewhat Puritannical [*sic*] valuation of the billboard in question. [. . . They] have not agreed on any statement of sociolinguistic value." Furthermore, he dubs Whalen's methodology "anti-empirical" and the studies she cites "marked by methodological sloppiness." In contrast, by criticizing Whalen, Bryant suggests that he is doing "good empirical research":

(17) [A] respondent claimed that I was "bending over backwards" to find possible motives for the auto dealer. I accept and applaud this characterization of good empirical research. I claim that this type of thoroughgoing critique of a theory is the only way to avoid canonizing one's theoretical and personal prejudices.

According to this version of reality, the billboard is defined as nonsexist, Whalen and her research efforts are discredited, and the author himself is credited with doing superior research, even though in actuality he has done nothing but post messages to Linguist. This is a blatant attempt by Bryant to twist the terms of the discourse to his own ends, and it is unfortunate that it stands as the last word in the *dog* discussion.

In summary, men in both discussions responded similarly to women's active participation: they first avoided addressing the women's expressed concerns; then, when women persisted, they turned on them with anger and accusations and finished off by co-opting key terms and definitions in the discussion, thereby reclaiming control of the discourse retrospectively.

Strategies for Empowerment

There is another side to these interactions, namely, the strategies employed by women to make themselves heard. Although women were ultimately silenced, for a time they were not silent at all. Moreover, MBU women were successful in effecting a temporary reversal of power relations, determining what was talked about, and how, for both women and men. In this final section we consider the strategies employed by women in the men's literature and *dog* discussions, why they were effective, and how they might have been maximized to bring about more successful outcomes.

First, and most important, women stepped out from the sidelines and attempted to communicate women-centered meanings in mixed-sex public forums. This required them to overcome the cumulative effect of past silencings—to try again even though they might feel discouraged or pessimistic about the eventual outcome. Nearly every woman who spoke out in the men's literature discussion also wrote of feeling tired or discouraged. As Shelley Maples expressed it:

(18) it's tiring to feel so continually on the defensive about our experience/perspective (our = women's). [... W]e all—men and women—want to be heard, but it gets wearing feeling like i'm so frequently, when speaking/politicizing my voice as "a woman" speaking on the defensive. [This is] why i suspect many of the women on line reading this have been silent, have no energy. feels too much like "one more time."

Nevertheless, a number of women did speak, even though it required them to engage in conflict, which many commented they found distasteful. Furthermore, women persisted in speaking, despite the resistance they encountered. When they were ignored or misconstrued the first time, they said the same thing again, rephrasing and elaborating, committed to getting their point across. Ultimately, persistence proved to be an effective tool of subversion, for in persisting, women made it difficult for men to ignore them or carry on with the dominant status quo. Indeed, had women continued to persist when instead they fell silent, the final outcome of the discussions might well have been different.

Persistence in these discussions meant not just continuing to speak out but keeping the discussion focused and on track despite attempts to dismiss, distort, and derail it. Women in both discussions were highly consistent in communicating the same primary message throughout the discussion, whether it be why they were concerned about the men's literature course or the sexist connotations of *dog*. By and large, they were also consistent in the direct, concerned, and matter-of-fact tone of their communication, especially compared with the men, whose messages ranged in tone from self-satisfied to patronizing to defensive to angry to contrite, and who repeatedly attempted to change the topic or go off on tangents.

Related to consistency of focus through time is solidarity or consistency of perspective across individuals. Remarkably, no woman disagreed with any other woman in either discussion.[10] Rather, women supported one another through their common stance in the discussion and through messages acknowledging and responding to what other women had said. An example of a supportive message of this type from each discussion is given below:

(19)   to Ellen Siegal:

   thank you for not speaking for but supporting and reflecting on the
   message i posted. i felt somewhat stunned by having it met with the
   response "a wee bit paranoid"
   what's next? hysterical? and does not such a response reinforce the
   point of concern both of us are expressing?
   again, many thanks.
   shelley

   [To Roberta Whalen:] Thanks for this interesting dialogue about
   yet another instance of offensive terms describing women.

The fact that women presented a unified front was no doubt responsible in part for men's accusations that they were being silenced or censored by a

"PC" force, even though in the case of the Linguist discussion only four women were involved, and three of them posted only once.

Finally, women on MBU were aware of silencing mechanisms used by men against them, and identified them when they occurred, constructing a metadiscursive commentary that proved to be a powerful form of resistance against silencing. Thus, when men initially ignored messages by women, Smythson and Maples posted messages pointing out that men were ignoring them. When men then responded patronizingly, Maples, Smythson, and others pointed this out as well and objected. When Bart intellectualized, Siegal accused him of intellectualizing. When three men threatened to unsubscribe from the list, Cass called it a power play and others (including many men) quickly followed suit; the men thus stood revealed and ultimately embarrassed by the irrefutable evidence of their attempts at suppression. Indeed the only silencing behavior the women did not name was co-optation, which was disguised in the form of agreement with feminist views, and their failure to do so ultimately led to their discursive gains being co-opted.

The presence of a feminist context facilitates the successful use of the naming strategy. MBU participants, steeped in feminism in their academic field, are sufficiently aware of the nature of discursive silencing to be able to recognize and name many of its manifestations, and most men express willingness to try to break out of traditional dominance patterns, making it possible for women and men to engage in metadiscourses about their own patterns of interaction. The situation is very different on Linguist. Few linguists understand or care about feminism, in part because mainstream linguistics has tended to marginalize discussion of language-related issues of social relevance. As a consequence, the female linguists who wish to engage with male colleagues about such issues have a difficult time; few terms are shared between them, and the women themselves may not be fully aware of how they are being silenced in Linguist interactions.[11] Linguist is also unusual by computer-mediated discussion-group standards in that it is virtually devoid of self-reflection or metadiscursive interaction; indeed, an attempt by a woman to respond metadiscursively in the *dog* discussion was preempted by the moderators of the list (see note 9). Yet the ability to draw attention to oppressive interactional patterns as they are taking place is a necessary prerequisite to changing such patterns.

Conclusion

In this paper, we have presented a close analysis of two computer-mediated mixed-sex discussions in which women participated actively. These discussions are of special interest in that they serve as test cases for the assertion that computer-mediated communication equalizes patterns of interaction between the sexes. Our analysis reveals that men in the groups employed numerous mechanisms to silence the women, including resorting to threats to withdraw from the group and cries of "This is too much!" when the amount of women's contribution to the discussion exceeded 30 percent. The men's reactions reveal clearly that women in such groups are not expected to take the lead in any topic of discussion, not even temporarily, let alone participate on an equal basis with men in the discourse of the group overall.

We believe that this finding helps to explain why many women on the Internet feel more comfortable in women-centered and women-only groups, and why men have no need for men-only groups: women-centered groups are the only places in which women set the terms of the discourse; men set the terms of the discourse everywhere else. That is, in keeping with the observation made by MBU women that all literature courses (except for specially labeled women's literature) teach men's literature, we suggest that all or most computer-mediated discussion groups (except for specially labeled women-centered groups) are men-centered. This state of affairs can be attributed in part to the ongoing success that men have had in defining computers and computer networks as male domains; it is more difficult for women to obtain access to computers, and women tend to feel less confident of their technical abilities even when they have used computers the same number of years as men,[12] although this may be changing for the younger generation (Kaplan & Farrell 1994). At the same time, the gender patterns found in computer-mediated interactions are so similar to those found in face-to-face interaction and in American culture at large that one cannot escape the suspicion that the electronic medium in fact changes things very little—its principal advantage may be in allowing users (and investigators) to see more clearly the asymmetrical aspects of communication that would otherwise go by in speech too quickly to be noticed.

Finally, and most important, the results of this study reveal that mutedness is not simply a condition assigned to women through early socialization nor an inevitable consequence of women's status as members of a culturally subdominant group but, rather, is actively constructed and enforced through everyday discursive interaction (cf. Houghton, this volume). The good news is that discursive oppression can be subverted assuming participants know what to look for. By recognizing and exposing silencing mechanisms in public conversation, we take the first step toward breaking the male stranglehold on control of public discourse on the Internet and elsewhere.

Acknowledgments

The present chapter is a revised and expanded version of Herring, Johnson, and DiBenedetto (1992). The authors wish to thank Dean Beverly Hendricks at California State University, San Bernardino, for making an Affirmative Action grant available to the first author to support the MBU research.

Notes

1. Examples of lists with a separatist philosophy are Systers, a list for female computer professionals; Sappho, devoted to discussion of issues of importance to lesbian and bisexual women; and SWIP, a discussion list for the Society for Women in Philosophy.

2. In response to an electronic survey administered to MBU subscribers and reported on in Herring, Johnson, and DiBenedetto (1992), 100 percent of respondents of both sexes said that they considered themselves to be feminists or strong supporters of feminist principles.

3. As of March 1994, the number of subscribers to both MBU and Linguist had more than doubled.

4. All names of MBU and Linguist participants that appear in this paper are pseudonyms.

5. The men's literature discussion extended from November 7 to December 15, 1991. It comprises 46,888 words contributed by 59 people in 242 messages. Broken down by gender, the proportions are as follows: words—men 70 percent, women 30 percent; participants—men 70 percent, women 30 percent; messages—men 64 percent, women 36 percent.

6. The *dog* discussion, which consists of three messages posted to Linguist on July 7, 1992, and eleven more between September 22 and October 19, 1992, comprises 6,322 words contributed by 10 people in 14 messages. Broken down by gender the proportions are as follows: words—men 41 percent, women 59 percent; participants—men 60 percent, women 40 percent; messages—men 57 percent, women 43 percent.

7. All messages are reproduced with the original spelling and punctuation preserved.

8. The remaining 19 percent of messages were directed to the group as a whole.

9. We later learned, through personal communication with the involved parties, that there was a suppressed sequel to this exchange. As it turns out, the woman who had supplied Whalen with the statistics was a graduate student, and the statistics were part of her master's thesis. This was her first public posting (in this case, indirectly posted) to a discussion group, and she was devastated by the mean-spirited tone of the men's responses. Her female supervising professor attempted to post a message to Linguist protesting the uncollegiality of the responses but was discouraged from doing so by the Linguist moderators, who no doubt wished to avoid provoking conflict on the list. Thus, to all public appearances women fell silent and implicitly acceded to the men's methodological criticisms, when in fact at least one protest was attempted but suppressed.

10. The only possible exception to this involved Siegal and a woman who posted a short message on MBU complaining about affirmative-action policies in university hiring; Siegal maintained that such policies were still necessary. This exchange, however, was not directly related to the men's literature course.

11. For example, when Linguist subscribers were asked in an anonymous electronic questionnaire why they had not contributed to a certain lively discussion, women and men gave identical reasons (nothing to add; not enough time), and both equally said they found it interesting. Nevertheless, men contributed 92 percent of the words in the discussion, and women only 8 percent—clearly something was very different about their experiences of the discussion. In interpreting these results, Herring (1993b) suggests that women felt excluded from what they perceived to be a male-male conversation.

12. Thus in a survey of Linguist subscribers, 13 percent of women reported feeling "hesitant" in using computers, compared with 0 percent of the men, even though respondents of both sexes had used computers for eleven years on the average (Herring 1992, 1993a).

References

Ardener, Edwin (1975). Belief and the problem of women. In Shirley Ardener (ed.), *Perceiving women*. London: Malaby. 1–17.

Ardener, Shirley (1975). Introduction. In Shirley Ardener (ed.), *Perceiving women*. London: Malaby. vii–xxiii.

Balka, Ellen (1993). Women's access to on-line discussions about feminism. *Electronic Journal of Communication* 3(1). Available from comserve@rpitsvm.bitnet.

Balsamo, Anne (1993). Feminism for the incurably informed. In Mark Dery (ed.), *Flame wars: The discourse of cyberculture*. Special issue, *South Atlantic Quarterly* 92(4): 681–712.

Broadhurst, Judith (1993). Lurkers and flamers: Why they do what they do. *Online Access* 8(3): 48–51.

Ebben, Maureen, and Cheris Kramarae (1993). Women and information technologies: Creating a cyberspace of our own. In H. Jeannie Taylor, Cheris Kramarae, and Maureen Ebben (eds.), *Women, information, technology, and scholarship*. Urbana, IL: Center for Advanced Study. 15–27.

Graddol, David, and Joan Swann (1989). *Gender voices*. Oxford: Basil Blackwell.

Hall, Kira (forthcoming). Cyberfeminism. In Susan Herring (ed.), *Computer mediated communication: Linguistic, social, and cross-cultural perspectives*. Amsterdam: Benjamins.

Herring, Susan (1992). Gender and participation in computer-mediated linguistic discourse. Washington, DC: ERIC Clearinghouse on Languages and Linguistics. Document no. ED345552.

——— (1993a). Gender and democracy in computer-mediated communication. *Electronic Journal of Communication* 3(2), special issue on computer-mediated communication, Thomas Benson (ed.). Available from comserve@rpitsvm.bitnet. Reprinted in Rob Kling (ed.), *Computerization and controversy*. 2d ed. New York: Academic Press (Forthcoming).

———— (1993b). Sex of linguists: Results of survey. *Linguist List* 4.517, June 30.

———— (1993c). Men's language: A study of the discourse of the Linguist list. In André Crochetière, Jean-Claude Boulanger, and Conrad Ouellon (eds.), *Les langues menacées: Actes du XVe Congrès International des Linguistes*, Vol. 3. Québec: Les Presses de l'Université Laval. 347–50.

———— (forthcoming a). Politeness in computer culture: Why women thank and men flame. In Mary Bucholtz, Anita Liang, Laurel Sutton, and Caitlin Hines (eds.), *Cultural performances: Proceedings of the Third Berkeley Women and Language Conference.* Berkeley: Berkeley Women and Language Group.

———— (forthcoming b). Posting in a different voice: Gender and ethics in computer-mediated communication. In Charles Ess (ed.), *Philosophical perspectives on computer-mediated communication.* Albany: SUNY Press.

———— (forthcoming c). Two variants of an electronic message schema. In Susan Herring (ed.), *Computer mediated communication: Linguistic, social, and cross-cultural perspectives.* Amsterdam: Benjamins.

Herring, Susan, Deborah Johnson, and Tamra DiBenedetto (1992). Participation in electronic discourse in a "feminist" field. In Kira Hall, Mary Bucholtz, and Birch Moonwomon (eds.), *Locating power: Proceedings of the Second Berkeley Women and Language Conference.* Berkeley: Berkeley Women and Language Group. 250–62.

Hiltz, Starr Roxanne, and Murray Turoff ([1978] 1993). *The network nation: Human communication via computer.* Reading, MA: Addison-Wesley.

Houghton, Cathryn (this volume). Managing the body of labor: The treatment of reproduction and sexuality in a therapeutic institution.

Kaplan, Nancy, and Eva Farrell (1994). Weavers of webs: A portrait of young women on the Net. *Arachnet Electronic Journal on Virtual Culture* 2(3). (FTP byrd.mu.wvnet.edu/pub/ejvc/KAPLANV2N3.)

Kiesler, Sara, Jane Siegel, and Timothy W. McGuire (1984). Social psychological aspects of computer-mediated communication. *American Psychologist* 39: 1123–34.

Kirkup, Gill (1992). The social construction of computers: Hammers or harpsichords? In Gill Kirkup and Laurie Smith Keller (eds.), *Inventing women: Science, technology, and gender.* Cambridge: Polity Press. 267–81.

Korenman, Joan, and Nancy Wyatt (forthcoming). Group dynamics in an e-mail forum. In Susan Herring (ed.), *Computer mediated communication: Linguistic, social, and cross-cultural perspectives.* Amsterdam: Benjamins.

Kramarae, Cheris (in press). A backstage critique of virtual reality. In Steven G. Jones (ed.), *CyberSociety: Computer-mediated communication and community.* Thousand Oaks, CA: Sage. 36–56.

Kramarae, Cheris, and H. Jeannie Taylor (1993). Women and men on electronic networks: A conversation or a monologue? In H. Jeannie Taylor, Cheris Kramarae, and Maureen Ebben (eds.), *Women, information, technology, and scholarship.* Urbana, IL: Center for Advanced Study. 52–61.

Lakoff, Robin (this volume). Cries and whispers: The shattering of the silence.

Lewis, Peter H. (1994). Persistent e-mail: Electronic stalking or innocent courtship? *New York Times*, Sept. 16: B18.

Linn, Pam (1985). Microcomputers in education: Dead and living labor. In Tony

Solomonides and Les Levidow (eds.), *Compulsive technology: Computers as culture.* London: Free Association Books. 58–101.

Selfe, Cynthia L., and Paul R. Meyer (1991). Testing claims for on-line conferences. *Written Communication* 8(2): 163–92.

Smith, Judy, and Ellen Balka (1988). Chatting on a feminist network. In Cheris Kramarae (ed.), *Technology and women's voices.* New York: Routledge & Kegan Paul. 82–97.

Spender, Dale (1979). Language and sex differences. *Osnabrücker Beiträge zur Sprach-theorie: Sprache und Geschlect* 2: 38–59.

Spender, Dale (1980). *Man made language.* London: Pandora Press.

Sproull, Lee (1992). Women and the networked organization. Presentation to Women, Information Technology, and Scholarship Colloquium, February 12. University of Illinois, Center for Advanced Study. [Cited in Ebben and Kramarae 1993.]

Sproull, Lee, and Sara Kiesler (1991). *Connections: New ways of working in the networked organization.* Cambridge, MA: MIT Press.

Sutton, Laurel (1994). Using USENET: Gender, power, and silence in electronic discourse. In Susanne Gahl, Andy Dolbey, and Christopher Johnson (eds.), *Proceedings of the Twentieth Annual Meeting of the Berkeley Linguistics Society.* Berkeley: Berkeley Linguistics Society. 506–20.

Taylor, H. Jeannie, and Cheris Kramarae (forthcoming). Creating cybertrust from the margins. In Susan Leigh Star (ed.), *The cultures of computing.* Oxford: Basil Blackwell.

Turkle, Sherry (1984). *The second self: Computers and the human spirit.* London: Granada.

Wajcman, Judy (1991). Technology as masculine culture. *Feminism confronts technology.* University Park: Pennsylvania State University Press. 137–61.

Wallwork, Jean (1978). *Language and people.* London: Heinemann Educational Books.

Wylie, Margie (1995). A man's world. *Digital Media* 4(8): 3–6.

4

The "Father Knows Best" Dynamic in Dinnertime Narratives

Elinor Ochs and Carolyn Taylor

Historical and sociological studies of gender have pursued the plethora of ways in which cultural concepts of gender impact social life, especially institutions such as the family, the church, the workplace, and the state. Of critical importance to all gender research is the idea that gender ideologies are closely linked to the management of social asymmetries. As Marie Withers Osmond and Barrie Thorne (1993:593) concisely put it, "Gender relations are basically power relations." Notions of patriarchy, male authority, male domination, and gender hierarchy have gained considerable intellectual vitality within feminist argumentation. The import of gender pervades all levels of analysis, from historical and ethnographic studies of gender ideologies, structures, and customs to interactional studies of gendered activities and actions. From a poststructuralist perspective, we need both macro- and microanalyses to illuminate continuity and change in the rights, expectations, and obligations vis-à-vis the conduct, knowledge, understandings, and feelings that constitute the lived experience of being female or male in society.

The present chapter addresses gender asymmetry in middle-class European American families through an examination of a single social activity: narrating a story or a report over family dinner. While recognizing that family interaction is socially and historically enmeshed in the prevailing interests of economic and political institutions (e.g., Hartmann 1981; Stack 1974), we offer a window into how family hierarchies are constituted in day-to-day family life. Our position is that family exchanges do not simply exemplify gender relations otherwise shaped by forces outside the family but, rather, are the primordial means for negotiating, maintaining, transforming, and socializing gender identities. Certainly from the point of view of a child, routine moments of family communication are the earliest and perhaps the most profound medium for constructing gender understandings (Cole & Cole 1989; Dunn 1984; Freud [1921] 1949; Goodwin 1990; Kohlberg 1966; Maccoby & Jacklin 1974; Schieffelin 1990). Awakenings to gender asymmetry may occur from infancy on, for example, in two-parent families, through such everyday activity as watching how mothers and fathers interact with each other and with their daughters and sons.

Our particular attention has been captured by the pervasiveness and importance of collaborative narration, wherein children interact with others in co-narrating, as a locus of socialization (Ochs, Smith, & Taylor 1989; Ochs & Taylor 1992a, b; Ochs, Taylor, Rudolph, & Smith 1992). In the present study, we examine how such narrative practices may instantiate gender-relevant narrator and family-role identities of women and men as mother and father, wife and husband, in white middle-class families in the United States.[1] Indeed, our observations of these households suggest that children are overhearers, recipients, and active contributors to gender-implicative, asymmetrical storytelling exchanges dozens of times in the course of sharing a single meal together.

One of the important tenets of this research is that all social identities, including gender identities, are constituted through actions and demeanors. Individuals come to understand a range of social identities primarily by learning, first in childhood, to recognize and/or display certain behaviors and stances that are permitted or expected by particular community members in particular activity settings. We suggest that, among other routes, children (and adults, taking on new roles as spouses and parents) come to understand family and gender roles through differential modes of acting and expressing feelings in narrative activity.

Another important perspective we propose to be essential to a fuller understanding of gender instantiation concerns the attention we place on family interactions—that is, families as multiparty activity systems (Engeström 1987). In gender research on social interaction, the exchanges analyzed have tended to be dyadic ones, i.e., female-male, female-female, or male-male interactions. This design lends itself to dichotomous comparisons between female and male conduct in these communicative arrangements. While two people may wear many hats within one dyad, which we also recognize, dyadic identity construction seems inherently less complex, less hierarchical than multiparty, and also less representative of the contexts in which most people are socialized into gender notions and roles.

Our study of family narrative-activity interactions examines multiparty two-parent contexts in which participants construct themselves and one another simultaneously as spouse, parent, child, and sibling—as mother and wife, father and husband, daughter and sister, son and brother. Within the variety of dynamics and alignments available, on the one hand, women and men may often work together to inquire about and control their children— and women can be seen as part of a dominating force. On the other hand, these parental alignments may co-occur with sustained internal-dyad exchanges wherein one spouse dominates the other—and women may regularly be part of (and a model for) the dominated.

We argue that the narrative practices of all family members in this study instantiate a form of gender asymmetry that we call a "Father knows best" dynamic. Within this dynamic, the father is typically set up—through his own and others' recurrent narrative practices—to be primary audience, judge, and critic of family members' actions, conditions, thoughts, and feelings as narrative protagonists (actors in the past) or as co-narrators (actors in the present). In our corpus, we are particularly struck by the practices of the women as mothers and wives that contribute to this dynamic, instantiating and modeling in their conduct as narrators a pervasive orientation toward fathers as evaluators. In this chapter, we focus especially on those specific practices.

The "Father knows best" ideology is usually associated with a prefeminist, presumably passé 1950s conceptualization of idyllic domestic order that was popularized and concretized by the television program of the same name. In that situation comedy, the title was often ironic, given that its episodes regularly served to point out that Father did not, in fact, know best but often learned that Mother had been right all along. Yet lip service to a "Father knows best" ideology was often maintained on the surface in that Mother would modestly defer to or indulge Father's ego. In the 1980s, variations on this formula for domestic gender relations included its extension to Black middle-class families, most popularly in *The Bill Cosby Show*. Our appropriation of this title is intended to suggest that the ideology may still be getting daily reinforcement in the everyday narrative practices of postfeminist 1990s American families—with considerable (perhaps unwitting) help from wives and mothers. Indeed, it seems to us that the ideology was instantiated even more strongly in the everyday dinnertime discourse in our study than it was or is in mass-media fictionalized versions of family life—that is, more implicitly and without the irony.

Database

For several years, we have been analyzing discourse practices in twenty middle-class, European American families, focusing especially on dinnertime communication patterns in narrative activity. The present study isolates a subcorpus of these families: seven two-parent families who earned more than $40,000 a year during the 1987–1989 period in which the study was conducted. Each family had a five-year-old child who had at least one older sibling.[2] Two fieldworkers video- and audiotaped each family on two evenings from an hour or so before dinner until the five-year-old went to bed. During the dinner activity, fieldworkers left the camera on a tripod and absented themselves.

The specific database for this study consists of the exactly one hundred past-time narratives (stories and reports) that the seven families told during thirteen dinners where both parents were present. As we elaborate in Ochs and Taylor (1992a, b) and Ochs, Taylor, Rudolph, and Smith (1992), we define a *story* as a problem-centered past-time narrative (e.g., the narrative activity eventually orients toward solving some aspect of the narrated events seen as problematic), whereas a *report* does not entail such a problem-centered or problem-solving orientation.

Narrative Instantiation of Gender Roles in the Family

The narrative roles that we address here as relevant to the construction of gender identities within families are those of *protagonist, introducer* (either elicitor or initial teller), *primary recipient, problematizer*, and *problematizee* (or *target*). Below we define each of these roles and discuss the extent to which that role was assumed by particular family members in our study.[3]

Protagonist

A *protagonist* is here defined as a leading or principal character in a narrated event. Our examination is limited to those narratives where at least one protagonist in the narrative is present at the dinner table, such as in (1), where the chief protagonist is five-year-old Jodie:

(1) Jodie's TB Shots Report (introductory excerpt)[4]

Participants:		———	
Mom		|	| Mom
Dad	Jodie |	| Dad
Jodie (female, 5 years)		———	
Oren (male, 7 years, 5 months)		Oren	

The following excerpt introduces the first past-time narrative told at this dinner, when the family has just begun eating.

Mom:	*((to Jodie))* =oh::You know what? You wanna tell Daddy what happened to you today?=
Dad:	*((looking up and off))* =Tell me everything that happened from the moment you went in - until:
	[
Jodie:	I got a sho:t?=
Dad:	=<u>EH</u> *((gasping))* what? *((frowning))*
Jodie:	I got a sho::t
	[
Dad:	<u>no</u>
Jodie:	*((nods yes, facing Dad))*
Dad:	*((shaking head no))* - Couldn't be
Jodie:	(mhm?) *((with upward nod, toward Dad))*
	[
Oren:	a TV test? *((to Mom))*
	(0.4)
Oren:	TV test? Mommy?
Mom:	*((nods yes))* - mhm
Jodie:	and a sho:t
Dad:	*((to Jodie))* (what) Did you go to the uh:: - *((to Mom))* Did you go to the ?animal hospital?
Mom:	mhh - <u>no:?.</u>
Dad:	(where)
Jodie:	I just went to the doctor and I got a shot
Dad:	*((shaking head no))* I don't believe it
Jodie:	<u>ri:?lly::</u> ...

Protagonist is an important role with respect to the "Father knows best" dynamic in that the protagonist is presented as a topic for comment (e.g., in Jodie's case above, for belief or disbelief) by family members. While being a protagonist puts one's narrative actions, conditions, thoughts, and feelings on the table as a focus of attention, this attention is not always a plus, given that protagonists' actions, thoughts, and feelings are not only open to praise but also exposed to familial scrutiny, irony, challenge, and critique. Furthermore, if there is asymmetric distribution in the allocation of protagonist status, one family member may be more routinely exposed to such evaluation by others than the rest, impacting the degree to which some members' identities are constructed as protagonists more than others. In our corpus, such an asymmetry existed, whereby children were the preferred narrative protagonists, as exemplified in the report of Jodie's activities in (1). Children composed nearly 60 percent of all family-member protagonists; mothers figured as protagonists 23 percent of the time; fathers, 19 percent.[5] Fathers' being least often in the role of protagonist meant that their past actions, thoughts, and feelings were least often exposed to the scrutiny of others and, in this sense, they were the least vulnerable family members.

Introducer

In light of the vulnerability of protagonists to familial scrutiny, an important factor to consider is the extent to which family members assumed this role through their own initiative as opposed to having this role imposed on them through the elicitations and initiations of other family members. To address this issue, we consider next how narratives about family members were introduced.

The narrative role of *introducer* is here defined as the co-narrator who makes the first move to open a narrative, either by elicitation or by direct initiation. We define these two introducer roles as follows. An *elicitor* is a co-narrator who asks for a narrative to be told. In (1) above, Jodie's mother assumes this role and, in so doing, introduces the narrative. An *initial teller* is a co-narrator who expresses the first declarative proposition about a narrative event. In (1), Jodie assumed this role but, because her mother had elicited her involvement, Jodie was not the narrative introducer per se. In unelicited narratives such as (2), the initial teller (in this case, the mother) is also the narrative introducer.

(2)   Broken Chair Story
       Participants:

Mom		Josh	
Dad		———	
Ronnie (male, 4 years, 11 months)	Ronnie |	| Mom
Josh (male, 7 years, 10 months)		———	
		Dad	

During dinner preparation, as Mom brings Ronnie a spoon to open a can of Nestlé Quik, she scoots Ronnie's chair in to the table. Josh is at his place; Dad is in kitchen area to the right of the table, as shown above.

Mom: Oh This <u>chair?</u> broke - today
                        [
                        ((microwave? buzzer goes off))
Dad: I? know=

((Mom heads back toward kitchen, stops by Josh's chair; Josh begins looking at Ronnie's chair and under table))

Mom: =I- no:: I mean it rea:?lly broke today
                                    [
Dad: I? know (0.2) I know?

Mom: Oh You knew that it was split?

Dad: yeah?,

Mom: the whole wood('s) split?

Dad: yeah,

Mom: Oh Did you do it?
       (0.4)

Dad: I don't know if I did? it but I saw that it wa:?s=
                                    [
Mom: (oh)

((Josh goes under table to inspect chairs; Mom bends over to chair))

Ron?: (what? where?)
       =[
Mom: yeah I sat down? in it and the whole thing split so I - I tie:d
                                                              [
Dad: ((with a somewhat taunting intonation))   (That's a)
       rea:l si:gn? that you need to go on a di:?et.

Ron?: ((going under table too)) (where)

Mom: hh ((grinning as she rises from stooped position next to Josh's chair))

Ron?: (where where where)=

Josh: =Mi:ne? broke?

Mom: I fixed it - I tied (it to the-)
                           [
Josh: mi:ne? I'm not gonna sit on that chair (if it's broken)

((Josh pushes his chair away and takes Mom's; Mom pushes Josh's chair over to her place, tells the boys to sit down; the subject of the broken chair is dropped))

The role of introducer is one that we see as pivotal in controlling narrative activity. The introducer nominates narrative topics, thus proposing who is to be the focus of attention (i.e., the protagonist), what aspects of their lives are to be narrated, and when. In (1), Jodie's mother directs the family's attention to Jodie at a particular moment in the dinner, suggesting that there is a narrative to be told as well as the tone, focus, and implicit boundaries of that narrative. For that moment, the introducer proposes what is important (to know) about that family member, as a protagonist. In addition, the introducer controls who is to initiate the narrative account itself, either self-selecting, as in (2), or eliciting a co-narrator, as in (1). Finally, introducers also exert control in that they explicitly or implicitly select certain co-narrator(s) to be primary recipients of the narrative (see following section). In both examples above, mother as introducer selected father as primary recipient.

Although the majority of the protagonists in our corpus were the children, the majority of the narrative introducers were the parents (who introduced seventy-one of the one hundred stories and reports), mothers more often than fathers. (Mothers and fathers *elicited* narratives from others almost equally; their difference derives from mothers' greater tendency to introduce by *direct initiation* as well—and often about others rather than about themselves.) All family members were vulnerable to having narratives about themselves introduced by others. Moreover, for parents, there was relative parity in this regard: for mothers and fathers equally, fully half of all narratives in which they figured as protagonists were introduced by themselves—and almost half by someone else.

A striking asymmetry exists, however, between parents and children. Only one-third of the narratives about children were introduced by the child protagonists themselves (for five-year-olds and younger, the figure was only one-quarter).[6] Children became protagonists chiefly because mothers introduced them as such and often by mothers' direct initiation of the narrative account. Thus, mothers were largely responsible for determining which children and which aspects of children's lives were subject to dinnertime narrative examination—and when and how. In light of this finding, we suggest that, for mothers, the role of introducer may be appropriated (at least in some family cultures and contexts within the United States) as a locus of narrative control over children—and, among family members, children may be particularly vulnerable in this sense.

Primary Recipient

The narrative role of *primary recipient* is here defined as the co-narrator(s) to whom a narrative is predominantly oriented. This role is a powerful one in that it implicitly entitles the family member who assumes it to evaluate the narrative actions, thoughts, and feelings of family members as protagonists and/or as narrators. Anyone who recurrently occupies this position is instantiated as "family judge." As noted earlier, the introducer is critical to the assignment of primary recipient. In some cases, as in (1) and (2), the introducer designated another family member to be primary recipient; in other cases, as in (3), an introducer may select herself or himself.

(3)   Lucy's Swim Team Report (introductory excerpt)
      Near the end of dinner, Lucy (9 years, 7 months) has been describing her swim class when Dad raises a new, related narrative.

   Dad: (Your) mother said you were thinking of uh: - getting on
           the swim team?

   Lucy: ((nods yes once emphatically))
           (1.0) ((Mom, who has finished eating, takes plate to nearby
           counter and returns))

   Dad: ((nods yes)) - (good) ...

Not surprising but nevertheless striking was the privileging of parents as primary recipients of dinnertime narratives: parents assumed that role 82 percent of the time. Within this privileging of parents as preferred audience, fathers were favored over mothers. Whereas fathers often positioned themselves as primary recipients through their own elicitation of narratives (as in example 3, above), in some families mothers regularly nominated fathers as primary recipients through their narrative introductions, such as in (1): *You wanna tell Daddy what happened to you today?* When we overlay this finding on those discussed above, the overall pattern suggests a fundamental asymmetry in family narrative activity, whereby children's lives were told to parents but, by and large, parents did not narrate their lives to their children.

This preference for fathers as primary recipients is partly accounted for by the fact that the father is often the person at the dinner table who knows least about children's daily lives. Typically, even the women who work outside the home arrived home earlier than their husbands and had more opportunity to hear about the events in their children's days prior to dinner. However, there are several reasons to see that being "unknowing" is an inadequate account for fathers' prominence as primary recipients in these narratives. First, in two of the thirteen dinners studied here, mothers knew less about their children's day that day than did fathers, yet we did not observe fathers nominating mothers as primary recipients of narratives about children (i.e., in this corpus, we did not find fathers saying, "Tell Mommy what you did today"). Second, child initiators oriented more narratives to mothers than to fathers in spite of the mothers' generally greater prior knowledge of children's lives. Third, mothers and children were typically as unknowing about fathers' reportable experiences as fathers were about theirs, yet fathers seldom addressed their lives to mothers or children as preferred recipients. (We also did not find mothers—or fathers—saying to each other the equivalent of "Honey, tell the children what you did today.") These considerations suggest to us that it was not simply being unknowing (about family members' daily activities) that determined primary-recipient selection but, perhaps, a matter of *who* was unknowing.

By considering who the initial teller was for each narrative (i.e., the one who was typically the first to address the primary recipient directly), we determined that it was neither children nor fathers themselves who accounted for fathers' assuming the role of overall preferred recipient. Instead, it was mothers who—in addition to often directing children to orient to fathers through elicitations (e.g., *Tell Daddy about ...*)—also directly initiated many narratives to fathers as primary recipients. In fact, mothers' direct initiation to fathers was the single greatest factor in accounting for fathers' privileging as preferred recipient. Mothers initiated twice as many narratives oriented to fathers as fathers initiated toward mothers. In light of these findings, we suggest that a gender-socialization factor entered into the nonequation, prompting mothers' elevation of unknowing fathers into primary recipients—and judges—of other family members' lives, unmatched by fathers' similar elevation of unknowing mothers to such status.

We have noted above that narrative introducers exert control by designating primary recipients, but here we emphasize that, at the same time, such designation passes control to the co-narrator who is so designated: the primary recipient is in a position to evaluate, reframe, or otherwise pass judgment on both the tale and how it is told. In our view, the role of primary recipient affords a panopticon-like perspective and power (Bentham 1791; Foucault 1979). The term *panopticon* refers to an all-seeing eye or monitoring gaze that keeps subjects under its constant purview (e.g., a prison guard in a watchtower). Similarly, we suggest that narrative activity exposes protagonists to the surveillance of other co-narrators, especially to the scrutiny of the designated primary recipient (see Ochs & Taylor 1992b). Given that this role was played mainly by the fathers in our data, we further suggest that it is potentially critical to the narrative reconstruction of "Father knows best" because it sets up the father to be the ultimate purveyor and judge of other family members' actions, conditions, thoughts, and feelings.

The family-role preferences we have found with regard to these first three narrative roles—protagonist, introducer, and primary recipient— already present an overall picture of the way in which narrative activity may serve to put women, men, and children into a politics of asymmetry. As noted earlier, in the family context, issues of gender and power cannot be looked at as simply dyadic, i.e., *men* versus *women* as *haves* versus *have-nots*. Rather, in two-parent families, women and men manifest asymmetries of power both dyadically as spouses and triadically as mothers and fathers with children. Although there *are* interesting dyadic observations here regarding women versus men (e.g., women tend to raise narrative topics; men tend to be positioned—often by women—to evaluate them), these apparently gender-based distinctions are part of a *triadic* interaction, or larger picture, wherein children are often the subjects of these narrative moves. Neither women's nor men's control is merely a control over each other but particularly encompasses and impacts children. Furthermore, a narrative role such as that of introducer (seen here to be more aligned with women, at least as initial teller) may have a complex relationship to power, both empowering the holder in terms of agenda-setting, choice of protagonist, and topic, but also disempowering to the degree that the introducer sets up someone else (here more often the man) to be ultimate judge of the narrated actions and protagonists.

Problematizer/Problematizee

The narrative role of *problematizer* is here defined as the co-narrator who renders an action, condition, thought, or feeling of a protagonist or a co-narrator problematic, or possibly so. The role of *problematizee* (or *target*) is defined as the co-narrator whose action, condition, thought, or feeling is rendered problematic, or a possible problem. As such, in this study, we consider only problematizing that targeted co-present family members.

An action, condition, thought, or feeling may be problematized on several grounds. For example, it may be treated as untrue, incredible, or doubtful, as when, in (1), the father problematized Jodie's TB shots narrative with mock disbelief (*no, couldn't be,* and *I don't believe it*). In other cases, it is problematized because it has or had negative ramifications (e.g., is deemed thoughtless or perilous), as when, in (2), the wife implicitly problematized her husband as thoughtless for not warning her about the broken chair (*Oh You knew that it was* _split!_).

We also see in (2) how an action, condition, thought, or feeling may be problematized on grounds of incompetence. When the husband indicted his wife for being overweight as the cause of the chair's breaking (*That's a* _rea:l_ _si:gn!_ *that you need to go on a* _di::!et._), we suggest he was implicitly problematizing her for lack of self-control. In (4), the same father again problematizes his wife, this time as too lenient a boss and thus incompetent in her workplace as well:

(4)   Mom's Job Story (excerpt)
       Same family as in (2). At the end of dinner, Mom is at the sink doing dish-
       es as Dad eats an ice cream sundae and seven-year-old Josh does home-
       work at the table opposite Dad. This excerpt comes near the end of a story
       about Mom's hiring a new assistant at work, which Dad has elicited and
       already probed considerably.

> Dad: *((eating dessert))* Well - I certainly think that - you're a- you
>   know you're a fair bo?ss - You've been working there how
>   long?
>
> Mom: fifteen years in June *((as she scrapes dishes at kitchen sink))*
>
> Dad: fifteen <u>years</u> - and you got a guy *((turns to look directly at Mom*
>   *as he continues))* that's been workin there a few <u>weeks?</u> and
>   you do (it what) the way <u>he</u> wants.
>
> Mom: hh *((laughs))*
>   (0.6) *((Dad smiles slightly?, then turns back to eating his dessert))*
>
> Mom: It's not a matter of my doin it the way <u>he: wa:nt -</u> It <u>does</u> help
>   in that I'm getting more <u>work?</u> done It's just that I'm workin
>   too <u>hard?</u> I don't wanta <u>work</u> so hard
>
> Dad: *((rolls chair around to face Mom halfway))* Well - You're the
>   <u>bo:ss</u> It's up to you to set the standards ...

Further grounds for problematizing were on the basis that an action is
out-of-bounds—e.g., unfair, rude, excessive. In (5), the father problematizes
his wife for her wasteful consumption (e.g., *You <u>had</u> a dress right?; Doesn't*
that sound like a - total: - w:aste?) and for her lack of consideration toward
his mother (e.g., *Why did you let my Mom get you something (that you) - ;*
Oh she just <u>got</u> it for you?):

(5)   Mom's Dress Story (Round 2 of two-round story)[7]
       Same family as in (1). The children have finished eating and just gone out-
       side to play; Dad is helping himself to more meat; Mom had begun a story
       about her new dress, interrupted by a phone call from his mother.

> Round 2 *((begins after Mom hangs up phone and sits at table))*
> Dad: So as you were saying?
> Mom: (As I was) saying *((turning abruptly to face Dad))* What was I
>   telling you
> Dad: I ?don't? know
> Mom: oh about the ?dress?
> Dad: (the) <u>dress</u>
>   (1.2) *((Mom is drinking water; Dad looks to her, to his plate, then*
>   *back to her))*
> Dad: You <u>had</u> a dress right?

Mom: *((nodding yes once))* Your <u>mo</u>ther bought (me it) - My
       mother didn't (like) it.
       (0.4) *((Mom tilts head, facing Dad, as if to say "What could I
       do?"))*
Dad: *((shaking head no once))* You're kidding
Mom: no
Dad: You gonna return it?
Mom: No you can't return it - It wasn't too expensive - It was
       from Loehmann's
       (0.8)
Mom: So what I'll probably do? - is wear it to the dinner the night
       before - when we go to the (Marriott)?
       (1.8) *((Dad turns head away from Mom with a grimace, as if he
       is debating whether he is being conned, then turns and looks off))*
Dad: (Doesn't that) sound like a - (total:) - w:aste?
Mom: <u>no?:</u>
Dad: no
Mom: *((with hands out, shaking head no))* It wasn't even that
       ex<u>pen?</u>sive
       (1.2)
Mom: *((shaking head no, facing Dad))* even if it were a com<u>plete</u>
       waste
       (0.4) *((Dad looks down at plate, bobs head right and left as if
       not convinced))*
Mom: but it's not. *((looking away from Dad))*
       (0.6) *((Mom looks outside, then back to Dad))*
Mom: (but the one) my mom got me is <u>gr:ea::t</u> -
                        [
                        *((Dad eats from son Oren's plate
                         next to him))*
Mom: (Is the *((inaudible))* okay?)
Dad: *((gesturing with palm up, quizzical))* (Well why did) you have -
       Why did you let my mom get you something (that you-)
Mom: Your <u>mo:</u>ther bought it - I hh-
Dad: Oh she just <u>got</u> it for you?
Mom: *((turning away from Dad, nodding yes))* (yeah)
Dad: You weren't there?
Mom: I was <u>there</u> (and your mom) said "No no It's great Let me
       <u>buy</u> it for you" *((turning back to face Dad))* - I didn't <u>ask</u> her
       to <u>buy</u> it for me?
       (5.0) *((Dad is eating more food from son's plate; Mom looking
       toward table))*

Dad: So they're <u>figh</u>ting over who <u>gets</u> you things?

Mom: ((nods yes slightly)) - ((smiling to Dad)) tch - (cuz I'm) so
         won?derful

         (9.0) ((no visible reaction from Dad; Mom turns to look outside;
         the subject of the dress is dropped))

In the narratives in our corpus, exactly half of them involved someone problematizing a family member at the dinner table. Those fifty narratives generated a total of 229 problematizations of oneself or, much more often, of another family member.[8] Problematizing displays the most significantly asymmetric narrator-role distribution found in this study and reveals a "Father knows best" dynamic in family interaction. Men took on the role of problematizer 45 percent more often than women did and 3.5 times as often as did children. Strikingly, this pattern was mirrored in female and male children's uptake of the problematizer role. Among children, boys did 50 percent more problematizing than girls (even though there were nine girls and eight boys in the corpus who were old enough to co-narrate). With regard to family members' role constitution vis-à-vis narrative problematizing, men were problematizers almost twice as often as they were problematizees; women were as often problematizees as problematizers; and children were predominantly positioned as problematizees.

Examining individual instances to assess who problematized whom (i.e., the preferred target for each family member), we found that the bulk of narrative problematizing occurred between spouses. In 80 percent of the eighty-four instances in which mothers were problematized, the problematizer was the husband. In 63 percent of sixty-seven instances in which fathers were targeted, the problematizer was the wife. Thus, although women also targeted their spouses, men did so 60 percent more often. The targeting of women by their husbands represents the largest allocation of problematizings in our corpus of narratives. The differential in both absolute numbers and percentages of cross-spousal problematizing suggests in more detail the across-the-board nature of men's domination.[9] That is, both women and men vastly outproblematized their children, but men also considerably outproblematized their wives. Examples (1), (2), (4), and (5) above illustrate how men problematized their spouse or their child.

In addition to this overall quantitative difference, there were differences as well in the qualitative nature of women's versus men's problematizations. Notably, there was a distinction in spouses' use of two domains of problematizing: the problematizing of someone's actions, thoughts, or feelings (in the past) as a protagonist versus the problematizing of someone's comments (in the present) as a co-narrator. The latter category includes counterproblematizing in self-defense, as a response to a previous problematizing (here, by the spouse). The distribution of cross-spousal use of these problematizing strategies indicates that husbands criticized their spouse as protagonist far more often than was the case for wives (thirty-six times versus fourteen times).

Many of the husbands' problematizings of wives as protagonists entailed targeting the wife on grounds of incompetence, as exemplified in (4), Mom's Job Story. In contrast, wives did not problematize husbands on the basis of incompetence as protagonists; as noted above, wives relatively infrequently problematized their spouses as protagonists at all. Rather, women most often problematized men as narrators and much of that was of the counterproblematizing type, either in self-defense or in defense of their children. In other words, fathers would target what mothers had done in the reported events and then mothers would refute the fathers' comments as co-narrators. Men's problematizing focused on "You shouldn't have done x"; women's problematizing was more a form of resistance—to being problematized. Women were more often saying in essence, "No, that's not the way it happened ... "; "Your interpretation is wrong ... "; "You don't see the context." Thus, women—to the degree that they are regularly targeted for problematization—may get the impression that they cannot *do* anything right (and wind up defending past actions, as seen in the Mom's Job and Mom's Dress Stories), whereas men—to the degree they are regularly targeted more for their comments as co-narrator—may get the impression that they can't *say* anything right.

Men's preeminence as problematizers is further seen in the fact that they problematized their spouses over a much wider range of narrative topics than did women. Wives' conduct and stance concerning child care, recreation, meal preparation, and even their professional lives were open to husbands' critiques. Narratives about men's workdays, however, were exceedingly rare and were virtually never problematized. This asymmetry, wherein men had or were given "problematizing rights" over a wider domain of their spouses' experiences than were women, further exemplifies how narrative activity at dinner may instantiate and socialize a "Father knows best" worldview; i.e., it is men as fathers and husbands who scrutinize and problematize everything.[10]

Given men's presumption to quantitative and qualitative dominance as problematizers *par excellence* in this corpus, an important issue to raise is the extent to which men's prominence as problematizers was related to their role as preferred primary recipients. There was clearly a strong link between the two roles for them: 86 of men's 116 problematizings occurred when they were primary recipients of the narrative. However, the status of primary recipient does not, in itself, completely account for who assumed the role of problematizer.

Three observations in particular dispute such an interpretation. First, men exploited the primary-recipient role to do problematizing to a far greater extent than other family members did. As primary recipient, fathers problematized a family member, on average, 1.6 times per narrative; women did so only 0.55 times per narrative, and children only 0.05 times per narrative. In both degree and range of problematizing, men used their recipient status distinctively. Second, the whole level of problematizing went up when the father/husband was primary recipient. Of the 229 problematizings in the corpus, 155 occurred when he was primary recipient, averaging 2.8 problematizings per narrative, considerably more than when either women or children were primary recipients (1.6 per narrative and 0.5 per narrative, respectively). As already suggested in the discussion of counterproblematizing, this heightened level of problematization overall occurred largely because men's problematizing of women (as protagonists) triggered women's own counterproblematizing of their husbands. As a result, women became problematizers much more often when men were primary recipients than when the women themselves were primary recipients (54 times versus 22 times). Third, we note that men problematized more than women did even in narratives where the woman was primary recipient (24 times versus 22 times).

For all these reasons, a primary recipient-becomes-problematizer explanation is too simplistic an account. Rather, our corpus suggests conceptualizations of recipientship that differentiate women, men, and children, i.e., differing dispositions and perhaps entitlements to problematize, with men in privileged critical positions. The role of problematizer seems to be a particular prerogative of the family role of father/husband, manifesting the ideology that "Father knows best," socializing and (re)constituting paternal prerogative and point of view in and through narrative activity.

Because an important issue we are pursuing here is women's role in establishing a "Father knows best" dynamic at the family dinner table and because we have seen that women's most notable narrative role was that of introducer, we examined the introducer-problematizer relationship to discover in particular the extent to which men's problematizings occurred in narratives introduced by women. Our finding is that women's introductions may indeed have triggered men's problematizations. First, when women introduced narratives, problematizing in general was more prevalent than when men or children did the introducing.[11] In narratives introduced by women, family members were problematized, on average, 3.4 times per narrative, considerably more than for narratives introduced by men (2.0 times) or by children (1.1). Second, the majority of men's problematizings (72 out of 116) occurred in narratives introduced by women. Men problematized other family members 1.8 times per narrative in those introduced by women, i.e., an even higher rate than we noted above when the factor of men's status as primary recipients was considered. Furthermore, men problematized more often in narratives introduced by women than in narratives they introduced themselves. This higher number of problematizations in narratives introduced by one's spouse might seem expectable but it was not matched by women, who wound up (counter)problematizing more often in the narratives they themselves introduced.[12] We see in these data an asymmetrical pattern wherein women's raising a topic seems to have promoted men's problematizing but not the reverse.

Women's assumption of the role of introducer co-occurred not only with increased problematization by men but also with increased targeting of women themselves. Women were problematized most often in the very narratives they introduced: 75 percent of all targetings of women occurred in those narratives, an average of 1.6 times per narrative. These figures contrast markedly with those for men: only 33 percent of the problematizings of men occurred in narratives they themselves introduced, an average of only 0.7 times per narrative.

These findings suggest that women were especially vulnerable to exposing themselves to criticism, particularly from their husbands, and thus may have been "shooting themselves in the foot" in bringing up narratives in the first place, as illustrated in (2), the Broken Chair Story, where a woman's designation (i.e., control) of narrative topic and primary recipient boomeranged in an explicit attack on her weight. In (1), Jodie's TB Shots Report, we see an example of how mother-introduced narratives also expose children to problematization by fathers. Reconsidering our earlier observation that women were problematized over a wider range of daily activities, including professional lives, than were men, we can posit that this may have resulted largely from women's introducing themselves as protagonists in a much wider range of contexts to begin with.

One final issue with regard to problematization concerns the extent to which family members self-problematized. In our corpus, women displayed the highest proportion of self-targetings and, in keeping with the findings just discussed, this was also associated with narratives that women themselves raised. Although such targetings account for a relatively small proportion (12 percent) of the targetings of women overall, and they came essentially from only two families, these female self-problematizings are noteworthy in their provoking of a "dumping-on" response. That is, when women did question their own past actions, it seemed to invite considerable additional problematizing by their husbands. As illustrated in (6), a wife problematizes herself as protagonist and her husband elaborates:

(6)   Bev Story (excerpt)
       This family consists of Mom (Marie), Dad (Jon), and four children (who at this point in the dinner have finished eating). Mom runs a day-care center in their home; she has been recounting to Dad how one of her day-care children's mothers, Bev, had given her more money than was owed for day-care services and that she had not accepted the extra money. She then recalled how Bev had not given a required two weeks' notice for withdrawing her daughter from day care, whereupon Dad problematized Mom's nonacceptance of the money as naive (i.e., incompetent).

       Mom: *((head on hand, elbow on table, facing Dad opposite her))* You know - Jon I verbally <u>did</u> tell Bev two weeks' notice Do you think I should've stuck to that? or just done what I did? (0.8) *((The children are standing by their seats, apparently listening))*

       Dad: When I say something I stick to it. unless <u>she:</u> - s-brings it up. If <u>I</u> set a policy - and a- - and - they accept that policy - unless <u>they</u> have reason to change it and and say something? <u>I</u> do not <u>change</u> it - I don't <u>auto</u>matically assume .h "We:ll it's not the <u>right</u> thing to do" If I were to <u>do</u> that e-I would be saying in the first place I should never have mentioned it I should never have set the policy if I didn't believe in it If I thought it was - a <u>hard</u>ship on people I shouldn'a brought it up? - shoulda kept my mouth shut .h If <u>I:</u> say there's two weeks' notice required - .h I automatically charge em for two weeks' notice without thinking twice? about it I say and i- "If you-you need - Your pay will include till such and such a date because of the two neek-weeks' notice that's required." - I:f <u>THE:Y</u> feel hardship it's on <u>thei:r</u> part - it's - <u>THEIRS</u> to say .h "Marie I really? - you know - I didn't expect this to happen 'n I'm *((softly))* sorry I didn't give you two weeks' notice but it was really <u>un</u> - a<u>void</u>able" - a:nd you can say "We:ll - okay I'll split the difference with you - it's har- - a <u>one</u> week's notice" - and then they s- then if they <u>push</u> it
                                        [
       Mom: See? you know in one way wi- in one (instance) *((pointing to Dad))* she <u>owed</u> me that money - but I just didn't feel right? taking it=
                                        [
       Dad: well you're - you

Mom:	=on that pretense because she (wanted) - <u>she</u> thought she was paying it for something ((*twirling her corncob*)) that (she didn't)

<pre>   [
Dad: You: give
     her the money and then you let it <u>bo</u>ther you then - you -
     get <u>all</u> ups-set You'll be upset for weeks
                    [
Mom: No no no - I'm <u>not</u> upset - it's just
</pre>

(0.4) ((*Mom plops corncob down, raps knuckles on table*))

Mom:	I guess I just wish I would have s:aid - I'm <u>not</u> upset with what happened - I just wanted- I think I - <u>would</u> feel better if I had said (something)....

In questioning her own actions as protagonist (*Do you think I should've stuck to that? or just done what I did?*), Marie invites her husband's evaluation and exposes herself to his critical uptake as he problematizes both her past actions (<u>*You:*</u> *give her the money*) and her present feelings (... *you let it* <u>*bother*</u> *you then - you - get* <u>*all*</u> *ups-set You'll be upset for weeks*). She is left to backtrack in self-defense, countering his portrayal of her present state and (re)defining her self-problematization on her own terms (... *I just wish I would have* ...), no longer as a question inviting further dumping on.[13]

In our corpus, the uptake on self-problematizing further distinguished women's and men's narrative practices; in contrast to this dumping-on response, women did not further problematize men after the men problematized themselves. When women took the opposite tack and presented themselves as problem-solvers rather than self-problematizers, another asymmetric practice entailed the husband's dismissing his wife's solution and problematizing it until she conceded at least partially. An example of this is seen in (5), Mom's Dress Story, when Mom offers her own solution to the two-dress situation (*So what I'll probably do? - is wear it to the dinner the night before* ...), to which Dad responds, "(Doesn't) that sound like a - (total:) - w:aste?" Mom initially rebuts (*no?:*) but, in the face of Dad's skepticism, concedes "... even if it were a com<u>plete</u> waste," thus implicitly problematizing herself by Dad's terms in acknowledging that she might have been wasteful.

Our data also suggest that women's self-problematizing may have socializing effects. This was vividly illustrated in a lengthy story focusing on a mother and her son in a restaurant (the same family as in Jodie's TB Shots Report and Mom's Dress Story). In this narrative, the son, Oren, recalls eating a chili pepper his mother thought was a green bean. Although Oren initially frames the experience as funny, his mother tells him it wasn't funny, that his mouth was burning and hurting. While problematizing his stance as narrator, she also implicates herself as a culprit, thereby self-problematizing as protagonist. In the course of the story, Oren eventually takes on his mother's more serious framing of events, to the point of shouting, "YOUR FAULT - YOUR FAULT." She agrees, nodding her head and saying, "It was my fault." While she is saying this, he leans over and pinches her cheeks hard. She gasps and pulls his hands away, saying, "OW That really hurts honey?" As she holds a napkin to her mouth and cheeks, her son comments, "Your fault - I get to do whatever I want to do once - (That was my fee?)," laughs, and adds, "Just like it happened to me it happens to you." Just as husbands piled on to wives' self-targeting, Oren thus follows up on his mother's self-problematizing, extending condemnation and executing punishment for her self-problematized actions. In so doing, he seems to be assuming a dramatic version of what, in this corpus, was a male narrator role.

This discussion calls attention to an appropriate ending caveat to our findings throughout this chapter. Namely, there is family variation even within this sample of seven families of similar socioeconomic status and racial-cultural background. There were men who took up the role of monitor and judge with what seemed almost a vengeance; there were others who displayed much less assertion of the prerogatives of power as primary recipient. Furthermore, we do not wish to fix particular men's (or women's) narrator personae based on two evenings in the lives of these families. Our aim is not to polarize the genders, but, rather, to shed potential new light on some underexplored aspects of gender construction and socialization in everyday narrative activity.

Conclusion

Synthesizing these findings—with the caveats noted above—we construe a commonplace scenario of narrative activity at family dinners characterized by a sequence of the following order. First, mothers introduce narratives (about themselves and their children) that set up fathers as primary recipients and implicitly sanction them as evaluators of others' actions, conditions, thoughts, and feelings. Second, fathers turn such opportunities into forums for problematizing, with mothers themselves as their chief targets, very often on grounds of incompetence. And third, mothers respond in defense of themselves and their children via the counterproblematizing of fathers' evaluative, judgmental comments.

In the first stage, we see mothers' narrative locus of power; in the second, however, we see that such exercise of power is ephemeral and may even be self-destructive by giving fathers a platform for monitoring and judging wives and children. In the third stage, we see mothers striving to reclaim control over the narratives they originally put on the table. Given our impression of the recurrence of these preferences and practices, it seems that the struggle of the third stage is not ultimately successful in that the fathers reappear as primary recipients and the cycle of narrative reenactment characterized by this generalized scenario prevails. It may be that all parties obtain a particular type of satisfaction or stasis through this interplay such that it serves underlying needs, self-conceptions, and communicative goals. However, in this generalized scenario, mothers seem to play a pivotal role in enacting and socializing a hegemonic activity system (Engeström 1987; Gramsci 1971) in which fathers are regularly reinstantiated as arbiters of conduct narratively laid before them as in a panopticon.

In the family interactions we observed, when women directed their narratives to their husbands (or when children directed their narratives, voluntarily or not, to their fathers), they disadvantaged themselves by exposing their experiences to male scrutiny and standards of judgment. They performed actions as narrators that rendered them vulnerable to repeated spousal/paternal criticism of them, especially as protagonists. Through such means and with such effects, "Father knows best"—a gender ideology with a deeply rooted politics of asymmetry that has been contested in recent years—is still in reverberating evidence at the two-parent family dinner table, jointly constituted and re-created through everyday narrative practices. In this chapter, we hope to have raised awareness of the degree to which some women as wives and mothers may wittingly or unwittingly contribute to—and even set up—the daily reconstruction of a "Father knows best" ideological dynamic.

Acknowledgments

This chapter is the result of the equal work of both authors. We are grateful for the support this research has received from the National Institute of Child Health Development (1986–1990: "Discourse Processes in American Families," Principal Investigators Elinor Ochs and Thomas Weisner, Research Assistants Maurine Bernstein, Dina Rudolph, Ruth Smith, and Carolyn Taylor) and from the Spencer Foundation (1990–1993: "Socialization of Scientific Discourse," Principal Investigator Elinor Ochs, Research Assistants Patrick Gonzales, Sally Jacoby, and Carolyn Taylor). We thank Marcelo Diversi for his assistance in editing the final version of this chapter. A preliminary version of this article appeared in the proceedings of the Second Berkeley Women and Language Conference (Ochs & Taylor 1992c).

Notes

1. Clearly, our findings are implicative for certain family cultures and are not inclusive of the range of linguistic, ethnic, economic, and other forms of group variation within the United States. This study is offered as a basis for possible future studies of family narrative activity as a medium for constituting gender relations in other socioeconomic and cultural settings for which we do not presume to speak here. At the same time, while we suggest a certain resonance in these findings, we recognize the limits of our corpus and do not wish to over-generalize regarding narrative practices even for white middle-class families.

2. This choice of five-year-olds follows from our interest in the roles played by children of an age to be fully capable of collaboration in family talk but still in their earliest, most pivotal years of language socialization (prior to much formal schooling). We also wanted at least one older child in the families so as to capture sibling as well as parent-child interaction.

3. For simplicity, we will often refer to participants by only one family role, e.g., to women as *mothers*, men as *fathers*, and girls and boys as *children*, but we note again, in keeping with our introductory perspectives, that at any one moment each participant may be constructing more than one family identity, e.g., also as spouses, as siblings, as females, as males.

4. All family names are pseudonyms. Transcription procedures are essentially those established by Gail Jefferson (see Atkinson & Heritage 1984:ix–xvi):

[	a left-hand bracket indicates the onset of overlapping, simultaneous utterances
=	two equals signs (latches) link utterances either by two speakers where the second jumps in on the end of the first, without any interval, or by the same speaker when lengthy overlap by another speaker requires that a continuous utterance be interrupted on the transcript to show simultaneity with another
(0.4)	indicates length of pause within and between utterances, timed in tenths of a second
a - a	a hyphen with spaces before and after indicates a short pause, less than 0.2 seconds
sa-	a hyphen immediately following a letter indicates an abrupt cutoff in speaking
(( ))	double parentheses enclose nonverbal and other descriptive information
( )	single parentheses enclose words that are not clearly audible (i.e., best guesses)
___	underlining indicates stress on a syllable or word(s)
CAPS	upper case indicates louder or shouted talk
:	a colon indicates a lengthening of a sound, the more colons, the longer
.	a period indicates falling intonation
,	a comma indicates a continuing intonation

?   a question mark indicates a rising intonation as a syllable or word ends

         Note: bounding question marks (e.g., *Did you go to the ¿animal hospital?*) are used (instead of rising arrows) to indicate a higher pitch for enclosed word(s).

h   an *h* indicates an exhalation, the more *h*'s, the longer the exhalation

.h   an *h* with a period before it indicates an inhalation, the more *h*'s, the longer

5. For tables detailing the quantitative findings of this study, see Ochs and Taylor (1992c).

6. For more detail and elaborated consideration of the roles of children in the narrative activity of this corpus, see Ochs and Taylor (1992b).

7. When a narrative is interrupted or dropped and taken up again after an interval of at least two other turns, we consider the restart to constitute a new "round."

8. Only 10 percent of all problematizations were "self-inflicted," meaning that 90 percent of the problematizations targeted others. The percentage of problematizing directed toward oneself was highest for women, although still only 12 percent. In keeping with our present focus on exploring women's roles in particular, we will discuss and illustrate these self-problematizations in more detail following our examination of cross-spousal problematizing.

9. Accounting for the percentage differential in cross-spousal targeting, the children, albeit infrequent problematizers, did twice as much targeting of fathers as they did of mothers.

10. Perhaps contrary to general expectation, spouses in our corpus did not tend to elicit narratives from each other about their workdays (Mom's Job Story being an exception), so that parental "what-my-day-was-like" narratives, unlike the narratives of children, tended to be directly self-initiated to the spouse without elicitation.

11. Out of the 39 narratives introduced by women, 62 percent included at least one instance of someone's problematizing a family member at the dinner table. In contrast, only 44 percent of the narratives introduced by men and 41 percent of those introduced by children evidenced such problematizing.

12. On average, men problematized in narratives that they introduced themselves only 1.2 times per narrative, i.e., less often than they problematized in narratives introduced by women (1.8 times per narrative). In contrast, women problematized in narratives that they introduced themselves 1.4 times per narrative, i.e much more often than they problematized in narratives introduced by men (only 0.5 times per narrative).

13. Regarding the roles and implications of problematization or challenges in co-narrators' theories of everyday events, and the potential here for Marie to incorporate her husband's challenge into something of a paradigm shift in her own stance, see Ochs, Smith, and Taylor (1989) and Ochs, Taylor, Rudolph, and Smith (1992).

References

Atkinson, J. Maxwell, and John Heritage (eds.) (1984). *Structures of social action: Studies in conversation analysis.* Cambridge: Cambridge University Press.

Bentham, Jeremy (1791). *Panopticon.* London: T. Payne.

Cole, Michael, and Sheila Cole (1989). *The development of children.* New York: Scientific American Books.

Dunn, Judy (1984). *Sisters and brothers.* Cambridge, MA: Harvard University Press.

Engeström, Yrjö (1987). *Learning by expanding: An activity-theoretical approach to developmental research.* Helsinki: Orienta-Konsultit Oy.

Foucault, Michel (1979). *Discipline and punish: The birth of the prison.* Translated by Alan Sheridan. New York: Random House.

Freud, Sigmund ([1921] 1949). *The standard edition of the complete psychological works of Sigmund Freud.* London: Hogarth Press.

Goodwin, Marjorie Harness (1990). *He-said-she-said: Talk as social organization among black children.* Bloomington: Indiana University Press.

Gramsci, Antonio (1971). *Selections from the prison notebooks of Antonio Gramsci.* Translated and edited by Quintin Hoare and Geoffrey Nowell Smith. New York: International Publishers.

Hartmann, Heidi I. (1981). The family as the locus of gender, class, and political struggle: The example of housework. *Signs* 6(3): 366–94.

Kohlberg, Lawrence (1966). *The development of sex differences.* Stanford: Stanford University Press.

Maccoby, Eleanor E., and Carol N. Jacklin (1974). *The psychology of sex differences.* Stanford: Stanford University Press.

Ochs, Elinor, Ruth Smith, and Carolyn Taylor (1989). Detective stories at dinnertime: Problem-solving through co-narration. *Cultural Dynamics* 2(2): 238–57.

Ochs, Elinor, and Carolyn Taylor (1992a). Science at dinner. In Claire Kramsch and Sally McConnell-Ginet (eds.), *Text and context: Cross-disciplinary perspectives on language study.* Lexington, MA: Heath. 29–45.

—— (1992b). Family narrative as political activity. *Discourse & Society* 3(3): 301–40.

—— (1992c). Mothers' role in the everyday reconstruction of "Father knows best." In Kira Hall, Mary Bucholtz, and Birch Moonwomon (eds.), *Locating power: Proceedings of the Second Berkeley Women and Language Conference.* Berkeley: Berkeley Women and Language Group. 447–62.

Ochs, Elinor, Carolyn Taylor, Dina Rudolph, and Ruth Smith (1992). Storytelling as a theory-building activity. *Discourse Processes* 15(1): 37–72.

Osmond, Marie Withers, and Barrie Thorne (1993). Feminist theories: The social construction of gender in families and society. In Pauline G. Boss, William J. Doherty, Ralph LaRossa, Walter R. Schumm, and Suzanne K. Steinmetz (eds.), *Sourcebook of family theories and methods: A contextual approach.* New York: Plenum Press. 591–623.

Schieffelin, Bambi B. (1990). *The give and take of everyday life: Language socialization of Kaluli children.* Cambridge: Cambridge University Press.

Stack, Carol (1974). *All our kin: Strategies for survival in a black community.* New York: Harper & Row.

5

—

Managing the Body of Labor

The Treatment of Reproduction and Sexuality
in a Therapeutic Institution

Cathryn Houghton

Recent commentators (e.g., Willis 1977) have stated that domination depends on the consent of the dominated. Such a view, though tragic, seems optimistic. It is optimistic in the sense that coercive force is no longer necessary, despite a long history that would attest otherwise, in the operations of a now-civilized state. It is tragic in the sense that consent increasingly depends on the thorough brainwashing of consenting parties. In this case, what is consent? What is freedom, autonomy, or independence, the values held so sacred by the citizens of a democratically ruled society? In a paradoxical way, state incorporation of coercive power presents a more optimistic outlook than that of symbolic power, or rule through the less readily perceived mechanisms of hegemonic control. The present chapter explores a case in which certain citizens do not subscribe to dominant values and the discourses through which they are articulated. Direct and indirect mechanisms of power are combined in manufacturing the consent of women who are designated for positions upon which industrial capitalism depends most: menial wage labor. Indeed, women increasingly represent the body of labor serving the forces of production and consumption, both nationally and internationally (see, for example, Ong 1987).

In disciplining the body of labor, institutions represent a state-sanctioned use of coercive power. Within the institution, rights become privileges, and freedoms that are taken for granted by ordinary citizens outside the institution are suspended (Basaglia 1987). In the institutions that serve as a basis of this study, therapeutic treatment functions as a means of behavioral management. In treating adolescent women removed from marginalized, predominantly Latino neighborhood communities, therapy involves an effort to address the resistance of young women to participating productively in the work force and to correct contraceptive problems and subsequent patterns of dependency on the state welfare system.

Culturally constructed ideas about the appropriate conditions for "normal" or "healthy" adolescent development inform decisions to remove women from previous living arrangements to the therapeutic institution. Intervention of social services is often due to school truancy or "overcrowded" or "unsanitary" living conditions. Given the institutional goals of "producing independently functioning and productive adult members of the community" (as stated on a program brochure), the therapeutic structure is intended to equip adolescent women with the skills of independent living and productive participation in the work force. School, vocational training, and part-time jobs are all components of treatment in the institution. On a more implicit level, therapeutic treatment is prescribed for those who do not subscribe to the dominant system of values, in which work, material acquisition, and productivity are an integral part of mainstream Western orientation.

In contrast to the women who embrace American ideals of autonomy, the rewards of work have little to offer the women who adhere to the values of traditional Latino communities. Such women often assume roles as principal caretakers enmeshed in an interdependence of community and familial relations. Perhaps due to the influence of the welfare system (see Piven & Cloward 1971), men seem to remain marginal figures in the communities where these women have been raised, and mother-daughter relationships, often labeled "codependent" in the therapeutic milieu, are among the most significant. It is also because of the relative absence of husbands and father figures that such family organization is determined to be less than appropriate according to the values of the dominant group. In addressing the values underlying such social arrangements, treatment must therefore involve more than the management of behavior through coercive means; the individual and cultural orientations unlikely to be effected through coercion must also be induced. In addressing resistance, therapeutic treatment must do more than prepare young women with vocational skills for the work force; it must first bring them to consent to the structures of production and consumption and their designated positions within them.

This chapter begins by addressing the role of power in language. The most powerful use of language is that of which we are least aware. In structuring the conditions conducive to the exercise of power through language, however, the role of coercive power cannot be overlooked. Although more readily apparent, the use of coercive power often remains invisible to citizens who are in compliance with mainstream values. Finally, the roles of power and resistance will be addressed, followed by a discussion of the limitations of their treatment in current social theory. Analysis is based upon recorded transcripts of interaction in group therapy sessions, and a two-year period of participant observation within several state-funded institutions. For the purposes of this study, the names of places and people mentioned herein are pseudonyms in order to protect individuals' identity and privacy.

Language and Linguistic Practices of Power

It is a firmly held tenet of clinical practice that internal change and ideological reorientation cannot be motivated by coercive measures alone, for although bodies can be controlled and regulated by external structures of control, minds cannot. To capture the words that reverberate throughout the therapeutic milieu, "You have to want to change." In efforts to bring patients to buy into the system, so to speak, and subscribe to the values of the producer- and consumer-oriented culture, the emphasis of therapeutic practice is on talk.

Much of the talk in the therapy sessions that I observed revolves around issues of female identity, interpersonal relationships, family planning, and sexuality. Patients do most of the talking, but the therapist actively controls the direction of talk. This control involves directing clients to formulate narratives of experience within the constraints of specified rules of language use. It is common in the course of client narratives for therapeutic authority to substitute for one word or one phrase of the client's another, more "appropriate," expression. A repeated case involves the imposition of the supposedly correct use of *I* in place of the second-person plural pronoun, *you*, which is viewed as incorrect as it is commonly used by the patient. For example:

(I)	I	Client:	You know how that is
	2		when you just want to have a baby,
	3		just something that is yours
	4		and belongs to you ...
	5	Therapist:	No Mirna,

6		we don't know what it is like.
7		Please tell us,
8		but don't say "you."
9		It is *your* experience,
10		not ours,
11		so you need to say "I" instead of "you."
12		"That is how *I* feel when *I* see a baby."
13	Client:	Okay. I.
14	Therapist:	So how does it feel to say "I"?[1]

Of course, it feels very different to say *I* instead of *you*. Client response to the correction is often an apathetic "I don't know," with a shrug and eyes cast to the floor. Following the correction, few individuals pick up the narrative line with their initial fervor, most likely because there is a significant distinction in meaning and intention between the use of *I* and *you* in this context. The use of *you* here is not the second-person singular, nor is it necessarily the second-person plural. Rather, it is a colloquial use that assumes experience in common with others present and may even serve to invoke the experience of women in general, thus functioning to construct alignment with other members of the group. Left unchallenged, such solidarity authorizes one's experience and views. The use of *you* constructs an alliance on the assumed basis of a common experience; the use of *I* breaks down potential alliance. The isolation of individual experience makes it easier for the therapist to identify a problem located in the individual, in this case the desire to have children, which can then become the focus of therapeutic effort. In establishing different relationships to the group, the two words construct alternate social realities: one supports and the other subverts the aims of institutional authority.

If the use of *you* is simply incorrect, there can be no suggested alternative for the originally produced meaning. Perhaps apathy rather than direct resistance is a characteristic response because of the elusive nature of the assumptions entailed in the use of *you*. To challenge the correction directly is difficult because the implicit differences in meaning between the two words are not simply differences in referential meaning. A conventional failure to acknowledge social and symbolic dimensions of language renders inaccessible the tools needed to challenge implicit constructions of meaning. Moreover, the use of *you* involves an unsubstantiated assumption of common experience. In short, the logistical and political complications involved in substantiating an assumption of common experience, of rendering explicit the implicit, are formidable.

Yet, language is based on assumptions of common meaning and experience. No two people experience anything in exactly the same way, and yet a system of communication is built more or less on an assumption that we do. To call into question the assumptions implicit in language is an act of power and dominance in which authority deconstructs, delegitimizes, defines boundaries, and allocates rights, privileges, and access to linguistic power. The therapist, for instance, retains the right to use *we*, such as in example (1) (*No Mirna, we don't know what it is like*). Such reference involves an assumption of the same sort a patient makes, not just an assumption of experience in common between individuals, but often one that additionally involves an implicit assumption of common agreement. If the same rules apply, for whom does the therapist speak? This case clearly presents a question not of grammatical correctness but of imposed meanings and assumptions. Here consent to the authority of a linguistic standard allows those in power to privilege one culturally recognized and legitimated system of meanings, interpretations, and social reality over another that is positioned as less valid.

This process of meaning-making may be illustrated by a second example. During a discussion of control in relationships, the therapist directs linguistic choice not by correcting but by interrupting to propose the completion of an unfinished sentence:

(2)	1	Therapist:	How was it in your relationships?
	2	Client:	Mine?
	3		Well at the beginning *I* had the control
	4		and then all of a sudden it's just like-
	5		<I>
	6	Therapist:	You lost it.
	7	Client:	I lost it. (clap clap)
	8		I completely lost it.

The client readily accepts the therapist's proposal, recycling it in her own speech (see Goodwin 1990) and adding claps for emphasis. A model of control is mutually built between client and therapist: control can be possessed like an object, and it can be lost by an agent. On the basis of this model, when in line 3 the client narrates from the position of the first-person singular in stating that "I" had the control, in line 6 the therapist is able to anticipate and propose an appropriate completion to the sentence: that the second-person singular, "you," lost control.

Due to its treatment in language, the concept of control is objectified through an attribution of material properties subject to cause-and-effect relationships, which can, for instance, be lost or possessed as the given responsibility of certain individuals, as we shall see below. Note what happens as the exchange continues:

```
(3)  7    Client:        I lost it. (clap clap)
     8                   I completely lost it.
     9    Therapist:     How did it happen?
    10    Client:        How?
    11                   <1.5>
    12                   (laughter)
    13                   <4>
    14                   Ha aha after the first time.
    15    Therapist:     After sex?
    16                   That's what happens.
    17                   That's one of the problems that=
    18    Client:        =then you don't have control anymore=
    19    Therapist:     =girls lose control once they agree to sex.
```

In line 18 the client interrupts the therapist's talk to anticipate the therapist's message. The therapist then affirms the client's statement of this message by recycling it in line 19. As may be noted in the shift between lines 18 and 19, relationships between structures are then further altered. The *you* in line 18 is replaced in line 19 by the general category of *girls*; *don't have control* becomes *lose control*, transforming a nonagentive subject in the former case to an active agent in the latter case; and *anymore* becomes the specific condition of *once they agree to sex*. Not only does the abstraction allow for the juxtaposition of the two categories of "having" and "losing" control, but the proposal of a cause-and-effect relationship equates a loss of control with having agreed to engage in sexual relations. Additionally, a relationship is posited between agents and things: one has to do something, or fail to do something, in order to lose control. A temporal sequence is thereby established. The agent is then the active subject in precipitating a chain of cause-and-effect relationships. Relationships between "facts," and between people and "facts," are constructed through the structures of specific speech forms. In such a manner, the particulars of individual experience are commonly transformed to represent a general statement about the world. The therapist abstracts from the client's statement the form of a general rule to be applied to specific circumstances, such as *Girls lose control once they agree to sex.*

Generalizations of this kind reproduce a discourse of sexuality that contributes to the regulation of populations according to the needs of the developing industrial complex (Foucault 1990). The institution in this case encourages women to delay pregnancies until they can acquire sufficient job skills and education to participate productively in the work force. Pregnancies are thus required to occur not only at what is deemed to be an appropriate period in a woman's life but also within an appropriate social context, namely, that of the nuclear family unit. Here the emotional and financial support of a male partner in fulfilling the roles of husband and father is emphasized. Alternative structures of support for women and their children (even when male partners are present), such as the extended family networks that many patients participate in, are not feasible in a society where work demands mobility. Resonating strongly with the Catholic backgrounds of many of the Latina patients, values promoting the nuclear family are framed within a context of moral choice concerning sexual abstinence, monogamy, and the avoidance of premarital sexual relations. Moreover, practices affiliated with ideals of women as mothers and caretakers in the domestic sphere are made to seem unappealing in contrast to the "choice," "freedom," and "independence" of contraceptive use and workplace production. Practices contributing to nuclear family structures are informed by related discourses of women's sexuality, power, and control, as in example (3) above.

The examples discussed so far cannot be explained simply in terms of the therapist's institutional identity and consequent ability to interrupt. Power, in this view, appears to be the product of rule-governed structures, allowing the intentions of some speakers to take precedence over others. The client, however, is not merely a passive recipient of power but an active contributor to the therapist's constructions. On the basis of several clues provided within the client's utterance, for instance, the therapist is able to build an appropriate completion of the client's sentence.

(4)	3	Client:	Well at the beginning *I* had the control
	4		and then all of a sudden it's just like-
	5		<I>
	6	Therapist:	You lost it.

Intonation and emphasis on *I* establishes a contrast between "I" and some other entity, "he" in this instance. The temporal markers *at the beginning* and *then* establish the basis for a cause-and-effect relationship. Finally, to have "had control" implies a relationship between agents and things, establishing the third set of contrasting elements: control can be possessed and lost. In complying with the structures of therapeutic authority, the client provides a foundation for the next interactional move of the therapist.

What might be seen as the therapist's interruptions throughout the exchange are the product not so much of violation as of invited collaboration in which the client not only consents to but, by providing the foundation upon which the therapist bases her actions, actively participates in the joint production of a shared social reality. In viewing utterances as the isolated, preformulated intentions located in the minds of individual speakers (Austin 1962; Searle 1970), conventional philosophical theories of language obscure a critical locus of social power. Speakers rely upon the cognitive work of hearers to attend to them actively in the formation of next interactional moves (Goodwin 1981). Power, from this perspective, is not the result of a predetermined, static structure existing "out there" but is considerably more complex, requiring examination in terms not of "dominators" but of the way in which the dominated contribute to the structures of their domination. To understand and address institutionalized power imbalances, we must examine not just the ways that women are silenced but how they contribute their own silencing (Lakoff 1992). Along these lines Elinor Ochs and Carolyn Taylor (this volume) analyze the processes whereby mothers construct their own weak positions within the context of family dinner conversations. Similar mechanisms are at work within the dynamics of group therapy, in which patients may be seen to produce the structures that constrain their actions.

The Power of Coercion

If clients play an active role in constructing relations of power through linguistic practice, it is not because they believe in the authority of therapists, older adults, professionals, or successful members of the white middle class. If this were the case, the women would not be institutionalized. The lack of subscription to the authority of the dominant group distinguishes voluntary clientele from involuntary patients, for whom treatment in therapy is a mandatory prescription. These individuals are identified, diagnosed, and subsequently treated for "problems with authority" precisely because they, unlike voluntary clients, do not subscribe to the dominant system of values, including those of professional therapeutic expertise. Indeed, there are commonly sharp disparities between the conflicting values of the staff and those of the population targeted for treatment, which account for a principal underlying tension in group therapy. These women would not be in therapy if they had a choice. But they do not have a choice. Whereas the therapeutic clientele is mainly represented by the white middle class, the institutionalized patients of therapy, unsurprisingly, are largely represented by cultural and economic "minorities." The coercive power that underlies this arrangement establishes conditions that are conducive to power exercised through discursive mechanisms. The distinction between the voluntary and involuntary patients of psychotherapeutic treatment is therefore an important starting point in identifying coercive power.

Once a patient is institutionalized, personal freedoms and choices that are often taken for granted by citizens who comply with mainstream values are contingent upon attendance and success in therapy. These freedoms often include the "privilege" of parenting one's children, for instance, or of reuniting with family members. Backed by legal jurisdiction, the regulation of the rights and privileges of minors (those under the age of eighteen) is more extreme. Noncompliance or refusal to cooperate with therapeutic authority results in penal consequences, at times involving placement in juvenile hall or in institutions that have "tighter structure," within which personal freedom is more regulated and restricted. Social workers relocate individuals geographically and thereby prevent them from interacting in community, family, and peer groups that potentially subvert mainstream values. Residents are often denied visitations with family because such visits are deemed likely to undermine "therapeutic progress." Isolation in addition to the regulation of group membership is a significant factor in the effort to reconstruct individual identity and self-image in the therapy group, where positive and negative sanctions for behavior often become highly significant to the individual (Goffman 1967). When clients have been removed from the sphere of influence of adult figures in previous living arrangements, they may invest the institutional staff with a certain authority. This is precisely what is intended, and this process is consolidated in therapist-client interaction in group therapy.

Despite the stated format of "free association" in which "we come together as equals to share informally," interaction in group therapy is in fact highly structured by enforced rules of communicative cooperation. Physical presence in therapy, for instance, is required and coercively enforced. In the ritual opening of each therapy group, rules to ensure some degree of communicative cooperation are explicitly stated. These include no interrupting, no "talking out of turn," no "put-downs," no swearing or "inappropriate language," no "side-talk," and no "mothering" (i.e., rephrasing of another person's words). A topic for discussion is proposed and the discussion must stay on topic. The circular arrangement of chairs must be maintained, and individuals are to remain seated. The circle does more than facilitate interaction; it makes silent resistance uncomfortable and difficult to sustain because there is little else to do but stare at other group members. Repeated violation of these rules results in the increased regulation of free time and free choice, either through structures already in place or through placement in alternative institutions with increased resources for the management of recalcitrant individuals. Enforcing the rules through coercive power assures a necessary degree of cooperation, particularly the presence of participants and a system of turn-taking. Language has little power in the present context of therapy if it is not spoken and heard. Coercive power therefore structures the conditions conducive to symbolic power as it is exercised through language and communication. In an effort to downplay the coercive role of authority, the structural constraints on behavior are ideologically removed from the human agency that creates and enforces them, in which rules and penal consequences for their violation are naturalized as the fixed conditions of "reality."

If the institutionally imposed rules are followed, and the patient is observed by the staff to make progress in therapy, increased privileges result, including time unsupervised by institutional staff and eventual release, or what is called "emancipation," from the institution. The incentive to cooperate with therapeutic authority is therefore strong. This cooperative stance is reflected in linguistic practice, particularly in consent and the adoption of the language of authority in order to exhibit an alignment with its values (see Cicourel 1968).

The highly structured format for interaction in group therapy is in keeping with stated objectives of preparing individuals for the work force by providing them with communication skills needed in the workplace—what can be said where, when, how, and to whom. For the "properly socialized," a deeply ingrained, tacit knowledge of language and social relations dictates that, for instance, one cannot hope to obtain a job in an interview by suddenly interrupting to demand why the interviewer is "so nosy." Group therapy is designed to provide an intensive apprenticeship opportunity in which social and linguistic practices are acquired in a context specifically constructed to sustain prolonged face-to-face interaction and to disregard breakdowns in communication. "We are giving them a language," in the words of a clinical director and therapist who once described this principal therapeutic objective. The appropriate language to be acquired, in other words, is one that involves rules of participation and cooperation according to the institutionalized structures of authority. Characterized by asymmetrical relationships of power and unequal control of the space of talk, the stated rules of interaction in therapy apply only to residents. Therapists retain the privileges of questioning and interrupting, and clients respond in limited ways deemed appropriate according to context.

Furthermore, common notions of communication obscure the power of the therapist by attributing to her or him the role of passivity, because the patient in therapy often assumes the active role of talking. In fact, the therapist, at least in theory, quite actively structures context and exercises control over the space of talk, the communicative outcome, and the conclusions patients reach "on their own." The cultural authority of clinical discourse and practice produces and reproduces reality through language that constructs, upholds, and at the same time veils the structures of domination and authority of the specific clinical institution and of the larger political-economic system of which clinical discourse is part.

The acquired practices of consent and powerlessness under such conditions serve to locate and perpetuate individual status within larger political-economic structures. These practices do not just reflect but also produce social hierarchy and a speaker's position within it. The structures of domination and cultural authority—that is, "reality"—in therapeutic treatment as in other forms of discourse are embedded and upheld in the structures of the institutionally defined appropriate language, both ideologically, as categorical propositions that are codified in the lexicon, and politically, in the sequential organization of talk. Cooperation in the authoritative context of therapy conditions residents not only to consent to but to produce a designated position within the specific social hierarchy of therapy, as well as the broader political-economic context. If not consent itself, what therapeutic treatment seeks to instill are the practices of consent upon which the established structures of power and domination depend.

The Power of Mystification

State-regulated residential institutions designed to treat "disturbed" or "problem" adolescents have high financial incentives to meet state-designated criteria for what is considered the "therapeutic treatment model." Treatment is achieved by providing "therapeutic structure" and, in particular, regular group and individual therapy sessions. Despite the emphasis on therapeutic treatment, however, an explicit definition of *therapy* or *therapeutic* is absent from program and social-services literature. Although elaborate and sophisticated definitions of psychotherapeutic theory and practice may be found by consulting the codified authority on clinical practice, common and informal professional knowledge of therapy provides a useful vantage point in the examination of the role of authority in cultural knowledge and practice. The questioning of therapeutic practice—what therapy is, what it does—is commonly viewed by clinical professionals and lay people alike as unnecessary. Yet, the logic and rational basis of what is essentially a "talking cure" remains obscure (Lakoff 1990). Such approaches to the human psyche and emotions have little to do with the physical domains of science, yet clinical ideology and discourse are authoritative by mere association with the institutions of science and medicine. Consider the common metaphors associated with therapeutic ideology and practice, such as *to let it out* or *talk it out*. In talking it out, words become invested with nearly magical properties. Problems are metamorphosed into words that are then somehow exorcised from the self through a process of articulation. It is good, according to the rationale, to talk it out between friends, but true therapy involves a professional, who from a more objective position can "bring it out of you" or help "bring you back to reality."

Indeed, as Thomas Scheff (1968) has suggested, interaction in psychotherapy can be viewed as an interactive negotiation of reality. In "bringing one back to reality," a basic "objective" premise in clinical treatment is that reality consists of fixed immutable conditions or facts to which individuals must adapt. Theoretical developments in the sociology of knowledge present a different perspective of reality, one that replaces questionable notions of objectivity with the concept of power. Reality in this view is not a fixed and immutable fact, as it is often presented in the discourse of authority, but a social construction in which social relations of power are directly implicated (Berger & Luckman 1967). Competing interests and the role of power in the therapeutic negotiation of reality become salient issues: Who has the power to construct and define reality, and to whose benefit? Here power and domination, which are involved in the social construction of reality, pose as an act of benevolence. This distortion is reflected in the common view that the purpose of therapy is to help individuals to "fit in": the problem is located in the individual, and it is the "problem individual" who therefore bears the responsibility to make whatever changes are necessary to adapt to the needs of inflexible social institutions. Yet, there is a failure to consider the larger social context of conditions into which the individual must fit.

Just as the decisions made by professional authority to remove young women from previous living arrangements are not objective but subjective determinations made on the basis of culturally informed values (such as in distinctions between *healthy* and *unhealthy*, *fantasy* and *reality*, *fit* and *unfit*), so too are decisions regarding the appropriate role of these women in society. Here the exercise of power and domination is explicit: the "real world" for which women are prepared in the institution is one in which they must come to terms with a system of inequality and the acceptance of one's position within it. Hard work and "luck," as the discourse goes, create the "privilege" of "opportunity," i.e., menial work in which the peak hours of a life are sacrificed for the agenda and profit of an often unknown and faceless other.

Patients are discouraged from developing other, "inappropriate," interests, because these often contribute to "unrealistic" goals, a determination based in part on professional assessments of scores on achievement, aptitude, and IQ tests. At the expense of developing other human potentials, the primary emphasis on the instrumentalization of women as products for the service and manufacturing sectors of the work force is justified because of the "limited time to get them on their feet," as a program director once commented. According to Goffman's (1961) observations in his study of asylums, the limitations of treatment are more convincingly attributed to the general conception commonly held by clinical and social workers: that the individuals categorized as residents have the potential to offer society little more than the functions for which they are trained.

Common metaphors employed by staff further reflect mechanistic views of the patients: in appeals for corporate funding and in the therapeutic milieu alike they are referred to as "investments," "insurance," and "products" that are "damaged," in need of "tune-ups" or "attitude adjustments" in order to "get into gear." Furthermore, the framing of social conditions and of the individual's position within them as natural constitutes a theme repeated throughout all contexts of therapeutic interaction. Although the program structure is an artificial construction that proposes to emulate the social conditions of "the real world out there," a point generally overlooked is that the social world is not natural, in the conventional sense of the term, but cultural and thus the product of human agency. The discourse of the natural is not specific to the therapeutic setting but is reproduced in it nonetheless, implying a certain inevitability and fixity of social structures, a belief upon which the status quo depends for its perpetuation. Such an orientation teaches the individual to accept rather than question and to conform rather than resist. There appears to be no choice but to live in the service of an amorphous and impersonal system.

The discourse of objectivity veils the role of power in social relations. Because perspectives are inherently situated within contexts of time, space, and power relations, there cannot exist a neutral, value-free, or "objective" perspective from which phenomena are observed. Feminist theorists (see for example Bordo 1987; Haraway 1989; Smith 1990) have pointed out that "objectivity" is a product of power relations and represents a formulation of experience grounded in dominant (and male-oriented) perspectives. The construction of objectivity as the self-professed and exclusive capability of professional expertise can therefore be viewed as a kind of advocacy in the promotion of dominant interests (Furner 1975). Yet, it is the reality constructed by the culture of the dominant group in Western society that distinguishes the sanctioned practices of teaching and socialization from cult indoctrination, of therapeutic treatment from ritual brainwashing, of legitimate from illegitimate uses of power. The authoritative practice of psychotherapy seeks to instill the dominant construction of reality, both ideological and political.

Conventional beliefs about language contribute to the discourse of objectivity, veiling the role of power in "healing through talk" as an apparatus of social control. Ideas about emotion, and about words that correspond with given emotions, contribute to further objective realities (Lutz & Abu-Lughod 1990). Emotions assume the properties of objects that are spatially located in individuals and temporally located in cause-and-effect sequences. This can be misleading. When "coming together to talk about our feelings" in group therapy, for instance, therapists state quite often that feelings belong to the individual (see Lutz 1985) and that "no one can tell you whether what you are feeling is right or wrong." Yet feelings do not exist independently; they are the reactive counterpart of culturally informed interpretations of experience. Narratives of experience are reconstructed, rephrased, and thus reformulated as a sensible coproduction of reality.

The Power of Resistance

Linguistic and paralinguistic mechanisms embedded within the structures of language and communication are difficult to identify and challenge. These are resources of power not just for authority but also for resistance. Restricted from access to equivalent resources of coercive power, individuals gain little from strategies of resistance that directly challenge the state-sanctioned use of coercive power. Authority is therefore challenged and subverted in ways that are difficult to confront. Resistance, like authority, relies upon indirect strategies. Therapists' avoidance of power through direct means represents an underlying tension in the group-therapy interaction, a dynamic characterized by the delicate and careful manipulation of surface meanings and appearances. The construction of symbolic authority through indirect mechanisms, however, depends upon the invisibility of coercion and its supporting mechanisms. This presents a resource for resistance: when the coercive mechanisms that symbolic authority attempts to downplay are made explicit, its legitimacy is seriously undermined. In relying on indirect means to expose direct means, resistance legitimates its own authority, problematizing notions of authority in competing constructions of legitimacy and illegitimacy.

Like authority, resistant power maintains a precarious balance between maneuvers that fail through explicit identification and those that effectively accomplish desired ends. Authority is challenged and subverted in ways that are difficult to identify and confront due to the implicit nature of resistance and opposition. (The institutional staff even have a specific phrase—to call on—for identifying and confronting such behaviors.) For instance, although you can't close your eyes in the therapy group, you can look down. You can't avoid sitting in your chair, whose rigid straight-back design already imposes restrictions on possible corporeal positions, but you can recline or slouch as far as physically possible, or tilt back to rock on two legs, using the chair in ways other than those originally intended.

Similarly, a common form of resistance involves mimicking the language or code used by the therapists in a way that accentuates the otherness associated with the relative formality, "nosiness," or "so-white" aspects of the therapist's conduct. If carefully executed, such behavior is not identified and disciplined because it can be somewhat difficult for therapists to discern the difference between a sincere cooperative effort and one of resistance. "How does that make you feel?" a client asks, after another client's tearful narrative, as if to serve as a reminder of the monitoring therapist's continual insincerity. The therapist often receives the general impression of resistance and subversion, but because it is difficult to identify explicitly the nature of the violations, resorting to coercive power appears irrational and thereby defeats the therapist in this game of verbal cunning. Those patients who actually adhere in earnest to the code of the therapeutic milieu become the focus of peer ridicule. This demonstrates not only the acute awareness patients have for differentiating between linguistic codes but the additional resource of peer pressure as a method to ensure the subversion of authority. Because the therapist does not share a common history of background knowledge and linguistic conventions that the patients draw upon, she or he often appears blundering, unaware, or naive, a situation that further undermines authority.

The implicit battle in which power alliances compete to construct symbolic authority is also evidenced in constructions of the context of interaction, and hence in control over topic and the rules of participation. That is, context shapes the interactional moves that in turn shape context (Gumperz 1990). Participants engage in cooperative efforts to redefine the therapeutic context according to what they call girl talk, a context of conversation that commonly occurs during "free time" in the smoking area on the back patio. The topics of girl talk—personal relationships and sexuality—are consistent with the proposed topics of group therapy, but its context is signaled and thus constructed through different cues (see Gumperz 1990). These include the initiation of long turns of talk begun by such words as *well* and *so*, and, in particular, the use of *like* to introduce quoted speech and enacted demonstrations.

In any context, relationships and the rules of participation may be implicitly redefined. This shift is signaled linguistically through communicative choices, such as in choosing between *you* and *I*, as in the example discussed previously, or paralinguistically through the cues of body language. In contrast to the hierarchical structure and relative formality of the therapeutic context, relationships between participants in the context of girl talk are relatively symmetrical. The format of girl talk typically involves the coproduction of narratives and results in the formation of an alliance that monopolizes the space of talk. Interruptions, questions, and the language of the therapist seem rude, irrelevant, or out of place.

Girl talk may be introduced into the therapeutic setting as a strategy of resistance. Residents may talk at length about the process of getting dressed that morning, for instance, and having to choose between the shoes with the purple laces or the shiny black flats. Therapists thus become engaged in an implicit struggle to get the group "back on topic" and into the format conducive to therapy. Authority has a vested interest in refraining from resorting to the mechanisms of coercive control, but such measures are often the only way to reestablish the practices of the therapeutic context. Therefore the therapist is usually caught trying to play along in a losing battle. Taking coercive action further undermines the authority of the therapist because it appears unreasonable. This is particularly the case when the therapist's reasons for imposing consequences (i.e., punishment) upon group members are difficult to make explicit; after all, under the guise of cooperative effort a stream of talk is being produced in place of recalcitrant silence. Oftentimes the resistant talk is even relevant to the topic. The objectives of therapy may never be realized as therapists remain engaged in an ongoing but implicit battle for the construction and legitimation of symbolic authority.

Mistakes represent yet another form of resistance that is difficult for therapeutic authority to "call on." Despite the constant correction in example (1), for instance, the patient persists in the "incorrect" use of *you*. Although this can be seen as an innocent mistake, attributable to the speaker's lack of access to standard or appropriate linguistic behavior (Bourdieu 1991), such an explanation is unconvincing. Indeed, although some residents are occasionally new enough to the group to be unfamiliar with the standard code in therapy, most of them are intimately familiar with the system and its language. Example (1) contrasts with example (2) discussed above, in which the client readily incorporates the therapist's proposals. In (1), once the use of *I* is proposed by the therapist, its abrupt incorporation into only a fragment of the patient's speech—*Okay. I.*— further suggests resistance. Repeated "mistakes" such as that illustrated in (1) can be explained in a more compelling way in terms not of incompetence but of strategy and appropriation, involving a dissociation from the language of authority in favor of an "illegitimate" language through which an alternate identity and affiliation are expressed and sustained.

Mechanisms of resistance extend beyond interaction in group therapy. Some patients "keep forgetting" to take birth-control pills or to use other contraceptives and thereby resist sacrificing their previous self-image and values associated with fertility and reproductivity for the values of productivity in the work force. Some clients exhibit lack of concentration and "learning deficits" and "have difficulty in applying themselves" to acquire necessary skills of menial labor. These problems vanish, however, when the same individuals confront the challenges of establishing more promising footholds to status and prestige within the hierarchy of power in illicit kinds of business. Still others simply refuse to dress "appropriately" or to stop saying things that are "inappropriate" or "incorrect." The sense of self affiliated with alternate cultural values seems to remain alive in individuals who cooperate in the collective adherence to the symbols of an alternate cultural reality.

Not all resistance is covert, however. On occasion therapeutic authority is overtly challenged by patients. The rules of conversation become the focus of discussion when patients demand of the therapist, for instance, "Why do you get to interrupt and I don't?" As a sincere question that is not in violation of the explicit rules of cooperation, the challenge cannot be "called on." Answers to the question are limited if the therapist is to avoid exposing the institutionally defined structure and the coercive power that backs it. To allow residents to apply the rules of cooperation symmetrically to all participants, however, involves the surrender of authority and undermines the objectives of therapy. The common strategy, to answer with another question, only temporarily evades exposing the underlying message of coercive power: "Because I am a therapist, and if you don't do as I say ..."

As the presence of institutions of social control attests, the expression of resistance persists despite the resources of control available to the authority of the dominant group. Yet, just as coercive mechanisms of power commonly remain invisible to citizens outside the institution, the power of resistance remains unacknowledged in some theories of power (e.g.,

Bourdieu 1977, 1991). Indeed, such theories may themselves contribute to the reproduction of the dominant discourses in which they are located. Oppositional linguistic and paralinguistic behavior attests to overt and conscious systems of resistance (Gal 1989; Woolard 1985), and this fact problematizes therapy as a process of instillation, inculcation, socialization, or cultural reproduction, involving the transmission of traditional cultural content. Such socialization theories are exemplified by the treatment of the "culturally deficient" (see, for example, Bernstein 1964), for just as language that does not adhere to the standard is "incorrect" and therefore "nonlanguage," alternatives to the dominant version of reality are simply nonreality. In contrast to this perspective, a theory that views actors as active agents in constructions of social reality, as the evidence in this chapter attests, challenges traditional notions of socialization as well as recent theories of cultural reproduction (e.g., Bourdieu 1991).

It has been sufficient for the purposes of the present chapter to make a relatively simplistic distinction in which authority is differentiated from resistance by legitimized access to resources of coercive power in the process of its construction. This schema raises a second set of theoretical problems, however, for it depends on a definition of authority that excludes the symbolic dimension: sustained by coercive power alone authority ceases to be, in the conventional sense. Additionally, conventional distinctions between resistance and authority inherently derive from and reproduce the dominant orientation and value system. In addressing these problems, Woolard's (1985) conceptual set of *status* and *solidarity* provides a useful point of departure. Woolard differentiates symbolic authority (status) from coercive domination (power). Such a distinction between solidarity and the authority of coercive power is succinctly captured in the words of a resident who remarked once, "I may do as you say, but I don't have to respect you."

Conclusion

Resistance prevails. Even institutions that make less than fifty percent of patients into productive and independently functioning individuals are considered model programs. Yet, the "successful" patients, those who seem to have internalized the values of authority, often have also internalized its problems. Disenfranchised citizens manifest a host of symptoms that are rooted in an insatiable hunger for the limited autonomy society affords the disenfranchised. There is a bitter side to the proliferation of the not-so-humorous slogans "Shop 'til you drop" and "I owe, I owe, so off to work I go" that points to certain contradictions and social tensions. Individuals seek a cure for the compulsive consumption of commercial products, for eating disorders, in which the body has become a symbolic war zone in the dialectic between individual and society (Bordo 1993), for compulsive spending, for unwanted pregnancy, and for drug addiction. They turn faithfully to an authority that cannot help with symptoms whose etiology remains "unknown" and therefore untreatable. Instead, individuals continue to be "therapized" by a society that "helps" the disenfranchised to come to terms with and accept contradictions of ideals and practices: of individual autonomy and subjection, free choice and no choice, the American dream and the American reality. With a certain irony, the producers and consumers keep the wheels of capitalism turning and perpetuate a system that seems to feed on itself and on the unacknowledged souls of human beings. From this perspective it can perhaps be understood how it feels "just to want something that is yours and belongs to you."

Note

1. Transcription conventions are as follows:
   - Italics indicate that what was said was emphasized in some way, e.g., through increased volume or stress.
   - Punctuation symbols are used not as grammatical markers but, rather, as intonation indicators:
   - A period indicates a falling contour.
   - A question mark indicates a rising contour.
   - A comma indicates a falling-rising contour.
   - An equal sign or = between words means that the talk is proceeding very rapidly, with the words joined by it almost running together.
   - Elements in parentheses are extralinguistic features and do not indicate speech.
   - Numbers contained within the marks <0.0> indicate periods of silence; the length of the silence is given by the numbers in terms of seconds.

References

Austin, John Langshaw (1962). *How to do things with words.* 2d ed. Oxford: Oxford University Press.

Basaglia, Franco (1987). *Psychiatry inside out: Selected writings of Franco Basaglia.* Edited by Nancy Scheper-Hughes and Anne M. Lovell. Translated by Anne M. Lovell and Teresa Shtob. New York: Columbia University Press.

Berger, Peter, and Thomas Luckmann (1967). *The social construction of reality: A treatise in the sociology of knowledge.* London: Penguin.

Bernstein, Basil (1964). Elaborated and restricted codes: Their social origins and some consequences. *American Anthropologist* 66(6, part 2): 55–69.

Bordo, Susan (1987). *The flight to objectivity: Essays on Cartesianism and culture.* Albany: SUNY Press.

——— (1993). *Unbearable weight: Feminism, Western culture, and the body.* Berkeley: University of California Press.

Bourdieu, Pierre (1977). *Outline of a theory of practice.* Cambridge: Cambridge University Press.

——— (1991). *Language and symbolic power.* Cambridge, MA: Harvard University Press.

Cicourel, Aaron Victor (1968). *The social organization of juvenile justice.* New York: Wiley.

Foucault, Michel (1990). *The history of sexuality. Vol. 1.* Translated by Robert Hurley. New York: Vintage.

Furner, Mary O. (1975). *Advocacy and objectivity: A crisis in the professionalization of American social science, 1865–1905.* Lexington: University of Kentucky Press.

Gal, Susan (1989). Language and political economy. *Annual Review of Anthropology* 18: 345–67.

Goffman, Erving (1961). *Asylums.* Chicago: Aldine.

——— (1967). *Interaction ritual: Essays in face-to-face behavior.* Chicago: Aldine.

Goodwin, Charles (1981). *Conversational organization: Interaction between speakers and hearers.* New York: Academic Press.

Goodwin, Marjorie Harness (1990). *He-said-she-said: Talk as social organization among black children.* Bloomington: Indiana University Press.

Gumperz, John J. (1990). Contextualization and understanding. In Alessandro Duranti and Charles Goodwin (eds.), *Rethinking context.* Cambridge: Cambridge University Press. 229–52.

Haraway, Donna Jeanne (1989). *Primate visions: Gender, race, and nature in the world of modern science.* New York: Routledge.

Lakoff, Robin (1990). *Talking power: The politics of language in our lives.* New York: Basic Books.

——— (1992). The silencing of women. In Kira Hall, Mary Bucholtz, and Birch Moonwomon (eds.), *Locating power: Proceedings of the Second Berkeley Women and Language Conference.* Berkeley: Berkeley Women and Language Group. 344–55.

Lutz, Catherine (1985). Depression and the translation of emotion words. In Arthur Kleinman and Byron Good (eds.), *Culture and depression: Studies in the anthropology and cross-cultural psychiatry of affect and disorder.* Berkeley: University of California Press. 63–100.

Lutz, Catherine, and Lila Abu-Lughod (eds.) (1990). *Language and the politics of emotion.* Cambridge: Cambridge University Press.

Ochs, Elinor, and Carolyn Taylor (this volume). The "Father knows best" dynamic in dinnertime narratives.

Ong, Aihwa (1987). *Spirits of resistance and capitalist discipline: Factory women in Malaysia.* Albany: SUNY Press.

Piven, Frances, and Richard Cloward (1971). *Regulating the poor: The functions of public welfare.* New York: Vintage.

Scheff, Thomas (1968). Negotiating reality: Notes on power in the assessment of responsibility. In John D. Stoeckle (ed.), *Encounters between patients and doctors: An anthology*. Cambridge, MA: MIT Press. 193–213.

Searle, John R. (1970). *Speech acts: An essay in the philosophy of language*. Cambridge: Cambridge University Press.

Smith, Dorothy E. (1990). *The conceptual practices of power: A feminist sociology of knowledge*. Boston: Northeastern University Press.

Willis, Paul (1977). *Learning to labor: How working class kids get working class jobs*. New York: Columbia University Press.

Woolard, Kathryn (1985). Language variation and cultural hegemony: Toward an integration of sociolinguistic and social theory. *American Ethnologist* 12: 738–48.

6

A Synthetic Sisterhood

False Friends in a Teenage Magazine

Mary Talbot

Feminist criticism with a poststructuralist perspective, as outlined by Chris Weedon (1987), takes language as the site of the cultural production of gender identity: subjectivity is discursively constituted. An individual's identity is constructed at every moment through subject positions. These positions are taken up by the language user in the enactment of discourse practices and are constantly shifting. From this view of subjectivity as a process, it is evident that a person's sense of identity is an "effect of discourse," which is therefore changeable: "A poststructuralist position on subjectivity and consciousness relativizes the individual's sense of herself by making it an effect of discourse which is open to continuous redefinition and which is constantly slipping" (Weedon 1987:106).

This poststructuralist perspective on identity, combined with a dialogic, or intertextual, view of actual texts, is what Julia Kristeva (1986a, b) proposed in her work in the late 1960s and early 1970s. According to Kristeva, a text consists of a mesh of intersecting voices. These voices can be viewed as an indeterminate "text population" (Talbot 1990, 1992, 1995). The metaphor is intended to capture the way any text is "populated" with a heterogeneous array of voices through which a language user's identity is built up. A text is therefore not the product of a single author; instead, the author her/himself is multiple, fragmented, and part of the population of the text. The same can be said of the reader. In reading a text, s/he is drawn into a complex of intersecting voices.

Like the other chapters in this section, this chapter examines the social reproduction of gender norms. My intention is to examine the mass media's contribution to the construction of a kind of femininity based on consumption. The material I focus on is a two-page consumer feature from a British magazine for teenagers called *Jackie* (which ceased publication in 1993). I outline the notion of women's magazines as a "synthetic sisterhood," which will involve an excursion into the history of magazines. I then concentrate specifically on one aspect of how this imaginary community is established: the simulation of a friendly relationship. I conclude with some discussion of how "unsisterly" this feature really is. Before attending to this synthetic sisterhood and its establishment, I need to consider some broader issues: the discursive organization of femininity and the nature of a reader's involvement in the mass media.

Femininity

What do we mean by *femininity?* The term refers to a conglomeration of concepts and themes, social relations and practices. It is a particular structuring of social space that spans across institutions and that is a key factor in the constitution of women's subjectivities. It discursively organizes women's lives, even impinging on their bodies. This discursively organized social space called femininity is articulated in commercial and mass-media discourses—especially in the magazine, clothing, and cosmetics industries. Such discourses shape the social practices that form women's identities and relationships. Social conditions bestow upon women feminine social identities and specific kinds of social relationships with other women and with men. Consumer femininity enters into women's daily lives in the resources they draw upon in spoken and written discourses and in nonlinguistic practices.

Dorothy Smith (1988) uses the conception of femininity as discourse to connect diverse phenomena in the economic and symbolic world: resources, women's work, and standards of appearance. Femininity informs the production and distribution of resources (such as clothes and cosmetics particularly, but also nonmaterial resources). Part of femininity as discourse relates to women's skills and work: "beauty work" and the activities surrounding it (planning, shopping for materials, and so forth). Most women are nonprofessional practitioners; their work on themselves has the status of a hobby (despite the fact that it is part of the good grooming necessary for entry into the job market).

According to Smith, femininity is a mass-media construction, a discourse realized through and on women's bodies. She stresses that femininity is not simply imposed on women by the mass media or by patriarchal social relations but that it is something in which women actively and creatively participate. It is manifested in women's activities, that is, in the practical skills cultivated, in the expenditure of money and free time, and also in patterns of friendship, especially among adolescents.[1] Women are actively involved in the construction of femininity; manufacturers and the mass media must be responsive to them. Their active participation is shaped by what manufacturers and the media have to offer:

> Women aren't just the passive products of socialization; they are active; they create themselves. At the same time, their self-creation, their work, the uses of their skills, are coordinated with the market for clothes, make-up, shoes, accessories, etc., through print, film, etc. This dialectic between the active and creative subject and the organization of her activity in and by texts coordinating it with the market is captured here using the concept of a textually-mediated discourse. (Smith 1988:39)

Manufacturing, advertising, and the fashion and magazine industries together shape fashion and beauty standards. Women's bodies, as Smith says, "always need fixing" (47), because without work they cannot approximate the kinds of appearance offered by images in the mass media. But in the process of her practical efforts, the woman becomes the object defined by the image. She feminizes herself. Smith insists that this is more than a matter of sexualization. In participating in feminine discourse, women construct their identities as women, not sex objects for the male gaze.[2]

This feminine discourse shapes women's experiences in diverse institutions: in their daily domestic activities, in their friendship relations, in the workplace, and so on. In the Foucauldian sense, femininity is not a discourse type in its own right but, rather, is articulated in different discourse types.

Discourse in the Mass Media and the Location of Power

As readers, our involvement in the processes of discourse is relatively passive. But we are still active participants. Reading takes place on readers' terms; they can stop whenever they want to, skip fragments, reread others, and so on. Readers are in control of the discourse. Readers are also active participants in the sense that they are actively involved in processes of interpretation. In their involvement in these processes, they are constructed as social subjects. But like any other language users, readers are both actively agentive and unwittingly acted upon. As readers, we are seldom aware of the resources we are drawing upon in investing texts with meaning. The sense of autonomy that we experience as readers is an illusion, implying a nonsensical ability to pull ourselves up by our own bootstraps. Readers are drawn into a kind of complicity with the texts they read. When meanings are simply obvious, that complicity and subjection are complete. Complicity is necessary for understanding; it is not inherently undesirable.[3]

In contrast with face-to-face interaction, media discourse is a one-sided affair. Producer and interpreter are sharply divided and distant from each other. Because of this distance, producers cannot shape their texts for their actual readers (Fairclough 1989). Addressing a mass audience imposes on mass-media producers the need to construct an implied reader (or viewer) as addressee. At the same time, it imposes on actual mass-media readers or viewers the need to negotiate with the constructed positions. Every text can be said to have such an implied reader, an imaginary addressee with particular preoccupations, values, notions of common sense, and so on. An actual reader who has a great deal in common with the imaginary ideal reader inscribed in a particular text is likely to take up the positions it offers unconsciously and uncritically. Conversely, of course, distance enables a reader to be more aware of the positioning, and perhaps more critical. Consider, for example, how differently a twelve-year-old girl and a forty-year-old man would respond to the following (taken from *Jackie*): "When you're trying to impress that hunk in the sixth form ... "

The need to construct an implied reader puts the producers of mass-media texts in a powerful position. They have the right to total control over production, including what kinds of representations of events are included. In the construction of an implied reader as an addressee, they are in a position to assign assumed shared experiences and commonsense attitudes as givens to a mass audience. In addition, the producers of mass-media texts, unlike their addressees, are professional practitioners. They do not work blindly in postulating subjects as addressees; mass-media discourse is targeted for specific audiences. These audiences have been measured by sophisticated market research practices, which are particularly scrutinizing kinds of discourse. As a result, actual addressees, in the targeted audience, are likely to take up the position inscribed, with its commonsense attitudes.

Mass Media and Communities: The Notion of Synthetic Sisterhood
The implied readers postulated by mass-media producers are constructed as members of communities. The targeted audience of women's magazines is represented, simply by virtue of its femaleness, as a single community:

> The picture of the world presented by women's magazines is that
> the individual woman is a member not so much of society as a
> whole but of *her* society, the world of women. It is to this separate
> community that these periodicals address themselves. Their spot-
> light is directed not so much at the wider "host" society, as at that
> host society's largest "minority" group: females. (Ferguson 1983:6)

This bogus social group has been described as a kind of surrogate sisterhood
by various writers (e.g., Ferguson 1983; McRobbie 1978; Winship 1987).
Within this female community, which appears to ghettoize women, magazines are targeted for different socioeconomic groups. *Jackie* magazine, for
example, had a predominantly working-class, young readership. (The target
audience was young teenagers, ages twelve to fourteen; its *actual* readership
was predominantly younger than this.)

Before going on to look at the synthetic sisterhood offered by women's
magazines, let me give some attention to the notion of imaginary communities, using advertisements as an example. As well as informing consumers
about what is available, ads also present to audiences the idea of communities based on the consumption of commodities. Ads offer consumers
membership in imaginary communities; to belong we need only to buy (and
presumably use) products. William Leiss, Stephen Kline, and Sut Jhally
(1986:53) explain that in the transition from industrial to consumer culture,
what they term *consumption communities,* "formed by popular styles and
expenditure patterns among consumers, became a principal force for social
cohesion in the twentieth century, replacing the ethnic bonds that people
had brought with them to the industrial city." Of course, being a certain kind
of consumer does not in itself form relationships; consumption communities cannot exist in the same way as real communities based on locality,
kinship, or work relations. They can provide a sense of belonging, of group
membership—no more. In the consumer feature that I am going to discuss,
producers and readers are set up in a synthesized sisterly relationship in a
community based on the consumption of lipstick.

An increasingly common feature of types of discourse used to address mass
audiences is a phenomenon sometimes called *synthetic personalization,*
which is designed by mass-media producers "to give the impression of treating each of the people 'handled' *en masse* as an individual" (Fairclough
1989:62). Synthetic personalization is extremely common in the media generally: in magazine advertisements and articles, front-page headlines, junk mail,
and so on. It involves the construction of an implied reader who is treated as
an actual individual. It also requires the construction of a persona for the

producers. An anonymous audience is addressed as thousands of identical *you*s, with attitudes, values, and preoccupations ascribed to them.

Synthetic Sisterhood

The roots of synthetic personalization as a gendered capitalist strategy lie in the history of women's magazines. A mixture of instruction and entertainment in publications specifically for women goes back to the late seventeenth century. A precursor of the modern women's magazine was a British publication for aristocratic women called *Ladies' Mercury*, which first appeared in 1693. This publication is generally considered the first women's magazine (Ferguson 1983; White 1970; Winship 1987). It contained a range of elements: fiction, readers' letters with editorial response, fashion articles and plates, educational tracts. In the mid-nineteenth century magazines aimed at a middle-class audience were produced. As Marjorie Ferguson remarks (1983:16), these publications "offered their readers—the socially climbing wives and daughters of the professional and business classes— guidance about what to buy, wear, and do to further their aspirations." The first women's magazine for a middle-class readership was *The Englishwoman's Domestic Magazine*, which began in 1852. Like its upper-class predecessors, it contained a mixture of fiction and nonfiction, written text and illustration. Unlike them, it dealt with activities and topics relating to women's unpaid work in the domestic domain of the home. The nonfiction element consisted of informative and facilitating features: recipes, instructions for knitting men's socks, articles on the management of servants, and so on.

Another new element was the presence of advertisements. Cynthia White (1970) reports that women's periodicals in 1800 carried very few ads, but by the end of the century, advertising was the main economic support of the magazine industry:

> The expansion of the women's periodical press was in fact being underwritten by advertisers from the 1880s onwards, and this dependency greatly enhanced the status of the advertising industry and modified editorial attitudes to advertising copy. The older generation of publishers had consistently frowned on advertising as an obnoxious nuisance and treated it with suspicion and contempt. (66)

As magazines became dependent on advertising revenue, editors were "forced into a position first of neutrality, then of concurrence, and finally of collusion" with the advertising industry (White 1970:115). In the late 1930s, magazines began to carry consumer features, in which advertising is presented as part of the editorial content. As this brief history suggests, the women's magazine has developed in the context of patriarchal and capitalist social relations.

The editorial shift that was precipitated by this economic restructuring can be seen in how the addresser-addressee relationship constructed in magazines changed over time. Janice Winship (1987:27) describes *The Englishwoman's Domestic Magazine* as "coolly formal and distant in tone" and contrasts it with the "more relaxed and less intimidating style" in publications in the 1890s that were aimed at the lower-middle-class end of the market. The change in tone was more than a matter of level of formality, however. The aim of achieving "an active and intimate relationship" with readers became specific editorial policy in a new publication in 1910 called *My Weekly* (produced, incidentally, by the same publisher as *Jackie*, namely D. C. Thomson). Looking at the preface of the first issue, which is quoted at some length below, we can see that the editor professes to know and understand the reader and offers her friendship, in order to encourage reader correspondence:

> My editorial experience has left me impressed with one thing in particular and that is the need for what is called the "personal note" in journalism.... I will try to appeal to readers through their human nature and their understanding of everyday joys and sorrows. For I know well that, in order to get into active and intimate relationship with the great public, one must prove oneself fully acquainted with its affections, sentiments and work. ... I understand, too, how that human nature is strangely and pathetically eager for friendship. I mean willingly to become the confidant of readers, young and old, rich and poor, who can safely trust me with their ideas and difficulties. (quoted in White 1970:88)

This change in the producer-audience relationship spread to other publications and is now a defining characteristic of women's magazines (Leman 1980).

The women's magazine, then, is a discourse type with historical continuity in an accumulated repertoire of practices. This historical context accounts for its conventional content and presentation. Interpersonally, magazines are informal and friendly, constructing a "tone of intimacy and confidentiality" (Leman 1980:63). The internal structuring of magazine texts follows an easily recognizable format in which the distribution of written text, photographs, and illustrations is highly conventional. Turning to content, one can see that the activities and topics taken up in magazines relate to women's domains of work

and leisure. Of particular relevance here is women's work on their own bodies
as objects to be looked at and their use of commodities, that is, women's activities as consumers who feminize themselves. Magazines for women contain
informative and facilitative elements on fashion and beauty products and their
use, which appear both in advertisements and in consumer features produced
by the editorial board. They are sites of the rearticulation of what Smith calls a
"discourse of femininity."

An important element of feminizing practices is the concept of a woman
as a visible object requiring work. In advertisements and do-it-yourself
sections of magazines for women, women's bodies are frequently itemized as
areas requiring separate attention with separate products. For new readers,
such a perspective may have the effect of actually creating new concepts:
"Are you doing enough for your underarms?" "How high is your bikini line?"
This itemization has been intensified by an endless proliferation of products
by manufacturers and accompanying distinctions among colors, skin types,
hair types, and so on.

The women's magazine as discourse type sets up subject positions for the
individuals it impinges upon. As mentioned earlier, interaction through
mass-media texts is asymmetrical and puts producers in the powerful position of setting up addresser and addressee. But it is difficult to determine who
this empowered producer really is. Who is it that actually wields the power
inhering in the construction of ideal subjects in magazines? The employees
who put the pages together work under specific editorial control. Any directives from the editor will have been informed in a more general way by
company policies shaping the production of the magazine, and ideological
positions are not questioned or examined (Leman 1980). The major determi-
nant is profit, which is earned through advertising revenue. Manufacturers,
in addition to buying space in magazines, also provide publishers with goods
and information about their products in return for free advertising in
commercial features. Magazines are therefore constructed within the relationship among staff, publisher, and manufacturers; more specifically,
among those who actually produce the magazines (the editor and her/his
staff, the story writers, photographers, and printers), the publishing company
management, and the promotion departments of manufacturing companies.
Hence the kinds of material made available to the copywriter and paste-up
artist on the editorial staff are not determined by the editor only. In the case
of *Jackie*, they were also determined by the relations in capitalism between
the publishers and manufacturers such as Gibbs Pharmaceuticals (makers of
acne cream who advertised regularly in *Jackie*), EMI (a record company that
provided exclusive interviews with pop stars), and so on.

Because magazine production is economically dependent on advertising revenue, in the 1950s editors were pressured by higher management into cooperating with advertisers in stimulating consumption. An (anonymous) employee interviewed by White in 1964 relates:

> Magazines have been forced to beg for advertising and to make concessions in return that would have been unheard of fifteen years ago. There has been a continual battle between management (run largely by accountants) and editors, who have the interests of their readers at heart and wish to retain their autonomy. The fight is a losing one. Content is planned with an eye on what will best serve the interests of the advertiser. ... The whole policy of a magazine is now dictated from above where only the advertiser counts. Because of the limitations on space, and the necessity of filling it to the advertiser's advantage, the order has gone out to dispense with "general interest" features in favour of "home service," because manfacturers do not like content which cannot be used to sell goods. An editor has to comply, despite the knowledge that readers' interests are much wider. (quoted in White 1970:206–7)

The women's magazine as a discourse type is not homogeneous. Publishers use sophisticated market research methods to provide manufacturers with profiles of readerships as consumption groups. Women, who have a lifelong concern with the marketplace as wives, mothers, and so on, are placed in the subject position of consumer in diverse discourses. This subject position is part of the femininity offered in women's magazines because feminizing practices involve the use of products. The definition of femininity as a mode of consumption has intensified in these publications since the consumer boom of the 1950s. One area of expansion was the cosmetics industry, another was the magazine industry itself. *Jackie* magazine appeared in 1964 when Scottish publisher D. C. Thomson picked up on the new teenage consumer market.

According to Angela McRobbie (1978:3; original emphasis), *Jackie* presented its teenage readers with a *"false* sisterhood" and imposed an ideology of femininity that isolated women from one another: "(1) The girls are being invited to join a close, intimate sorority where secrets can be exchanged and advice given; and (2) they are also being presented with an ideological bloc of mammoth proportions, one which *imprisons* them in a claustrophobic world of jealousy and competitiveness, the most unsisterly of emotions, to say the least." She asserts that *Jackie* "addresses 'girls' as a monolithic grouping," so that differences in the social conditions experienced by actual readers became obscured. The magazine presented its readers with an ideology of adolescent femininity in which the emotional was of paramount importance. Following Roland Barthes (1967), McRobbie picks out four semiological codes to characterize this ideology: romance, personal life, fashion and beauty, and pop music. As part of the semiological "raw material" (12) in the production of *Jackie*, they were drawn from a preexisting culture of femininity that already impinges upon girls' lives. By means of the codes, girls were addressed as a group with shared interests in romance, makeup, fashion, and so on. The codes thus constructed a teenage-girl grouping, and their mere presence in the magazine is the main substantiation for McRobbie's declaration that *Jackie* offered an "invitation" to its teenage readers to join a bogus social group. Apart from this she refers, in an impressionistic and unsystematic way, to the "tone" of the codes at specific points. More generally, she refers to the informal " 'lightness' of tone" (9) characteristic of the magazine and the "sisterly" social position taken up by the producer.

By *lightness of tone* McRobbie means those properties of *Jackie* that mark it as a magazine rather than a serious text: the presence of advertisements, use of color, choice of layout, and so forth. She also refers to informality and an unserious attitude toward subject matter, which presumably contribute to *Jackie*'s tone, although she does little more than suggest these in passing, forcing her readers to try to draw them out for themselves from the occasional fragments of text given as examples.

The main example McRobbie gives of a sisterly relationship is in the problem pages, which she discusses in her chapter on the code of personal life. The characters set up as counselors replying to readers' letters (Cathy and Claire at the time of the study) are likened by McRobbie to older sisters. She refers to the tone of the letters as "friendly and confidential" and describes the replies to them as "both jolly and supportive" (27).[4] In the problem pages in general, she observes "a tone of secrecy, confidence, an intimacy evoking a kind of female solidarity, a sense of mutual understanding and sympathy" (29). She identifies Cathy and Claire as part of girls' feminine education, their function being to advise the less experienced by distributing "useful feminine knowledge" about how to behave (29).

McRobbie's references to sisterliness are frequent. My own sample text is a beauty page, so for a further example I will look at the sisterliness she observes in the code of fashion and beauty. The beauty pages contribute to feminine education, giving instructions for essential beauty work. As McRobbie points out, this training is necessary for girls' future entry into the job market. She also notes that in learning self-maintenance, girls lift part of the load of domestic reproduction from their mothers. The beauty pages provide a kind of do-it-yourself manual, educating girls in self-maintenance, or grooming, which includes becoming a feminine consumer:

> Here the girls learn how to apply mascara correctly, pluck their eyebrows and shave their legs. Each of these tasks involve *labour* but becomes fun and leisure when carried out in the company of friends, besides which when the subject is the self, and when "self-beautification" is the object, narcissism transforms work into leisure. Nonetheless, this labour, carried out in the confines of the home (bedroom or bathroom) does contribute, both *directly* and *indirectly*, to domestic production, itself the lynchpin upon which the maintenance and reproduction of the family depends. (41; original emphasis).

The anonymous authors pass on essential knowledge about using artificial aids to match up to accepted standards of feminine appearance (which are standards of beauty). McRobbie notes "a tone of hesitancy and apologetics" about the skills being passed on. She puts this tone down to an openly acknowledged double-edged guilt surrounding the inevitable failure, on one hand, to match up to conventions of beauty without resort to cosmetics and the dishonesty, on the other hand, of achieving it with them. In the beauty pages she studied, the skills that were transmitted concern "how girls can get the best of both worlds by deceiving men into believing they are naturally lovely, whilst subtly hiding their own flaws" (40). The authors pass on this guilty knowledge with a combination of "sisterly resignation" and reassurance, followed by the offer of specific actions as practical solutions, actions involving the use of commodities. McRobbie is deeply critical of these pages for offering consumption as the only way of compensating for inevitable failure in the natural beauty stakes, and their lack of any discussion of "*why* women feel ashamed or embarrassed by this 'failing'" (40; original emphasis). This kind of neglect is certainly unsisterly, and is probably more harmful than the enticement to competitiveness and mistrust that McRobbie asserts she observes in *Jackie*.[5] The next section develops her loose observations about *Jackie*'s offer of a "false sisterhood," detailing the linguistic means by which a close relationship is simulated in my sample text. I return to the issue of unsisterliness in the conclusion.

Synthetic Personalization and Friendship in a Magazine for Teenagers

How do we establish friendship? In part, by communicating, "I know what you're like, and I'm like that too." This kind of friendly behavior, the signaling of closeness and interest in another person, is sometimes known as being "positively polite" (Brown & Levinson 1987). It involves the participants' attention to "positive face": their need to be liked, approved of, flattered, or thought of as interesting. It is referred to as positive politeness, not in an evaluative sense, but to distinguish it from the kind of politeness, used predominantly among strangers and to superiors, that attends to "negative face" needs: participants' need for freedom from imposition and harassment. Positive politeness is probably central to the well-documented cooperativeness of women. For example, Janet Holmes (1990, 1993) presents a detailed picture of New Zealand women's use of politeness strategies. These are mostly positive (affective tags and other hedges, boosting devices, compliments), but some are negative (e.g., apologies).[6]

Positive politeness is very much in evidence in the mass media, and magazines are no exception. Certain kinds of linguistic features that are common in advertising and the mass media in general contribute to synthetic personalization and the establishment of an informal friendly relationship between the producers of mass-media texts and their audience. I concentrate on the mass-media producer's persona as a friend and the synthesized friendly relationship set up between producer and audience in a single sample of mass-media discourse, a consumer feature from *Jackie*. I shall briefly present two examples of synthesized positive politeness: the simulation of friendship and the simulation of reciprocal discourse.

The Simulation of Friendship

Aspects meriting attention in examining the producer's construction of a friendly persona for herself are the use of the pronouns *we* and *you*, relational and expressive values of lexis and punctuation, the setting up of shared presuppositions and projected facts (beliefs attributed to the reader, to "us," or just to common sense),[7] and, a variant of this, negating the reader's supposed assumptions. In focusing on these specific linguistic features, I attend to the way the producer realizes her simulation of friendly interaction with her audience, how she shows she knows who the reader is, and how she establishes herself as a member of the same social group. The entire consumer feature is reproduced in Figure 6.1. The column of text on the history of lipstick reads as follows:

Ask any clever advertiser how to suggest femininity with a product, and he'll probably tell you "a kissprint." Lipstick on a collar, a glass, his cheek—they all suggest that a woman was there. When men think of make-up, they think of lipstick.

It's hardly a modern invention—women have been adding artificial colour to their lips for centuries now. Before the days of lipstick as we know it, ladies used vegetable or animal dyes like cochineal—beetle's blood—to colour their lips.

The reason behind it wasn't simply to make themselves more beautiful—superstition lingered that the devil could enter the body through the mouth, and since red was meant to ward off evil spirits "lipstick" was put around the mouth to repel his evil intentions!

These days there are more complicated (and ruder!) theories. Experts in human behaviour say that it's all to do with sex (what else?!).

Other "experts" claim that the shape of your lipstick can reveal a lot about your character—i.e. if you wear the end flat you're stubborn, if it's round and blunt you're fun-loving etc. etc.—but don't seem to take into consideration the fact that each brand of lipstick is a different shape to start with and it's easiest just to use it accordingly. So much for the experts!

What *is* interesting is the way that fashions in lipsticks have changed over the years. When lipcolour first came into fashion at the beginning of this century, dark colours and the style of "drawing" on little pursed lips meant that women looked cutesy and doll-like. Later on, in the forties, film stars wanting to look lovable and "little-girl"ish continued this, while the newer breed of dominant, business-like women opted for a bolder look, colouring right over the natural "bow" in the lips. By the sixties "women's lib" was in style and most girls abandoned lipstick altogether, or used beige colours to blank out the natural pink of their lips, and concentrated on over-the-top eye make-up and face painting instead.

Now, in the eighties, there are more colours available than ever before—right down to blue, green and black! "Glossy" lips, popular for a while in the seventies, are out again, and the overall trend is for natural pink tints, with oranges and golds in summer, on big, full lips.

Large cosmetic manufacturers will have upwards of 70 shades available at a time, introducing a further three or four shades each season to complement the fashion colours of that time. And with some companies churning out batches of lipstick at a rate of 9,000 an hour, that's an awful lot of kisses to get through ... !

LIP

Ask any clever advertiser how to suggest femininity with a product, and he'll probably tell you 'a kissprint'. Lipstick on a collar, a glass, his cheek — they all suggest that a woman was there. When men think of make-up, they think of lipstick.

It's hardly a modern invention — women have been adding artificial colour to their lips for centuries now. Before the days of lipstick as we know it, ladies used vegetable or animal dyes like cochineal — beetle's blood — to colour their lips.

The reason behind it wasn't simply to make themselves more beautiful — superstition lingered that the devil could enter the body through the mouth, and since red was meant to ward off evil spirits 'lipstick' was put around the mouth to repel his evil intentions!

These days there are more complicated (and ruder!) theories. Experts in human behaviour say that it's all to do with sex (what else?!).

Other 'experts' claim that the shape of your lipstick can reveal a lot about your character — i.e. if you wear the end flat you're stubborn, if it's round and blunt you're fun-loving etc etc — but don't seem to take into consideration the fact that each brand of lipstick is a different shape to start with and it's easiest just to use it accordingly. So much for the experts!

What is interesting is the way that fashions in lipsticks have changed over the years. When lipstick first came into fashion at the beginning of this century, dark colours and the style of 'drawing' on little pursed lips meant that women looked cutesy and doll-like. Later on, in the forties, film stars wanting to look lovable and 'little-girl'ish continued this, while the newer breed of dominant, business-like women opted for a bolder look, colouring right over the natural 'bow' in the lips. By the sixties 'women's lib' was in style and most girls abandoned lipstick altogether, or used beige colours to blank out the natural pink of their lips, and concentrated on over-the-top eye make-up and face painting instead.

Now, in the eighties, there are more colours available than ever before — right down to blue, green and black! Glossy lips, popular for a while in the seventies, are out again, and the overall trend is for natural pink tints, with oranges and golds in summer; on big, full lips.

Large cosmetic manufacturers will have upwards of 70 shades available at a time, introducing a further three or four shades each season to complement the fashion colours of that time. And with some companies churning out batches of lipstick at a rate of 9,000 an hour, that's an awful lot of kisses to get through . . .!

MARGARET (15)
"I wear it all the time, because I always wear make-up. My favourite shade's a sort of brown-and-red mixture — I usually buy Boots 17 or Max Factor lipstick. I got my first one when I was 10, for Xmas — it was a sort of pink colour, I think it was just for me to play with."

EMILY (12)
"Usually I just wear lipstick when I'm going out, but sometimes for school, I like pinks, oranges and plain glosses. I was about 7 when my mum gave me a bright red lipstick to experiment with — I think I've worn it ever since!"

CLARA (wouldn't tell us her age!)
"I always wear red — dark red — and usually from Mary Quant or Estée Lauder. I don't know if I can remember my first lipstick — wait! yes I can! It was called "Choosy Cherry" by Mary Quant — everyone used to ask me if I was ill when I was wearing it!"

RHONA (18)
"I like pinks and deep reds. I don't wear it all that often. My first lipstick? I stole it from my sister's drawer — I was about 12 — dying to look grown-up even then!"

GOLD SPOT
STOPS YOUR MOUTH
FEELING LIKE A...

GOLD SPOT

Figure 6.1 The Consumer Feature

Pronouns. In the column there is an example of the inclusive *we*, referring to both producer and audience together: *lipstick as we know it*. Elsewhere in the feature, use of exclusive *we* (i.e., the editorial *we*) contributes to setting up the producer as a team; the anonymous group voice is a friendly gossip in the orientation beneath the title (see Figure 6.1).

Pronominal reference to the reader as if she were an individual addressee is quite frequent. An example of it occurs in the first sentence in the

column of text: *Ask any clever advertiser how to suggest femininity with a product and he'll probably tell you a "kissprint."*

Relational and expressive values of lexis and punctuation. The informality of some lexical terms contributes to the construction of a youthful female identity for the writer, matching the targeted audience by approximating the sort of vocabulary that teenagers might be supposed to use among themselves (e.g., *awful, cutesy*, in the column). The frequent exclamation marks add expressive value, attributing to the writer a friendly, enthusiastic emotional state. They seem to be the strongest boosting devices in this particular magazine feature. (Other boosting devices in this and similar magazines include *really, brill, well-trendy, mega*). The use of scare quotes contributes to setting up the familiar and the normal for the reader: the writer makes out that she knows what is and is not normal usage for her readers.

Common ground: projected facts and presuppositions. In the column of text in Figure 6.1, the writer negates an assumption attributable to the reader concerning the modernity of lipstick: *it's hardly a modern invention.* Similarly, in a set of instructions (reproduced below; see Figure 6.1 for the accompanying photographs), the writer challenges the reader's assumed pessimism about using lipstick successfully: *you* can *achieve a long-lasting look!*

LIP TRICKS!

Choosing the right shade of lipstick is easy—making it stay on is a bit more tricky. But by applying lipcolour correctly, you *can* achieve a long-lasting look!

1. Outline the lips with a toning lip-pencil—this will help stop your lipstick from "bleeding" around your mouth (a touch of Elizabeth Arden's Lip-Fix Creme, £4.95, provides a good base to prevent this, too).

2. Fill in using a lip brush loaded with lipstick—a lip brush gives you more control over what you're doing, and fills in tiny cracks more easily.

3. Blot lips with a tissue, dust over lightly with face powder, apply a second layer and blot again.

The writer is represented as the reader's friend and as knowing what the reader thinks. She minimizes the social distance between herself and her readership, claiming common ground and a social relation of closeness. With her implicit claims to common ground in presuppositions and projected facts, she sets herself up as a member of the same social group as her readers. So, for example, two agreed-upon and interesting facts in the column are that each brand of lipstick is a different shape, and that fashions in lipstick have changed over the years. These are projected by the fact-nouns *fact* and *way*, respectively. The writer assumes shared knowledge that relates to historical details about "breeds" of women, kinds of "looks," fashion changes, choice and ownership of lipstick, details relating to lipstick as a commodity that is subject to fashion change, the dullness of experts, and so on.

The Simulation of Reciprocal Discourse

Various features that are used to simulate reciprocal discourse contribute to constructing relationships on the advertisement page: response-demanding utterances (commands and questions in particular), adjacency pairs, and interpolations.[8]

Producer-audience. Response-demanding utterances directly addressed to the reader occur notably in the instructions text. These commands requiring action as response are highly conventional in instructions scripts.

[stage 1]	"Outline the lips with a toning pencil....
[stage 2]	Fill in using a lip brush....
[stage 3]	Blot lips with a tissue, dust over lightly ... apply a second layer ... blot again"

In the column, the writer begins with a command addressing the reader: *Ask any advertiser...*. In the same text, she interpolates her own statements twice:

Statement:	"... ladies used animal dyes like cochineal
Interpolation:	—beetle's blood—
(Statement):	to colour their lips"
Statement:	"These days there are more complicated
Interpolation:	(and ruder!)
(Statement):	theories."

Another interpolated remark occurs in the caption of a testimonial in the same feature: *CLARA (wouldn't tell us her age!)*

Representations of dialogue. The opening sentence of the column places the reader in an imaginary dialogue with a male advertiser. This dialogue consists of a two-part question-answer exchange, in which the reader asks the advertiser for information and he provides it:

Question:	"... how to suggest femininity with a product
Answer:	...'a kissprint.'"

Although reciprocal discourse is commonly constructed between writer and audience, in the sample I have chosen, the simulation of two-way discourse is most striking between the writer and various characters set up in the text. The effect is an impression of overhearing gossip. Simulation of reciprocal, two-way discourse is particularly noticeable in the testimonial section of the *Jackie* consumer feature. These testimonials are reproduced below (see Figure 6.1 for the accompanying snapshots):

MARGARET (15)

"I wear it all the time, because I always wear make-up. My favourite shade's a sort of brown-and-red mixture—I usually buy Boots 17 or Max Factor lipstick. I got my first one when I was 10, for Xmas—it was a sort of pink colour, I think it was just for me to play with."

EMILY (12)

"Usually I just wear lipstick when I'm going out, but sometimes for school, I like pinks, oranges and plain glosses. I was about 7 when my mum gave me a bright red lipstick to experiment with—I think I've worn it ever since!"

CLARA (wouldn't tell us her age!)

"I always wear red—dark red—and usually from Mary Quant or Estee Lauder. I don't know if I can remember my first lipstick—wait! yes I can! It was called 'Choosy Cherry' by Mary Quant—everyone used to ask me if I was ill when I was wearing it!"

RHONA (18)

"I like pinks and deep reds. I don't wear it all that often. My first lipstick? I stole it from my sister's drawer—I was about 12—dying to look grown-up even then!"

To make any sense of these statements at all we need to postulate a set of questions or first pair-parts that were asked by an interviewer but that do not appear on the page. They are interviewee responses to three reconstructable questions: *How often do you wear lipstick? What's your favorite shade? When did you get your first lipstick?* Notice the echoing repetition of the question in the fourth testimonial.

Interestingly, although the whole consumer feature establishes a friendly relationship between apparently like-minded people, as I have indicated, it is particularly in these testimonials that positive politeness strategies of the kind used by women in face-to-face interaction are prominent. The high proportion of hedges (*sort of, I think, about*) contrasts sharply with the authority of the editorial voice in the other sections. The editorial voice is that of the expert with special knowledge. The interviewees do not always use the modality of categorical certainty, as the editorial voice does; in fact, the only things they are not tentative about are their color preferences. But of course the interviewees' supposed "own words" have been structured by the interests of the editor-as-interviewer (present only as the shadow cast by her questions), who has set the agenda and constructed these interviews with "ordinary" people. The hedging presumably contributes to the simulation of informal speech.

Conclusion

In concluding, let me emphasize that I am not presenting the readers of publications for women as passive receptors and ignorant dupes. This simplistic view of readers as gullible consumers has been most determinedly and effectively challenged by ethnographic work on readers of romance novels (Owen 1990; Radway 1987), which has shown us that readers are not simply taken in by the fiction they read, at least not in any straightforward way. Romance readers use fiction strategically—to escape family demands, for instance—and are quite capable of spotting poor writing and of challenging stereotypes. The readers of *Jackie* magazine cannot be dismissed as fools, either. As McRobbie (1991) demonstrates, the magazine was used oppositionally, as a challenge to teachers and parents. Such publications for teenagers, along with other elements of nonschool culture, provide strategies of resistance for low achievers in school. Like Radway's romance readers, teenagers use reading deliberately to cut themselves off from the rest of the world and the obligations it tries to impose on them. Actual readers of the sample text analyzed in this chapter would have taken up multiple, and almost certainly contradictory, subject positions. At most, one can say they may have been simultaneously both duped and not duped, so to speak.

Perhaps I had also better make it quite clear that lipstick per se is not under criticism here and no disparagement of lipstick wearers is intended (or indeed of practitioners of any of the other feminizing practices available to us). It is not a matter of repressing the pleasures of self-beautification. What I have been investigating are some of the mechanisms by means of which consumer femininity intrudes into the subjectivities of women.[9] Women actively construct their own femininity, but this frequently means drawing on resources supplied by the magazine, clothing, and cosmetics industries. The femininity available to women is articulated principally in commercial and mass-media discourses. This very fact has certain consequences that are not beneficial to women and girls.

The audience of the feature analyzed here is offered sisterhood in consumption. Synthetic personalization and the need for adult femininity catch readers up in a bogus community, in which the subject position of consumer is presented as an integral part of being feminine. Members of this community other than the reader and her friendly editorial big sister are media celebrities, the testimonial givers, and other wearers of lipstick.

In the beauty feature, womanhood is a pattern of consumption. Teenagers aspire to adulthood. What girls aspire to be as women is presented for them as a matter of what kind of look they will opt for. The beauty feature is not a piece of sisterly advice or an exchange of sisterly secrets; it is covert advertising: a consumer feature. Its producers' aim, apart from filling two pages in the magazine inexpensively, is to promote lipstick as a commodity. The advice that it does provide for readers—that is, the instructions for professional application of lipstick—is curiously inappropriate for the age range. These instructions seem to be calculated to encourage experimenters to consume extravagantly by playing at being movie star and beautician rolled into one.

Girls need peer-group membership; they turn to other girls for friendship and to learn how to behave like teenage girls. Consumer femininity is a real part of adolescent patterns of friendship. The consumer feature, however, offers no real human relationship. The testimonials are an example of how, at puberty, girls are drawn into synthetic consumption communities of commodity users. Whether based on actual interviews or invented altogether, they are manipulative. Cosmetics use is presented as a natural part of a woman's identity, making demands on her discernment, her creative energies, and her time. In reading the feature, girls "associate" with business people. Fashion and beauty alone are newsworthy. The only practices cultivated relate to being a competent consumer; in fact, readers are encouraged to ridicule the scientific and analytical.

The sisterhood offered in the consumer feature is also unsisterly because it is patriarchal. The feature makes a small contribution to the shaping of the "paradigms for women's production of appearances" (Smith 1988:43) that are formed for women by the manufacturing, advertising, fashion, and magazine industries. In the opening paragraph of the column, in which the kissprint is presented as a symbol of femininity, this symbol is provided by a male character. It is a man who is the authority on femininity. The same passage goes on to present lipstick smudges as indices of a woman's presence. These are located on a man; to be feminine is to be (hetero)sexual. Feminine identity is achieved in consumption and in relationships with men. The friendly older sister writing for *Jackie* magazine (who could perfectly well be a man, of course) betrays her young readers, tying up their self-definition with external patriarchal standards of femininity. Given the poststructuralist vision of identity with which I opened, however, we need not view these readers as deterministically positioned in the act of reading this feature. Identity is not fixed but constantly in flux, being constructed moment by moment in the complexes of intersecting voices, or text populations, with which we engage in reading.

Notes

1. See, for example, Angela McRobbie (1978) and Leah Cohen (1984), both of whom are cited by Smith.

2. Smith is here taking issue with assertions made by other theorists of femininity. For Catharine MacKinnon (1982:530–31), for example, femininity is first and foremost a matter of sexualization: "Socially, femaleness means femininity, which means attractiveness to men, which means sexual attractiveness, which means sexual availability on male terms. What defines woman as such is what turns men on.... Gender socialization is the process through which women internalize (make their own) a male image of their sexuality *as* their identity as women. It is not just an illusion."

3. The subject positioning of readers is an issue I consider in more detail in an analysis of fiction in which I examine its potential for both socially reproductive and socially subversive tendencies (Talbot 1995).

4. Martin Barker (1989) observes that *Jackie*'s predecessors were more overtly dictatorial. Most notable was *Marilyn*, which ran a feature entitled "Mum Knows Best."

5. Barker (1989) finds McRobbie's justification for this claim very tenuous.

6. Hedging and boosting devices are kinds of modals, that is, elements that modify the force of a statement (Holmes 1984, 1993). Hedges (e.g., *sort of, kind of, rather, about*) are used to avoid making categorical statements by adding an impression of tentativeness. Tags (e.g., *isn't it?, don't you?*) sometimes function as hedges. Boosters, in contrast, serve as intensifiers and are used in expressions of interest or enthusiasm (e.g., *I'm so glad we came, we had a really good time*).

7. Projected facts and presuppositions are both kinds of external, prior text embedded in another text (Talbot 1990, 1995), but whereas projections are formal metalinguistic devices (Halliday 1985), presuppositions cannot be accounted for as formal features because they may be triggered by a wide variety of textual elements (Levinson 1983). Both projected facts and presuppositions tend to be backgrounded ideas that are noticeable only when assumptions of shared knowledge are erroneous.

8. Adjacency pairs are utterances that occur in pairs, forming small two-part exchanges such as question-answer (Schegloff 1968; Schegloff & Sacks 1973). The first pair-part sets up an expectation of the second pair-part. In simulations of interaction in written discourse, a first or second pair-part may be present without its partner.

   In a study of the language of a disc jockey on BBC's *Radio 1*, Martin Montgomery (1988:94) notes how frequently the DJ uses utterances requiring responses and observes that these utterances are contributing to a "sense of reciprocity" in the one-way discourse of the radio. Other features he observes contributing to this sense of two-way talk are short shifts in speaker role, which he refers to as *interpolations*. They are often response-demanding or expressive utterances. *Jackie* frequently contained bracketed remarks that seem to be simulations of such interpolations.

9. Cathryn Houghton (this volume) analyzes other discursive mechanisms that impose the capitalist agenda on teenage girls.

References

Barker, Martin (1989). *Comics: Ideology, power, and the critics.* Manchester: Manchester University Press.

Barthes, Roland (1967). *Elements of semiology.* London: Jonathan Cape.

Brown, Penelope, and Stephen Levinson (1987). *Universals in language usage: Politeness phenomena.* Cambridge: Cambridge University Press.

Cohen, Leah (1984). *Small expectations: Society's betrayal of older women.* Toronto: McClelland & Stewart.

Fairclough, Norman L. (1989). *Language and power.* London: Longman.

Ferguson, Marjorie (1983). *Forever feminine: Women's magazines and the cult of femininity.* London: Longman.

Halliday, Michael A. K. (1985). *An introduction to functional grammar.* London: Edward Arnold.

Holmes, Janet (1984). Hedging your bets and sitting on the fence: Some evidence for hedges as support structures. *Te Reo* 27: 47–62.

———— (1990). Politeness strategies in New Zealand women's speech. In Allan Bell and Janet Holmes (eds.), *New Zealand ways of speaking English.* Clevedon: Multilingual Matters. 252–76.

———— (1993). New Zealand women are good to talk to: An analysis of politeness strategies in interaction. *Journal of Pragmatics* 20: 91–116.

Houghton, Cathryn (this volume). Managing the body of labor: The treatment of reproduction and sexuality in a therapeutic institution.

Kristeva, Julia (1986a). The system and the speaking subject. In Toril Moi (ed.), *The Kristeva reader.* Oxford: Basil Blackwell. 24–33.

———— (1986b). Word, dialogue and novel. In Toril Moi (ed.), *The Kristeva reader.* Oxford: Basil Blackwell. 34–61.

Leiss, William, Stephen Kline, and Sut Jhally (1986). *Social communication in advertising.* New York: Methuen.

Leman, Joy (1980). "The advice of a real friend": Codes of intimacy and oppression in women's magazines, 1937–1955. *Women's Studies International Quarterly* 3: 63–78.

Levinson, Stephen (1983). *Pragmatics.* Cambridge: Cambridge University Press.

MacKinnon, Catherine A. (1982). Feminism, Marxism, method, and the state: An agenda for theory. *Signs* 7(3): 515–44.

McRobbie, Angela (1978). *Jackie:* An ideology of adolescent femininity. Occasional paper. University of Birmingham: Centre for Contemporary Cultural Studies.

———— (1991). *Feminism and youth culture: From* Jackie *to* Just Seventeen. London: Macmillan.

Montgomery, Martin (1988). D-J talk. In Nikolas Coupland (ed.) *Styles of discourse.* London: Croom Helm. 85–104.

Owen, Mairead (1990). Women's reading of popular romantic fiction: A case study in the mass media. A key to the ideology of women. Ph.D. diss., University of Liverpool.

Radway, Janice (1987). *Reading the romance: Women, patriarchy and popular literature.* London: Verso.

Schegloff, Emanuel (1968). Sequencing in conversational openings. *American Anthropologist* 70:1075–95.

Schegloff, Emanuel, and Harvey Sacks (1973). Opening up closings. *Semiotica* 8: 289–327.

Smith, Dorothy (1988). Femininity as discourse. In Leslie G. Roman and Linda K. Christian-Smith (eds.), *Becoming feminine: The politics of popular culture.* New York: Falmer Press. 37–59.

Talbot, Mary M. (1990). Language, intertextuality and subjectivity: Voices in the construction of consumer femininity. Ph.D. diss., University of Lancaster.

——— (1992). The construction of gender in a teenage magazine. In Norman L. Fairclough (ed.), *Critical language awareness.* London: Longman. 174–99.

——— (1995). *Fictions at work: Language and social practice in fiction.* London: Longman.

Weedon, Chris (1987). *Feminist practice and poststructuralist theory.* Oxford: Basil Blackwell.

White, Cynthia (1970). *Women's magazines, 1694–1968.* London: Michael Joseph.

Winship, Janice (1987). *Inside women's magazines.* New York: Pandora.

Part Two

Agency

through

Appropriation

7

Language, Gender, and Power

An Anthropological Review

Susan Gal

For a number of years now, issues of language have been at the forefront of feminist scholarship. This has been as true in psychology, anthropology, and history as in literary theory and linguistics. Yet, oddly, the studies that result often seem to have little in common. Psychologist Carol Gilligan writes about women's "voices," historian Carol Smith-Rosenberg wants to hear "women's words," anthropologists Shirley Ardener and Kay Warren discuss women's "silence and cultural muteness," literary critics from Elaine Showalter to Toril Moi explore "women's language and textual strategies." But it is not at all clear that they mean the same thing when they say *voice, words, silence,* and *language* as do the linguists and anthropologists who study women's and men's everyday conversation, who count the occurrence of linguistic variables, analyze slang and euphemisms, or examine the linguistic expression of solidarity in same-sex groups.

To be sure, we share a broad frame of reference, a capacious scholarly discourse that provides a fundamental coherence. First, in all feminist scholarship an initial and often remedial focus on women—their roles and stereotypes—has been replaced by a more sophisticated notion of gender as a system of relationships between women and men (Connell 1987; Gerson & Peiss 1985). As a corollary, gender relations within any social group are seen to be created by a sexual division of labor, a set of symbolic images, and contrasting possibilities of expression for women and men. A second source of coherence within feminist discourse has been the continuing argument about the relative importance of *difference*—between women and men, and among women—as opposed to *dominance* and *power*, in our understanding of gender relations. The contrast between approaches focused on difference and those centered on dominance remains important in orienting debates, and feminist scholars increasingly argue that we need to move beyond such static oppositions (di Leonardo 1987; Scott 1988).

Despite these important commonalities, however, a dilemma remains. On opening a book with a title such as *Language and Gender*, one is likely to find articles on pronouns, pragmatics, and lectal variation jostling unhappily with articles on textual gynesis, Arabic women's poetry, and the politics of gender self-representation. What exactly do such studies have in common? Certainly, a major strength of feminist scholarship is exactly the involvement of many disciplines and their divergent terminologies and interests. But I believe it is important to make some of these very different kinds of scholarship on language and gender speak more cogently to each other.

My aim here is twofold. First, I want to give an example of how two apparently divergent types of research on language and gender can complement each other, indeed must learn from each other. Second, I want to argue that a conceptualization of *power/domination* that is different from our usual, traditional assumptions promises an even broader integration, one that is already under way in much exciting recent work and that allows feminist research to criticize and rethink received notions about power.

Sociolinguistics and Cultural Studies

First then, the two types of research on language and gender that ought to embrace each other: I will call them, for convenience, variationist sociolinguistics and symbolic or cultural studies. Variationist studies of urban communities have provided some powerful insights about the internal and external forces operating in language change, and the central role of gender differences in these processes. But variationists have too often counted linguistic variables, correlated these with sex of speaker, and then merely speculated about why urban Western women usually choose more standard, "prestigious" forms and urban men of all classes evaluate working-class features more positively than women do. Usually, sociolinguists have resorted to universal sexual propensities, or global differences in power, to explain their findings (e.g., Labov 1972; Trudgill 1975). Similarly, other sociolinguists have located and counted moments of silence in female-male talk, or apparent interruptions, and have tried to read off power relations directly from these linguistic asymmetries.

What is missing in such work is the understanding that the categories of *women's speech*, *men's speech*, and *prestigious* or *powerful speech* are not just indexically derived from the identities of speakers. Indeed, sometimes a speaker's utterances create her or his identity. These categories, along with broader ones such as *feminine* and *masculine*, are culturally constructed within social groups; they change through history and are systematically related to other areas of cultural discourse such as the nature of persons, of power, and of a desirable moral order.

As we know, directness and bluntness are understood in some cultures to be styles appropriate to men, elsewhere to women. In some cultures verbal skills are seen as essential for political power, in others as anathema to it. The links between gender, status, and linguistic practices are not "natural" but culturally constructed (Borker 1980). Indeed, women's forms are sometimes symbolically opposed to men's forms, so that the values enacted by one are denied by the other. A classic case is that of the Malagasy: women's speech is blunt and direct, men's speech veiled and restrained (Keenan [1974] 1989). What "counts" as opposite is culturally defined, and such definitions affect the *form* of the differences between the sexes. In such cases we might even speak of "anti-languages" in Halliday's (1976) sense. Speakers often attribute the differences to the different "natures" of women and men. Nevertheless, historical analysis shows that much ideological work is required to create cultural notions that link forms of talk to social groups in such a way that speakers come to think the relationship is natural.

Silence is a familiar example. The silence of women in public life in the West is generally deplored by feminists. It is taken to be a result and a symbol of passivity and powerlessness; those who are denied speech, it is said, cannot influence the course of their lives or of history. In a telling contrast, however, we also have ethnographic reports of the paradoxical power of silence, especially in certain institutional settings. In religious confession, modern psychotherapy, bureaucratic interviews, oral exams, and police interrogation, the relations of coercion are reversed: where self-exposure is required, it is the silent listener who judges and who thereby exerts power over the one who speaks (Foucault 1979). Silence in American households is often a weapon of masculine power (Sattel 1983). But silence can also be a strategic defense against the powerful, as when Western Apache men use it to baffle, disconcert, and exclude white outsiders (Basso

1979). And this does not exhaust the meanings of silence. For the English Quakers of the seventeenth century, both women and men, the refusal to speak when others expected them to marked an ideological commitment (Bauman 1983). It was the opposite of passivity, indeed a form of political protest. (For other related views on silence, see the articles by Lakoff and Mendoza-Denton in this volume.)

Silence, like r-dropping, o-raising, interrupting, or any other linguistic form, gains different meanings and has different effects within specific institutional and cultural contexts, and within different linguistic ideologies. And these meanings can, of course, be changed. A telling example is the dilemma of elite women during the French Revolution, as described by Dorinda Outram (1987) and Joan Landes (1988). Elite writings during the French Revolution glorified male vertu, and identified the influence of women with the Old Regime's system of patronage, sexual favors, and corruption in which elite women had actively participated. Revolutionary theorists deliberately committed themselves to an antifeminine logic: political revolution could take place, they argued, only if women and their corrupting influence were excluded from public speaking and from the exercise of power. In part as a result of this new conceptualization, the famous and powerful political participation of upper-class women during the Old Regime was replaced, in the era of the revolution, with vigorous attacks on female political activists. In the new ideology, elite women's public speech and activities brought their sexual virtue into question: for a woman, to be political was to be corrupt. The famous revolutionary calls for universal equality applied only to men. Thus, politically active women such as Jeanne Roland could organize influential forums at which men debated the issues of the day, but her memoirs and letters reveal that this demanded a painful compromise. To retain her dignity she herself had to remain utterly silent.

This example briefly illustrates the contingency of women's silence in Europe, as well as the complex, mediated relationship of women to public speech. It highlights as well the strength of cultural definitions, and that they are not simply the product of nature or some age-old and monolithic male dominance. In this case we can watch them emerge articulately in the writings of the revolutionary theorists and Enlightenment philosophers who were doing the ideological work of formulating, explaining, justifying, and naturalizing the constraints on women's speech.

Returning now to variationist sociolinguistics, I suggest we take a hint from students of culture. For instance, the well-known affinity of the United States and British urban men for working-class speech variants should be seen within a broader cultural and historical frame. The linguistic evidence is strikingly congruent with a general symbolic structure in which manliness is associated with "toughness" and with working-class culture, not only in language but in other cultural spheres such as dress and entertainment. Femaleness, in contrast, is associated with respectability, gentility, and high culture. Surely, it is not accidental that just these oppositions emerged in literature, popular culture, and scientific discourse on both sides of the Atlantic in the nineteenth century and continue to be one component of current gender images (e.g., Halttunen 1982; Smith-Rosenberg 1985). The enactment of this opposition in linguistic practices strengthens and reproduces it; the encoding in prescriptive grammars and etiquette books institutionalizes it (Kramarae 1980). But it is the broader symbolic opposition itself that makes the linguistic variants meaningful, and allows them to be exploited for ironic play, parody, and ambiguity.

If variationists have neglected such ideological symbolic aspects of talk—the cultural constructions of language, gender, and power that shape women's and men's ideas and ideals about their own linguistic practices—a parallel neglect is apparent on the other side. Some of the anthropologists and others who have found that the women they study are "mute" or "uncommunicative" have often not attended to the contexts of talk, the constraints on the interview situation, and the communicative conventions of the people they study. The situatedness of communication of all kinds is a commonplace for sociolinguists. But it is not so self-evident, for instance, to students of popular culture.

Janice Radway (1984) has shown that if we look only at the content of American pulp romance novels, it is hard to avoid the conclusion that the women who read them are passive consumers masochistically drawn to images of female victimization and male brutality. But Radway examines not just the content of the novels but, inspired by sociolinguistics and the ethnography of speaking, the event of reading itself, its immediate context and meaning for the women who do it. For many romance readers the act of reading, often done in stolen moments of privacy, counts as educational and socially useful, and as something these women do for themselves. It is a way of fighting for a modicum of autonomy and against the usual self-abnegation of their lives. Thus, attention to the immediate performative or receptive context expands the understanding of popular culture, just as attention to the larger symbolic context allows for the interpretation of sociolinguistic variation. Clearly, these kinds of studies should be much more closely integrated with each other.

Although such mutual exchange of analytic strategy is very advantageous, an explicit discussion of what we mean by power promises to be even more so. Traditional views of power emphasize access to resources and participation in decision-making (see Lukes 1974). Certainly, linguistic and interactional factors are often intimately related to such access. But these views of power mask the important relationship between two quite different phenomena, both currently studied under the polysemous rubric of *women's words*.

Unlike linguists and sociolinguists who examine the phonological, semantic, syntactic, and pragmatic details of everyday talk, anthropologists, historians, psychologists, and literary critics often use terms like *voice*, *speech*, and *words* as a powerful metaphor. This usage has become extraordinarily widespread and influential in social science. Such terms are routinely used not to designate everyday talk but, much more broadly, to denote the public expression of a particular perspective on self and social life, the effort to represent one's own experience rather than accepting the representations of more powerful others. Similarly, *silence* and *mutedness* are used not for inability or reluctance to create utterances in conversational exchange but for failure to produce one's own separate, socially significant discourse. Here, *women's words* are a synecdoche for *gendered consciousness* or for *a positioned perspective*. Thus, although studies of gender differences in everyday talk focus on formal properties of speech or interaction, studies of women's voice have focused more on values and beliefs, asking whether women have cultural conceptions or symbolic systems concerning self, morality, or social reality different from those of men or of some dominant, official discourse.

Power and Domination

It is not only that sociolinguistic studies on the one hand and studies of women's values and beliefs on the other are mutually illuminating, as I argued above. More important, the two are inextricably linked. They both investigate how gender is related to power—with power redefined as *symbolic domination*.

In the familiar, classic cases of symbolic domination, some linguistic strategies, variants, or genres are more highly valued and carry more authority than others (e.g., Bourdieu 1977; Lears 1985). What makes this domination, rather than just a difference in form, is that even those who do not control these authoritative forms consider them more credible or persuasive, more deserving of respect than the forms they do control. As a corollary, people denigrate the very forms they themselves know and identify with. Archetypal examples include standard languages vis-à-vis minority languages or racial/ethnic vernaculars, and ritual speech vis-à-vis everyday talk. But respected, authoritative linguistic practices are not simply forms; they also deliver, or enact, characteristic cultural definitions of social life. When these definitions are embodied in divisions of labor and in social institutions such as schools, they serve the interests of some groups better than others. It is through dominant linguistic practices (such as a standard language, for instance) that speakers within institutions such as schools impose on others their group's definition of events, people, actions. This ability to make others accept and enact one's representation of the world is another, powerful aspect of symbolic domination. Domination and hegemony are matters of expressive form as well as cultural content. Thus, the notion of symbolic domination connects the concerns of linguists and sociolinguists with the broader cultural questions posed by social scientists studying gendered consciousness.

But it is important to remember that domination and power rarely go uncontested. Resistance to a dominant cultural order occurs in two ways: first, when devalued linguistic forms and practices (such as local vernaculars, slang, women's interactional styles or poetry, and minority languages) are practiced and celebrated despite widespread denigration and stigmatization. Second, it occurs because these devalued practices often propose or embody alternate models of the social world. The control of representations of reality occurs in social, verbal interaction, located in institutions. Control of such representations, and control of the means by which they are communicated and reproduced, are equally sources of social power. The reaction to such domination is various: it may be resistance, contestation, conflict, complicity, accommodation, indirection.

This general insight about domination and resistance is articulated in one way or another in the writings of a number of influential social theorists—Gramsci, Bourdieu, Foucault, among others, although they have not always applied it to language. Missing from these theories, however, is a concept of gender as a structure of social relations that is reproduced and sometimes challenged in everyday practice. That is why the emerging work on resistance to gender domination—especially the important work on linguistic resistance—is a powerful critique of social theory.

This returns us to the feminist debate about difference and dominance: if we understand women's everyday talk as well as women's linguistic genres and cultural discourses as forms of resistance, then this implies that difference and dominance are always intertwined. We hear, in any culture, not so much a clear and heretofore neglected "different voice," certainly not separate female and male cultures, but rather linguistic practices that are more ambiguous, often contradictory, differing among women of different classes and ethnic groups and ranging from accommodation to opposition, subversion, rejection, or autonomous reconstruction of reigning cultural definitions. But such practices always occur in the shadow of domination and in response to it. Finding the attempts at resistance will tell us about where and how power is exerted, and knowing how institutions of power work will tell us where to look for possible signs of resistance (Abu-Lughod 1990).

Two examples should clarify these general statements. The first is Carol Edelsky's (1981) intriguing study of different kinds of "floor" in mixed-sex faculty meetings at an American college. Two sets of implicit rules seemed to regulate the length and quality of contributions to the meeting. In episodes characterized by the first kind of floor, speakers took longer and fewer turns, fewer speakers participated overall, they did not overlap much, there were many false starts and hesitations, and speakers used their turns for reporting facts and voicing opinions. The other kind of floor occurred at the same meetings but during different episodes. It was characterized by much overlap and simultaneous talk but little hesitation in speaking, and by more general participation by many speakers who collaboratively constructed a group picture of "what is going on." In the second kind of floor many speakers performed the same communicative functions, such as suggesting an idea, arguing, agreeing, joking, and teasing. It was men who monopolized the first kind of floor by taking longer turns. In the second kind of floor everyone took shorter turns and women and men participated in similar ways in the communicative functions performed. Importantly, the first, more formal kind of floor, in which women participated less, occurred vastly more frequently, at least in this institutional setting. And it was the accepted norm. It is noteworthy that explicit and tacit struggles between speakers about how meetings are to be conducted are not idle; they are conflicts about the control of institutional power, about who will get to speak, and with what effect. Even among status equals, as in this example, the interactional contraints of institutional events such as meetings are not gender-neutral but weighted in favor of male interactional strategies.

I suggest it is useful to reinterpret Edelsky's work within the view of power I have been outlining. As in all the classic cases of symbolic domination, the organization of the meeting masks the fact that speakers are excluded on the basis of gender, while it simultaneously accomplishes that exclusion. But we can also ask about the implicit worldview or value system that is enacted by the different kinds of floors. And then we see the two not as simply different but as mutually dependent, calling on different values within American culture, values conventionally seen as opposed to each other. The kind of floor more congenial for male strategies of interaction depends on images of heroic individuality, competition, and the celebration of planning and hierarchy. The second kind of floor is implicitly a critique of the first because it enacts values of solidarity, simultaneity, and collaborative cooperation. When women constructed the second kind of floor, they were resisting the dominant floor both as form and implicitly as enactment of cultural values. Note that the way in which one set of values is linked to one gender and the other set is associated with the other gender is not explored here. It is an ideological and interactional process that deserves much more attention by social scientists (see Ochs 1992).

My second example draws on the oral lyric poetry performed among intimates by the Bedouin of Egypt's Western Desert. In describing these delicate, brief, and artfully improvised performances, Lila Abu-Lughod (1986) stresses that the dominant ideology, what she calls (metaphorically) the "public language," of the Bedouin is one of honor, autonomy, self-mastery, personal strength, and sexual modesty. The poems directly violate this code of honor and implicitly criticize it by expressing the feelings of dependency, emotional vulnerability, and romantic longing condemned by the official view. The poetry constitutes what Abu-Lughod calls "a dissident or subversive discourse . . . most closely associated with youths and women, the disadvantaged dependents who least embody the ideals of Bedouin society and have least to gain from the current social structures. Poetry is the discourse of opposition to the system and of defiance of those who represent it" (251).

But the poetry is anything but a spontaneous outpouring of feeling. Indeed, its formal properties and context of performance enhance its ability to carry subtle messages that run counter to official ideals. It is formulaic, thereby disguising the identities of poet, addressee, and subject. It is fleeting and ambiguous, performed by women and youths among trusted intimates who can decipher it precisely because they already know the reciter well. Yet, this poetry of subversion and defiance is not only tolerated but culturally elaborated and admired because of the paradoxical intertwining of official and dissident discourse. The oral poetry reveals a fundamental tension of Bedouin social and political life that, while valuing and demanding autonomy and equality between families and lineages, demands inequality between the genders and generations within families. This verbal genre of women and youths reveals the contradictions of the ruling ideology.

Conclusion

In sum, I have been arguing that power is more than the chance to participate in decision-making—what early feminist theorists sometimes call *informal* or *micropolitics* (e.g., Rosaldo 1974). The notions of domination and resistance alert us to the idea that the strongest form of power may well be the ability to define social reality, to impose visions of the world. And such visions are inscribed in language and, most important, enacted in interaction. Although women's everyday talk and women's voice or consciousness have been studied separately, I have argued that both can be understood as strategic responses, often of resistance, to dominant hegemonic cultural forms. Thus, attention to linguistic detail, context of performance, and the nature of the dominant forms is essential to both endeavors. The precise form of questions and turn-taking is crucial in understanding the construction of different floors in American meetings (that is, in everyday talk); the exact formal conventions of intimate Bedouin poetry (expressive genre) are indispensable to understanding how it is suited to the expression of vulnerability and dependence. Although the linguistic materials are quite different, both collaborative floors and intimate poetry locate an opposition or contradiction in dominant conceptions and try to subvert the dominant through rival practices. One undermines the hierarchical form and ideology of meetings that favor men's expertise in competitive talk; the other is seen as the opposite of ordinary talk and undermines the cultural rule of honor, threatening to reveal the illegitimacy of elder men's authority.

This returns us to the cultural constructions about women, men, and language with which I began. These cultural constructions are first of all linguistic ideologies that differentiate the genders with respect to talk. It is only within the frame of such linguistic ideologies that specific linguistic forms such as silence, interruption, or euphemism gain their specific meanings. Like all ideologies, these are linked to social positions, and are themselves sources of power. These ideas are enacted and sometimes contested in talk. I believe that the research I have discussed marks a very productive path for future studies of language and gender, one informed by sociolinguistics at least as much as by cultural studies and social theory.

The chapters in this section explore just this terrain of linguistic ideology, and women's diverse forms of contestation and resistance to dominant definitions of gender categories and of women's speech. For example, the chapters by Laurel Sutton and Shigeko Okamoto remind us that we cannot take for granted the social meanings of individual linguistic forms. Speakers redefine and play with language so that within particular social contexts (and within implicit counterideologies) demeaning lexical items can be recast as terms of solidarity. Similarly, stereotypically or prescriptively "male" forms, when used by women, can index youthfulness, liveliness, and nonconformity. Although socially rather homogeneous, Shigeko Okamoto's sample of Japanese college women nevertheless shows impressive linguistic diversity in the use of forms usually associated with "masculine" speech. This leads Okamoto to question the analytical category of *women's speech.* The fundamental insight is not so much that this analytic category is unduly monolithic but, more important, that it is not an analytical category at all. It also forms part of a larger ideological framework linking language, class, region, and gender, a framework whose historical formation can be located in the Meiji era. As Okamoto shows, it is against the backdrop of this complex ideology that contemporary Japanese women strategically fashion new identities in talk.

The historical construction of identities in talk is also the theme of Anna Livia's chapter on the fictional representation of butch and femme speech. Here it is obvious that direct correlations between some essentialized category such as *sex of speaker* and the linguistic forms they produce will be of little analytical significance. Livia asks, instead, how *feminine* and *masculine* are constructed in the fictional material she analyzes, and how these images play against, comment upon, contradict, parody, or reinforce ideologies about female/male speech. Livia's work is particularly sensitive to the disjunctures between ideology, representation, and everyday practice. In fictional representations of butch and femme speech, she finds not a simple imitation of everyday talk or even an instantiation of stereotypes but, rather, the use and ironic reuse of earlier literary examples.

In a different vein, Kira Hall discusses the use of women's language as sexual commodity. As in my examples above, it is not only the sexual content of the talk produced by women in the "adult message industry" that is sex-typed but the forms of conversational exchange as well. Using exactly the stereotyped and stigmatized forms of "women's speech" that many investigators have described, the women on those "fantasy phone lines" owned and operated by women nevertheless see themselves as feminists in control of their work and their lives. What might have seemed at first glance (and according to earlier analyses) to be powerless, sexualized language is economically powerful for these women because it provides a safe, flexible, and relatively lucrative income during hard times. Linguistic forms gain their value, their social meaning and social effect, within specific institutional contexts. As Hall carefully points out, however, this is not some simple reversal in which women unexpectedly gain powerful speech. The women know they must reproduce their clients' negative images of women in the very act of gaining their own relative distance from those stereotypes.

Finally, Bonnie McElhinny's rich ethnographic description of female police officers in Pittsburgh raises important issues about the local definitions and imbrication of emotions such as sympathy or anger, linguistic strategies such as "facelessness," and the subversion of assumptions about femininity and masculinity. Indeed, contrary to much research on language and gender, McElhinny shows that gender is not always equally relevant; it can be submerged by actors in some institutions and thus can be made variable in its salience in interaction. Because the linkages between linguistic forms or strategies and gender categories are ideologically constructed, female police officers can start to reconstruct femininity and masculinity in their own lives, as they manage their everyday interactions.

As these chapters amply demonstrate, the study of language and gender is significantly enhanced by simultaneous attention to everyday practices on the one hand, and on the other to the ideological understandings about women, men, and language that frame these practices and render them interpretable in particular social contexts, historical periods, and social institutions. These chapters move beyond the notions of "women's and men's speech" or the "difference versus dominance" controversy to analyze the hegemonic power of linguistic ideologies and the ways in which speakers attempt to parody, subvert, resist, contest, or in some way accommodate these positioned and powerful ideological framings.

Acknowledgments

A somewhat different and much longer version of the argument outlined here appeared in Micaela di Leonardo (ed.) (1991), *Gender at the Crossroads of Knowledge*, Berkeley: University of California Press, 175–203.

References

Abu-Lughod, Lila (1986). *Veiled sentiments*. Berkeley: University of California Press.

———(1990). The romance of resistance: Tracing transformations of power through Bedouin women. *American Ethnologist* 17: 41–55.

Basso, Keith (1979). *Portraits of "the Whiteman": Linguistic play and cultural symbols among the Western Apache*. New York: Cambridge University Press.

Bauman, Richard (1983). *Let your words be few: Symbolism of speaking and silence among seventeenth-century Quakers*. New York: Cambridge University Press.

Borker, Ruth (1980). Anthropology: Social and cultural perspectives. In Sally McConnell-Ginet, Ruth Borker, and Nelly Furman (eds.), *Women and language in literature and society*. New York: Praeger. 25–46.

Bourdieu, Pierre (1977). The economics of linguistic exchanges. *Social Science Information* 16(6): 645–68.

Connell, R. W. (1987). *Gender and power.* Stanford: Stanford University Press.

di Leonardo, Micaela (1987). The female world of cards and holidays. *Signs* 12(3):440–53.

Edelsky, Carol (1981). Who's got the floor? *Language in Society* 10(3): 383–422.

Foucault, Michel (1979). *Discipline and punish.* New York: Vintage.

Gerson, Judith, and Kathy Peiss (1985). Boundaries, negotiation, consciousness: Reconceptualizing gender relations. *Social Problems* 32(4): 317–31.

Hall, Kira (this volume). Lip service on the fantasy lines.

Halliday, Michael (1976). Anti-languages. *American Anthropologist* 78: 570–84.

Halttunen, Karen (1982). *Confidence men and painted women.* New Haven: Yale University Press.

Keenan, Elinor ([1974] 1989). Norm-makers and norm-breakers: Uses of speech by men and women in a Malagasy community. In Richard Bauman and Joel Sherzer (eds.), *Explorations in the ethnography of speaking.* 2d ed. New York: Cambridge University Press. 125–43.

Kramarae, Cheris (1980). Gender: How she speaks. In E. B. Ryan and Howard Giles (eds.), *Attitudes towards language variation.* London: Edward Arnold. 84–98.

Labov, William (1972). *Sociolinguistic patterns.* Philadelphia: University of Pennsylvania Press.

Lakoff, Robin Tolmach (this volume). Cries and whispers: The shattering of the silence.

Landes, Joan (1988). *Women and the public sphere in the age of the French Revolution.* Ithaca: Cornell University Press.

Lears, Jackson (1985). The concept of cultural hegemony: Problems and possibilities. *American Historical Review* 90: 567–93.

Livia, Anna (this volume). "I ought to throw a Buick at you": Fictional representations of butch/femme speech.

Lukes, Steven (1974). *Power: A radical view.* London: Macmillan.

McElhinny, Bonnie S. (this volume). Challenging hegemonic masculinities: Female and male police officers handling domestic violence.

Mendoza-Denton, Norma (this volume). Pregnant pauses: Silence and authority in the Anita Hill–Clarence Thomas hearings.

Ochs, Elinor (1992). Indexing gender. In Alessandro Duranti and Charles Goodwin (eds.), *Rethinking context.* Cambridge: Cambridge University Press. 335–58.

Okamoto, Shigeko (this volume). "Tasteless" Japanese: Less "feminine" speech among young Japanese women.

Outram, Dorinne (1987). Le langage mâle de la vertu: Women and the discourse of the French Revolution. In Peter Burke and Roy Porter (eds.), *The social history of language.* New York: Cambridge University Press. 120–35.

Radway, Janice (1984). *Reading the romance.* Chapel Hill: University of North Carolina Press.

Rosaldo, Michelle (1974). Women, culture, and society: A theoretical overview. In

Michelle Rosaldo and Louise Lamphere (eds.), *Woman, culture, and society.* Stanford: Stanford University Press. 17–42.

Sattel, Jack W. (1983). Men, inexpressiveness and power. In Barrie Thorne, Cheris Kramarae, and Nancy Henley (eds.), *Language, gender, and society.* Rowley, MA: Newbury House. 119–24.

Scott, Joan (1988). *Gender and the politics of history.* New York: Columbia University Press.

Smith-Rosenberg, Carol (1985). *Disorderly conduct: Visions of gender in Victorian America.* New York: Oxford University Press.

Sutton, Laurel (this volume). Bitches and skankly hobags: The place of women in contemporary slang.

Trudgill, Peter (1975). Sex, covert prestige, and linguistic change in urban British English of Norwich. *Language in Society* 1: 179–96.

8

Lip Service on the Fantasy Lines

Kira Hall

When the deregulation of the telephone industry co-occurred with a number of technological advances in telecommunications in the early 1980s, American society witnessed the birth of a new medium for linguistic exchange—the 900 number. On the fantasy lines, which generate annual revenues of more than $45 million in California alone,[1] women's language is bought, sold, and custom-tailored to secure caller satisfaction. This high-tech mode of linguistic exchange complicates traditional notions of power in language, because the women working within the industry consciously produce a language stereotypically associated with women's powerlessness in order to gain economic power and social flexibility. In this chapter, I refer to research I conducted among five women-owned fantasy-line companies in San Francisco in order to argue for a more multidimensional definition of linguistic power, one that not only devotes serious attention to the role of sexuality in conversational exchange but also recognizes individual variability with respect to women's conversational consent.

The linguistic identification of women's language as "powerless" and men's language as "powerful" has its origins in early readings of the work of Robin Lakoff (1975), who argued in *Language and Woman's Place* that sex differences in language use both reflect and reinforce the unequal status of women and men in our society. After identifying an array of linguistic features ideologically associated with women's speech in American English—among them lexical items associated with women's work; "empty" adjectives such as *divine, charming,* and *cute;* tag questions in place of declaratives; hedges such as *sort of, kind of;* and *I guess;* intensifiers such as *so* and *very;* and hypercorrect, polite linguistic forms—Lakoff suggested that the association of indirect speech with women's language and direct speech with men's language is the linguistic reflection of a larger cultural power imbalance between the sexes. Her treatise, packaged beneath the unapologetically feminist photograph of a woman with bandaged mouth, has inspired two decades of heated debate among subsequent language and gender theorists. A number of feminist scholars have argued that Lakoff's identification of women's language as culturally subordinate serves to affirm sexist notions of women as deviant and deficient, and sociolinguists steeped in Labovian empirical argumentation have dismissed her claims altogether as quantitatively invalid (see Bucholtz & Hall, this volume).

I have no desire to reopen the academic wounds of what remains a divisive subject among language and gender theorists, but a discussion of my research on the discursive fictions produced by phone-sex employees in San Francisco would be incomplete without reference to Lakoff's early description of "women's language." The type of language that these employees consider sexual, and that for them is economically powerful, is precisely what has been defined by language and gender theorists since Lakoff as "powerless." The notion that behavior that is perceived as powerless can, in certain contexts, also be perceived as sexual may be old hat to anthropologists and sociologists, but language theorists have yet to address this connection explicitly. The very existence of the term *sweet talk*—an activity that, in the American heterosexual mainstream, has become associated more with the speech patterns of women than with men[2]—underscores the ideological connection between women's language and sexual language. By taking on the outer vestments of submissiveness and powerlessness, or, rather by appropriating the linguistic features culturally associated with such a posture, the female "sweet-talker" projects a certain sexual availability to her male listener so as to further her own conversational aims. Her use of this discursive style, which in its sexualized duplicity might more appropriately be dubbed the *Mata Hari technique,* is itself powerful; the speaker is not the naive, playful, and supportive interactant her male audience has taken her to be but a mature, calculating adult with a subversive goal in mind.³ Perhaps in an effort to underscore this very duplicity, Kathleen K. (1994), author of a recent book on her experiences as a phone-sex worker in the Pacific Northwest, chose the title *Sweet Talkers: Words from the Mouth of a "Pay to Say" Girl.*

In this chapter, I address the superficial conflict in the use of submissive speech for reasons of power. The adult-message industry has enjoyed considerable financial success during the past decade, grossing well over $3 billion since its national debut in 1983.⁴ As fear of the AIDS epidemic and the accompanying interest in safe sex spreads throughout the culture at large, the demand for women's vocal merchandise promises to expand into the next millennium. The growing success of this discursive medium in the marketplace calls for a new interpretation of the place of women's language in contemporary society. Its easy marketability as a sexual commodity and the profits it reaps for the women who employ it suggest that the study of cross-sex linguistic exchange must acknowledge the more subversive aspects of conversational consent.

Antipornography Feminists Meet the Legislative Right

The growing demand for fantasy-line services in American society has prompted the U.S. Congress to examine the legality of vocal pornography,⁵ an undertaking that is perhaps not surprising, given the phone-sex industry's organizational similarity to prostitution. Live-conversation services, now available mainly through credit cards, allow the caller to engage in a live verbal encounter with a speaker who is paid by the minute to fulfill a phone fantasy. The customer calls the fantasy line and speaks directly to a switchboard operator who then processes his fantasy request. After screening his credit card number, the operator calls one of her home-based employees, explains the requested fantasy to her, and gives her the choice of accepting or rejecting the work. In a sense, then, the encounter mimics conventional sex work except that it is conducted entirely within the vocal sphere. In layperson's terms, the john calls the conversational brothel, files his request with the phone pimp, and gets connected to the oral prostitute of his choice. In contrast, prerecorded services, also referred to more colloquially as *dial-a-porn*, offer the caller a choice of predetermined sexually explicit messages, accessible through the appropriate button on the touch-tone telephone. The caller is greeted by a recorded woman's voice that informs him that he must be at least eighteen years of age in order to continue the call and then outlines the currently available fantasies. One service that advertises monthly in *Hustler*, for example, offers a choice of "oral fantasies," "oriental girl fantasies," "housewives fantasies," "lesbian fantasies," "Swedish mistress fantasies," and even "women-in-jail fantasies."

In April of 1988, an upset Congress responded to complaints about the unregulated nature of prerecorded services, amending section 223(b) of the Communications Act of 1934 to impose a complete ban on both indecent and obscene interstate commercial telephone messages—a proposal referred to in the legal literature as the *1988 Helms Amendment,* after its author Senator Jesse Helms (R-N.C.). In the battle that ensued between Sable Communications of California and the Federal Communication Commission, the FCC attempted to justify the ban on indecent messages by arguing in a U.S. district court that mass telephone message systems are analogous to public radio broadcasts. The government relied on *FCC v. Pacifica Foundation* (438 U.S. 726 (1978)), in which the Supreme Court, in response to a father's complaint against a radio's afternoon broadcast of George Carlin's "Filthy Words" monologue, ruled that the FCC could in fact regulate indecency over the airwaves on a nuisance basis. The plaintiff, on the other hand, compared dial-a-porn to the private medium of cable television, which a number of courts have declared may broadcast obscene and indecent materials. The district court found that the provision dealing with dial-a-porn was severable, deciding that although the First Amendment did not protect *obscene* messages, it did protect *indecent* ones. But because the official legal definitions of obscenity and indecency remained vague,[6] adult services that believed their messages to be indecent and not obscene could continue to transmit messages. In 1989 Congress amended section 223(b) a second time, requiring telephone companies to establish presubscription policies. Three years later, President Bush signed into law the Telephone Disclosure and Dispute Resolution Act, which, in broad terms, not only establishes uniform standards for the pay-per-call industry at the federal level but also ensures that consumers who call such services receive adequate information before they are charged any money.[7]

Congressional debates on the legality of this controversial form of communication coincided with recent feminist discussions on what has been called, since the 1982 Barnard College Politics of Sexuality Conference, the *pleasure/danger controversy.* Feminists like Andrea Dworkin (1981, 1988), Sheila Jeffreys (1990, 1993), Catharine MacKinnon (1987, 1993), and Diana Russell (1993), who stress the sexual danger brought on by male pornography, oppose feminists like Susie Bright (1992) and Pat Califia (1994), who emphasize the need for freedom of speech in the pursuit of women's sexual desire, embracing as powerful what has been traditionally thought of as "feminine" sexuality.[8]

Catherine MacKinnon in particular, in her argument that "pornography, in the feminist view, is a form of forced sex" (1987:148), blurs the division between representation and act, defining depictions of sex as synonymous with actual sex. Her arguments have unfortunately been appropriated by conservative legislators led by Helms who back the U.S. obscenity law, deeming images obscene either because they cause real-life effects (or in legal terms, appeal "to the prurient interest in sex of the average person"[9]) or because they depict sexual acts that are illegal under other sections of the criminal code. To make their case against photographer Robert Mapplethorpe, for instance, legislators cited the MacKinnon/Dworkin amendments to the Minneapolis antipornography ordinance in their own bill to set restrictions on the kinds of representations fundable by the state (Butler 1990). The strength of this discursive alliance between antipornography feminists and conservative legislators, albeit a superficial one, led the Senate to pass a bill forbidding the National Endowment for the Arts to fund artistic projects that depict "obscenity," which became law in September 1989. Additional legal equations of representation and act could have implications for the adult-message industry, where the representation, though vocal, invites comparison with actual prostitution. As the mediums by which people gain access to obscene and indecent material change (the most recent form being computer pornography, which provides formats for exchanging sexual messages and conducting on-line "modem sex"), courts and legislatures will have to determine which types of representation (e.g., visual, verbal, vocal) more closely approximate, or affect, reality.

Dworkin and MacKinnon are especially concerned with the issue of pornography because for them, sexuality is the basis for the constitution of power relations in our society; in MacKinnon's (1987:3) often-quoted words, "The social relation between the sexes is organized so that men may dominate and women must submit. This relation is sexual—in fact, is sex." But other feminists have argued that in their arguments against pornography, Dworkin and MacKinnon construct a definition of sexuality in terms of oppression, a definition that, in the words of Judith Butler (1990:113), "links masculinity with agency and aggression, and femininity with passivity and injury." Theorists such as Alice Echols (1983) and Gayle Rubin (1984), and more recently Marianne Valverde (1989), Carla Freccero (1990), and Lynne Segal (1993), have argued that in defining female sexuality as uniformly powerless and constructed by men, Dworkin and MacKinnon leave no room for women to construct their own sexual desires, much less to reclaim patriarchal ones.

Central to the work of these latter theorists is the notion that sexual oppression, though certainly important, should not be emphasized to the exclusion of economic and social oppression. Freccero's (1990) work speaks to this claim directly as she criticizes North American mainstream feminism for its almost exclusive preoccupation with pornography. Arguing that sex workers, because they focus on the sex industry from the point of view of its labor force, "provide an important corrective to the middle-class intellectual feminists' debates about pornography and sexuality," Freccero asserts that feminism should be concerned neither with "the commodity itself (pornography) nor the 'private' sexual practices of individuals, but rather, their convergence in the marketplace" (316). The marketplace is also of central concern to phone-sex employees in San Francisco, who see parallels between their own situation and that depicted by contributors to collections such as Gail Pheterson's (1989) *A Vindication of the Rights of Whores* and Frederique Delacoste and Priscilla Alexander's (1987) *Sex Work: Writings by Women in the Sex Industry*. Because pornographic representation is an essential ingredient of their own economic livelihood, fantasy-line operators have necessarily had to ally themselves with pro-pornography activists. It is not my intention in this chapter to side with "pro-pornography" feminists as opposed to "antipornography" feminists; my own experiences with feminist activism in San Francisco have shown me that this division is itself superficial. Rather, I wish to suggest that the ongoing feminist debate over the notion of power can contribute to the study of conversational interaction, particularly as it points to the importance of contextualizing any definition of power within an array of intersecting influences.

Fantasy and the Telephone

The telephone, as a medium that excludes the visual, allows for the creation of fantasy in a way that face-to-face interaction cannot. In the absence of a visual link, the speaker is able to maintain a certain anonymity that can potentially allow for a less self-conscious and, in the appropriate circumstances, more imaginative presentation.[10] On the 900-lines, where the sense of anonymity is of course heightened by the fact that the two interactants have never met, callers must construct their conversational partner visually. Once they have created such a representation, they have already entered into a fantasy world of sorts, and the construction of any additional representations is facilitated by this entry. Although the majority of communication studies in the 1970s (e.g., Cook & Lallgee 1972; Goddard 1973; Rutter & Stephenson 1977; Short, Williams, & Christie 1976;) support the assertion that the telephone's lack of visual access restricts individual expression, it seems that today's users find that this lack in fact encourages creativity—a change of attitude that might explain the dramatic increase in phone-related devices, among them answering machines, cellular mobile telephones, cordless telephones, dial-up teleconferencing facilities, and electronic mail, not to mention the numerous varieties of 900 and 976 services. Even though the telephone has been around for more than a hundred years, it is only in the past twenty years that the system has undergone what G. Fielding and D. Hartley (1987:11) refer to as "explosive growth," both in quality and scope. The advent of telephone deregulation in the United States and the increasing availability of the mobile telephone have prompted telecommunication theorists like Frederick Williams (1985:191) to argue that the telephone is shifting "from a 'home' or 'business' based communications link to an individual, personal based one." This shift is nowhere more apparent than in the advertising strategies of the telephone industry itself, which regularly appeals to the personal, private, and expressive contact that it affords. With just one thirty-second AT&T telephone call, clients can find a long-lost friend, pacify a weeping mother, or "reach out and touch" that special someone. Perhaps it is not so strange after all to see advertisement after advertisement on late Saturday-night television for "romance lines," "friendship lines," "party lines," "psychic lines," "teenage date lines," "therapy lines," and "confession lines."

Adult-message services have clearly capitalized on this shift as well, appealing to the private and expressive nature of the medium in their own advertising strategies. The company Call Girls offers "live conversation with a personal touch," Linda's Lip Service declares that it is "friendly, personal, and unhurried," and ABC International features "completely private, one to one, adult conversations." Most services appearing on the back pages of *Hustler* and *Penthouse* advertise their numbers visually—with pictures of naked women in provocative poses talking on the telephone—but an increasing number of services are advertising themselves verbally, perhaps in an effort to represent a more personal, involved, and creative relationship between seller and consumer. The company Terry's Live Talk, for instance, advertises its number in the form of a typewritten letter, urging its readers to call its "very personal" service and concluding with the intimate salutation "Love XOXOXOXOXO." The service Nicole Bouvier, which reserves an entire page in *Penthouse* for its letter of advertisement, opens romantically with a reference to the senses, equating phone talk with touch, smell, and taste and shunning the need for sight altogether: "My love, it doesn't matter if you can't see me. You can touch me ... smell me ... taste me ... and then you will *know* and always *remember* me." Still other services choose to imitate the written format of the newspaper personals, listing prose descriptions of their fantasy-line operators (which are presumably fictional because most employers have never met their employees face-to-face) in an effort to set their employees apart from the generic phone-sex model.

Dial-a-porn clients use a medium that is intensely public, with one line potentially servicing as many as fifty thousand calls an hour in an anonymous fashion,[11] in order to engage in a subject matter traditionally thought of as intensely private. The unnaturalness of this interaction must be rectified by the fantasy-line performer, who presents herself through a unique mixture of public and private discourse. Lakoff (1990), differentiating genres of discourse with reference to these two dimensions, argues that participants in private discourse tend to express themselves with shared allusions, jointly created metaphors, and telegraphic references, promoting feelings of intimacy and trust. Participants in public language, on the other hand, because they cannot count on shared allusions, tend to express themselves in an explicit, concrete manner so that the larger public can understand. Because the fantasy-line operator has never met her male client, she clearly lacks the frame of reference necessary for private conversation; instead, she must create a feeling of intimacy by evoking a frame of reference that the majority of her male callers will understand and be familiar with—namely, that of male pornography. Within this rather limited field of discourse, she and her client are able to express themselves with the shared allusions, jointly created metaphors, and telegraphic references necessary for private communication, however stereotypical they may be.

For fantasy to be effective, it must somehow parallel reality, and if its intended audience is the culture at large, it must necessarily prey on certain cultural perceptions of what the ideal reality is. To sell to a male market, women's prerecorded messages and live conversational exchange must cater to hegemonic male perceptions of the ideal woman. The training manual for operators of 970-LIVE, a male-owned fantasy-line service based in New York City, instructs female employees to "create different characters" and to "start with one that resembles the ideal woman"—as if this is a universal, unproblematic concept. To train women to fulfill this ideal, the manual gives additional details on how to open and maintain conversations while preserving "professionalism":

> *Create different characters:*
> Start with one that resembles the ideal woman. Move on to bimbo,

nymphomaniac, mistress, slave, transvestite, lesbian, foreigner, or virgin. If the caller wants to speak to someone else, don't waste time being insulted. *Be someone else.* You should be creative enough to fulfill *anyone's* fantasy.

To start a conversation:
"What's on your mind?" "What would you like to talk about?" "What do you do for fun?" "What are you doing right now?"
Remember: Never initiate sex. Let the caller start phone intimacy.

Ways to keep callers interested:
Tell them crazy fantasies: Jell-O, honey, travel, ice cream, lesbian love, orgies. If conversation stays clean, tell them an interesting story: movies, TV, books, etc. Make it sound like it really happened. *Insist* that it happened.

Professionalism:
Do not talk to *anyone* besides a caller when taking a call. Always be bubbly, sexy, interesting, and interested in each individual caller. Remember, *you* are not your character on the phone.

[Reprinted in *Harper's Magazine*, December 1990, 26–27.]

What makes the ideal woman from a verbal point of view is reminiscent of Pamela Fishman's (1978) definition of *maintenance work*: encouraging men to develop their topics by asking questions (*What's on* your *mind? What would* you *like to talk about? What do* you *do for fun?*), showing assent (*Always be bubbly, sexy, interesting and interested in each individual caller*), and listening (*Don't talk to* anyone *besides a caller when taking a call*). Because the conversation will be meaningless unless it in some way approximates the male caller's understanding of reality, what becomes critically important to its success is for it to "sound like it really happened"—for the woman to "*insist* that it happened." This realization, coupled with the fact that many clients may be calling the lines in response to the increasing threat of AIDS, has even led some companies to practice "safe phone sex." The number 1-900-HOT-LIPS, for instance, which advertises as a "steamy safe-sex fantasy number," has all of its fantasy-line operators "carry"—in the verbal sense, that is—condoms and spermacides to their vocal sexual encounters. The suggestion that an interactant might need to practice safe sex over the telephone wires is of course ludicrous; by overtly referencing this practice in its advertisement, however, the message service suggests that there is a very real physicality to the medium and simultaneously alludes to its inherently "safe" nature.

The Prerecorded Message

The language promoted in the trainer's manual is precisely the kind of language sold by the prerecorded services—language that, through extensive detail and supportive hearer-directed comments, presents a certain reality. The two-minute prerecorded message reproduced below in (1) is played daily on a national fantasy line that advertises as "girls, girls, girls." The speaker is unquestionably the perfect woman: she loves to shop, she wears feminine clothes, she likes to look at herself in the mirror, and she lies in bed half the day fulfilling male fantasies.[12]

(1)   oo::f:: - i'm so ((in breathy voice)) ex<u>ci</u>ted. - i just got a <u>hot</u> new job. (0.8) well, - ((in slight Southern accent)) i've been bored lately. .hh - i live in a small town and my husband travels a lot, (0.5) i have lots of time on my hands. - .hhh of course, i've always managed to stay busy. (0.4) lots of girlfriends, you know, - ((whispered)) i love to <u>shop</u>, - i ((laugh)) ^<u>pract</u>^ically live at the mall it seems, but still- .hhhh (2.0) <u>any</u>way. - this friend told me about this job i can do at <u>ho</u>me. - all i need is a <u>pho</u>ne. - and a lusty imagination. ((laugh)) yeah, you've got it - .hh i'm doing <u>h::ot</u> sexy phone calls these days. (0.5) i <u>rea</u>lly get into it <u>too</u>. - .hhh i love that sexy hot fellows from all over the country call me and enjoy my ((whispered)) voice and my fantasies. (0.4) i like to <u>dress</u> the part too. - i went to my favorite lingerie ((in hoarse, breathy voice)) store, - victoria's secret? - and bought <u>s::a</u>tin bikinis, <u>l::ac</u>y thong underwear, - a tight black corset - and fishnet stockings, (1.0) ((in lower voice)) and a <u>dan</u>gerous pair of <u>red</u> ((whispered)) <u>spiked heels</u>. ((smack)) - <u>um</u>hmm:::: .hhh - then. when i'm in a dominant mode? .hh i have this leather g-string and bra and thigh-high boots. - ooh <u>ba</u>by. ((giggle)) (0.5) when i dress up and look in the mirror, ((slower, breathy voice)) i - get - so - <u>crazy</u> .hhhh i just can't wait for that first ca::ll. (0.6) <u>then,</u> - i assemble all my favorite little (0.3) <u>toys</u> all around me, (0.4) lie back on my big bed with <u>s::a</u>tin sheets .hhhh (1.0) and live out my fantasies with some my<u>ste</u>rious stranger .hhhhhhh oo::::::h <u>hea</u>ring those voices. .hh - those excited whispers and moans, ((in breathy voice)) u::h, it gets me so- .hhhh - well, - you know. (2.0) then (0.5) i just go <u>wi::ld</u>, - i have <u>so</u> many great <u>idea::s</u>. - they come fa::st and furious, (in hoarse voice)) oo::h, i can't get enough. -.hh each call makes me hot- ter, - i just keep going, <u>o</u>ver and <u>o</u>ver, ((gasping)) ^<u>o:h</u>^ - .hhh <u>yea:h</u> <u>ba</u>by do it a<u>gain</u> - ^oo^:::f, .hhhhhhh - <u>well</u>. (2.0) i <u>love</u> my workday - ^but^ - by the time I put in a few hours on the phone? - i'm so re<u>la:xed</u> hh, - and when my husband gets home ((smack)) - <u>oo::</u>h - he gets the treatment. - he lo:ves it. - .hh but (1.0) shhh. ((whis- pered)) don't tell. - it's <u>our</u> secret.

In the absence of a visual link, this ideal is created solely through language (as the speaker herself says, "All I need is a phone and a lusty imagination"). She begins by constructing a visual image of herself with words popularly thought of as feminine: *girlfriends, lusty, lacy, lingerie, satin,* and *secret.* Her voice is dynamic, moving from high-pitched, gasping expressions of pleasure to low-pitched, breathy-voice innuendoes. Although this is unidirectional discourse, she makes it quite clear that she would be an admirable conversational partner in any female-male dyad—she "just can't wait for that first call" so that she can respond supportively to all those "voices" and "excited whispers." Additionally, she sets up her monologue so as to establish an exclusive intimacy with her absentee partner, referring to their conversational relationship as a passionate "secret" that should be kept from her husband.

Particularly telling is what happens at the end of this fantasy, when the speaker's verbal creativity comes to represent the sex act itself: *I have so many great ideas. They come fast and furious—ooh, I can't get enough!* An equation of the spoken word with the sex act is a common element in such messages, a fitting metaphorical strategy given the nature of the exchange. Often in the beginning of the fantasy scenario, the speaker will be reading a book at a library, selling encyclopedias door to door, or taking a literature course at the local college. By the end of the scenario, swayed by the voice and intellect of the suitor in question (who is often identified with the caller so as to bring him directly into the fantasy), she has discarded her books, her encyclopedias, and her academic pretensions for the bedroom.

In the fantasy reproduced below, for example, the speaker projects the persona of a young college student who is obsessed with her English professor. Having established the power imbalance inherent to this scenario—she, the eager coed; he, the aloof, self-involved intellectual—the student develops a preoccupation with her professor's voice, describing how it repeatedly "penetrates" her during lecture:

(2) ^hi. - my name's vicky^, – and i <u>guess</u> i'm in <u>deep</u> trouble in one of my <u>classes</u> at college. (1.5) ((whispered)) it's my english professor. - he's got me <u>cra::</u>zy, (0.5) and i think i'm losing my <u>mi:nd</u>, – he's really (0.4) not handsome or anything, - it's the way he talks, (1.0) his voice gets deep inside me where it counts, - turns me to jelly, (1.5) i sit at the front of the class, - and i just can't seem - to keep ^<u>still</u>^, (1.5) i remember the first day, i wore jeans and a sweater. (0.5) and my long blond hair up in a bun. (0.6) i felt pretty studious, - but the moment i started <u>listening</u> to him, i knew i was gonna

change - all - that. (2.0) and the next session, i showed up in the shortest mini-skirt i could find. (0.5) ^i'm real tan^ ((in breathy voice)) and in real good shape. (0.5) and i knew i looked pretty good in that mini-skirt. - i wore a silk blouse that ((slowly)) should have had his eyes riveted on me, - instead - he hardly ^no^ticed, (1.0) ^o:::h^ i was getting so ^cra::^zy. (2.0) well - after a few weeks, - the weather changed and it got real hot, - so i started wearing shorts and this great little halter top, (1.5) i know i looked okay, because guys in the class were stumbling over themselves to sit next to me. - but my professor - there he was, just a few feet away, and hardly a ^glance^. (1.0) and still i go back to my dorm room and lay in my bed, and dream about that voice, ((in breathy voice)) all of me reponds to it, (2.0) ((sigh)) hhhhh it's as if he's penetrated me, ((slowly)) reached the depths of my soul and won't let go. (1.0) i dream about the moment - when we'll be alone, - maybe it'll be after class, (1.5) maybe it'll be a chance meeting at a coffee shop or something, but when that moment comes, (0.5) i know i'm going to tell him what he does to me, - and i don't think he'll be surprised, - because i ^think^ he already knows.

The speaker begins the fantasy by establishing that she is attracted to this particular professor not because of his physical appearance but because of the "way he talks": *His voice gets deep inside me where it counts, turns me to jelly.* After several unsuccessful attempts to impress the professor by relaxing her studious stance and gendering herself with the appropriate apparel, the speaker goes back to her dorm room so that she can at the very least "dream about that voice." She concludes the fantasy by exclaiming, rather emphatically, that she becomes powerless before the sound of it: *All of me responds to it, it's as if he's penetrated me, reached the depths of my soul and won't let go.* Although in this particular text it is the speaker, not the hearer, who is the owner of the fantasy, the one-sided nature of the created exchange (that is, even though the coed talks incessantly in the hopes of attracting her professor's attention, he fails to offer her any individualized verbal acknowledgment) parallels the real-life interaction between operator and client. The caller, unable to respond to the emotional desires of a prerecorded voice, easily assumes the role of the coed's nonresponsive superior.

As this scenario nicely illustrates, the reality presented on the message line presents an interactive inequality between the sexes, portraying men as dominant (penetrating, powerful, intellectual) and women as submissive (penetrated, powerless, emotional). To have a successful conversation, the fantasy-line recording must affirm this inequality, for it is essential to the frame of male pornographic discourse. Rosalind Coward (1986), with reference to visual pornography, argues that although images of women are never inherently pornographic, they necessarily become so when placed within a "regime of representations" (i.e., a set of codes with conventionally accepted meanings) that identify them as pornographic for the viewer. The captions and texts that surround such images identify them explicitly as figures for male enjoyment, affirming the differential female-as-object versus male-as-subject. In vocal pornography, because there is no visual link, this differential must be created through voice and word alone. The fantasy-line operator has been assisted, of course, by the many advertisements in adult magazines that have already situated her within this frame, but she must still actively assume a submissive position in the conversation. In the telephone advertisement below, for example, offered by a message service as a "free phone-job sample," the speaker sells the number by highlighting this very inequality:

(3)   ((in quick, low, breathy voice)) baby I want you to listen closely, - dial 1-900-884-6804 <u>now</u> for <u>hard</u> love, - for <u>tough</u> love, - for girls who <u>need</u> <u>men</u> to <u>take</u> contro::l. - dial 1-900-884-6804, - for women who aren't afraid to say what they <u>rea::</u>lly want, - for girls who need <u>powerful</u> men to open their deep desires, dial 1-900-884-6804, and go all the way. (0.5) <u>deep</u> into the secret places for a fantasy experience that just goes <u>on</u> and <u>on</u> and <u>on</u>, - dial 1-900-884-6804, and get a girl who wants to give <u>you</u> the ultimate pleasure, 1-900-884-6804, ((quickly)) just half a dollar a minute, forty the first. (0.5) <u>now</u> I can tell <u>you</u> everything, now i can give you everything you want, <u>all</u> you desire, i can do it now, i <u>want</u> to, i <u>have</u> to, ((giggle)) dial 1-900-884-6804.

In a low, breathy voice, the operator explains that the women who work at this particular company will provide the "love" (which is here overtly sexualized with the modifiers *hard* and *tough*) if the caller provides the "control." They are women who need "powerful men to open their deep desires"—who not only *want* to submit and give their callers "the ultimate pleasure" but *"have* to" do so.

Bonnie McElhinny (this volume) refers to Rosabeth Kanter (1977) and Arlie Hochschild (1983) in order to discuss the gendered division of emotional labor that characterizes corporate workplaces. Certain types of work structures, particularly those that involve women in typically feminine jobs, require female employees to perform emotional labor for their bosses. As Catherine Lutz (1986, 1990) and other anthropologists have pointed out, such divisions follow from the way emotion has been constructed along gender lines within Western society, so that men are expected to be rational and women emotional—a construction that has effects on women's language and on societal perceptions of what women's language should be. What is noteworthy with respect to the present discussion is the way in which fantasy-line operators consciously appropriate ideologies of emotional language and sexual language (which are not always entirely distinguishable) in order to intensify the perceived power imbalance. As one fantasy-line operator explained, "My job is kind of a three-conversation trinity—one part prostitute, one part priest, and one part therapist."

Interviews with San Francisco Fantasy-Line Operators

The eleven women and one man interviewed for this study, all residing in the San Francisco Bay Area and working for services that advertise to a heterosexual male market,[13] were aware of the recent feminist controversy over pornography and were highly reflective of their position within this debate. Each of them had reinterpreted this debate within the vocal sphere, perceiving their position in the linguistic exchange as a powerful one. Their positive attitude may have much to do with the fact that in San Francisco, many of the adult message services are women-owned and -operated, with a large percentage of employees identifying themselves as feminists and participating actively in organizations such as COYOTE, Cal-Pep, and COP—political action groups established for the purpose of securing rights for women in the sex industry. For these individuals, many of whom are freelance artists, fashion designers, graduate students, and writers, work on the telephone brings economic independence and social freedom. To them, the real prostitutes in our society are the women who dress in expensive business suits in the financial district, work fifty hours a week, and make sixty-five cents to a man's dollar. They understand the adult-message industry as primarily a creative medium, viewing themselves as fantasy tellers who have embraced a form of discourse that has been largely ignored by the women of this sexually repressed society. Moreover, they feel a certain power in having access into men's minds and find that it empowers them in their everyday cross-sex interactions.

Before embarking on this study in 1991, I informed the San Francisco Sex Information Hotline of my project and asked for assistance in locating phone-sex workers who might be interested in being interviewed. Over the next few months I spoke with twelve people, including nine "call-doers" (as fantasy makers are sometimes called), two managers, and a woman who is co-owner of one of the oldest phone-sex companies in the United States (K. G. Fox). Most of the interviews were conducted anonymously by phone because many of the participants did not wish to have their names publicized. Approximately half of the interviewees allowed me to record our interviews over the telephone. The race, age, sex, and sexual-orientation backgrounds of the operators I spoke with were roughly equivalent to those of employees working for women-owned and -operated services in San Francisco.[14] Six of the employees I interviewed were heterosexual, three bisexual, and three lesbian; eight were European American, two Latino, one African American, and one Asian American. The employees who granted me interviews ranged in age from twenty-three to forty-six; they were generally from middle-class backgrounds, college-educated, and supportive of the industry. Many of these women had sought employment with women-owned services in reaction to the poor treatment they had received from various men-owned services in the city, among them the financially successful Yellowphone.[15]

At the beginning of each interview I explained that I was writing an article on the phone-sex industry from the point of view of its labor force; only at the end of the interview did I disclose my particular interest in language use. The female participants all believed that both the antipornography feminism of Dworkin, Jeffreys, and MacKinnon and the pro-freedom feminism of Bright prioritize an issue that most of the women in this country— because they suffer from serious economic and social oppression—do not have the privilege of debating. The most important issue to the women I interviewed is not whether pornography is oppressive or whether women's sexuality is repressed but, rather, how they, as a group, can mobilize for a better work environment so that the job they have chosen will be as nonoppressive as possible. They spoke of the need for a sex-workers' union, for health-care benefits, and for approval from people working outside the industry. Each of them chose her or his line of work initially for the economic freedom and social flexibility it offered. Like the fantasy-line operators quoted in excerpts (4) through (6) below—who variously identify themselves as *militant feminist, humanist,* and *feminist most definitely*— they regard the issue of sexual oppression as comparatively unimportant to the other types of economic and social oppression they have suffered.

(4)   Yes, in one word, the reason I got involved in this work is Reaganomics. It doesn't filter down to people like me. I'm an artist. I refuse to deal with corporate America. I'm an honest person. I

have integrity. I work hard. There's no place in corporate America for me.... About a year and a half ago when the economy really started to go sour, I started thinking, well, I'm going to have to get a part-time job. I looked around at part-time jobs and it was like, you want me to dress in $300 outfits when you're paying me six bucks an hour? Excuse me, but I don't think so. And I saw an ad in the *Bay Guardian* for a fantasy maker, and I thought about it for months, because I had an attitude that it was really weird and I was concerned that I would end up really hating men, and finally it got down to, well, you can go downtown and spend a lot of money on clothes, or you can check this out.

(5)   I moved out here a couple of years ago from Ohio, and one of the main reasons I moved out here is so I could still be as strange as I am and do a job. I have piercing - body piercing, facial piercing - and I have tattoos, and I'm an insurance adjuster. And I wanted to come out here and get the piercings, and I'd been having to wear make-up over the [tattoo] ring on my finger, and that kind of thing. And I thought, well, god, San Francisco! If I can't get away with it there, then where can I? Well, I couldn't get away with it here either - not in the financial district. So I started watching *SF Weekly* and the newspapers, and I originally went to a company called [deleted]. And they told me it was a chat line and there'd be a few fantasy calls and not to be surprised by that. And oh boy, I was like, yeah, this is great money, I love it! And so I said sure. And that's basically how I got into it.

(6)   For me, I can work at home, I can make my own hours. If I want to take off and go on vacation on last minute's notice and be gone for a month, I can do that and know that my job is there. And I like that flexibility and I like the idea of not really having a boss to answer to. In some ways, it's powerful and in some ways it's definitely not. [We're] people who are sort of marginalized, [there's a lot] that we don't have access to- like health care. It's like forget it, you get sick and you don't have insurance. We don't have any kind of union. I think it would be great if we could have some kind of sex workers' union. So it's a mixed bag, but I guess for me, in light of what the options would be for me to make a living at this point in time, it seems like the best thing I can do for myself. Definitely one of the best compared to the options I see out there, I'm pretty damn lucky with what I'm doing. Because I've tried to have a few sort of semi-straight normal jobs and I didn't cut it very well. I

don't deal very well with authority, especially if I feel like the person is not treating me with the respect that I deserve, and that I'm not getting paid what I deserve for the quality of work that I'm putting out- like I have to dress a certain way that I'm uncomfortable in.

All three women have balanced the patriarchal oppression found in corporate America against the patriarchal oppression in a capitalist enterprise like pornography and have opted for the latter (although they made it quite clear that the women-owned services treat them much more kindly than those owned by men, especially with respect to advertising technique[16]). The first of these women entered the industry for economic security in a reaction to "Reaganomics," but the other two did so primarily for social flexibility. When the final operator speaks of the phone-sex industry as a *mixed bag*, she is not referring in any way to the sexual subordination that such a job might require of her but, rather, to the subordination required by a society that has marginalized her line of work: she has no benefits, no sex workers' union, no societal support.

Because the income of these women is entirely dependent upon verbal ability, they are very conscious of the type of language they produce and often explain specific linguistic qualities that make their language marketable. The features that make the prerecorded message persuasive are the same features that these operators choose to emphasize in their live-conversation exchanges: those that have been defined by linguists working in the area of language and gender as powerless. They explained that they make frequent use of feminine lexical items, incorporate intensifiers into their conversation whenever possible, regularly interrupt their narrative with questions and supportive comments, and adopt a dynamic intonation pattern.

One operator, a thirty-three-year-old European American heterosexual who calls herself Rachel, pointed out that "to be a really good fantasy maker, you've got to have big tits in your voice." She clarified this comment by explaining that she creates sexy language through lexical choice, employing "words which are very feminine":

(7)   I can describe myself now so that it lasts for about five minutes, by using lots of adjectives, spending a lot of time describing the shape of my tits. And that's both - it's not just wasting time, because they need to build up a mental picture in their minds about what you look like, and also it allows me to use words that are very feminine. I always wear peach, or apricot, or black lace- or charcoal-

colored lace, not just black. I'll talk about how my hair feels, how
curly it is. Yeah, I probably use more feminine words. Sometimes
they'll ask me, "What do you call it [female genitalia]?" And I'll say,
well my favorite is *the snuggery*....And then they crack up, because
it's such a feminine, funny word.

Rachel initiates conversation on the fantasy lines by creating a feminine
image of herself through soft words like *curly* and *snuggery* together with
nonbasic color terms such as *peach*, *apricot*, and even *charcoal* instead of
black—a creation markedly reminiscent of Lakoff's (1975:8) early assertion
that women are thought to use "far more precise discriminations in naming
colors" than men. Another operator, a European American self-identified
butch bisexual whom I will call Sheila, defines what makes her language
marketable as an intonational phenomenon. When she explains that she
"talks in a loping tone of voice" with a "feminine, lilting quality," she alludes
to a vocal pattern identified by Sally McConnell-Ginet (1978) almost two
decades ago as characteristic of women's speech:

(8)   I feel like definitely the timbre of my voice has a lot to do with it.
       I don't know, the ability to sound like, I hate to say it, feminine and
       kind of that lilting quality, and to sound like you're really enjoying
       it, like you're turned on and you're having a good time. I think that
       has a lot to do with it because they're always telling me, "Oh yes,
       you have such a great voice! God, I love listening to your voice!" I
       think that's a big part of it, it's just the sound of the person's voice.
       Some people will tell you that they really like detail and lots of
       description, and so I can provide that too. But I think so much of
       it is the way that you say things, more than what you're actually say-
       ing. That's kind of funny, you know- sort of an inviting tone of voice.

A third operator, Samantha, a manager of a San Francisco company
established in 1990 by a woman and her male-to-female transsexual partner, emphasizes the maintenance work she uses to engage her male callers
in a more collaborative exchange, mentioning that she tries to draw out
shy callers with supportive questions and comments ("I stop a lot to say
things like, 'Oh, do you like that?' You know, that kind of thing. I try to get
them to talk as much as I can, because some of these people would sit here
and not say one word. And if I get one of those, from time to time I say,
'Hello? Are you still there?'"). K. G. Fox alludes to the importance of maintaining this conversational attentiveness when she explains, "You got to
be in the moment, you got to pay attention, you got to keep it fresh. It's a

performance and you have to stay in time with your audience. After all, it's really a one-person show." To make the fantasy effective, then, these fantasy makers consciously cater to their clients by producing a language that adheres to a popular male perception of what women's speech should be: flowery, inviting, and supportive.

Even though an attentive and nurturing discursive style seems to be the primary posture adopted by the women I interviewed, many of them additionally explained how they embellish this style by incorporating more individualized linguistic stereotypes of womanhood, particularly those of age and race. Samantha, for instance, makes her voice sound "sexy" by performing four different characters: (1) herself, whom she calls Samantha; (2) a girl with a high-pitched eighteen-year-old voice who fulfills the "beach bunny" stereotype; (3) a woman with a demure Asian accent whom she calls Keesha; and (4) a dominating "older woman" with an Eastern European accent whom she calls Thela. That these performances serve to approximate linguistic stereotypes rather than reflect any particular linguistic reality is underscored by Sheila in her discussion below; she identifies the irony in the fact that European American women are more successful at performing a Black identity on the phone lines than African American women are:

(9)   Most of the guys who call are white, definitely, and for them talking to someone of a different race is exotic and a fetish, you know. So it's really weird. They have this stereotypical idea of how, like, a Black woman should sound and what she's gonna be like. So frequently, we'd have women who were actually Black and we'd hook them up, and they wouldn't believe the woman, that she was Black, because she didn't <u>sound</u> like that stereotype. So conversely, what we had to do- I remember there was this one woman who did calls and she had this sort of Black persona that she would do, which was like the total stereotype. I mean, it really bugged me when I would hear her do it. And the guys loved it. They <u>really</u> thought that this is what a Black woman was!

Sheila's irritation with her colleague's performance points to the restrictive nature of the discourse; operators must vocalize stereotypes that cater to the racist assumptions of their clients. Because the vast majority of male callers request European American women, Sheila explains that operators must also know how to sound "white" on the telephone. That women of color are often more successful than white women at doing so is underscored by the remarks of a second manager I interviewed, who acknowledged that "the best white woman we ever had here was Black." Certainly this is a very different realization of ethnic "passing" than that discussed by Mary Bucholtz (this volume), whose interviewees overtly resist such stereotypes, voicing their own assertions about their identity rather than affirming the expectations of the observer. On the fantasy lines, in contrast, we have the somewhat unusual situation of speakers' being able to perform others' ethnicities more "successfully" than their own. This fact not only points to the strength of stereotyping in the realm of fantasy but also demonstrates the inseparability of race and gender in the public reception of an identity.

This inseparability is particularly evident in the phone-line performances of Andy, a thirty-three-year-old Mexican American bisexual who poses as a female heterosexual before his male callers. As with the women interviewed for this study, Andy finds that his conversations are well received when he projects a cultural stereotype of vocal femininity: not only is he attentive to the desires of his unsuspecting caller, but he also projects a "soft and quiet" voice.

> (10) Believe it or not, it's important to them that you're basically in the same mood as they are, that you're enjoying it too. So if you can sound like you <u>are</u>, then that's the better, that's <u>always</u> the better. And the other thing I've found over the years is it's better to sound soft and quiet than loud and noisy ... if you're a woman. ... [It's] better to sound ((whispered)) soft, you know, softer. ((in natural voice)) You know, like whispering, rather than ((in loud voice)) OH HO HO HO, ((in natural voice)) really <u>loud</u>, you know, and <u>scream-</u>ing. 'Cause basically you're in their ear. And physically that's a very strange thing also. Because with the phone, you know, you <u>are</u> in somebody's ear.

To convince callers of his womanhood, Andy style-shifts into a higher pitch, moving the phone away from his mouth so as to soften the perceived intensity of his voice. This discursive shifting, characterized by the performance of the vocal and verbal garb associated with the other sex, might more appropriately be referred to as *cross-expressing*.[17] The parallel between such an undertaking and the more visual activity of cross-dressing becomes especially apparent in the excerpt below, when Andy performs a European American woman whom he calls Emily:

> (11) So here, I'll give you the voice, okay? Hold on. (4.0) ((in high pitch, soft whisper)) Hello. (2.0) Hello? (2.0) How are <u>you</u>? (1.5) This is <u>Emi</u>ly. ((in natural voice)) See? It's more- it's more nostrily. I higher the phone- I lift the phone up. Right now I'm just talking regular but

I do have the phone lifted up higher. ...And then I lower my vocals (3.0) ((inhales, then in slow, high, breathy voice)) Hello::. Hi::. ((gasps)) Oh yes! (0.5) I'm so horny right ^no^::w.... ((in natural voice)) It's funny how I've actually taped myself and then played it back, and it's actually two separate voices.

Andy's use of the term *the voice* for his female persona is telling. On the phone-sex lines, person and voice are indistinguishable, with the latter coming to substitute for the former. He begins the conversation by tailoring it to his interactant's state of mind (*Hello. Hello! How are you?*), even before offering up his own name. The phone receiver itself becomes an extension of his vocal apparatus, as he moves it away from his mouth and simultaneously lowers his voice so as to achieve the varied pitch range he associates with European American women's speech.

But female heterosexuality is one of the few constants in Andy's cast of phone-sex characters. He presents himself variously as Asian, Mexican, African American, and Southern, catering to the desires of individual callers. As with his performance of women's language, he garnishes his speech with features hegemonically associated with particular ethnic groups.

(12)   And then when I put the other little things into it, like- if I want an Oriental, then I have to put a little- you know, then I have to think Oriental sort of ((laughs)) and then it comes out a little bit different. Well it's- for example, okay- (1.0) ((in alternating high and low pitch)) hull^o^::. ^hi^i:::, ^how are^ you::? This is Fong ^Su^u:. ((in natural voice)) See? Then you give them like- I think like I'm ((laughs)) at a Chinese restaurant, and I'm listening to the waitress- you know, take my order or something. And then the Hispanic is more like ((clears throat, in high breathy voice)) He:llo:::, this is Ésta es Amelia, cómo estás? (.hhhhh) o:::h lo siento bien, (1.0) rica. ((in natural voice)) Then I think I'm like watching Spanish dancers or Mexican dancers- you know, with their big dresses? ((sings)) da:: dadada da:: dadada- the mariachis. (1.5) And then the Black is a little bit- you know, on and on it goes. [My Black name is] Winona- Winona. Like from the Jeffersons? No, I mean- not the Jeffersons, it was uh- the one guy, Jay-Jay? I can't remember the show name, but anyways the sister was named Winona or Wilona or something like that. And then there's the Southern sound, you know, and then like I say, there's a British sound and a French sound. For the Southern woman I'll use, like, Belle, ((laughs)) something Belle. ((laughs)) Oh, I play right up to it sometimes. ...You definitely have

to use ((in slow Southern accent, with elongated vowels)) a
Sou:::thern a::ccent. ((laughs, in natural voice)) Abso<u>lute</u>ly, that has
to come through. Shining. So that's a real concentrator, I have to
really- you know, be really quiet.

Andy models his Asian persona on a submissive waitress, adopting a quiet
voice that serves to highlight the inequality between himself and his conversational master; his voice, perhaps in attempted imitation of a tonal
language, moves back and forth between two distinct pitches. His Mexican
voice, in contrast, which he models on a flamboyant Spanish dancer, is more
overtly sexual; with breathy inhalation and emphatic pronunciation, he
manages to eroticize a number of very common Spanish expressions.
Because the success of the interaction depends on the middle-class white
male caller's ability to recognize the fantasy frame, the operator's language
tends to recall dominant instead of localized gender and race ideologies—
ones often deemed highly offensive by the group to whom they are ascribed.

In accordance with this outlook, most of the women I spoke with
described their work first and foremost as artistic. Sheila calls herself a *telephone fantasy artist*. Rachel, whose self-definition is reproduced below,
describes what she does for a living as *auditory improvisational theater on
the theme of eros*:

Yet the fantasy maker, while admitting the often degrading nature of such
an enterprise, nevertheless views her employment of this language as powerful and identifies her position in the conversational exchange as superior.
The operators who participated in the study reported that they are
completely in control of each conversation: they initiate and dominate the
conversational exchange; they are creators of the fantasy story line and
scenario; they can decide what kind of fantasies they will entertain; and they
can terminate the conversation with a simple flick of the index finger.
Indeed, Natalie Rhys (1993), a phone-sex worker in San Francisco who
recently wrote about her experiences in the book *Call Me Mistress: Memoirs
of a Phone Sex Performer*, comments that the real victims in the exchange
are the customers, who feed their time, energy, and money into a noncaring
enterprise that exploits them: "To the workers, pornography is a job no more
exciting than any other job. To the owners and managers, it's a business.
Both feel superior to the customers. If this attitude seems calloused, consider
that it's difficult to have much respect for someone when the only contact
you have with him is when you're exploiting his neediness. You might have
compassion for him, but not respect" (119).[18]

In accordance with this outlook, most of the women I spoke with
described their work first and foremost as artistic. Sheila calls herself a *telephone fantasy artist*. Rachel, whose self-definition is reproduced below,
describes what she does for a living as *auditory improvisational theater on
the theme of eros*:

(13) I'm a good storyteller. A lot of what I do is wasted on most of
these people. They're not bright enough to know some of the
words I use. And then about every fifteenth call is one that makes
it worthwhile. Because it's someone who will go, "God, you're really good at this! You really use language well! This is fun! I was
expecting this to be really weird, but you're cool!" I have a large
vocabulary. I read a lot and I'll use other words. I don't own a television. I think that's a big part of my greater command of language
than the average human being. And since I've gotten into this, I've
also decided that if I'm going to be a storyteller, I'm going to study
more about storytelling. I've listened to Garrison Keillor for years,
and in the last year or so, I've taped him several times and listened
for the devices that he's using to be a more effective storyteller.

This particular operator has written erotica for a number of years and identifies herself primarily as a *good storyteller*. She explains that she actively
incorporates storytelling techniques into her own fantasy creations, imitating Garrison Keillor of *Prairie Home Companion*, as well as a number of
other well-known storytellers. She and the other fantasy makers would often
jokingly refer to themselves as *phone whores* and their switchboard operators as *phone pimps*, but they did not perceive the conversational exchange
as representative of any particular asymmetrical sexual reality. Like the
woman in this excerpt, who mentions her "large vocabulary" and her
"greater command of language than the average human being," the operators
interviewed felt that they were so superior linguistically to the average man
who called the service that male power was just not an issue. The only
exchanges they did perceive as asymmetrical, and in which they consequently did not like to participate, were those domination calls where the
male caller overtly restricted their freedom of expression by limiting their
feedback to a subservient *yes sir* and *no sir*. Many of the women refused to
take these calls altogether, although one operator did say that these low
verbal expectations did at least allow her to get a lot of dishes done.

Still, the same fantasy operators would readily admit that they had to
subdue their own creativity in order to please a comparatively uncreative
audience. The fantasy maker above who considers herself a storyteller, for
instance, explained that her linguistic creativity makes her less popular
than some of the other fantasy operators because she often refuses to adopt
the expected "stupid, pregnant, and dumb" voice:

(14) If I'm in a surly mood and I get a call from a guy who sounds like
he just let go of his jackhammer and graduated with a 1.2 average,

you know, I have a hard time with those guys. I mean, they need love too, but jesus! Dumb people bug me.... It's hard to realize that you're a lot smarter than whoever it is you're dealing with, and number one, if you're really bright then you won't let them know it, and number two, if they do figure it out, then you're in trouble, because they don't like it, especially if it's a man. I mean, that's just the way it is. Girls are supposed to be stupid and pregnant, or just dumb, so that the testosterone type can get out there and conquer the world for you, or whatever it is that they do. ... I'm approaching this from the angle that I want to be a better storyteller, I want to increase my linguistic abilities. But that isn't what the average customer wants.

Another operator similarly explained that she had to "be constantly walking that line" between embracing a sexuality for herself and catering to customer expectations of her sexuality. Interesting in her interview, reproduced in excerpt (15), is that she describes her clients' perception of women's language as a submissive sexual position:

(15) I wonder if it really is women's language or is it mostly that we're repeating what it is that the men want to hear and want to believe that women like and think. I think it's more what's in their heads. You know, scenarios where I'm being mildly submissive, even though they don't call it that, and they're like calling me a slut and a horny little bitch.... It's a total turn off, I never think of myself that way. And that definitely goes through their heads.... So having to sometimes sort of like repeat their ideas back to them because it's what they want to hear can be a drag. So sometimes it's more my idea than my language and sometimes it's there and it's what they're reading out of these stupid magazines, you know, that they really want to believe women are like.... It's interesting to be constantly walking that line where you're trying to make sure they're happy and please them and get them off and at the same time- you know, for me, I want to do my best not to perpetuate all the bullshit that goes on in their minds. It is a difficult task sometimes. It's a challenge to come up with ways that you can still turn them on without perpetuating all the bullshit about women that they believe.

She realizes that the male fantasy of female sexuality is so firmly rooted within our culture that even though she tries not to perpetuate it, there is little she can do to dispel it. Her feeling is also shared by Andy. He states that being a man has given him more liberty to speak against such degradation, yet he also recognizes the negative influence such attitudes have had on him as an individual:

(16) What I think has bothered me over the years more than anything about it has been the degradation of women that I've had to kind of feel because of the way [men] think and feel towards women - a lot of them. You know, there is a lot of degradation involved and basically it filters over to you if you're not careful, and you could yourself either feel degraded or degrade others. [I think I notice this] more than the girls, because the girls are interested, I think, in just pleasing, you know, and trying to do the best they could on the call, whereas I feel that I'm beyond doing good on the call.

Both Sheila and Andy speculated that for the male callers this interactive fantasy was in some sense very real, evidenced by the dismay of those callers who for some reason came to suspect that the voice on the telephone was not the beautiful young blonde it presented itself to be.[19] It seems that although these employees are aware of and wish to break away from the negative stereotypes about women's language and sexuality, they are restrained by their clients' expectations of the interaction, and they must therefore try to strike a balance between employing a creative discourse and a stereotypical one.

Conclusion

What exists on the adult message lines is a kind of style shifting that is based primarily on gender and secondarily on variables of age, class, geography, and race. When on the telephone, the fantasy-line operators in this study, whether Asian American, African American, European American, or Latino, switch into a definable conversational style that they all associate with "women's language." Bourdieu (1977) might argue that these women, as "agents continuously subjected to the sanctions of the linguistic market," have learned this style through a series of positive and negative reinforcements:

Situations in which linguistic productions are explicitly sanctioned and evaluated, such as examinations or interviews, draw our attention to the existence of mechanisms determining the price of discourse which operate in every linguistic interaction (e.g., the doctor-pateint or lawyer-client relation) and more gener-

ally in all social relations. It follows that agents continuously
subjected to the sanctions of the linguistic market, functioning as
a system of positive or negative reinforcements, acquire durable
dispositions which are the basis of their perception and appreciation of the state of the linguistic market and consequently of their
strategies for expression. (654)

According to Bourdieu, speakers develop their strategies for expression
through their experiences within the linguistic market, a notion that he refers
to elsewhere as *habitus*. In their interactional histories (e.g., at school, in the
family), the female fantasy-line operators have received positive reinforcement for this particular style of discourse and are now, through additional
reinforcement within the workplace, selling it back to the culture at large for
a high price. Like examinations and interviews, fantasy-line conversations are
situations in which linguistic production is explicitly sanctioned and evaluated. If the operator fails to produce the appropriate discursive style (one that
is feminine, inviting, and supportive), she will lose her clients and therefore
her economic stability. But for such a style to be so overtly reinforced within
this particular medium of discourse, the same reinforcement must exist
within the larger public, so that women at a very early age begin to, in the
words of Bourdieu, "acquire durable dispositions" toward this particular strategy of expression.

The question then follows: How can current definitions of linguistic
power account for the fact that on the fantasy lines, speech that has been
traditionally thought of as "powerless" suddenly becomes a very powerful
sexual commodity? Many of the authors represented in this volume have
followed Penelope Eckert and Sally McConnell-Ginet (1992, this volume)
in arguing that discussions of gender should be located within particular
communities of practice. By studying the local meanings attached to interactions, researchers will develop a more flexible understanding of gender—
an understanding that allows for variability of meaning within and among
communities. These San Francisco-based fantasy-line operators challenge
theories that have categorized women's language as powerless and men's
language as powerful. Within the context of the adult-message industry,
women have learned that manipulating the female conversational stereotype can in fact be powerful, and sometimes even enjoyable. It potentially
brings them tens of thousands of dollars; it allows them to support themselves without having to participate in a patriarchal business structure; it
lets them exercise sexual power without fear of bodily harm or judicial retri-
bution. Clearly, there is another dimension to power besides the dichotomy

of oppressor-oppressed. To say that all women are powerless in sexual inter-action, as MacKinnon does, or to say that all women are powerless when they assume a role traditionally thought of as subordinate in a conversation, denies real women's experience of their situation. The women quoted in this chapter view the success of their exchange in terms of how creative they can be in fulfilling a fantasy. Although they recognize that they often have to perpetuate the girly-magazine stereotype of women to maintain a clientele, they consider the men who require this stereotype so unimagina-tive that to attribute any power to them in the conversational exchange is ludicrous. This somewhat ironic state of affairs indicates that any theory of linguistic power in cross-sex interaction must allow for a variety of influ-ences with respect to individual consent.

Acknowledgments

An earlier version of this chapter was presented at the 1992 Berkeley Women and Language Conference and appeared in the conference proceed-ings. I would like to express my gratitude to the very diverse group of people who supported this undertaking: Andy, the Berkeley Women and Language Group, Mary Bucholtz, Beth Daniels, Brad Davidson, Penny Eckert, K. G. Fox, Good Vibrations, Jeanne Hall, Deena Hill, Leanne Hinton, Jacob Javitz, Robin Lakoff, Veronica O'Donovan, Pam, Jo Anna Pettit, Mo Phalon, Roxie, San Francisco Sex Information Hotline, Sharon, Style, Laurel Sutton, Quinton Tuck, and especially Anna Livia. Above all, I would like to thank the fantasy-line owners, managers, and operators who participated in these interviews, trusting me to maintain their confidentiality and present their experiences fairly.

Notes

1. This figure is given in Maretz (1989); it is quite likely that today's revenues are significantly higher.
2. Compare the less-sexualized term *smooth talk*, which is often used in refer-ence to the genteel flattery employed by a participant in a business transaction. The term can of course be sexualized in certain situations, but it is usually men, not women, who are said to have "smooth-talked" their partners into bed. Similarly, when the term *sweet talk* is used in reference to men, it often implies that the goal of the talk, rather than the talk itself, is sexual. See Smitherman (1994) and Major (1994) for commentary on the use of this expres-sion in the African American tradition.
3. Mata Hari, whose original name was Margaretha Geertruida Zella, acted as a

spy for the Germans during World War I. She hid her middle-class Dutch origin from her French audience, representing herself instead as the daughter of an exotic dancer in Southern India. By learning a vast repertoire of sultry dances with erotic movements, Mata Hari became so successful as an espionage agent that her name has become a synonym for the beautiful *femme fatale* who uses sex appeal to extract military secrets from men. I am grateful to Anna Livia for suggesting this parallel.

4. This estimate is somewhat conservative. I have based it on a 1988 estimate (134 *Congressional Record* E271, daily ed., February 17, 1988) that the dial-a-porn industry grossed $2.4 billion between 1983 and 1988. Even with the 1992 governmental regulations, which according to Stern (1993) caused 900-number revenue to drop from a reported $980 million to $540 million, more than $270 million of this is nevertheless attributable to the phone-sex industry. The industry is clearly continuing to thrive. An article in the *Economist* (July 30, 1994, p. 64), for example, reports on the expansion of the phone-sex industry overseas; telephone companies earned $900 million in 1993 from international services, around 90 percent of which was phone-sex lines.

5. I have used the term *vocal* throughout this chapter when referring to telephone discourse in order to underscore the oral nature of this type of pornographic representation, distinguishing it from both visual representation (e.g., adult videos, adult photography) and writing.

6. That an obscenity judgment is necessarily subjective is nicely illustrated by Justice Stewart's well-known observation: "I shall not today attempt further to define the kinds of material I understand to be embraced within that shorthand description; and perhaps I could never succeed in doing so. But I know it when I see it" (*Jacobellis v. Ohio*, 378 US 184, 197 [1964]).

7. For an outraged critique of the Supreme Court reception of the 1989 amendment, see the article by pro-pornography activist Pat Califia (1992). Recent legal reviews of the decisions surrounding the phone-sex industry include Burrington and Burns (1993), Davis (1993), Dee (1994), and Woolfall (1994).

8. The antagonism between these two views is said to have divided American feminism into the misleadingly labeled camps of "antipornography" radicalism and "pro-sex" liberalism. I have simplified the history and import of this theoretical division considerably; see Bacchi (1990) for an illuminating discussion of these two strands of feminist thought.

9. In accordance with the definition of obscenity established in *Roth s. United States* (354 US 476 [1957]) and refined in *Miller v. California* (413 US 15 [1973]), the Minneapolis code defines *obscene* as the following: "(i) That the average person, applying contemporary community standards, would find that the work, taken as a whole, appeals to the prurient interest in sex of the average person; (ii) That the work depicts or describes, in a patently offensive manner, sexual conduct specifically defined by the clause (b) [clause (b) includes representations of sexual intercourse, "actual or simulated," "sadomasochistic abuse," "masturbation," and "physical contact or simulated physical contact with the clothed or unclothed pubic areas or buttocks of a human male or

female."]; (iii) That the work, taken as a whole, lacks serious literary, artistic, political or scientific value."

10. This potential is pointed out by the female character in Nicholson Baker's (1992) best-seller *Vox*, a novel that has as its story line a single conversation between a female caller and a male caller to an adult conversational service: "Well, I like [the telephone] too," she said. "There's a power it has. My sister's little babe has a toy phone, which is white, with horses and pigs and ducks on the dial, and a blue receiver that has no weight to it at all, and I find there is an astonishing feeling of power when you pretend to be talking to someone on it. You cover the mouthpiece with your hand and you say in this dramatic whisper, 'Stevie, it's *Horton the Elephant* on the phone. He wants to speak to you!' and you hand it over to Stevie and his eyes get big and you and he both for that second believe that Horton the Elephant really is on the phone" (58).

11. This information is quoted in Potter (1989:453); the original source is *Carlin Communications, Inc. v. FCC*, 749 F2d 113, 114 (2d Cir 1984).

12. The transcription conventions used in this chapter are adapted from Gail Jefferson (1984):

h	an *h* indicates an exhalation (the more *h*'s, the longer the exhalation)
.h	an *h* with a period preceding it indicates an inhalation (the more *h*'s, the longer the inhalation)
(0.4)	indicates length of pause within and between utterances, timed in tenths of a second
a - a	a hyphen with spaces before and after indicates a short pause, less than 0.2 seconds
sa-	a hyphen immediately following a letter indicates an abrupt cutoff in speaking
(( ))	double parentheses enclose nonverbal movements and extralinguistic commentary
( )	single parentheses enclose words that are not clearly audible (i.e., best guesses)
[ ]	brackets enclose words added to clarify the meaning of the text
___	underlining indicates syllabic stress
CAPS	upper case indicates louder or shouted talk
:	a colon indicates a lengthening of a sound (the more colons, the longer the sound)
.	a period indicates falling intonation
,	a comma indicates continuing intonation
?	a question mark indicates rising intonation at the end of a syllable or word
^ a ^	rising arrows indicate a higher pitch for enclosed word(s) or syllable(s)
...	deletion of some portion of the original text

13. There are a significant number of services that advertise to the gay male market, and still others that advertise to the transgender market; only a limited

number of services advertise to women. For a lively analysis of gay male phone-fantasy production, see Miller (forthcoming).

14. Because these services normally hire their employees by telephone instead of in person, precise statistics on employee identity are unavailable. The manager of a company established in 1990 estimated that the employees at her company were equally divided between European Americans and African Americans, as well as between heterosexuals and lesbians. In contrast, K. G. Fox, who has been involved with the San Francisco phone-sex industry since 1981, indicated that San Francisco employees tend to be middle-class white women, college-educated, between the ages of twenty-five and thirty-five; she estimated that 20 to 30 percent of them identify as lesbian and 60 to 70 percent as bisexual or heterosexual.

15. It is quite possible, indeed probable, that the women who did refuse me interviews felt more negative about the industry; for a less optimistic account, see Danquah (1993). Still, the perceptions of the phone-sex workers I interviewed in San Francisco are strikingly similar to those of the twenty operators interviewed by Simakis (1990) for the *Village Voice*, who, for the most part, speak positively about their experiences in the industry.

16. The advertising strategies chosen by the men-owned services tend to be much more pornographic and sexually degrading to women than those chosen by the women-owned services. As one manager explained of her own company, "Since there's a woman owning it and another woman managing it, even though we advertise in *Hustler*, we have probably the most tasteful ads in it. The model has on a bikini-type thing, long blond hair, and she's not showing anything. But the rest of them are like, open wide! So there's a little class in it. And [the last four digits of] our number is KISS. So it's presented a little softer, a little nicer." The advertising strategies used by K. G. Fox's company are often subtle as well; one of the company's most successful ads was nothing more than a photograph of a telephone with the phrase *SEX OBJECT* underneath.

17. Barrett (forthcoming a, b) has noted a comparable instance of discursive style shifting among a community of African American drag queens. Anthropological discussions of analogous performances include Gaudio's article (forthcoming) on Hausa-speaking *'yan daudu* and Hall's (1995a, b, forthcoming a) work on Hindi-speaking *hijras*. For a discussion of verbal cross-expressing in computer-mediated interaction, see Hall (forthcoming b).

18. A very different perspective on the power differential between caller and operator is offered by Harry Goldstein (1991) in his sort article "The Dial-ectic of Desire": "The psychological effects of performing as a tele-sex operator are comparable to, if not more insidious than, being a flesh and blood prostitute, simply because working as a disembodied masturbation enhancement device denies the worker all sense of individuality and a large measure of control. ... Though most operators cling to the illusion that they control the call, in reality it is the man at the other end of the line, fingering his Gold Card and stroking himself to glory, who wields the mental paint brush, rendering his Perfect Woman on the blank canvas of the operator's voice" (33).

19. In support of this statement, I had an interesting interaction, at the time I was

conducting this study, with my next-door neighbor, who in response to my project told me about "all the sexy women" he had seen in the 900-number advertisement section of *Penthouse*. When I later told him that all the women in my study had been hired by voice alone and had never met their employers, he responded in disbelief, "What? You mean it's all a scam?"

References

Bacchi, Carol Lee (1990). The sexuality debates. *Same difference: Feminism and sexual difference*. Boston: Allen & Unwin. 202–27.

Baker, Nicholson (1992). *Vox: A novel*. New York: Random House.

Barrett, Rusty (forthcoming a). "She is *not* white woman": The appropriation of (white) women's language by African American drag queens. In Mary Bucholtz, Anita Liang, Laurel Sutton, and Caitlin Hines (eds.), *Cultural performances: Proceedings of the Third Berkeley Women and Language Conference*. Berkeley: Berkeley Women and Language Group.

———— (forthcoming b). The homo-genius community. In Anna Livia and Kira Hall (eds.), *Queerly phrased: Language, gender, and sexuality*. New York: Oxford University Press.

Bourdieu, Pierre (1977). The economics of linguistic exchanges. *Social Science Information* 16(6): 645–68.

Bright, Susie (1992). *Susie Bright's sexual reality: A virtual sex world reader*. Pittsburgh: Cleis Press.

Bucholtz, Mary (this volume). From mulatta to mestiza: Passing and the linguistic reshaping of ethnic identity.

Bucholtz, Mary, and Kira Hall (this volume). Introduction: Twenty years after *Language and Woman's Place*.

Burrington, William W., and Thaddeus J. Burns (1993). Hung up on the pay-per-call industry?: Current federal legislative regulatory developments. *Seton Hall Legislative Journal* 17: 359–99.

Butler, Judith (1990). The force of fantasy: Feminism, Mapplethorpe, and discursive excess. *Differences: A Journal of Feminist Cultural Studies* 2(2): 105–25.

Califia, Pat (1992). Is their number up? The Supreme Court pulls the plug on phone-sex-line operators. *Advocate*, March 10: 61.

Califia, Pat (1994). *Public sex: The culture of radical sex*. Pittsburgh, PA: Cleis Press.

Cook, M., and M. L. Lallgee (1972). Verbal substance for visual signals. *Semiotica* 3: 212–21.

Coward, Rosalind (1986). Porn: What's in it for women? *New Statesman*, June 13.

Danquah, Meri Nana-Ama (1993). Hanging up on phone sex. *Washington Post*, June 13: C1.

Davis, Christian A. (1993). Revisiting the lurid world of telephones, sex, and the First Amendment: Is this the end of dial-a-porn? *Widener Journal of Public Law* 2: 621–69.

Dee, Juliet (1994). "To avoid charges of indecency, please hang up now": An analysis of legislation and litigation involving dial-a-porn. *Communications and the Law* (March): 3–28.

Delacoste, Frédérique, and Priscilla Alexander (eds.) (1987). *Sex work: Writings by women in the sex industry.* Pittsburgh: Cleis Press.

Dworkin, Andrea (1981). *Pornography: Men possessing women.* New York: Perigee.

Dworkin, Andrea (1987). *Intercourse.* New York: Free Press.

Echols, Alice (1983). Cultural feminism: Feminist capitalism and the anti-pornography movement. *Social Text* 7: 34–53.

Eckert, Penelope, and Sally McConnell-Ginet (1992). Think practically and look locally: Language and gender as community-based practice. *Annual Review of Anthropology* 21: 461–90.

——— (this volume). Constructing meaning, constructing selves: Snapshots of language, gender, and class from Belten High.

Fielding, G., and P. Hartley (1987). The telephone: A neglected medium. In Asher Cashdan and Martin Jordin (eds.), *Studies in communication.* New York: Blackwell. 110–24.

Fishman, Pamela (1978). Interaction: The work that women do. *Social Problems* 25: 397–406.

Freccero, Carla (1990). Notes of a post-sex wars theorizer. In Marianne Hirsch and Evelyn Fox Keller (eds.), *Conflicts in feminism.* New York: Routledge. 305–25.

Gaudio, Rudi (forthcoming). Not talking straight in Hausa. In Anna Livia and Kira Hall (eds.), *Queerly phrased: Language, gender, and sexuality.* New York: Oxford University Press.

Goddard, J. B. (1973). *Office linkages and location: A study of communications and spatial patterns in central London.* New York: Pergamon.

Goldstein, Harry (1991). The dial-ectic of desire: For women at the other end of the phone sex line, some fantasies ring painfully true. *Utne Reader* (March/April): 32–33.

Hall, Kira (1995a). A third-sex subversion of a two-gender system. In Susanne Gahl, Andy Dolbey, and Christopher Johnson (eds.), *Proceedings of the 20th Annual Meeting of the Berkeley Linguistics Society.* Berkeley: Berkeley Linguistics Society. 220–33.

——— (1995b). Hijra/hijrin: Language and gender identity. Ph.D. diss., University of California, Berkeley.

——— (forthcoming a). Shifting gender positions among Hindi-speaking hijras. In Victoria Bergvall, Janet Bing, and Alice Freed (eds.), *Language and gender research: Theory and method.* London: Longman.

——— (forthcoming b). Cyberfeminism. In Susan Herring (ed.), *Computer mediated communication.* Amsterdam: Benjamins.

Hochschild, Arlie Russell (1983). *The managed heart: Commercialization of human feeling.* Berkeley: University of California Press.

Jeffreys, Sheila (1990). *Anticlimax: A feminist perspective on the sexual revolution.* London: Women's Press.

——— (1993). *The lesbian heresy: A feminist perspective on the lesbian sexual revolution.* North Melbourne, Australia: Spinifex.

K., Kathleen (1994). *Sweet talkers: Words from the mouth of a "pay to say" girl.* New York: Masquerade Books.

Kanter, Rosabeth Moss (1977). *Men and women of the corporation.* New York: Basic Books.

Lutz, Catherine (1986). Emotion, thought, and estrangement: Emotion as a cultural category. *Cultural Anthropology* 1(3): 287–309.

———— (1990). Engendered emotion: Gender, power and the rhetoric of emotional control in American discourse. In Lila Abu-Lughod and Catherine Lutz (eds.), *Language and the politics of emotion.* Cambridge: Cambridge University Press. 69–91.

MacKinnon, Catherine (1987). *Feminism unmodified: Discourses on life and law.* Cambridge: Harvard University Press.

———— (1993). *Only words.* Cambridge: Harvard University Press.

Major, Clarence (1994). *Juba to jive: A dictionary of African-American slang.* New York: Penguin.

Maretz, Heidi S. (1989). Aural sex: Has Congress gone too far by going all the way with dial-a-porn? *Hastings Communications and Entertainment Law Journal* 11: 493.

McConnell-Ginet, Sally (1978). Intonation in a man's world. *Signs* 3: 541–59.

McElhinny, Bonnie S. (this volume). Challenging hegemonic masculinities: Female and male police officers handling domestic violence.

Miller, Edward David (forthcoming). Inside the switchboards of desire: Storytelling on phone sex lines. In William L. Leap (ed.), *Beyond the lavender lexicon: Authenticity, imagination, and appropriation in lesbian and gay language.* New York: Gordon and Breach Press.

Pheterson, Gail (ed.) (1989). *A vindication of the rights of whores.* Seattle: Seal Press.

Potter, Robert D. (1989). Constitutional law—the regulation of telephone pornography. *Wake Forest Law Review* 24: 433–79.

Rhys, Natalie (1993). *Call me mistress: Memoirs of a phone sex performer.* Novato, CA: Miwok Press.

Rubin, Gayle (1984). Thinking sex: Notes for a radical theory of the politics of sexuality. In Carole Vance (ed.), *Pleasure and danger: Exploring female sexuality.* Boston: Routledge & Kegan Paul. 267–319.

Russell, Diana E. H. (1993). *Against pornography: The evidence of harm.* Berkeley: Russell Publications.

Rutter, D. R., and G.M. Stephenson (1977). The role of visual communication in synchronising conversation. *European Journal of Social Psychology* 7: 29–37.

Segal, Lynne (1993). Introduction. *Sex exposed: Sexuality and the pornography debate.* New Brunswick: Rutgers University Press. 1–11.

Short, John, Ederyn Williams, and Bruce Christie (1976). *The social psychology of telecommunications.* New York: Wiley.

Simokis, Andrea (1990). Telephone love. *Village* Voice, July 17. 35–39.

Smitherman, Geneva (1994). *Black talk: Words and phrases from the hood to the amen corner.* New York: Houghton Mifflin.

Stern, Christopher (1993). Expectations lowered for 900 numbers. *Broadcasting and Cable* 123(43): 40.

Valverde, Marianne (1989). Beyond gender dangers and private pleasures: Theory and ethics in the sex debates. *Feminist Studies* 15(2): 237–54.

Williams, Frederick (1985). Technology and communication. In Thomas W. Benson (ed.), *Speech communication in the 20th century*. Carbondale: Southern Illinois University Press. 184–95.

Woolfall, Brian D. (1994). Bond requirement for dial-a-porn: Exploring the need for tighter restrictions on obscenity and indecency. *California Western Law Review* 30: 297–311.

9

Challenging Hegemonic Masculinities

Female and Male Police Officers Handling Domestic Violence

Bonnie S. McElhinny

An important part of feminist strategy has been to distinguish between the biological attributes of women and men (*sex*) and the social, cultural, and psychological significance attached to those differences (*gender*). Although different feminist theorists have drawn the distinctions between sex and gender in different places and different ways, most have agreed that the distinction is important to make as part of a challenge to entrenched views that naturalize divisions between women's and men's activities, propensities, characters, and appearances. As Linda Nicholson (1994) has argued, however, this distinction still allowed many theorists to view biological differences between women and men as a base upon which specific gender characteristics were built (the "coat-rack" approach to gender). The coat-rack view allowed feminists to discuss both commonalities and differences among women, but it prevented feminist theorists from "truly understanding differences among women, differences among men, and differences regarding who gets counted as either" (Nicholson 1994:82). As Nicholson goes on to point out, it also prevented theorists from seeing that social variations in women and men are connected to social constructions of the body.

In sociolinguistics and ethnomethodology an increasingly influential model for understanding gender seems, at first, to circumvent the problems of the coat-rack model. Candace West and Don Zimmerman (1991) argue that gender is something one *does* rather than something one *has*: "Doing gender involves a complex of socially guided perceptual, interactional, and micropolitical activities that cast particular pursuits as expressions of masculine and feminine 'natures'" (14). This model reverses the way that the relationship between gender and sex is understood: sex differences are here inferred from gender differences (see also Butler 1990). It also suggests the ways that gender may vary according to context and activity, and thus provides a strong recommendation for a research program: sociolinguists should be investigating the way that gender and language covary in an array of speech events and activities (e.g., Eckert & McConnell-Ginet 1992; Goodwin 1990).

Yet West and Zimmerman's account is still closely linked to the dichotomous view of gender, which itself is derived from a kind of biological foundationalism that the rest of their work repudiates. West, for instance, in a recent article coauthored with Sarah Fenstermaker (1993), uncritically cites Harold Garfinkel's (1967) and Erving Goffman's (1971) argument that when people interact with one another, they take for granted that each has an essential womanly or manly nature. Although West and Zimmerman (1991) argue that femininity and masculinity are not invariant and that gender norms are not templates for behavior, they still insist that "it does not seem plausible to say that we have the option of being seen by others as female or male" (18). By assuming that there is one "commonsensical" view that allows people to organize their understandings of the world, the authors do not question the hegemonic understanding of gender. Their view occludes subversive perceptions of gender arrived at by subcultural groups, among them feminists and queer theorists, who might celebrate gender ambiguity or recognize a greater range of diversity.[1]

Although postmodern social theory has barely touched sociolinguistic analyses of gender (or indeed sociolinguistic analyses of any other social category—see McElhinny 1993:18–48), it may provide a partial solution to the problems engendered by the ethnomethodological model. For instance, Judith Butler (1990:17) retains the insight of gender as performative while asking us to consider what is at stake in the tendency of the hegemonic view to ignore genders that are not culturally intelligible (i.e., those where sex, gender, and sexual practice and desire are not "coherent" or continuous). She focuses on the need to investigate the costs of this view for individuals whose "aberrant" genders are understood as inhuman, as well as the costs for individuals who suppress such aberrant identities within themselves in order to conform to prevailing cultural norms. Similarly, Andrea Cornwall and Nancy Lindisfarne (1994) suggest that researchers separate investigations of "feminine" and "masculine" from womanhood and manhood, and that they consider female and male versions of both femininities and masculinities. Investigations of gender should not focus exclusively on differences between women and men, they argue, but also on how hegemonic femininities and masculinities produce subordinate and subversive femininities and masculinities. The investigation of gender thus becomes the investigation of the existence and competition of different feminine or masculine identities in any given context.

Postmodern feminists' insights may not, however, provide a complete solution. Although the recommendations given above imply that gender hierarchies have marked costs, including economic ones, for the people at the bottom of them, on the whole postmodernist feminists have focused little attention on gender and political economy, leading some critics to charge postmodern feminism with understanding politics as primarily and simply a matter of subverting or transforming representational practice. Feminists whose focus is primarily on economic inequalities or institutional practices often judge postmodernism as irrelevant to, or as undermining, materialist concerns (cf. Bordo 1990; Walby 1992).

Postmodernist and materialist approaches to the study of gender are not, however, fundamentally incompatible. To say that gender is performed is to say that it is constructed through activities. The notion of activity has recently proved fruitful for linguists in demonstrating how cognitive skills develop in participation through social activities, such as children's play (Goodwin 1990), the socialization of children in households (Ochs 1988), and participation in political events (Duranti 1994). Studies of language as activity in the workplace return us to the materialist theory of the relationship between social life, language, and activity. As Raymond Williams (1977:38–39) writes, "Language ... is saturated by and saturates all social activity, including productive activity"; thus, the social creation of meaning through language is "literally, a means of production."

In this chapter I investigate the gender performances required of women moving into traditionally masculine, all-male, working-class jobs. In particular, I focus on the activities of female police officers, for such women provide a challenge to the ethnomethodological account of gender. Because the job of policing is understood as masculine (as I will demonstrate below), a female police officer may, at any given moment, be perceived as a woman, as a man, or simply as a police officer. The decisions that an officer herself makes also contribute to the construction of a revised notion of police officer. In an examination of how female and male police officers handle domestic violence, I argue that female officers do not, counter to the expectations of some, produce the empathetic warmth associated with many traditionally female jobs (such as mothering, secretarial work, and social work). Instead, they choose to embody an image of police officers as rational, efficient, and professional. In doing so they challenge the hegemonic definition of a police officer (and of working-class masculinity) as centered on displays of physical force and emotional aggression and replace this image with a more middle-class masculine norm. The presence of female officers on the force significantly transforms the kind of masculinity displayed there, but does not present the more radical revision of policing that would center it around, for instance, the interactional norms of social work.

Reconciling Being a Woman with Being a Police Officer

Creating spaces for women in nontraditional workplaces like police departments is half of a two-pronged approach adopted by feminists to redress income inequities between women and men. The other prong is comparable worth, or challenging the low value attached to traditional women's work. Because ideas about the labor power of women and men are gender differentiated into jobs understood as "heavy" and "light," cultural stereotypes about gender often lead potential employers to dismiss some female applicants. Advocacy groups attempt to counter the effects of these stereotypes by encouraging women applying for traditional blue-collar jobs to demonstrate in their interviews the courage, aggressiveness, and strength the job requires (Weston 1982). Women are frequently coached, for instance, to wear long-sleeved shirts and bulky sweaters to suggest upper-body strength, and well-worn boots to suggest familiarity with doing "hard" work; they are told to take along a toolbox even if they don't expect to use it, making sure that the tools look used rather than new. The symbolic manipulation of gender markers, then, gives skilled women a chance to demonstrate their competence; in effect, women perform gender so gender will be ignored. Symbolic manipulation of this kind can mean the difference between having a job or not having one, between a poverty-level paycheck and a living wage, between harassment from coworkers and a peaceful work environment.

In Pittsburgh, a strong affirmative action program for police officers has not obviated any such need for symbolic manipulation. In 1975 a court injunction was issued to the City of Pittsburgh requiring each incoming class of police recruits to be evenly split between women and men, and between Blacks and Whites. This quota-hiring system has led to a slow, steady increase of White women, African American women, and African American men, so that now women and African Americans each compose approximately 25 percent of the force. This represents a larger percentage of female police officers than is found in any other major U.S. city but Detroit, and the percentage of African American officers matches the percentage of African Americans in the Pittsburgh population at large (U.S. Department of Justice 1987a, b).[2] However, as we shall see, female police officers must still engage in interpretive and symbolic work in order to reconcile others and themselves to their presence in the police department.

Policing has traditionally been regarded as "men's work," especially White men's work. Despite increasing numbers of women working on the police force in Pittsburgh during the past two decades, this attitude holds true not only among many of the city's citizens but also among both female and male police officers—even the female officers who consider themselves and other women to be very good at what they do. In general, blue-collar jobs like policing are thought to be more masculine than white-collar ones, and blue-collar jobs that require, or are thought to require, the exercise of strength or violence are perceived as more masculine than those that do not. The gender of a workplace is determined not only by the presence, or even predominance, of women or men in it but also by cultural norms and interpretations of gender that dictate who is best suited for different sorts of employment.[3]

Susan Martin (1980:89) has provided a psychosocial explanation for why certain working-class jobs are interpreted as masculine, suggesting that "for blue collar men whose jobs often do not provide high incomes or great social prestige, other aspects of the work, including certain 'manly' features, take on enormous importance as a means through which they confirm their sex-role identity." Her work has been critiqued by Barbara Ehrenreich (1983), who convincingly argues that explanations that focus on the psychological inadequacies of working-class men, even if seemingly sympathetic to the lack of prestige or pay associated with their work, still participate in a somewhat contemptuous dismissal of working-class styles of masculinity as *overly* masculine when compared to a middle-class norm. Such explanations stereotype blue-collar men as culturally retrograde hard-hats, and allow middle-class men to excuse themselves from examination or transformation of their own kinds of sexist behavior. Ehrenreich argues that working-class masculinity, rather than being obsolete, dysfunctional, or immature, can instead be understood as a way of generating power in workplace confrontations with management and concludes that "'working-class male chauvinism' might be an expression of class rather than gender antagonism" (135). Because men have been more likely to have unionized jobs that have stylized and formalized workplace confrontations in particular ways, the kinds of resistance and "masculine" display described by Ehrenreich are more likely for men.[4] We need to investigate, then, what happens when women are admitted to such jobs, while at the same time recognizing that different kinds of working-class masculinity are required in different kinds of workplace situations.[5]

Police work is defined, in public representations and in many male police officers' minds, by the situations in which officers are required to exert physical force to keep the peace. Male officers who do not believe women should be on the job often argue that women cannot handle these conflictual situations. Most female police officers, while recognizing differences in physical ability between themselves and men, question the significance of those differences. They argue that on serious calls one rarely needs to act without backup and can cooperate with other officers to bring the situation under control. Female police officers also tend to distinguish between physical strength (which most agree they do not have) and institutional force (which they argue that they do have). As one woman put it, "It's never just a fight between a man and a woman—it's a fight between a man and a *police officer.*" Her comment points out that police officers have special resources—tools, training, the power to arrest, and radio access to "the largest gang in the city," as one officer put it—which should be considered in any definition of *strength*. Female police officers describe, in matter-of-fact voices, the ways they handle situations using these resources. Naisha, for instance, one of the first two women in the city to work as a plainclothes detective and the first African American woman to do so, described cornering a man with a gun in a dead-end street with her partner:

(1)   I had my badge out, my gun out, cause we cornered him. We heard
       he had a gun, he had his hand in his pocket, he turned around like
       that, I told him, "You make one more move and I'm gonna blow
       your head off."[6]

A European American police officer, Georgia, casually mentioned a call that required her to deal with two men at once. She grabbed one, handcuffed him, and had the other over the hood of the car before she called the police dispatcher to say she needed backup. Her principal point in telling me this story was not to display bravado but, rather, to say that no police officer should ever have to work alone, and that the radio dispatcher should have been censured for not obtaining an accurate description of the situation and for endangering her by sending her alone to a conflictual call.

Images of female police officers in popular culture, by contrast, tend to support the male officers' views on the centrality of physical force and women's inability to exercise it in moments of crisis. This was highlighted by the airing of the prime-time television show *Sirens* the year after I did my fieldwork (in 1992–1993). The show centered on the lives of four female police officers who were, ironically enough, fictionally based in Pittsburgh. In one episode a rookie Black female officer was riding with a seasoned white male officer. She was unable to open the door of a wrecked car to rescue the driver inside, so her male partner ripped the door off its hinges, lifted the man in his arms, and carried him to the paramedics' rolling bed. She was unable to overtake a criminal running down the street, but the older officer quickly ran past her and nabbed the criminal. When she began to despair about whether she was suited for policing, her kindly partner continually reassured her that she was indeed police material, and that she would have a chance to prove she could handle the tough stuff. Finally, she was given her chance at the end of the show by comforting a grieving woman to whom she had just broken the news of her husband's death.

In discussing similar situations with me, female officers, who are well aware of these cultural and media stereotypes, regularly noted that there are some frightened, weak, do-nothing men on the job—an implicit retort to male officers that women should not be regarded as a group but rather as individuals. They pointed out how unlikely it would be that a slightly overweight man in his fifties would outrun a fit woman in her twenties in a chase. Female and male officers alike ridiculed the image of a police officer ripping off a car door and pointed out that there is no need to carry a man to a medic's trolley when the trolley can be rolled to him, and that one does not even need to lift people onto trolleys since medics' trolleys are designed to fold down to the ground so one can gently ease patients onto them. Some female officers and many male officers, however, nevertheless agreed with a portrayal of a woman as better suited to deal with a victim's grief.

Some female police officers believe women are better at the job because they are more likely to stay calm and cool in conflictual situations—precisely because they cannot as easily resort to force and must use talk as a tool instead. Serissa, an African American officer, told me, "To tell you the truth the best officers that I know ARE women. . . . Most situations, they keep their cool in certain situations, whereas I have seen plenty of men just kinda lose their tempers." The few officers who were identified by others as likely to "go off" (i.e., to escalate too quickly into the use of force) were mostly men. Other officers regarded these individuals negatively, believing that they endangered themselves and their partners by embroiling them unnecessarily in physical conflicts. The few female police officers who were labeled as masculine by female or male officers were those who were perceived as getting too angry too fast, as "not treating people right," and as using "too much" profanity. Contrary, perhaps, to what has been found in other situations (cf. Devor 1989), it was not the appearance of female officers that defined them as masculine, but their actions; women who were conventionally feminine in their appearance could also be labeled masculine.

There are other differences in how women and men interpret the job of policing. In addition to redefining strength as institutional rather than physical, and emphasizing the importance of using talk before physical force, many female officers point out that most police work does not entail handling conflictual situations but taking reports. After telling me with pride and in considerable detail about a report she wrote that convicted a rapist, Georgia concluded, "Report writing, it's just a proven fact, women are just much better and that, that builds your court case." More women than men emphasize the importance of report writing in getting convictions. Men who object to women's presence on the job are likely to say, "I will give them that—they're good report writers"—a backhanded compliment because these men often accord little importance to report writing. But many women tend to believe that it doesn't matter what you do on the streets if you don't write it up properly. Joi, for instance, an African American woman who was a street-trainer for rookies, told me with a laugh that all new officers should take a creative writing course. When I asked her why she said:

> (2)   You should learn just how to tell your story, a flowing story, a chain
>   of events.... Here this attorney has your report in front of him
>   and he's reading it and y'know he can tear you apart if you're tes-
>   tifying to something entirely different. A lot of things you remem-
>   ber but you don't write it down. I try to tell <<rookies>>, Write
>   down EVERYthii::ng that you remember at the time so if you hap-
>   pen to say something he'll say, "Well that's not in the report" and
>   you'll say, "I just remember."

Because policing is so strongly associated with a certain kind of masculinity, women who work as police officers are often assumed to have either a certain kind of personality (tomboyish or tough) or a particular sexuality (lesbian). In fact, there is no distinguishable personality trait that is common to all female police officers, although there are important similarities in why women become police officers. The first female officers were often working-class women who found themselves in financial difficulties and therefore welcomed the relative security and adequate pay of policing: some had recently been divorced and were suddenly single mothers; others had husbands who lost their jobs in the steel mills during the spate of deindustrialization in the 1970s and 1980s. Most of these officers reported that they had just happened to see advertisements for female officers. A number of the younger women, by contrast, grew up wanting to be police officers. Some cited the influence of popular media on their career decisions, such as Angie Dickinson's portrayal of a policewoman or the television program *Charlie's Angels*.

An Economy of Affect: Emotional Requirements of Policing

I now turn to a more detailed analysis of the interactional performance of gender in police work, focusing on the construction of emotionlessness and objectivity. The projection of emotion is a type of work that often goes unrecognized and uncompensated even though it is a crucial part of the definitions of some jobs. The display of positive affect, for instance, is required in traditionally female jobs, such as being a secretary (Kanter 1977) or a flight attendant (Hochschild 1983). Indeed, Arlie Hochschild reports that half of women's jobs require the performance of emotional labor, and only one-quarter of men's jobs require it. Moreover, the jobs that require men to perform emotional labor often demand displays of negative instead of positive affect (for example, bill collectors are taught to threaten customers who have delinquent bills).

The emotion work that policing exacts is quite different from that of typically feminine and female jobs. Janie, a European American rookie and former teacher, describes how she adapted to workplace interactional norms (my questions and comments are in italics):

(3)   *Do you think women who come on this job start to act in masculine ways?*
Umhm. Un-huh.

Like what are some of the things you see?
Your language. I know mine changes a lot. When I'm at work I always feel like I have to be so gruff, you know. And normally I'm not like that. Sometimes I try to be like such a hard ass. I don't smile as much. . . . I think it's mostly language. Mine's atrocious sometimes. I've toned it down a lot. When I first started you know cause I worked with a lot of guys it seemed like- They didn't- may not even have swore but I felt like I had to almost like be tough or something around them. And that was my way of being tough.

Is it mostly profanity, or do you do it with tone of voice or something?
Little bit of both. Like I said I've toned down my profanity a lot. I just
kinda use it to describe things now, like I don't call people names and
stuff. Like I said about how Black women were able to kinda command respect from people in the projects, I try to like pick up some
of their slang, either their slang or their tone, something. Then I like
I listen to myself sometimes. I'm like god I sound like you know hhh
I sound like a HILL person <<a person who lives in a largely Black,
largely poor area of Pittsburgh>>. And then I think I should just be
able to be me. I shouldn't have to be everybody else.

This police officer feels that her occupational persona is a mask: *I should
just be able to be me. I shouldn't have to be everybody else.* This sort of
alienation from the emotional labor required by a job was also widespread
among the flight attendants interviewed by Hochschild (1983): the ways
that they were required to act had little to do with how they themselves
felt. Janie's experience demonstrates that her occupational persona is
shaped by both her interactions with the public and her perception of the
expectations of other police officers. The result is that she smiles less, acts
gruffer and tougher. When I asked her why smiling mattered, she responded
that when a person smiles she drops her guard. Letting down your guard
means that someone can challenge you, test you, or hurt you.

Many officers believe that some sense of reserve or emotional distance is
the only way to survive on the job; otherwise, it is too stressful. Naisha,
who had been on the job for twelve years, reported the high rates of alco-
holism, divorce, and suicide among officers. She described her reaction to
seeing her first bad accident and explains her way of coping with this and
other traumatic scenes:

(4)   So my first dead body, which was one that was a girl that was very
      young. . . . There was all this blood. The lieutenant called me, he said
      okay okay kid this is your first (.) time for a dead body I want you
      to take a look at this. Think you can handle it? And I see this body
      covered up. And I see ALL this- this pool of blood came all the way
      down and made a huge pool at the end of the street. So much
      blood. And I said I don't know if I can handle it or not boss, I never
      seen one before. Said okay, said if you think you're gonna throw up,
      turn around and don't throw up on my shoes. I remember him say-
      ing that. DON'T THROW UP ON MY SHOES! So he pulls back the
      sheet and I look at this and I was SOOO FASCINATED. . . . I was
      TOTALLY fascinated and he said THAT'S ENOUGH. He said ARE

YOU GETTING SICK? I said NOOO! He said SOMETHING'S WRONG WITH YOU KID—he said YOU SEEN ENOUGH. He put the sheet back on her. After I went and got in the car and I sat there my stomach started to eew, heave-ho, started to heave a little bit, but I wouldn't let on. That is when I looked and decided that was not a person. They were no longer people if they were dead to me. I didn't get involv- think of them as people. I didn't think about her as having a family, as having a full life, you know, anything. If I did it would kill me. . . . I don't get emotionally involved. In anything. I just think—they're like clients. I don't get emotionally involved. And I don't have nightmares. I know guys that have nightmares. That's because you take it PERSONALLY. You see the baby with the cigarette burns and you get all emotional. You can't do that. You always have to be impartial. You can never allow your opinion—you can't you can't be opinionated. You are an impartial person. So that's just the way I do it. And it works for me. I don't have to drink myself to sleep at night.

A sort of commodity logic (Strathern 1988) governs the way Naisha and other police officers talk about the offering of emotion. Emotion is a limited commodity and using it means losing it; offering sympathy to others means losing a piece of oneself, which then requires bandaging through alcohol or drugs. Naisha believes that if an officer does not hold herself aloof from the emotionally traumatized people she meets on the job, she will become damaged herself. Being emotionally distant is not only personally crucial but also professionally proper: impartiality and objectivity are characteristics the new generation of police officers shares with other middle-class bureaucrats and professionals, such as coroners, physicians, and lawyers. Because police officers' experiences differ from those of most other citizens, citizens often believe their predicament merits a different reaction from the one that police officers deem appropriate or wise.

The result of these experiences is the development of an occupationally conditioned *habitus*, the notion proposed by Pierre Bourdieu to describe how experience constructs interactional behavior. According to Bourdieu (1977:82–83), habitus is "a system of lasting transposable dispositions which, integrating past experiences, functions at every moment as a matrix of perceptions, appreciations and actions." In other words, interactional experiences are incorporated into memory to form commonsense expectations and reactions.

Although interactional histories are shaped by any number of social circumstances and accidents, Bourdieu's theory identifies speakers' experiences in families, schools, and workplaces as most influential. In practice, however, he has focused most attention on the first two of these sites.[7] My use of Bourdieu's notion of habitus brings the labor market back into focus as a source for shaping adults' speech styles and creating norms for the expression of affect. The traumatic, dangerous, and hostile interactions that police officers regularly experience produce what I call an *economy of affect*. The term *economy* is a reminder that this style is shaped by the officers' involvement in the labor market. It also suggests that officers are economical (in the sense of thrifty) in their expenditure of (especially positive) affect with citizens. This is because police officers understand the expenditure of positive affect in terms of a closed economy: a significant expenditure of sympathy or grief on others means that less is available for themselves.

Police officers do express positive affect on the job, but they choose the situations in which they do so carefully, as if they were on a limited budget. They will often invest emotion where a payoff seems most likely—with children, for example, or with an individual who is clearly asking for help or recommendations. Some officers choose particular kinds of people, such as the family of a homicide victim, or particular individuals, like a slightly retarded homeless woman, as the focus of their sympathy and attention. But most emphasize that they cannot serve as social workers and also do their job.

Because most officers budget their affective resources, and because the experiences the police have had are quite different from those of most other citizens, complainants often expect more sympathy from officers than they in fact receive. Police officers learn to act like "tough cops" who limit their conversation to the formalities of the investigation, because increased interaction offers further opportunities for excuses, arguments, or complaints (Rubinstein 1973). If they are unable to minimize the amount of interaction or contact, they can at least engage in the interaction as little as possible— with terse comments, a body position half turned away, or lack of eye contact. Such behaviors are typical on buses or in elevators where passengers must come into close physical contact (Goffman 1971), but police evince such reactions in situations of emotional crowding rather than physical crowding.[8] Reducing the amount of interaction affords others some personal space in what is often an intrusively intimate, albeit necessary, interaction with a stranger. Milgram (1988) points out that urban dwellers, when required to engage in unpleasant interactions with strangers, often assume unfriendly countenances and brusque manners; police officers seem to accentuate this conversational style. Because the situations in which most complainants meet police officers are characterized by high emotional intensity, the businesslike way that officers set about taking their reports is likely to strike complainants as cold or heartless. The possibility for miscommunication is immanent, given the differing Western interpretations of *unemotional* as either calm and rational or withdrawn and alienated (Lutz 1986, 1990): that which police officers interpret as the first, citizens may interpret as the second.

Facelessness in Face-to-Face Interaction

I turn now to a detailed consideration of two police calls that exemplify the different ways that police officers and complainants can approach an interaction. Both of the following calls were described by the police dispatcher as a *violent domestic*, but by the time the police arrived on the scene the actors had fled. I attended the first call with an African American woman who had been on the force for twelve years, the second with an African American man who had been on for about a year. I chose these two incidents because their similarity makes a comparison of the two officers' behavior possible. Often calls are so different that this is impossible. I was not able to record the first call but was able to take detailed field notes while the officer herself was taking notes for the report. The second call was audiotaped. The first call takes place in an affluent, largely white area of the city; the second takes place in one of the city's largely Black housing projects.

Call #1

When the complainant sees the police car pulling up, she comes out of the house with blood dripping from her mouth down her chin. The officer sees her and says simply, "Oh." Once we go into the house, the woman starts telling her story rapidly and breathlessly. It is difficult at first to sort out what has happened.

(5)   The father of my daughter's son, he just got out of jail for threatening someone with a gun, he lives out there in a stolen car with stolen plates, his mother won't let him live there, but his father keeps getting him out, my daughter lives with me with the baby, I told him not to come back, I came out, he came towards me, I pushed, he punched me in the mouth.

The woman repeats this story, over and over. Gradually it becomes clear that her daughter's boyfriend punched her when she asked him not to return to her house. The officer says very little, aside from getting the woman's address, date of birth, and other information necessary for the incident report. The woman says over and over, "I don't know if I can have [my daughter] back. I know nothing's gonna come of this. I don't know what to

do. I don't know if she'll come back." The officer replies to none of this for
the first fifteen minutes of the call, so that at one point the complainant
even says in some frustration, "You don't say much." Not until all the
necessary information has been obtained and the officer has moved to the
door does she offer some advice:

> (6)   Officer: Next time he comes back, call 911—that's an
>   emergency. Call him in for trespassing, to prevent
>   all this pushing, verbal confrontation. We'll be
>   right here.
>   Complainant: I don't know if she'll come back.
>   Officer: I've got a daughter too—she'll come back. How
>   old is she?
>   Complainant: Nineteen.
>   Officer: She'll do what she has to do.
>   Complainant: I don't know if she'll be back.
>   Officer: She'll be back.

As we leave, the daughter returns to the house and emphatically declares
that her boyfriend did not punch her mother. She states that her grandmother was trying to punch her, but hit her mother instead. When we are
back in the car the officer says rather bemusedly, "Grandma might have
done it—she never did come out of the kitchen." She adds, "See what I
mean. I was on the mother's side, but you just don't know."

This episode characterizes several aspects of police-citizen interaction on
report-taking calls. The officer concentrates on obtaining the information
needed in the incident report; she does not react with horror or sympathy, as
others might in the same situation. In this case, the woman's remark that
the police officer doesn't "say much" is a mitigated complaint that she does
not say enough. Often, however, as a police officer is leaving, she or he will
offer some advice or make a personal comment. These personal comments
are not always integrated into the rest of the interaction; rather, they constitute a marked break from a report-taking frame to a counseling frame
(Goffman 1977; Tannen 1984). In this instance, the officer puts away her
notes for the incident report and moves to the doorway, so that she is
literally speaking from a different, liminal point of view when she offers her
remark: *I've got a daughter too.* The police officer's final, more personal
comments, while removing some of the impersonality of the encounter, also
serve to highlight the distinction between the two frames of interaction.
Occasionally, a complainant will explicitly ask for these personal comments.
In one case a pregnant woman, who had been beaten up by her boyfriend,

refused to allow a female police officer to take a report. Instead she asked the officer what she should do. The officer at first demurred, saying that she didn't offer advice, but the woman persisted: "Take off your uniform, just for a minute—what would you do?" The officer finally replied, "No one hits me. I get paid to get hit—that's all." Again, this incident reveals that personal comments are not perceived as coming from the police officer but from the person inside the uniform.

Finally, we should note that the officer's need to suspend judgment and remain impartial during Call #1 means that she never ratifies the account of the complainant. She produces few, if any, of the minimal responses like *umhm* or *right* that are common features of conversation. Daniel Maltz and Ruth Borker (1982) have argued that women and men interpret such responses differently, with women using them to indicate "I'm listening" and men using them to mean "I agree." The female officer's abstention from the use of these minimal responses shows that she is well aware of their polysemy, and that the importance of maintaining a professionally objective stance outweighs any desire to display attentiveness.

The return of the daughter at the end of the call with her own story reinforces the officer's belief that this withholding of judgment is the appropriate strategy. In a training tape that officers were shown on how to testify in a courtroom, being professionally impartial was repeatedly emphasized. "Present the facts," the narrator said, "not your conclusions and not your opinions. You're a fact-finder, not a judge." These instructions should be seen not only as directives for police behavior but also as a distillation of officers' experiences of what works, which is then encoded in their training. In keeping with this advice, in the incident report the female officer included both the mother's and the daughter's versions of the incident.

Call #2

As the officer and I walk into the apartment building, a man salutes us with "Hi, how you doin'?" The police officer responds, continues upstairs, and immediately discovers that this man is the one who assaulted the caller. Had this been a more dangerous situation, the officer would have unknowingly come face-to-face with someone desperate to escape. Experiences like these train officers to be wary of all people around the scene of even the most innocuous call. The woman who made the call proceeds to tell her story. The domestic dispute apparently took place after the woman, who had found out that she had contracted a venereal disease, tried to talk to her longtime partner about it. She asked him if he had been fooling around and asked him to seek treatment. He responded by punching her.

For me, as participant and observer, the most striking aspect of the subsequent exchange between the police officer and the woman was again the near-complete absence of responses, including back-channelers, to the complainant's ongoing description of the incident, to her description of her feeling of betrayal, and especially to her direct, repeated questions as to whether she was right to feel this way (see examples (7), (8), (11), and (12)). I was reluctant to respond, in part because I wanted to see how the officer would respond and in part because I didn't want the officer to perceive me as interfering. Clearly, the woman expected some response; more than once she waited for one through a long pause, or insistently repeated her question, sometimes eliciting a response from me (usually a barely audible back-channeler like *umhm* or *yes* produced after a noticeable delay, as in examples (9) through (12)).

(7)   Complainant: This is the point don't, if somebody care about you, DON'T HURT the people who care about you. (10.0) Okay I know. I have nobody now. (9.0)

(8)   Complainant: I'm so good to him he never want for ANYthing and I'm gonna really- You understand? (5.0) I want something out of life. I thought I had it.

(9)   Complainant: You know we just having- I was sitting right there, he was sitting there and we just- if you CARE about somebody, don't you think you can talk to them about situations? (2.0)
      Bonnie: umhm

(10) Complainant: When he knocked me down on the bed and stuff I don't even know how it happened. (1.0) I just can't believe it. (1.0) I just don't want my son over here. He'll tear him up. (2.0) It's (1.0) I just thought I had it MADE. (1.0) Ever love anybody?
      Bonnie: <<barely audible>> umhm
(11) Complainant: I mean that's what hurts, when you try to be honest with somebody, and they just gonna punch you in the face. You see this. You see it! (1.0)
      Bonnie: umhm (1.0) I see it (6.0)

(12) Complainant: I can't say that he's transmitting shit out there. I know what I caught. I know that I don't DEAL. (4.0) And it hurts. I was only trying to talk to him about that. "Oh you drunk bitch. You wanna talk shit." It's not fair. If I didn't care about him, you think I would TALK to him about it? (2.0) You think I would?

Bonnie: <<barely audible>> hm.

During the interval that the police officer is taking the report (the first twenty minutes or so of the call) he produces no responses to the woman's questions. All his comments are guided by the script of the incident report. Sometimes this script leads to interruptions of the woman's ongoing account:

(13) Complainant: I mean I just wanted- I mean you go to the health depart-

Police officer: <<interrupting>> Spell your name for me.

In other instances, his responses to her questions and remarks, while not actually interrupting her in midclause, still constitute an interruption because he fails to respond to a question or abruptly changes the topic (Murray 1985), as in examples (14) and (15) below:

(14) Complainant: You know and all of a sudden he said old drunken bitch. I said what're you talking about. I said (1.0) we're together, we gotta help each other. You know?

Police officer: What's your date of birth?

(15) Complainant: I said something's going ON here. I said I'm gonna tell you what I'm gonna do for you. . . . I cannot—me, have a disease <<incredulously>>. Now wouldn't you be honest if you got something for somebody

Bonnie: (1.0) umhm

Complainant: and not be shooting drugs? I don't shoot drugs! I don't play it! I don't have it in my house! (6.0) And I hurt.

Police officer: What color was his pants?

These interruptions might be perceived as inattentiveness to the complainant's account. In fact, at one point it does become clear that the officer hasn't heard all that she has said: he asks what her relationship is with the assailant at the point where the report form dictates that question, although she had told him earlier that her boyfriend had done it. In at least one case, however, the officer's interruption is an attempt to accord the woman some privacy by preventing her from sharing personal and perhaps painful intimate details that he may not need to know for his report:

(16) Complainant: The point is, I tell you what this started from. . . .
                        he's been messing with other women and
      Police officer: <<interrupting>> Okay, just have a seat there.

As before, however, the frame break at the end of the call provides an opportunity for the officer to respond to the woman's questions. Although throughout the call he has been seated across the room from the woman, head bent to his writing, at the end of the call he gathers his papers together, stands up, goes over to her side of the room, tells her he does indeed understand, and asks if she will be okay for the rest of the evening (examples (17) and (18)). This response can also be seen as a very belated production of a response to the woman's repeated questions about whether he understands her suffering.

(17) Complainant: Can you understand how that makes me feel?
      Police officer: I understand. I understand perfectly how you feel.
      Complainant: If you can't talk to somebody that you care about,
                        about transmitting disease, then what is it.
      Police officer: I understand exactly what you're saying. . . . He
                        had no reason to hit you either. Nope, I under-
                        stand exactly what you're saying. You guys are
                        grown, you should be able to sit down and talk-

(18) Police officer: Sure you're okay now, don't need anything?
      Complainant: No no I'm all right.

This increased intimacy allows the woman to ask how he would react in a similar situation—to treat him, that is, like a man rather than a police officer:

(19) Complainant: You know, if I was your woman, and you was
                        messing around

Police officer:	I don't do
Complainant:	would you want me to tell you?
Police officer:	No. <<silent laughter>>
Complainant:	(3.0) No seriously.
Police officer:	The reason why I'm laughing is because see I don't do that and I don't beat on women. I mean I you know it's it's not funny but I don't do that.
Complainant:	It hurts. (1.0)
Police officer:	I understand.
Complainant:	You take someone into your heart like that, you know, I was in my glory. You know, that hurts. I'm hurting. (1.0)
Police officer:	Well if he's downstairs I'm taking him with me.

The officer's immediate response is to try to recreate emotional distance between himself and the complainant with quick laughter, a quick apology, and an insistence that he does not act like the assailant. The point at which the woman focuses on the police officer's maleness (*You know, if I was your woman, and you was messing around would you want me to tell you?*) instead of his professional identity is the only point where the officer's speech contains any false starts. He quickly returns to his professional role by emphasizing the action he will take if he finds the man lurking downstairs: *Well if he's downstairs I'm taking him with me.*

Police officers in such situations display behavior similar to that of other powerful speakers. In many institutional settings like confessional booths, psychotherapy sessions, classrooms, bureaucratic interviews, job interviews, and even family dinner tables (Foucault 1978; Gal 1991; Gumperz 1982a, b; Ochs & Taylor, this volume; Sattel 1983), a more powerful speaker asks listeners to expose themselves to an interlocutor who has the power to judge and act upon their account. The ability to remain silent and require justification of behavior is a prerogative of the powerful. Speakers use inexpressivity in order to make their behavior appear to be the result of unemotional rationality, forestalling unwanted challenges and questions about their own actions or the actions of the institution they are associated with. Douglas Biber and Edward Finegan (1989) use the term *faceless* for texts like newscasts, newspapers, professional letters, and official documents characterized by the absence of markers of affect and evidentiality; in popular usage, this sort of language is called *bureaucratese*. This concept can be extended to the linguistic style of both female and male officers in taking reports: because they have the same experiences and tasks and interpret them similarly, they resort to the same linguistic style when taking reports. Their discourse management techniques—long silences, nonresponsiveness, interruptions, frame breaks, and nonproduction of preferred seconds in adjacency pair sequences—mark their language as a sort of bureaucratese, or *facelessness in face-to-face interaction.*

Objectivity, Contested Masculinities, and the Bureaucratization of the Police Force

Police officers in the 1990s are associated with considerably less physical violence than in the 1960s, partly in response to widespread public protests about police action after conflicts with the community in the 1960s and 1970s. Today's police officers, although still required upon occasion to exert physical force, are increasingly required to act as bureaucrats. This marks a change in the role of policing in American society: as other parts of American bureaucracy grow, police officers' tasks as clerical workers increase. The growth of insurance companies in particular has contributed to this change, because police officers are required to complete complicated police forms for every robbery, burglary, and car theft. Increasing restriction and supervision of police action, as well as increases in the number of civil suits filed against police officers, has led to requirements for written documentation of each act of force. "God forbid you fire your gun," said one officer. "You might as well hire a novelist."[9]

The hiring of women, and to a lesser extent of minority men, is both an effect and a cause of the increasing bureaucratization of the police department. To retain its authority as an objective arbiter of community conflict, the police department had to hire officers that represent the community more accurately. The large-scale inclusion of women and minorities changed the meaning and organization of police work. For instance, a seniority system was instituted for choosing shifts, patrol partners, and patrol areas almost immediately after the first large hiring of women and minorities, when women and Black men complained that the White men who had been hired at the same time were being accorded special privileges from commanders. Commanders had up until then always had the option of singling out certain officers for favored jobs. The seniority system ensured equality between genders and races. Although it also provided older White men who had been hired earlier with a domain of privilege, others were content because it promised them similar privileges in the future.

I have focused in this chapter on similarities among officers during a single kind of call: taking a report of domestic violence. The production of uniformity should be understood as one of the effects of bureaucratization.

This focus is not meant to obscure how and where differences exist among police officers. Such differences do of course manifest themselves in certain kinds of policing situations. For instance, police officers have very different attitudes toward residents of housing projects, different reactions to police behavior in the beating of Rodney King, and different attitudes toward how to engage in the "war" on drugs (McElhinny 1993). However, report taking is the single most common duty of police officers, and it is defined by an orientation toward a bureaucratic ideology that, according to Weber (1968:975), explicitly deemphasizes the traits of the individual occupying the slot and the individual receiving bureaucratic services:

> Bureaucratization offers above all the optimum possibility for carrying through the principle of specializing administrative functions according to purely objective considerations. . . . "Objective" discharge of business primarily means a discharge of business according to calculable rules and "without regard for persons." . . . Bureaucracy develops the more perfectly, the more it is "dehumanized," the more completely it succeeds in eliminating from official business love, hatred, and all purely personal, irrational, and emotional elements which escape calculation.

For bureaucratic decisions to be considered legitimate, argues Weber, they must be rational and objective, not personal and discretionary. Weber's remarks are as much normative as descriptive, as numerous critiques of bureaucratic gatekeeping interactions have demonstrated (e.g., Ferguson 1984; Gumperz 1982a, b; McElhinny 1994; Savage & Witz 1992). Nevertheless, to the extent that bureaucrats adhere to the ideology of objectivity and impersonality in practice, we want to ask what strategic ends they gain by doing so. In reacting to domestic violence it may be particularly important for police officers to distinguish themselves maximally from the perpetrators of domestic violence—who are often seen as persons "out of control"—by themselves demonstrating a kind of professional control.[10] Such an explanation explains, in part, the discomfort of the male officer in example (19) above when he is associated with the class of men who abuse women.

Bureaucratization requires a change in the pattern of gender relations on several levels. Although it enables women to become police officers, it also effects a change in the normative pattern of masculinity—from physical aggressiveness to technical rationality and calculation (Connell 1987). The workplace may well be perceived as less masculine than before not only because it includes women but also because an emphasis on emotionless rationality rather than physical ability weakens the perception of the job as masculine. Rationality and emotional control are, however, still gendered masculine in American culture by virtue of their contrast with the emotionality associated with women (Lutz 1990).

It may appear that female police officers, like other women who move into powerful and masculine institutions, simply adopt the interactional behavior characteristic of these institutions without subverting it, but the truth is more complex. The process by which women enter a masculine workplace necessarily includes some adoption, as well as adaptation, of institutional norms. Because female officers may draw on contrasting definitions of masculinity and effective policing, their decision to orient toward a "professional" rather than a "physical" norm must be understood simultaneously as adaptation to one hegemonic masculinity and contestation of another. By resisting the definition of policing as an occupation centered on exertion of physical force and aggressiveness and by offering an alternative definition of policing that centers instead on mental ability and cool efficiency, female police officers create a space for themselves in a formerly all-male and currently still largely masculine occupation. They contest ideologies of "working-class" masculinity with a kind of "middle-class" masculinity that, although valued in the wider society, is subordinate within cultural definitions of policing. In their interactions, female police officers construct a kind of masculinity that is simultaneously hegemonic, subordinate, and subversive.

This chapter has shown that a model of gender that assumes that all individuals will be perceived as female or male is overly simple because gender is not only the attribute of individuals, or even constituted by the activities of individuals, but is also part of institutional definitions, structures, and tasks. In my analysis I have extended postmodern insights about the "incoherence" of sex, gender, and sexual practice to an instance of "incoherent" sex, gender, and institutional practice. Female officers' actions simultaneously affected the construction of their workplace and of their own ever-changing gender identities. Of course, "interpretations of maleness, manhood, or masculinity are not neutral, but rather all such attributions have political entailments. In any given situation, they may align men against women, some men against other men, some women against other women, or some men and some women against others. In short the processes of gendering produce difference and inequality" (Cornwall & Lindisfarne 1994:10). In the Pittsburgh police department, the choices available to women who seek to be accepted as police officers align them with younger or college-educated male officers who also orient toward middle-class professional norms, and against the many older male officers who orient toward working-class definitions of their workplace. The cost of professionalization to citizens (female and male) may be the absence of freely offered sympathy at some of the most stressful moments of their lives.

Acknowledgments

I gratefully acknowledge the financial and institutional support given to this project by the National Science Foundation, the Wenner-Gren Foundation for Anthropological Research, the Stanford Humanities Center, the Mellon Foundation, and the Women's Studies Program at the University of Pittsburgh. Commanders Freeman, McComb, Patterson, and Wind graciously allowed me to patrol with officers under their command and thus made this project possible. The generous cooperation of the officers themselves made it worthwhile. Earlier versions of this paper have benefited from the questions and comments of participants in the Stanford Sociolinguistics Rap Session, the University of Pittsburgh Women's Studies Lunch Series, the Swarthmore Linguistics and Psychology Department Colloquia, and the Kristiina-Instituuti for Women's Studies at the University of Helsinki. For detailed comments, I thank Niko Besnier, Mary Bucholtz, Penny Eckert, Gregory Guy, Kira Hall, Shirley Brice Heath, and John Rickford.

Notes

1. For example, Judith Butler (1990) focuses on the parodic element in drag, cross-dressing, and the sexual stylization of butch-femme identity; Andrea Cornwall (1994) describes prostitution and *travestis*; Nancy Lindisfarne (1994) documents the cultural construction and reconstruction of a virgin's hymen in the Mediterranean and Middle East; Holly Devor (1989) is interested in women often mistaken for men; Marjorie Garber (1989, 1991) investigates cross-dressing; and Sally Stone (1989) and Judith Shapiro (1989) consider transsexuals.

2. See McElhinny (1993) for a more extended description of the police department, the quota-hiring system, and the fieldwork I conducted in Pittsburgh.

3. First appearances embody and reinscribe notions about who police officers are and what they do. The dark blue uniform is more masculine than feminine, more militaristic than bureaucratic. It has a stripe down the seam on the outside of each pant leg, back pockets with top buttons, sharp pointed collars (rather than large round or squared ones), and ties and tie pins (rather than scarves or decorative pins). The gun belt is wide, heavy, and leather, and carries the radio, nightstick, blackjack, and revolver or semiautomatic. Bulletproof vests square off body outlines, and according to regulations, hair is supposed to

be short, or pulled up above the collar, though not all female officers regularly heed this regulation. Most female police officers have been addressed as *sir*.

4. The predominance of men in unionized jobs in the United States is itself a result of a complicated interaction of class and gender dynamics, and is not, as it is often interpreted, simple evidence for working-class chauvinism. See Elizabeth Garnesey (1982) and Jane Humphries (1982) for further discussion.

5. The normative masculinities associated with the Pittsburgh police department seem to be understood by police officers and citizens as White, and many Black officers assimilate to these norms, although some Black male officers do develop alternative philosophies.

6. The transcription conventions used in this chapter are as follows:

italics	researcher's questions
(6.0)	pauses, timed in seconds.
(text)	barely audible speech for which the transcription is uncertain
<<comment>>	transcriber's commentary
TEXT	increased volume
re::::ally	lengthened syllables
Twel-	cut-off word (often, a self-interruption)

    All names of people and places are pseudonyms.

7. See Kathryn Woolard (1985) for a compelling critique of this position.

8. Similarly, although all police reports require officers to obtain information on the complainant's age, address, employment, and so on, one officer told me that she had decided to stop asking about employment because it was none of her business anyway. Other officers say the same about age, especially the age of women. One officer, when he got to that part of the form, would cup his hand around his mouth and drop his voice to a whisper as if asking for secret information.

9. The war on drugs embodies the countertrend to this longer trend of professionalization and bureaucratization. This "war" strongly emphasizes physical force and requires guerrilla-style policing. All of the officers chosen to serve on the elite Drug Task Force in Pittsburgh were young men.

10. Feminist analyses have challenged this picture of domestic-violence perpetrators, arguing instead that violence is often a quite systematic attempt at being "in control."

References

Biber, Douglas, and Edward Finegan (1989). Styles of stance in English: Lexical and grammatical marking of evidentiality and affect. *Text* 9(1): 93–124.

Bordo, Susan (1990). Feminism, postmodernism, and gender-scepticism. In Linda Nicholson (ed.), *Feminism/Postmodernism*. New York: Routledge. 133–56.

Bourdieu, Pierre (1977). The economics of linguistic exchanges. *Social Science Information* 16(6): 645–68.

Butler, Judith (1990). *Gender trouble: Feminism and the subversion of identity.* New York: Routledge.

Connell, Robert W. (1987). *Gender and power: Society, the person and sexual politics.* Stanford: Stanford University Press.

Cornwall, Andrea (1994). Gendered identities and gender ambiguity among *travestis* in Salvador, Brazil. In Andrea Cornwall and Nancy Lindisfarne (eds.), *Dislocating masculinities: Comparative ethnographies.* New York: Routledge. 111–32.

Cornwall, Andrea, and Nancy Lindisfarne (1994). Dislocating masculinity: Gender, power, and anthropology. In Andrea Cornwall and Nancy Lindisfarne (eds.), *Dislocating masculinities: Comparative ethnographies.* New York: Routledge. 11–47.

Devor, Holly (1989). *Gender blending: Confronting the limits of duality.* Bloomington: Indiana University Press.

Duranti, Alessandro (1994). *From grammar to politics: Linguistic anthropology in a Western Samoan village.* Berkeley: University of California Press.

Eckert, Penelope, and Sally McConnell-Ginet (1992). Think practically and look locally: Language and gender as community-based practice. *Annual Review of Anthropology* 21: 461–90.

Ehrenreich, Barbara (1983). *The hearts of men: American dreams and the flight from commitment.* New York: Doubleday.

Ferguson, Kathy (1984). *The feminist case against bureaucracy.* Philadelphia: Temple University Press.

Foucault, Michel (1978). *The history of sexuality.* Vol. 1. New York: Pantheon.

Gal, Susan (1991). Between speech and silence: The problematics of research on language and gender. In Micaela di Leonardo (ed.), *Gender at the crossroads of knowledge.* Berkeley: University of California Press. 175–203.

Garber, Marjorie (1989). The chic of Araby: Transvestism, transsexualism, and the erotics of cultural appropriation. In Julia Epstein and Kristina Straub (eds.), *Body guards: The cultural politics of gender ambiguity.* New York: Routledge. 223–47.

——— (1991). *Vested interests.* New York: Routledge.

Garfinkel, Harold (1967). *Studies in ethnomethodology.* Englewood Cliffs, NJ: Prentice-Hall.

Garnesey, Elizabeth (1982). Women's work and theories of class and stratification. In Anthony Giddens and David Held (eds.), *Classes, power, and conflict.* Berkeley: University of California Press. 425–46.

Goffman, Erving (1971). *Relations in public.* New York: Harper & Row.

——— (1977). *Frame analysis.* New York: Harper & Row.

Goodwin, Marjorie Harness (1990). *He-said-she-said: Talk as social organization among black children.* Bloomington: Indiana University Press.

Gumperz, John (ed.) (1982a). *Language and social identity.* Cambridge: Cambridge University Press.

——— (ed.) (1982b). *Discourse strategies.* Cambridge: Cambridge University Press.

Hochschild, Arlie (1983). *The managed heart: Commercialization of human feeling.* Berkeley: University of California Press.

Humphries, Jane (1982). Class struggle and the persistence of the working-class family. In Anthony Giddens and David Held (eds.), *Classes, power, and conflict*. Berkeley: University of California Press. 470–90.

Kanter, R. M. (1977). *Women and men of the corporation*. New York: Basic Books.

Lindisfarne, Nancy (1994). Variant masculinities, variant virginities: Rethinking "honour and shame." In Andrea Cornwall and Nancy Lindisfarne (eds.), *Dislocating masculinities: Comparative ethnographies*. New York: Routledge. 82–96.

Lutz, Catherine (1986). Emotion, thought, and estrangement: Emotion as a cultural category. *Cultural Anthropology* 1(3): 287–309.

——— (1990). Engendered emotion: Gender, power, and the rhetoric of emotional control in American discourse. In Catherine Lutz and Lila Abu-Lughod (eds.), *Language and the politics of emotion*. Cambridge: Cambridge University Press. 69–91.

Maltz, Daniel, and Ruth Borker (1982). A cultural approach to male-female miscommunication. In John Gumperz (ed.), *Language and social identity*. Cambridge: Cambridge University Press. 196–216.

Martin, Susan (1980). *Breaking and entering: Policewomen on patrol*. Berkeley: University of California Press.

McElhinny, Bonnie (1993). We all wear the blue: Language, gender, and police work. Ph.D. diss., Stanford University.

——— (1994). An economy of affect: Objectivity, masculinity, and the gendering of police work. In Andrea Cornwall and Nancy Lindisfarne (eds.), *Dislocating masculinities: Comparative ethnographies*. New York: Routledge. 159–71.

Milgram, Stanley (1988). The urban experience: A psychological analysis of urban life. In George Gmelch and Walter Zenner (eds.), *Readings in urban anthropology*. Prospect Heights, IL: Waveland. 53–62.

Murray, Stephen (1985). Toward a model of members' methods for recognizing interruptions. *Language in Society* 14(1): 31–40.

Nicholson, Linda (1994). Interpreting gender. *Signs* 20(1): 79–105.

Ochs, Elinor (1988). *Culture and language development*. Cambridge: Cambridge University Press.

Ochs, Elinor, and Carolyn Taylor (this volume). The "Father knows best" dynamic in dinnertime narratives.

Rubinstein, Jonathan (1973). *City police*. New York: Farrar, Straus & Giroux.

Sattel, Jack (1983). Men, inexpressiveness, and power. In Barrie Thorne, Cheris Kramarae, and Nancy Henley (eds.), *Language, gender, and society*. Rowley, MA: Newbury House. 118–24.

Savage, Mike, and Anne Witz (eds.) (1992). *Gender and bureaucracy*. Oxford: Basil Blackwell.

Shapiro, Judith (1989). Transsexualism: Reflections on the persistence of gender and the mutability of sex. In Julia Epstein and Kristina Straub (eds.), *Body guards: The cultural politics of gender ambiguity*. New York: Routledge. 248–79.

Stone, Sandy (1989). The Empire strikes back: A posttranssexual manifesto. In Julia Epstein and Kristina Straub (eds.), *Body guards: The cultural politics of gender ambiguity*. New York: Routledge. 280–304.

Strathern, Marilyn (1988). *The gender of the gift.* Berkeley: University of California Press.

Tannen, Deborah (1984). *Conversational style: Analyzing talk among friends.* Norwood, NJ: Ablex.

U.S. Department of Justice (1987a). *Profile of state and local law enforcement agencies.* Washington, DC: Office of Justice Programs, Bureau of Justice Statistics.

—— (1987b). *Police departments in large cities.* Washington, DC: Office of Justice Programs, Bureau of Justice Statistics.

Walby, Sylvia (1992). Post–post-modernism? Theorizing social complexity. In Michèle Barrett and Anne Phillips (eds.), *Destabilizing theory: Contemporary feminist debates.* Stanford: Stanford University Press. 31–52.

Weber, Max (1968). Bureaucracy. In Guenther Roth and Claus Wittich (eds.), *Economy and society: An outline of interpretive sociology.* New York: Bedminster Press. 946–1005.

West, Candace, and Sarah Fenstermaker (1993). Power, inequality, and the accomplishment of gender: An ethnomethodological view. In Paula England (ed.), *Theory on gender/Feminism on theory.* New York: Aldine de Gruyter. 151–74.

West, Candace, and Don Zimmerman (1991). Doing gender. In Judith Lorber and Susan Farrell (eds.), *The social construction of gender.* Newbury Park, CA: Sage.

Weston, Kath (1982). *The apprenticeship and blue collar system: Putting women on the right track.* Sacramento: California State Department of Education.

Williams, Raymond (1977). *Marxism and literature.* Oxford: Oxford University Press.

Woolard, Kathryn (1985). Language variation and cultural hegemony: Toward an integration of sociolinguistic and social theory. *American Ethnologist* 12: 738–48.

10

"I Ought to Throw a Buick At You"

Fictional Representations of Butch/Femme Speech

Anna Livia

I fear a Man of frugal Speech-
I fear a Silent Man-
Haranguer -I can overtake-
Or Babbler-entertain-

But He who weigheth- While the Rest-
Expend their furthest pound-
Of this Man- I am wary-
I fear that He is Grand-

—Emily Dickinson, c. 1862

Fiction and Reality

In a "two-cultures" model of cross-sex talk, where does lesbian butch/femme dialogue fit? Because both parties are women, one might expect their conversation to reflect the findings for same-sex conversation. Yet the dichotomous nature of the butch/femme dyad suggests that butch discourse will share many of the features that recent linguistic research shows to be typical of men, and that femme discourse will be similar to feminine linguistic behavior. Do butch lesbians talk like men and femmes like women, or is butch-femme talk an autonomous realm independent of heterosexual models? How do lesbians *think* they talk? In this chapter I will be concerned not with the linguistic production of real lesbians but with fictional representations of butch/femme speech. What are the models for butch fictional dialogue, and is the femme simply the butch's conversational opposite? Literary texts present strong clues to popular perceptions, which are often very different from linguistic realities.

As one of the tools that creates and reproduces ideology, language is an important site for the construction of gendered identities. Fictional representations of starkly dichotomous identities, such as the butch/femme couple, are particularly interesting in that they refer at once to lived reality and to other fictional texts; they are unique artistic creations, and yet they build on literary traditions, genres, and conventions. The relationship between reality and its reflection in art can never be stated precisely, though many speakers (including linguistic theorists) invoke fictional characters as if they were real. I will argue that it is the intertext (the semiotic codes set up by the referential links between one text and another) rather than the co-text (the situation of a particular text in the material site of its creation) that most informs the production of the butch/femme identity. One of the main goals of this chapter will be to locate the speech of fictional butches and femmes in its own literary history.

Verbosity and Interruption

Since the publication of Robin Lakoff's groundbreaking *Language and Woman's Place* (1975), the conversational interaction of women and men has been placed under intense scrutiny by linguists. A large number of research projects were conducted on cross-sex discourse in the seventies and eighties. From these studies clear pictures emerged, first of popular conceptions of the speech characteristics of each sex, and then of the actual state of affairs. English speakers were found to believe, for example, that men's speech is "forceful, efficient, blunt, authoritative, serious, effective, sparing, masterful" and that women's speech is "weak, trivial, ineffectual, tentative, hesitant, hyperpolite, euphemistic and often marked by gossip and gibberish" (Spender 1980:33, quoting Kramer 1977). The use of the adjective *sparing* to qualify men's speech is interesting because it suggests that men speak little, weighing their words, and that women are garrulous and verbose. In keeping with this suggestion, many articles on sex differences begin with a sample of proverbs suggesting that women talk too much, as in the following examples:

> Women's tongues are like lambs' tails, they are never still. (England)
>
> The tongue is the sword of woman, and she never lets it become still. (China)

Nothing is so unnatural as a talkative man or a quiet woman.
(Scotland)

The North Sea will sooner be found wanting in water than a woman
at a loss for words. (Jutland) (Swacker 1975:76)

Many women, many words; many geese, many turds. (England) (Coates
1986:31)

When both husband and wife wear pants it is not difficult to tell them
apart—he is the one who is listening. (James and Drakich 1993:281)

It seems from these sayings that the popular perception of women is that they talk without stopping (their tongues are never still), that their talk is either inconsequential (like lambs' tails or geese droppings) or aggressive (like a sword). Delivered as statements of fact and therefore descriptive (women's words are as abundant as the waters of the North Sea), such proverbs also have a prescriptive function, warning women that if they talk too much, they will be considered at best frivolous, at worst nags, usurping the man's role (the pants).

The portraits drawn by linguists of female and male conversants are very different from these caricatures. In the research, men were shown to talk far more than women; indeed, one experiment showed men speaking for an average of thirteen minutes to women's three, with three of the male subjects talking until the thirty-minute tape ran out altogether (Swacker 1975). In a study conducted by Don Zimmerman and Candace West (1975), men interrupted 96 percent of the time to women's 4 percent. Women suggested more topics, yet men controlled topic choice. Dale Spender (1980:46) reports on a workshop on sexism and education at which there were only five men and thirty-two women, but the men talked for more than 50 percent of the time and, once again, controlled topic choice by "remaining aloof," not offering examples from personal experience. Thus, men interrupted women; men silenced women either by interruption or by ignoring them; men would not express their feelings; men dominated discussion by insisting that their subject be taken up. Women did the conversational service work by providing backchannel support, expressing agreement, linking apparently disparate conversational contributions, and suggesting topics to fill awkward silences.

The heady generalizations of the radical seventies and eighties has given way, in the more pragmatic nineties, to a nuanced approach. Long gone are the days of Valerie Solanas's SCUM Manifesto, with its glorious, outrageous, hyperprovocative vituperations:[1]

> To be male is to be deficient, emotionally limited; maleness is a
> deficiency disease. . . . The male is completely egocentric, incapable
> of empathizing or identifying with others. He is a completely
> isolated unit, . . . trapped in a twilight zone halfway between
> humans and apes. (Solanas [1968] 1983:1–2)

In the late eighties and early nineties, feminist rage has quietened, become scholarly. The studies conducted by earlier researchers have undergone reevaluation, careful verification, fine-tuning of hypotheses, and restatement of the parameters of investigation. Do men talk more in every context, or is their greater verbosity linked to particular situations, registers, or topics? What constitutes an interruption? Is it always tantamount to verbal hijacking? Is silencing active or passive? What are its effects?[2]

In a comprehensive survey, Deborah James and Janice Drakich (1993) review sixty-three studies discussing the question of gender differences in amount of talk that appeared between 1951 and 1991. Of these studies, twenty-four found that men talked more than women overall; ten found that in some circumstances men talked more and in other circumstances there was no difference; three found that in some circumstances men talked more than women and in others the positions were reversed; one found that sometimes men talked more, sometimes women talked more, and at other times the sexes talked the same amount; sixteen found no differences between the sexes; and only two found that women talked more than men. Thus, a more complex picture emerges. Yet, it is nonetheless notable that twenty-four studies found that men talked more than women, and only two found the reverse to be true. Even among the studies reporting mixed results, the findings are weighted toward men's talking more since in ten studies men either talked more or the same amount as women.

James and Drakich then ask, what are the circumstances in which men talk more than women? They analyze the findings of the previous surveys in terms of status characteristics, that is, the kinds of status involved in different social interactions. They then classify the studies according to type of task involved. Formal tasks (e.g., faculty or hospital staff meetings, a mock jury) involve high-status talk, which is goal-oriented and tends to take longer than informal tasks (e.g., "just getting to know each other"). People who have high status tend to participate more in more formal tasks. In the studies involving formal tasks, thirteen out of twenty-four found men to talk more than women, whereas only one found women to talk more. Of the sixteen studies that involved neither formal task-oriented activities nor formally structured interactions, five found men to talk more and eight found no difference between the sexes. Only one study found women to talk more. The formality of the task was shown to have a direct effect on the difference between amount of women's talk in comparison to men's talk, informal tasks tending to shorten the gap between the sexes. Although James and Drakich prefer to emphasize the different cultural expectations of amounts of talk from women and men in different contexts, deculpabilizing men by showing the cultural construction of speech rather than the inherent power imbalances, the findings of the 1970s and 1980s are still borne out in their study. Despite the popular image of the nagging wife and her taciturn husband, men tend to talk more, in almost all discourse environments, than women.

In their review of the research conducted on interruptions and gender, Deborah James and Sandra Clarke (1993) point out that although it has frequently been asserted that men interrupt women more than the other way around, in fact seventeen of thirty-two studies found no significant difference between the sexes in this regard; five found that women produce more interruptions, and only ten found men to produce more interruptions. The authors quote research showing that simultaneous talk and interruption are not necessarily the same thing (see, for example, Coates 1986). Simultaneous talk may be collaborative and supportive, or simply a matter of mistiming, rather than an attempt to seize the floor. Changing the criteria somewhat and asking whether men's interruptions are more likely to be dominance-related, James and Clarke (1993) looked at twenty-one studies that examined whether women have more interruptions directed at them than men. Of these, thirteen found that women were interrupted more often than men; only two found the opposite to be true. Women's speech was found to be significantly more "affiliative" and "facilitating," and to include "more positive socioemotional acts" (258). Although James and Clarke state, "The majority of studies have found no significant differences between the sexes" (268), I read their survey to indicate that the difference between the sexes with regard to interruption is indeed significant. Men interrupt women more often than the other way round, particularly when the discourse context involves status and competition.

Deborah Tannen (1990) offers an interpretation of the linguistic data in terms of cross-cultural differences between women and men. She argues that the two sexes have been brought up to have different expectations of conversation, so different that it is as though they come from different cultures and are acting on entirely separate sets of cultural understandings. Women, she writes, talk primarily to establish connections and negotiate relationships, and men talk to prove their independence and maintain status; she dubs these conversational styles *rapport-talk* and *report-talk*, respectively. Men speak more in the public domain, women in the private. The wife's cry, "Put down that paper and talk to me," the title of Tannen's chapter 3, represents a woman frustrated not at her inability to get a word in but at her husband's silence. Although not supporting the finding that men are more verbose regardless of context, this situation nonetheless coincides with the perception that men are reluctant to talk about personal relationships and emotional issues. Indeed, Tannen reports the case of a teenage boy who learned which college his best (male) friend was going to only after reading the school yearbook, even though the two boys spent many hours a day in each other's company.

Robin Lakoff (1992) reanalyzes the silencing of women in both the public and the private spheres, showing that the gap between the two domains is not as great as has been supposed. Because the public arena is seen as belonging to men, and women more easily occupy the private sphere, a "two cultures, mutual misunderstanding" model might have explained women's public silence. Lakoff's argument shows, however, that this cannot stand as sole explanation. The silencing of women, she argues, is directly related to the allocation of power. Noting also that women often silence other women, or become complicit in their own silence, Lakoff states, "Silencing is always political" (345). In some circumstances women's silence can become deafening, as in the silencing of Anita Hill during the Clarence Thomas confirmation hearings, for example, which exploded into a mass speak-out on sexual harassment.[3] Silence, then, can be double-edged. When its techniques are laid bare, it can work against its creator. Although women as well as men are responsible for its perpetration, the silencing of women by men still seems to preponderate over the silencing of men by women.

The Butch Model T

It is clear from the foregoing discussion that generalizations of the type *Men talk more than women; Men interrupt women; Men silence women;* and *Men do not talk about their feelings* do not reflect the situation adequately. Yet, there nevertheless emerges a picture of female/male conversational interaction in which men's talk is aimed more at establishing dominance and status, whereas women's talk is intended to build community and connection. In formal situations, where social power is at stake, men will dominate discussion; in informal situations, although the difference between the sexes is less stark, women will still perform more service work than men. With these patterns of interaction in mind, I turn to an examination of butch/femme interaction in fiction. Are butch lesbians portrayed as hogging the conversation, interrupting the femme when she tries to get a word in edgewise, silencing her when she begins to talk, changing the subject toward task-oriented discourse rather than social chitchat—a stereotyped caricature of masculine conversational behavior based loosely on the findings of linguistic research? Or is the butch lesbian taciturn and circumspect, the strong silent type that emerges from popular sayings and proverbs?

Shannon Bell (1993) describes going to a workshop entitled "Drag-King For-A-Day" at which participants are to be taught to pass as a man by Diane (Danny) Torr, a butch lesbian who frequently passes as a man. The flyer advertising the event promises, "You will learn specific gestures, phrases and tones-of-voice; and you'll be coached on the best ways to convincingly DRESS/ACT/TALK/WALK/STAND/MOVE/DANCE ETC LIKE A REAL MAN" (92). After their day of training, participants are to go to a "passing event" to see whether members of the general public will accept them as men. The bulk of the article is devoted to sartorial matters; Bell describes her own costume choices in lavish detail. When it comes to speech, their instructor advises that they should adopt "an authoritative low command-ing voice," and "take all the time in the world, talk low, say few words" (92). Torr explains that her own inspiration for the quintessential male was George Bush, then President of the United States. She watched him closely during his State of the Union Address, wondering what it was he was doing with his body to convey importance and authority when the content of his speech was so idiotic. She realized that his body language was opaque: "You can't read him."

It is ironic that Torr chose this particular role model, since Lakoff (1990:273) has described Bush as the "modern Tiresias." Lakoff points out that at the beginning of his presidency Bush's gestures and speech were so effeminate (he frequently left his sentences unfinished, used colloquial expressions in formal situations, and hedged many of his statements instead of making straightforward assertions) that his aides had to coach him into a more masculine self-presentation. The irony is that a group of butch women are being taught to talk like men by a woman who passes as a man and who gets her image of quintessential male speech from a man who had to be taught how to talk like a man by his own aides—whether female or male I know not.[4] According to Torr, men speak slowly, in low voices, and spar-ingly; their gestures are few, they communicate little with hands or face. Male dance, we are told, is "all about holding your hips still." Sneering too is apparently an important factor in the making of a male persona. Bell and

her lover "sneer at each other a few times; say 'yep' and 'nope'" (95); she
sneers at the sushi makers in a Japanese restaurant a couple of times in
order to set them at ease, as though to say, "Yep, I'm a guy." Male language,
then, as reconstructed in this workshop, is a series of short grunts accompanied by open displays of contempt or one-upmanship (that is, sneering).[5]
During her passing activity, Bell is approached by two lesbians who ask
questions that demand a response longer than three words. This blows her
cover since she replies in a long sentence; she ends up taking off her mous-
tache because, as she says, "I want to talk" (95). Real conversation, Bell
implies, is not possible as a man, though whether this is simply because
protracted talk would reveal her higher vocal register, or because real men
don't talk, is left ambiguous.

In her introduction to *The Persistent Desire: A Femme/Butch Reader*,
Joan Nestle (1992:14) characterizes femme/butch traits as "flamboyance
and fortitude—not poses, not stereotypes, but a dance between two different
kinds of women." The femme is flamboyant, spectacular, showy, highly
ornamented in dress, mannerisms, and speech, while the butch, her opposite, exhibits moral strength and stoicism, for fortitude is one of the cardinal
virtues. Interestingly enough, however, fortitude is also a passive virtue,
meaning not active courage but the ability to endure in the face of adver-
sity. "At the crux of the modern discussion about butch-femme identity is
the question of its autonomy," Nestle asserts, using the term *identity* in
place of the more common *roles*, as in the expression "butch/femme role-
playing" (14). Her book serves as an argument for the authenticity of
butch/femme characteristics; it is not an anthology or a collection but a
"reader" with explicit didactic intent. Rather than argue against the perni-
cious strength of heterosexual gender polarization, as some theorists have
done,[6] Nestle sees butch/femme identities as serving as a radical critique of
traditional gender constructs. "Many of the women who speak in this book
believe in the originality of their choices," she observes. Of a butch lesbian
who dies as "an unidentified man," Nestle remarks, "Her butch self was
not a masquerade or a gender cliché, but her final and fullest expression of
herself" (19).

Nestle's choice of words is telling. Eschewing expressions like *pose*,
masquerade, *stereotype*, and *cliché*, with their suggestions of falsity and illusion, of something copied, Nestle describes the phenomenon as a kind of
dance, an identity, an original choice, a well-rounded expression of self. If it
is a dance, it is not static or isolate; if it is original, it was there from the
beginning, fresh, new, independent, and yet in all Nestle's descriptions butch
and femme are dependent on each other for definition and even existence.

Madeline Davis (1992:268–69) similarly shrugs off the idea of role-playing: "Roles? I don't know anyone who's 'playing.'" She describes "our own special femme strength" as "surely not 'playing' but, as for our butches, truly who we are." Writing of the 1940s and 1950s, Elizabeth Kennedy and Madeline Davis (1992:62) state, "Butch-femme roles were a deeply felt expression of individual identity and a personal code guiding appearance and sexual behavior." What emerges from these different descriptions is the insistence at every turn that butch and femme lesbians' self-presentation is simply a question of their own personal identity; they walk the way they walk and talk the way they talk because that is what it is natural for them to do. Their behavior springs from within, an authentic expression of their unique selves.

"If the butch deconstructs gender, the femme constructs gender," writes Nestle (1992:16). Exactly what is meant by this statement is unclear, but its wording is nevertheless important. The two personality types are once again cast as each other's opposite. Whereas the display of masculine characteristics in a woman might disturb essentialist notions that regard masculinity as simply the sum of traits belonging to men, the extravagant ("flamboyant") femme personality picks the elements of her self-expression from among those usually attributed to women, creating unusual effects from familiar pieces. "Butch-femme self-expression [is] a lesbian-specific way of deconstructing gender," Nestle states elsewhere (14). This time the phrase *deconstructing gender* is applied to the couple as a whole instead of only to the butch, while the femme is seen as responsible for construction. The contradiction between the two statements is expressive of a contradiction in Nestle's argument. In its appeal to theories of gender construction for validation, her contention that the butch/femme dyad should be accepted as authentic and natural suffers from a built-in, no doubt unintended, irony. According to recent gender theorists, gender must at each moment be constructed. It is, as Judith Butler (1990) has pointed out, performative in the Austinian sense: a speech act that "does something." In Austin's (1962:6) own words, the term *performative* "indicates that the issuing of an utterance is the performing of an action"; that is, to say is to do, saying is an action in and of itself. The term *utterance* has been expanded to refer to any semiotic system, not just language. Gender is performed by the selection of particular semiotic items encoding gender information; it is not natural or innate; it does not spring full-grown from within. Instead it is a highly sophisticated learned behavior. Nestle's presentation of the femme/butch dyad is essentialist, but the deconstruction of gender entails a radically antiessentialist critique. A deconstructionist approach to the linguistic studies referred to at the beginning of this chapter would involve asking not how women and men interact in conversation, labeling the discourse habits of women *feminine* and the discourse habits of men *masculine,* but rather how "the feminine" or "the masculine" is constructed without tying it necessarily to one gender or another. Such an approach would allow for the possibility of butch women and femme men.

If masculinity is learned behavior that either women or men can exhibit, where is butch conversational behavior learned? Gayle Rubin (1992:467) states explicitly that *"Butch* is the lesbian vernacular term for women who are more comfortable with masculine gender codes, styles, or identities than with feminine ones." Kennedy and Davis (1992) note in their study of the Buffalo lesbian bar community that butches cultivated masculine mannerisms including tone of voice, surrounding themselves not with camp humor (as did gay men) but with an aura of solemnity (a term that echoes Nestle's "fortitude"). Butches projected an image of toughness: if they were in a bar and someone called their name, they would not turn around smiling, because such a reaction would have been interpreted as sissy behavior and they would have lost face. This cult of emotionless and expressionless masculinity bears a stronger resemblance to the ethos of the Drag-King-For-A-Day workshop than it does to the findings of the various studies done on female-male conversational interactions quoted earlier.

The Persistent Desire intermingles theoretical articles with excerpts from short stories and novels.[7] The implicit message is that fictional representations and personal accounts give equally valid testimonies of authentic butch and femme speech. In her incisive and cogently argued article "Of Catamites and Kings: Reflections on Butch, Gender, and Boundaries," Rubin (1992:469) examines the iconography of the butch paragon in contemporary lesbian periodicals, a character who is, she notes, "semiotically related to a long line of images of young, rebellious, sexy, white working-class masculinity." Rubin mentions various well-known butches from lesbian classics to show the range of butch lesbianhood, such as Ann Bannon's Beebo Brinker, heroine of four novels first published in the fifties and sixties, and Stephen Gordon of Radclyffe Hall's *The Well of Loneliness,* first published in England in 1928. Many of the nonfiction contributors to the anthology also call on images from popular novels or films to clarify points they make about real-life women. Rita Laporte (1992:209), for example, remarks that if a strange butch says hello to another's "chick," she gets slugged "in the best barroom brawl tradition." It is important to note that the "tradition" referred to here is not one from the author's own personal experience but from Hollywood westerns featuring classic film stars like

John Wayne. Lyndall MacCowan (1992:315) laments, "I might wish for a butch lover like Beebo Brinker, but butch in the seventies was a cartoon. Mighty Mo from Rita Mae Brown's *Rubyfruit Jungle* is a "diesel dyke" whose approach is to "barrel down . . . slam on the brakes . . . and bellow." Of a former lover Madeline Davis (Davis, Hollibaugh, & Nestle 1992:261) says, "Her name was Dawn, but she was Beebo Brinker," identifying the woman completely with the fictional character. She mentions Beebo Brinker twice more on the same page—"I was in love with Beebo Brinker"; "She was . . . a short chunky version of Beebo Brinker"—and another speaker comments, "Old Beebo really didn't come through with it." In "A Letter," Judy Lederer (1992:96) relates how she summoned up the courage to go to her first gay bar, dressed as butch as she could manage, only to be greeted by a howl of "Oh my God, Millie, it's Prince Valiant." Prince Valiant is the hero of a cartoon strip from the 1930s, featuring a medieval Briton. Thus, the real-life butch is continually compared with Hollywood characters and other fictional images. Often, the comparative element is lost and the description stands not as a simile but as an existential: *It's Prince Valiant*; *She was Beebo Brinker*. Is the construction of femme and butch fictional characters based correspondingly on reference to real-life heroines and heroes, the characters' speech a recognizable imitation of that of idealized women and men?

The Butch Grunt Syndrome

An analysis of the portrait of Miss Ogilvy in the white upper-class British writer Radclyffe Hall's ([1926] 1992) short story "Miss Ogilvy Finds Herself" (first published in 1926 and reprinted in *The Persistent Desire*) reveals much about the fictional butch. After a glorious but all too brief career as the lieutenant commander of a unit of female ambulance drivers during the First World War, Miss Ogilvy returns to England and a more sedate existence as a relatively impoverished, unmarried gentlewoman with two unmarried sisters. In the opening scene, Miss Ogilvy listens to one of her "girls" complaining in a "high, rather childish voice" about the breakup of the unit. To this Miss Ogilvy responds merely, "Oh," with rising intonation which is, we are told, "her method of checking emotion" (25). Emotion is for femmes (the "girls"); the butch must make an effort to stifle hers. Instead, she pats her car "as though she would say: 'Yes I know how it feels—never mind, we'll go down together.'" Unspoken communication with her beloved and trusty car must take the place of real verbal interaction with her former subordinates. In this she conforms well to the finding of studies showing that men prefer not to talk about emotions, engaging instead in task-oriented talk. Even when not in the grip of some powerful emotion, Miss Ogilvy finds it hard to talk to other women: "Towards young girls and women she was shy and respectful, apologetic and sometimes admiring" (27). She prefers the company of men, wanting to share their sport and business interests. Like the male participants in the studies quoted above, Miss Ogilvy is more comfortable in the formal or public arena.

Grown used to the unhedged imperatives of military commands, Miss Ogilvy continues to use this form back home with her sisters. "'Stop sneezing!'" she orders, "in the voice that had so much impressed the Unit." When her sisters tell her to grow her hair, she responds with her famous "Oh?" silencing them and putting an end to further discussion. There is a stark contrast between her mother's and sisters' way of articulating requests and her own. Her mother uses modalized expressions like "You might see to that"; "I wish you'd go down" (personalized in terms of her mother's desires); "Do run over" (the intensifier *do* betraying a lack of power, an admission that an imperative will not be heeded on its own), and her sisters phrase their request in terms of a question, "Will you let your hair grow again?" Now that Miss Ogilvy is no longer in the public arena, however, her status as an officer and honorary gentleman is eroded. Unhedged imperatives are out of place from a sister among sisters, and Miss Ogilvy begins to "insist" instead of order. She forgets "to say 'Oh?' quite so often as expediency demanded" (30) and enters into domestic disputes with the same venom and pettiness she has previously attributed to her sisters: when they tell her they are now vegetarians she calls them "two damn tiresome cranks!" (29). She feels her self-respect being whittled away by the necessity to speak like a woman and comes to question whether she had indeed ever "issued orders."

One day Miss Ogilvy abruptly announces "I'm off" (31), the grunting monosyllables indicating that she has retained something of her former butch persona and must leave before the rot goes too far. She returns to an Anglo-Saxon tribe of cavemen with blue tattoos and "extremely hairy legs" (34). Now at last she—or rather *he*, for Miss Ogilvy has become "a young man"—can speak the way she was intended to. Hurling a stone, for example, he comments tersely, "Good! Strong!" (34). When his woman fashions a pretty speech culminating in a pretty little harvest metaphor, "For you. All of me is for you and none other. For you this body has ripened," he replies with a bipartite grunt: "You . . . woman." Fortunately the narrator is on hand to explain Miss Ogilvy/the young man's intent: "His speech was slow and lacking in words when it came to expressing a vital emotion, so one word must suffice" (35). The word *woman*, we are told, meant "little spring of exceedingly pure water" (or innocence, perhaps); "hut of peace for a man after battle" (or rest and recreation); "ripe red berry sweet to the taste" (sex); "happy small home of future generations" (fertility) (35). Because of their love for each other, his woman understood all this too. "With her it was different, love had taught her love's speech." She is therefore able to command much more complicated registers of language and emotion. "My master; blood of my body," she croons happily at one moment, darkening this joyful image later with the worrisome thought, "My father is a still black cloud full of thunder." In contrast, the young man's finest expression of love is the double-headed snort "You . . . mine." This so impresses him with its emotional intensity that instead of speaking out clearly, he is impelled to stammer.

Although separated by nearly sixty years, Frenchy, the butch heroine of white working-class American Lee Lynch's (1985) *The Swashbuckler*, bears a strong family resemblance to Miss Ogilvy, especially in regard to her speech patterns. Just as Miss Ogilvy prefers to discuss sport with the men, so Frenchy likes to talk baseball with the other butches. Like Miss Ogilvy, Frenchy's "shyness with the other girls" contrasts markedly with her self-confident, authoritative behavior on what she considers her own turf. For Miss Ogilvy this "home turf" was, paradoxically perhaps, First World War France; for Frenchy it is the gay bars of Greenwich Village where she is "a prince, a sharp dancer, a big tipper" (3). Frenchy and her butch friend Jessie are adept at sexual conquest (like the caveman/Miss Ogilvy) but lousy at small talk, and feel out of place in a group of women. Jessie wishes she could get a job loading trucks, sighing that at her job, typing for an insurance company, "Alls I do is listen to the girls gossip." Frenchy agrees, "I know what you mean. The other cashiers never shut up" (5).

The language Frenchy uses with regard to femmes is that of sexual innuendo, conquest, and possession. Describing the women she works with, she tells Jessie, "'There's a cute new girl. . . . A little blonde. Wears these tight black sweaters. . . . Wish I could make her.' She grinned lasciviously" (5). Flirting with her femme, Frenchy grins, "I wouldn't mind a night locked up with you, beautiful." This contrasts strongly with her tongue-tied silence in the face of female gossip. Frenchy's relationship with her girlfriend Donna is described in terms of personal property, not dissimilar to Miss Ogilvy's "you . . . mine" approach. "'I don't want you fooling around like that.' 'Why not? It's a free country.' 'Yeah, but you're my girl'" (12). Flirting lazily with Frenchy's femme, the waitress asks, "Still got the shackles on Donna, huh?" She tells Donna to let her know when she's free, but turns immediately to Frenchy to reassure her, "I wouldn't touch her" (11). Donna is Frenchy's property and no other butch can touch her; to be found even casually talking to her could cause trouble. Like Miss Ogilvy, Frenchy does not discuss, she relies on the sparser vocabulary of social gesture. Frenchy gets jealous, despite the fact that she is planning to break up with Donna that night anyway. "Let's dance," she says to Donna; the suggestion is more of an order, accompanied as it is by a rough tug pulling Donna from the booth onto the floor. Once again, the butch does not discuss her feelings, but transforms them into action, in this case a public display of possession.

To convey the mood for this situation Little Anthony and the Imperials sing "Tears on My Pillow." When Jessie announces her breakup with her girlfriend, she expresses her feelings of loss by reference to another popular hit. "It's like that song, 'It's all in the game,'" she says. Frenchy agrees, "Love is some game," and the subject is changed. Later that night, when Frenchy finds a new femme, she sings "Will You Still Love Me Tomorrow?" to herself, the adverb *tomorrow* implying that she will sleep with the woman that night (17). Not mentioned, but undoubtedly familiar to both Frenchy and her girlfriend, is another line of this well-known Carole King song, *Tonight you're mine completely*, making Frenchy's song a song of triumph. Again, instead of creating her own original discourse, Frenchy relies on cultural commonplaces to speak for her. The playing of the popular music of the day turns out to be an important part of butch/femme courting. Merrill Mushroom (1993), in her short story "How to Engage in Courting Rituals 1950s Butch-style in the Bar," specifically mentions "Ritual #3: The Playing of the Jukebox" as "an especially good ritual if you are not ready to approach the woman directly" (214). The fictional butch is, it seems, rarely ready to approach the woman directly, if *approaching* means 'talking to.'

The linguistic attributes of the butches and femmes in *The Swashbuckler* are repeated in each of the other fictions analyzed in this chapter. The butches speak little, much less than their femme counterparts; frequently limit their responses to monosyllabic grunts or use physical gestures instead of words to convey their meaning; are chary of expressing emotion, often letting song lyrics speak for them; and their vocabulary as concerns femmes is one of possession and sexual innuendo. The use of song lyrics to convey emotions that the butch is unable to express is particularly noticeable in (Irish/Filipino American) Chea Villanueva's (1992) short story "In the Shadow of Love." Two girls are making out on the sofa while the father of one of them sleeps in front of the television. Fearful of waking the father, the girls cannot talk; instead, from the TV Diana Ross and the Supremes sing "Whisper you love me, boy . . . you know how to talk to me, baby" (222). It is particularly ironic in this example that the boy addressed by Diana Ross is told that he knows how to talk to his girlfriend, but at the same time seems to need instructions on what to say, while the song itself stands for what the butch lover cannot say to her woman. When the relationship is discovered, the butch is sent to reform school, and the femme remains at a convent. The butch escapes and goes to wait for her femme. "Ain't no mountain high enough, ain't no valley low enough, ain't no river wide enough to take me away from you," she sings to herself, with all the wishfulness and bravado she is unable to voice. After the breakup of the relationship, the butch mourns as she listens to Carole King singing, "Tonight you're mine completely, you give your love so sweetly," with its sad chorus, "Will you still love me tomorrow?" (224). The manipulation of the lyrics of popular songs of the sixties can be quite subtle, the same lines quoted in different contexts to very different effects. Where Frenchy in *The Swashbuckler* uses "Will You Still Love Me Tomorrow?" as her triumph song, the butch of "In the Shadow of Love" (itself another song title) finds the same words full of loss and longing.

There are variations on the popular lyric as emotional expression theme. In Nisa Donnelly's (1989) *The Bar Stories*, the white butch Babe who "talked like a longshoreman" (a stereotype of working-class male speech) is continually unfaithful to her long-suffering femme, Sharon. Sharon imagines turning the tables, making Babe be the one to wait long, anxious hours until she gets home, but even in her fantasy Sharon is still left "waiting for the words from Babe that wouldn't come" (348). She finds Babe at the bar, where *The Maltese Falcon* is playing on the television. Together they sit quietly "watching Humphrey Bogart playing a deadly game." Finally Sharon tells Babe her fears: "I woke up and you were gone . . . and . . . for the first time I was afraid, really afraid you were gone." To this touching speech, Babe replies with the usual butch monosyllables ("usual" in terms of fictional butches, that is), "Not gone, just not home." In this case it is scenes from *The Maltese Falcon* that fill in for Babe's silence (the reference to film noir will be discussed further on). Sharon's frustration is vividly presented: "Sharon pressed, prodding, trying to find the point that would prick this flatness that had settled over Babe's face, trying to make her bleed, scream, do anything but sit there as quietly frozen as Humphrey Bogart's Maltese Falcon" (351), echoing, in heightened form, the classic situation depicted in Tannen's (1990) *You Just Don't Understand* in which the husband picks up the paper and refuses to talk to his wife (a running theme of Tannen's Chapter 3). Like a reluctant hippopotamus giving in to pressure, Babe tells Sharon shortly that she loved some of the women she had affairs with, but never as she loved Sharon. Then, moving from terse speech to action, she offers Sharon a drink, a gesture that Sharon recognizes as "a signal the conversation was over." When contemplating a sexual conquest, on the other hand, Babe shows herself to be slick-tongued and quick-witted. Marty, a new barmaid, is studying women's studies, occasioning Babe's comment, "I've been studying women most of my life. You need a teacher at that college of yours?" Marty asks her what her field is. "Pussy," Babe replies. Marty jokes that Babe wants to tutor her, to which Babe responds, "Think you need it?" Then, "without a word," Babe reaches over and takes Marty's hand in her own. "When can you start?" she asks (210). Where the femmes' speech is original, articulate, and emotional, the butches' is conventional, restricted.

Beebo Brinker, a character frequently exalted as the image of the perfect butch, is less provocatively coarse-tongued than Babe, her banter more teasing. "Sweet sixteen and never been kissed," she laughs lightly at her friend Laura. Laura corrects her with a snap, "Twenty." "Your innocence is getting tedious, lover," responds Beebo. At which Laura explodes, "Beebo, I don't like you. I don't like the way you dress, or the way you talk or the way you wear your hair. I don't like the things you say" (Bannon [1959] 1986:84). What Laura doesn't like, it seems, is Beebo's straightforward expression of sexual desire. On occasion Beebo is capable of forceful, pertinent rejoinders, as when Laura screams, after the two of them have slept together, "You're nothing but a dirty animal." "What were you last night, Miss Prim?" Beebo snaps back. "You were panting at me like a sow in rutting season" (97). At other times, however, Beebo, like the other butches discussed here, lapses into silence. Laura turns on Beebo: "You're ridiculous. You're a little girl pretending to be a little boy. And you run an elevator for the privilege. Grow up, Beebo. You'll never be a little boy. Or a big boy. . . . You can wear pants till you're blue in the face and it won't change what's underneath" (175). This time, Beebo just stares at Laura, and leaves in silence.

Butch Al, a character who features prominently in Leslie Feinberg's (1993) *Stone Butch Blues*, is "gruff" with the heroine Jess, a much younger butch, as well as short of speech, but her rich repertoire of physical gestures is easily interpretable. She musses the kid's hair, hugs her shoulders, whistles in appreciation of a new sports coat. When Jess asks Butch Al's femme to dance, Butch Al merely lets her shadow fall across the kid, saying nothing, and when another butch taunts Jess's lack of sexual prowess with the sneer, "Hey, femme, wanna dance with a real butch?" Al hits the contemptuous outsider, holding her for Jess to do likewise. In a butch father-to-son talk about the correct use of dildos, the dialogue begins promisingly:

"You know what that is?"
"Sure."
"You know what to do with it?"
"Sure."
(30)

It is Al's femme, Jackie, who has to explain what the mysterious "noon and midnight" stuff is all about. Jackie bursts out laughing, "You can't learn to fuck from reading *Popular Mechanics*," an incisive comment on her butch's hydraulic explanations. She proceeds to let the young and innocent Jess in on a few femme secrets about women's feelings and the need for respect. Later Butch Al is arrested by the police in a routine raid on the local gay bar and subsequently raped and beaten. Al refuses to talk about her experience. Once again it is Jackie's role to explain, "It's hard for Al to say everything she feels" (37). This is quite an understatement, for Butch Al never says anything about her feelings in the whole of the story.

A champion of the butch grunt syndrome is the narrator of Sally Bellerose's (1992) short story "Redheads." Her conversation with her girl-friend's husband is a three-line classic of the genre. The husband's car has a dead battery and the narrator offers to jump-start it, whereupon they "start talking cars":

"Nice car," he says.
"Thanks," I say.
"69?" he asks. (356)

After this intricate piece of butch/male bonding the two new buddies go off to the bar leaving a two-grunt note for the girlfriend/wife who is toiling with the groceries. "Next door," it says, gnomically. There is enough in the tone of these interchanges to suggest that Bellerose may have in mind a gentle parody of the butch/femme genre. The narrator and her femme book into the "Jungle Room" at a motel and proceed to call each other *Tarzan* and *Jane* in recognition of their hypermasculine and hyperfeminine roles. But the life-sized cheetahs who chase each other around the wallpaper are a little too exaggerated, a little too camp, for a straightforward portrait of a butch/femme couple. An analysis of the techniques used in parody will prove useful in our examination of the linguistic models upon which butch/femme conversational interaction is based.

The depictions of butch and femme speech characteristics in the fictional works analyzed above (with the exception of Bellerose's short story) are intended as sincere expressions of real-life talk. Yet, they portray butches as predominantly silent, emotionally mute, but sexually aggressive types who are quicker with their fists and other physical gestures than with words, and who speak mostly to claim possession of their femmes. Although some of these traits do correspond to an admittedly exaggerated portrait of male speech as constructed by linguistic studies, they are more of a stereotype than an actuality and in one important particular contradict those findings. The majority of studies show that men talk, in all circumstances, more than women. The silent man is a statistical rarity; how then did taciturn masculinity come to figure so prominently in the portrayal of butch lesbian characters? Nonfictional accounts of butch/femme speech present rather different conversational traits than those seen in fictional representations. Reminiscing about a past relationship, Sky Vanderlinde (1992) observes that at the beginning she (the femme) was wary of expressing her feelings and her butch interpreted her emotions. Four times in two pages Vanderlinde recalls this butch lover talking about her past: "Blue began telling me her stories"; "Blue continued to woo me with the stories of her life"; "more stories of her life in New Orleans"; "I relived the stories of her life" (231–32). Her new friend is, in fact, so chatty that people call her "the lesbian mayor of New York" and she stops at the corner of nearly every street to say hello to someone. Clearly, in real life the butch partner may talk far more than her femme lover.

The image of butch talk as full of sexual innuendo and stories of recent conquests is, likewise, not borne out by butches' own accounts. In their investigation into the Buffalo lesbian community, for example, Kennedy and Davis (1992:71) note that one particular butch was adamantly against "men's locker room talk about women: Even though they talk to me as a butch or a man . . . they will not talk to me the way they talk to their locker room buddies. . . . I don't want to hear that. . . . I wouldn't allow it for a minute. . . . I am a woman and you're gonna treat me like one." This woman refuses to listen to stories of sexual prowess and speculation not just out of chivalry for "the weaker sex" but because she would feel herself implicated in it. "I am a woman," she insists, despite her butch appearance. In her account of her "woman poppa" (an ultrabutch characterization) Nestle (1992) relates how her lover drives a forklift and is obliged to listen to the anti-Semitic, racist, misogynist jokes of her male coworkers. When they start on rape jokes, she speaks out: "Don't talk that shit around me" (348). Rubin (1992:469) points out that "there are at least as many ways to be butch as there are ways for men to be masculine," and Nestle herself lists some of the variations: the courtly butch, the femme wife, the punk femme, the butch bottom, the femme slut, the street butch, the bulldagger and her lady, the lesbian-feminist femme, the movement butch, the tomboy, and the stone butch. However, as we have seen above, very few of these possibilities make their way into fiction, which is mostly limited to versions of the bulldagger and her lady. In parody, however, new images emerge, many stating explicitly both their origin and their import.

One of the stories included in Nestle's anthology, "Jacky and the Femme" by Lee Lynch (1985) (who also wrote *The Swashbuckler*, discussed above), works as a parody of lesbian-feminist ideas that would condemn butch/femme behavior as an imitation of the heterosexual model and criticize the vocabulary of sexual possession as exploitative. The white heroine, Jacky, is first seen eating a "gardenburger" and drinking Red Zinger herbal tea, both semiotically marked as hyperhealthy but dull and therefore feminist food choices. Jacky can't help noticing that the cook at the diner looks like a man and calls Jacky's girlfriend *babe*. "You mind me giving your lady a squeeze?" the cook asks her. Jacky is affronted that the cook not only looks like a man but thinks and talks like one too. "What a sexist thing to ask," she protests, "like I own you." She discovers during the short pages of this short short story that she rather likes the butch/femme way of doing things. "Oh Goddess," she says in horror, "what if it's not being sexist I'm afraid of at all? ... what if I'm just plain afraid of being a real queer?" Although Jacky is a parody of feminist righteousness (the feminized exclamation *Oh Goddess*, the Red Zinger, and the gardenburger are a mite too much to take seriously), the cook's speech is that of a classic fictional butch. Jacky's exclamation underlines the notion of authenticity that is one of the *raisons d'être* of Nestle's anthology: real queers divide off into butch/femme units, and real butches talk like the cook.

The butch/femme conversational practice examined so far appears more in the work of white lesbian writers; Black women writing on lesbian themes do not seem to use the same forms of dialogue in their fiction. Audre Lorde (1982) reports in *Zami* that in 1956 most Black lesbians she knew of were in the closet due to the pressures of racism and homophobia, so those who were out felt "you'd better come on so tough that nobody messed with you" (224). This suggests that tough speech was a reaction to an oppressive situation, not an innate characteristic or a way of distinguishing masculine from feminine lesbians. Lorde often felt intimidated by butch self-presentation. She expresses the fear that "the black women I usually saw around the Bag [Bagatelle—a gay bar] were into heavy roles," and sees these roles as forced on the Black women concerned "by white america's racist distortions of beauty." "Black women playing 'femme' had very little chance in the Bag. Butches wanted the most gorgeous femme, as defined by white male standards," Lorde explains (224). Though she mentions that she and her friends owned some "well-thumbed copies" of Ann Bannon's Beebo Brinker novels, the conversational interchanges recorded in Lorde's "biomythography" do not reflect butch/femme discourse.

In Ann Allen Shockley's (1982) *Say Jesus and Come to Me* the Reverend Myrtle Black, a charismatic Black preacher, and Travis Lee, a Black jazz singer, become lovers. They are not out in their community, the Universal Church for All People, and the gay bar scene does not feature in the novel. In the face of such remarks as "Lesbians are something that can't be dealt with in the black community," Myrtle feels it is safer to keep her own sexual orientation hidden. Her seduction speech to Travis is not butch but biblical: "I will save you. . . . Come to Him through me. . . . Praise the Lord—Travis Lee is one of us!" (146–47). Their consequent bed dialogue is more egalitarian than butch/femme, each woman echoing the other:

> "I want to take you to bed," says Myrtle.
> "I want you to," says Travis.
> "I can't get enough of you."
> "Nor I of you." (157–58)

Myrtle is the more commanding of the two: "We'll do it this way—first," she says (157), the first-person plural masking a unilateral decision on her part. "'We are going to do it another way,' she commanded softly" (160). Here the narrator's use of the verb *commanded* makes it clear that this constitutes an order, despite the use of the first-person plural, but the adverb *softly* mitigates its force and it has none of the unquestionable authority of Miss Ogilvy's *Stop sneezing!*

The main characters of Jewelle Gomez's (1991) *The Gilda Stories* are Black lesbian vampires, and their conversation follows the protocol of the undead rather than that of twentieth-century butch/femme convention.[8] When Effie confronts Gilda with her own desires ("You are scampering around inside of your own thoughts when you should be joining with mine" (212)), Gilda makes no answer, allowing the words of one of her own songs to speak for her. The song includes the line "You are the life I've searched for and found" (201), an affirmative answer to Effie's request. Gomez's vampires are, however, scrupulously egalitarian, more so even than Shockley's Reverend and her jazz singer, and it would be hard to say one character was more butch or femme than another. Lapsing into silence at moments of emotional intensity and allowing the words of a song to speak for one, a feature typical of many of the butch characters in the novels by white writers examined so far, has another significance in a different ethnic setting.

Gomez's (1993) story "Don't Explain" makes this clear. Letty and Delia are both Black waitresses at a diner. One evening, Delia invites Letty to come over to meet a few friends and play cards. When she arrives, Letty realizes from the way the women are absorbed in each other that they, like her, are lesbians, although no one mentions this fact. She sits on a sofa with another Black woman and listens in silence to the Billie Holiday song "Don't Explain." As Billie sings, "Hush now, don't explain / Just say you'll remain," even though Letty has heard this song a hundred times before, "They both listened to Billie together, for the first time" (282). This silence does not come from an inability to speak, to find the right words, or to express oneself emotionally, but from a participation in the music, which lifts these two individual Black lesbians into the strength, legend, and tragedy of Billie Holiday. Letty becomes a larger, richer character from her intertextual ties not only to Gilda, another Black blues singer, heroine of Gomez's *The Gilda Stories*, but also to Travis Lee, the Black blues singer of Shockley's (1982) *Say Jesus and Come to Me*. Although there may be traces here and there of butch and femme dialogue among these novels by African American female writers, the stronger links are to other patterns of discourse—the preacher, for example, or the jazz singer.

Parody

Alongside the "sincere" presentations of butch/femme conversation by white lesbian writers is a whole subgenre of parodic versions such as Anna Wilson's (1984) short story "The Reach"; Claire Macquet's (1991) "The Sparrow"; Mary Wings's (1992) *Divine Victim*; and Ellen Galford's (1994) *The Dyke and The Dybbuk*. The most explicit of these in its parodic intentions is "The Reach," in which Elizabeth, a worldly London lesbian, goes to a more remote part of the country and is picked up in a bar by Amy, "a very, very butch dyke." The story's opening line is a skillful imitation of a Raymond Chandler opening, or rather a pastiche of various of his opening lines: "She was the kind of dyke you can identify at a thousand paces—or could anyway if you weren't heavily myopic as I am, and knew a thousand paces when you see them, which I never have" (9). Like "The Reach," Chandler's *The Pencil* ([1959] 1971) begins with a third-person cataphoric pronoun for which an identifying description must be sought further on in the text: "He was a slightly fat man with a dishonest smile that pulled the corners of his mouth out half an inch." The use of a cataphor (*she* in "The Reach," *he* in *The Pencil*) as the first word of a work of fiction is a broad hint to the reader that the character referred to thereby will be of great importance in the story, especially if the story itself is told in the first person, as both "The Reach" and the Chandler mysteries are. The narrator, Elizabeth, assumes enough familiarity with the character introduced that the pronominal reference, with its high presuppositional status (the use of a pronoun *presupposes* the existence of a referent, as opposed to stating it) will be adequate for identification. The reader is thus asked to behave as though she or he is likewise already familiar with the character, to put a pin in the slot occupied by the pronoun and await further information.

Another Chandler ([1933] 1956) title, *Blackmailers Don't Shoot*, begins, "The man in the powder-blue suit—which wasn't powder blue under the lights of the Club Bolivar—was tall." In its immediate negation of the proposition it has just presented, this opening also parallels that of "The Reach." The first character presented in Wilson's story was, we are told, "the kind of dyke you can recognize at a thousand paces," except that the person telling us this is unable to recognize a thousand paces and is, what's more, very short-sighted. Chandler's "man in the powder-blue suit" is, similarly, not really wearing a powder-blue suit at all at the time when our informant first sets eyes on him. The effect in Chandler's novel is to inform the reader that she or he is privy to the thoughts of an extremely smart observer, so smart that he is able to tell the real color of the suit despite the bad lighting under which he first sees it. The effect of Wilson's parody, on the other hand, is to tell the reader that the narrator is not necessarily a reliable witness, an idea that would be intolerable in Chandler's description of master private eye Philip Marlowe. It is her careful imitation and deliberate undermining of Chandler's style that makes Wilson's work a parody, and a very successful one. The knowledgeable reader is able to recognize both the model and the deviation.

But why is Wilson parodying Chandler in her comic version of the butch heroine? Chandler scarcely mentions lesbians in his depiction of the underworld sleuthing of his macho superdetective. Why does Wilson not imitate and subvert some of the classics of the butch/femme genre discussed above? The reason is complicated, going back to the roots of the genre itself. Wilson does indeed poke gentle fun at images of stereotypically butch lesbians and her heroine's attraction to just those qualities. "We all know that dykes aren't allowed to be like that anymore. We put our collars and ties away when enlightenment came and followed our fresh-faced little sisters into utility clothing and combat boots," says the narrator (9–10), recounting the ideological move from the role-playing of the forties and fifties to the egalitarian feminism of the sixties and seventies. The exaggerated term *enlightenment*, used to describe this sociopolitical development, is a clue that the account is intended as a parody rather than a sincere report. "She probably went home at night and whipped her wife," thinks Elizabeth (11), making a reference to extreme depictions of butch/femme relationships as sado-masochistic. The lack of quotation marks around the term *wife* is, again, a sign that the reader should not take this statement as an accurate reflection of Elizabeth's thoughts and beliefs concerning the unknown butch in the bar. She is mocking the whole situation and, in particular, the polarity between her own position as a lesbian feminist and the assumed position of the other woman as a butch who is still "identifying with the guards as though there were no tomorrow" (10). The point of the parody becomes clear at the end of the story when it is revealed that the unknown butch has deliberately taken on a recognizably lesbian appearance in order to entice Elizabeth to come home with her to a secret lesbian-separatist community. The other members of the community openly laugh at the butch's success-ful disguise. "Still falling for the old dyke routine, are they?" they joke, and turning to Elizabeth, "Do you normally fancy very very butch dykes?"

In Wilson's short story there are continual references to the butch's odd speech habits and to the whole setup as reflective of some fictional conven-tion. Elizabeth, musing on the possibility that the locals would kill her cat or chickens if she had any, cheers herself up with the reflection that this may be a "Hollywood concept" that has not yet reached these parts. Elizabeth asks Amy, "Where are you taking me?" and reflects, "It was irritatingly reminis-cent of the script as given to helpless kidnapped damsels." *Kidnapped damsels* is hardly a contemporary reference but, rather, part of medieval legend and the knights of the Round Table. Elizabeth is told she is being taken home to meet "us" and comments, "There was her odd language," and again later, "There was that script" (15)—the term *script* suggesting that Amy's language is not simply her natural form of expression but, indeed, a prewritten speech according to established convention.

Amy's script is unusual. Despite her leather jacket and untipped Players (both of which serve as semiotic references to working-class masculinity: Players were seen as masculine, he-man cigarettes, especially when smoked without filters), Amy does not talk the way the fictional butch should talk. After losing a game of pool to Amy (theirs is clearly not a butch/femme encounter because the femme is supposed to watch the butch play, not take her on), Elizabeth revises her assumptions about the way Amy should speak. Informed that Amy has chosen her own name instead of keeping the one her parents gave her, Elizabeth tries to fit the name change to her idea of the usual motivation for such an act: lesbian feminists' dropping their fathers' surnames in favor of less patriarchal ones. This doesn't work either, however. "I'm poet and outrider," Amy explains, "so the name fits."

Elizabeth makes a mental note to herself, "I had a feeling that I should be paying attention to what she was saying. It didn't seem to be quite what I expected" (13). It is not quite what the reader is expecting either. This serves as a message to the reader to watch for the script, to be aware of literary conventions and of fictional characters as participating in those conventions. The short story ends with a framing device that makes explicit reference to its status as a work of fiction: "The foregoing fragment is transcribed from the first few pages of a notebook found on a rain-soaked rubbish tip" (i.e., a garbage heap). The fictional butch, then, is a literary convention, her dialogue every bit as stylized as the "helpless kidnapped damsel" who wails hopelessly, "Where are you taking me?"

References to other literary genres and conventions as models for butch/femme representations abound in the parodies of butch/femme fiction. In Mary Wings's (1992) *Divine Victim*, for example, the heroine ends up in what appears to be the only gay bar in the whole of Montana. Regaled at the door by a Latino Shirley MacLaine, a white Roberta Flack, and a Carol Channing look-alike doing a lip-synched rendition of "Hello Dolly," the heroine sighs, "I miss San Francisco. None of these drag queens have beards." She is promptly chastised by one of the barmen, "What's the matter? You only take queens as cultural commentary?" The male drag queens in the bar base their speech on that scripted for Hollywood actresses in hyperfeminine roles, dressing like female singers and mouthing the lyrics of popular songs. The sophisticated heroine, representing the sophisticated reader, expects these displays of archfemininity to be undermined by some essentially masculine item, such as a beard. The *camp talk* of gay men[9] is characterized by imitation of the stereotypically feminine and then undermined by a solely masculine reference. In *Another Mother Tongue*, for example, Judy Grahn (1984:32), recounts being arrested during a police raid on a bar; in the holding cells the queens defended themselves with camp theatricality, "Alice Blue Gown [a camp term for a police officer] tried to sit on *my* nightstick but I said, 'No. You dirty boy! I know you're menthrating!'" The humor of this remark lies in its mixing of feminine and masculine codes. The drag queen is lisping (the /s/ of *menstruating* becomes a /θ/—pronounced *th*—and the second syllable is lost) in a representation of the effeminate, yet the mention of his nightstick—the penis—is a purely masculine image; moreover, the male police officer is given the feminine name *Alice* and is said to be bleeding like a woman.

Although there are references to gangster movies in Ellen Galford's (1994) *The Dyke and the Dybbuk*—for example, Anya, the antiheroine, has a "gun straight out of a B-movie props department" (214)—the dominant frame of reference is that of a cowboy film. Like the typical fictional butch, Anya is monosyllabic and unemotional, but unlike the typical portrayal, this speech representation makes clear its origin in the dialogue of cowboys in Hollywood westerns, with a little extra hardness thrown in from mobster films by way of reinforcement. Anya is also referred to in passing as *James Cagney*. Having saved Rainbow, the heroine, from drowning, Anya "adjusts her mirror-lensed sunglasses, yanks down her hat brim," and shrugs off Rainbow's gratitude with the unemotional "Well, I'll be off" that we have come to expect of the fictional butch. Rainbow and her dybbuk (a kind of personalized devil from Jewish legend) follow the prints of Anya's "richly tooled cowboy boots" not to a tethered horse "as we are somehow both expecting" but to a small car. "Something familiar about that one," Rainbow comments. "Yep," the dybbuk replies, "last seen riding into town in *A Fistful of Dollars*" (170). The conventions of a Hollywood western are clearly evoked; indeed, Anya is later referred to as *Clint*, after Clint Eastwood, star of the film the dybbuk mentions. Referring to the features of butch speech, Rainbow reminds herself, "The first thing she learned in Baby Dyke school . . . was Never Gush." Both she and Anya "snort" and guffaw" together; they are above anything "so trillingly femme as a girlish giggle" (184). It is clear that Galford, like Wilson and Wings, intends to represent a stereotype with which her readers will be familiar. Anya is described as the "stereotypical dyke's delight" (191), and an "identikit old-fashioned dyke" (204).

In Claire Macquet's (1991) short story "Sparrow," the young school-teacher Pattie, the innocent sparrow of the title, meets "Cleo Cadaverous," a dominatrix who refers to her sexual proclivities as *theatre*. "Can you imagine how many times I've played that little piece of theatre with how many pretty girls?" she asks Pattie wearily (51), surrounded by the whips and blindfolds of her trade. Galford's novel gives Clint Eastwood, John Wayne, and James Cagney as models for the butch character. It is not the screen character who is invoked but the real-life actor who plays him, so that the artifice is clearly underlined. Macquet's story, on the other hand, makes explicit intertextual reference to earlier lesbian novels. Pattie remembers how her friend Eugenie "had once talked about strange things in Paris a long time ago, where, in salons dripping in gold leaf and lilies, women poets in monocles conducted secret liaisons with the daughters of defunct royal houses" (47). This description connects Macquet's text with novels like Radclyffe Hall's *The Well of Loneliness*; indeed, the salon Eugenie describes could be that of Valerie Seymour, Hall's portrait of Natalie Barney, a real flesh-and-blood American who ran a literary salon in Paris for almost fifty years (Barney 1992).

Because Wilson and to a lesser extent Wings and Galford make their style a clear parody of Raymond Chandler's, and the hardboiled detective is one of the models cited for butch lesbian speech, it may prove fruitful to look at some dialogue from one of Chandler's ([1939] 1989) most famous novels, *The Big Sleep*. Philip Marlowe's speech to the female characters often sounds similar to that of the butches we have come across. His barked threat, "I'll give you three minutes to get dressed and out of here. If you're not out by then, I'll throw you out—by force. . . . Now—get started" (174), resembles Anya's order and her insistence that it be carried out immediately: "Get in here. Both of you. . . . Call in and tell them you're on an all-day job out-of-town. Now" (210). Both Marlowe's *get started* and Anya's *Get in here* feature the unhedged imperative we have seen before with Miss Ogilvy. Chandler's women, on the other hand, tend to speak more like drag queens. Or perhaps it would be truer to say that drag queens copy some of the discourse features of Chandler's female characters. "You're just a big tease," says Carmen; "You're awfully tall"; "'You're cute,' she giggled, 'I'm cute too.'" (19). This barrage of impertinent physical description, or "personal remarks," categorizes these comments as feminine since men are perceived to be less comfortable with the personal. The lines of Chandler's character Vivian Regan are gloriously outrageous in the best camp tradition: "I loathe masterful men. I simply loathe them" (35); "Hold me close, you beast" (165); and the prize, "My God, you big dark handsome brute! I ought to throw a Buick at you!" (35).

Intertextuality

It is in theories of intertextuality that we discover the key to the speech of butch and femme characters in fiction, whether female or male, for as Julia Kristeva (1974) (among others) has shown, all semiotic systems, including language itself, rely for a large part of their message on the intertextual level of discourse that relates the meaning of one text to those of other texts that have come before them. In this way, every text may be said to quote, or at least echo, previous texts. The meanings of one text are, indeed, enriched by this polyphonous network.

If some of the best camp and butch dialogue was written by Raymond Chandler, what models are there for the speech of Chandler's characters? A very interesting interchange between Vivian Regan and Philip Marlowe sketches the beginnings of an answer to this question. Vivian is wearing "brownish speckled tweeds, a mannish shirt and tie, hand-carved walking shoes" (67), a description that would not be out of place if transposed to the heroine of Hall's *The Well of Loneliness*. When the private detective finally shows up, late, for an appointment with his client, Vivian opens the conversation with "I was beginning to think you worked in bed like Marcel Proust" (67). The sophisticated reader will recognize Vivian's mention of Proust, coupled with her "mannish shirt" and sensible shoes, as a homosexual signal. Unlike the reader, however, Marlowe the macho has never heard of the Parisian writer, for that kind of knowledge would compromise his masculinity. "Who's he?" he asks bluntly. "A French writer, a connoisseur in degenerates. You wouldn't know him," Vivian replies (67), reinforcing Marlowe's heterosexual status in her assumption that he would not be familiar with Proust's work.

This brief dialogue is a prefiguring of what will happen between the detective and his client later in the novel. Vivian undermines her own distant stance and butch image as she starts a conversation with the man she has hired by imagining him in bed. At first Vivian the mannish is hostile toward Marlowe's manly charms: *I loathe masterful men* (35). But her style is overblown, more personally involved than a true fictional butch would permit herself: *I ought to throw my Buick at you* (35). The adjective *masterful* shows that Vivian has noted Marlowe's ability to dominate and confers upon it a covert admiration. The exaggeration inherent in the image of Vivian throwing a car at Marlowe shows that she cannot possibly be serious and must therefore mean something like the opposite of what she is saying. Later she and Marlowe engage in a passionate kiss. At the level of the plot the reference to Proust is thrown out seemingly just to tease the reader, a *sexualization* of Vivian Regan rather than a *homosexualization*. Yet at the metadiscourse level, the reference to Proust fulfills an extremely important intertextual function by making explicit the connection between Chandler's very heterosexual novel and earlier homosexual authors. The hypermasculinity of Marlowe's speech provides a model for the butch lesbian discourse of later lesbian novels, and the hyperfeminine speech of some of Chandler's female characters can be seen in gay male camp. By citing the works of Marcel Proust, Chandler acknowledges a debt, ironic though it may be, to one of his own sources, for without homosexuality, conscious heterosexuality would be impossible.

The overwhelmingly intertextual nature of butch/femme discourse should now be clear. Whether they are aware of it or not—the "sincere" authors like Radclyffe Hall and Lee Lynch seem to be unaware; the parodic writers like Anna Wilson and Ellen Galford seem not only to be aware of it but to revel in it—the femme and butch lesbians of fiction talk not like real women and men, nor even like stereotyped versions of women and men, but like other femmes and butches in earlier fictions, whether female or male. That this is the case is confirmed by an examination of the many parodies of butch/femme conversation patterns in lesbian novels of recent years that explicitly mention the sources on which they are drawing. John Wayne, Philip Marlowe, and James Dean have contributed more to butch conversational ideologies than has any lived experience of male bosses, fathers, or colleagues. The semiotic pathways do not simply stop at this juncture, however, for, as I have shown, Chandler cites Proust, who refers to the work of the nineteenth-century decadents including Baudelaire, just as Radclyffe Hall's mannish women have appeared before in earlier works, in Gautier's Mademoiselle de Maupin, for example.

In the dialogue of the Black lesbian characters studied, it is the lyrics of jazz and blues songs and the discourse style of evangelical preachers that provide the intertextual links connecting otherwise disparate works and enriching them with an echoic structure. Intertextuality, as Norman Fairclough (1992) makes plain, usually entails an emphasis on the hetero-geneity of texts, caused by the polyphonic or echoic effect whereby the citation is read simultaneously both in its current contexts and in its previous manifestation in an earlier text (or texts). This device is frequently used with ironic intent (hence the prevalence of parody in the fiction discussed here) or to add cultural richness and a sense of deeply rooted history to specific social customs. Because of the emphasis on orig-inality and authenticity in the presentation of butch and femme charac-ters—both in the theoretical discussion concerning them and often in the texts themselves—instead of an opening up of the works to a multitude of complex readings that transcend the plot and characters presented, there results a forced closing, a limitation in the number of possible readings, so that the novel or short story must be read as a personal testimony, the char-acters identified as representing the speech of real individuals. The insis-tence on the authenticity and originality of butch/femme identities is not simply demonstrably incorrect but serves to impoverish the fictional work. Limiting the meanings of the speech of Miss Ogilvy by a too-close identifi-cation with that of the author, Radcyffe Hall, declaring it the natural expres-sion of an early-twentieth-century butch lesbian, for example, deprives it of the richness it acquires when seen in relation to the work of Chandler and Proust.[10]

Although the findings presented here are limited to the portrayal of butch/femme characters in fiction, linguists sometimes draw upon fictional representations of dialogue as though they were expressive of the speech of real people. This is clearly a dangerous practice if performed with the naive expectation that fiction can accurately represent reality, but I suggest that intertextual references and polyphony may be as common in real-life conversation as they are in fiction. An awareness that a given piece of discourse may be a citation (conscious or unconscious) could usefully inform any work on cross-sex talk.

Notes

1. This sounds even better in Italian:

   Essere maschio significa essere tarato, emotivamente limitato; la virilità è una tara. . . . Il maschio è totalmente egocentrico, intrappolato in se stesso, incapace di trasporto, di identificazione con gli altri. . . . È un'individualità isolata, incapace di communicare. . . . Il maschio è intrappolato in una zona d'ombra a metà strada tra l'essere umano e la scimmia. (Solanas 1988:11, 12)

   It is my own, entirely idiosyncratic, belief that Italian is the language for which the SCUM Manifesto was intended. Translation theorists take note.

2. For summaries of the various studies on amounts of talk and further references, see Dale Spender (1980:41–51), Jennifer Coates (1986:31–34), and especially Deborah James and Janice Drakich (1993). For more on interrupting and nonresponse as forms of silence, see Pamela Fishman (1983), Candice West and Donald Zimmerman (1983), all of the articles in *Discourse and Society* 2(2), and especially Deborah James and Sandra Clarke (1993).

3. Because both Lakoff and Norma Mendoza-Denton discuss the Clarence Thomas confirmation hearings in this volume, I will not discuss this case further here. I am cheered to see such cogent and well-substantiated commentary on the hearings; Hill's enforced silence is doubly avenged, by women drawing courage from it to speak out on sexual harassment and by feminist linguists analyzing its discourse pragmatics.

4. Kira Hall (MS) makes a similar point. Because this observation seems to have come out of conversations between the two of us, we both take credit for it. Hall uses it in a rather different context, however.

5. Torr makes no attempt to distinguish between types of men, lumping them all together regardless of age, race, class, or cultural background. She seems to have in mind the generic white male of the seventies' cigarette commercials.

6. See, for example, Sheila Jeffreys (1987), who uses the cutting phrase *gender fetishism* to describe role-playing.

7. I quote this anthology with great frequency in this chapter because, although I have some quarrel with its theoretical underpinnings, it is nevertheless an extraordinarily rich undertaking, bringing together a wealth of material, including previously unpublished personal accounts of butch/femme in the forties and fifties.

8. Lesbian vampires, however, do not all speak the same. See, for example, Kerry in Pat Califia's (1993) "The Vampire," who snarls and grunts, beats a man within an inch of his life, but utters scarcely a word, strong and silent to the last. At one point she blurts out, "What the hell are you talking about?" then bites her lip and repents "not keeping silent," while the femme, Iduna, explains

her to herself: "You haven't fed for months now. You still draw blood, but you don't allow yourself to taste it" (312). Or my own, very different, portrait of Natalie Clifford Barney as a vampire bitterly berating herself for her spoiled night of love with Minnie:

> It was dreadful and it was my fault. Sheer bloody-minded, insensitive boorishness. She is my perfect beautiful darling and I treated her shamefully. . . . She was sitting on the sofa, right where I am now. I still smell the essence of camellia from the bath oil. There she was, beside me, her plump soft arm almost touching mine. And . . . I talked to her. I don't know what got into me. I talked to her for hours. I used her as a sounding board for everything that was on my mind. (Livia 1991:173–75)

The description of the second vampire represents a pastiche of the values of the first. Vampires should be strong and silent, creatures of few words and enormous appetites (whether sanguine or sexual). That a vampire should show a sensitive side, a desire to talk, to discuss emotional problems, is clearly to defame the time-honored traditions of vampirehood. Any genre with clearly defined conventions and conversational roles lends itself to parody.

9. A classic, though now somewhat dated, account of camp is to be found in Susan Sontag's "Notes on Camp," first published in 1964, republished in *A Susan Sontag Reader* (1983). I also thoroughly recommend the anthology *The Politics and Poetics of Camp*, edited by Moe Meyer (1994), and particularly Cynthia Morrill's contribution, "Revamping the Gay Sensibility: Queer Camp and *Dyke Noir*." Morrill discusses the dyke noir style of contemporary lesbian mysteries as a camp discourse, particularly from the point of view of its gallows humor. Another useful anthology on the subject is *Camp Grounds*, edited by David Bergman (1993).

10. Too close an identification between the speakers of a language and fictional representations of these speakers also impoverishes analysis of real speech, and may help to obfuscate the fact that speakers also continually quote one another in a ventriloquous game of which they may be entirely unaware. Originality is not necessarily a virtue; most statements have been made before. The real skill is often in fitting quotation to occasion.

References

Austin, John (1962). *How to do things with words*. Cambridge, MA: Harvard University Press.

Bannon, Ann ([1959] 1986). *I am a woman*. Tallahassee: Naiad.

Barney, Natalie Clifford (1992). *A perilous advantage: The best of Natalie Clifford Barney*. Translated and edited by Anna Livia. Norwich, VT: New Victoria.

Bell, Shannon (1993). Finding the male within and taking him cruising: Drag-king-for-a-day. In Arthur Kroker and Marilouise Kroker (eds.), *The third sex*. New York: St. Martin's Press. 89–103.

Bellerose, Sally (1992). Redheads. In Joan Nestle (ed.), *The persistent desire*. Boston: Alyson. 355–59.

Bergman, David (ed.) (1993). *Camp grounds: Style and homosexuality*. Amherst: University of Massachusetts Press.

Butler, Judith (1990). *Gender trouble.* New York: Routledge.

Califia, Pat (1993). The vampire. In Pam Keesey (ed.), *Daughters of darkness: Lesbian vampire stories.* Pittsburgh: Cleis. 167–83.

Chandler, Raymond ([1933] 1946). Blackmailers don't shoot. In *Red wind: A collection of short stories.* New York: World. 69–124.

———— ([1959] 1971). The pencil. In *The midnight Raymond Chandler.* Boston: Houghton Mifflin. 163–200.

———— ([1939] 1989). *The big sleep.* San Francisco: North Point Press.

Coates, Jennifer (1986). *Women, men, and language.* London: Longman.

Coates, Jennifer, and Deborah Cameron (eds.) (1988). *Women in their speech communities.* London: Longman.

Davis, Madeline (1992). Roles? I don't know anyone who's "playing": A letter to my femme sisters. In Joan Nestle (ed.), *The persistent desire.* Boston: Alyson. 268–69.

Davis, Madeline, Amber Hollibaugh, and Joan Nestle (1992). The femme tapes. In Joan Nestle (ed.), *The persistent desire.* Boston: Alyson. 254–67.

Donnelly, Nisa (1989). *The bar stories.* New York: St. Martin's Press.

Fairclough, Norman (1992). *Discourse and social change.* Cambridge: Polity Press.

Feinberg, Leslie (1993). *Stone butch blues.* Ithaca: Firebrand.

Fishman, Pamela M. (1983). Interaction: The work women do. In Barrie Thorne, Cheris Kramarae, and Nancy Henley (eds.), *Language, gender, and society.* Rowley, MA: Newbury House. 89–102.

Galford, Ellen (1994). *The dyke and the dybbuk.* Seattle: Seal Press.

Gomez, Jewelle (1991). *The Gilda stories.* Ithaca: Firebrand.

———— (1993). Don't explain. In Margaret Reynolds (ed.), *The Penguin book of lesbian short stories.* London: Viking. 273–83.

Grahn, Judy (1984). *Another mother tongue: Gay words, gay worlds.* Boston: Beacon Press.

Hall, Kira (MS). Gender identity and linguistic appropriation. Department of English, Rutgers University.

Hall, Radclyffe ([1926] 1992). Miss Ogilvy finds herself. In Joan Nestle (ed.), *The persistent desire.* Boston: Alyson. 24–38.

———— ([1928] 1990). *The well of loneliness.* New York: Doubleday.

James, Deborah, and Sandra Clarke (1993). Women, men, and interruptions: A critical review. In Deborah Tannen (ed.), *Gender and conversational interaction.* Oxford: Oxford University Press. 231–80.

James, Deborah, and Janice Drakich (1993). Understanding gender differences in amount of talk: A critical review of research. In Deborah Tannen (ed.), *Gender and conversational interaction.* Oxford: Oxford University Press. 281–312.

Jeffreys, Sheila (1987). Butch and femme: Now and then. *Gossip* 5: 65–95.

Kennedy, Elizabeth Lapovsky, and Madeline Davis (1992). "They was no one to mess with": The construction of the butch role in the lesbian community of the 1940s and 1950s. In Joan Nestle (ed.), *The persistent desire.* Boston: Alyson. 62–80.

Kramer, Cheris (1975). Women's speech: Separate but unequal? In Barrie Thorne and Nancy Henley (eds.), *Language and sex: Difference and dominance*. Rowley, MA: Newbury House. 43–56.

——— (1977). Perceptions of female and male speech. *Language and Society* 20(2): 151–61.

Kristeva, Julia (1974). *La Revolution du langage poétique*. Paris: Seuil.

Lakoff, Robin (1975). *Language and woman's place*. New York: Harper & Row.

——— (1990). *Talking power*. New York: Basic Books.

——— (1992). The silencing of women. In Kira Hall, Mary Bucholtz, and Birch Moonwomon (eds.), *Locating power: Proceedings of the Second Berkeley Women and Language Conference*. Berkeley: Berkeley Women and Language Group. 344–55.

——— (this volume). Cries and whispers: The shattering of the silence.

Laporte, Rita (1992). The butch–femme question. In Joan Nestle (ed.), *The persistent desire*. Boston: Alyson. 208–19.

Lederer, Judy (1992). A letter. In Joan Nestle (ed.), *The persistent desire*. Boston: Alyson. 95–97.

Livia, Anna (1991). *Minimax*. Portland, OR: Eighth Mountain.

Lorde, Audre (1982). *Zami, a new spelling of my name*. Freedom, CA: Crossing Press.

Lynch, Lee (1985). *The swashbuckler*. Tallahassee: Naiad.

MacCowan, Lyndall (1992). Re-collecting history, renaming lives: Femme stigma and the feminist seventies and eighties. In Joan Nestle (ed.), *The persistent desire*. Boston: Alyson. 299–330.

Macquet, Claire (1991). Sparrow. In *The flying hart*. London: Sheba. 44–58.

Mendoza-Denton, Norma (this volume). Pregnant pauses: Silence and authority in the Anita Hill–Clarence Thomas hearings.

Meyer, Moe (ed.) (1994). *Camp grounds: The politics and poetics of camp*. London: Routledge.

Morrill, Cynthia (1994). Revamping the gay sensibility: Queer camp and *dyke noir*. In Moe Meyer (ed.), *Camp grounds: The politics and poetics of camp*. London: Routledge. 110–29.

Mushroom, Merril (1993). How to engage in courting rituals 1950s butch-style in the bar. In Margaret Reynolds (ed.), *The Penguin book of lesbian short stories*. London: Penguin. 213–18.

Nestle, Joan (1992). Flamboyance and fortitude: An introduction. In Joan Nestle (ed.), *The persistent desire*. Boston: Alyson. 13–22.

Rubin, Gayle (1992). Of catamites and kings: Reflections on butch, gender, and boundaries. In Joan Nestle (ed.), *The persistent desire*. Boston: Alyson. 466–82.

Shockley, Ann Allen (1982). *Say Jesus and come to me*. Tallahassee: Naiad.

Solanas, Valerie ([1968] 1983). *Scum manifesto*. London: Matriarchy Study Group.

——— (1988). *SCUM Manifesto per l'eliminazione dei maschi*. Translated by Adriana Apa. Milan: Studio Editoriale.

Sontag, Susan ([1964] 1983). Notes on camp. In *A Susan Sontag reader*. New York: Vintage Books. 105–19.

Spender, Dale (1980). *Man made language*. London: Routledge & Kegan Paul.

Swacker, Marjorie (1975). The sex of the speaker as a sociolinguistic variable. In Barrie Thorne and Nancy Henley (eds.), *Language and sex: Difference and dominance*. Rowley, MA: Newbury House. 76–83.

Tannen, Deborah (1990). *You just don't understand*. New York: Ballantine.

——— (ed.) (1993). *Gender and conversational interaction*. Oxford: Oxford University Press.

Thorne, Barrie, and Nancy Henley (eds.) (1975). *Language and sex: Difference and dominance*. Rowley, MA: Newbury House.

Thorne, Barrie, Cheris Kramarae, and Nancy Henley (eds.) (1983). *Language, gender, and society*. Rowley, MA: Newbury House.

Vanderlinde, Sky (1992). Loving Blue. In Joan Nestle (ed.), *The persistent desire*. Boston: Alyson. 226–33.

Villanueva, Chea (1992). Excerpts from "In the Shadows of Love." In Joan Nestle (ed.), *The persistent desire*. Boston: Alyson. 220–24.

West, Candace, and Don Zimmerman (1983). Small insults: A study of interruptions in cross-sex conversations between unacquainted persons. In Barrie Thorne, Cheris Kramarae, and Nancy Henley (eds.), *Language, gender, and society*. Rowley, MA: Newbury House.102–17.

Wilson, Anna (1994). The reach. In Lilian Mohin and Sheila Shulman (eds.), *The reach and other stories: Lesbian feminist fiction*. London: Onlywomen Press. 9–21.

Wings, Mary (1992). *Divine victim*. New York: Dutton.

Zimmerman, Don, and Candace West (1975). Sex roles, interruptions and silences in conversation. In Barrie Thorne and Nancy Henley (eds.), *Language and sex: Difference and dominance*. Rowley, MA: Newbury House. 105–29.

11

Bitches and Skankly Hobags

The Place of Women in Contemporary Slang

Laurel A. Sutton

"I mean, just how many ugly ... names *do* men have for women, anyway?"
—Luba, a character in the comic book *Love & Rockets*, 1985

A great deal of work has been done on the "ugly names" for women. Researchers have pointed out that in English there are many more negative terms for women than for men—a quick look in a thesaurus will confirm that—and that negative terms, which almost always carry sexual connotations, reflect the status of women in Western society, that is, as identified in terms of the men they relate to (Lakoff 1975). These terms have probably been in common use since the advent of Modern English and show up most recently in several slang surveys conducted in California in the past several years. Although there does not seem to be much change in the "ugly names" men have for women, there are some interesting developments in the terms that *women* use for women.

Background

Robin Lakoff has pointed out that pairs of words in English carry vastly different meanings for women and men: *master/mistress*, *gentleman/lady*, *bachelor/spinster*. The terms for women all have sexual definitions, that is, a woman is defined by her sexual relation to men. Muriel Schulz (1975:135) examined a huge range of words and discovered, not surprisingly, that "again and again in the history of the language, one finds that a perfectly innocent term designating a girl or woman may begin with totally neutral or even positive connotations, but that it gradually acquires negative implications, at first perhaps only slightly disparaging, but after a period of time becoming abusive and ending as a sexual slur." Schulz concludes that pejorative terms for women are created by men because of their sexual fear of women, which threatens male hegemonic power.

Paula Treichler (1989) argues that selected meanings of terms for and about women are "authorized" by dictionary makers—those in "authority"—and that this authority may be central to the way we construct and interpret concepts and use them in discourse. She finds that "dictionaries have generally excluded any sense of women as speakers, as linguistic innovators, or as definers of words ... they have perpetuated the stereotypes and prejudices of writers, editors, and language commentators, who are almost exclusively male. At no point do they make women's words and women's experiences central" (60). Treichler's examples show that from the selection of words to the sentences given to illustrate definitions, women are relegated to secondary, nonmale status, defined by their relations to men.

The vast landscape of language, then, seems to be a male construct in which women are talked about and talked to but do not themselves speak. Shifting the focus to words that specifically refer to women in their sexual relationship to men, words that do not pretend to be otherwise, Julia Penelope (1977) found two hundred expressions and Schulz another one hundred that describe women's availability to men as sexual objects; these were primarily male slang, a set that changes constantly and can be viewed as the cutting edge of language. Penelope (1990) refers to this collection as "Paradigmatic Woman: The Prostitute" and sets up parameters that define *woman* in a male world: cost, method of payment, and length of contact. All women exist only to provide sex for men; "no man perceives consenting sex with a woman as free, [and] the only question in his mind is how much it will cost him to get a woman into bed with him" (121). *Slut* and *whore* are often applied to women who have sex with different partners (without charging them). They are the worst insults that can be hurled at women, because "a woman who thinks so little of herself as to not get something in exchange for sex is perceived as pitiful, the lowest of the low" (Penelope 1990:121).[1]

Referring to women by synedoche, reducing the being to the body part, is also among the worst of insults. Calling a man a *dick* is something of a standard insult term; one even finds it on television in mutated forms, such as *dickweed* and *dickwad*. But one will never hear a woman called a *cunt* on television. And although *dick* (or its "cuter" form, *weenie/wiener*) seems to be used by women as well as men, it is extremely rare to hear one woman refer to another as a *cunt*. There seems to be very little or no work on the words that women have for women. In fact, in an informal survey of my female friends and acquaintances, there was only one word used to insult a woman: *bitch*.

The word *bitch* is the prime example of a subclass of women-as-sex-objects terms, that of women as animals. C. R. Whaley and George Antonelli (1983) provide a deft and thorough analysis of this linguistic area, pointing out that because the Western mind generally values humans over animals, most animal comparisons express negative attitudes toward the person so compared. In a few cases positive values are found in animals that are considered "noble, courageous, assertive, clever, or sexually powerful" (Whaley & Antonelli 1983:219). But none of them can be applied to women: *lion-hearted, a real moose, Italian stallion, young buck*. Those that are positive are, again, admirable from a male viewpoint: *fox, foxy lady, kitten, Playboy bunny*.

Whaley and Antonelli assert that by examining this set of terms, "we may discover a basis for the concept of woman as male chattel; themes of male conquest, domination, and exploitation; and the roots of the idea that 'woman's place is in the home'" (220). Using the categorization of animals into four classes—pets, pests, cattle, and wild animals—Whaley and Antonelli make the case that because women are equated with animals in the minds of some men, "when men use animal metaphors to refer to women, they reveal a set of assumptions, a kind of regard, and the relation-ships with women they prize and despise" (222). Echoing Penelope's point, Whaley and Antonelli demonstrate that terms like *pig* and *cow* show that women are thought of as sexually accessible if the male pays for them (or "feeds" them). Women are viewed as either domesticated animals or pets—soft, affectionate, easily controlled. But there are also women who can be classed as wild animals, like *fox* or *wildcat*. "Their value exists in their rela-tive scarcity, superior physical appearance, independence, the challenge of exploiting them sexually, and the possibility that they may steal the male's resources without giving reciprocity.... Foxes are desired as trophies" (225). And then there is the case of the domesticated animal that has gone wrong, that bites the hand that feeds it. A female dog in heat or protecting her young will growl, threaten, or even bite her owner; she has reverted to her wild state; she is a *bitch*, uncontrollable.

Slang

Woman-as-animal metaphors are most commonly expressed in slang. Slang in general is a rich source of timely and creative metaphors; if language in general is indeed man-made and man-authorized, it is no surprise that the images of slang are those from the male point of view. This is true for the slang used a hundred years ago and for what is spoken on the street or in the classroom today. The slang I examine here is some of the most up-to-date available.

Until recently, most studies of slang—and, indeed, of language innovation in general—have seen women as linguistic conservatives (that is, as adhering closely to the "standard" form of speech) and at the same time as linguistic deviants (which is obvious, if "men's speech" is taken as the norm); much of the latter view can be traced back to Otto Jespersen's (1921) chapter "The Woman" in *Language: Its Nature, Development and Origin.* Other studies that have looked at social stratification and gender as linguistic variables (for example, Labov 1966, 1972; Trudgill 1974; Wolfram 1969) assert that women tend to use more prestige linguistic features than men of similar social backgrounds. They attribute this disparity to the fact that women's social positions are less secure and women are more sensitive to the social significance of language, as well as the fact that the "working-class vernacular" (which includes slang and other kinds of group-related jargon) has a covert prestige that appeals more to male speakers.

David Graddol and Joan Swann (1989) provide a thorough criticism of the assumptions that underlie these theories, pointing out that women cannot simply be assigned the same social class as their husbands and fathers, and that women and men interact—and thereby construct their social identity—in different ways.

> In several respects, sex differences in the use of language varieties parallel those in voice quality. Social significance is visible in the interplay between the indexical and symbolic associations of different voices and of different language varieties. And evaluations of both aspects of speech involve complex notions of femininity and masculinity within which many individual attributes can be distinguished. Whereas voice qualities are particularly linked with biological notions of gender and sexuality, the study of language varieties introduces strong elements of class associations, and of economic and social conditions that relate to gender divisions. (68)

Graddol and Swann also emphasize the effect of interviewer bias and the fallacy of a single continuum of style that encompasses all vernacular and prestige varieties—a continuum that is supposed to hold for women and men in all contexts. More recent work has shifted the focus of inquiry to the contexts themselves, acknowledging the very different styles of interaction within mixed-sex and single-sex groups. This issue is especially relevant for studies of slang and other types of "nonstandard" speech that serve largely to distinguish one group from another. If it is true that adolescents use a great deal of slang because they want to show that they are a solid group apart from adults and children, it follows that slang is also used to establish other aspects of social identity, such as ethnicity and (importantly for adolescents) sexuality.

The studies that have been undertaken on sexual slang have shown that men "outscore" women in their ability to generate or report words and phrases. Michael Gordon (1993) cites several studies conducted in the 1970s that support this finding, including Foote and Woodward (1973), Walsh and Leonard (1974), Sanders and Robinson (1979), and, into the 1980s, Johnson and Fine (1985). But Gordon's own work on terms for masturbation (for which there is considerable overlap in lists of frequently used words by women and men, but much more variation by gender in complete lists of words) shows that sexual slang (and, by extension, slang in general) cannot be treated as a unitary category and that "the results of this study tell little about gender differences in *spoken* patterns of sexual slang nor about recognition of such terms when used by others" (20).

It seems clear that women know slang used primarily by men, but if they use it, when do they do so? My own study reveals only a glimpse of actual patterns of use; more work and more thorough work needs to be done before we can make any definitive pronouncements.

Data

The first group of slang data I consider comes from work done by Pamela Munro and her graduate students at the University of California at Los Angeles (UCLA) during 1988, much of which was later published as Munro (1989). Florie Aranovich (MS) reports that most of the words used to describe women can be grouped into several basic categories: *women as objects, women as prostitutes, women as dumb,* and *women as rude and evil.* Although she does not provide figures, Aranovitch mentions that most of the insulting or negative terms are used by men in conversation. She notes that even though words could be classed as positive if they referred to a woman as attractive, the term itself might still be demeaning: *filet* ('cute girl'), *freak* ('attractive girl'), *treat* ('cute girl'), and *goddess* ('female achiever') are all compliments, yet they still define women in relation to men—as meat, as abnormal, as prizes, and as untouchable.

Aranovitch concludes that almost 90 percent of the words for women in the UCLA slang list describe women in a negative way, compared to only 46 percent of the words for men. None of the positive words for men are demeaning (Aranovitch compares the corresponding terms for men, *adonis* and *god*, and says that their connotations are quite different from *goddess*), and the negative words do not focus on attractiveness to women. Even a term rated as negative may still imply desirable qualities: *mr. groin* ('promiscuous male') is rather cute and funny, but *roadwhore*, *skag*, and *wench* (all meaning 'promiscuous female') are all clearly insults.

From the negative terms for women in the UCLA slang list, we might conclude that the following are "bad" for women to be: fat (*heifer*), unattractive (*skank*), dumb (*dimbo*), too free sexually (*turboslut*), assertive (*bitch*), and prudish (*nun*); a woman should not display interest in a man without following through, that is, having sex (*trap*). Conversely, it is "good" to be attractive (*betty, filet, freak, treat, wilma*). Unless women are seen by men as attractive, they are fat, dumb, evil, and sexually promiscuous. No such restrictions are placed on men, according to the UCLA slang list; there are no words for fat, assertive, or dumb men, and only one word each for ugly men (*lou*) and sexually promiscuous men (*mr. groin*). The word *barney* is defined as 'person who's not with it, nerd' and only secondarily as 'ugly guy' (Munro 1989:28). Clearly, there is some linguistic sexual dimorphism going on.

The data I have been working with from undergraduates at Berkeley show much the same results. The slang terms were collected from undergraduates in a large lecture class in linguistics, held in fall 1991 and spring 1992. The students were representative of the diverse student body and its many varieties of speech. They were not asked to specify their ethnicity or social background for this assignment, but data collected from the same students for other surveys indicate that they represent a wide range of ethnic groups.

Students were told to collect ten slang terms that they or their friends used frequently, and to write down definitions and example sentences. They turned their assignments in to their graduate-student instructors, who in turn gave copies to the small group of graduate students processing data for the class. The assignments were then coded and entered into a database. For the fall semester 1991, the complete database consisted of 1,528 terms, reported by 139 students. Collapsing the multiple reports of a single word, we ended up with a total of 1,205 terms. For spring semester 1992, 2,260 terms from 226 students were collected, reflecting the higher enrollment in the course. For both semesters, the ratio of female to male students was about one to one. Definitions were provided by the students themselves; we did not attempt to impose judgment. It is important to bear in mind that the students were not told what categories of words to report; their choices reflect their own intuitions about what words they used most frequently.

Here is a raw listing for the collected terms (student definitions are given in Appendixes A, B).

FALL 1991. A total of 79 terms for and about women, collapsed to 66 different terms.

Women. 55 terms. Excluding the terms for ugly women, we are left with terms for women who are sexually loose, spiteful, fat, and attractive. The first group, of course, is the largest: *bait, beddy, ho, hooker, hootchie, nocturnal, parnass, scud, sex [trip], skank, skank ho, skankly hobag, skanky, skeezer, slag, slam hole, slut, squid bait, stimey hole, strawberry, tramp, tuna, whore.* Spiteful or malicious women: *bitch, biscuit, CWA* (chick with an attitude), *yatch.* Fat women: *feet, heifer.* Finally, some attractive women: *around the way girl, babe, Betty, chack, chubby, dinghy, fawn, GK, honey, hoogie, hottie, nectar, tender.* There were also a few words that seemed to be insults; they referred to women specifically by their sexual organs: *box, clam, hole, hootchie, hot dog bun, pink taco, software.* Finally, there were some terms that singled women out for appearance or behavior (there were no corresponding terms for men): *barker, glamour bitch, jailbait, lush, sober-chick.* One term that did have a male corollary was *guidette.*

Ugly People. 11 terms. The nouns referring to ugly people were all for women, except one: *barney* "stupid or ugly guy." This reflects the importance of women's looks over almost everything else about them, except sexual activity: *butch, GG* (gangster girl), *heifer, hellpig, hiddie, hobag, scud, tuna, UFO, un-K.* Some of the terms also indicated that the woman could be fat as well as ugly.

SPRING 1992. A total of 87 terms for and about women, collapsed to 61 different terms.

Women. Again, words for promiscuous women led the pack, with 14: *bambi, ho, hobag, hoochie, hoogie, pelt, skank, skank-ho, skankly ho, skeezer, slut, strawberry, thumper, trinket.* Spiteful or malicious women: *apple, bitch, catty, wicked witch of the west.* Fat women: *ewok, heffa, swamp sow, tetunca, thunderthighs, tug boat, yeti.* Attractive women: *betty, bitty, box, bytches, cheesecake, elegant, freak, MILF* ('older attractive woman'), *peach.* Genitalia: *bearded clam, beaver, cheesehole, clam, cooch, coota, poon tang, tuna.* Ugly women: *mud-duck, mutt, roll, scud, sea-hag, shark, six pack beauty queen, stank.* Terms that singled out women for appearance or behavior: *barbie, cha cha, cracker, duck, guidette, hyper-hootch, skeezy.* There were some words that were just defined as 'women': *fluke, hole, puddy.* There was only one word that was a verb rather than a noun: *slime* (meaning, as one student explained, "the act of a woman walking home after a night of partying with a man"), which evokes images of filth and implies that women's sexual organs are unclean, or perhaps like slugs or snails.

Immediately we can see that this group of Berkeley slang follows the pattern of the UCLA slang very closely. There is a higher percentage of negative words for women than positive, and the positive words all focus on the attractiveness of women to men as sexual partners. The animal references fit perfectly in Whaley and Antonelli's (1983) framework, and some are especially creative, like *hellpig,* which combines the domesticated animal metaphor (sexually available) with a strong contradictory image of demons or nightmare. *Nocturnal,* too, implies a woman who lives in darkness and preys on others—a wild animal, uncontrollable. *Heifer* fits the domestic animal paradigm, also implying youth and possibly virginity due to unattractiveness; a cute and submissive timid woman is a *fawn.* Another interesting variation is *swamp sow,* combining both the domestic animal image and the image of nastiness.

Some other animal references are more obscure. *Duck* and *mud-duck* are probably formed from *lame duck,* and this is confirmed in the meaning given by the student for *duck,* "a lame girl." (*Lame* is a common slang term meaning something like 'loser' or 'in a sorry state'.) Both *bambi* and *thumper* are references to media, and fit Whaley and Antonelli's (1983) class of women as pets (cute, cuddly, with large eyes and high voices). *Puddy* might be a mutated form of *pussy,* but it is hard to tell whether this is a reference to genitalia or to cats. *Mutt* is a common term for ugly women, perhaps less aggressive than *bitch* but still on the animal scale.

Jailbait has been around for a long time and is straightforward in construction (*bait* that will send you to *jail*), and from that comes the shortened form *bait*; there is also *squid bait,* 'a woman who tries to attract men in the navy'. In a slightly different aquatic realm, we have *tuna* and *clam* (also *bearded clam*), reflecting men's perceptions of the appearance and "odor" of women's genitalia. More creative terms for women's genitalia are food images—*hot dog bun, pink taco*—and as the students explained, such terms are often extended to refer to women themselves, not just their genitals. There are several terms built on *hole: cheesehole, slam hole, stimey hole.* These terms support Penelope's (1990:120) observation of the paradigmatic woman as "holes, receptacles, containers—things they [men] can or want to fuck."

Terms for attractive women parallel Aranovitch's findings. Women are considered attractive only if men find them sexually desirable, and even then they are still viewed as objects, especially as food: *cheesecake, honey, nectar, peach.* The other terms can still be seen as offensive, with one exception: *elegant.* The acronym *MILF* ('mother I'd like to fuck') is particularly interesting, because it singles out older women and expresses the condescension of men toward them.

The terms for a promiscuous woman are similar, based on either *skank* (also said to refer to marijuana) or its variation *stank* and the word *ho* (also *hobag*; one student reported that this term was derived from *bag lady*). Women who have sex frequently are also reduced to their genitals: *hootchie, pelt, slam hole, stimey hole, tuna.* The one word offered as a male parallel to *hobag* was *hoebuck.* This seems a prime example of the kind of radical difference in meaning that we saw earlier with *master/mistress. Buck* has entirely positive connotations—man as an animal with strength, speed, and aesthetic value; *bag* is either the common word for 'old woman', or, more likely, from *douchebag.* A man who has sex often is to be admired; a woman, despised.[2]

Once again, the conclusions drawn are the same as from the UCLA slang: it is acceptable to be thin, smart (not too smart), passive, and sexually available (but not sexually promiscuous). It is not acceptable to be fat, ugly, aggressive, or sexually unattractive to men. As Lakoff pointed out, women are still defined by their sexual relation to men.

Some Observations

Because we also had a database of student personal information in both semesters, I was able to match up terms with the ethnicity of the students who reported them. The breakdown for fall 1991 was 23 by Asian Americans, 4 by Latinos, 17 by European Americans, 8 by mixed, and 26 not identified; for spring 1992, 54 by Asian Americans, 6 by Latinos, 24 by European Americans, 3 by mixed, and 1 not identified. Surprisingly, there were no students who identified themselves as African Americans, although there were several in both classes.

For fall 1991, 32 terms were reported by women and 47 by men; for spring 1992, 32 terms were reported by women and 56 by men. When entering the data into the database, I paid special attention to the terms that women reported. Although women sometimes specified that the terms were used only by men, most said that they themselves used the slang with their friends (this appears in the "Comments" column in the Appendixes as *college students*). Some even gave examples using a female speaker.

For fall 1991, two words were reported by women as being used exclusively by men (*barker* and *fawn*), and three as exclusively used by women (*nectar, parnass, slag*). Men reported that three words were used only by men (*babe, betty, chubby*) and none only by women. In spring 1992, women reported that five terms were used only by women (*barbie, catty, heffa, hoochie, trinket*) and nine by men only (*apple, betty, box, clam, peach, shark, skanky ho, slime, troll*). Men said that six terms were used exclusively by men (*betty, clam, ho, hyperhootch, tetunca*), and none only by women. All other terms were not specified as being used by one sex or the other.

One very interesting fact came up in the data. Several of the women reported that *ho* and *bitch* were used between women as terms of affection, but were never used by men in this way. This was true only for *ho* itself, and not for any of its other forms (*hobag, skank ho*). To verify this, I conducted a small survey with students enrolled in the course during the spring semester, in which I asked them if they used *bitch* and *ho*, and if the terms had positive or negative meanings. I also asked them to identify themselves by sex. Thirty females responded; of these, twenty said that both *bitch* and *ho* had negative meanings, and they did not use them as terms for or about women except as insults. Of the remaining ten, two said that although they did not use either of the words, which have a negative meaning to them, they would not be insulted because "it is used among friends. No offense will be taken— just teasing." Six of the remaining eight said that they used *bitch* to their female friends as "joke insults," but all eight said they used *ho* and some specified that it is "just another name," "a neutral word," or that it "doesn't really mean anything." This corroborates the information taken from the slang assignments during the same semester, in which women mentioned that they used *ho* but not *bitch* as a term of endearment among friends. As one woman put it, "When talking about women it's negative, but when talking to women it's a joke."

It is possible that we can attribute the use of some of these insult terms as affectionate terms to the influence of Black English Vernacular (BEV) on mainstream youth culture. Robert Chapman's (1986) etymologies in *New Dictionary of American Slang* show that BEV is an important source of slang in general, and this is reflected in many of the items that turn up in Munro's list as well as in my own.[3] It has been established that signifying, the verbal art of insult in which a speaker humorously puts down the listener, is a feature of BEV (Smitherman 1977), and some of the non-Black students mentioned that their slang was taken from rap or hip-hop music, or from the speech of their Black friends. The covert prestige of BEV for white youth is well known and growing, and appearing cool and hip is definitely a priority for students on the Berkeley campus. Certainly, not all of the women who reported using *ho* and *bitch* are Black.

Is this an appropriation of "masculine speech"? I am uncomfortable with the notion that women want to talk "like men," or "like African Americans" (if they are not Black), or like anyone besides other women. I argue that the slang used by young women to address one another is part of their search for identity as individuals and as a group (women) in a male-dominated world. Using *ho* and *bitch* as a signal of solidarity between women is, I think, much like the use of *nigga* (not *nigger*, which is always considered offensive) between African Americans—it's OK for us to do it, but definitely *not* OK for an outsider to call us that. It also has parallels with the use of *queer* within gay communities, although neither *bitch* nor *ho* has undergone the kind of wholesale reclamation of *queer*. (I don't see NOW changing its name to *Bitch Nation*, for example.)

Rather than say that young women are "talking like men," I see these women as imitating other *women*, whom they want to be like and who are different from the stereotypical image of *woman*. They see themselves, as individuals and as a group, as different from what they are supposed to be— and other research has shown that this is not an isolated event. Shigeko Okamoto (this volume) examines the use of masculine sentence-final forms by younger Japanese women and finds that although "moderately masculine forms" are now viewed as neutral, "strongly masculine forms" are used less frequently and for specific effect—"to make their conversation more interesting, fun, and spirited," that is, to enhance group solidarity. These Japanese women are aware of the prescribed behavior for women and choose to flout it within their own group, where they feel they are secure. (Okamoto mentions that these "strongly masculine forms" are not used with outsiders, especially older people.)

This behavior is, in Susan Gal's (this volume) framework, a strategic response to dominant hegemonic cultural forms:

> Resistance to a dominant cultural order occurs in two ways: first, when devalued linguistic forms and practices (such as local vernaculars, slang, women's interactional styles or poetry, and minority languages) are practiced and celebrated despite widespread denigration and stigmatization. Second, it occurs because these devalued practices often propose or embody alternate models of the social world.

Adolescent slang, then, may serve radically different functions for female and male youths. For both, it establishes an identity separate from adults and children, and allows them to feel as if they have some control over as least one aspect of their lives. This feeling of control and belonging can be seen as their alternate model of the social world. Young men, however, in continuing to devalue women through language, reinforce the dominant cultural order in which they are the holders of power, thus establishing an important part of their social identity. Perhaps women, in contrast, go even further in constructing an alternate model of the social world by choosing language that deliberately runs counter to societal expectations of women's behavior (or, more specifically, middle class white women's behavior). They are not trying to appear "like men"; rather, both Okamoto's informants and the women I surveyed are trying to construct a new societal identity that does not conform to traditional definitions of femininity. In contrast, Bonnie McElhinny (this volume) shows that the female police officers she studied are redefining femininity and masculinity through their use of language and behaviors usually linked with men in their profession. Through resistance comes redefinition.

I don't really know why we can call each other *ho* (never *whore*) and *bitch*, as opposed to any other slang terms. (For a defense of *bitch* as a positive label, see Spender 1992.) Maybe when we call each other *ho*, we acknowledge that we are women who have sex and earn our own money, too; when we call each other *bitch* we acknowledge the realities of this man-made world and affirm our ability to survive in it. Without revolution, resistance to and redefinition of long-held concepts of femininity and masculinity can be a long, hard process. Perhaps being a ho or a bitch is a start.

Appendix I

Terms for Women, Defined by Linguistics 55 Students, Fall 1991

Lexical entry	Meaning	Student comments about slang users or usage	Sex	Ethnicity
airhead	a perky, unintelligent female	Southern California	f	Latino
around-the-way girl	an attractive girl		f	0
babe	really good-looking girl	guys, especially in groups	m	Asian
bait	sexually loose woman	used by Korean Southern California high school students	m	Asian
barker	a woman who makes a lot of noise having sex	related to living conditions in a fraternity	f	European
beddy	a promiscuous girl	students in Southern California	f	Mixed

Term	Definition	Note		
Betty	an exceptionally good-looking female	male high school and college students	m	0
Betty	a good-looking girl	students in the Philippines	f	Mixed
Betty	an attractive female	a character in "The Flintstones" Used mainly by high-school and college students	f	
Betty	pretty girl	surfers in Southern California	f	0
biscuit	lewd, immoral or spiteful, malicious, and domineering woman		f	0
bitch	lewd, immoral or spiteful, malicious, and domineering woman		f	0
box	n. a woman's vagina, female genitals	used in reference to an attractive, desirable woman	f	0
box	female genitals	semantic shift, used by high-school students	m	Asian
box	n. a woman's vagina, female genitals	used in reference to an attractive, desirable woman	f	European
butt	an ugly girl usually	shortening of butt ugly; used by my co-workers and me	m	European
chack	an attractive female		m	Asian
chavala	a girl, but used mostly in reference to males	from Spanish, used mostly by Mexican youths	m	Asian
chubby	a very beautiful girl who makes you feel tingly	Wilson High School students (male)	m	Latino
clam	a derogatory term for the female gender	private and public schools in Philadelphia	0	0
CWA	"chick with attitude," a hard-to-get-along-with girl	college and high school students	m	Asian
dinghy	a perky, giggly, naive girl	Southern California	f	Latino
fawn	good-looking girl	men	f	Asian
feet	very fat woman	students in Hawaii	f	European
freak	girl, girlfriend	Rap, hip hop, neighborhoods of cities like Chicago	m	Asian
GK	a very attractive girl		m	0
glamour bitch	female with very long, manicured nails, hair-sprayed hair, too much makeup, and a low IQ	same as Guidette, but does not refer specifically to an Italian	f	European
Guidette	a Guido's girlfriend	ethnic identification; derived from Guido; used by non-Italian high school students in New York's suburbs.	f	European
hairbear	a girl who uses a lot of hairspray	students in Northern California	f	Mixed
heifer	extremely ugly teenage female, almost always overweight	high school students	f	European
heifer	a very overweight female	Texas	m	Asian
heifer	a fat girl	students in California and Maryland	m	0
heifer	an unattractive girl, generally large or overweight		f	0
hellpig	an unattractive female	high school seniors from Southern California	m	Asian
hiddie	an unattractive person, especially a girl	shortening of hideous; Orange County high school students	m	Asian
ho	a girl who submits to sex often and with anyone	whore; pronunciation from Black English	f	European
ho	promiscuous woman		f	Asian
ho	a derogatory term used to accuse a girl of promiscuity		f	0
ho	promiscuous female		f	0
ho	a bitch; a girl who sleeps with everybody short version of whore; used by most people		m	Asian

hole	insulting term for woman; also used for mouth	refers to vagina; used by my co-workers and me	m	European
honey	an attractive girl (generally plural)		f	0
hoochie	promiscuous female		f	0
hoochie	female genitalia, pussy	*hooch* refers to the person with the hoochie	m	European
hooker	promiscuous female		f	0
hot-dog bun	female genitalia		f	0
hottie	very attractive female	ethnic identification: hip hop (Black)	m	0
hyna	female, used often to describe unfamiliar females	borrowed from Spanish, used by Mexican youths	m	Asian
jailbait	a woman considered too young for sexual activity		m	European
jailbait	a girl below the legal age of sexual consent	teenagers and college students	f	Asian
lush	heavy drinker, female	students	f	Asian
nectar	a good-looking guy or girl	sorority	f	Mixed
nocturnal	(of a woman) sexually promiscuous	used in Los Angeles	m	European
parnass	a female who has large breasts and is sexually promiscuous	sorority	f	Mixed
pink taco	female genitalia		f	0
scud	a girl who looks good from far away, but is mufugly close up	"Saturday Night Live" audience	0	0
sex trip	a person (usually female) who is a tease or a slut	Philippines	f	Mixed
skank	promiscuous female		f	0
skank ho	a slut; a woman who sleeps around	made up; used by most African Americans	f	Mixed
skanky	a tramp, slut, or sleazy woman	University of California at Berkeley band members	f	Asian
skate betty	girl who skates	skateboarders	m	Asian
skeezer	promiscuous female		f	0
slag	an overweight female who is sexually promiscuous	sorority	f	Mixed
slam hole	promiscuous female	*slam* = to have sex with and *hole* = the vagina	m	European
slut	(n.) slovenly or promiscuous woman		m	Asian
slut	promiscuous female		f	0
sober chick	an extremely drunk girl on the point of passing out	used to someone who insists she's not drunk	f	European
software	vagina or a woman's breasts	her boyfriend	f	Latino
squid bait	a girl acting flirtatiously in order to attract a squid (i.e., a Navy man)	people from large military communities	m	0
stimey hole	a sleazy girl	*hole* means female genitalia, *stimey* means disgusting	f	European
strawberry	a woman who sells sex for crack		m	Asian
tender	a very beautiful girl	Berkeley	m	European
tramp	promiscuous female		f	0
tuna	(1) whore, prostitute (2) promiscuous woman		m	Asian
tuna	ugly girl	students in Hawaii	f	European
UFO	"unidentified female object," an unattractive female	senior students of Bellaire High School in Houston	m	Asian
Un-K	a most unattractive female		m	0
whore	promiscuous female		f	0
yatch	n. a malicious, heartless woman; bitch	my old high school jazz group	m	Asian

Appendix II

Terms for Women, Defined by Linguistics 55 Students, Spring 1992

Lexical entry	Meaning	Student comments about slang users or usage	Sex	Ethnicity
apple	girl who is evilish, cruel	Northern California college students, frats	m	0
bambi	female slut	association with *thumper*; high school	f	Asian
barbie	girl who acts superficial	high school and college girls	f	European
bearded clam	pussy or vagina	waterpolo players	m	Asian
beaver	female organ for sexual intercourse	high school boys	f	Asian
betty	attractive female	male college and high school students	f	European
betty	girl who is extremely beautiful	males of all ages	m	Asian
betty	beautiful girl	teenagers and young adult males	m	Asian
bitch	person with no regard for others (usually a woman)	used by everyone	m	Asian
bitch	girl with a very bad attitude	college students	m	European
bitty	attractive girl	from *betty*; New York City	m	Mixed
box	good-looking girl	frat guys	f	0
bytches	good-looking females	East Coast	m	European
catty	girls who backstab or don't get along with other girls	used by girls	f	Asian
cha cha	a girl with a lot of make-up		f	Asian
cheesecake	very good looking female	college students	f	Asian
cheesehole	slut	dorm at the University of California at Berkeley	m	Asian
clam	female	male college students	m	Asian
clam	female	Philadelphia males	f	Asian
coota	cunt, in a foreign language		f	Asian
cracker	ordinary, common girl	coined by Eddie Murphy in "Raw"; high school students	m	Asian
duck	lame girl	used in Seattle	f	Asian
elegant	extremely beautiful (usually a woman)	college students	m	Asian
ewok	very fat unattractive girl	South San Francisco high school	m	Asian
fluke	female	Southern California football players	f	European
freak	slut, nasty		f	Asian
freak	attractive girl, sometimes slutty or promiscuous	Hispanic college students	m	Latino
freak	beautiful girl	Los Angeles	m	Asian
freak	cute girl or boy	Black college students	m	Asian
guidette	female guido	New York City	m	Mixed
heffa	fat girl	from *heifer*; used by Black girls	f	European
ho	loose or slutty girl	high school and college students	f	Asian
ho	slut, girl who is promiscuous	high school and college students	f	Asian
ho	promiscuous woman	New York	m	Asian
ho	promiscuous woman	male high school and college students	m	Asian
ho	cute girl who is very promiscuous	college students	m	European
hobag	female who readily surrenders her body for sex	teenagers and college students	m	Asian
hobag	slutty woman, whore	college students	f	Asian
hobag	promiscuous woman	University of California at Berkeley students	m	Latino
hobuck	womanizer	teenagers and college students	m	Asian
hole	woman	high school in Pennsylvania	m	European
hoochie	prostitute, whore	college students	m	Asian
hoochie	slut, ho	used by women	f	European
hoochie	ho, promiscuous woman	Black college students	m	Asian
hoogie	slut	rap/hip hop music	f	European

hyperhootch	outgoing, loud, annoying female	male college students	m	Asian
hyperhootch	overly excitable female	teenagers at the Univ. of California at Berkeley	f	Asian
MIF	"mother I'd fuck," extremely attractive older woman	Marin [California] males	m	Asian
MILF	"mother I'd like to fuck," attractive older woman	college students from East Contra Costa [California]	m	European
mud-duck	girl who is extremely ugly, to the point of nausea	Hispanic college students	m	Latino
mutt	ugly girl	Los Angeles	m	Asian
mutt	very unattractive girl	college students	m	European
nectar babe	pretty girl	radio station	f	Asian
peach	girl who is very sweet, charming, soft, lovely	Northern California college students, frats	m	0
peach	beautiful girl	high school and college students	m	Asian
pelt	pretty and notoriously easy girl	Massachusetts boarding school	f	European
poon tang	vagina	college students	m	Latino
puddy	girl	New York	m	Asian
putang	vagina	some guy just made it up; college students	m	Asian
scud	ugly, undesirable girl	college students	m	Asian
sea-hag	thin unattractive girl	South San Francisco high school	m	Asian
shark	ugly girl	used in dorms and frats	m	0
six-pack beauty queen	unattractive woman	college students	f	Latino
skank	nasty, cheap	skaters	f	Asian
skank	flirtatious girl	Los Angeles	m	Asian
skank	extremely ugly girl, who is also promiscuous	college students	m	European
skank	dirty, nasty, unprincipled (woman)	Black/Hispanic college students	m	European
skank-ho	very ugly person who is also promiscuous (female)	New York	m	Asian
skankly ho	slut, ugly girl	Los Angeles guys	f	European
skeezer	filthy, slutty person	high school and college students	f	European
skeezy	gross, nasty		f	Asian
slime	the act by a female of walking home from a boy's house after a night of partying	frat guys	f	0
slut	easy girl, willing to put out	high school students	m	European
stank	ugly girl	college students	m	Mixed
strawberry	girl who sleeps around to obtain drugs	college students	m	Asian
strawberry	prostitute who works for drugs	street term	m	Asian
swamp sow	fat unattractive girl	South San Francisco high school	m	Asian
tetunca	very fat girl	Indian word for buffalo; frat guys	m	
thumper	promiscuous female	from a movie; high school	f	Asian
thunderthighs	fat female wearing a short skirt	teenagers	m	Asian
trinket	slut	freshman girls in high school	f	Asian
troll	ugly girl	frat guys	f	
tug boat	fat and ugly girl	Los Angeles	m	Asian
tuna	a slut	teenagers in Hawaii	m	Asian
tuna	slut, whore, or just a derogatory term for females	Hawaiian high school students	f	Asian
wicked witch of the west	mean woman	college students	m	Asian
yeti	big girl	high school in Pennsylvania	m	European

Notes

1. For an excellent discussion of the metaphor of *woman as dessert*, an extension of this concept, see Caitlin Hines (forthcoming).

2. It is worth noting that many of the insults reported for men meant 'homosexual'. For men to have sex with women is acceptable, but sex with men reduces men to the level of women (and therefore as subject to insult). This finding probably indicates that the majority of students in the class identify as heterosexual, at least in the context of the class. Slang used by gays and especially lesbians is an area largely unexplored by linguists.

3. See also the dictionaries by Clarence Major (1994) and Geneva Smitherman (1994).

References

Aranovitch, Florie (MS). The portrayal of women in the UCLA slang list: a reflection of women's status in society. University of California, Los Angeles, Department of Linguistics.

Chapman, Robert L. (1986). *New dictionary of American slang*. New York: Harper & Row.

Foote, R., and J. A. Woodward (1973). A preliminary investigation of obscene language. *Journal of Psychology* 83: 263–75.

Gal, Susan (this volume). Language, gender, and power: An anthropological review.

Gordon, Michael (1993). Sexual slang and gender. *Women and Language* 16(2): 16–21.

Graddol, David, and Joan Swann (1989). *Gender voices*. Oxford: Basil Blackwell.

Hernandez, Gilberto (1985). The reticent heart. In *Tears from heaven*. Vol. 4 of *Complete Love & Rockets*. Seattle: Fantagraphic Books.

Hines, Caitlin (forthcoming). "Let me call you sweetheart": The WOMAN AS DESSERT metaphor. In Mary Bucholtz, Anita Liang, Laurel Sutton, and Caitlin Hines (eds.), *Cultural performances: Proceedings of the Third Berkeley Women and Language Conference*. Berkeley: Berkeley Women and Language Group.

Jespersen, Otto (1921). *Language: Its nature, development and origin*. New York: Norton.

Johnson, F. L., and M. G. Fine (1985). Sex differences in uses and perceptions of obscenity. *Women's Studies in Communication* 8: 11–24.

Labov, William (1966). *The social stratification of English in New York City*. Washington, DC: Center for Applied Linguistics.

——— (1972). *Sociolinguistic patterns*. Philadelphia: University of Pennsylvania Press.

Lakoff, Robin (1975). *Language and woman's place*. New York: Harper & Row.

Major, Clarence (1994). *Juba to jive: A dictionary of African American slang*. Harmondsworth: Penguin.

McElhinny, Bonnie S. (this volume). Challenging hegemonic masculinities: Female and male police officers handling domestic violence.

Munro, Pamela (1989). *Slang U*. New York: Harmony Books.

Okamoto, Shigeko (this volume). "Tasteless" Japanese: Less "feminine" speech among young Japanese woman.

Penelope [Stanley], Julia (1977). Gender marking in American English: Usage and reference. In Alleen Pace Nilsen, Haig Bosmajian, H. Lee Gershuny, and Julia P. Stanley (eds.) *Sexism and language.* Urbana: National Council of Teachers of English. 43–74.

———. (1990). *Speaking freely.* New York: Pergamon Press.

Sanders, J. S. and W. Robinson (1979). Talking about and not talking about sex: male and female vocabularies. *Journal of Communication* 29: 22–30.

Schulz, Muriel R. (1975). The semantic derogation of women. In Barrie Thorne and Nancy Henley (eds.), *Language and sex: Difference and dominance.* Rowley, MA: Newbury House. 64–73.

Smitherman, Geneva (1977). *Talkin and testifyin.* Boston: Houghton Mifflin.

———. (1994). *Black talk: Words and phrases from the hood to the amen corner.* Boston: Houghton Mifflin.

Spender, Dale (1992). Information management: Women's language strengths. In Kira Hall, Mary Bucholtz, and Birch Moonwomon (eds.), *Locating power: Proceedings of the Second Berkeley Women and Language Conference.* Berkeley: Berkeley Women and Language Group. 549–59.

Treichler, Paula A. (1989). From discourse to dictionary: How sexist meanings are authorized. In Francine W. Frank and Paula A. Treichler (eds.), *Language, gender, and professional writing: Theoretical approaches and guidelines for nonsexist usage.* New York: Modern Language Association. 51–79.

Trudgill, Peter (1974). *The social differentiation of English in Norwich.* Cambridge: Cambridge University Press.

Walsh, R. H., and W. M. Leonard (1974). Usage of terms for sexual intercourse by men and women. *Archives of Sexual Behavior* 3: 373–76.

Whaley, C. R., and George Antonelli (1983). The birds and the beasts—woman as animal. *Maledicta* 7: 219–29.

Wolfram, Walt (1969). *A sociolinguistic description of Detroit Negro speech.* Washington, DC: Center for Applied Linguistics.

12

"Tasteless" Japanese

Less "Feminine" Speech Among Young Japanese Women

Shigeko Okamoto

It's Tasteless—Women's Use of Men's Language

In addition to the use of childish words and final rising intonations, young women have even started using men's language. Speaking in men's language is one thing, but there are girls who even use dirty words such as "*Aitsu, nani nebokete yagandai. Bakkeyaroo. Fuzakenjanee yo*" ['That guy, is he sleeping or something? You fool. Cut the crap'], which makes me wonder how in the world their parents and teachers are raising them. But then, their mothers are also actively using men's language. On TV, I even saw a female professor using men's language proudly; I felt it was deplorable and questioned her educational level. It is difficult to judge whether they are trying to be like men even in language because men and women have equal rights or whether it is a fad influenced by the mass media. In either case, for men it seems as taste-less as eating sand or grafting bamboo on a tree. It sets my teeth on edge like eating a sour apple. In Japan there is an attractive and adorable women's language. If we teach men's language to female foreigners, we will inevitably end up teaching the wrong Japanese culture.

—Letter from a fifty-nine-year-old man
to the readers' columns,
Asahi Shinbun, November 2, 1992;
translated from the Japanese original.

Japanese norms of behavior have traditionally been highly gendered. The Japanese language has also been characterized as having distinct female and male speech registers or "languages," and the gender differences are usually deemed more extensive and more rigid than those in English and other European languages. Descriptions of Japanese female and male speech differences are abundant in the literature (e.g., Ide 1979, 1982, 1990; Jugaku 1979; Kindaichi 1957; Mizutani & Mizutani 1987; Ohara 1992; Reynolds 1985; Shibamoto 1985, 1990; Smith 1992a, b); the most frequently cited differences include women's and men's divergent uses of self-reference and address terminology, sentence-final particles, honorifics, pitch ranges, and intonation.[1] Compared to "Japanese men's language" (*otoko-kotoba* or *dansei-go*), "Japanese women's language" (*onna-kotoba* or *josei-go*) has been described as polite, gentle, soft-spoken, nonassertive, and empathetic (e.g., Ide 1979, 1982, 1990; Jugaku 1979; Mizutani & Mizutani 1987; Reynolds 1990; Shibamoto 1985; Smith 1992a, b). These characteristics are often interpreted as reflecting women's lower social status or powerlessness (e.g., Ide 1982; Reynolds 1985; Smith 1992a, b).

Recently, however, newspapers and other publications within and outside Japan have been reporting anecdotally that some Japanese women, particularly younger women, are abandoning "traditional women's language" or stereotypical feminine speech patterns:

Women's Language

There are other signs of change, particularly among younger Japanese [women]. Suzuko Nishihara [an administrator at the National Language Institute in Tokyo] said that her two college-age daughters use more neutral, less polite and even mildly masculine forms of speech. Instead of ending their sentences with the feminine *wa yo*, they use *da yo* (the masculine form) when they are speaking with their classmates, male or female. Toward their elders, they end their verbs with *-masu* instead of the more polite *gozaimasu*. (Ellen Rudolph, *New York Times*, September 1, 1991)

Women's Language is Disappearing

"*Omee nani yatte n da yo!*" ('What the hell are you doing!'), "*Urusee naa. Monku yuu n ja nai yo.*" ('Shut up. Don't grumble'.), "*Oi, ore kono mondai tokeda zo.*" ('Hey, I solved this problem'.), "*Maji ka yo. Iya na yatsu.*" ('Are you serious? Disgusting guy'.). In classrooms of junior and senior high schools now, conversations like these are flying around among female students. Expressions like these make even male students feel embarrassed and are causing adults to lament, "Recently, girls' speech has become *ranboo* 'rough'." (*NHK Jissen Hanashi Kotoba*, October 1991–March 1992; translated from the Japanese original)[2]

These casual observations suggest that there may exist wide synchronic and diachronic variations in Japanese women's speech styles. If so, such practices would undermine essentialist assumptions about Japanese women's speech as constituting a discrete, homogeneous category. At the same time, these observations suggest the need for careful empirical studies of variations in Japanese women's speech, together with analyses that consider social diversity among Japanese women. In her critical overview of the literature on Japanese women's language, Eleanor Jorden (1990:2) pointedly asks, "How much actual correlation is there between *onna-rashii* ['womanly'] language and the broad spectrum of language used by the Japanese woman of today?" Katsue Reynolds (1990), discussing "deviant" cases of Japanese women's language, emphasizes the need to analyze such phenomena because such cases may eventually lead toward female-male linguistic equality. To date, however, only a few studies have examined variation in female speech patterns (Kobayashi 1993; Takasaki 1993).

Against this background Shie Sato and I (Okamoto & Sato 1992) carried out a preliminary study, examining tape-recorded conversations of fourteen Japanese women in three age groups. (All but two of the subjects were living in the United States.) Results of the study revealed great variation in speech styles across the three age groups, as well as among individuals within each age group. The present chapter, an extension of this earlier study, examines the speech styles of female college students living in Tokyo, focusing specifically on their employment of sentence-final forms. Three interrelated issues are of principal concern: (1) How and to what extent do the speech styles of young Japanese women differ from the stereotype known as *Japanese women's language*? (2) Does "Japanese women's language" reflect real language practices or the linguistic ideal for Japanese women? (3) Why and under what circumstances do Japanese women use or not use stereotypical "women's language"?

Consideration of these issues requires a reexamination of our thinking about the relation between language and gender. Previous studies of language and gender—in particular, the two opposing theories often referred to as the *dominance approach* (e.g., Fishman 1983; Lakoff 1975; O'Barr & Atkins 1980; Trudgill 1975; West & Zimmerman 1983) and the *difference* or *cultural approach* (e.g., Maltz & Borker 1982; Tannen 1990a, b)—have made important contributions, raising our awareness of how language reflects the social inequalities or cultural differences between women and men.[3] Many of these studies, however, are based on static binary opposi- tions and abstractions, such as *women* versus *men, powerless* versus *power- ful,* and *women's speech* versus *men's speech* (Eckert & McConnell-Ginet 1992). Recently, a number of researchers have emphasized the importance of investigating local linguistic practices and recognizing the multiplicity, contextuality, ideologies, and historicity involved in the relation between language and gender (Cameron & Coates 1988; Eckert & McConnell-Ginet 1992; Gal, this volume; Ochs 1993). Such an approach pays close attention to the diversity and heterogeneity of women and stresses women's agency in their linguistic practices. It enables us to identify the meanings of women's linguistic choices in specific sociocultural and historical contexts (e.g., Brown 1990; Cameron, McAlinden, & O'Leary 1988; Eckert 1989; Gonzales Velásquez, this volume; Goodwin 1988, 1992; Nichols 1983; Ochs 1987; Thomas 1988).

The present study examines Japanese women's speech from this new perspective. Although previous research has concluded that the linguistic differences between Japanese women and men are extensive, most resorts to overgeneralizations based on the static dichotomous categories of *women's language* and *men's language*—an approach that tends to represent and rein- force stereotypes or linguistic norms. Many of these studies also suffer from methodological weaknesses in that they rely on either the researchers' introspection or self-report surveys that do not accurately capture actual speech practices. In contrast, the present study analyzes tape-recorded actual conversations in order to explore the meanings of the linguistic choices that young Japanese women make in specific sociocultural and historical contexts.

Method

The data for the present study, collected in September and October 1992, consist of five tape-recorded informal conversations, each between two close friends. A total of ten female college students, ages eighteen to twenty, participated as subjects. All were born in Tokyo and still reside there, are from middle- or upper-middle-class backgrounds, and speak standard Japanese. The subjects were asked to tape-record their *oshaberi* 'chat' with their close friends.[4] Each conversation, with the exception of the first five minutes, was transcribed to obtain 150 consecutive sentence tokens for each speaker.[5]

The analysis focused on sentence-final forms, each of which was identified as *feminine, neutral,* or *masculine.* Feminine forms are those traditionally considered to be used primarily by women; masculine forms, by men; and neutral forms, by both women and men. This identification was based mainly on the classification given in the literature (e.g., McGloin 1990; Mizutani & Mizutani 1987; Shibamoto 1985).[6] Feminine and masculine forms were further subdivided into *strongly feminine* or *strongly masculine* forms and *moderately feminine* or *moderately masculine* forms; forms traditionally considered to be used exclusively by women or by men are classified respectively as strongly feminine or strongly masculine. The following list exemplifies the gender classification of sentence-final forms used in the present study (the list is not exhaustive; see Okamoto & Sato 1992 for a more detailed list). It is to be underscored that this classification is used only as a reference point and is by no means absolute.

Gender Classification of Sentence-Final Forms

Feminine forms
- The particle *wa* (with rising intonation) for mild emphasis or its variants (*wa ne, wa yo, wa yo ne*)

  Example: *Iku wa.* ['I am going.']

  Classification: strongly feminine
- The particle *no* after a noun or *na*-adjective in a statement

  Example: *Ashita na no.* ['It is that it is tomorrow.']

  Classification: strongly feminine
- The particle *no* after a plain form of a verb or *i*-adjective for emphasis or explanation in a statement

  Example: *Iku no.* ['It's that I'm going'.]

  Classification: moderately feminine
- The particle *no* followed by *ne* or *yo ne* for seeking confirmation or agreement; the particle *no* followed by *yo* for assertion

  Example: *Ashita na no ne?* ['It's that it's tomorrow, isn't it?']

  Classification: strongly feminine
- The auxiliary *desho(o)* for expressing probability or for seeking agreement or confirmation

  Example: *Iku deshoo?* ['You are going, aren't you?']

  Classification: moderately feminine
- The particle *kashira* ['I wonder']

  Example: *Kuru kashira.* ['I wonder if he is coming.']

  Classification: strongly feminine

Masculine forms

• The particles *ze* and *zo* for assertion
<blockquote>
Example: *Iku ze.* ['I'm going, I tell you.']
Classification: strongly masculine
</blockquote>

• The particle *yo* after a plain form of a verb or *i*-adjective for assertion
<blockquote>
Example: *Iku yo.* ['I'm going, I tell you.']
Classification: moderately masculine
</blockquote>

• The auxiliary verb *da* alone for declaration (or its variants *da ne, da yo,* or *da yo ne*)
<blockquote>
Example: *Ashita da.* ['It's tomorrow.']
Classification: moderately masculine
</blockquote>

• The plain imperative form of a verb alone or followed by *yo*
<blockquote>
Example: *Ike.* ['Go.']
Classification: strongly masculine
</blockquote>

• The phonological form *ee* instead of *ai* and *oi*
<blockquote>
Example: *Shiranee.* (*Shiranai.*) ['I don't know.']
Classification: strongly masculine
</blockquote>

• The verb *-oo ka* for an invitation or offer
<blockquote>
Example: *Ikoo ka?* ['Shall we go?']
Classification: moderately masculine
</blockquote>

Neutral forms

• The plain form of a verb or *i*-adjective for assertion
<blockquote>
Example: *Iku.* ['I'm going.']
</blockquote>

• The particle *yo* followed by *ne* for seeking agreement or confirmation
<blockquote>
Example: *Iku yo ne?* ['You are going, right?']
</blockquote>

• The negative auxiliary *ja nai* for mild assertion or to seek agreement
<blockquote>
Example: *Ashita ja nai?* ['It's tomorrow, isn't it?']
</blockquote>

• The negative auxiliary *jan* (a contracted form of *ja nai*) for mild assertion or to seek agreement
<blockquote>
Example: *Ashita jan?* ['It's tomorrow, isn't it?']
</blockquote>

• The particles *ka na* 'I wonder'
<blockquote>
Example: *Iku ka na.* ['I wonder if he is going.']
</blockquote>

• The gerundive form of a verbal alone or followed by the particle *ne* or *sa* (when accompanied by a sentence-final intonation and/or semantic completeness)
<blockquote>
Example: *Ikoo to omotte (ne/sa).* ['I thought I would go.']
</blockquote>

• The exclamatory particle *naa*
<blockquote>
Example: *Ii naa.* ['How nice.']
</blockquote>

After the gender style of each sentence token was identified, the total number of sentence tokens in each style for each speaker and for the entire group were tallied, and the percentages of each style for each speaker and the whole group were calculated.

Less "Feminine" Speech Styles Among Female College Students

Table 12.1 shows the distribution of gendered sentence-final forms for all ten subjects combined. Although this distribution varies from individual to individual,[7] the speech styles of the participants in this study are hardly feminine in the traditional sense.

Table 12.1 Use of Gendered Sentence-final Forms for All Ten Subjects (ages 18–20)

Sentence-final Forms	Total Tokens Used (%)
Feminine forms	12.3
• Moderately feminine forms	7.8
• Strongly feminine forms	4.5
Masculine forms	18.9
• Moderately masculine forms	17.5
• Strongly masculine forms	1.4
Neutral forms	68.8
Total	100.0

Note: Total number of tokens = 1,500 (150 tokens for each subject)

All of the speakers used neutral forms most frequently,[8] and all except two used masculine forms more often than feminine forms. Moreover, the majority of the feminine forms used by the subjects were moderately feminine forms, the most common being the verb or *i*-adjective *no*, appearing in 55 tokens, and the auxiliary *desho(o)*, appearing in 40 tokens, as illustrated in the sentences reproduced in (1) and (2):

(1)   (Speaker 4, referring to her trip to Europe)
      Uun, ichi-gatsu ni wa moo kaette kuru no.
      'No, I will already be back in January'.

(2)   (Speaker 3)
      Shoogaku-juken desho.
      'That's an entrance exam for elementary school, right?'

The use of strongly feminine forms was infrequent, appearing in only 34 percent of all feminine tokens. The forms used most frequently were *no ne*, appearing in 42 tokens, and *na no*, appearing in 15 tokens. It is worth noting that the particle *wa* (with rising intonation) and its variants, often cited in the literature as the most typical feminine forms, were used only twice in the entire data set. The particle *kashira*, another ending perceived as strongly feminine, was used only once; in its place subjects employed the neutral form *ka na*. There was not a single instance of the (noun/*na*-adjective) *yo* with rising intonation (e.g., *Ashita yo* 'It's tomorrow'), which is also considered a typical feminine ending. Note, however, that in addition to the two instances of the feminine particle *wa* just mentioned, there were six other instances of the feminine particle *wa* in the data set. Interestingly, these were all part of speakers' quotations of older women (for instance, their mothers or female teachers), as in examples (3) and (4).

(3)   (Speaker 4, quoting her female teacher)
      Sono roku-nin ni wa moo kekkoo gooka-na mono agechau wa yo to ka ittee.
      'She said, "I will then give quite luxurious things to those six people."'

(4)   (Speaker 8, quoting her mother)
      Sore okaasan ni hanashitara, ja watashi ga morau wa yo to ka itte.
      'When I told that to my mother, she said, "Then I will get it."'

Most of the masculine forms used by the subjects were moderately masculine forms, appearing in 93 percent of all masculine tokens. The two forms used most commonly were the auxiliary verb *da* and its variants (e.g., *da yo*, *da yo ne*), used in 263 tokens, and the particle *yo* (preceded by a plain form of a verb or *i*-adjective), used in 69 tokens. These uses are exemplified in sentences (5) and (6), respectively.

(5)   (Speaker 6, talking about reading books)
      Jaa kore wa pittari da yo.
      'Then this (book) is perfect (for you)'.

(6)   (Speaker 7, discussing skiwear)
      Demo ryuukoo wa [oe] owanai hoo ga ii yo.
      'But it's better not to follow the fashion'.

The subjects did use strongly masculine forms, though on a very limited basis; such forms appeared in only 21 tokens of the entire data set. Three of these uses are reproduced in examples (7) through (9).

(7)　(Speaker 1, discussing the location of an office)
　　　Iya datte tooi zo.
　　　'But it's far away'.

(8)　(Speaker 4, correcting the interlocutor's mispronunciation)
　　　Gondoro ja nee, gondora (laughter).
　　　'It's not *gondoro*, it's *gondora* (gondola)'.

(9)　(Speaker 10, responding to the interlocutor's teasing remark)
　　　Katte ni itte ro tte.
　　　'Say whatever you want to say'.

In addition to the instances of strongly masculine sentence endings, subjects also used other expressions commonly perceived as strongly masculine or vulgar: e.g., *aitsu* 'that guy', *bakayaroo* 'stupid', *dekai* 'humongous', *kuu* 'eat/chow down', *nukasu* 'say', *yabai* 'troublesome', *yatsu* 'that guy/thing', and *yatsu-ra* 'those guys'.

In sum, the speech styles of the speakers observed in this study are hardly feminine but, rather, neutral to moderately masculine. The following excerpt from the data set, a conversation between two participants about a part-time job, illustrates the speakers' unfeminine conversational styles:

(10)　Speakers 3 and 4, discussing a part-time job that involves collect-
　　　ing questionnaires (neutral and masculine forms are underlined)
　　　SP 4:　*Baito.*
　　　　　　'It's a part-time job'.
　　　SP 5:　*Baito ka. Ii jan, sore.*
　　　　　　'Oh, it's a part-time job. That's good, isn't it?'
　　　SP 4:　[laughter]
　　　SP 5:　*Nani, yareba ii jan.*
　　　　　　'What? You should do it, don't you think?'
　　　SP 4:　*Iya, hyaku-nin da yo.*
　　　　　　'But I have to ask 100 people'.
　　　SP 5:　*Un, karui mon jan.*
　　　　　　'Yeah, it's easy, isn't it?'

SP 4:   *Iya, hyaku-nin de ichi-man-en <u>da</u> <u>yo</u>.*
         'But it's (only) 10,000 yen for (asking) 100 people'.
SP 5:   *Ichi-man-en? Ichi-man-en kaa.*
         '10,000 yen. Oh, it's 10,000 yen'.
SP 4:   *Hyaku-nin yaru no wa muzukashii tte yuu uwasa <u>da</u> <u>yo</u>.*
         'I heard that it's difficult to get 100 people'.

All the sentences in the exchange reproduced in (10) end with either a masculine or a neutral form, not with a feminine form; such a conversation is typical of those appearing in the data set.

It is interesting to compare these results with those obtained by Okamoto and Sato (1992). The earlier study examined the speech styles of three age groups: 18–23 (seven subjects, all college students), 27–34 (three subjects, all homemakers), and 45–57 (four subjects, all professional women). Except for two subjects in the oldest age group, all were Japanese women living in the United States; the subjects in the two youngest age groups came to the United States no more than 18 months before the time of data collection. Table 12.2 summarizes the results of the study.

Table 12.2 Use of Gendered Sentence-final Forms (Percentages)

Sentence-final Forms	7 subjects ages 18–23	3 subjects ages 27–34	4 subjects ages 45–57
Feminine forms	14	24	50
• Moderately feminine forms	10	13	23
• Strongly feminine forms	4	12	28
Masculine forms	29	14	6
• Moderately masculine forms	24	14	6
• Strongly masculine forms	5	0	0
Neutral forms	57	62	44
Total	100	100	100

Note: Total number of tokens = 1,820 (130 tokens for each subject)

Source: Shigeko Okamoto and Shie Sato, "Less Feminine" speech among Young Japanese Females," in Kira Hall, Mary Bucholtz, and Birch Moonwomon (eds.), *Locating Power: Proceedings of the Second Berkeley Women and Language Conference* (Berkeley: Berkeley Women and Language Group, 1992).

The speech styles of the youngest subjects in the 1992 study, whose sentence-final forms are itemized in the first column, closely resemble those of the participants in the present study. The styles of younger women, then, appear to be much less feminine than the styles of older women, although there are of course individual differences among the speakers within each age group.

"Japanese Women's Language" and Gender Ideologies

The results of the present study and the 1992 study illustrate the great variations in the speech styles of Japanese women, an observation also recently noted in studies by Mieko Kobayashi (1993) and Midori Takasaki (1993). Kobayashi reports that the self-report surveys and analyses of conversations she and her colleagues conducted show generational differences among women: older speakers (grandmothers and mothers) used more "feminine" expressions (i.e., sentence-final forms, indirect expressions, honorifics) than younger speakers (students) did. Takasaki's analysis of conversations of women in different occupations shows that homemakers used more "feminine" linguistic features (such as sentence-final particles, interjections, and honorifics) than students did, and that female office workers used features such as honorifics and the polite prefix o- much more than professional or self-employed women did.[9] These findings suggest that the common sex-based category *women's language*, as opposed to the category *men's language*, is too static and monolithic to capture variation in the speech styles of Japanese women.

Because the attributes associated with "Japanese women's language" include politeness, formality, empathy, soft-spokenness, indirectness, and nonassertiveness, it could be said to function to create an image of powerlessness, social sensitivity, and femininity. A textbook example of this style surfaced in the speech of one of the older speakers in the 1992 study, designated as Speaker 2 in Table 12.3.

The majority of the forms used by Speaker 2 were feminine forms (70 percent), many of them strongly feminine forms; only rarely did she employ masculine forms (1 percent). In addition, the pitch level of her speech was very high; when she was a small girl, she told me, her mother used to chide her whenever she spoke with a low voice because it was *gehin* 'vulgar, unrefined'. She was raised in an upper-middle-class family in Tokyo and graduated from a prestigious university for women; she has been living in the United States for more than twelve years, having very little contact with other Japanese.

Table 12.3 Use of Gendered Sentence-final Forms for Individual Speakers in the Oldest Age Group, 45–57 (Percentages)

Sentence-final Forms	SP 1	SP 2	SP 3	SP 4	All
Feminine forms	50	70	55	24	50
• Moderately feminine forms	22	33	21	12	22
• Strongly feminine forms	28	37	34	12	18
Masculine forms	6	1	3	15	6
• Moderately masculine forms	6	1	3	15	6
• Strongly masculine forms	0	0	0	0	0
Neutral forms	44	29	42	61	44
Total	100	100	100	100	100

Note: Speakers 1 and 2 = U.S. residents; Speakers 3 and 4 = Tokyo residents

Source: Shigeko Okamoto and Shie Sato, "Less Femine" Speech among Young Japanese Females," in Kira Hall, Mary Bucholtz, and Birch Moonwomon (eds.), *Locating Power: Proceedings of the Second Berkeley Women and Language Conference* (Berkeley: Berkeley Women and Language Group, 1992).

One would rarely encounter such a stereotypical feminine speech style among contemporary young women. Even many of the older women in the middle classes do not use such feminine speech styles, as exemplified by the less feminine style of Speaker 4 in the same study. For this speaker, only 24 percent of the forms were feminine; 15 percent were masculine. Nor do women living in farming and fishing communities seem to use hyperfeminine speech styles. Chisato Kitagawa (1977:292) points out, "The sexual distinction in speech style in Japan has been more of an urban phenomenon than a rural one." (See also Kindaichi 1957.) In this connection, the gender differences in regional dialects also seem to be less distinct than those in the standard dialect, which may be due to the historical fact that the use of "women's language" was particularly encouraged in the Meiji era (the late nineteenth century to the early twentieth century), along with the standardization of Japanese. In Tokyo itself there are two regions, *Yamanote* 'the hillside' and *Shitamachi* 'the downtown', but the boundaries are not as clearcut today as they once were. In the words of Dorinne Kondo (1990:57), *Yamanote* is "the mainstream, modern ideal," the domain of white-collar workers, whereas *Shitamachi* "conjures up images of the merchant, the artisan, the small family business." The two groups are said to speak different "languages": *Shitamachi kotoba* and *Yamanote kotoba*. In contrast to the former style, which is thought to be "rough," "direct," and "vulgar"

(Kondo 1990), *Yamanote kotoba* is thought to be "soft-spoken," "indirect," and "refined"—or, rather, the language that encompasses the feminine ideal.

In light of these observations, it is uncertain to what extent the label *Japanese women's language* reflects the actual language practices of Japanese women. Speech styles of Japanese women are not, as frequently implied, consistent across different age groups, classes, occupations, regions, and situations. Where, then, does the stereotype of Japanese women's language come from? As pointed out in Okamoto and Sato (1992), "Japanese women's language" is a construct based largely on the speech style of traditional women in the middle and upper-middle classes in Tokyo, corresponding to the "ideal feminine" variety in *Yamanote kotoba*. Sachiko Ide (1979) notes that her characterization of Japanese women's language is based on the variety spoken by people in the middle class or above in Tokyo, in particular the variety *Yamanote kotoba*. Miyako Inoue (forthcoming) explains that modern perceptions of Japanese women's language were shaped and promoted during state formation and industrialization in the Meiji era, when government officials and intellectuals sought to standardize the language and to discipline women according to the ideal of *ryoosai kenbo* 'good wife and wise mother'. Women's language, thus identified, was viewed as the "natural" speech of the Tokyo elite. Today's notion of Japanese women's language can be seen as a lasting legacy of this historical enterprise.[10] Along with other symbolic systems (e.g., clothes, bearing), it constitutes an ideal for the traditional, proper, or *onna-rashii* 'feminine' Japanese woman. It is thus culturally and ideologically constructed, both class-related and normative.

Elinor Ochs (1993:149) asserts that "language is a source and moving force of gender ideologies" and that "we should expect language to be influenced by local organizations of gender roles, rights, and expectations." Similarly, Susan Gal (this volume) argues that categories such as *women's speech* and *men's speech* are "culturally constructed within social groups; they change through history and are systematically related to other areas of cultural discourse such as the nature of persons, of power, and of a desirable moral order." Thus "Japanese women's language" is not simply a result of overgeneralization in linguistic description; rather, it is a reflection of the dominant gender ideologies embedded, even today, in Japanese culture and society. Inoue (forthcoming) argues that the modern "Japanese women's language" is a result of "a political project to construct a norm or ideology of women's language." To regard a particular feminine variety as belonging to Japanese women's language is, then, to advance certain gender ideologies.

To disregard all unfeminine or less feminine language practices as deviations serves to marginalize the meanings women express through these practices. Such ideological conflict is well illustrated by this chapter's epigraph.

As emphasized by Penelope Eckert and Sally McConnell-Ginet (1992), ways of being women and men are diverse and continually changing, and so are ways of talking. In contrast to the images projected by stereotypes, particularly those advanced by cultural essentialism,[11] Japanese women are socially and ideologically diverse and constantly changing (Brinton 1993; English Discussion Society 1992; Inoue & Ehara 1991; Iwao 1993; Kondo 1990; Lebra, Paulson, & Powers 1976; Roberts 1994; Tamanoi 1990; Uno 1993). In 1990, for example, more than half of all Japanese women were in the labor force (Lam 1992); working mothers now outnumber full-time homemakers (Inoue & Ehara 1991). Expectations in connection with gender roles and the images of ideal Japanese women (and men) are also changing, as the following excerpts demonstrate:

> In a society where it is difficult for women to gain economic independence, it has been thought that marriage is the place of life security for women, and that child rearing after marriage is the woman's way of living. But recently, along with women's advancement in the society, more people think that [a woman] need not necessarily get married if she can be independent. [According to government polls, in 1972, 13 percent of women and 7 percent of men agreed with this view; in 1987, 24 percent of women and 16 percent of men supported the same view.] (Inoue & Ehara 1991: 14–15)

> According to the opinion survey on women released by the Prime Minister's Office on January 13, 1991, 34 percent of men and 43 percent of women disagreed with biological division of labor. In the previous survey, 20 percent of men and 32 percent of women were opposed. (English Discussion Society 1992:79)

> Mom is jogging and Dad is cleaning. That is an illustration used in a new elementary school home economics textbook. ... Some [illustrations] which imply reversed sex roles or images have appeared in the textbooks which are to be used from '92. (English Discussion Society 1992:80; original from *Asahi Shinbun*, February 3, 1992)

> New models of manhood are constantly being proffered. *Nikkei Woman* magazine, the bible for working women in Japan, exhorted its readers this year to seize the advantage and settle for nothing less

than a "Goat Man." Like the animal regarded in Japan as gentle but
strong, the Goat Man is a mate of intelligence and wide interests
who doesn't look to his wife as substitute mother and who likes
household chores and child care. (Teresa Watanabe, *Los Angeles
Times*, January 6, 1992)

Women's linguistic practices, particularly their use or disuse of stereotypical
Japanese women's language, may reflect or "index" (Silverstein 1976, 1985)
differences in gender ideologies like those alluded to in these passages. This
observation has prompted analysts like Eleanor Jorden (1990:3) to call for
more study of variation in Japanese speech styles: "Assuming that Japanese
women are expected to use a gentle, empathetic style more commonly than
men, it becomes important to identify the image and the message they
communicate when they do *not* speak in this register." But such images and
messages can be identified only if variation and change are examined vis-à-
vis dominant norms and expectations at a given time, with reference to their
sociocultural and historical significance. Such a study entails the investigation of actual language practices in diverse communities and contexts.

Identities, Interpersonal Relations, and Speech-Style Strategies
Why and under what circumstances, then, do Japanese women choose to
use or not use stereotypical women's language, or, more appropriately,
certain speech styles? As the traditional classification of sentence-final
particles illustrates, certain Japanese linguistic forms have often been
regarded as gendered. Such a treatment views the relation between language
and gender as a simple straightforward mapping of linguistic forms to the
speaker's sex (Ochs 1993). Clearly, however, this view cannot account for
the speech styles of the subjects in this study. Rather, as argued by Ochs
(1993:146), it is more helpful to view the relation between language and
gender not as directly indexical, but as "constituted and mediated by the
relation of language to stances, social acts, social activities, and other social
constructs." For example, it is often said that compared to masculine forms
such as *zō* and *da*, particles such as *wa* (with a rising intonation) and *no* are
gentle, nonassertive, or empathetic, and hence convey a sense of femininity
or politeness (Ide 1979, 1982, 1990; McGloin 1990; Reynolds 1985; Smith
1992b; Uyeno 1971). In other words, these linguistic indexes are best
regarded as expressions of pragmatic meanings, such as gentleness and
empathy, which in turn may relate to gender images or "the preferred
images of men and women" and hence may "motivate their differential
uses by men and women" (Ochs 1993:151).

To go a step further, the choice of speech styles or certain linguistic forms can be considered a matter of the speaker's "strategic choice" (Brown 1980), based on the kind of pragmatic meanings she (or he) wishes to convey. Not all Japanese women may wish to project the image of "traditional" femininity. Japanese women (and men) choose particular speech styles to communicate certain pragmatic meanings that are appropriate for expressing and constructing their identities in specific relational contexts. These choices, then, require the context-specific consideration of multiple social attributes associated with the speaker's identity and interpersonal relationships (such as gender, age, occupation, intimacy), as well as the speaker's knowledge and evaluation of the relevant linguistic norms. It is to be emphasized that one's identity is dependent on specific relationships and sociocultural contexts (Bachnik 1994; Kondo 1990; Rosenberger 1992); Japanese women's speech styles reflect their understanding of themselves as certain kinds of Japanese women (e.g., young unmarried women, homemakers, managers) interacting in specific contexts. Thus, gender cannot be viewed in the abstract, as independent of identity and relationships. Rather, gender and other social attributes jointly and interactively construct women's identities and their relationships, thereby affecting their choice of speech styles.

Age, for example, may be an important aspect of a Japanese woman's identity, affecting her way of relating to others and hence her choice of speech style or linguistic form. It is often said that Japanese women, in particular young women, are becoming more assertive (English Discussion Society 1992; Iwao 1993)—a perception supported by an *NHK* survey conducted in 1979:

> Among teens and those in their early '20s, more women than men regarded themselves as "the main speaker" in casual conversations, but the opposite was the case in older generations. Further, in the case of younger generations, the portion of those who regarded themselves as "likely to insist on their opinions against others" was about the same among men and among women, but in middle-age or older generations the portion of men who held this view was two or three times that among women. (Hiroshi Ishino, *Kotoba* 4, no. 4, (1980):34–37; translated from the Japanese original)[12]

A 1992 article in *Asahi Shinbun*, in reference to the speech of young female employees newly entering a company, similarly reported: "[Their speech] has a positive aspect: they are able to speak without hesitation" (October 8, 1992). In an interview with the *Los Angeles Times* during the same year, a board member of the International Community Association in Tokyo attributed the success of his matchmaking firm to this same assertiveness, declaring that "Japanese women today are not like women":

> When you look at it from a Japanese male perspective, Japanese women today are not like women," Omura sighed. "They're too self-assertive. They won't listen to men. They used to be more submissive and weaker. Women have changed. But men haven't. So these men who haven't changed can't find women. (Teresa Watanabe, *Los Angeles Times*, January 6, 1992)

College-age women frequently use sentence-final forms traditionally deemed masculine, that is, more direct or assertive styles, but they use the feminine particle *wa* when quoting their mothers and female teachers.

Other linguistic features that characterize the informal speech styles of young women include the contracted sentence-final form *jan* (see example (10)) instead of the more formal form *ja nai*, a prolonged sentence-final (and medial) rising intonation (e.g., the final *ittee* in example (4)), faddish slang and coinages (e.g., the prefix *choo-* 'super-', *suggee* 'awesome', *tame* 'agemate', *kakyoo* from *kateikyooshi* 'tutor'), and quick conversational tempos (*Asahi Shinbun*, October 8 and 14, 1992, October 20, 1993; Kashiwagi 1991). These features seem to create an image of playfulness and youthfulness. A number of young women I talked with emphasized the importance of these features as a marker of youth; regarding tempo, for example, they characterized their mothers' speech as slow. The differences in speech among age groups seem rather important in Japanese, as the term *sedai-hoogen* 'generation dialect' suggests. A newspaper reporter writes, "It's gotten so that I could be told by young people 'You (the chief) have a strong *yonjyuu-namari* ('a forty-something accent')'" (*Asahi Shinbun*, October 14, 1992). When I showed the reader's letter in *Asahi Shinbun*— this chapter's epigraph—to two young Japanese women, one of them immediately responded that she was not using men's language but "*waka-mono no kotoba*" 'the language of young people'. It seems that the use of such speech styles by young women, particularly in conversation among peers, serves to convey an image of youthfulness, to differentiate younger from older women, and thus to establish solidarity.

A woman's occupation and position, as they relate to her relative power, may also affect her choice of speech styles in certain situations. In Okamoto and Sato (1992), the speech of the youngest group, all of whom were students, was less feminine than the second youngest group, all of whom were homemakers (see also Takasaki 1993). Here, the fact that communities of students are not as clearly differentiated in gender roles as communities of homemakers may account for some of the difference. In this connection, we may note that the use of the first-person masculine pronoun *boku* is not uncommon among high school girls in Japan. Akiko Jugaku (1979:80) reports that high school girls explained that they use *boku* because if they use the first-person feminine pronoun *atashi* they cannot compete with boys. According to Reynolds (1990:140), girls are "aware of the disadvantage of female speech in school situations where they are expected to compete with boys for good grades and choose to ignore traditions openly."

Reynolds (1990:138) also discusses the conflict between traditional female speech expectations and the need for professional women to communicate more assertively: "Female informal speech, which has long been limited to private discourse among women, does not work in the same way as male informal speech in public environments. For a woman teacher to be successful under the present circumstances, she has no choice but to use defeminized patterns to strengthen solidarity with her students without losing authority." Prominent female politicians are frequently reported as defying traditional speech conventions, as in the following reference to Takako Doi, the current Speaker of the House of Representatives in the National Diet:

> Takako Doi, who recently resigned as head of the Socialist Party and is one of the most visible women in Japan, succeeds in breaking many of these rules [for Japanese women's speech]. Her voice is always low, even when she is passionately pressing a point. She uses honorifics much less often than most women, and she employs the masculine form, *de arimasu*, instead of the more polite, and thus feminine, *de gozaimasu*, meaning "to be." Most noticeable is a bit of unusual body language: she always looks the listener straight in the face when speaking. (Ellen Rudolph, *New York Times*, September 1, 1991)

Gender differences in speech also seem less distinct in rural areas, perhaps in part because "in farming communities, women constitute an important labor force, and thus are not as dependent on men as their urban counterparts" (Kitagawa 1977:292); they need not behave as powerlessly as urban homemakers.

All these examples show that Japanese women at times employ unfeminine speech styles—that is, speech styles that are less formal and more direct—in order to express power or to empower themselves. Such linguistic behaviors may be considered "marked" (Ochs 1993:154) against the normative behaviors, insofar as they are viewed as unfeminine or incongruous with expectations of gender practices. Although such a culturally marked strategy may be found appropriate by some women in certain domains, others may prefer to exert more gender-appropriate strategies to express and gain power. Janet Smith (1992a) discusses two such strategies that women in positions of authority sometimes employ in giving directives: *motherese*, based on forms that mothers commonly use in speaking to their children, and *passive power*, based on relatively passive or indirect forms. The former recalls the authority of the Japanese mother while simultaneously invoking family-like solidarity; the latter exploits the normative expectations for Japanese women's interactional behaviors. Yukako Sunaoshi (1995, forthcoming) supplies empirical data for the effective use of these two strategies as well as several others used to create rapport in the context of power relations. Thus, gender, relative power, norms, and expectations interact in complex ways, and Japanese women select the strategies—whether marked or unmarked—that they find most appropriate for expressing and constructing their identities and relationships.

The nature of the relationship between conversational partners (e.g., degree of intimacy) and the formality level of the conversational situation also affect a woman's choice of speech style. For example, both in the present study and in Okamoto and Sato (1992), the subjects' use of strongly masculine or vulgar speech styles was limited in frequency and reserved for certain interlocutors. Some of the subjects explained that they use strongly masculine or vulgar expressions only with close peers or *"kokoro no tsuujiru aite"* ('those who can understand each other well') as *"aijoo no hyoogen"* ('expressions of affection'). When compared to the use of moderately masculine forms, the use of strongly masculine forms seems to be a highly conscious decision. In both studies subjects often qualified strongly masculine expressions by giggling (as in example (8)) or using hedges, such as a quotative *tte* 'that' (as in example (9)) or the expression *mitai na* 'like': e.g., *shiranai no ka yo mitai na* 'It's like, "don't you know?"' (Okamoto & Sato 1992:486). Such devices indicate that the speakers are aware of the markedness of these vulgar forms and do not see them as part of their normal speech style. Yet, they elect to use them, to break the norms, in an attempt to reinforce solidarity. The participants used strongly masculine forms particularly for emphasis (example (7)), when telling a joke (example (8)), or when criticizing or protesting (example (9)). Their employment therefore functions to increase the expressiveness of an utterance, making the conversation between peers "more interesting and spirited," as several participants remarked in the Okamoto and Sato study (1992:487).

Note also that the youngest group in the 1992 study used many more masculine forms, including strongly masculine forms, than the subjects in the present study. One of the reasons for this difference may be related to the fact that the present study was carried out in a more formal context than the earlier one: the subjects were asked to cooperate by their professors at Japanese colleges; the subjects in the 1992 study, conducted at an American college, were asked to participate by a student or professor who did not know them. The style differences observed in the two studies, particularly regarding the use of strongly masculine styles, may reflect not only the participants' awareness of speech norms for women but also their desire to employ speech styles most appropriate to the situation. Their discursive choices are perhaps influenced by notions such as *uchi* 'inside/private' versus *soto* 'outside/public', and *tatemae* 'social surface' versus *honne* 'real feelings'—distinctions essential to understanding Japanese behaviors (Bachnik 1992, 1994; Kondo 1990; Tobin 1992). Dorinne Kondo (1990:141) explains that *uchi* "instantly implies the drawing of boundaries between us and them, self and other," and that "*soto* means the public world, while *uchi* is the world of informality, casual behavior, and relaxation. *Soto* is where one must be attentive to social relationships, cultivating one's *tatemae*, whereas in the *uchi* one is free to express one's *honne*." In a setting of *soto*, then, young women may be inclined to use more feminine or polite speech styles, and in a setting of *uchi*, where solidarity and casualness are important, they may find such styles inappropriate. As several young women in the study explained, feminine speech styles in the latter situation sound "*aratamatta*" ('formal') and "*kidotta*" ('prudish').

Nobuko Uchida (1993) offers further evidence for the influence of social relationships on the choice of speech styles. She and her colleagues examined dyadic conversations of forty female and male college students (in which each pair of speakers was meeting for the first time) as well as conversations on television interviews. Her analysis revealed that in mixed-sex conversations between college students, both women and men used facilitative questions and interjections frequently—a finding that suggests speakers are more relaxed with same-sex interlocutors. In the television conversations, the relative status between speakers affected the occurrence of features such as interruptions, indirect expressions, and honorifics. Moreover, the male college students in her study used the first-person masculine pronoun *ore*—a form regarded as more masculine/informal than another masculine first-person pronoun, *boku*—more frequently in mixed-sex conversations than in same-sex conversations. Uchida concludes that the choice of speech style is regulated by the psychological distance that the speaker feels toward the interlocutor; speakers monitor their linguistic behaviors according to how they view themselves and how others view them.

In sum, the discussion in this section demonstrates that the use of Japanese women's speech is not directly derived from the gender of the speaker; rather, its employment is dependent on multiple social factors relating to the speaker's identity and relationships.

Conclusion

In this chapter I have presented empirical evidence for variations in Japanese women's speech and argued that the category commonly delineated as *Japanese women's language*—a culturally and ideologically constructed, class-based norm—is too static and monolithic to account for the varied speech styles of Japanese women. Rather than correlating speech styles directly with the speaker's sex, I have tried to demonstrate that Japanese women select their speech styles by considering multiple social attributes associated with identity and relationships and by evaluating the linguistic norms in the relevant communities. Based on a context-specific assessment of these interrelated factors, Japanese women strategically choose particular speech styles to communicate desired pragmatic meanings and images of self. In other words, the choice of speech styles is a means by which women express and construct their identities and relationships. Young women's use of unfeminine or direct speech styles in informal conversation is not simply an exception to "Japanese women's language" but a meaningful choice based on their understanding of themselves as young unmarried female students situated in specific interpersonal relationships and sociocultural contexts.

Although the preceding discussion has focused on synchronic divergence, the variation in Japanese women's speech styles is also diachronic and its careful investigation is imperative. The perception that the speech styles of Japanese women are becoming less feminine often leads to a second generalization about Japanese women's speech that is equally essentialist: the idea that the speech styles of all Japanese women are changing from feminine to masculine. The speech styles of Japanese women are diverse, and the use of ideal feminine styles or "Japanese women's language" has been far from universal among Japanese women. Thus, when we discuss diachronic change, it is important to examine which kinds of women are adopting which kinds of change.

For example, with regard to the "defeminization" phenomenon, it may be helpful, as a start, to narrow our attention to the speech styles of middle-

and upper-middle-class women in Tokyo and ask to what extent defeminization, if in fact it is occurring, is advancing: is it mostly limited to young women or is it affecting older women as well? The differences among age groups summarized in Table 12.2, for example, may reflect a broad defeminization process—related to changing gender roles and ideologies—that most strongly affects the younger generation; on the other hand, the same differences may point to a feminization process that individual women may experience as they grow older (due to societal pressures deriving from employment, marriage, and so on); alternatively, and perhaps most likely, both processes may coexist. Jennifer Coates's (forthcoming) study of the talk of teenage girls in London shows significant changes in discourse styles during adolescence (from ages twelve to fifteen); in particular, innovations and agency in discourse declined as the girls in her study grew older. A similar kind of developmental change may explain, at least in part, the age-group differences shown in Table 12.2. Several working women in their late twenties also told me that since they started working, their ways of talking have changed, and that they have come to use less rough (*"ranboo na"*) expressions and have become more careful about the use of honorifics. Furthermore, although the data set is limited, the results of this study and of Okamoto and Sato (1992) suggest that there are wider variations in speech styles among older women as compared with younger women. Perhaps defeminization and feminization are highly individualized, affecting different women to different degrees. It is interesting to note here that Speakers 1 and 2 in Table 12.3 have been living in the United States for nineteen years and twelve years respectively, and have therefore not experienced the change in women's speech styles in Japan. In fact, Speaker 2, who used the most feminine style of all participants, said that when her older sister and mother visited her from Japan, she felt that their language had become *kitanai* 'dirty'.

Finally, it has been noted by some that neutralization of Japanese women's and men's speech may be taking place, with masculinization occurring in women's speech and feminization occurring in male speech (Kobayashi 1993; Reynolds 1985).[13] Jorden (1990:2–3) also observes, "Some patterns continually described as *onna-rashii* now turn up frequently in examples of men's speech." What may be occurring, then, is a shift in cultural stereotypes of women's speech and men's speech, so that the linguistic forms previously identified as feminine, masculine, or neutral no longer convey the same meanings among modern-day speakers. A growing number of young women do not perceive certain moderately masculine forms to be masculine at all; their changing attitudes may in turn affect the dominant linguistic norms of speech for Japanese women and men. Surely, not only women's speech patterns but men's as well will continue to adapt to the ongoing changes in Japanese gender roles and gender ideologies. However, we must also recognize that systematic research on change in Japanese women's and men's speech is virtually nonexistent. Before drawing conclusions about the process of neutralization as a universal linguistic phenomenon among Japanese, we must closely examine the linguistic practices of women and men in diverse communities across time. In particular, speakers who have remained "invisible" behind "representative" Japanese (e.g., farmers, blue-collar workers) must be included in our studies. We need to identify the nature of linguistic change, the types of speakers most likely to adopt it, and the social conditions that encourage it. Only then can we begin to understand fully the meanings of specific changes in Japanese women's and men's speech.

Acknowledgments

This paper is a revised and expanded version of a paper originally presented at the 1994 Berkeley Women and Language Conference, which will be included in the conference proceedings (Okamoto forthcoming). The study was partly supported by a California State University research grant. I am very grateful to those who helped me with the data collection, in particular Akiko Honjo, Sachiko Kamei, and Yoko Tada, and those who participated in recording the conversations. I would also like to thank Mary Bucholtz, Penelope Eckert, Susan Ervin-Tripp, Per Gjerde, Kira Hall, Peter Hedrix, Sachiko Ide, Miyako Inoue, Karen Mistry, Yukiko Morimoto, Shie Sato, and Janet Smith for their valuable comments, discussions, and encouragement.

Notes

1. In addition to these differences, Shibamoto (1985, 1990), based on her analysis of naturalistic speech data, demonstrates that female and male speech also differs syntactically with regard to the ellipsis of subject nominals, word order, and the ellipsis of case particles, among other features. Smith (1992b) analyzes gender differences in the use of "secondary modality."

2. I thank Miyako Inoue for providing me with this material. The acronym *NHK* stands for *Nippon Hoosookyookai* 'Japan Broadcasting Association'.

3. See Coates (1988) and Uchida (1992) for an overview and critical discussion of these approaches.

4. This study employs basically the same method of data collection and analysis that was used in Okamoto and Sato (1992), so as to enable comparisons of the results obtained in the two studies. All ten subjects were attending private

colleges: Speakers 1–8 were attending a two-year women's college, and Speakers 9 and 10 a four-year coed college (see Table 12.4 in note 7). Topics for conversation were not specified, although sample topics were suggested, among them school matters, friends, shopping, and travel. I chose to record informal conversations rather than administer interviews for two reasons: first, female–male differences in sentence-final forms appear most clearly in familiar conversation, not in formal conversation; second, it seems that young women gravitate toward an unfeminine speech style particularly with their close peers in informal situations.

5. Such tokens do not include the following types of sentences or fragments: (1) interrupted or incomplete sentences, (2) neutral interrogative sentences (e.g., *Iku?* 'Are (you) going?'), (3) neutral fillers (e.g., *A soo* 'Is that right?'), (4) direct and indirect quotations, except for the direct quotations of the speaker's own speech, and (5) expressions repeated for emphatic purposes (e.g., *Takai, takai* 'Expensive, expensive'). The final forms of interrogative sentences and fillers are normally neutral, and these neutral forms were excluded because their inclusion would have skewed the data for those participants who tended to be listeners and asked questions or used fillers constantly. Further, dependent clauses were ignored unless they were used sentence-finally with semantic completion. In the case of so-called right dislocation (of a phrase or clause), the final form of the sentence in the "original" word order was considered because it is the part that is gendered.

6. For the forms for which classification was not available in the literature, we made our own judgments, making reference to women's and men's conversational data.

7. The distribution of gendered sentence-final forms for each speaker is shown in Table 12.4.

Table 12.4 Use of Gendered Sentence-final Forms for Individual Speakers (Percentages)

Form	SP1	SP2	SP3	SP4	SP5	SP6	SP7	SP8	SP9	SP10	All	Range
F	13	15	12	13	13	16	8	19	5	10	12	5–19
•MF	8	9	10	10	9	10	5	7	3	8	8	3–10
•SF	5	7	2	3	4	6	3	12	2	2	5	2–12
M	11	17	25	17	19	25	17	13	23	23	19	11–25
•MM	8	15	25	16	19	22	15	13	21	21	18	8–25
•SM	3	1	0	1	1	3	2	1	2	1	1	0–3
N	77	68	63	71	68	59	75	68	73	67	69	59–77
Total	100	100	100	100	100	100	100	100	100	100		

8. Among the neutral forms, the most commonly used (appearing in more than one hundred tokens) were plain forms of verbs and *i*-adjectives (e.g., *soo omotta* 'I thought so'), the gerundive forms (... *itte* ' ... said'), and the base of *na*-adjectives and nouns by themselves (e.g., ... *juuyoo* ' ... is important').

9. Takasaki (1993) analyzes transcribed conversations published in a journal

between 1951 and 1988. She compares the speech of working and nonworking women, but it seems that the comparison cannot be made straightforwardly because the conversational situations for the two groups differ in formality, which strongly affects the use of features such as honorifics and sentence-final particles.

10. The concept of *women's language* existed in premodern Japan (Ide forthcoming; Kindaichi 1957; Kitagawa 1977). However, Inoue (forthcoming) asserts that what is now thought of as modern "Japanese women's language" is a recent historical product and discontinuous with the premodern women's "voices."

11. See Minear (1980) and Tamanoi (1990) for criticisms of cultural essentialism in Japanese studies.

12. I thank Miyako Inoue for providing me with this material.

13. See Ogawa and Smith (forthcoming) for a discussion of the feminization of men's speech in gay Japanese couples in Tokyo and Osaka.

References

Bachnik, Jane (1992). *Kejime*: Defining a shifting self in multiple organizational modes. In Nancy Rosenberger (ed.), *Japanese sense of self*. Cambridge: Cambridge University Press. 152–72.

———— (1994). Introduction: *Uchi/Soto*: Challenging our conceptualizations of self, social order, and language. In Jane M. Bachnik and Charles J. Quinn, Jr. (eds.), *Situated meaning: Inside and outside in Japanese self, society, and language*. Princeton: Princeton University Press. 3–37.

Brinton, Mary C. (1993). *Women and the economic miracle: Gender and work in postwar Japan*. Berkeley: University of California Press.

Brown, Penelope (1980). How and why are women more polite: Some evidence from a Mayan community. In Sally McConnell-Ginet, Ruth Borker, and Nelly Furman (eds.), *Women and language in literature and society*. New York: Praeger. 111–36.

———— (1990). Gender, politeness, and confrontation in Tenejapa. *Discourse Processes* 13(1): 123–41.

Cameron, Deborah, and Jennifer Coates (1988). Some problems in the sociolinguistic explanation of sex differences. In Jennifer Coates and Deborah Cameron (eds.), *Women in their speech communities*. New York: Longman. 13–26.

Cameron, Deborah, Fiona McAlinden, and Kathy O'Leary (1988). Lakoff in context: The social and linguistic functions of tag questions. In Jennifer Coates and Deborah Cameron (eds.), *Women in their speech communities*. New York: Longman. 74–93.

Coates, Jennifer (1988). Introduction to part 2. In Jennifer Coates and Deborah Cameron (eds.), *Women in their speech communities*. New York: Longman. 63–73.

———— (forthcoming). Discourse, gender, and subjectivity: The talk of teenage girls. In Mary Bucholtz, Anita Liang, Laurel Sutton, and Caitlin Hines (eds.),

Cultural performances: Proceedings of the Third Berkeley Women and Language Conference. Berkeley: Berkeley Women and Language Group.

Eckert, Penelope (1989). The whole woman: Sex and gender differences in variation. *Language Variation and Change* 1: 245–67.

Eckert, Penelope, and Sally McConnell-Ginet (1992). Communities of practice: Where language, gender, and power all live. In Kira Hall, Mary Bucholtz, and Birch Moonwomon (eds.), *Locating power: Proceedings of the Second Berkeley Women and Language Conference.* Berkeley: Berkeley Women and Language Group. 89–99.

English Discussion Society (1992). *Japanese women now.* Kyoto: Women's Bookstore Shoukadoh.

Fishman, Pamela M. (1983). Interaction: The work women do. In Barrie Thorne, Cheris Kramarae, and Nancy Henley (eds.), *Language, gender, and society.* Rowley, MA: Newbury House. 89–101.

Gal, Susan (1992). Language, gender, and power: An anthropological view. In Kira Hall, Mary Bucholtz, and Birch Moonwomon (eds.), *Locating power: Proceedings of the Second Berkeley Women and Language Conference.* Berkeley: Berkeley Women and Language Group. 153–61.

——— (this volume). Language, gender, and power: An anthropological review.

Gonzales Velásquez, María Dolores (this volume). Sometimes Spanish, sometimes English: Language use among rural New Mexican Chicanas.

Goodwin, Marjorie Harness (1988). Cooperation and competition across girls' play activities. In Alexandra Dundas Todd and Sue Fisher (eds.), *Gender and discourse: The power of talk.* Norwood, NJ: Ablex. 55–94.

Goodwin, Marjorie Harness (1992). Orchestrating participation in events: Powerful talk among African American girls. In Kira Hall, Mary Bucholtz, and Birch Moonwomon (eds.), *Locating power: Proceedings of the Second Berkeley Women and Language Conference.* Berkeley: Berkeley Women and Language Group. 182–96.

Ide, Sachiko (1979). *Onna no kotoba, otoko no kotoba* (Women's language and men's language). Tokyo: Keizai Tsushinsha.

——— (1982). Japanese sociolinguistics: Politeness and women's language. *Lingua* 57: 357–85.

——— (1990). How and why do women speak more politely in Japanese? In Sachiko Ide and Naomi Hanaoka McGloin (eds.), *Aspects of Japanese women's language.* Tokyo: Kuroshio. 63–79.

——— (forthcoming). Women's language in women's world. In Mary Bucholtz, Anita Liang, Laurel Sutton, and Caitlin Hines (eds.), *Cultural performances: Proceedings of the Third Berkeley Women and Language Conference.* Berkeley: Berkeley Women and Language Group.

Inoue, Miyako (1994). Gender and linguistic modernization: A historical account of the birth of Japanese women's language. In Mary Bucholtz, Anita Liang, Laurel Sutton, and Caitlin Hines (eds.), *Cultural performances: Proceedings of the Third Berkeley Women and Language Conference.* Berkeley: Berkeley Women and Language Group.

Inoue, Teruko, and Yumiko Ehara (1991). *Josei no deeta booku* (Women's date book). Tokyo: Yuhikaku.

Iwao, Sumiko (1993). *The Japanese woman: Traditional image and changing reality*. New York: Free Press.

Jorden, Eleanor H. (1990). Overview. In Sachiko Ide and Naomi Hanaoka McGloin (eds.), *Aspects of Japanese women's language*. Tokyo: Kuroshio. 1–4.

Jugaku, Akiko (1979). *Nihongo to onna* (The Japanese language and women). Tokyo: Iwanami.

Kashiwagi, Hiroshi (1991). *Oyaji-gyaru-teki gengo kuukan* (Linguistic space of oyaji-gal). *Gengo* 20(1): 42–47.

Kindaichi, Haruhiko (1957). *Nihongo* (The Japanese language). Tokyo: Iwanani.

Kitagawa, Chisato (1977). A source of femininity in Japanese: In defense of Robin Lakoff's *Language and Woman's Place*. *Papers in Linguistics* 10(3/4): 275–98.

Kobayashi, Mieko (1993). Sedai to Josei-go: Wakai sedai no kotoba no "chuusei-ka" ni tsuite (Generation and women's language: On the "neutralization" of the speech of the young generation). *Nihongo-gaku* 12(6): 181–92.

Kondo, Dorinne K. (1990). *Crafting selves: Power, gender, and discourses of identity in a Japanese workplace*. Chicago: University of Chicago Press.

Lakoff, Robin (1975). *Language and woman's place*. New York: Harper & Row.

Lam, Alice C. L. (1992). *Women and Japanese management: Discrimination and reform*. London: Routledge.

Lebra, Joyce, Joy Paulson, and Elizabeth Powers (eds.) (1976). *Women in changing Japan*. Boulder: Westview Press.

Maltz, Daniel N., and Ruth A. Borker (1982). A cultural approach to male-female miscommunication. In John Gumperz (ed.), *Language and social identity*. Cambridge: Cambridge University Press. 196–216.

McGloin, Naomi H. (1990). Sex difference and sentence-final particles. In Sachiko Ide and Naomi Hanaoka McGloin (eds.), *Aspects of Japanese women's language*. Tokyo: Kuroshio. 23–41.

Minear, Richard H. (1980). Orientalism and the study of Japan. *Journal of Asian Studies* 39(3): 507–17.

Mizutani, Osamu, and Nobuko Mizutani (1987). *How to be polite in Japanese*. Tokyo: Japan Times.

Nichols, Patricia C. (1983). Linguistic options and choices for Black women in the rural South. In Barrie Thorne, Cheris Kramarae, and Nancy Henley (eds.), *Language, gender, and society*. Rowley, MA: Newbury House. 54–68.

O'Barr, William M., and Bowman K. Atkins (1980). "Women's language" or "powerless language"? In Sally McConnell-Ginet, Ruth Borker, and Nelly Furman (eds.), *Women and language in literature and society*. New York: Praeger. 93–110.

Ochs, Elinor (1987). The impact of stratification and socialization on men's and women's speech in Western Samoa. In Susan Philips, Susan Steele, and Christine Tanz (eds.), *Language, gender, and sex in comparative perspective*. Cambridge: Cambridge University Press. 50–70.

——— (1993). Indexing gender. In Barbara Diane Miller (ed.), *Sex and gender hierarchies*. Cambridge: Cambridge University Press. 146–69.

Ogawa, Naoko, and Janet S. (Shibamoto) Smith (forthcoming). The gendering of the gay male sex class in Japan: A preliminary case study based on "Rasen no Sobyo." In Anna Livia and Kira Hall (eds.), *Queerly phrased: Language, gender and sexuality*. New York: Oxford University Press.

Ohara, Yumiko (1992). Gender-dependent pitch levels: A comparative study in Japanese and English. In Kira Hall, Mary Bucholtz, and Birch Moonwomon (eds.), *Locating power: Proceedings of the Second Berkeley Women and Language Conference*. Berkeley: Berkeley Women and Language Group. 469–77.

Okamoto, Shigeko (forthcoming). "Gendered" speech styles and social identity among young Japanese women. In Mary Bucholtz, Anita Liang, Laurel Sutton, and Caitlin Hines (eds.), *Cultural performances: Proceedings of the Third Berkeley Women and Language Conference*. Berkeley: Berkeley Women and Language Group.

Okamoto, Shigeko, and Shie Sato (1992). Less feminine speech among young Japanese females. In Kira Hall, Mary Bucholtz, and Birch Moonwomon (eds.), *Locating power: Proceedings of the Second Berkeley Women and Language Conference*. Berkeley: Berkeley Women and Language Group. 478–88.

Reynolds, Katsue A. (1985). Female speakers of Japanese. *Feminist Issues* 5: 13–46.

——— (1990). Female speakers of Japanese in transition. In Sachiko Ide and Naomi Hanaoka McGloin (eds.), *Aspects of Japanese women's language*. Tokyo: Kuroshio. 129–46.

Roberts, Glenda S. (1994). *Staying on the line: Blue-collar women in contemporary Japan*. Honolulu: University of Hawaii Press.

Rosenberger, Nancy R. (ed.) (1992). *Japanese sense of self*. Cambridge: Cambridge University Press.

Shibamoto, Janet S. (1985). *Japanese women's language*. New York: Academic Press.

———. (1990). Sex related variation in the ellipsis of *wa* and *ga* in Japanese. In Sachiko Ide and Naomi Hanaoka McGloin (eds.), *Aspects of Japanese women's language*. Tokyo: Kuroshio. 81–104.

Silverstein, Michael (1976). Shifters, linguistic categories, and cultural description. In Keith H. Basso and Henry A. Selby (eds.), *Meaning in anthropology*. University of New Mexico Press. 11–55.

——— (1985). Language and the culture of gender: At the intersection of structure, usage, and ideology. In Elizabeth Mertz and Richard J. Parmentier (eds.), *Semiotic mediation: Sociocultural and psychological perspectives*. New York: Academic Press. 219–59.

Smith, Janet (Shibamoto) (1992a). Women in charge: Politeness and directive in the speech of Japanese women. *Language in Society* 21: 59–82.

——— (1992b). Linguistic privilege: "Just stating the facts" in Japanese. In Kira Hall, Mary Bucholtz, and Birch Moonwomon (eds.), *Locating power: Proceedings of the Second Berkeley Women and Language Conference*. Berkeley: Berkeley Women and Language Group. 540–48.

Sunaoshi, Yukako (1995). Japanese women's authoritative speech in their communities of practice. Paper presented at the 1995 Annual Meeting of the Linguistic Society of America, New Orleans.

———— (forthcoming). Mild directives work effectively: Japanese women in command. In Mary Bucholtz, Anita Liang, Laurel Sutton, and Caitlin Hines (eds.), *Cultural performances: Proceedings of the Third Berkeley Women and Language Conference*. Berkeley: Berkeley Women and Language Group.

Takasaki, Midori (1993). Josei no kotoba to kaisoo (Women's language and social strata). *Nihongo-gaku* 12(6): 169–80.

Tamanoi, Mariko A. (1990). Women's voices: Their critique of the anthropology of Japan. *Annual Review of Anthropology* 19: 17–37.

Tannen, Deborah (1990a). *You just don't understand: Women and men in conversation*. New York: Morrow.

———— (1990b). Gender differences in topical coherence: Creating involvement in best friends' talk. *Discourse Processes* 13(1): 73–90.

Thomas, Beth (1988). Differences of sex and sects: Linguistic variation and social networks in a Welsh mining village. In Jennifer Coates and Deborah Cameron (eds.), *Women in their speech communities*. New York: Longman. 51–60.

Tobin, Joseph (1992). Japanese preschools and the pedagogy of selfhood. In Nancy Rosenberger (ed.), *Japanese sense of self*. Cambridge: Cambridge University Press. 21–39.

Trudgill, Peter (1975). Sex, covert prestige, and linguistic change in the urban British English of Norwich. *Language in Society* 1: 179–95.

Uchida, Aki (1992). When "difference" is "dominance": A critique of the "anti-power-based" cultural approach to sex differences. *Language in Society* 21: 547–68.

Uchida, Nobuko (1993). Kaiwa-koodoo ni mirareru seisa (Gender differences in conversation). *Nihongo-gaku* 12(6): 156–68.

Uno, Kathleen S. (1993). The death of "good wife, wise mother"? In Andrew Gordon (ed.), *Postwar Japan as history*. Berkeley: University of California Press. 293–322.

Uyeno, Tazuko (1971). A study of Japanese modality: A performative analysis of sentence particles. Ph.D. diss., University of Michigan.

West, Candace, and Don H. Zimmerman (1983). Small insults: A study of interruptions in cross-sex conversations between unacquainted persons. In Barrie Thorne, Cheris Kramarae, and Nancy Henley (eds.), *Language, gender and society*. Rowley, MA: Newbury House. 102–17.

Part Three

Contingent Practices

and

Emergent Selves

13

"Are You With Me?"

Power and Solidarity in the Discourse of African American Women

Michèle Foster

The study of the language behavior of African Americans that has been conducted over the past thirty years has produced a substantial body of research describing and analyzing the linguistic, sociolinguistic, and metalinguistic aspects of the community. In the main, these studies have disregarded variations in gender and social class. Most of the early work dealt with the language behavior of groups within the African American community which deviates most from the standard—the exotic, male-dominated street language of males and adolescents (Abrahams 1964; Folb 1980; Kochman 1972; Labov 1972a, b)—while ignoring the language behavior of "drylongso" (Gwaltney 1980), ordinary Black people, who make up the largest segment of the community. Although some of the early studies (Mitchell-Kernan 1971; Ward 1971) considered the language of children and the language of women, they are relatively rare.

If African American women have been overlooked in language studies of the African American community, they have also been neglected in research by feminist scholars. By centering almost exclusively on middle-class white women, feminist scholarship, including research on the language behavior of women, has marginalized African American women of all social-class backgrounds. One reason for this oversight could be the misconception that as they ascend the social ladder, individuals forfeit not only their identification with the community but their communicative competence in the norms of the African American community as well. The segment of African Americans who have not learned African American English natively may be increasing, but this is a relatively new phenomenon that in itself does not necessarily signal disidentification with the African American community (Baugh 1992). As several African American feminist scholars have demonstrated, severing ties with the African American community, its cultural norms, community practices, and political interests need not be an inevitable outcome for middle-class African American women (Carothers 1990; Collins 1990; Etter-Lewis 1993; hooks 1989).

Whatever the reasons for the inattention to issues of gender and social class, the result is that we know comparatively little about the language behavior extant in the broader African American community, about the language behavior of African American women in particular, and about how social class and gender interact to produce variations within the African American speech community. According to Marcyliena Morgan (1991), studies of African American women's speech behavior are central to a complete understanding of how the community expresses its reality because it is women who have historically been responsible for the language development of children and consequently the community. This chapter examines specific linguistic forms and discourse features used by African American women to express and invoke solidarity, power, and community. Although the investigation considers linguistic factors, they are analyzed in light of their social and cultural meaning. Finally, the chapter explores some of the factors that seem to affect the choice of a particular style of speaking and analyzes the roles that particular styles play in promoting and maintaining a shared identity by reinforcing culturally valued attitudes, beliefs, and mores.

This chapter is grounded in the empirical, conceptual, and philosophical scholarship undertaken by African American women over the past decade that places African American women at the center of its inquiry. Some of this research is linguistic in nature; much of it is not. Nonetheless, the nonlinguistic research is topically and conceptually linked to the linguistic data reported on in this chapter. One important link is the leadership role of African American women as teachers in their communities. In one of many conceptual articles on Black feminism, bell hooks (1989) pays tribute to Miss Annie Mae Moore, one of the progressive middle-class African American teachers in the segregated community of her childhood. According to hooks, Miss Moore was passionate in her teaching, confident that her work was a pedagogy of liberation (words she would not have used but lived instinctively), one that would address and confront our realities as black children growing up in the segregated South, black children growing up within a white-supremacist culture. Miss Moore knew that if we were to be fully self-realized then her work, and the work of all our progressive teachers, was not to teach us solely the knowledge in books, but to teach an oppositional world view—different from that of our exploiters and oppressors, a world view that would enable us to see ourselves not through the lens of racism or racist stereotypes but one that would enable us to focus clearly and succinctly, to look at ourselves, at the world around us, critically—analytically—to see ourselves first and foremost as striving for wholeness, for unity of heart, mind, body, and spirit. (49)

In her work on Black feminist thought, Patricia Hill Collins (1990) offers another view of African American teachers. Locating them within the larger community context, she illustrates the myriad ways that middle-class African American teachers have served as "othermothers" to children in the communities. The lack of linguistic data notwithstanding, the work of Collins and hooks complements the ever-growing scholarship undertaken by African American women to study formally the linguistic and communication styles of their African American sisters. Many of these studies examine the language behavior of middle-class African American women (Etter-Lewis 1993; Foster 1987, 1989; Morgan 1989, 1991, 1993; Nelson 1990, Stanback 1985). Together they form the conceptual base that undergirds the analysis of this chapter.

Setting and Methodology

For seven years I have been engaged in studying the lives, experiences, and practices of African American teachers. The linguistic material analyzed in this chapter is drawn from two speech situations—the interview and the classroom—that vary on several dimensions. One difference between these contexts is that the investigation in the classroom was limited to the language behavior of one individual; the interviews, on the other hand, encompassed a group of women. A second difference is that whereas the primary focus of the classroom inquiry was on communicative processes, the main point of the interviews was the exploration of social themes. The final difference concerns my role in the communicative event. Being one individual in an audience of twenty people in the classroom precluded me from structuring the teacher's discourse, which was rarely addressed exclusively to me. In fact, the teacher seemed oblivious to my presence in the classroom. This inattentiveness is evident in the transcript of one of the first classes where she interrupts her customary discourse to comment on my presence, then continues with her talk:

(1)

Morris:	Un huh managers have to be able to think on their feet
	Oh I didn't see you there Michèle// how are you?
Michele:	Fine//
Morris:	I wanted to call your test and I look up and saw it was you//Mr. Gomez /Lugo Gomez/ not here today. I am a little bit disappointed in him too.

In contrast to the classroom setting, the discourse in the interviews was structured as a set of verbal exchanges between two interlocutors. My active role in the interviews enabled me to influence and shape them. Where interviewee and interviewer come from different backgrounds including class, race, ethnic, and gender differences, and these differences produce dissimilar communicative norms, interviews are likely to be strained. On the other hand, where interviewer and interviewee have a background in common and possess similar norms of communication, the strain, though not obliterated, may be minimized. Although many of the narrators were initially reluctant to be interviewed, when the session ended, most commented that the interview had been more enjoyable and more like a conversation than expected and that they were surprised that they had so much to say. Statements such as these were more likely to be made by women than man, a point taken up later in this chapter.

The adequacy of the interview for eliciting reliable sociolinguistic data has been discussed by Nessa Wolfson (1976), who argues that the nature of the interview constrains the production of certain forms that might occur in an ordinary conversation. Charles Briggs (1986), however, adopts a more flexible approach, maintaining that understanding the communicative context of the interview is essential not only to the kind and quality of social-science data collected but also to comprehending fully the themes that emerge. He argues further for the need to understand interviews as speech events in their own terms, a position that mirrors my own, and one that is reflected in the way I approached the analysis of the interview data.

Theoretical Underpinnings and the Significance of Performance

The classroom analysis was informed by performance theory, a field that gained ascendancy in the late 1970s and early 1980s as anthropologists became interested in the role of verbal art in social interaction and as some folklorists shifted their attention from text as item to text as performance (Bauman 1977; Hymes 1975). Those working within this new tradition understood performances to be a specific category within the field of ethnography of communication, a special kind of communicative event in which there is a particular relationship among stylized material, performer, and audience. These theorists argued that just as a system of speaking varies from one speech community to another, so too do the nature and extent of stylized communication, or performance. Rules governing performance can be expected to vary from one community to another. Different speech communities will have their own rules regarding who can assume the role of performer, which speech acts and genres can be performed, which institutions are suitable contexts for performances, and the extent to which performances are expected, permitted, or even required in day-to-day interactions. The verbal and nonverbal means utilized by performers to signal that they are performing and displayed by audiences to indicate they understand the performers' intentions will also vary across speech communities (Hymes 1972, 1974, 1975). Consequently, according to performance theorists, the complex relationships among context, audience, performer, and stylized material that produce performances can be established only emically, that is, by reference to the particular community in question (Bauman & Briggs 1990; Briggs & Bauman 1992). In their writing on intertextuality and genre, Charles Briggs and Richard Bauman (1992) suggest that genres should be approached synchronically and diachronically. By combining these two approaches to analyzing genres, performance theorists call for the merging of microanalytic approaches to investigating discourse with the macroanalytic issues of the larger social structures of power, as well as the way that particular genres and the interrelationship among them both shape and are shaped by factors such as gender, class, and ethnicity.

To my knowledge, this study is the first to have explicitly utilized performance theory to examine the communication patterns of an African American woman or to investigate the classroom interaction between an African American teacher and students from the same speech community. In other writings (Foster 1987, 1989, 1992), I have argued that performance theory is useful for understanding many of the everyday interactions that take place across various institutional contexts within the African American community. Unfortunately, like much of the other research conducted in the African American community, studies that have considered performances have tended to focus exclusively on those of men, while largely ignoring women's performances. Conducted in the classroom of a community college, my own research has demonstrated how one African American woman incorporated familiar ways of speaking into her classroom and used performances to engage students in classroom discussion, reinforce group identity and values, and promote solidarity with her predominantly African American students.

Performance was one of five discrete events that occurred regularly in this classroom. At the beginning of each class, the teacher opened the class with a greeting. Despite their brevity and formulaic nature, greetings served an important social function. Students in this classroom were quick to point out that the greetings signaled the teacher's attempts to reduce the social distance between her and themselves. Brief announcements concerning on- and off-campus events, reminders or extensions of assignment due dates, or the date and scope of an upcoming test generally constituted the content of announcements. Following announcements, the teacher commented extensively on class assignments or tests. Only after greetings, announcements, and comments on student performance did the instructional event of the classroom begin. The teacher officially signaled the end of the instructional part of each class with a closing, which typically consisted of an expression of leave-taking accompanied by a call to action or an evaluation of the class. The following closing is representative: "Class is over? I just got started. Thank you for your attendance. Good class. Have a good weekend. Turn in your papers, and hit those books this weekend."

The teacher was most likely to "break into performance" when attempting to clarify a concept that students had encountered in a text or a lecture. As if to decrease the distance between herself and her students, create greater intimacy, increase the interaction between performer and audience, and signal an incipient performance, the teacher would often remove the lectern behind which she usually lectured, and place it on a chair beside her desk.

Typically, a performance was preceded by a sequence in which the teacher read from her notes or students were asked to read a passage directly from the text. Consider the following excerpt taken from a longer sequence,[1] in which the teacher is trying to help students understand the budgeting process, a concept they have encountered in their textbooks. To elicit student participation, she begins by asking students about their own budgeting procedures:

(2)

Morris:	ah Miss Summer/ um ah. not even based on the book what do you know about budgets
Summer:	what do I know about budgets?
Morris:	I'm looking for everybody's collective conscious-ness of what they know about budget making? you have one? you got a budget?
Summer:	yes
Morris:	how do you do it?
Summer:	|:my house
Morris:	your house:|
Summer:	my money
Morris:	no/ I don't know a house a money that a budget?
Summer:	yeah/ yeah I have a budget
Morris:	{[acc:] you have a master pla:n to beat this eco-nomic system?
Summer:	no/ not yet (laughs)
Morris:	well, that's what a budget is umh/
Summer:	I was referring to budgeting money to for payin' the bills runnin' my my house//
Morris:	unhuh// that's a budget//
Summer:	yes/ it works//
Morris:	you're sure?
Summer:	yes/ |:it works//
Morris:	it works:|
Summer:	for me//
Morris:	for you:| ok// somebody else who wanna share their ideas about budget// I want to make sure everybody understands what a budget is before we go on// yes, Miss Goins//
Goins:	I was just makin' mines up this morning// it has (class laughs) un/where who I have to pay up and you know/ how much money do am I gonna gonna get and how much money do I have to pay off everybody and everything and how much money will I have left and how much money will I put in the bank// that's basically what my budget is.

Compared to other speech events in the class, the talk during performances is embellished by a number of African American stylistic devices:

manipulation of grammatical structure, repetition, use of symbolism and figurative language, and intonational contours, including vowel elongation, and changes in meter, tempo, and cadence. These linguistic devices serve as framing devices to distinguish performances from other kinds of classroom talk. Not only do these features mark a different classroom genre, they also seem to signal a change in social relations that is manifest in subsequent verbal interactions. Talk during the performance genre is more symmetrical than other talk in this classroom. In one instance, for example, students and teacher have an equal number of turns, the students speaking almost as much as the teacher, 211 words to her 296. This contrasts sharply with other speech events that are teacher-dominated and highly asymmetrical; in one case the teacher speaks 23 times as much as the students. Unlike other speech events, in which the teacher dominates the interactions, students are expected to participate in performance sequences; indeed, they frequently and spontaneously interject unsolicited comments into the ongoing talk. Occasionally, the teacher specifically calls for audience response and the class responds in unison. At other times, however, the teacher uses a more subtle mechanism—cross-speaker anaphora—to elicit additional student comments. Cross-speaker anaphora is the repetition or transformation of a previous speaker's contribution; in either case the words are uttered with rising intonation. Two segments from the longer transcript illustrate the phenomenon:

(3)

| Summer: | \|: my house |
| Morris: | \|your house:\| |

(4)

Summer:	yes/ |: it works//
Morris:	it works:|
Summer:	|: for me//
Morris:	for you :|//

The performance genre requires the active participation of students in order to develop. Several times during these sequences, the teacher chastises the class for failing to respond to an incipient performance, and sometimes after receiving no response, she suggests lecturing as a less desirable alternative. As used in this classroom, performances are intended to evoke personal knowledge, which becomes the vehicle through which students get meaning from and make sense out of academic content. Moreover, there is some evidence, though slight, that performances served a mnemonic function for students. Students were more likely to remember information conveyed through performances than they were to remember information not encoded in this way, as verified by analysis of student tests.

Other speech events in this classroom stress conformity to rules, allow almost no student input, and are regulatory and institutional. Performances, on the other hand, are creative, humorous, interactive events that allow for student contribution. In performances, there is a shift away from mainstream language to language and behavior that is more Black. The resulting talk is more participatory, with students contributing spontaneously. Despite its resemblance to play, the focus of these performances is instructional, the content intellectual, and it is through them that explanations and learning take place. In the performance genre, by deliberately manipulating rhythm, grammatical structures, and intonational patterns, and by using images, symbolism, and gestures, the teacher shifts from a mainstream to an African American discourse style to accomplish certain communicative ends.

Although in this context the performance genre is used to index a particular ethnic identity, performance can also be used to index or appropriate the ethnic and gender identities of the other, as illustrated in this volume by Mary Bucholtz's chapter on American women and girls of mixed cultural heritage, and Bonnie McElhinny's chapter on the discursive practices of female police officers.

Metaphors

One feature of the performance genre is the use of metaphor. However, performances are not distinguished by this single aspect alone. Over the course of the semester the teacher employed several metaphors and created an extended metaphor that enabled her to talk to students effectively and enabled them to communicate with one another within the same framework. Early in the semester, the teacher began using the metaphor of *F-troops* to refer to students who because of insufficient effort were not making satisfactory progress in classroom work and were therefore in danger of receiving a failing grade. The F-troop metaphor was derived from a television series of the same name, which portrayed a fictional U.S. cavalry unit whose members, because of lack of discipline, poor planning, and ineptitude, were unable to carry out even the simplest tasks. Without exception, students in this class understood the use of the innuendo as the teacher intended it—a joke with a hidden meaning, not something to be offended by or to take personally. At midterm the teacher divided the class into four cooperative work groups. Named after three local Black community businesses and one state agency whose characteristics were familiar to students, these groupings formed a metaphorical system that could be invoked throughout the semester. On the day the groups were established the teacher told the class:

(5)

> I don't want the Bank of Commerce to get swelled heads. Now don't get swelled heads because you if you want to remain, if you want to be in the Bank of Commerce and if you give someone in Cruz Construction Company a hard time you may end up in that group. Now I want some competition in here, I'm gonna give you a class project. You all are gonna be managers and um this state agency the Division of Employment Security if you don't want to be unemployed you gonna be fighting to get jobs in Cruz Construction and ah hunh Western Union in order to keep your position. I'm gonna have you do a class project in here. So, if you don't like the company or the state agency you work for you gonna have to do something about your grades. I'm not gonna be tellin' you it anymore. So, I'm gonna let you sit with your most deserved group.... Oh, yeah, I pick on DES (Division of Employment Security), I pick on the DES un and the Bank of Commerce a lot. I'm gonna call on them for all my questions. (Foster 1987, 1989)

Later in the day she draws on the metaphor to exchange jokes with students:

(6)

Morris:	Is this the group with all the money? You'd better give me a house loan.
Student:	Depends on how good your credit rating is.
Morris:	I have an excellent credit rating. (Foster 1987, 1989)

In the classroom, the metaphor functions on multiple levels. Because the class is a management class, a business metaphor such as this one is ideal, thus creating one layer of meaning. The fact that all of the businesses are Black-owned and operate within the Black community adds a second layer of significance. Finally, the particular circumstances of the companies add another dimension to the metaphor. These circumstances include that the Bank of Commerce, reorganized from another bank that closed because of insolvency, has become successful; that Cruz Construction Company, one of the most successful minority-owned businesses in the community, was formed by a common laborer; and that although Western Union provides a crucial service for community residents, it charges stiff fees for its check-cashing service. The resulting metaphor is elaborate, intertwined with multiple levels of meaning that allow for the relationship and interplay among ideas.

Talking through the metaphor creates a discontinuous speech event that classroom participants can invoke at will. Throughout the semester, the teacher called on the metaphor to nominate students, urge them to do their best on an assignment, quiz or compliment them. Although the teacher generally used the metaphor to communicate directly with students, the students quickly embraced it for their own use; only four days after it was introduced, students began using the metaphor to communicate with one another and thereafter often used it to talk among themselves. Two examples illustrate this use. A male student who normally would not approach a particular female student commented to her in the elevator, "You'd better study if you want to stay in the Bank. I'm planning to get a job in the Bank." In another instance, I was interviewing a student who used the metaphor to explain why she had to study harder in school: "I didn't come to school to be unemployed," she informed me.

An analysis of the events in which the metaphor is used is instructive because it shows that in addition to being used to compliment or admonish students, the metaphor is also used to encourage competition between groups and individuals. Ordinarily the teacher does not promote competition, and students rarely compete with one another. Within the metaphorical frame, however, a key aspect of business is introduced and competition becomes acceptable. Because they are spoken and heard within the metaphorical frame, student challenges such as those quoted above are acceptable, whereas outside the frame, remarks such as these would not be uttered; indeed, competitive comments such as those above would be deemed inappropriate.

Employed in this manner, this use is consistent with Max Black's (1962) analysis of metaphor. According to Black, metaphors can be used to suppress, select, or organize features of the principal subject by applying statements about it that normally apply only to a secondary subject, using a set of "associated implications." In this setting, the characteristics associated with the business world—such as competition to get ahead—are assigned to a typically noncompetitive classroom to encourage academic achievement. As used in this classroom, the metaphor serves two principal purposes. First, students are permitted to compete with and challenge one another through the frame of the metaphor while still maintaining their personae of noncompetitiveness. Second, it allows participants to take one another's comments figuratively instead of literally, resulting in a kind of indirection characteristic in Black communities (Mitchell-Kernan 1971; Morgan 1991; Smitherman 1977).

To summarize, metaphor and performance are two of the genres used in this African American teacher's classroom. These genres are bounded by particular linguistic features that set them apart from other kinds of discourse, and they create indexical connections that extend beyond the immediate context. Metaphors operate at multiple levels of indexicality and can be initiated by any member of the classroom. The performance genre is marked by linguistic features that signal a shift from standard English to a more Black style of discourse, a style that manipulates grammatical structures; exploits cadence, meter, and vowel lengthening; utilizes pitch, stress, intonation, and repetition; and employs figurative language, symbolism, and gestures. Embellished prosodically as well as gesturally, performances are highly stylized speech events. Unlike other speech events that do not encourage students to participate, the shift to performance elicits active student participation. The teacher, moreover, depends on student participation to construct the meaning to be derived from the text. In this class, performances are used to relate academic concepts to everyday events and incidents. Performances spark personalized accounts and vivid illustrations, and through them subject matter is linked to real life. Performances are important organizing principles in many other African American speech events as well, such as in the interactions between preacher and congregation in African American churches. Some or all of the stylistic features identified in these classroom performances are also evident in the stories and play songs of Black children; in the sounding, rapping, toasts, and verbal art of Black adolescents and adult males; in Black music and Black preaching styles (Abrahams 1970; Abrahams & Bauman 1971; Chernoff 1979; Davis 1985; Heath 1983; Keil 1972; Kochman 1970; Mitchell-Kernan 1971; Smitherman 1977; Szwed 1969; Waterman 1952).

Before I conclude this analysis, let me discuss the significance of classroom performances from the teacher's perspective. This teacher's self-described style has developed out of her involvement with the Black church. Though unable to name particular features of a Black sermonic tradition, she emulates African American preachers and believes they are effective because "they are able to take complicated theological material and break it down to the ordinary person; teach, preach, entertain, and keep the people's attention" (cf. Mitchell 1970:100). Likewise, using stylized speech events, the teacher creates intertextual links between the public knowledge of textbooks and personal experience rendered through narrative. Through her use of performance, moreover, the teacher signals and affirms her voluntary affiliation with the African American community and its values (Blom & Gumperz 1972). With these code and style changes, she shifts between multiple identities and roles while at the same time demonstrating her ability to negotiate the superordinate community and her proficiency in adhering to its norms. Using these code shifts, she demonstrates that participation in both communities is possible. Taking on multiple roles increases her chances of being understood and appreciated by the students and at the same time demonstrates her ability and willingness to take on the various identities required by each community.

This study contests and corrects much of the research on language practices in the African American community. Earlier studies, by ignoring the communication practices of middle-class African American women, have tended to dichotomize along hegemonic conceptions of gender and class the language use both of women and men and of individuals from different class backgrounds. What the present study demonstrates is not only that this teacher possessed a broad linguistic repertoire that included Standard English and a range of African American English forms but that she appropriated so-called masculine African American English forms, using them as tools for learning in order to enhance her own self-expression, power, and effectiveness in the classroom.

Codeswitching in Interviews

The remainder of this chapter deals with the codeswitching behavior of women who are participants in an ongoing study of African American women. The principal linguistic data come from the interviews of four women who are part of a larger study of African American teachers (Foster 1990, 1991a, b). The linguistic data of these four women are contrasted with those of two women in a related study of thirty African American women by Linda Williamson Nelson (1990). In both studies the researchers made sure that our interviewees, or narrators, were aware of our shared background. Because I was dealing with strangers, I emphasized these shared characteristics to my narrators in initial letters and in subsequent telephone conversations to set up interviews. However, I did not initiate the use of Black vernacular forms in my interviews. Nelson, on the other hand, did not hesitate to demonstrate her fluency in the vernacular and sometimes codeswitched into the vernacular before her narrators did.

In both Nelson's study and my own, the narrators switched from Standard English to African American English at some point during the interview.

Perhaps because I did not initiate codeswitches, in my study, codeswitches never occur in the beginning of the interview. In fact, the earliest appearance of any codeswitch is thirty-five minutes into the interview. In Nelson's study, codeswitches occurred early in the interviews with either interlocutor initiating the switch from standard to vernacular forms.

Even though there are a number of syntactical variants that characterize Black English, all of the codeswitches in my study were instances of multiple negation. There were no instances of the use of the invariant *be* and no nonoccurrences of the copula, the third-person singular, or the possessive. Though sporadic, the use of multiple negation is systematic, occurring intersententially and frequently functioning as a narrative device. The three examples that follow are illustrative:[2]

(7) JV: I find myself addressing character and self-image, much more than I did before. Constantly reiterating the fact that you can do it. I must say that fifty times a day or more. "You know you can do it. Do it a little faster. Let me see if you can try your next sentence. Try something harder. Try that book." I find myself doing that more and more than ever. I find myself trying to encourage them to do things on their own rather than say, "Have your mother help." I never say, "Have your mother help," cause the mother might not be there. "Miss Vander, *I don't have no mother.*" What can you say to that? "*I don't have no ... my father ain't there.*"

(8) MBM: Oh yes, more times than not. More times than not and then, you have to be even more entertaining, so they don't get discouraged. And you have to tell them that you know they don't know; it's not their fault. They say, "Miss Miller, I can't read." I say, "I know that. Now come on and try." But you can't say, "Now what's the matter with you, boy?" or any of those things. All that has to go out of your mind. And when they tell you that you can't say, "There's no such a word as *can't.*" Say, "I know you can't do it, but now we're gonna try some more." Because there is a can't. There're a whole lot of reasons you can't do something. But we keep telling children that lie. "*Ain't no such word as* can't." Yes, there is.

(9) RF: And do you know we have only one white teacher that will teach Black history. Only one, only one. She doesn't mind

teaching the Black history, but the rest of them say, "*I don't know nothing about it!*" You see, "I don't know enough about it to teach it. I leave that with Miss Ruthie." It isn't that. I think they do not want to acknowledge the achievements that have been done by Black men alone, you understand?

In the preceding examples, the narrators use an African American English variant specifically to report the speech of others. In some instances, they reported their students' speech using negative concord. At other times, they used the Standard English variant to report the speech of others. Of course, it is impossible to know whether the quoted speech is being reported as spoken or whether it is being highlighted for emphasis. In example (9), for instance, it is unclear whether the white teacher whose speech the narrator is allegedly reporting used multiple negation or whether she is using the African American English variant as a strategic device. That she immediately rephrases the statement in Standard English suggests that she is calling attention to the comment by setting it off using the African American English variant.

Codeswitching is sometimes used for allusion or emphasis. My narrators used multiple negation more frequently to highlight a particular statement than they did when quoting someone. In fact, there were twice as many instances of the former as of the latter. In contrast to quotations, this type of switch occurred intrasententially. It is illustrated in examples (10), (11), and (12):

(10) RF: You see, there were Blacks all over there back in times before. Not owned by all whites. But now it's all white. Understand? All this over here that is developed—we call it—what do we call it—Palmetto? I think that's what they call that beach—Palmetto Beach. Dr. Burney's group from Sumter and Columbia. Blacks that own that beach. All right, the whites wanted it. All right, so then they put the taxes so high that their heirs couldn't pay it. So, after they wouldn't sell it to them. They put it on auction. So we had a group of men—doctors and lawyers and undertakers. They all got together. Blacks. And, they said they were gonna save it. So that Monday when I got the paper and the lady who was in New York, Miss Lilly, who was paying the taxes, *she didn't know nothing* about it because they didn't take the paper.

(11) MG: No, no, no, no, no. If you make the highest score on the test
           that's your seat. So, remember, Friday, you've still got to make
           the highest grade to keep your seat.

      MF: That's what I'm saying. So, you can lose your seat.

      MG: Yeah. Sometimes, *don't nobody sit at the table.*

      MF: Why not? Somebody must have had the highest score?

      MG: You *can't get no fifty* and sit at a table. You've got to make an
           A or a B.

(12) RF: Thurgood Marshall and Perry and all.

      MF: Oh, it was Thurgood Marshall.

      RF: Oh yeah, they were the ones that handled that case. Perry.
           And, they sat there and when he would just tell them the
           number of the page and what the law was. And they knew.
           They knew what they were doing. Hear? They had to pay
           that girl for time that she was off.

      MF: That they didn't hire her?

      RF: And they wanted to reinstate her, but she said, "NO." She
           went to New York and got a job in New York. She wouldn't
           go back in the school. But, she got the money!

      MF: She got the money.

      RF: And they won the case. And from then on, *we didn't have no
           more trouble.* But that was, that was a sight to see.

There are a few intriguing points about the codeswitching behavior in
these interviews. The first is that irrespective of the reason for codeswitching, at most it involves a single clause or sentence. Multiple negation is
always embedded in longer stretches of Standard English, which highlights
the contrast even more. Also, codeswitching is used both as a device to set
off reported speech and as a means to highlight a particular statement.
Almost without exception, the frequency and use of codeswitching varies
according to the region in which the narrators spent their childhoods. The
two narrators who grew up in the North, attended desegregated schools, and
resided there at the time of the interviews codeswitched less frequently and
almost invariably used this device when quoting someone else's speech. On
the other hand, the two women who grew up in segregated communities and
attended segregated schools codeswitched twice as often, and their switches
were almost always used for emphasis. The length of the interview did not
affect the number of switches.

In an article analyzing the social and structural factors affecting
codeswitching, Carol Myers-Scotton (1993) distinguishes between non-

marked and marked codeswitching: unmarked speech is the particular code that is expected in any given interaction, whereas marked speech is any code that is unexpected in a particular interaction. She notes that marked codeswitching occurs in all kinds of interactions, even formal ones like interviews. Several points in Myers-Scotton's discussion about the differences between marked and unmarked codeswitching are relevant for this chapter. One is that marked codeswitching is always an attempt to alter the social relationship and that the social significance of marked codeswitching rests on a single switch from one code to another. The second is that marked codeswitching is typically highlighted phonologically and is more likely to occur intersententially rather than intrasententially. Using marked speech to report the remarks of others is a common verbal strategy in narrative performances (Wolfson 1976). Consequently, it is arguable whether when the teachers used marked speech to quote the words of others, their shifts were deliberate choices intended to change the social relationship.

This analysis has concentrated solely on the manipulation of grammatical structures, but there are undoubtedly other equally important features of codeswitching such as vowel elongation, manipulation of meter rhythm, cadence, and repetition that may signal and be understood as a shift to a discourse style that is more Black. For example, in Nelson's (1990) study, in addition to the use of multiple negation, the narrators employed aspects of a preaching style—responses in repetitive parallel clause structures that are commonly used for emphasis in the Black church tradition. Thus, in response to Nelson's question inquiring what it means to be a Black married woman, Sara, one of her narrators, provides an extended reply, part of which is excerpted here:

> It is pain, suffering, determination, perseverance.... It means a lot of heartache. It means achievement. It means a struggle, not for freedom, but for an identity, for that identity that is yours, that identity that says you don't have to have hair down your back, straight; you don't have to have blue eyes; you don't have to have a pencil point nose; you don't have to have razor thin lips; you don't have to be coy and cute in order to be attractive. (147)

The interviews in Nelson's study thus have a definite performance component. Narrators manipulate words to enhance their utterances. They frequently repeat phrases for emphasis. Changes in pitch, meter, and cadence evident in these narratives resemble the performances described earlier. Moreover, throughout their interview Nelson and Sara interact spontaneously, using both verbal and nonverbal means of communication. The interlocutors' statements are punctuated by responses and comments in the form of what Nelson calls *cosigns* and *completers*. In cosigning, the listener expresses an affirmation, an agreement with the speaker. In a completer the response completes the caller's statement. Sometimes this is an answer to a rhetorical question and sometimes it involves spontaneously talking along with the speaker. Dynamic interaction of this kind, along with shifts into performance and codeswitching at the grammatical level, can be drawn upon as a resource for establishing identity.

The extent to which gender influences the social relationship and governs codeswitching at all linguistic levels is worth investigating further. The studies presented in this chapter examine the language behavior between African American women, but the interviews between me and my male informants are qualitatively different. The men speak for longer stretches at a time and there are fewer instances of codeswitching, a pattern noted by others who have investigated interactions between African American women and men (Stanback 1985). This suggests that gender plays some part in facilitating or inhibiting codeswitching behavior and cannot be ignored.

The present study challenges the idea that regardless of context African American women's speech is always closer to Standard English than the speech of African American men. It also questions previous claims that African American teachers are rigid, uncompromising, and prescriptivist in their language attitudes. Rather, it argues for including the dynamic of gender as one of many influences that facilitates or constrains linguistic displays of solidarity and in-group identity among African Americans.

Conclusion

It is not possible to give a complete account of the reasons or the conditions under which African American women appropriate features of an African American discourse style. In this chapter I have attempted to present some examples of this behavior and to demonstrate that in the case of interviews and classroom discourse codeswitching is a deliberate and systematic practice intended to express the speakers' identities and influenced by the social relationships between participants. In some contexts—my own interviews, for instance—the social relationship is not established immediately. Rather, it is negotiated throughout the interview and not until the narrators feel comfortable do they codeswitch. It is unlikely that these narrators would codeswitch with outsiders, who would probably misunderstand it. Because both Nelson's and my own study of codeswitching examine speakers' behavior only in interviews, which represents merely a slice of our informants' daily interactions, the conclusions that can be drawn must be provisional. It is worth asking in which other contexts besides interviews and classrooms narrators might codeswitch.

Some researchers contend that teachers generally uphold norms of middle-class speech, that women adhere to the prestige code more than men, and that middle-class African American speech more than that of working-class African Americans is likely to conform to Standard English norms (Labov 1969). The narrators in all these studies belong to at least two of these three supposedly "unvernacular" groups. These facts notwithstanding, this chapter makes clear not only that African American women of the middle class and in the teaching profession retain their ability to communicate in the African American vernacular but that through their use of African American discourse they index a social identity and communicate a particular stance or point of view that cannot be expressed in Standard English. African American English enables these women to communicate cognitive, affective content not available in the standard form of the language, to create and maintain social relationships and express solidarity with listeners.

Although the particular features analyzed in this chapter represent important characteristics of African American discourse, there are other features not discussed here that may also signal and be understood as a shift to speech that is more Black (Foster 1989). Morgan's (1989) study of the discourse of three generations of African American women examines forms of indirection, which she argues is a counterlanguage through which African Americans assess speakers' intentionality. Taken together, my own studies and those of Nelson (1990) and Morgan (1989, 1991, 1993) argue for a broadened conception of codeswitching, one that takes into account all levels of language—phonology, semantics, syntax, and other discourse strategies—that characterize a particular speech community.

This analysis is narrow in scope, but it reveals that in even in the relatively formal context of interviews and classroom discourse, African American middle-class women do codeswitch into Black vernacular forms. I believe that their codeswitching behavior is an expression of solidarity and shared identity through which they express their power and challenge the hegemony of public discourse.

Notes

1. See Foster (1987, 1989) for a complete transcript. Transcription conventions are as follows:

    /   pause
    //   long pause
    |: :| repeated material
    :   long vowel
    ::   longer vowel
    [acc.]   accelerated speech
    { }   range of speech over which a description in brackets applies
    ...   ellipsis

2. Grammatical structures under discussion are italicized in the excerpts.

References

Abrahams, Roger D. (1964). *Deep down in the jungle: Negro narrative folklore from the streets of Philadelphia.* Chicago: Aldine.

——— (1970). *Positively black.* Englewood Cliffs, NJ: Prentice-Hall.

Abrahams, Roger D., and Richard Bauman (1971). Sense and nonsense in St. Vincent: Speech behavior in a Caribbean community. *American Anthropologist* 73: 762–72.

Baugh, John (1992). Hypocorrection: Mistakes in production of vernacular African American English as a second dialect. *Language and Communication* 12(3/4): 317–26.

Bauman, Richard (1977). The nature of performance. In Richard Bauman (ed.), *Verbal art as performance.* Rowley, MA: Newbury House. 3–58.

Bauman, Richard, and Charles Briggs (1990). Poetics and performance as critical perspectives on language and social life. *Annual Review of Anthropology* 19: 59–88.

Black, Max (1962). *Models and metaphors: Studies in language and philosophy.* Ithaca: Cornell University Press.

Blom, Jan-Petter, and John Gumperz (1972). Social meaning in linguistic structures: Code switching in Norway. In John J. Gumperz and Dell Hymes (eds.), *Directions in sociolinguistics.* New York: Holt, Rinehart & Winston. 404–34.

Briggs, Charles L. (1986). *Learning how to ask: A sociolinguistic role of the interview in social science research.* New York: Cambridge University Press.

Briggs, Charles, and Richard Bauman (1992). Genre, intertextuality, and social power. *Journal of Linguistic Anthropology* 2(2): 131–72.

Bucholtz, Mary (this volume). From mulatta to mestiza: Passing and the linguistic reshaping of ethnic identity.

Carothers, Suzanne (1990). Catching sense: Learning from our mothers to be black and female. In Faye Ginsburg and Anna L. Tsing (eds.), *Uncertain terms: Negotiating gender in American culture.* Boston: Beacon Press. 232–47.

Chernoff, John Miller (1979). *African rhythms and African sensibility: Aesthetics and social action in African musical idioms.* Chicago: University of Chicago Press.

Collins, Patricia Hill (1990). *Black feminist thought: Knowledge, consciousness, and the politics of empowerment.* Boston: Unwin Hyman.

Davis, Gerald L. (1985). *I got the word in me and I can sing it you know: A study of the performed African-American sermon.* Philadelphia: University of Pennsylvania Press.

Etter-Lewis, Gwendolyn (1993). *My soul is my own: Oral narratives of African-American women in the professions.* New York: Routledge.

Folb, Elizabeth (1980). *Runnin' down some lines: The language and culture of black teenagers.* Cambridge, MA: Harvard University Press.

Foster, Michèle (1987). "It's cookin' now": An ethnographic study of a successful Black teacher in an urban community college. Ph.D. diss., Harvard University.

———— (1989). "It's cookin' now": A performance analysis of the speech events of a Black teacher in an urban community college. *Language in Society* 18:11–29.

———— (1990). The politics of race: Through African teachers' eyes. *Journal of Education* 172(3): 123–41.

———— (1991a). Constancy, connectedness and constraints in the lives of Black women teachers: "Some things change, most stay the same." *NWSA Journal* 3(2): 233–61.

———— (1991b). "Just got to find a way": Case studies of the lives and practice of exemplary Black high school teachers. In Michèle Foster (ed.), *Qualitative investigations into schools and schooling.* New York: AMS Press. 273–309.

———— (1992). Sociolinguistics and the African American community: Implications for literacy. *Theory into Practice* 31(4): 303–11.

Foster, Michèle, and Jeanne Newman (1989). "I don't know nothin' about it": Black teachers' code-switching strategies in interviews. *Working Papers in Educational Linguistics,* Spring: 1–10.

Gwaltney, John Langston (1980). *Drylongso.* New York: Random House.

Heath, Shirley Brice (1983). *Ways with words: Language, life and work in communities and classrooms.* New York: Cambridge University Press.

hooks, bell (1989). *Talking back: Thinking feminist, thinking black.* Boston: South End Press.

Hymes, Dell (1972). Contribution of folklore to sociolinguistics. In Antonio Paredes and Richard Bauman (eds.), *Toward new perspectives in folklore.* Austin: University of Texas Press. 124–34.

———— (1974). *Foundations in sociolinguistics: An ethnographic approach.* Philadelphia: University of Pennsylvania Press.

———— (1975). Breakthrough into performance. In Dan Ben-Amos and Kenneth Goldstein (eds.), *Performance and communication.* The Hague: Mouton. 11–74.

Keil, Charles (1972). Motion and feeling through music. In Thomas Kochman (ed.), *Rappin' and stylin' out.* Champaign-Urbana: University of Illinois Press. 83–100.

Kochman, Thomas (1970). Toward an ethnography of Black American speech behavior. In Norman Whitten and John Szwed (eds.), *Afro-American anthropology: Contemporary perspectives.* New York: Free Press. 145–62.

———— (ed.) (1972). *Rappin' and stylin' out.* Champaign-Urbana: University of Illinois Press.

Labov, William (1969). Some sources of reading problems for Negro speakers of nonstandard English. Joan C. Baratz and Roger W. Shuy (eds.), *Teaching black children to read*. Washington, DC: Center for Applied Linguistics. 29–67.

———— (1972a). *Language in the inner city*. Philadelphia: University of Pennsylvania Press.

———— (1972b). *Sociolinguistic patterns*. Philadelphia: University of Pennsylvania Press.

McElhinny, Bonnie (this volume). Challenging hegemonic masculinities: Female and male police officers handling domestic violence.

Mitchell, Henry (1970). *Black preaching*. Philadelphia: Lippincott.

Mitchell-Kernan, Claudia (1971). *Language behavior in a black community*. Working Paper No. 23. Berkeley: Language Behavior Research Laboratory, University of California.

Morgan, Marcyliena (1989). From down South to up South: The language behavior of three generations of Black women residing in Chicago. Ph.D. diss., University of Pennsylvania.

———— (1991). Indirectness and interpretation in African American women's discourse. *Pragmatics* 1(4): 421–51.

———— (1993). The Africanness of counterlanguage among Afro-Americans. In Salikoko S. Mufwene (ed.), *Africanisms in Afro-American language varieties*. Athens: University of Georgia Press. 423–35.

Myers-Scotton, Carol (1993). Common and uncommon ground: Social and structural factors in codeswitching. *Language in Society* 22(4): 475–503.

Nelson, Linda Williamson (1990). Codeswitching in the oral life narratives of African-American women: Challenges to linguistic hegemony. *Journal of Education* 172(3): 142–55.

Smitherman, Geneva (1977). *Talkin and testifyin*. Detroit: Wayne State University Press.

Stanback, Marsha H. (1985). Language and black woman's place: Evidence from the black middle class. In Paula A. Treichler, Cheris Kramarae, and Beth Stafford (eds.), *For alma mater: Theory and practice in feminist scholarship*. Urbana: University of Illinois Press. 177–93.

Szwed, John (1969). Afro-American musical adaptation. *Journal of American Folklore* 82: 112–21.

Ward, Martha (1971). *Them children: A study in language learning*. New York: Holt, Rinehart & Winston.

Waterman, Richard (1952). African influence on the music of the Americas. In Sol Tax (ed.), *Acculturation in the Americas*. Chicago: University of Chicago Press. 81–94.

Wolfson, Nessa (1976). Speech events and natural speech: Some implications for sociolinguistic methodology. *Language in Society* 5: 189–209.

14

From Mulatta to Mestiza

Passing and the Linguistic Reshaping of Ethnic Identity

Mary Bucholtz

> There was a campus orientation for new students of color. A black woman slowly approached me and as she hesitated, I knew she was going to ask the inevitable question. After struggling with it for a few seconds, she finally blurted out, "What are you . . . ? I mean, where do you come from?" Then instead of waiting for me to answer, she showed that she already knew and said, "Your mama is Black, right?" I nodded in agreement and then I realized that she had said everything in Spanish.
>
> —Kristal Brent Zook, "Light Skinned-ded Naps"

The act of passing usually refers to the ability to be taken for a member of a social category other than one's own. The very term, like the practice, is viewed negatively in most studies of ethnicity. But in other areas of cultural studies, most prominently in queer theory as it has emerged from poststructural feminism, the notion of passing—together with its associated concepts, masquerade and mimesis—has become a crucial theoretical tool (e.g., Butler 1990, 1993; Silverman 1992). Indeed, this difference in perspective is one of the fundamental divisions between multicultural feminist theory and those strands of feminism that focus primarily on sexuality.

Why is a concept that is considered invaluable for understanding certain social categories rejected as a way of understanding others? The answer can be found in the eagerness with which poststructural feminism has declared the end of identity and the destruction of social categories. This event has not been met with answering cheers from all quarters, a reticence that is due to the fact that the implosion of sexual categories authorized by queer theory has not yet been matched by the eradication of racial and ethnic categories. The subversive appeal of queer identities lies precisely in their ability to be disguised. Metaphors of theater, parody, and drag permeate postmodern feminist writing, with little recognition that disguises cannot be as easily assumed by members of social groups whose identities have been imposed rather than assumed or appropriated—namely, members of nonwhite racial and ethnic groups. The categorizing power of skin color, hair, and facial features remains a reality for most Americans of non-European background, a fact that is often overlooked by white poststructural feminists. Whereas gender theorists celebrate passing as an achievement, a transcendence of sexual difference, in ethnic studies the phenomenon is generally considered an evasion of racism, an escape that is available only to individuals who can successfully represent themselves as white.

Nevertheless, both passing and poststructuralism may be rehabilitated for use in studies of ethnicity. After all, a major contribution of scholars of race and ethnicity has been to destabilize these social categories, an activity that is quintessentially poststructuralist in spirit. Such scholars demonstrate that the assignment of race to particular body types is without scientific basis. Instead, racial categorization authorizes social divisions on the basis of purported scientific divisions (Outlaw 1990). The ethnic paradigm, for its part, is no more valid. Ethnic theory replaces science with social science as its justifying discourse, arguing that racial characteristics are part of a larger set of social behaviors like language and custom. But this strategy fails as well because it obscures the phenomenon of racism by attributing all social inequalities to the cultural values of minority ethnic groups (Omi & Winant 1994).[1]

The assumption that an essential core, whether biological or social, determines one's race and ethnicity promotes the belief in ethnic authenticity. Authenticity—that is, the legitimacy of one's claim to ethnicity—underlies the traditional definition of passing given above, which posits a recategorization of the passing individual from her "own" ethnic group to another that is not her "own." The framework of authenticity is especially difficult to sustain, however, in the case of individuals of ambiguous or mixed ethnic background, for when multiple identities are available it is not at all clear which identity takes precedence. As I use the term for the remainder of this chapter, then, *passing is the active construction of how the self is perceived when one's ethnicity is ambiguous to others.* From this perspective an individual may in certain contexts pass as a member of her "own" or biographical ethnic group by insisting on an identity that others may deny her. Furthermore, passing of this kind is not passive. Individuals of ambiguous ethnicity patrol their own borders, using the tools of language and self-presentation to determine how the boundaries of ethnic categories are drawn upon their own bodies.

In the following pages I support these claims, using evidence drawn from twelve interviews with women of ambiguous or mixed ethnicity.[2] Interviews were conducted with individuals from a wide range of ethnic backgrounds, and it should therefore be kept in mind that speakers were in many ways more different than similar.[3] Nevertheless, the breadth of ethnicities represented in the data provides a sense of the scope of the issue of passing and its various meanings in women's lives.

Passing in Queer Theory and Practice

Just as movement across ethnic borders casts doubt on the biological basis of race and ethnicity, so too does movement across gender borders interrogate the rigidity of sexual categories. A striking example of this process is provided in the early ethnomethodological literature, in Garfinkel's (1967) study of Agnes, a young adult who looked female to outward appearances but had male genitalia. She insisted that she was neither male nor hermaphroditic but lived as female and therefore sought a sex-change operation. Garfinkel's study, carried out in collaboration with Robert Stoller, was undertaken in order to decide whether the operation should be done; such an extreme measure, it was felt, could be justified only if Agnes really was who she claimed to be: a woman. Extensive psychological and physical testing supported Agnes's assertion, and she steadfastly refused to provide the researchers with any information about herself that might undermine her claim to femaleness. On the strength of Agnes's normative femininity, the operation was authorized. It was not until eight years later that Agnes offhandedly revealed that she had in fact been born biologically male and had achieved her female shape by taking her mother's estrogen pills since the age of twelve.

Garfinkel seems to have received this revelation good-naturedly, even appreciatively; although his opponent has bested him, he expresses admiration for her skills. The irony of the situation was not lost on him: the operation, meant to "right" a biological "wrong," succeeded in erasing altogether the maleness that Agnes had already partly obscured. The weight of social norms, in the end, overwhelmed the objective tests of medical science. Agnes's strategic deployment of cultural stereotypes of feminine linguistic and social practices can therefore be seen as simultaneously subversive and constitutive of the social order.[4]

On the basis of his work with Agnes, Garfinkel argues that passing is not a one-time event but a never-completed process of achieving a position in a recognized social category: "members' practices alone produce the observable-tellable normal sexuality of persons, and do so only, entirely, exclusively in actual, singular, particular occasions through actual witnessed displays of common talk and conduct" (181). The ethnomethodological perception of identity as emergent in practice is in many respects compatible with the view put forward by poststructuralist queer theorists. Elizabeth Grosz (1994), for example, suggests that lesbian and gay identities, unlike all others, are based on practice rather than essence. Grosz's contention leads her to assert that sexual identities can be effaced or obscured far more readily than other identities: "It is this split between what is and what one does that produces the very possibility of a notion like 'the closet.' . . . It also accounts for the very possibility of coming out—after all, a quite ridiculous concept in most other forms of oppression. This is what enables homosexuals to 'pass' as straight with an ease that is extraordinarily rare for other oppressed groups" (151). But, with the important caveats already given, most other identities can indeed be separated in the same way; as the case of Agnes proves, if femininity is displayed and performed, an individual does not need to be a woman to be taken for a woman. Such disjunctions may be relatively rare, but they do occur. The calculated use of social practices, including linguistic practices, allows an individual to mark out an identity that may not correspond to biology or biography.

Linguistic Studies of Passing

The fact that language use is instrumental to the projection of social identity is widely recognized by sociolinguists, but studies of the relationship between language and passing have been undertaken only recently. The work that has been done thus far focuses primarily on gender and sexual identity rather than on ethnicity. This work corroborates nonlinguistic research on queer subversions of gender categories in that it demonstrates that parody, as much as passing, is the goal of such subversions. This parodic element, identified for example by Judith Butler (1990), has often limited the utility of poststructuralist insights for multicultural scholarship. Yet, to distinguish sharply between gender and ethnicity in the deconstruction of social categories is to overlook that both parody and passing are acts of performance. The recognition of ethnic identity as performance allows researchers in this area to gain valuable insights from queer theory.

Most important from a linguistic perspective, the new work on gender-bending convincingly demonstrates that language may be a crucial resource for moving from one social category to another. Recent ethnographic work in non-Western cultures, for example, indicates that the construction of a female identity by biological males and intersexed individuals takes place in large part through the strategic deployment of stereotypically feminine speech features (Gaudio forthcoming; Hall 1995, forthcoming). Similar observations have been made regarding the phenomenon of drag in North American society. Anna Livia (this volume) recounts the experiences of a butch lesbian who attended a workshop for aspiring drag kings, in which students were trained in the linguistic features associated with masculinity. The test of the workshop's efficacy came when each participant attended a "passing event" in the guise of a man.

These discussions do not explicitly address ethnic issues, but other studies do incorporate ethnicity. For example, in Rusty Barrett's (forthcoming) research on the performances of African American drag queens in gay bars, the performers made no pretense of being female, although they employed stereotypically feminine speech features. Indeed, as Barrett's nuanced analysis shows, such use of middle-class white "women's language" by lower-class Black gay men is a political statement that is designed not to efface but to highlight disjunctions of ethnicity, class, and gender.

Kira Hall's (this volume) discussion of phone-sex workers also contributes to this line of research. Hall offers several examples of the uses of ethnically stereotyped language by both female and male phone-sex workers to project a variety of feminine personas. In these instances, the performance of ethnicity is not designed to be recognized as such, and must therefore count as passing. Both studies make clear that social boundaries may be transgressed, whether overtly or covertly, using the tools of language.

Language and Ethnicity

As Hall's study (this volume) suggests, the ideological link between language and ethnicity is so potent that the use of linguistic practices associated with a given ethnic group may be sufficient for an individual to pass as a group member. In support of this fact, numerous studies have found that speakers may be able to pass linguistically even if they lack the ability to pass physically. Ronald Butters (1984) cites an unpublished study of a European American child whose peer group was African American; based on tape-recordings of her speech, more than forty native speakers of African American Vernacular English judged that she was African American. Additionally, Howard Giles and Richard Bourhis (1976) found that a majority of third-generation West Indians in Cardiff were heard as "white" in a judgment test involving both white and Black judges. It is important to note that in these studies the speakers were not attempting to represent themselves as members of another ethnic group; indeed, in the Giles and Bourhis study the ethnic identity of speakers who were judged to be white did not differ in any apparent way from that of the other speakers. In short, linguistic ability is not a reliable predictor of ethnicity or of ethnic identity.

However, it is by no means exceptional for individuals to be perceived as outsiders in an ethnic group if they lack the requisite linguistic skills. This linguistic metric of ethnic authenticity is exemplified nowhere better than in the writings of William Labov. In his pioneering sociolinguistic research Labov (1972a) held speakers to stringent standards of vernacular language use, seeking methodologies that would elicit the purest and most authentic varieties of nonstandard dialects. For this reason he elected to use teenage male street gang members for his investigation of African American Vernacular English (Labov 1966, 1972b), a method that necessarily eliminated the linguistic practices of female speakers, as well as those of male adults and middle-class African Americans. This important criticism of Labov's research has been issued by Michèle Foster (this volume) and Marcyliena Morgan (1991). Indeed, given his well-known insistence that women's speech is more standard than men's (Labov 1991), we might infer that for Labov female speakers in general are linguistically inauthentic. Thus one of the "linguistic consequences of being a lame," to borrow Labov's (1973) title, is to be excluded from sociolinguistic research.

The women in the present study are likewise atypical group members, "lames" in the parlance of the street gang members Labov studied, who lack complete knowledge of the vernacular of at least one of the groups with which they are associated. Labov views such individuals with suspicion, for their "connection to the vernacular is one of wishful approximation" (1972b:xviii). The women I interviewed, however, did not seem to harbor any idealistic nostalgic feelings for their vernacular languages; instead, they clearly recognized their limited knowledge of such varieties as an inevitable consequence of their marginal position in vernacular-speaking communities. Ursula,[5] for example, a twenty-four-year-old whose mother is African American and whose father is European American, explained her linguistic situation not wistfully but matter-of-factly: "In a sense I was brought up pretty much in white culture so that's where my identity comes from. I use the language of white culture. . . . When we [studied] the Black English thing in school I had just as much problem as anybody else."

Labov is not alone in linking language use to group membership. A large body of sociolinguistic and social psychological research argues that language is frequently a central component of ethnic identity; in fact, language is often a primary criterion of the definition of ethnicity itself.[6] Hence ethnic identity is especially sensitive to language issues, as Gloria Anzaldúa (1990:207) confirms: "Ethnic identity is twin skin to linguistic identity—I am my language." Moreover, for individuals who have access to multiple linguistic codes, as many of the interviewees do, language choice is inevitably an act of self-presentation. María Dolores Gonzales Velásquez (this volume) makes this same point in her analysis of Spanish, English, and codeswitching as three functionally different linguistic varieties in New Mexico. Language becomes a powerful tool in the display of the ethnic self, a tool that can either reinscribe or subvert the ethnic identities assigned by outsiders.

Traditional Perspectives on Passing

In the epigraph of this chapter Kristal Zook (1990), a light-skinned Black woman, describes how language can be mined for the materials of identity. Yet, Zook's expression of ethnicity through language use differs from those already discussed in that she is not biographically a member of the ethnic group with which she identifies; language is the glue that binds her to her ethnic identity. Zook describes the effort required to gain access to her adopted community, and the motivation for this effort:

> Due to a complex combination of socio-economic circumstances, I happened to find a kind of psychological shelter in Latino heritage and even grew to identify more with *it* than with my own culture(s). . . . It wasn't until years later that I realized why I had such an obsessive drive to learn Spanish and why I felt so at ease, relaxed and at home in Spain, a country whose people had the *exact* same skin color I did. I had simply been searching for a kind of psychic shelter, wherever I could find it. (92)

Coincidentally, another essay (Creef 1990) published in the same collection also emphasizes the appeal of Latino culture as a place of ethnic security and certainty:[7]

> When I am thirteen, I bury my mother once and for all and decide to go Mexican. It makes a lot of sense. I am no longer Elena, I am now Elaina and I begin insisting I am Mexican wherever I go. With my long black hair, my sun-darkened skin, and my new name, I can pass and I am safe. I obsessively hide my Japanese mother and deny my Japanese roots. . . . I love it when people ask if I am Español, because it is safe, because it means I do not stand out. (82–83)

Like Zook, Elena Creef undergoes a linguistic makeover (in this case an unofficial name change) in order to shore up the ethnic claims she is able to make on the basis of her physical appearance. The two passages are also similar in their description of the labor that goes into the construction of a new identity: both authors employ the term *obsessive* in reporting this process. In these reminiscences, being of ambiguous ethnicity presents psychological difficulties. Precipitated by the insensitive remarks of outsiders, the desire to pass offers itself as a temporary solution to racism and rejection. At the conclusion of both essays, however, the authors return to their biographical ethnic origins.

This perspective is corroborated by Erving Goffman (1963), whose sociological study of passing relies heavily on autobiographical materials. Goffman discusses the phenomenon of passing not only across racial boundaries but also between the worlds of the insane and the sane, the deaf and the hearing, the blind and the seeing, the gay and the straight. This rather bizarre taxonomy collapses diverse groups into a single dichotomy that separates "normals" from the stigmatized; the stigma can be escaped, Goffman suggests, by passing as "normal." In his data passing is viewed merely as a stage that the individual can transcend through self-acceptance. He reports that "in the published autobiographies of stigmatized individuals, this phase in the moral career is typically described as the final, mature, well-adjusted one, a state of grace" (101–2). George Kich (1992), in his research on biracial identity, presents a similar developmental account: in his three-stage model, passing occurs in Stage 2, a period during childhood and the teen years in which the individual seeks the approval of others; self-acceptance comes with adulthood in Stage 3, when the biracial identity is embraced. In such frameworks, passing is tantamount to pathology. An individual cannot be psychologically healthy or whole unless her or his entire ethnic heritage is acknowledged.[8]

The autobiographical emphasis on psychological problems is also common in literary treatments of racial ambiguity, but happy endings such as those reported above are rare in literature. Whereas the autobiographies emphasize that passing may represent a search for a sense of belonging, the evidence of early-twentieth-century novels suggests that it is a rejection of one's true community. In fiction, passing from one ethnic group into another is most often represented as a symptom of confused identity and denial of one's heritage. This pattern was established early on in literature on passing. In the context of American race relations, the phenomenon was usually restricted in the literary imagination to the movement of people of mixed African American and European American ancestry from Blackness to whiteness.[9] Although permanent changes in identity were in reality very rare (Spickard 1989), this sort of passing provided dramatic tension for novelists. In most fictional accounts, the figure of the "tragic mulatto," the mixed-race individual, suffered an untimely demise for her or his transgression of racial borders. For white novelists projecting their own racist fears onto the pages of their texts, this trope was a useful warning of the dangers of miscegenation. For Black novelists the issues were more complex because passing could allow an individual to avoid racism and garner economic advantages, but only at the price of rejecting her or his community. Thus even in novels by African Americans, mixed-race characters who were spared the fate of death nevertheless ended their lives unhappily. James Weldon Johnson's ([1912] 1990) fictional *Autobiography of an Ex-Colored Man*, for example, concludes with the narrator, a Black man who has lived his life as white, lamenting, "I have sold my birthright for a mess of pottage" (154).[10] And in Nella Larsen's ([1929] 1986) novella *Passing* the mulatta who moves between the world of her white husband and the Black New York of the Harlem Renaissance inexplicably falls to her death upon her husband's discovery of her racial background.

As Anna Livia (this volume) points out, literature should be used as a source of information not about social realities but about dominant ideologies. Hence we may understand from these and other novels that the hegemonic cultural belief about passing is that it is a deliberate and permanent project of identity transformation that yields economic or social benefits in exchange for heavy psychological costs. My own study suggests a mismatch between the novels and autobiographies on the one hand and the narratives of the women I interviewed on the other. Passing does not always emerge from an identity crisis or a sense of alienation. Moreover, it is very rarely a long-term undertaking; it is far more commonly temporary and most of the time it is unintentional. In short, women may pass in a number of ways and for a number of reasons, not all of them negative. It is necessary, therefore, to expand the notion of passing to incorporate the entire range of the phenomenon. At the same time, it is important to note that most of the interviewees did not use the term *passing* to describe their experiences, and some explicitly rejected the term. Thus Paige, a twenty-three-year-old Filipina, commented:

> The thing was, when someone would ask me what I was I would tell the truth. . . . I was always curious to see if I could get away with being, you know, something else, but then I thought, "Why pretend to be something I'm not?" I'm proud of who I am, so there's no reason for me to lie, which is flat-out what it is when you pass for something else.

Paige is responding here to the traditional, essentialist definition of passing. But what should count as passing becomes more complex when individuals of mixed ethnicity are involved. Unsurprisingly, then, revised understandings of passing come from mixed-race theory, an emerging branch of ethnic studies.

Mixed-Race Perspectives on Passing

In early 1995 *Newsweek* magazine dedicated its cover story to the topic of mixed race in the United States. This event represented a milestone in public awareness of the issue, coming as it did on the heels of the publication of two autobiographies—both quite well received on the talk-show circuit—by authors of mixed race whose families were split by "the color line" (Haizlip 1994; Williams 1995). The category of *mixed* itself has slowly begun to enter the public discourse as well: in commenting on the O. J. Simpson trial in March 1995, an event in which racial issues are paramount, a talk-radio host in San Francisco remarked that the jury included seven Blacks, two whites, two Latinos, and one person of mixed race. The recent shift in popular thinking about mixed race is due in large part to the efforts of mixed-race activists and academics, whose undertakings include high-profile lobbying for a *mixed* ethnic category on the next U.S. census form. Theorists of mixed-race identity have also sought to challenge earlier analyses of multiracial heritage as a psychological burden or as a romanticized symbol of racial harmony. In addressing these issues, such theorists have inevitably turned to the issue of passing.

It is possible that mixed-race theory leads other theories of ethnic identity in the analysis of passing because, as Carla Bradshaw (1992:80) remarks, "The only people capable of racially passing, and the only people to whom the concept can realistically apply, are multiracial ones." Some of the newer theories of passing echo traditional analyses in suggesting that passing is a denial of identity, but where earlier commentators often viewed passing as a rejection of one's true ethnic group, mixed-race theorists now advocate a mixed-race identity in which no single ethnic category is paramount. Nonetheless, several scholars have recognized the potential for a positive understanding of the phenomenon. Naomi Zack (1993), for example, points out that individuals who are able to pass may draw upon a variety of flexible identities to their own advantage. Additionally, in a recent collection of essays on mixed-race Americans, Reginald Daniel (1992) argues that passing may be viewed as a subversive exercise of agency, and Cynthia Nakashima (1992:177) suggests that passing should be seen as a way of selecting an identity: "An interesting twist on the phenomenon of 'choosing' occurs when a multiracial person chooses to be a different race or ethnicity altogether—for example, an Asian-White person who identifies as Hawaiian, Samoan, Native American, or Latino." As Nakashima's comment indicates, the new theories recognize that passing is not simply a movement into whiteness; individuals may pass as belonging to another race or ethnicity, or as having a mixed ethnic background.

This fact is illustrated in my own research: none of the interviewees reported being taken for white; instead, the ethnicities ascribed to them by outsiders ranged from South Asian to Polynesian to Cuban to Native American. For example, Shaneinei, a twenty-two-year-old of Japanese and Latin American descent, recalls:

> I remember one time in high school within the distance of just a few feet I got asked by different people. "Are you Hawaiian?" And then the next stop, "Are you Filipino?" And then, what was the next one? Filipino and then, oh, "Samoan?" "No." And then I kept walking and someone else asked me if I was Mexican.

Regardless of category, choice is also at issue when an individual refuses an assigned or ascribed ethnicity. Paige, the Filipina who commented above on her unwillingness to represent herself as a member of another ethnic group, describes such a situation involving an encounter with a young boy in an airport waiting room:

> And then he says, "What are you?" ... He said it really brashly. And I was thinking, "Where are you coming off?" And I said, "Well, I'm American," because I am. And he said, "Are you Chinese?" And I said, "No," and he said, "Are you Mexican?" "No." And it was weird because the way he was talking he assumed that I wasn't American, that I couldn't speak this language. And here I am talking to him! ... He was asking me these questions like, "Do you speak Chinese?" or "Do you speak another language?" ... And I said to him, "Never make assumptions based on what someone looks like.... Don't ever assume that someone can't speak English if they have black hair and slanted eyes."

Paige's rejection of imposed ethnic categories intersects with the reinterpretations of passing offered above in demonstrating how individuals actively construct contested identities. Moreover, her comments point to one important facet of this process that is rarely discussed at length in the scholarship on mixed race: the contribution of language to the projection and ascription of ethnic identity.

Ideologies of Language

In the interview data I collected, ethnic identity is a site of struggle. Respondents reported that although their physical appearance violated the standards of their biographical ethnic groups, language could be instrumental in challenging the assumptions triggered by their appearance. For example, some participants in the study took steps to reclaim a lost language of heritage as part of their display of an ethnic identity. Hence Paige bought a book on Ilokano—one of her family's languages of heritage—and searched for classes in the language, and Shaneinei attended twelve years of Japanese school and majored in Japanese in college. As she reports, her efforts made her feel more authentic than the other students, who had two Japanese parents:

> When I was growing up I felt sometimes like I was in a way more Japanese than the Japanese American kids were, just because they were trying so hard to forget their Japanese and I was trying so hard to learn Japanese. Just language! Not even, you know, cultural aspects, although of course you get that with language too. Like sometimes I felt like I understood some Japanese things better or, or like I don't know if *appreciated*, but somehow I felt more Japanese than they were sometimes. Which, now that I think about it I don't know if I could get past just because of how I looked. I don't think I felt like I really could ever admit that openly to anybody just cause I didn't look Japanese.

Shaneinei's statement illustrates the dissonance between the possibilities of language and the perceived limitations of the physical self. Even as Shaneinei's appearance renders her inauthentic in the eyes of others, she constructs her ethnic authenticity through language.

Over and over again, the women in these interviews use language to challenge external perceptions and to lay claim to their own definition of ethnic identity. For example, Kavita, a thirty-year-old of mixed European American and African American ancestry, explains how she resists being the subject of racist stereotypes about African Americans: "I work hard to be articulate and to come off as intelligent, to be sort of upstanding." Kavita's definition of her own ethnic identity runs counter to the expectation that nonwhite ethnic groups will be lower-class speakers of a nonstandard variety, for she explicitly defines her "articulate" speech style as standard English. Similarly, Claudia, a twenty-one-year-old Mexican American, distances herself from users of nonstandard Spanish, or "slang": "People say things and I don't understand. . . . I've never been around people who speak that way, and I was told not to use slang when I was growing up." Although both Kavita and Claudia report being teased by others for their "proper" speech, they have made no effort to adopt vernacular speech community norms. As Kavita emphasizes, language and identity are intimately connected: "I don't alter my language the least bit. What you hear is what I am inside."

Although it is clear that the ability to speak like members of a group enhances the likelihood of being included by group members, the comments of Kavita and Claudia suggest that the inability to speak a particular way may be effective in challenging ethnic expectations. In her study of bilingual children of Japanese and American ancestry, Teresa Kay Williams (1992:295) likewise describes a type of linguistic passing predicated not upon language ability but upon inability: "Many ... learned when to keep quiet about their knowledge of the *other* language and when to disclose it. Sometimes Amerasians pretended they could not speak either language, to get special attention or for mere convenience." An example of this phenomenon in the present study is offered by Shaneinei, who occasionally refuses to engage in interaction in Spanish, a language in which she is fluent. As she explains, she does so in order to resist the imposition of an identity she views as problematic:

> Latino people speak to me in Spanish. Sometimes, I don't know, it's really bad of me, and it makes me feel like a hypocrite because ... I don't like to look down on people but I guess I do because sometimes I won't answer in Spanish, I'll just answer in English. I guess from when I was a kid it was kind of bad to be Latino because you know just this big stereotype of Latino and Chicano people being so, like, dirty or bad or lazy or blah blah blah, whatever bad or negative stereotypes. I think that's partly why I still say the Latin American part of me is second because you know I identify more with the Japanese part and plus that's, like, the better side. You know, follow the existing stereotype.

Shaneinei's analysis of her own behavior is sensitive to the complex hierarchy of American racisms, which ranks ethnicities differentially based on stereotypes of class, color, and other factors.[11] Unwilling to be boxed into a category that carries with it the racist beliefs of the dominant culture, she averts the situation by not revealing her linguistic knowledge.

Ideologies of Gender

In resisting ethnic stereotypes, the women in this study resisted gender stereotypes as well. Indeed, Barrett's (forthcoming) research on drag queens and Hall's (this volume) work on phone sex, discussed above, indicate that ethnicity and gender are not separable parameters: any performance of gender is always simultaneously a performance of ethnicity. Conversely, as my interview data suggest, any performance of ethnicity is always simultaneously a performance of gender. Violations of one social category may be attributed to violations of the other; hence, Claudia ascribes her atypical ethnic identity to atypical gender arrangements in her family:

> My father died when [my twin sister and I] were a year old, so my mother raised us by herself. And I think that had a lot to do with different things, because my father's side of the family was very … traditionally Mexican where they live together in the same community, they like to stick together, with the male dominating view on the culture.

Under the guidance of their mother and older sister, Claudia and her twin were discouraged from embracing the markings of a stereotypical Mexican American female identity, in short, from being "cholas," or gang-identified.[12] The nexus of ethnicity and class thus also inescapably involves gender, for gender norms are linked to class positions. It is important to keep in mind that all the interviewees were students or recent graduates of a prestigious university and thus in violating expectations of gendered ethnicity they may be distancing themselves from lower-class status. In the passage below, Claudia describes the factors that make her ethnically ambiguous. Strikingly, none of the features she lists is associated with her skin color or facial features; the markers of ethnicity, as she describes them, are language and self-adornment:

> I think it has a lot to do with how you present yourself. And if I don't have an accent, if I don't use slang a lot, if I don't dress a certain [way], they tend to think, "You know, she could be something else." Because if I had a perm, if I had, like, a plaid shirt with jeans … they would know right off [that I was Mexican].

Several of the badges of ethnicity that Claudia cites are also badges of gender: specific hairstyles, distinctive clothing (she comments elsewhere that dark colors in particular point to a Chicano identity). These details are enumerated by Paige as well, in a parallel discussion of her own resistance to the stereotyped image of her ethnic group: "I avoided stuff that made me look typically Filipino, like big hair and lots of eyeliner." The ethnic stereotypes that Paige mentions, cosmetics use and hairstyle, are also gender stereotypes. The passages suggest that one cannot be merely Filipino or Chicano; like the forms of these words themselves, one must be marked for gender as well, as a Filipina or a Chicana.

The pressure to display an ethnically appropriate persona is motivated in part by expectations of normative heterosexuality. Ursula, who is of African

American and European American heritage, reports that in her experience this pressure has been exerted primarily by men:

> I remember one instance I was on a bus in Rhode Island and I was just dressed the way I normally dress, you know, sort of Gap basic clothes, and there was this Black guy and white guy, they were friends obviously, sitting behind me, and the white kid was asking the Black guy, "Well, how come you wear that kind of scarf and that kind of hat?" which is sort of the Islamic kind of hat and Arab scarf. And he said, "Well, I feel it's part of my culture and part of my heritage, and I just want to say that I'm identifying with that and I'm not buying into the white culture." And the kid's saying, "Oh, that's really interesting," and then this Black guy behind me says, "You know, you see that girl sitting in front of us, she's obviously not in touch with her roots." And I felt so mad, but being the little female I didn't stand up and say anything to him.

Ursula's violation of ethnic expectations by dressing "white" is also a violation of gender expectations, and thus she experiences herself in this incident as the object of specifically male scrutiny. Men's evaluations may extend to other areas of women's lives as well: Ursula notes that she is often criticized for dating white men. But male disapproval is not the sole province of any particular ethnic group. As she remarks, "Men feel territorial, just in general."

Because ethnicity, gender, and sexual identity are so tightly bound up together, however, it is not always easy to determine which factor is uppermost when women withdraw their participation in culturally expected practices. Thus, Kavita could not decide whether her racial background or her emerging recognition of her lesbianism was the reason that she did not date as an undergraduate at a predominantly white university. At the same time, she reports that in her own life sexuality takes precedence over race as a way of organizing identity and community. She explains, "The bonds don't come from race, they come from shared experience."

Yet, this assertion does not mean that racial or ethnic concerns are absent altogether. On the contrary, the interview data attest to the complexity of Kavita's ethnic identity: within the space of an hour-long conversation she offers at least three ways of understanding her ethnic self:

> "Mostly, when I feel like I'm being myself I feel like I'm acting like a middle-class white person."

> "I identify as black, but there's kind of a dissonance or something. It's like having two identities, basically."

> "I just don't see myself as white or black."

Kavita's shifts in self-definition imply not the fragmentation or incoherence of her identity but the multiple perspectives that are available to her from moment to moment. Just as significant to the presentation of self are the labels that individuals reject; Paige, for instance, does not allow herself to be labeled *mixed* although she acknowledges that her ancestry is technically multiracial (Spanish and Filipino). She reports with some amusement that another woman tried to befriend her on the basis of their assumed shared experience as mixed-race individuals. As Kavita notes earlier, however, shared racial background does not necessarily yield commonalities of experience.

Nevertheless, rejecting particular practices or labels does not entail rejection of the biographical ethnicity. In fact, interviewees tended to assert their biographical identity precisely because observers frequently failed to recognize this identity. Embracing a contested ethnicity when it is called into question in this way, insisting on its authenticity, is, in effect, an act of passing.

Acting and Passing

To assume one's biographical identity when it is in dispute is not acquiescence to a default category but active resistance to the way one's body is read by a stranger. It often involves subverting hopeful expectations of the exotic: Ursula reports being asked if she is Azorean, commenting, "People don't think I'm Black. They'll choose something way out there." Disappointment often greets the revelation of ethnic identity, as noted by both Claudia, who is commonly taken for an Italian or a Middle Easterner, and Paige, who (until she cut her hair) reported being mistaken for a Native American. "Oh, did I let you down?" is the way Paige summarizes her feelings to such reactions.

Even when an individual elects to exploit ethnic ambiguity in the direction of another ethnic group (that is, the traditional sense of passing), she may undermine this representation of herself in order to complicate the easy assumptions of outsiders. The extended passage below shows how the conflict of workplace demands, employer racism, and ethnic expression may be reconciled through creative linguistic work:

> I used to work as Princess Jasmine [from the film *Aladdin*] at Disneyland. And that was interesting. And for a while Disneyland didn't want—they were debating whether they should have an ethnic-looking person for this ethnic character, because they never did [for] a face character like Snow White who talks, and Belle [from *Beauty and the Beast*], things like that.... For a while, like for a month, they

had a white girl....They used her for a while but she didn't look like her at all. And I think I look [like Princess Jasmine]. I mean once you put the wig on, things like that, you look like the character. But it was funny how they didn't want to use [a nonwhite actress]....And then when guests, the people at the park, with kids would come, Spanish-speaking kids [would say], "Oh, Jasmine!" ...We could speak to them in Spanish if we wanted to, any language if we knew different languages. And they were really surprised and you know, "Are you [Latino]?" And people did think that I was maybe Arabic and they would try to talk to me. That was funny, so depending on where you are you can look like different things, and [it's funny] what benefits you can get or can't get.

Claudia gains access to the financial opportunity that the Disneyland job represents precisely because of her ethnic ambiguity, because she can pass as Arab. Yet by drawing upon her Spanish ability (an ability that, she reports elsewhere, she is normally reluctant to use in public), Claudia calls attention to her ethnic identity as a Mexican American. This maneuver challenges the racist belief of her employers that white actors should play the parts of nonwhite characters. In asserting herself as an "ethnic" Princess Jasmine, Claudia also delights Spanish-speaking children who visit the theme park and thereby subverts racist social arrangements that dictate that Latinos must be in invisible or subservient positions. Yet she accomplishes this reversal by playing to gender stereotypes; the character wears a bikini top and diaphanous full pants, and is hardly a feminist role model. The situation recalls Hall's (this volume) study of the appropriation of feminine speech features by phone-sex workers: by drawing on existing ideologies of gender, individuals may overcome economic—and in Claudia's case, racial—barriers. Such strategies at once preserve and subvert the social order. Although actual identity practices may be fluid, social categories themselves are rigid ideologies. Claudia plays off these ideologies and reaps economic and symbolic benefits by constructing her identity—and deconstructing Princess Jasmine—through language.

But deconstruction cuts both ways. If women of mixed racial background can appropriate ethnic categories, so too can other individuals. In particular, white women may co-opt other ethnicities for their own use; this may occur because European Americans are often viewed as lacking an ethnicity. Laying claim to another ethnic group may allow whites to "become ethnic." Such a situation is exemplified in my data by my interview with Julia, a European American woman of Celtic descent. Julia contacted me by telephone about the study because, she said, she is often asked if she has Asian ancestry. When we met in person, however, I was surprised to find that, at least as far as I could see, she was unambiguously white. Julia explained that in some situations, especially photographs, people remark that her eyes look Asian. Moreover, sometimes people ask her whether she is of African American descent because of her curly hair. She states that these questions, which are exclusively from European Americans, surprise her: "I don't look anything but white, to me anyway." Such comments, she goes on to suggest, are potentially insulting, although she does not take offense at them. In fact, she reports that she herself is often the one to joke about being racially mixed.

Julia takes great pride in her Irish heritage, and makes no claims to an Asian American or African American identity. She suggests that one reason for her ethnic pride is that she has always lived in ethnically diverse areas; as she was growing up, most of her friends were Asian American. Her insistence on her potentially ambiguous ethnicity should be read in juxtaposition to this fact. She feels that white ethnic pride is often trivialized or labeled racist; in this context a claim to Asianness or Blackness may provide a sort of ethnic legitimacy that even Irishness does not offer.

Julia's situation calls to mind a similar and widely debated issue in feminist circles: the issue of European American women's co-optation of Native American identities. For example, some non-Native women use sacred symbols on clothing, jewelry, and in other contexts that Native Americans view as sacrilegious. Some white feminists have even invoked a part-Native American ancestry to argue that they have a legitimate right to practice indigenous people's spiritual traditions. Still others have suggested that spiritual practices should be open to all interested individuals. These arguments overlook the fact that racial differences produce power differences, and that in taking up the practices of other groups, well-meaning whites may strip these groups of an important source of their own power and identity. As such situations indicate, the politics of deconstruction, by eradicating social categories like ethnicity, gender, and so on, leads inevitably to the politics of appropriation. Despite the many contributions of poststructuralist theories to ethnic studies of language and gender, these theories should be scrutinized carefully for what they may, perhaps unwittingly, authorize.

Conclusion

Cookie Stephan (1992:62) has asserted, on the basis of her research with individuals of mixed race, that "regardless of number of identities, ethnic identities do not seem to involve conscious selection. One does not experience electing to be Hispanic, for instance, but instead experiences being Hispanic." But as I have argued in this chapter, ethnic identity, especially for those of ambiguous ethnicity, is a consciously constructed product of self-presentation. The fluidity of ethnicity means that individuals can authenticate themselves in a variety of ways, and language use is a particularly effective tool in this process. As Ursula aptly puts it, "If you have the ability to use either [ethnicity] then you use them in situations to get what you can. I'm sorry to say it's not any kind of deep ideology, it's just kind of like, I mean, you look out for yourself." The renovated notion of passing contributes greatly to such an enterprise.

Poststructuralist feminism and ethnic studies converge in the notion of passing, whether sexual or ethnic, as performance. Moreover, performance is not limited to gender subversions any more than it is limited to individuals of mixed race. Just as issues of gender ambiguity highlight the strategies of all gendered persons, so does attention to individuals at the boundaries of ethnic categories illuminate the ethnic work that all speakers do. Finally, as Penelope Eckert and Sally McConnell-Ginet (this volume) demonstrate, social categories like gender and class—and, I would add, ethnicity and sexuality—are not separable, nor are they separate from language. Speakers cannot abstain from affiliating themselves with a social identity in their linguistic choices, for identity in all its facets is largely constructed through language.

Acknowledgments

I would like to thank Kira Hall, Robin Lakoff, Jon McCammond, Norma Mendoza-Denton, and Pam Morgan for suggestions and comments on earlier versions of this chapter. I would also like to thank the participants in the study for their stories and insights.

Notes

1. To deny the coherence of race and ethnicity as categories is not to deny their ongoing relevance in interaction as well as their utility for social and political organization. For further discussion see Bucholtz (forthcoming).

2. Although it is widely recognized among sociolinguists that speakers' reports of their language use reflect idealized rather than actual usage, these disparities can be scrutinized for information about speakers' ideologies and identities (Blom & Gumperz [1972] 1986). Such data are therefore crucial in a study of this kind, which focuses on how language is deployed in self-representation and representation.

3. Because all the interviewees were affiliated with the same California university as students, recent graduates, or staff members, they had in common their

membership in the academic community, as well as a general middle-class identity. Their age range (eighteen to thirty-two) was also fairly narrow. Three men were also interviewed for the study, but their comments are not presented here because the small number of male participants precludes meaningful comparative analysis.

4. Many of the linguistic devices that Agnes used correspond to the features of "women's language" described by Robin Lakoff (1975, 1982), including intensifiers and emphatic stress: "Oh, everything was just so wonderful"; "It was the best job I *ever* had" (Garfinkel 1967:167). Agnes also managed information about her private life by using feminine conversational strategies to draw out other speakers, especially men (P. Fishman 1983), and to avoid talking about herself.

5. Interviewees were asked to select their own pseudonyms.

6. See J. Fishman (1977) and Gudykunst and Schmidt (1988) for overviews.

7. The security afforded by a Latino identity is not universally agreed upon. As I will describe later, the interview data suggest that the pressure of racist stereotypes can make this identity problematic for some individuals of Latino descent.

8. The utility of such models for some individuals should not be dismissed. Their danger lies in the potential to label as developmentally backward an adult who chooses not to embrace a multiracial identity. Conversely, Maria Root (1990) offers a nonlinear model of multiethnic identity that views a number of solutions as equally acceptable over a lifetime, but passing does not figure into her account.

9. The opposite type of passing, from white to Black, is a literary rarity, although Goffman (1963) briefly mentions it as a possibility. The most famous documentation of a white man passing as Black (Griffin 1960) denaturalizes the process by suggesting that it is achievable only through scientific intervention. In consultation with a doctor, Griffin took pills and used ultraviolet light to darken his skin for what he calls the "experiment."

10. The very possibility of a man who looks white but is classified as Black is a quirk of the American system of race: the existence of a single Black ancestor has historically been sufficient to classify an individual as legally Black. In 1986 the U.S. Supreme Court refused to reject this definition of Blackness, often termed the *one-drop rule*. The case, *Doe v. State of Louisiana* (479 US 1002), involved a woman who sought to change her parents' race, as recorded on her birth certificate, from *colored* to *white*; the classification had been made on the basis of the fact that her great-great-great-great-grandmother was Black (United Press International, December 8, 1986). The state court had denied the claim in part because the "fact that family members describe themselves as 'white' did not prove error on document designating their parents as 'colored' " (479 So. 2d 370 [1985]).

11. Like the topic of mixed race, issues of colorism, that is, of bias based on skin color, have recently come to the fore in the popular press (Russell, Wilson, & Hall 1992), as well as in activist writings (Camper 1994; Featherston 1994).

12. The term *chola/-o* has a wide variety of meanings that almost always have

negative connotations. The term may designate a range of sexual, racial, and class positions ('mestizo', 'pretty boy', 'hick', etc.) that often suggest outsider or stigmatized status. See Polkinhorn, Velasco, and Lambert (1986).

References

Barrett, Rusty (forthcoming). "She is *not* white woman": The appropriation of (white) women's language by African American drag queens. In Mary Bucholtz, Anita Liang, Laurel Sutton, and Caitlin Hines (eds.), *Cultural performances: Proceedings of the Third Berkeley Women and Language Conference.* Berkeley: Berkeley Women and Language Group.

Blom, Jan-Petter, and John J. Gumperz ([1972] 1986). Social meaning in linguistic structures: Code-switching in Norway. In John J. Gumperz and Dell Hymes (eds.), *Directions in sociolinguistics: The ethnography of communication.* New York: Blackwell. 407–34.

Bradshaw, Carla K. (1992). Beauty and the beast: On racial ambiguity. In Maria P. P. Root (ed.), *Racially mixed people in America.* Newbury Park, CA: Sage. 77–88.

Bucholtz, Mary (forthcoming). Theorizing African American women's linguistic practices. In Victoria Bergvall, Janet Bing, and Alice Freed (eds.), *Language and gender research: Theory and method.* London: Longman.

Butler, Judith (1990). *Gender trouble: Feminism and the subversion of identity.* New York: Routledge.

—— (1993). *Bodies that matter: On the discursive limits of "sex."* New York: Routledge.

Butters, Ronald R. (1984). When is English "Black English Vernacular"? *Journal of English Linguistics* 17: 29–36.

Camper, Carol (ed.) (1994). *Miscegenation blues: Voices of mixed race women.* Toronto: Sister Vision.

Creef, Elena Tajima (1990). Notes from a fragmented daughter. In Gloria Anzaldúa (ed.), *Making face, making soul/Haciendo caras.* San Francisco: Aunt Lute. 82–84.

Daniel, G. Reginald (1992). Passers and pluralists: Subverting the racial divide. In Maria P. P. Root (ed.), *Racially mixed people in America.* Newbury Park, CA: Sage. 91–107.

Eckert, Penelope, and Sally McConnell-Ginet (this volume). Constructing meaning, constructing selves: Snapshots of language, gender, and class from Belten High.

Featherston, Elena (ed.) (1994). *Skin deep: Women writing on color, culture and identity.* Freedom, CA: Crossing Press.

Fishman, Joshua A. (1977). Language and ethnicity. In Howard Giles (ed.), *Language, ethnicity, and intergroup relations.* New York: Academic Press. 15–57.

Fishman, Pamela (1983). Interaction: The work women do. In Barrie Thorne, Cheris Kramarae, and Nancy Henley (eds.), *Language, gender, and society.* Rowley, MA: Newbury House. 89–101.

Foster, Michèle (this volume). "Are you with me?": Power and solidarity in the discourse of African American women

Garfinkel, Harold (1967). Passing and the managed achievement of sex status in an "intersexed" person: Part 1. In *Studies in ethnomethodology*. Cambridge, MA: Polity Press. 116–85.

Gaudio, Rudi (forthcoming). Not talking straight in Hausa. In Anna Livia and Kira Hall (eds.), *Queerly phrased: Language, gender, and sexuality*. New York: Oxford University Press.

Giles, Howard, and Richard Y. Bourhis (1976). Voice and racial categorization in Britain. *Communication Monographs* 43: 108–14.

Goffman, Erving (1963). *Stigma: Notes on the management of spoiled identity*. New York: Simon & Schuster.

Gonzales Velásquez, María Dolores (this volume). Sometimes Spanish, sometimes English: Language use among rural New Mexican Chicanas.

Griffin, John Howard (1960). *Black like me*. Boston: Houghton Mifflin.

Grosz, Elizabeth (1994). Experimental desire: Rethinking queer subjectivity. In Joan Copjec (ed.), *Supposing the subject*. London: Verso. 133–57.

Gudykunst, William B., and Karen L. Schmidt (1988). Language and ethnic identity: An overview and prologue. In William B. Gudykunst (ed.), *Language and ethnic identity*. Philadelphia: Multilingual Matters. 1–14.

Haizlip, Shirlee Taylor (1994). *The sweeter the juice: A family memoir in black and white*. New York: Simon & Schuster.

Hall, Kira (1995). Hijra/Hijrin: Language and gender identity. Ph.D. diss., University of California, Berkeley.

——— (forthcoming). Shifting gender positions among Hindi-speaking hijras. In Victoria Bergvall, Janet Bing, and Alice Freed (eds.), *Language and gender research: Theory and method*. London: Longman.

——— (this volume). Lip service on the fantasy lines.

Johnson, James Weldon ([1912] 1990). *The autobiography of an ex-colored man*. Harmondsworth: Penguin.

Kich, George Kitahara (1992). The developmental process of asserting a biracial, bicultural identity. In Maria P. P. Root (ed.), *Racially mixed people in America*. Newbury Park, CA: Sage. 304–17.

Labov, William (1966). *The social stratification of English in New York City*. Washington, DC: Center for Applied Linguistics.

——— (1972a). *Sociolinguistic patterns*. Philadelphia: University of Pennsylvania Press.

——— (1972b). *Language in the inner city: Studies in the Black English Vernacular*. Philadelphia: University of Pennsylvania Press.

——— (1973). The linguistic consequences of being a lame. *Language in Society* 2: 81–115.

——— (1991). The intersection of sex and social class in the course of linguistic change. *Language Variation and Change* 2(2): 205–51.

Lakoff, Robin (1975). *Language and woman's place*. New York: Harper & Row.

——— (1982). Some of my favorite writers are literate: The mingling of oral and literate strategies in written communication. In Deborah Tannen (ed.), *Spoken and written language: Exploring orality and literacy.* Norwood, NJ: Ablex. 239–60.

Larsen, Nella ([1929] 1986). *Passing.* In Deborah E. McDowell (ed.), *Quicksand* and *Passing.* New Brunswick, NJ: Rutgers University Press. 143–242.

Livia, Anna (this volume). "I ought to throw a Buick at you": Fictional representations of butch/femme speech.

Morgan, Marcyliena H. (1991). Indirectness and interpretation in African American women's discourse. *Pragmatics* 1(4): 421–51.

Nakashima, Cynthia (1992). An invisible monster: The creation and denial of mixed-race people in America. In Maria P. P. Root (ed.), *Racially mixed people in America.* Newbury Park, CA: Sage. 162–78.

Omi, Michael, and Howard Winant (1994). *Racial formation in the United States: From the 1960s to the 1990s.* 2d ed. New York: Routledge.

Outlaw, Lucius (1990). Toward a critical theory of "race." In David Theo Goldberg (ed.), *Anatomy of racism.* Minneapolis: University of Minnesota Press. 58–82.

Polkinhorn, Harry, Alfredo Velasco, and Malcolm Lambert (1986). *El libro de caló: The dictionary of Chicano slang.* Rev. ed. N.p.: Floricanto Press.

Root, Maria P. P. (1990). Resolving "other" status: Identity development of biracial individuals. In Laura S. Brown and Maria P. P. Root (eds.), *Diversity and complexity in feminist therapy.* New York: Harrington Park Press. 185–205.

Russell, Kathy, Midge Wilson, and Ronald Hall (1992). *The color complex: The politics of skin color among African Americans.* New York: Harcourt Brace Jovanovich.

Silverman, Kaja (1992). White skin, brown masks: The double mimesis, or With Lawrence in Arabia. In *Male subjectivity at the margins.* New York: Routledge. 299–338.

Spickard, Paul R. (1989). *Mixed blood: Intermarriage and ethnic identity in twentieth-century America.* Madison: University of Wisconsin Press.

Stephan, Cookie White (1992). Mixed-heritage individuals: Ethnic identity and trait characteristics. In Maria P. P. Root (ed.), *Racially mixed people in America.* Newbury Park, CA: Sage. 50–63.

Williams, Gregory Howard (1995). *Life on the color line: The true story of a white boy who discovered he was black.* New York: Dutton.

Williams, Teresa Kay (1992). Prism lives: Identity of binational Amerasians. In Maria P. P. Root (ed.), *Racially mixed people in America.* Newbury Park, CA: Sage. 280–303.

Zack, Naomi (1993). *Race and mixed race.* Philadelphia: Temple University Press.

Zook, Kristal Brent (1990). Light skinned-ded naps. In Gloria Anzaldúa (ed.), *Making face, making soul/Haciendo caras.* San Francisco: Aunt Lute. 85–96.

15

"Nobody Is Talking Bad"

Creating Community and Claiming Power on the Production Lines

Tara Goldstein

The walls of the classroom begin to shake as the tow motor speeds by on the old wooden floor.[1] The truck is transporting down to the production floor raw materials needed by some of the assembly-line workers. The assemblers themselves, however, are not on the lines. It is lunchtime, and they are sitting in the English classroom waiting for the noise to pass and for the teacher to begin speaking again. The line workers are all women, and most of them are first-generation immigrants from Portugal. The noise dies down, and the teacher continues his lesson on polite ways of asking coworkers for tools while working on the line. The women smile in amusement, look at each other, laugh quietly, and start talking to each other in Portuguese. The teacher is puzzled and waits for someone to tell him what is funny about talking politely on the lines. Fernanda[2] looks at the teacher, smiles, and tells him that on the lines no one has to be polite. They are all "sisters," and sisters don't have to be polite when asking each other to pass over tools. What Fernanda does not tell the teacher, and what he does not know, is that on the lines, the workers not only do not have to be polite with one another; they do not speak English. The majority of the women working on the lines in this Canadian workplace, like the majority of the women in the English class, are Portuguese. And on the lines, the communicative tasks that make up the curriculum the teacher is using in his workplace-English language class, tasks such as asking a coworker for tools, are not performed in English. They are performed in Portuguese.

Current English as a Second Language (ESL) curriculum for immigrant workers in Britain, Canada, and the United States is often centered on the need to learn English to carry out tasks and assume greater responsibility at work. The use of English is associated with both economic survival and economic mobility. However, as the incident reported above reveals, not all immigrant workers working in English-speaking countries need to learn and speak English to perform everyday work tasks. Furthermore, the ability to speak English is not necessarily linked to getting ahead in the workplace. In fact, for many working-class immigrant women in Canada, the use of English at work may be associated with economic and social costs rather than benefits (Goldstein 1991, 1994a, b).

Statistics show that many immigrants living in Canada do not speak either of the country's official languages (English and French) at all, and even fewer use them at home. For example, statistics on the Portuguese community in Canada show that 15 percent of all those who identify themselves as having a single Portuguese origin (that is, as having two parents of Portuguese origin) do not speak English or French at all, and 64 percent use only Portuguese at home (Statistics Canada 1989). These figures are actually low estimates because they are based on self-reported data. As an indication of the differences between women and men in this group, statistics show that although 12 percent of all single-origin Portuguese men do not speak either French or English, 18.2 percent—almost one in five—of single-origin Portuguese women do not speak one of the official languages (Statistics Canada 1989). Although some women may simply not have access to formal English- or French-language training or to informal opportunities for language learning, others do but choose not to take advantage of such opportunities or choose not to use the English or French they have learned. To understand these choices, we need to reexamine our assumptions about the use of official languages and access to opportunities that are associated with economic and social advancement.

Bilingual Life and Language Choice on the Production Floor

Portuguese immigrant workers who do not have access to English-speaking networks and/or ESL classes upon their arrival in Toronto, Canada, are able to find and keep jobs by relying on Portuguese network ties and the Portuguese language. In the production department at Stone Specialities, the factory in which the study described in this chapter was undertaken, twenty-four out of twenty-seven Portuguese workers surveyed (88 percent) found a job at the company through a "friend," that is, a relative, the friend of a relative, or the relative of a friend. Others found work at the company by responding to an ad placed in a Portuguese church newspaper or by following up on information proferred by a Portuguese church worker. The majority of the Portuguese employees working in the production department work on assembly lines. Almost all of the assembly-line workers are women, and most of them have been with the company for sixteen to twenty-two years.

The company's use of Portuguese networks and churches to recruit employees for work on the production floor can be related to the labor shortages it periodically experiences. At the time when most of the Portuguese production workers at Stone were hired (in the late 1960s and early 1970s), the company was in competition with fast-food restaurants and local hotels for "cheap labor." Portuguese immigrants who did not speak English would work for low wages on an assembly line because it was not possible to get a better-paying job off the lines without English-language skills or additional job training or education. Stone Specialties could hire Portuguese workers who did not speak English because they had bilingual English-Portuguese supervisors on the staff who could convey information in Portuguese to those workers, an arrangement that continues today.

The company's practice of hiring Portuguese family and friends to work on the production floor and the Portuguese community's practice of finding work through community networks have led to the creation of a Portuguese "family" or community in the production department. Although some members of this Portuguese "family" are actual kin related by blood ties, others are not, but most think of one another as family. People call each other *sister*, *brother*, *daughter*, and *marida*, which is an invented feminine derivation of the Portuguese word for 'husband', *marido*. A problem involving a worker who is unhappy about the boss she is working for is referred to as a "family problem." Thus, for most Portuguese workers on the production floor, work conditions at Stone Specialties are lived and represented as family and community relationships.

The use of Portuguese functions as a symbol of solidarity and group membership in the "family" on the production floor. Portuguese is associated with the rights, obligations, and expectations that members of the community have of one another at work.[3] Members of the "family" who work on assembly lines are expected to help one another "keep the line up." If one person on a line is ahead because her particular task is easier and takes less time to complete, she is expected to help someone else whose work is piling up. Similarly, if a person needs to leave the line, someone else is expected to pitch in and help do that person's work while she is gone.

Making friends, thereby ensuring access to assistance in case an employee's work piles up or she needs to leave, depends on knowing how to talk to people on the line. Furthermore, talk that provides access to friendship on the lines and thus to assistance is in Portuguese. Women, including those whose first language is not Portuguese but Spanish or Italian, use Portuguese on the lines to gain access to friendship and assistance when they need it.[4]

(1)

Tara:	If I am on the line with you and I want to be your friend, what should I do to be your friend on line?
Angela:	So all you have to do is talk with us. And if we see you can't do the job properly, then we will help you.
Odile:	We will help show you what you have to do. And you need to talk to the others, so we can know about yourself.
Tara:	What kind of things are important to know about me? What should I tell you about myself?
Odile:	We would like to know where you worked before. If you like to work with us. We will help you to get your hands on the work so you won't feel nervous on the line.
Tara:	What kind of things do people talk about on the lines?
Angela:	Mostly family problems or they talk about their sons and daughters. Family matters.
Augusta:	Sometimes they talk about cook[ing], movies.
John:	If you're married. If you're single. If you're dating. They all want to know that kind of stuff. Or why aren't you married?
Lidia:	You talk about your recipes or ask about a person who everyone is talking about. People talk about who's sick, events in people's lives.
Raquel:	Some talk every day about the cook[ing]. Some girls they talk about their husbands. Every day about the kids. Shopping. Everything. Everything.
Tara:	This is mostly in Portuguese.
Raquel:	Yeah.

Women's formation of friendships through talk to each other has been documented by other sociolinguists studying the relationship between language and gender (e.g., Coates 1988; Jones 1980). On the production floor, the value of friendship and assistance at work is not to be underestimated. When asked what advice she would give me if I were new to the company and wanted to make friends on the lines, one of the line workers, Raquel, replies, "If you have a good job already, don't come here. Because this is a change and you have to make other friends." Friendships at work are valuable—valuable enough not to leave a job and risk not finding them elsewhere. Without friends on the line, without access to assistance, assembly workers run the risk of losing their jobs for not being able to meet efficiency standards.

As a language that is associated with the performance of a work role on the production lines, Portuguese is associated not only with finding a job through networks in the community but with keeping a job and getting a paycheck as well. For Portuguese immigrant women who have had no prior access to English-speaking networks or ESL classes, the use of Portuguese is the only accessible linguistic means to economic survival and gain in Canada. There are social and economic benefits associated with the use of Portuguese on the lines that are not associated with the learning and use of English. Moreover, there are risks to using English at work.

Line workers who do not understand English report that they feel "like it's an insult" when a Portuguese speaker speaks to them in English, because the speaker knows Portuguese. They also report that they tell such speakers to "talk in Portuguese." Accommodating the preference for Portuguese on the line is important for members of the Portuguese "family" who are able to speak English. Using English with workers on the lines is risky; if people do not understand exactly what a speaker saying, they may assume she is talking about them and may feel insulted. The following quotation describes how one worker felt when a Portuguese speaker addressed her in English before she had acquired enough of the language to understand what was being said to her. It illustrates how angry people can become if they think others are talking about them in English.

(2)

> Before I'm mad because I don't speak English. I don't understand the people who talk English. It make me crazy because maybe they talk about me.... Now, I don't care. Before I don't understand.... Now, I don't speak very, very good, but I understand.

The use of English on the production lines, then, is associated with social and economic risks for many of the Portuguese line workers. Line workers who depend on their "sisters" for assistance in "keeping the line up" and meeting efficiency standards cannot risk making others "mad" and losing their friendship by using English.

"Talking Bad"

As important as the use of Portuguese is to gain access to friendship and assistance, the content of talk is also interesting in this regard. As Lidia reports in (1) above, on the lines people talk about one another and the events going on in one another's lives. These data support Deborah Jones's (1980) claim that gossip between women has to do with personal experience. It also fits Jennifer Coates's (1989:97) finding that discussion in all-women groups typically involves "people and feelings." On the lines, such talk or gossip provides individuals with information that is needed for "talking bad" about others. Talking bad is an important sociolinguistic act on the lines; it provides people with a way of asserting social control and managing conditions of subordination associated with the everyday activities of doing production-line work.

One of the values and goals held by workers on the line is that of distributing work tasks as fairly as possible so that some workers do not always take on heavier and more tiring work tasks than others. After many years on the lines, the workers know which jobs are more difficult than others and how job tasks can be distributed fairly. To illustrate, in an exchange with Rosa, Cecília talks about how many pieces need to be produced before the run (the total number of pieces that need to be produced in order to fill the company's orders) is finished and how work for the woman at the end of the line would be more comfortable and more fairly distributed if the supervisor had another worker share her job task:[5]

(3)

> Havia de ser vinte mil, agora cinquenta mil. Cinquenta mil para a gente descansar daqui para fora. Se ela deitar duas mulheres no fim da linha é é mais comodo.
>
> *Should be twenty thousand, now fifty thousand. Fifty thousand until we can rest. If she puts two women at the end of the line it is more comfortable.*

Trying to ensure that work tasks are as comfortable as possible is one way workers deal with the physical demands of working on an assembly line. Ensuring that all line workers get their fair share of difficult tasks is another. If a worker looks down the line and discovers that someone else has a less difficult task, she may engage in talking bad about the worker in the easier position. Example (4) provides an illustration of this phenomenon. Cecília is at the front of the line. The assembly job consists of filling different-colored plastic containers with a number of small plastic animals. One of the tasks consists of putting a cover on each container that comes down the line. It is considered an easy task and Lúcia is the worker who has been assigned to it.

(4)

Cecília (to line):	A Lúcia é que está fechando?
	Is it Lúcia who is closing [the containers]?
Raquel:	Yes! São muito bons de fechar.
	Yes! They are very good [easy] to close.
Cecília:	São bons, por isso é que ela foi para lá!
	They are good [easy], that's why she went there.
Lúcia:	Também podes vir para aqui se quiseres.
	You can also come here if you want.
Cecília:	Ai, Lúcia! Ningúem está falando mal. Olha que tu também!
	Ai, Lúcia! Nobody is talking bad. See that you too. [You are always waiting for people to talk bad about you. / See that you don't either.]

In this exchange Lúcia, who has overheard Cecília and Raquel talking about her, responds with *"You can also come here if you want."* This is interpreted by Cecília as a defensive response to the others' talking bad. Having publicly pointed out to those within hearing distance that Lúcia has the easiest job on the line—making it difficult for her to have the easiest job the next time around—Cecília distances herself from her remarks; she, too, needs to keep up friendships on the lines, by denying that she was talking bad and by insisting that Lúcia is always waiting for people to talk bad about her or that Lúcia shouldn't talk bad about others (*"See that you don't either"*) by accusing them of talking bad about her when they were not. (The meaning of *Olha que tu também* in this exchange was interpreted differently by two different translators. One thought it meant, "You are always waiting for people to talk bad about you"; the other thought it meant "See that you don't [talk bad] either.")

Talking bad is a powerful means of effecting social control among members of the "family." For example, immediately before the exchange in (5), Olga notices when Luísa, the supervisor of the line, passes by that her eyes are red. Aloud, she wonders why. Fatimá suggests it might be because someone has "talked bad" to Luísa and that her eyes are red because she has been crying. When Olga disagrees, Fatimá restates her opinion that being the target of talking bad can make someone cry:

(5)

Fatimá:	Eu digo-te uma coisa se me disserem uma simple palavra que não me caia bem eu sou capaz de estar o dia inteiro a chorar, sinto-me tanto, tanto, tanto de uma me palavra que me deem.

> *I'm telling you something if someone tells me one simple word*
> *that doesn't feel good I'm able to cry all day I feel so much,*
> *much, much one bad word that is said to me.*

Olga: Tu sentes-te muito, mas se tu tiveres uma pessoa íntima
               doente, muito doente, tu não choras com mais dor que
               se já qualquer coisa que te digam aqui.

> *You feel it a lot, but if you have a close person who is ill, very*
> *ill, don't you cry with more pain than about something that*
> *they say to you here?*

Talking bad, then, is language behavior that is powerful enough to make an
individual "cry all day"; it has the power to inflict pain comparable to that
of having a close friend or family member fall very ill. It also has the power
to assert social control on the lines, which is used to manage local, everyday
work activities that must be completed in order to bring home a paycheck.

It is interesting to note here that all instances of talking bad in the data
can be attributed to women. It is possible that talking bad is a gendered
linguistic practice that is performed solely by women. Unfortunately, interactional data of men's linguistic practices on the production floor, which are
needed to support such a hypothesis, were not collected. This is because all
interactional data between Portuguese workers were tape-recorded off the
production lines and no men were assigned to the lines during the period of
tape-recording. The male production workers were busy transporting raw
materials and finished goods to and from the lines. If data on male interactional practices had been collected and had demonstrated that the act of
talking bad was indeed a gendered linguistic practice, then the strategy of
talking bad could be linked to the management of activities and relations
associated with women's subordinate position as production-line workers.
Such evidence would provide support for Susan Gal's (1989) argument that
women's "special verbal skills" can be seen as strategic responses to positions of powerlessness.

Nevertheless, even in the absence of data linking the practice to gender,
talking bad can still be seen as an act to claim power in a position of subordination. Interpreted in this way, the practice of talking bad challenges the
notion that all-female interaction can always be characterized as "tentative," "powerless," or—in a more positive vein—"cooperative."[6] In the
public domain of the production floor, working-class Portuguese women
talk bad to each other to manage conditions of subordination at work.
Unlike talk that takes place within the private domain, in informal conversations between middle-class female friends (Coates 1989), talk on the lines
is not necessarily cooperative, for it can be used to injure or to assert

control. When tested against the parameters of ethnicity, class, and domain, then, the assertion that women's language is always cooperative does not hold up. The data presented in this chapter suggest that any analysis of women's language needs to be located in a larger analysis that examines relations of power, that is, "in a framework which acknowledges dominance and oppression as relevant categories" (Coates 1989:120).

In her zygotic[7] study on language use in the bilingual community of Barcelona, Kathryn Woolard (1985, 1989) has argued that subordinate languages (such as Portuguese in Canada) can be used as a symbolic means of resisting unequal relations of power. On the production floor at Stone Specialities, however, the use of Portuguese does not seem to function in this way. Instead, Portuguese and the particular practice of talking bad seem to be used as means of coping with conditions of subordination associated with the everyday activities of doing production-line work. Portuguese is thus used as a language of solidarity, but this in turn is motivated by the unequal power relations between Portuguese and English. R. D. Grillo (1989) points out that where substantial labor migration has brought linguistically diverse populations together, the official languages of the receiving or host society have greater authority than the languages of the immigrants. Speakers of languages other than those of the receiving or host society usually occupy subordinate social, cultural, economic, and political statuses. Languages of solidarity are often used by speakers of subordinate, powerless groups as part of a survival strategy. On the lines at Stone Specialities, asserting social control and easing work demands by "talking bad" in Portuguese is a linguistic practice that can be seen as part of such a strategy.

Language Choice, Ethnicity, Class, and Gender

People's language choices on the production floor are further illuminated when they are examined in terms of the cultural values and practices they symbolize and the economic arrangements and possibilities that govern speakers' lives. Most of the women on the lines who choose to use Portuguese at work are from rural villages in the Azores, an archipelago of nine islands that lies 1,223 kilometers east of Lisbon in the Atlantic Ocean. During the period of heaviest migration to Canada, rural life in Portugal was still characterized as a traditional "peasant" society with a light local and family-oriented economy (Higgs 1982). Dependence on the family as the basic unit of economic and emotional security in Portugal has been understood as a legacy of the country's feudal heritage and historic impoverishment. Familial bonds are formed not only within the immediate family but also outside it through godparent arrangements. The appointment of godparents links the families of the godchild and godparents and "they become like family" (Anderson 1974).

Born into a traditional rural society based on an economic and emotional dependence on family network ties, raised to expect favors from relatives and to assume obligations toward them in return, those who first emigrated from Portugal to Canada in the 1950s were responsible for bringing over many others from their native communities. Ever since the early 1960s, Portuguese immigration into Canada has been mostly a product of extensive family and community links. The strong ties of rural and small-town Portugal that bring people to join friends and neighbors are renewed within the Portuguese communities in Canada. As in Portugal, such ties—and the commitments they entail—are basic resources for economic survival and prosperity. For the women in this study such commitments are represented in their decisions not go to school to learn English upon their arrival in Canada but to find work to "help friends" and "start a new life."

The discussion undertaken so far has attempted to demonstrate how and why Portuguese may be used by some immigrant workers as part of a survival strategy in a new English-speaking setting. However, it is important to remember that there are certain economic gains associated with English, which is the dominant way of communicating in the factory. Better-paying jobs off the lines, such as the job of quality-control inspector, require a good command of English. Why, then, do production-line workers who have come to Canada to improve their economic circumstances choose to speak Portuguese over English when English would provide them with access to better-paying jobs? How do we make sense of the ways people choose to communicate on the production floor?

Most Portuguese workers who have been able to move into higher-paying jobs off the lines are individuals who have had access to English-speaking contacts and, in some cases, English literacy skills prior to joining the company. Importantly, the differences between those who bring prior English language skills with them to the factory and those who do not are not arbitrary. Generally, men and those women who immigrated to Canada under the age of sixteen bring prior English-speaking network ties with them to the workplace and have access to jobs off the lines. Women who immigrated to Canada over the age of sixteen do not.

Five of the six Portuguese men working on the production floor came to the factory with prior English-speaking ties, and four of the six have higher-paying jobs off the lines as maintenance man, production-line supervisors, and quality-control inspector. Conversely, only three out of thirty women had some command of English when they began to work at the factory, and only four out of thirty now have better-paying jobs as supervisors and quality-control inspectors. The three women who brought some English language skills to the factory had all immigrated to Canada under the age of sixteen and spent some time in an English-Canadian high school. Although they all left school at sixteen to go to work and help their families financially, they did have an opportunity to develop English literacy skills.

The reasons that Portuguese men have more access to English-speaking ties and better-paying jobs have to do with the way linguistic resources are distributed in Portugal and within the Portuguese community in Toronto. Julio, the maintenance man, reports that he learned English in Portugal by talking to American soldiers stationed at the army base on the island of Terceira. He also had the opportunity to speak English when he was a soldier stationed in Mozambique, which at the time was still a Portuguese colony. Tony and Peter, the production-line supervisors, report that for six months they attended all-day English-language classes held at a local community college five days a week. Although both men believe that their formal English language training gave them "a start," they also believe that most of the English they have learned has been by "just talking with people" at work. Tony and Peter have had the opportunity to "just talk with people" because of the nature of the jobs they have held at the factory. Welding (Peter was a welder for the company before he became a supervisor) and supervisory jobs off the lines provide access to English-speaking ties that jobs on the lines do not:

(6)

> Peter: Most of the other welders were not Portuguese. One or two of them were. And when I was welding, we worked in an area by ourselves, so that also forced me to communicate without having to ask for translation. It was a separate area away from the production area. You know what I mean.
>
> Tara: In the production area, it's much easier to find someone to translate for you.
>
> Peter: Yes. That's what I think. But sometimes when you're, not really by yourself, but, you know, working away, I think you really are forced to learn how to communicate in English.

Portuguese women working on the production floor at the factory did not have the opportunity to learn English by talking to American soldiers in Portugal and they did not travel to places like Mozambique, where they could practice English. In Toronto, the majority of the women who were over the age of sixteen and were therefore not forced by Canadian law to attend school also lacked access to formal language training, which gave Tony and Peter the "start" they needed to secure jobs as welder and supervisor. One obstacle to obtaining formal ESL training is described by Augusta, who reports that her father did not permit her to attend language classes because of the presence of men —"so many boys"—in the classroom. Other obstacles are revealed in the conversations below:

(7)

Tara:	Some people go to school when they come from another country. Did you have a chance to go to school when you first came?
Olga:	Yes. When I came [to Canada], my husband come with me to the employment insurance [Canada Employment Centre] and for make a card for a social insurance number. And the girl [asked me if] I am so young why I don't go to the school? I had nineteen years old when I came. I say no, I came for work. I make a life. I think I make big mistake, but I never go.
Tara:	Did you ever think that you would like to go to night school? Or it was too hard working and coming home?
Olga:	I think it's hard, because after four years here I have my son. And for working the day and then the night go to the school.... I have to pay to the babysitter, and the night maybe again. It's very hard for my son, and very hard for me.

(8)

Tara:	Did you think about going to school when you first came here?
Luísa:	I was scared to walk on the streets at night. Because I came in August and in September the school starts. And I was scared because I hear so many strange things.
Tara:	So you never wanted to go to night school.
Luísa:	I want to go, but I was scared.
Tara:	And day school?
Luísa:	I had to help my friends because we had to start a new life.

(9)

Tara:	When there's two Portuguese speakers speaking English and you are there, what do you think?
Angela:	I would like to know English to talk to them. I have a Spanish lady telling me that I could go for six months and learn

English and get paid by the government. But I didn't want to
at the time.... I was not feeling optimistic, so I didn't want to
go to school.

(10)

Tara: You didn't at that time think about going to school?

Fernanda: No, at that time I don't think to go school, because I don't
           have a father. Me and my mother had to work alone. My
           [younger] brothers went to school.

As mentioned earlier, in order to move into a higher-paying job off the
line, production workers need a good command of English. Specifically,
they require a Canadian grade-12 education or at least English language
skills equivalent to those of a Canadian grade-12 graduate. This kind of
training is beyond the realm of possibility for most, if not all, working-class
women, who have only four years of schooling in Portugal, do not have
access to evening ESL classes, and perceive the two weekly hours of ESL
they do have access to at work primarily as a social activity, that is, as a
chance to spend extra time socializing with coworkers during their lunch
break. As Virginia explains, the women on the lines do not have "enough
school" to compete for a job off the lines and "see nothing better" than the
line work that they currently do—work that is associated with the use of
Portuguese. Thus, the language choices the line workers make, on the basis
of the linguistic resources to which they have access, can be linked to the
gendered structure and dynamics of the Portuguese family and the class
positions the workers hold within the Canadian political economy.

Toward a Curriculum of Empowerment for Women Learning ESL

English-language training is not always necessary for economic survival in
English-speaking countries, nor does it always provide access to economic
mobility, but there may still be good reasons for women whose daily activities are in languages other than English to participate in English-language
classes. In a society where English is the dominant language, not speaking
English may limit the control people have over everyday living conditions
and relationships. For example, Virginia tells the story of relying on a
Portuguese dental assistant to translate for her during an operation for gum
surgery being performed by an English-speaking dentist. After the assistant
explained the surgical procedure to her, Virginia agreed to undergo the operation but told the assistant that she wanted to go to the bathroom before the
dentist started the procedure. When the assistant translated for Virginia, she
told the dentist that Virginia was going to the bathroom because she was

frightened of the operation and wanted to run away. Virginia, having spent some time in an English high school, understood everything the assistant said. She was so angry at the assistant's attempt to humiliate her that she decided to use English and speak to the dentist herself. Similarly, Portuguese parents who do not speak English and need to obtain the services of English-speaking doctors and lawyers will sometimes ask their children to act as language brokers for them. Grace Anderson and David Higgs (1976) report that Portuguese children who translate for their parents at doctors' and lawyers' offices become privy to all kinds of secrets from which they may have normally been excluded. They also report that parents find it "much more difficult" to discipline children who act as language brokers because they are dependent on them for translation services and discretion outside the family. By increasing the control people have over everyday living conditions and relationships, English-language training can provide people with expanded possibilities for functioning as members of English-speaking societies. For example, participation in English-language classes may enable people to participate more fully in their children's social lives, intervene at school on behalf of their children's interests, participate in a union, or deal with corporate and government bureaucracies on behalf of their own interests.[8] Finally, immigrant workers who do not speak English may be vulnerable to unemployment during times of economic hardship when ethnic networks fail to help them find work. Workers who get jobs in recessionary times have a variety of skills they can draw upon. The possession of English-language skills may enhance workers' chances of finding new employment in case of layoff.

English-language instruction for economic protection and control over everyday living conditions and relationships must be understood differently from the way current workplace English-language training is often viewed. To differentiate between the two types of practices, the term *critical pedagogy of ESL* is used in contrast to the terms *job-specific language training, vocational ESL (VESL), industrial English-language training, ESL training, ESL instruction, ESL teaching, English-language training, English-language instruction,* and *English-language teaching,* all of which are currently used in the field of workplace ESL. As mentioned earlier, these latter terms often refer to curriculum that is centered around the need to learn English to carry out work tasks and assume greater responsibility at work.

Following Roger Simon and Don Dippo (1986), the word *critical* in *critical pedagogy of ESL* refers to an understanding of ESL practice as transformative. Like job-specific English-language training, much of which is based on the teaching of English for everyday use and mobility in workplace situations, a critical pedagogy of ESL takes as its starting point the reality that we teach ESL to immigrant workers in an ethnically stratified society where members of different ethnic groups have differential access to valued resources and power. However, unlike the ideology underlying much job-related language training, the discourse of a critical pedagogy of ESL does not see job-specific English-language training as an unproblematic means of gaining access to valued resources and power. As discussed above, English-language training cannot generally initiate change in the lives of many working-class immigrant workers because of structural processes and constraints (for example, lack of a high school education) that limit possibilities for workers in our society. Instead, a critical pedagogy of ESL attempts to challenge immigrant workers' subordinate status by providing students with a means of thinking about their position in their communities and society and with ways of increasing their access to economic, social, and personal power. As will be discussed below, such thinking can be encouraged by giving ESL learners opportunities both to talk about their work and life experiences and to reflect on the way they talk about them.

The word *pedagogy*—as opposed to *training, instruction*, and *teaching*—in *critical pedagogy of ESL* refers to the distinction Roger Simon (1988) makes between teaching and pedagogy in his work on "the pedagogy of possibility." As conceptualized by Simon, *teaching* refers to the specific strategies and techniques educators use in order to meet predefined, given objectives. Simon considers such strategies and techniques insufficient, however, for constituting a practice that strives to increase students' access to power or, in his words, "a practice whose aim is the enhancement of human possibility." What is required is "a discourse about practice that references not only what we as educators might actually do, but as well, the social visions such practices would support.... Pedagogy is simultaneously about the details of what students and others might do together *and* the cultural politics such practices support" (2; original emphasis).

A critical pedagogy of ESL is close in vision and spirit to Bronwyn Peirce's (1989:401) "pedagogy of possibility in the teaching of English internationally." Peirce challenges what she calls "the hegemony of communicative competence" as an adequate set of principles on which to base the teaching of English internationally. Developed by sociolinguist Dell Hymes (1972), the notion of communicative competence refers to the intuitive mastery native speakers possess to use and interpret language appropriately in the process of interaction and in relation to social context. In Hymes's words, communicative competence is knowing "when to speak, when not, and ... what to talk about with whom, when, where, [and] in what manner" (227).

The concept of communicative competence has been widely accepted in language-teaching circles in recent years and has led to a strong interest in teaching learners appropriate language use in addition to correct grammatical or phonological use. Peirce, however, raises questions of the central role given to the concept of communicative competence in language teaching and argues that the teaching of English can open up possibilities for students by helping them explore what might be *desirable* as well as "appropriate" uses of English.

In developing her argument, Peirce begins by suggesting that the phenomenal spread of the English language throughout the world has led to the perception that it is the world's first truly global language. Peirce points out that English is also a subject of controversy. Some writers have argued that communicative competence in English provides linguistic power (Kachru 1986), but others have characterized the language as a "cultural intrusion" that is "the property of elites" and that expresses "the interests of the dominant classes" (Cooke 1988:58–59). In an attempt to work through the role that teachers of English play in producing and perpetuating inequalities in the communities in which they teach, Peirce draws upon Simon's theoretical work on the pedagogy of possibility (Giroux & Simon 1984; Simon 1987, 1988). She reconceptualizes the teaching of English as a pedagogy that opens up possibilities for students not only in terms of material advancement but in terms of the way they perceive themselves, their role in society, and the potential for social change. Like Peirce's pedagogy of possibility in the teaching of English internationally, a critical pedagogy of ESL seeks to provide opportunities for immigrant English-language learners to explore these issues.

A critical pedagogy of ESL is also close in vision and spirit to the "problem-posing" approach associated with the work of Brazilian educator Paulo Freire (1970, 1971, 1973, 1985) and the work of progressive North American ESL educators who believe that problem-posing is particularly relevant to immigrant and refugee ESL learners who often have less control over their lives than they would like to have (Auerbach & Wallerstein 1987; Barndt, Cristal, & marino 1982; Bell & Burnaby 1984; Crawford-Lange 1981; ESL Core Group 1983; Moriarty & Wallerstein 1979; Pratt 1982; Sauvé 1989; Unda 1980; Wallerstein 1983).

An ESL curriculum is centered on talk about shared conflicts and problematic interactions. Such talk enables learners to envision different working and living conditions and to generate an individual or community response to problems (Auerbach & Wallerstein 1987). An important part of this work involves providing learners with the linguistic resources they need to make positive changes in their working and living environments: language and linguistic strategies for dealing with government bureaucracies (McDonald 1992a, 1993; McDonald & Zuern 1994); for undertaking social activism (McDonald 1992b; Shiller 1993); for ensuring health and safety at work (Auerbach & Wallerstein 1987; Wallerstein 1983); for challenging barriers of racism and discrimination in gaining employment (Brand, Gallaugher, & Langevin 1992; Guy 1990; Lee 1993); and for participating in a union (Auerbach & Wallerstein 1987; Metro Labour Education Centre 1992; Wallerstein 1983).

The substance of a critical pedagogy of ESL that emerges differs depending on the gender of the learner. Women have special concerns because of their social and economic situations. To illustrate, taking the issue of health and safety at work as an example, many women (like Olga in this study) carry the double duty of paid work and responsibilities at home, which makes it more difficult to get involved in after-work meetings about working conditions. Women often have low seniority or jobs that place them in caretaking roles or require close working relationships with their bosses, all of which make them hesitant to bring up complaints about workplace safety hazards.

Feminist Studies and ESL

Other health and safety issues that might be particularly relevant and important to women in ESL classes concern pregnancy on the job, maternity leave, and sexual harassment and assault. This is where educational material written from a feminist perspective has much to offer a critical pedagogy of ESL for female workers. Although it is beyond the scope of this chapter to explore deeply the many ways in which feminist political activity, analyses, research, materials, and resources may inform ESL education, I will briefly focus on one issue—the issue of sexual harassment and assault. I have chosen to focus on this particular issue for two reasons. First, it is an issue that has been linked to immigrant women's personal safety on the job, and as such, it is an extremely important issue to take up. Second, in examining public-education materials concerning sexual harassment at work and school, it is clear that part of the challenge to harassment and assault is located in a woman's ability to use language effectively. In the Canadian multilingual workplace, safety from harassment and assault may require the ability to use English (or French) to respond to a harasser or to make an official complaint about harassment.

English for Personal Safety

Although factory settings present their own unique problems for women's safety at work, it may be instructive to look at general issues of workplace safety by considering a case that has recently come to my attention at the University of Toronto, where I am a faculty member. The university initiated an English-language program for workers in the Buildings and Grounds Services Division after one of the caretaking staff, an older woman who did not speak English as a first language, was assaulted at work. The worker was unable to attract attention or use the telephone to call the police because she had lost her ability to use English in the panic she felt at the time of the assault (Susan Addario, personal safety officer, University of Toronto, personal communication).

As a result of that incident, a task group was formed to look at ways to increase the personal safety of the buildings and grounds staff. Initiatives resulting from the task group's work included modifying the emergency telephone system so that a caller's location would come up on a computer screen when s/he dialed the emergency number; eliminating the night shift (because staff working the night shift were particularly vulnerable to assault); and starting up a language program for staff who wanted to improve their communication skills in English (Philip Garment, director, Buildings and Grounds Services, University of Toronto, personal communication). Materials introducing the program to staff members were presented in Polish, Greek, Ukrainian, Italian, and Portuguese, as well as English, and when the program began in the fall of 1992, one hundred staff members (both native and nonnative users of English) signed up. In addition to its focus on the use of English for personal safety at work, the program also addressed some of the workers' other English-language needs such as English for promotion at work, for improving service to customers, and for reading their children's report cards. Such a program, cosponsored by the University of Toronto and the Metro Labour Council (through its Labour Education Centre) is an example of a program that provides learners with the opportunity to explore what might be "desirable" as well as "appropriate" uses of English, in addition to linking the issue of personal safety to the ability to use the dominant language.

The Centrality of Language in Challenging Sexual Harassment and Assault

The connection between language and safety is not only important for workers; it has consequences for women in all public situations. An examination of the recommendations for dealing with sexual harassment in a number of Canadian public-education materials demonstrates the importance of being able to use language effectively in challenging harassment at work and at school:

(11) What Can a Student Do? First, say "No!" loud and clear to the harasser. It is important to say very clearly that the harassment is unwelcome and that you want it to stop at once. (Aggarwal 1985)

(12) What can *you* do to stop sexual harassment? Say NO clearly and directly. (George Brown College Advisory Committee for Equity 1990)

(13) What to Do in a Sexual Harassment Emergency: Simply tell the person, "What you are doing makes me uncomfortable." Perhaps describe in words what is happening while it is happening, for example, "You have your hands on my shoulders" or "This is the third time today that you have brushed against my body when you walked by." (Ontario Institute for Studies in Education [OISE] Women Students' Sexual Harassment Caucus poster)

(14) Writing a letter to the harasser about the harassment helps the victim handle it herself. By taking an active role, she gains a sense of being in charge of what is "happening" to her. She is control of her own destiny. (Bernice Sandler, quoted in Aggarwal 1985:27)

Speaking out by talking or writing a letter to the harasser is not the only recommendation these guides and pamphlets make for dealing with sexual harassment. Other recommendations include keeping a record of what happened, finding out about the organization's policy on sexual harassment, talking to the organization's sexual harassment officer if one exists, talking to others in authority if there is no sexual harassment officer associated with the organization, and contacting the Canadian Human Rights Commission, which can provide advice concerning legal action against the employer. All of these actions are likely to require the ability to use English or French because they are the dominant languages in Canadian schools and workplaces. However, taking action is not always easy for women, whether they use English as a first, second, or other language. In a book called *Let's Talk About Sexual Assault*, written for young women between the ages of thirteen and nineteen, the Victoria Women's Sexual Assault Centre (1984:10) asserts, "As young women, most of us have been taught to bow to the wishes of others, often against our own interests. We need to learn and practice assertiveness." An important part of learning and practicing assertiveness for protection against sexual harassment and assault, for both immigrant and Canadian-born women, has to do with learning how to say "No." In this regard, feminist educational materials and resources that can be used to provide women with opportunities to learn and practice the language, tone of voice, and physical posture associated with saying "No" have much to contribute to an ESL curriculum for protection and control at work. Other helpful feminist analyses are those that encourage women to name and understand the myths that support discrimination and harassment in the workplace, myths such as: women invite sexual harassment by their dress or behavior; women sleep their way to the top or for good grades; most harassers don't intend harm, they're just complimenting women (Freada Klein, in Boston Women's Health Collective 1992). Naming and rejecting such myths is an important aspect of education about sexual harassment because part of being afraid to say "No" or to speak out has to do with women's fear that they are somehow responsible for the sexual harassment they experience or that they will not receive help in facing possible retaliation. Feminist insights that encourage women to examine critically what they have learned about their behavior at work allow them to explore concerns, goals, and available courses of action with greater awareness of their right to work in a harassment-free environment.

In my own work as an ESL educator, I have come across two sets of ESL materials that have included activities for talking about and dealing with sexual harassment. Elsa Auerbach and Nina Wallerstein's (1987) *ESL for Action* and Florence Guy's (1990) *Working Skills for Immigrant Women* both have lessons that examine the issue of sexual harassment in the workplace. The texts recognize the importance of providing women who are learning ESL not only with opportunities to learn and practice the language they need to respond to sexual harassment but with opportunities to discuss attitudes toward sexual harassment and strategies for dealing with it.

This process is extremely important because the way learners of ESL will choose to deal with sexual harassment on the job depends on many factors, including how much they can afford to risk losing their jobs, whether they believe they can get support from their coworkers, and whether they believe they can get any organizational support from their administrators, managers, union stewards or officials, or personnel or equal-opportunity/employment-equity counselors (Alliance Against Sexual Coercion, in Boston Women's Health Book Collective 1992). Furthermore, many workplace language classes operate through the cooperation of administrators, managers, and supervisors, who may remove their support and cancel classes if they do not think the issue of sexual harassment is "appropriate" in language learning. Both learners and teachers in the workplace language class, then, need to evaluate different options when considering a desirable response to sexual harassment on the job. Such an evaluation needs to be informed by the learners' and teachers' primary concerns and goals, the courses of action that are available, and the possible outcomes and risks of each action (Alliance Against Sexual Coercion, in Boston Women's Health Book Collective 1992).

A particularly helpful analysis for exploring what courses of communicative action are available to women in situations of harassment is that of Sue Wise and Liz Stanley (1987). Wise and Stanley state that women may respond by (1) reacting against the harassment in an active attempt to rebuff the intrusion; (2) joining in, in order to neutralize the imposition of sexual harassment; (3) letting it pass and pretending that the harassment is not occurring; and (4) avoiding it. In contrast to reacting against the harassment, the other strategies can be seen as colluding, not fighting back. However, these choices may be important survival tactics for a woman whose job may be jeopardized by more direct action. Knowledge about sexual harassment and where it occurs allows women to make their own (though admittedly limited) choices as to how much risk they will allow themselves to endure. What is important about the preceding analysis for teachers and learners of ESL is the amount and variety of language learning and practice involved in experimenting with different strategies of challenging sexual harassment. Even the strategy of avoiding sexual harassment involves a great deal of language practice in that it involves talking about when, where, and how to avoid sexual harassment at work.

Conclusion

This chapter has documented women's language behavior at work, attempted to interpret what this behavior might mean in light of the background knowledge women bring to their talk, and briefly examined how women's language practices may be related to their experience at work and opportunities in life. It has been argued that the use of English in the multicultural and multilingual workplace may be associated with costs as well as benefits and that immigrant workers may resist using the language when these costs are perceived to be too high. Educators who wish to facilitate opportunities for immigrant women workers through the provision of English-language training must understand the nature of these costs and understand in what ways language training may or may not assist their students. In the hope of encouraging our students to see and achieve "something better," we must be sensitive to the social, political, economic, and historical circumstances that have shaped their lives. A critical ESL curriculum that acknowledges the social conditions of work can greatly benefit from feminist material and resources that consider women's work issues.

These materials and resources not only help women understand the myths that support discrimination and harassment against women in the workplace, they can also help them conceptualize, develop, and practice a communicative competence for gaining protection and a sense of control at work.

Notes

1. This paper is based upon research I undertook for my doctoral thesis study. I would like to acknowledge and thank my thesis supervisor, Dr. Monica Heller, and the members of my committee, Dr. Roger Simon and Dr. Barbara Burnaby, for their interest and expert guidance. I would also like to acknowledge York University for its financial support and for making research funding available to part-time faculty. I must also acknowledge the important contribution made by Dora Matos, my research assistant, whose warmth and ability to relate to the Portuguese workers who participated in this study was invaluable to the data-collection stage of the project. Dora's work as linguistic and cultural interpreter also significantly contributed to the sociolinguistic analysis of language use on the production floor of the factory. Finally, I would like to express my appreciation to Mary Bucholtz and Kira Hall for their editorial expertise and assistance. Their work helped to sharpen the analysis and clarify the points I wanted to make.

   The title of this paper refers to a comment made by one of the participants in the study to her coworker on the production line. It foreshadows the analysis I present in this chapter and points to the different ways working-class women use Portuguese at work. It is important to note at the outset that the women's use of Portuguese to "claim power" on the production lines occurs as a response to their positions of subordination at work and is best understood as a means of coping with these conditions. I do not mean to imply that Portuguese is a language of power or dominance in the Canadian workplace described in this study.

2. The names of the participants and the name of the manufacturing company in this study have been changed to maintain the anonymity of the participants.

3. The study of language choice in this chapter is rooted in the field of interactionist sociolinguistics. An interactionist approach to the study of language choice makes use of anthropological research perspectives and traditions to investigate what makes individuals in a multilingual society choose to use one language or language variety rather than another in a particular instance. For other interactionist studies on the social significance of language choice and codeswitching (the use of more than one language in the course of a single communicative episode) refer to Jan-Petter Blom and John Gumperz (1972); Michèle Foster (this volume); Susan Gal (1979); María Dolores Gonzales Velásquez (this volume); John Gumperz (1982a, b); Monica Heller (1988a, b, c); Kathryn Woolard (1989).

Velásquez (this volume); John Gumperz (1982a, b); Monica Heller (1988a, b, c); Kathryn Woolard (1989).

4. The following is a collage of data obtained from separate interviews with Portuguese line workers. The interviews were undertaken in both English and Portuguese, that is, some workers chose to use English in the interview sessions and others chose to use Portuguese. During this part of the research project, I worked with a fluently bilingual Portuguese/English research assistant, Dora Matos. At the time, Matos was teaching ESL and Portuguese literacy classes for immigrant women and men from Portugal and the Azores, but she was not one of the teachers working in the workplace ESL program at the factory. Although she speaks standard Portuguese, she understands and was able to translate the Azorean variety as a result of her work with her students.

My work with a bilingual/bicultural research assistant during the interviews requires some discussion. As a nonspeaker of Portuguese, I was dependent on Matos's interpretation of what participants were saying in their interviews. Although working with a linguistic and cultural interpreter meant working with two layers of interpretation (a characteristic of my work that may be seen as a limitation by some readers), it has also provided me with the sociocultural and sociolinguistic background knowledge necessary for understanding Azorean workers' talk. This knowledge, whose importance and complexity have been discussed by sociolinguists interested in intercultural interview situations (e.g., Belfiore & Heller 1992; Gumperz 1992), would have been inaccessible to me otherwise; Matos's assistance has strengthened my analysis immeasurably.

5. A translation of a Portuguese speaker's utterance(s) appears immediately below the utterance(s) and is *italicized*. Any additional information needed to make the meaning of the speaker's words clear to the reader appears in brackets ([ ]).

6. See Jennifer Coates (1988) for a review of work on this topic. Cooperative talk is usually characterized by collaborative topic development; minimal responses that signal active listenership and support for the speaker; mitigating modal forms that respect the face of speakers; and simultaneous speech, which gives the floor to more than one speaker at a time.

7. The word *zygotic* is used here instead of *seminal*. Both terms mean 'having the possibility of future development'. Unlike *seminal*, however, the metaphor underlying the use of *zygotic* does not make the male contribution to reproduction central. A zygote is a cell formed by the fusion of two reproductive cells.

8. See Mary Ellen Belfiore and Monica Heller (1992) and Belfiore (1993) on the need to assist ESL learners with language for dealing with bureaucracy.

References

Aggarwal, Arjun (1985). *Sexual harassment on campus: A guide for students and teachers.* Thunder Bay, Ont.: MM Publications.

Anderson, Grace M. (1974). *Networks of contact: The Portuguese and Toronto.* Waterloo, Ont.: Wilfrid Laurier University.

Anderson, Grace M., and David Higgs (1976). *A future to inherit: The Portuguese communities of Canada.* Ottawa: McClelland & Stewart.

Auerbach, Elsa Roberts, and Nina Wallerstein (1987). *ESL for action: Problem posing at work.* Reading, MA: Addison-Wesley.

Barndt, Deborah, F. Cristal, and dian marino (1982). *Getting there: Producing photo-stories with immigrant women.* Toronto: Between the Lines.

Belfiore, Mary Ellen (1993). The Changing World of Work research project. *TESL Talk* 21(1): 2–20.

Belfiore, Mary Ellen, and Monica Heller (1992). Cross-cultural interviews: Participation and decision-making. In Barbara Burnaby and Alistair Cumming (eds.), *Sociopolitical aspects of ESL.* Toronto: OISE Press. 233–40.

Bell, Jill, and Barbara Burnaby (1984). *A handbook for ESL literacy.* Toronto: OISE Press.

Blom, Jan-Petter, and John Gumperz (1972). Social meaning in linguistic structures: Codeswitching in Norway. In John Gumperz & Dell Hymes (eds.), *Directions in sociolinguistics: The ethnography of communication.* New York: Holt, Rinehart & Winston. 407–34.

Boston Women's Health Collective (1992). *The new our bodies/ourselves.* New York: Simon & Schuster.

Brand, Merrilee, Annemarie Gallaugher, and Donna Langevin (1992). *"I can do the job very well": A collection of job search stories by adult ESL learners.* Toronto: Board of Education for the City of Toronto, Continuing Education.

Coates, Jennifer (1988). Gossip revisited: Language in all-female groups. In Jennifer Coates and Deborah Cameron (eds.), *Women in their speech communities: New perspectives on language and sex.* London: Longman. 94–122.

Cooke, David (1988). Ties that constrict: English as a Trojan horse. In Alistair Cumming, Antoinette Gagné, and Janet Dawson (eds.), *Awarenesses: Proceedings of the 1987 TESL Ontario Conference.* Toronto: TESL Ontario. 56–62.

Crawford-Lange, Linda (1981). Redirecting second language curricula: Paulo Freire's contribution. *Foreign Language Annals* 14(4/5): 257–68.

ESL Core Group (1983). *Themes for learning and teaching.* Toronto: ESL Core Group.

Foster, Michèle (this volume). "Are you with me?": Power and solidarity in the discourse of African American women.

Freire, Paulo (1970). *Pedagogy of the oppressed.* New York: Seabury Press.

——— (1971). To the coordinator of a cultural circle. *Convergence* 4(1): 61–62.

——— (1973). *Education for critical consciousness.* New York: Seabury Press.

——— (1985). *The politics of education.* South Hadley, MA: Bergin-Garvey.

Gal, Susan (1979). *Language shift: Social determinants of linguistic change in bilingual Austria.* New York: Academic Press.

——— (1989). Between speech and silence: The problematics of research on language and gender. *Papers in Pragmatics* 3(1): 1–38.

George Brown College Advisory Committee for Equity (1990). *What you can do to stop sexual harassment.* Toronto: George Brown, The City College.

Giroux, Henry, and Roger Simon (1984). Curriculum study and cultural politics. *Journal of Education* 166: 226–38.

Goldstein, Tara (1991). Immigrants in the multicultural/multilingual workplace: Ways of communicating and experience at work. Ph.D. diss., University of Toronto.

———— (1994a). Bilingual life and language choice on the production floor. *Multilingua* 13(1/2): 213–24.

———— (1994b). "We are all sisters, so we don't have to be polite": Language choice and English language training in the multilingual workplace. *TESL Canada* 11(2): 30–45.

Gonzales Velásquez, María Dolores (this volume). Sometimes Spanish, sometimes English: Language use among rural New Mexican Chicanas.

Grillo, R. D. (1989). *Dominant languages: Language and hierarchy in Britain and France*. Cambridge: Cambridge University Press.

Gumperz, John (1982a). *Discourse strategies*. Cambridge: Cambridge University Press.

———— (ed.) (1982b). *Language and social identity*. Cambridge: Cambridge University Press.

———— (1992). Interviewing in intercultural situations. In Paul Drew and John Heritage (eds.), *Talk at work: Interaction in institutional settings*. Cambridge: Cambridge University Press. 302–7.

Guy, Florence (1990). *Working skills for immigrant women*. Toronto: Working Skills Centre of Ontario.

Heller, Monica (1988a). Introduction. In Monica Heller (ed.), *Codeswitching: Anthropological and sociolinguistic perspectives*. Berlin: Mouton de Gruyter. 1–24.

———— (1988b). Strategic ambiguity: Codeswitching in the management of conflict. In Monica Heller (ed.), *Codeswitching: Anthropological and sociolinguistic perspectives*. Berlin: Mouton de Gruyter. 77–96.

———— (1988c). Speech economy and social selection in educational contexts: A Franco-Ontarian case study. *Discourse Processes* 12(3): 377–90.

Higgs, David (1982). *The Portuguese in Canada*. Ottawa: Canadian Historical Association.

Hymes, Dell (1972). On communicative competence. In J. B. Pride and Janet Holmes (eds.), *Sociolinguistics: Selected readings*. Harmondsworth: Penguin. 269–93.

Jones, Deborah (1980). Gossip: Notes on women's oral culture. In Cheris Kramarae (ed.), *The voices and words of women and men*. Oxford: Pergamon Press. 193–98.

Kachru, B. J. (1986). *The alchemy of English: The spread, functions, and models of non-native Englishes*. Oxford: Pergamon Press.

Lee, Enid (1993). Displacement and discrimination: A double burden for workers of colour. Interviewed by Jennifer Shields. *TESL Talk* 21: 102–17.

McDonald, Valerie (1992a). *English language activities for a changing world of work*. Toronto: Ontario Ministry of Citizenship.

——— (1992b). Coping with unemployment. *Ontario Times and Teachers' Notes* 6(2): 1-4–1-12.

——— (1993). Raising the issue of unemployment in the ESL classroom. *TESL Talk* 21: 120–26.

McDonald, Valerie, and Guenther Zuern (1994). *Finding a job: Language skills and strategies for ESL learners*. Toronto: Ontario Ministry of Citizenship, Program Development Branch.

Metro Labour Education Centre (1992). *It's our union too!* Toronto: Metro Labour Education Centre.

Moriarty, Pia, and Nina Wallerstein (1979). Student/teacher/learner: A Freire approach to ABE/ESL. *Adult Literacy and Basic Education* 3(3): 193–200.

Peirce, Bronwyn (1989). Toward a pedagogy of possibility in the teaching of English internationally: People's English in South Africa. *TESOL Quarterly* 12(1):3–89.

Pratt, Sydney (1982). ESL/literacy: A beginning. *TESL Talk* 13(3): 401–20.

Sauvé, Virginia (1989). Power and presence: Reconceptualizing the work of the ESL teacher. *TESL Talk* 19(1): 118–32.

Shiller, Maureen (1993). ESL for a real purpose: Advocacy. *TESL Talk* 21: 136–40.

Simon, Roger (1987). Empowerment as a pedagogy of possibility. *Language Arts* 64: 370–83.

——— (1988). For a pedagogy of possibility. *Critical Pedagogy Networker* 1(1): 1–4.

Simon, Roger, and Don Dippo (1986). On critical ethnographic work. *Anthropology and Education Quarterly* 7: 195–202.

Statistics Canada (1989). *Profile of ethnic groups: Dimensions—Census of Canada 1986*. Ottawa: Statistics Canada.

Unda, Jean (1980). An approach to language and orientation. *TESL Talk* 11(4): 33–40.

Victoria Women's Sexual Assault Centre (1984). *Let's talk about sexual assault*. Victoria: Victoria Women's Sexual Assault Centre.

Wallerstein, Nina (1983). *Language and culture in conflict*. Reading, MA: Addison–Wesley.

Wise, Sue, and Liz Stanley (1987). *Georgie Porgie: Sexual harassment in everyday life*. New York: Pandora.

Woolard, Kathryn (1985). Language variation and cultural hegemony: Toward an integration of sociolinguistic and social theory. *American Ethnologist* 12(4): 738–48.

——— (1989). *Double talk: Bilingualism and the politics of ethnicity in Catalonia*. Stanford: Stanford University Press.

16

Reproducing the Discourse of Mothering

How Gendered Talk Makes Gendered Lives

Jenny Cook-Gumperz

"I was always glad that I was a girl. I cannot ever remember wanting to be a boy."
—Margaret Mead, *Blackberry Winter*

"When I grow up and you grow up we'll be the bosses."
—One four-year-old girl to another

This chapter is based on a paradox that recurs repeatedly in feminist writings. It deals with one of the major puzzles in the establishment of gender identity: how it is that although young children experience the mother's role as all-powerful and important, little girls still grow up into young women who publicly carry through roles, activities, and talk that allow them to be placed in a secondary position. The paradox of this publicly demonstrated powerlessness was described by Simone de Beauvoir in *The Second Sex*:

> If the little girl at first accepts her feminine vocation, it is not because she intends to abdicate; it is, on the contrary, in order to rule; she wants to be a matron because the matron's group seems privileged; but, when her company, her studies, her games, her reading, take her out of the maternal circle, she sees that it is not the women but the men who control the world. It is this revelation— much more than the discovery of the penis—that irresistibly alters her conception of herself. (quoted in Chodorow 1989)

Nancy Chodorow, in her work on the growth of gender identity and the reproduction of mothering, suggests that girls' gender identity has more continuity than boys' throughout childhood and into young adulthood. Yet, as she points out, girls' gender identity is more difficult to achieve because there is no clear break or choice of identification, which boys must make in switching from the loved mother to the competing but companionable father. Girls continue to identify with and support their mothers while entering into an alliance to attract their fathers (Chodorow 1976). Girls' understanding of the mother role is based in large part on their perception of everyday life where the activities of mothering surround them, a fact that is underlined by the child-rearing and family practices in many different societies.

In her more recent work, Chodorow sees the self-perpetuating cycle of female deprecation described by de Beauvoir as arising in part from the essential ambivalence of girls' position in the family dynamic, where young girls first become aware of the responsibilities and burdens of motherhood (Chodorow 1989). She sees these responsibilities as integral to the Western idealization of the mother, which rests on an opposition between the nurturance of mothering and blaming the mother for any perceived shortcomings of children. Chodorow relates the overwhelming "Momism" of American social ideology to the Western history of mother idealization and to the assumption that the moral worth of future generations depends on the activities of the ideal mother (Bloch 1978). In her exploration of the history of the normative ideal of mother love, Yvonne Schutze (1987) demonstrates the extent of the ideological constraints that are put on women to attempt to live up to the ideal of the "good mother." Such normative constraints place mothers in a preeminent position of child nurturance, and so essentially isolate them by putting them in a separate sphere of relationship with their children. In this way the idealization of the mother can cut the early mother-child relationship off from other sources of sociability and support and so threaten the existence of the mother's own individuality outside of the exclusive mother-child relationship. One direction of feminism in the 1960s took the form of an angry response to the isolation this idealization produces, seeing in it a direct manipulation of a more natural mother-child relation by the patriarchal dominance of Western society (Chodorow & Contratto 1982). At the same time, such reasoning also serves to exclude an adequate consideration of the active role children themselves have in establishing their own gender identity in interaction with a world "beyond Mom." However, young girls within the daily dynamic of the family can see, even early in life, some of the constraints and responsibilities that motherhood entails as a threat to their own gender development.

The problem posed by work on gender identity takes on a new look if we go beyond the mother-centeredness of many theories to consider other social and cultural influences on children's development. Although the mother's part in the growth of gender identity is still seen as primary, the social lives of children are also an important part of their developmental cycle, as Chodorow has recently discussed from the perspective of psychoanalytic theory. The need to make a transition from absorption of personality in the mother to an independent being, that is, to find the individuated self, requires a psychic space to be created where the self can develop. Some areas of psychoanalytic theory suggest that children's play makes available just this kind of psychic space (Winnicott 1971).

However, the statement above by de Beauvoir, even in brief quotation, gives clues to other explanations of this problem. De Beauvoir indicates that it is not the deep psychic struggles over envy or fear of the other that shape young girls' lives, at least not in a way of which they are conscious, but the need to continue to explore the ambiguity of women's gender roles. Girls must go from experiencing a model of all-powerful womanhood that mothers offer their daughters, that is, from an expectation of powerfulness, to finding that adult women's lives offer models of subordination. To come to such a realization is to find one's expectations seriously compromised.

The Reproduction of Mothering Talk

The central theme of this chapter is that gender relations are constituted in and through daily talk. By focusing on the talk and communication of girls (and boys) we are provided with a basis for understanding the daily social construction of gender in children's lives. Through discourse practices, social gender becomes an integral part of children's developing identity. As Elinor Ochs (1992:336) has pointed out, "Conversational practices are primary resources for the realization of gender hierarchy." Through detailed incidents in children's play conversation, I will demonstrate how gendered lives begin with the playful exploration of the woman's role as a mother before the new sociability of girlhood is entered. It is at this time in early childhood that very young girls apprentice themselves to their mothers, helping, studying this role, and reproducing in their play some of the essential elements of "motherness" that they have perceived. Later on, by age seven or eight, they begin to enter into another social world, the peer-dominant world of girlhood. The period of peer support provides exploration and consolidation of a gender identity that is established through a communicative system that is built up through the sharing of secrets and peer bonding. The communicative approach to adult social gender identity is rooted in children's critical experiences of girlhood and boyhood. Daniel Maltz and Ruth Borker (1982), building on Marjorie Goodwin's detailed studies of children's talk with peers from the ages of seven until well into adolescence (collected in Goodwin 1990), suggest that miscommunication between women and men is due to different cultural assumptions that find expression in differing styles of interaction and talk. Crossing the gender divide is made difficult by differing cultural and conversational norms, which are interactionally supported.

I will return to the discussion of peer-group talk later. First we must examine the process by which young girls come to consider the "powerful mother" as a woman who manages and controls resources for all family members. The significance of the model is evident in the fact that girls reproduce this control during play in their recreated conversational practices. Elinor Ochs and Carolyn Taylor (this volume) suggest that European American middle-class mothers project a subordinate image through their conversational styles because they are predominantly the accommodating party in interactional exchanges with their children. In spite of this apparent accommodation, mothers ultimately control and manage goods and services—such as snacks and food, entertainment and rewards, even love—as part of the repertoire of activities on which children's well-being depends. In the middle-class family, then, the mother could be described as a "mistress of ceremonies." Mothers may voluntarily relinquish center stage in family conversational dramas, but they still powerfully determine the parameters of the scenes, props, and actors. The voluntary choice of accommodation puts the chooser in a role of nominating the positions to be held by other conversational partners, and so the chooser is ultimately in the more powerful situation of "leading from behind." Children respond to the underlying dynamic of mothers' control and resource management. It is this powerful management style with all its possibilities that young girls produce in their play as the reproduction of mothering talk.

The dilemma or paradox of women's position first becomes apparent to children when their peer and outside influences show that women outside their domestic scene may not have as much control or choice of action as they have in the family. Family talk and interaction, and by extension other close-knit social groups, provide women with opportunities for the establishment of their own linguistic management styles. It is often suggested that it is for these reasons that women's language is characterized as less appropriate to the establishment of interpersonal control in life outside the "domestic sphere," in arguments that continue to seem persuasive to many (Tannen 1994). Therefore, before looking at children's socialization influences we must make a brief digression to recap some of the arguments that have been put forward about the nature and character of women's language that have led to the present interest in children's play talk.

Women's Speech in the Home and in the Larger Society

Discussions of women's language, now well into their second decade, have their beginnings in the work of Robin Lakoff (1975) and Dale Spender (1980), both of whom focus in different ways on how language usage and a genderized lexicon present women with a continually compromised position in the world of men. The issues of power, domination, and the difference between women's and men's uses of language provided the focus for the first decade of research (Thorne & Henley 1975). Researchers frequently looked for universals in the communication of gender through language. Much of this research concluded that within the prevailing gender ideology of most societies, the social discourses of gendered languages presented women as mute, domestically or socially reclusive members of their social group, placed in a secondary position (Ardener 1975). During this time, however, anthropologists often noticed that women in the course of their daily activities, whether within the "domestic world" that is usually viewed as the woman's domain or in other ceremonial duties in the wider social world, did not display powerlessness in actions or words. In many ways women's sociability and linguistic resources have been seen as creating a social network that can substitute for any lack of influence or power outside this network. Nevertheless, the limitations placed on women in the public domain can still seem at odds with their sociolinguistic skills and social network activities in the private sphere (Rosaldo 1974).

An exploration of why on the one hand we have demonstrated lexical and interactional powerlessness in women's speech yet on the other hand we have discovered the powerful discourse of women at work within their own constructed discourse occasions suggests a wider problem than local differences. Michelle Rosaldo (1980), revising her own analysis of the women and society paradigm described above (Rosaldo 1974), postulates that a Western bias makes the implications of different practices hard to acknowledge. She points to the inherent ambiguity in much of the discourse of gender if women's social tasks are examined comparatively.

More recent work in language use and gendered communication looks at the specific character of the many communicative differences in discourse in wider ranges of situations and societies. Differences in genre and pragmatic forms are linked to both social structural differences and different social occasions of use. As Susan Philips (1987) suggests, a new approach to gendered language focuses on the variety of ways in which gender is constructed through different genres of talk.

Gender as Conversational Style

In recent work (Philips, Steele, & Tanz 1987; Tannen 1993a), researchers have explored particular strategies of language use and the different ways that specific discourse occasions are realized as talk. Women's sociocultural styles are linked to conversational strategies and interactional routines, a method that makes for a much more specific, genre-based exploration of the more general findings from previous research. Penelope Brown (1990), who looks in sociolinguistic detail at women's politeness strategies in arguments in Tenejapa, Mexico, comments that her study helps "make sense of the widespread finding in language and gender research that women interact more co-operatively than men do, at least on the surface; that a patina of agreement is put over women's interactions in many contexts and in different societies" (140). In the same publication Tannen goes one step further and suggests that we consider the two genders as operating like two cultures that are made easily visible through two different conversational styles.

Yet, although the new research on women's language points to the usefulness of exploring gendered interactional and conversational styles in children's activities, considering these to be a posssible grounding for future adult interactions, as Maltz and Borker (1982) originally suggested, it does not assume that there is a direct relationship between specific features of linguistic style and broad cultural differences. Both Susan Gal (1989) and Elinor Ochs (1992) comment on the lack of direct indices of gender difference in the grammar and pragmatics of adult women's language. No single feature can be found, verbal or nonverbal, universally to characterize women's speech across different cultures. Different cultural traditions contextualize speech differently and hence evaluations are culturally specific. As Rosaldo suggested as long ago as 1974, it is not different practices that make for difference but the ideological principles by which these practices are judged. The interactional sociolinguistic argument developed here suggests that what is at issue is how differences, which are not hard and fast distinctions, are negotiated and become contextually significant features of discourse and action. Through daily practices, certain words or grammatical expressions become the bases of discourse differences that both create and recreate the situations of gendered lives. Detailed, contextually based arguments of this kind are part of the revaluation of women's speech within their own communities of practice (Eckert & McConnell-Ginet, this volume).

Play Talk and Gender

We can now find other reasons for exploring children's play as a particularly fruitful approach to understanding how gendered lives come to be. Play has been recognized as the window into the cultural life of societies and as a social and personal source for the development of cultural metaphors (Bateson 1970; Bruner, Jolly, & Sylva 1976). The play and social life of children therefore provide communicative contexts for realizing the scenes of everyday life.

Most of the work on play has yet to be influenced by feminist theory. Instead, research on play more often places gender as an issue within the biological determinism of sex differences. Girls' play is seen as different and by contrast often inferior to or less exciting than that of boys, that is, girls' activities are seen as residual. Traditionally, boys' play is characterized as exploratory, inventive, fast-paced, inclusive of a range of peers, and often involving some risk to person or property, even if only in getting grubby. Girls' play is characterized as the opposite: careful; focused on small events, objects, or relationships; quiet; and mostly clean and tidy. These attributes could be summed up by saying that boys "do" and girls "do not" (Lever 1976). More recent feminist-inspired work by Barrie Thorne (1993) on the games of nine- and ten-year-olds has taken a social-constructivist approach to girls' gender roles, exploring the ways tomboy girls define their activities when they cross the gender divide. In the study of very young children's early understandings of gender identity, however, fantasy or pretend play is an obvious resource.

The scenarios of fantasy play as talked and enacted scenes provide compact vignettes of gender understanding and gendered talk that other occasions of daily life with young children rarely provide. They give glimpses into fantasy, which is motivated by deep, unconscious responses as well as by the needs of the present activities (Kelly-Byrne 1989). But most of all these games and play practices present sets of verbally (and nonverbally) communicated scenarios that can be described as narrative constructions of self. They provide insight into the development of a gendered self.

The Play Narrative—The Voicing of Gender

Pretend or make-believe games are spontaneous speech in which children blend talk and social and physical action into a developing series of events that have a meaning and an internal coherence as well as an often satisfactory social outcome. Such games can involve two or several children. The relation of talk to action and the interpretation of intent inherent in the discourse do not appear particularly to worry children in game talk.

Contrary to what happens in adult-dominated talk, children pay little attention to potential miscues; they appear to respond to any previous cue or to take any response as adequate. In fact, the specific feature of these pretend games is their fluency; game solutions are verbally defined, negotiated, or solved within the continuity of the game. Game discourse also has a naturally progressive quality. Games are necessarily concurrent stretches of speech and social actions organized into a sequence that is meaningful and coherent for the participants, even if the cohesive qualities expected of adult conversation are not apparent on the surface of the interaction.

Pretend games have several forms, but a common feature of those for children from three to seven years old is that there must be some plot development: one event follows another and the transition from one event to the next must be verbally accomplished, that is, spoken out loud. I refer to such games as *narrative games,* for children not only adopt different voices to differentiate characters but, as my analysis will show, also construct a narrative level of game planning, which describes the details of the game's actions. Such a description may be dismissed as an analyst's construct, but the discovery of discourse genres in play has been illustrated in several studies (e.g., Attwater 1986). Studies of this kind give us independent evidence that children themselves recognize distinctions similar to those recognized by the analysts. Even young children can recognize and use intonation contours to mark genres of discourse and thus enact distinctive voices as part of a monologue of recollections spoken aloud.

A Narrative Game of "Mummies and Babies"

The game to be examined is a complex and rapid game of "Mummies and Babies" between two three-and-a-half-year-old girls, Lucie and Susie, for whom this game and its variations are a regular part of their play repertoire. In the game, which lasts about twenty minutes, twenty-six separate events can be identified in the stream of action from the audiotape recording. The first question to ask, which on reflection is far from simple, is how, given the verbal ability of such young children, they can keep such a concentrated oral narrative performance going. What verbal, pragmatic, and paralinguistic strategies do they use to get the game started and continue it for such length?

Two issues of discourse planning need to be discussed here. We must consider first the choices by which the speaker creates a pattern of expectations for the listener. These enable the listener both to process the information being received and to prepare for her turn as the speaker. The second consideration is the speakers' more immediate problem of encoding their own talk, the need both to talk and to plan ahead in order to maintain the right to speak and sustain the pace and flow of speech. The first issue, speaker/hearer expectations, can be looked at in three ways: (1) expectations set up by prosodic contours in certain linguistic environments; for example, a rising intonation indicates that more is to come in some contexts or signals a question in others; (2) expectations set up by syntax; these may be set up by utterance strings that break off before a clause is complete, by varied repetitions, by use of cohesive markers such as *but* and *because*, or by anaphoric devices such as pronouns; (3) expectations set up by what is known about thematic structures or discourse frames, such as knowledge that a story requires and will be given an ending.

The second issue, speech planning, can be looked at in two further ways: in terms of the rhythm and pace of exchanges, and in terms of the speaker's ability to maintain the flow of her talk. Neither of these is an easy task for young children.

Both of these planning problems are of particular importance in studying young children, whose control over the grammar and lexicon is still limited. What is more, the issue of fluency and effectiveness of production within social interaction is something that has been too often overlooked. One of the reasons that these self-organized games stand out from the more usual child-language corpus is the amount of speech that even very young players produce and the richness of its content and fluency. Clearly, game situations, in which children control their own social interaction, can provide sociolinguistic experiences that demand more from the interactants than exchanges with accommodating adults. This chapter may give the impression, because it considers the language of very young girls, that girls' talk is more intense or fluent than boys' talk. However, it can be shown that in game talk both girls and boys have the ability to generate fast, fluent talk. Two particular issues will be explored in the game material under consideration here: (1) the progression of the narrative and the development of themes throughout the game; and (2) the levels of the narrative, the ways in which the participants structure the discourse (and thus the game world) for themselves through their speaking performances, that is, through giving special significance to prosodic and rhythmic distinctions that become markers of the different game levels.

A great deal of thematic content and action is generated in these games. Given that the game under study is marked by frequent shifts in thematic focus, I was able to recognize twenty-six event phases. It seems evident, then, that talk must play a key role in the realization of the game's action. The result is that these games may strike the adult listener as strangely fast-paced and somewhat confused narratives that are talked out as they occur.

Figure 16.1 (based on Cook-Gumperz 1985) describes the twenty-six distinguishable phases of the game's action. Because the events are not necessarily entailed by previous events, arrows show the direction in which they
were sequenced. At the end of the game (item 24) the participants provide
alternate game-plan scenarios and follow two different courses of narrative
action sequence. (The figure also describes the discourse level at which each
game event is accomplished, and which participant initiates the event. See
below for the full description of the discourse of the game.)

The progression of events takes place both within and across speaker
turns. Speakers make suggestions about the direction of play through their
contributions, and listeners respond to these suggestions by using or adding
to the information provided. In this way, the progression of events appears
to be smoothly negotiated by the two participants. Even in episodes 24 and
26, in which the two participants have differences over the use of pins and
their Babies, the disagreement is resolved by one participant's persuasive
strategies. There is no evidence that the two have different expectations.
Throughout the game, each of the girls seems to be quite prepared to accept
and respond to the other's contributions to the plot and to recognize any
change in discourse level when it occurs.

In adult discourse the absence of overt markers of cohesion across turns
makes thematic connections difficult to see; for the two little girls this
does not present any problems. Fluency and coherence are achieved and
maintained through the use of a series of different voices that serve to mark
different levels of the game. These voices are established through
prosodic/intonational cues that, when co-occurring with certain lexical
characteristics, mark the different voices. Prosodically, a rhythmic and
metrical formula is developed by the two girls, which then provides a
frame into which further contributions can be placed. This formula
provides a metrical beat that appears to mark the pace of the action.
Although such stylistic devices also occur in adult talk (Tannen 1989), they
are used here in quite distinctive ways by very young children. Children
also provide signaling cues to set up the context, so that each utterance can
be placed within the narrative progression. As is generally true with very
young children, these are exclusively prosodic cues. Most listeners will
readily recognize these cues as marking different voices. In studies of
pretend play, it is usually assumed that these voices indicate different characters or roles. However, as I worked at the transcription, I realized that the
different voices did not merely mark in-character/out-of-character speech,
as I had first assumed, but constituted a series of organizational levels in
the performance—that is, different discourse contexts. These voices are of

1	2	3	4	5
The Babies are given a drink	One Baby is sick	One Baby is shouting at Sandra	One Baby spills the tea	One Baby is pushing
Narrative	Mummy to Baby	Mummy to Baby	Mummy to Mummy	Mummy toMummy
Susie	Lucie	Lucie	Lucie	Susie
→	→	→	→	→

6	7	8	9	10
The Baby is put to bed for pushing	The Baby spills her Falalanga and spits it out	One Baby spits at the other Baby	The Baby is sent to bed	One Baby is given a drink
Mummy to Baby	Narrative	Mummy to Mummy	Mummy to Mummy	Mummy to Mummy
Susie	Lucie	Lucie	Lucie	Lucie
→	→	→	→	→

11	12	13	14	15
One Baby wets	One Baby cries	Mummy decides to take Babies for a walk	The Babies are given drinks	The Babies are held by the Mummies
Mummy to Baby	Mummy to Mummy	Narrative	Mummy to Babies	Mummy to Mummy
Lucie	Lucie	Lucie	Lucie	Susie
→	→	→	→	→

16	17	18	19	20
One Mummy takes Babies and Sandra is to follow	A lid is put on the juice bottle	One Baby is put down for a nap	The Mummies get strollers	One Mummy is Mary; the other is Sandra (old information)
Mummy to Baby	Mummy to Baby	Mummy to Baby	Real life	Narrative
Lucie	Lucie	Lucie	Unclear who initiates	Susie
→	→	→	→	→

21	22	23	24	25
One Mummy will buy a diaper	The drinks can be replenished at the park	The Mummies and Babies have a picnic in the park	One Mummy needs a pin for her Baby	The Baby needs to go to the doctor because it has a pin stuck in it
Mummy to Baby	Mummy to Mummy	Mummy to Baby	Narrative	Narrative
Lucie	Lucie	Lucie	Lucie	Susie
→	→	→	→ ↓	→

26
One Mummy tries to procure pins
Mummy to Mummy
Lucie

Figure 16.1 Progression of Events in the "Mummies and Babies" Game.

four kinds: in-character speech from Mummies to Babies; in-character speech from Mummies to Mummies; off-record speech (real-life talk or organizational comment with Lucie and Susie in their real-life characters as themselves); and narration (description of things and events in the game). By utilizing these voices to mark the game's different organizational levels, the children structure their performance through discourse strategies and conventions of their own making.

The level of narrative talk, which is the focus of this chapter, is distinguishable by its prosodic form as well as by a kind of rhythmic patterning with made-up words that fit a metrical slot. For example, the made-up words *maccacamba*, *falalanga*, and *sallalanga* are used to continue or complete both an utterance and an activity. These "words" are produced to fill out a rhythmic pattern and do not appear to have any specific propositional content to an adult hearing this game.

Description of the Game

The game consists of fast-paced described action; that is, little action physically occurs, but the girls describe activities like going to the park, visiting a doctor, putting Babies to bed, getting them up and letting them interact with each other, Babies' spitting, and so on. The physical action comprises choosing dolls, putting them into toy beds and baby strollers (push chairs in the game), dressing and undressing them, and feeding them from toy cups. The two participants, Lucie and Susie, refer to themselves when they are in the Mummy role by first names that they suggest during the game, Mary for Lucie and Sandra for Susie. These names do not stay constant, however, for at another time the name *Sandra* is used by Lucie to refer to herself.

The two girls are both younger siblings, and the families of both girls belong to the British middle class. Their mothers work part-time: Lucie's mother is a teacher who is studying at present for an advanced degree, and Susie's mother is a professional translator who works at home. On alternate afternoons after morning preschool, the two girls are looked after at either Lucie's or Susie's house, allowing both mothers time for their work; the girls have been regular playmates for a year. This game takes place in Lucie's home. The play occurs in a small area off the main breakfast room, which is outside the kitchen—an area separate from but visible to the mother in the kitchen. The recording was made as a part of a longer-term project with Lucie's mother, who recorded her daughter's afternoon play sessions.

Game Voices: Characterization of Different Voices

Within the two types of in-character speech, differences exist between Mummy-to-Mummy and Mummy-to-Baby speech. Mummy-to-Baby talk normally has a relatively low pitch register as well as a characteristic sing-song rhythm. One type of this speech has tensing of vowels with a marked sing-song rhythm; when a much higher pitch is used, the vowels become sharp. For example, in *Come on let's carry you* the final word is almost a squeak, with a much higher-pitched voice than usual. The more usual Mummy-to-Baby talk is lower in tone and noticeably rhythmic, with some of the reprimands in a loud voice. For example, *All right baby I'll give you a drink of. Look baby don't spit it out* is said in a loud voice with a steady crescendo. Mummy-to-Mummy speech, on the other hand, uses a higher pitch than normal voice with a sharpening of vowels and a shortened, clipped enunciation, as in *Sandra do you have pins?*

Real-life speech, in which the children talk to each other as Lucie and Susie, includes things unrelated to the game (*You like that one, don't you, Lucie*), as well as discussion of mechanical aspects of the game, i.e., of how x in the real world is related to y in the game world (*I'm not having mine to be the golliwog*). Here the voice quality is perhaps nearest to the children's ordinary voices in other than play contexts, although when there is an alternation in tone, it is in the direction of "being whiny." Since off-record talk is used for negotiations that cannot be settled in any other way, there is often a tone of urgency about real-life talk, e.g., *NO that's my cup* (here *cup* is lengthened and there is a heavy stress on *my*); or *NO I want it there*, which has lengthening of *there* and a slight whiny tone. Another possibility is conciliatory tone, the tone of voice closest to the orderly talk outside play contexts, although sometimes the voice quality shifts in the direction of a whiny drawl. For example, *Cause you like this one don't you, don't you Lucie?* has a staccato rhythm and *don't you* is repeated with a pleading tone, relatively low-pitched.

Finally, narrative or planning speech, which organizes things in the game world without reference to things in the real world, includes naming the actions and reactions of Mummies (*I* and *you*) and Babies, planning the plot, and so on: e.g., *And they sit on our lap with us.* The voice quality here is often close to an ordinary tone. Narrative talk is mostly distinguished by special formulaic features: the use of *and* to introduce comments, often in conjunction with a *because* clause to add additional information or explanation, as in *I hold my baby . . . cause she was crying for me.* The narrator's tone is more measured and in some ways more like a reading tone, with even intonation and spaced word enunciation. When I was transcribing the discourse of this game, I relied on formulaic features such as the use of *and*, tag phrases, and the present tense, particularly when these were found in conjunction with a measured voice, for distinguishing the narrative speech. Everyday speech, by contrast, has a flexible use of prosody.

It is by means of these voices that children transform everyday reality into a game world and so create an everyday ritual event. The discourse-planning issue is further resolved by the use of rhythmic formulas. These formulas help the fast-paced games to continue by introducing made-up words and exchanges into a metric slot in the game talk, as discussed above. It must be remembered that the girls are only three and a half years old, and therefore their vocabulary and grammatical ability are still limited. The pace and fluency of the game shows how creative the two are in their language use.

Narrative Strategies

The development and distinguishing of the narrative level of the game is very important for game organization. It shows some specific aspects of the children's understanding of discourse, including the fact that they can make both a semantic and a prosodic separation of these different levels. Below are some of the examples of narrative utterances:

(1) L: And we sit down and have a glass of orange juicy
    S: And they sit on our laps with us
    L: The babies don't like it
    S: No the babies don't like maccamba

The first two utterances are typical of the narrative level—that is, they are introduced by *and* as a narrative-coherence marker. In the last utterance, a made-up word is used and the voice quality serves to distinguish this as a narrative utterance rather than speech of Mummies to each other. Example (2) illustrates the switch back and forth between in-character speech and the narrative or planning level, which is again distinguished by *and*:

(2) L: And baby spilt her Falalanga . . . Look baby don't spit it out
        (Mummy to Baby)

The planning speech occurs to move the game forward into another activity and is often announced and then acted out, as in the following:

(3) S: And my my my baby goes to bed there don't she
    L: And give her a drink of sallalanga
    S: Not that babe . . . I'll give her some . . . Shh tea (Mummy to Mummy)

Narrative level is used in the development of the game as in example (4), where Lucie uses the Mummy voice to introduce the idea of a pin stuck in a Baby and Susie gives a further explanation and plan for the game action in the narrative style:

(4) L: My baby needs a pin stuck in her (Mummy to Mummy)
     S: Why (Mummy to Mummy)
     L: Have you got a pin? ... (Mummy to Mummy)
     S: Um, my my baby has got a a pin stuck in her and because
            we have to go to the doctor's don't we (Narrative)

The narrative style, though used to plan ahead, always uses present-tense verbs. Narrative utterances sometimes provide more than an additional piece of game information that is acceptable to both sides or that develops a theme already in existence. In some cases, the narrative level is used to make an indirect command or to insist on the speaker's plans against the other person's plans. In the following example, Lucie moves into narrative-level speech to try to resolve a difficulty about who should have the push chair that has been carried on in off-the-record talk.

(5) L: You have that (Off-record) And you have you can can
            carry it like that quicker and I can't (Narrative)

Planning speech can also be used to counter what someone has just done and alter the course of the action without a direct off-the-record disagreement.

(6) S: I've finished (drinking sound) (Mummy-to-Mummy)
     L: No, no you shouldn't drink it You should you should leave
            it in until we get to the park
     S: And then there's another tap at the park

In this case, the new piece of information, "going to the park," is introduced at the narrative level. Previously, the children had planned an imaginary walk and the new information leads to an alteration of Susie's game plan. The narrative level can also be used as an occasion to rehearse and plan out what is to be enacted more directly, as in the following examples:

(7a) S: You're called Mary and I'm called Sandra
     L: Yes

(7b) L: Now you say "Sandra have you got pins" and I say "Yes"

The statement in (7b) appears to reverse the decision in (7a) but no disagreement follows.

The narrative voice is also used to get back into the game after a long period of off-the-record disagreement and negotiation, as in the resolution of the push-chair difficulty:

(8) L: Anyway Susie you know, you you can go to the park
           quicker and I can't

The distinguishing of a narrative level in these games has some very important implications for children's understanding of language-in-use, which I can only briefly summarize here. In previous research (Cook-Gumperz 1981, 1986), I have explored some of the consequences of children's rhetorical uses of language as a force to shape and control interpersonal relations. Here, we see the separation of the narrative level as commentary upon the action itself, showing the children's recognition of the need to stay within the game world yet still to reflect or act reflexively upon the course of the action. The creation of the narrative level of the game discourse shows the ability to move the game events forward through use of this special metaprocedural level of discourse that frames sequences of talk (Goffman 1974).

Furthermore, the recognition of the prosodically different voices suggests even more clearly that the game event is separated off as a ritual transformation from everyday talk. However, there is a flow back and forth between daily talk, as Lucie and Susie use their own voices as well as a narrative channel to construct the game world through talk. In this way, game ritual performances are similar to those recognized by Charles Briggs (1988) as the fuzzy fringes where performance styles shift back and forth between daily talk and special performance discourse. The shift into performance is also explored by Michèle Foster (this volume).

It is in looking at the child as a performer of speech in action and at how the child's social world is constructed through talk that we gain a notion of the communicative range possessed by children and, perhaps even more important, the purposes for which these skills are used. One prominent function of the game is to allow the two girls, in their game talk, to explore their gender role as women. Their games show a discourse complexity that would previously have been considered far in advance of their three-year-old grammatical and communicative abilities. We can see in the examples from the game that Lucie and Susie present several levels of mothering talk. The structure of the narrative events involves the Mummies in organizing the life of their Babies. The Babies are fed, given drinks, put to bed, taken to the park, and given fresh diapers and exercise. The Babies are scolded, soothed, cajoled, cosseted, and disciplined. The Mummies' talk to the Babies is always aimed at putting right something the Babies have done.

The Mummies' talk to each other also involves organizing their own lives in relation to the Babies, but the Babies do not talk. The Babies are embodied characters moved around in space and time, but they are not given a voice, not even a coo or a shout, in spite of the fact that the Mummies report to each other on the Babies' naughty behavior, e.g., *My baby's spitting at your baby*. One interpretation of this finding would be that children see mothers as so powerful that children are less important and therefore voiceless. However, this is contradicted by the other finding, that at the level of Mummy-to-Baby talk the voice moves through a greater prosodic range than for any other narrative level, expressing a gamut of emotions from exasperation and annoyance to cajoling and sympathy. The Babies are clearly the central part of the game, the reason for the Mummy-to-Mummy and narrative talk to exist at all. The narrative is constructed around the Babies as the little girls play out their understanding of women's gender role, to which children are central. They use their knowledge of the world in which having children makes a woman a Mummy and in which being a Mummy, controlling the resources and destiny of others, makes women powerful. The narrative game of Mummies and Babies gives a particular, dramatized voice to gender identity.

Conclusion: Why Women Before Girls

The game's narrative themes show some of the ways in which little girls come to terms with early gender understanding of powerful mothers. Little girls use their available mother knowledge to work out the consequence of gender identification; they must learn about being women before they can become girls. Girlhood will present other gender issues through the sociability of alliances with other girls and the ability to discover gender together. It is this peer exploration of gender that is described by Maltz and Borker (1982) as shaping a communicative culture of gender. In girlhood, gender identities are consolidated through a new sense of the possibilities and boundaries of gender roles. These roles are practiced together and developed through a process of group inclusion and exclusion. However, it seems from this inquiry that we can suggest that an initial generalized gender identity that can form a basis for later social gender identity is gained by early role-playing and understanding of the role of mother/woman.

References

Ardener, Shirley (1975). *Perceiving women*. London: Malaby.
Attwater, Manfred (1986). Development of communicative skills. In Jenny Cook-

Gumperz, William Corsaro, and Jurgen Streek (eds.), *Children's worlds and children's language*. Berlin: Mouton de Gruyter. 205–30.

Bateson, Gregory (1970). *Steps to an ecology of mind*. New York: Ballantine Books.

Bloch, Ruth (1978). American feminine ideals in transition: The rise of the moral mother, 1785–1815. *Feminist Studies* 2: 100–26.

Briggs, Charles (1988). *Competence in performance*. Philadelphia: University of Pennsylvania Press.

Brown, Penelope (1993). Gender, politeness and confrontation in Tenejapa. In Deborah Tannen (ed.), *Gender and conversational interaction*. New York: Oxford University Press. 144–62.

Bruner, Jerome, Allison Jolly, and Kathy Sylva (eds.) (1976). *Play: Its social and developmental importance*. London: Penguin.

Chodorow, Nancy (1976). *The reproduction of mothering*. Berkeley: University of California Press.

——— (1989). *Feminism and psychoanalytic theory*. New Haven: Yale University Press.

Chodorow, Nancy, and Susan Contratto (1982). The fantasy of the perfect mother. In Barrie Thorne and Marilyn Yalom (eds.), *Rethinking the family: Some feminist questions*. New York: Longman. 34–75.

Cook-Gumperz, Jenny (1981). Persuasive talk. In Judith Green and Cynthia Wallat (eds.), *Ethnography and language in educational settings*. Norwood, NJ: Ablex. 25–50.

——— (1985). Text and context in children's language socialization. In Deborah Tannen and James Alatis (eds.), *Languages and linguistics: The interdependence of theory, data, and application*. Washington, DC: Georgetown University Press. 337–56.

——— (1986). Caught in a web of words. In Jenny Cook-Gumperz, William Corsaro, and Jurgen Streek (eds.), *Children's worlds and children's language*. Berlin: Mouton de Gruyter. 37–65.

Eckert, Penelope, and Sally McConnell-Ginet (this volume). Constructing meaning, constructing selves: Snapshots of language, gender, and class from Belten High.

Foster, Michèle (this volume). "Are you with me?": Power and solidarity in the discourse of African American women.

Gal, Susan (1989). Between speech and silence: The problematics of research on language and gender. *Papers in Pragmatics* 3(1): 1–31.

Goffman, Erving (1974). *Forms of talk*. Philadelphia: University of Pennsylvania Press.

Goodwin, Marjorie Harness (1990). *He-said-she-said: Talk as social organization among black children*. Bloomington: Indiana University Press.

Kelly-Byrne, Deborah (1989). *A child's play life*. New York: Teacher's College Press.

Lakoff, Robin (1975). *Language and woman's place*. New York: Harper & Row.

Lever, Janet (1976). Sex differences in games children play. *Social Problems* 23: 478–83.

Maltz, Daniel, and Ruth Borker (1982). A cultural approach to male-female miscommunication. In John J. Gumperz (ed.), *Language and social identity.* New York: Cambridge University Press. 196–216.

Ochs, Elinor (1992). Indexing gender. In Alessandro Duranti and Charles Goodwin (eds.), *Rethinking context.* New York: Cambridge University Press. 335–58.

Ochs, Elinor, and Carolyn Taylor (this volume). The "Father knows best" dynamic in dinnertime narratives.

Philips, Susan (1987). Introduction. In Susan Philips, Susan Steele, and Christine Tanz (eds.), *Language, gender and sex in comparative perspective.* New York: Cambridge University Press. 1–11.

Philips, Susan, Susan Steele, and Christine Tanz (eds.) (1987). *Language, gender and sex in comparative perspective.* New York: Cambridge University Press.

Rosaldo, Michelle (1974). Women, culture, and society: A theoretical overview. In Michelle Rosaldo and Louise Lamphere (eds.), *Woman, culture, and society.* Stanford: Stanford University Press. 1–16.

—— (1980). The use and abuse of anthropology: Reflections on feminism and cross-cultural understanding. *Signs* 5(3): 389–417.

Schutze, Yvonne (1987). The normative model of mother love. Paper given at the International Conference on Child Development, Trondheim, Norway.

Spender, Dale (1980). *Man made language.* Boston: Routledge & Kegan Paul.

Tannen, Deborah (1989). *Talking voices.* Cambridge: Cambridge University Press.

—— (1990). *You just don't understand.* New York: Morrow.

—— (ed.) (1993a). *Gender and conversational interaction.* New York: Oxford University Press.

—— (1993b). Editor's introduction. In Deborah Tannen (ed.), *Gender and conversational interaction.* New York: Oxford University Press. 3–13.

—— (1994). *Talking from nine to five.* New York: William Morrow.

Thorne, Barrie (1993). *Gender play: Girls and boys in school.* New Brunswick, NJ: Rutgers University Press.

Thorne, Barrie, and Nancy Henley (1975). *Language and sex: Difference and dominance.* Rowley, MA: Newbury House.

Winnicott, Douglas (1971). *Playing and reality.* New York: Basic Books.

17

Sometimes Spanish, Sometimes English

Language Use among Rural New Mexican Chicanas

María Dolores Gonzales Velásquez

Since the 1970s the sociolinguistics of women's language use has focused on monolingual American and British English-speaking women (e.g., Cameron & Coates 1989; Kramarae 1981; Lakoff 1975; Spender 1980; Thorne, Kramarae, & Henley 1983). The few studies on the linguistic behavior of Chicanas,[1] African American women, and Native American women (Castro 1982; Foster, this volume; Galindo 1992; Galindo & Gonzales Velásquez 1992; Gonzales Velásquez 1992; Medicine 1987; Nichols 1983; Yañez 1990) support the notion that women's use of language reflects their socioeconomic status, experiences, social networks, strategies, and linguistic options. Because Chicanas belong to a minority group that historically has been relegated to a lower social and economic status, it is erroneous to assume that all women are homogeneous, that women of color share the same life experiences as white, middle-class women, or that their language use will be identical when in fact it is quite distinct (cf. Foster, this volume). Some Chicanas may be middle class and belong to monolingual English-speaking or bilingual communities, whereas others may be working class and live in monolingual Spanish or bilingual speech communities (Galindo & Gonzales Velásquez 1992; Yañez 1990). Given the heterogeneity and diversity exemplified within the Chicana community, the study of language use is complex and intertwined with a myriad of social variables. Thus, Chicanas sometimes use Spanish, sometimes English, and sometimes they codeswitch (that is, they alternate between Spanish and English words, phrases, and sentences).[2]

In this chapter, I discuss innovative and conservative language use among three generations of Chicanas belonging to a rural community in northern New Mexico. My analysis is based on the notion that Chicanas in this stable bilingual community have developed strategies in order to survive economically, linguistically, and culturally, and that their role as agents of social change (Medicine 1987) is obvious in their linguistic interactions in both public and private domains. What will be evident at the end of this discussion is that the Chicanas in this speech community are a heterogeneous group and their linguistic behavior is influenced by various social factors including age, education, occupation, nativity, and residence.

Setting
Córdova is a rural community of seven hundred inhabitants, only two of whom are Anglos. The uniqueness of this speech community lies in its tight-knit social structure, which has survived since the mid-eighteenth century and which continues to function as a norm-enforcement mechanism for the maintenance of the vernacular, Spanish. The stability of the dense and multiplex social structure has also created a strong sense of in-group cohesiveness and linguistic security. Furthermore, although the community language is Spanish, Córdova is a fairly stable bilingual community.

Design of the Study
The design of this study was based on the assumption that the linguistic patterns of the respondents could not be understood independently of social and cultural patterns and vice versa. Thus, an ethnographic approach was used to examine the use of Spanish, English, and codeswitching among Cordovan women. This ethnographic approach involved my living in Córdova for ten weeks to gain entry and ultimately become a participant in women's social interactions. Respondent 3B, who was a student of mine at the University of New Mexico, introduced me to the respondents who participated in this study as well as to other community members. To gain an overall perspective of language use within this speech community, general observations of the language behavior of all members, both female and male, adults and children, were documented. However, the focus remained on same-sex linguistic interactions.

Data Collection

The data collection took place over a ten-week period. Formal interviews and observation of language use of the nine respondents were conducted in two contexts: intragroup and intergroup situations. These events included an anniversary party, a bridal shower, a family reunion, and a wedding. *Intragroup interaction* is defined as the linguistic interaction that takes place among individuals belonging to a specific speech community or ethnic group (Sherif 1966). In the present study, discourse between members of this community (the ingroup) is referred to as intragroup interaction. *Ingroup* is defined as those individuals belonging to an ethnic group who share the same language and cultural identity (Sherif 1966). The women in this study, when speaking Spanish, identify themselves as *Mexicanas* who speak *Mexicano*. *Intergroup interaction* is defined as the interaction that occurs, collectively or individually, between members of two distinct groups (Sherif 1966). In this case, persons not residing in Córdova are considered outgroup members regardless of their ethnic background.

The formal interview was based on questions that were divided into three categories. The first category included twelve questions concerning demographic information such as date and place of birth, educational background, and family history. The second category consisted of eight open-ended questions that required self-reporting and evaluation regarding the respondent's use of Spanish and English. The last six open-ended questions were focused on attitudes related to the use and maintenance of both Spanish and English. These open-ended questions produced a vast and dynamic range of responses that helped in explaining women's use of English and/or Spanish in different settings.

The formal interview, which lasted between one and two hours, was tape-recorded in the respondents' homes, as was the informal discourse that occurred between women. The self-reported and self-evaluation information pertaining to language use was compared with observed linguistic interactions so as to confirm the general speech patterns and language use of the respondents.

To obtain these linguistic interviews it was possible to draw on my own experiences and memories of having been a resident of a small village in northern New Mexico. I knew that the most important task was not to be viewed as an "outsider." I was aware that being an urban, middle-class, educated Chicana could create unfriendliness, distrust, and rejection. Nevertheless, my cultural, ethnic, and linguistic background permitted me to establish rapport with the women in the community. Rather than employing a traditional interview primarily as a device for obtaining information in the least amount of time and with the least amount of personal contact, I concentrated on the interview process as a communicative event, that is, I functioned as a coparticipant in the dialogue and discourse that occurred between the respondents and other women. This participation contributed to rapport-building speech events that helped decrease the distance between the cultural and communicative norms of the researcher and those of the respondents. This friendly atmosphere prevented a hiatus from occurring that could have generated interpersonal tensions and misinterpretation in the interviewing process (Briggs 1986).

Cordovan Women: A Description

The respondents were chosen on the basis of their interest in participating and their availability. The most important factor was the presence in the community of three generations of the family: daughter, mother, and grandmother. The ages of the respondents ranged from three to ninety-six (see Table 17.1). The families are identified as Family A, Family B, and Family C, and within each family the individual women are identified by generational number only.

Table 17.1 Ages of Women in Three Cordovan Families, by Generation

Generation	Family A	Family B	Family C
1	79	96	46
2	52	65	26
3	25	23	3

Because there were four generations available in Family C, I included second-generation Respondent 1C as part of the first generation, rather than her mother, age seventy-five, in order to observe linguistic interaction with and by a three-year-old, Respondent 3C. Observing the three-year-old's linguistic behavior allowed me to determine whether Spanish was being transmitted to the younger generation.

Language Proficiency

The language proficiency and use of language by the women varied. Respondents 1A and 1B are both monolingual in Spanish. The other respondents are bilingual, Spanish-dominant, except for respondents 3A and 3B, who are bilingual, English-dominant. Respondents 2B, 1C, and 2C codeswitched more often than the other respondents.

These patterns can be explained by educational attainment and contact with English. Respondents 1A and 1B had little education and minimal contact with the English-speaking society. The other respondents, in contrast, had encountered mandatory-English policies in their schools and they currently have relatively frequent contact with the dominant group. Respondents 2B, 1C, and 2C, who have the highest rates of codeswitching, have an equal amount of contact with the three speech communities (Spanish, English, and codeswitching). This contact influences them to accommodate to different linguistic situations. Viewing codeswitching within a style/strategy framework, we may say that these three respondents alternate strategically between English and Spanish when interacting with individuals who may codeswitch, or they switch for stylistic purposes (Giles 1978).[3]

The patterns summarized above suggest that domain is an important means of predicting language choice in bilingual/bicultural settings. The concept of *domain* follows closely that elaborated by Joshua Fishman (1966:980), who identifies family, friendship, employment, education, government, and religion as typical and appropriate clusters of settings and relationships affecting language choice for most bilinguals: "Domains are defined, regardless of their number, in terms of institutional contexts and the congruent behavioral co-occurrences. They attempt to summate the major clusters of interaction that occur in clusters of multilingual settings and involve clusters of interlocutors." Congruent behavior is that which occurs when individuals interact in appropriate role relationships with one another, in appropriate locales for those relationships, and discuss topics appropriate to their role relationships. In keeping with Fishman's paradigm, interactions that occur in the intimate setting, the home, and the informal intragroup interactions that take place with family members, friends, neighbors, and community are classified in this study as belonging to the private domain. The clusters of interaction within the public domain take place in settings outside the community, such as government, educational, and employment locales. In view of the isolation and the tight-knit social structures present in Córdova, I have included the community setting as a component of the private domain.

With the parameters of *domain* well defined, it is necessary to discuss the linguistic options available to the respondents within their speech community. These include English, Spanish, and codeswitching. During the study, in some situations only English was used, in others only Spanish was used, and in others all three (Spanish, English, and codeswitching) were utilized. Having these three codes available also produced other patterns of language use. The other linguistic options involved the use of both languages but with clear separation of the two codes depending on the domain. Some speakers used equal amounts of Spanish and English, and others used primarily English with some Spanish, or primarily Spanish with some English, but without alternation of the two languages in a single situation. Finally, speakers could separate by domain the use of Spanish and codeswitching, or the use of English, Spanish, and codeswitching. The following discussion of respondents' language proficiency and language use will clarify these patterns.

As expected, given their minimal contact with English speakers, Respondents 1A and 1B spoke only Spanish in both the private and public domains. In the second generation, language choice became more varied. Respondent 2A spoke only Spanish in the private domain, and in the public domain she spoke Spanish with some English. For example, if she interacted with English-speaking individuals in the public domain, she would speak English, but at her place of employment she spoke mostly Spanish because her coworkers were also Spanish speakers. By contrast, her daughter, Respondent 3A, used both English and Spanish in the private domain, and especially Spanish with the elderly. When interacting with her peer group, she used mostly English. This pattern was much the same in the public domain. With everyone other than the elderly, Respondent 3A used English.

Respondent 3A's accommodation to her interlocutors was a phenomenon found in other speakers' language use as well. Respondent 2B used Spanish, codeswitching, and some English in the private domain and all three varieties in the public domain; her language use in both domains was determined by her interlocutors' language use. Respondent 3B, on the other hand, used mostly Spanish with some English in the private domain, and in the public domain mostly English with some Spanish.

Although the increasing use of English over generations often points to linguistic assimilation, speakers may consciously resist such a tendency. For this reason, Respondent 1C's and Respondent 2C's language proficiency was identical. They used Spanish, codeswitching, and some English in both the private and the public domains. As Respondent 1C explained, "I prefer Spanish, and if I don't have to use English, I don't." Finally, Respondent 3C used Spanish with some English in both the private and public domains. Her language proficiency can best be explained by the fact that she is only three years old and Spanish is her mother tongue. She is being reared by her grandparents and does not attend a day-care center. The English she knows is limited, but she does watch *Sesame Street* and other television programs in English.

For the Cordovan women English and Spanish are kept separate in most situations. In other words, subdomains can be established and the appropriate code is selected for that domain. For example, Respondents 3A and 3B used English with high school friends and Spanish with family members when interacting within the community. It is not uncommon for the respondents to have their language choice influenced by interlocutors when in the private or public domain, as we will see later in this chapter.

Another important option available to most of the respondents is codeswitching. Although codeswitching is often misinterpreted as evidence of a lack of linguistic ability or deterioriation of one or both languages, recent research confirms that codeswitching plays an important role in social and discourse functions (Sánchez 1983; Zentella 1987). Not only are some of the respondents in the present study proficient in two languages, English and Spanish, but they are also proficient in codeswitching. Furthermore, they exhibit an impressive knowledge of grammar in their switching behavior. The respondents may codeswitch intersententially or intrasententially; when codeswitching intersententially, they may speak several sentences in one language and then add a sentence in the other, whereas when codeswitching intrasententially, they will alternate words in English and Spanish within the same sentence. In both types, codeswitching is done not haphazardly but, rather, according to grammatical structure. It is considered a variety of speaking that is appropriate in certain domains or subdomains and with certain interlocutors.

Education
The Public Education Act was introduced in the Territory of New Mexico in 1891 (Milk 1980), but did not have an impact on Córdova until the 1930s, when the first public school was established. Thus Respondents 1A and 1B, who were of school age in the early 1900s, attended the community elementary school, where classroom instruction was conducted in Spanish. Eventually, a standardized curriculum and textbooks in English became mandatory. Bilingual teachers were hired and classroom instruction was conducted in both Spanish and English until the early 1940s; thereafter, primarily English was used. The paving of the roads in 1953 improved accessibility to junior high and high schools in neighboring communities (Briggs 1986), permitting the isolated villagers to have greater contact with outside groups, including Anglos and more urbanized Chicanos.

Reflecting the diversity of educational attainment, Respondents 1A and 1B did not attend school beyond the third grade, whereas the women of the second and third generations received high school diplomas. Respondent 3B, the only college graduate, was in the process of finishing her master's degree in communications disorders at the University of New Mexico, and Respondent 3C was just beginning Head Start, a federally funded program for low-income children.

Respondents 2A, 3A, 2B, and 1C all attended English-speaking boarding schools in the neighboring areas. Respondents 3B and 2C attended the public high school located in Española, fifteen miles from Córdova. Educational experiences were not always positive. For example, Respondent 2A dropped out of the mission boarding school after her sophomore year, in 1952, and later earned her high school equivalency degree. She had always used Spanish until she left the community to attend school as an eighth grader. When she arrived at the boarding school, she was expected to use English; however, she chose to speak Spanish whenever she could. She recalled, "I was always given demerits for speaking Spanish." Her behavior was considered a sign of defiance, but despite the strong pressures to give up her native language, Respondent 2A remained loyal to Spanish.

This language behavior was influenced by the speaker's need for identity and solidarity with her ethnic group. Respondent 2A's experiences have analogies in the history of government educational policy for Native Americans in the early 1900s. According to David Wallace Adams (1988), this policy was based on civilizing the children for American progress by removing hereditary customs and manners, and language was the most important element. Thus, English was imposed on students in boarding schools and use of the native language was punished. Bea Medicine (1987:160) argues that "the introduction of the majority language— English—placed and continues to place a heavy burden on Indian women because adopting the English language often has meant losing linguistic symbols of culture." It is precisely this kind of loss that Respondent 2A prevented in her refusal to abandon Spanish.

Family Size

Because women's lives are greatly influenced by their ability or inability to control their fertility, it is important to consider the outcomes in women's lives if they choose to limit the size of their family. The smaller the family the greater the options—social, economic, and educational. This pattern was evident in the contrast of family size between the first and second generation of women in this study. Respondent 1A had eight children; her daughter, Respondent 2A, had one child. Respondent 1B had ten children; her daughter, Respondent 2B, had five children. Respondent 1C's mother had six children, and she had three. For the younger generations, exercising more control over their fertility meant having more control over their own lives (Whiteford 1980), thereby increasing their feelings of efficaciousness in helping determine their family's future.

The social changes occurring during the 1940s in Córdova propelled the second generation of women toward innovation. Innovation is "the recombination or redefinition of options, invention of new options, or taking advantage of new options" (Whiteford 1980:120). The Cordovan women now had access to the educational system, which would eventually affect their lifestyles through employment outside the home, social mobility, and a decrease in family size. In the process of adapting to these new changes the women became more adept in participating in the public domain, the dominant society, which included the use of English.

Thus, the women of the second generation functioned as "cultural brokers" (Medicine 1987). Cultural brokers are defined by Bea Medicine as women who have the role of mediator between their own community and white society; "they are often vested with this role because of their facility with the English language" (162). This new role for the second generation required the "crossing of borders" (Anzaldúa 1987), both linguistically and culturally. Their educational achievement and knowledge of English permitted them to become gainfully employed outside the community. However, to maintain their ethnic identity, they countered the rapid current of these cultural and linguistic changes by performing a balancing act in two separate realities. Functioning in the dominant society did not interfere with maintaining the traditional role of wife and mother or the transmitting of traditional values, culture, and language to their children. For example, Respondent 2B had a variety of jobs, such as cosmetologist, social worker, and emergency technician, and she received an associate's degree in social work through a correspondence course program from a nearby college, yet she still managed to raise her five children traditionally and to pass on the Spanish language.

Employment

The inhabitants of Córdova, like those of other *Hispano* villages in northern New Mexico that began with community grants, survived for two centuries by living off the land and depending on a barter system, a cooperative exchange of goods and services meeting most needs. The decreasing land base became a problem for *Hispano* villagers when traditional avenues of expansion were cut off by the effect of Anglos on their economic base (Deutsch 1985). After the land base contracted, the subsistence-based economy collapsed. The change in subsistence patterns forced the *Hispano* to become dependent upon the political economy of the Anglo. To cope with the change from a barter system to a predominantly cash economy, the imposition of land taxes, and the replacement of locally produced with mass-produced goods, Cordovans were forced to turn to various types of migratory wage labor. Although a majority of the community members adapted to outside employment, the Great Depression of the 1930s forced many to return and make do with what the land and the community could provide for survival. Shortly thereafter, World War II brought additional changes within the community. New job opportunities came with the establishment of the nearby Los Alamos National Laboratory and with improved transportational accessibility to urban centers and to other rural northern communities (Briggs 1986).

Today the majority of Cordovans who belong to the work force are employed in Los Alamos, Española, or Santa Fe. Those employed at Los Alamos work at the laboratory, the branch campus of the University of New Mexico, and the Pan Am Corporation, which provides maintenance, construction, and security services for government housing. The Cordovan women who are employed at the laboratory are mostly blue-collar workers unless they have educational credentials that allow them to obtain secretarial positions. Employment in Santa Fe is available through government agencies or public services. The Cordovan women who work in nearby communities are teachers, teacher aides, social workers, bank tellers, or secretaries and receptionists.

Córdova offers some employment opportunities, but the only residents who have secure jobs are the three grocery store and gas station owners. Approximately thirty-five residents are *santeros*, who market their wood carvings of religious icons to tourists visiting the small village or at art expositions throughout New Mexico (Briggs 1986). However, for the majority of *santeros* these funds provide supplementary rather than primary employment.

Though rural in composition, Córdova tends to manifest class differences. Rather than the typical three-tier stratification system (upper class, middle class, and working class), two classes within the working-class rubric, one upper and one lower, appear to exist. The upper working class comprises landowning families and families in which both spouses have obtained high school diplomas or have taken some college courses and are or have been employed outside the community in service jobs. The lower working class includes those who did not complete high school and are employed as custodians, domestics, construction workers, bus drivers, and similar blue-collar labor.

First-generation women in this study primarily worked in the home and community in the production, preparation, and distribution of food, as well as in communal labor such as plastering, adobe making, sewing, and mattress making (Deutsch 1985). Prior to becoming a *santera*, Respondent 1C worked as a housekeeper in a private home in Los Alamos. She then devoted herself full-time to wood carving, a skill she had learned as a child from her parents and grandparents. Her workshop is next to her home, and she works there on a daily basis.

The women of the second and third generation are or have been employed both in their homes and outside the community, primarily in service and blue-collar jobs. Respondent 2A is employed at Los Alamos National Laboratory as a custodian and works the evening shift. Prior to this job she held primarily factory jobs in nearby communities or out of state. Her daughter, Respondent 3A, is also employed outside Córdova, as a bank teller. Respondent 2B is now retired, but her work experience included working with the elderly and the disabled. She functioned as mediator and interpreter between community members and such government agencies as Social Security, Medicare, and Medicaid. She was also a certified emergency technician and worked with the ambulance services that served several communities in the area. Respondent 3B fulfilled her course requirements for a master's degree from the University of New Mexico in 1990. She is employed in Albuquerque as a speech pathologist. Respondent 2C has been employed in blue-collar jobs outside the community. However, after her divorce she became unemployed, and she currently receives Aid for Families with Dependent Children (AFDC). As is evident, Cordovan women have been on the cutting edge. They have played the role of innovator and cultural broker by working outside the home and by having contact with the larger society while playing the role of enforcers of tradition and guardians of culture (Zentella 1987).

Drawing on the language-maintenance and language-shift framework (Fishman 1966, 1972; Stevens 1986), we are able to correlate Cordovan women's language use with their educational and employment status as well as their residence. Studies have shown that residents in rural areas, with greater isolation and less contact with the English-speaking community, have a tendency to retain the mother tongue to a greater extent and for more generations (Lewis 1971; Myers 1973; Spolsky 1969; Thompson 1974). Córdova was settled between 1725 and 1743, and for many generations this village was isolated from the dominant society; thus, Spanish was maintained as the community language. For employment and educational achievement, more knowledge of English was required. The acquisition of the English language therefore became the vehicle for upward mobility for some of the women, whereas the absence of English ability restricted socioeconomic movement for others. According to Rosaura Sánchez (1983), in most situations where language contact exists, structural institutions (labor processes) and cultural institutions (social processes) can be instrumental in the maintenance or the loss of the mother tongue:

> Social contact is of course determined by the class factor, by the labor process and the relations of production. Participation in the labor process with a given income and occupation in turn determines the area of residence, the people with whom one socializes, educational goals, consumption of commodities and ideology, all factors which determine one's continued use or non-use of the Spanish language. (64)

It is obvious that social and economic factors have determined the functions of Spanish and English in this speech community as well as the domains in which they are used. Geographic and social isolation from the dominant group, however, has limited contact with the English-speaking society and English-speaking institutions, thereby contributing to the retention of the mother tongue in intimate and informal functions. Nonetheless, many individuals have enough contact with English to acquire some degree of bilingualism.

Consequently, two questions emerge regarding the linguistic behavior of the Cordovan women in this study. Why do they choose to speak Spanish rather than English, or vice versa, in certain linguistic interactions? What factors influence their linguistic choice in both intragroup and intergroup situations? The variables I considered—ethnicity and identity, solidarity, accommodation, age, respect, and social networks—were constrained by the community status of interlocutors (ingroup versus outgroup) and the location of the interaction. These factors yielded four interaction types: (1) interaction among community members in Córdova (intragroup interaction in the private domain); (2) interaction among community members away from Córdova (intragroup interaction in the public domain); (3) interaction with noncommunity members in Córdova (intergroup interaction in a noncongruous domain situation, the private-cum-public domain); and (4) interaction with noncommunity members away from Córdova (intergroup interaction in the public domain). Discussion regarding these categories follows.

Interaction Among Community Members in Córdova

When the respondents interacted with one another or with other community women—that is, when they interacted in the private domain—Spanish was almost always used. The wide use of Spanish may be explained using the social network framework (Milroy 1992). Lesley Milroy maintains that network participation, rather than external social variables, is the pertinent element in language use. Within a close-knit network structure, speakers are able to create solidarity, which strengthens their resistance to linguistic and social pressure from the dominant group. In Milroy's terms, the number of social contacts between various members of a community is its density. Contacts can occur through personal networks of friends, relatives, and neighbors and through participation in religious activities and specific group membership (e.g., clubs or choirs).

In the case of Córdova, the size of the village, its historical background, and the social networks, such as *comadrazgo*[4] and church-related functions, established during the agricultural era, are density factors that have contributed to the transmission of cultural and linguistic patterns from one generation to another. Furthermore, strengthened and sustained density patterns have influenced the retention of Spanish. An example of the social networks in Córdova is as follows: Family A is related to Family B because the husband of Respondent 1A is the uncle of Respondent 1B's husband, and these respondents are also neighbors; Respondent 2A is employed at Los Alamos, where the husbands of respondents 2B and 1C worked until they retired; Respondents 3B and 2C attended the same high school as did Respondents 2A and 1C; and the former husband of Respondent 2C is cousin to Respondent 3A. A looser-knit network with less multiplex linkage almost certainly would have permitted a more dramatic language shift from Spanish to English over time.

Four exceptions to the dominant use of Spanish surfaced in ingroup situations within the community. These exceptions involved Respondents 3A, 3B, 1C, and 2C. Respondents 3A and 3B belong to the same generation and are identified as English-dominant bilinguals. English has become the usual language for Respondent 3B since she began living in the city and attending the university, and Respondent 3A has daily contact with English-speaking institutions through her employment. When Respondents 3A and 3B interacted with each other, they used mostly English with some Spanish. Respondent 3B was also observed speaking with younger teenage cousins in English, but she used Spanish with two older cousins who were approximately thirty-five or forty years old. English was probably used because the younger generation is bilingual and comfortable speaking both languages, whereas the older generation is generally Spanish-dominant and more at ease speaking Spanish. This linguistic behavior may be attributed to a weakened network structure and to the amount of contact both of these respondents have with English. Sánchez (1983:63) suggests that "the more contact with the English-speaking community, the more likelihood there is of bilingualism or monolingualism in English. The greater the social distance and the more limited the contact with English institutions, the more probability that Spanish will retain intimate and informal functions."

The other two exceptions involved codeswitching by Respondents 1C and 2C. Their codeswitching is best explained by the notion of accommodation, which is a process whereby individuals adapt or converge to one another's speech (Giles 1978). In this case both respondents converged toward the speech style of their interlocutors, who, according to the respondents, always codeswitch. The first interaction was observed between Respondent 1C and her cousin. The cousin is the same age as Respondent 1C and works as a social worker in Española, where codeswitching is widely used. In the other instance, the interlocutor of Respondent 2C was a twenty-four-year-old from a nearby community where codeswitching is always used. Consequently, codeswitching dominated in these two interactions.

As discussed earlier, codeswitching is a linguistic option available to these respondents because they are proficient in Spanish and English. Codeswitching functions as part of their verbal repertoire, as do English and Spanish. The respondents have acquired the three codes and use them appropriately in different interactions and linguistic settings. This practice can be interpreted as innovative behavior by Cordovan women. In my observations of their language use, the respondents were cognizant of a need to change speech styles in different situations with different interlocutors. The altering of their speech styles can be explained as a strategy in crossing linguistic borders. However, codeswitching can also be explained as the beginning of a language shift to English. Sánchez (1983:142) points out that

> two of the factors that affect the degree of code-switching and the extent of loss of functions for a language are nativity and generation. For a segment of the younger generations of Chicanos today, English has begun to assume all of the functions of Spanish. Spanish language maintenance is strongest among the older generation. Thus a significant number of younger people seem to be shifting from Spanish to English as their primary language. The intermediate step is often code-switching.

Despite this observation, I believe the emphasis on innovation rather than deterioration is more appropriate for the community under study.

Interaction among Community Members away from Córdova

In almost all (fifteen of eighteen) linguistic interactions between the respondents and community members in public domains, Spanish was the dominant language, and language choice was most heavily influenced by identity and ethnicity. Of the remaining three interactions, English was utilized in one, Spanish and English in another, and codeswitching in the third.

Observations of ingroup behavior indicate that the sense of solidarity and identity functions equally outside and within the community. Spanish is used among ingroup members. The best example of this linguistic and social behavior was observed during wedding activities that were held in the city. Although the women were not in their community environment, they continued to function as if they were. The presence and the number of family and community members (approximately one hundred) contributed to the creation of a private domain within a public domain. The need to identify as a speech community as well as an ethnic group influenced the language choice of Cordovan women in this setting.

Ninety percent of the wedding guests were from Córdova and neighboring communities and were predominantly bilingual. The priest, the choir, the musicians, and the women who helped with the reception came from the Córdova area. Because the wedding took place in the public domain, I assumed that English would be the language choice of the respondents. However, we will see that the respondents' role as cultural brokers was evident in this situation and influenced language use.

After the mass, a receiving line was formed outside the church. The bride's employers and colleagues were all Anglo-American. Respondent 2B, the mother of the bride, converged toward the speech behavior of these guests, who spoke English. With first-generation guests from Córdova and other villages who were monolingual Spanish speakers, she converged and used Spanish. Many of the second-generation women codeswitched; thus Respondent 2B converged toward their speech style. Respondent 3B spoke Spanish with elderly guests from Córdova and other communities. With all other guests she converged to their language choice.

The use of Spanish on the part of Cordovan women at this event reveals how they interact with one another in public domains. The women adhered to community norms by not deviating from the use of Spanish. This linguistic behavior may be explained within the intergroup-distinctiveness framework. Henri Tajfel (1974) suggests that when members of different groups are in contact they compare themselves on dimensions that are important to them (such as personal attributes, abilities, and material possessions) and that will lead them to differentiate themselves favorably from the outgroup:

"Interpersonal social comparisons will lead individuals to search for, and even create, dimensions on which they can make themselves positively distinct from the outgroup" (68). All observed nonconvergent linguistic behavior at the wedding was in reaction to an interlocutor's use of English. This pattern may be interpreted as a powerful symbol whereby the Cordovan women displayed their intention of maintaining their identity, cultural distinctiveness, and group solidarity. Divergence on the part of the women of this speech community can also be interpreted as a means of resistance or as an expression of pride in their language and their ethnic identity. By distancing themselves linguistically, they are able to resist assimilation and at the same time maintain their group distinctiveness. It is also plausible that the respondents wanted not merely to maintain their own speech style but to emphasize it in interaction with others. This ingroup behavior reinforces their positive social identity as well as their satisfaction with ingroup membership by demonstrating their competence in community norms (Tajfel 1974).

Interaction with Noncommunity Members in Córdova

Of the twenty interactions, English was present in half. English was used in only three interactions, English with an equal amount of Spanish was used in five interactions, and three interactions included mostly Spanish with some English. Codeswitching dominated in one situation and was occasionally used in another.

English only was used in three interactions, two of those by Respondent 2B. The first instance took place in the respondent's home with an Anglo nun from Santa Cruz. Because Respondent 2B and her husband were the *mayordomos* (overseers) of the community church and were also choir members, the discussion centered on religious activities. Although the nun knew some Spanish, this conversation was entirely in English. The reason for her choice of English may have been that she was aware that she was an outsider, as an English-dominant speaker, and was therefore uncomfortable speaking in Spanish with the respondent and her husband. An alternative explanation may be that English was already the established language of their interactions, because they had known one another for many years. In support of this second explanation, I observed the nun interacting with Respondent 1B in both the private and public domain and in some situations she did use Spanish with the respondent.

The second and third situations were similar. The second involved a tourist inquiring about visiting the Córdova church; Respondent 2B replied using only English. The third occurred between Respondent 1C and an

English-speaking friend from Santa Fe. These three instances are examples of noncongruent situations: that is, the interactions occur in a setting and involve topics that are characteristic of the intimate domain, but because the interlocutors are English-speaking, the situations are altered and become more like a public domain.

English with an equal amount of Spanish was used in four interactions. The first interaction took place when I met Respondent 3A at her grandmother's home. At first she spoke primarily in English with me, yet she spoke to her grandmother in Spanish. After two hours of becoming acquainted, she began to use Spanish with me as well, although she kept both codes separate. It seemed that certain topics related to the community or the elderly precipitated the use of Spanish.

The other interactions that included equal amounts of Spanish, English, and codeswitching involved Respondents 2B and 3B. They took place in a private domain, on a Sunday afternoon in the front yard of Respondent 2B's home in Córdova. Her three daughters had been home for the weekend and were preparing to leave for the city. Respondent 2B used only Spanish with her oldest daughter, codeswitched with the other two daughters, and used English with her seventeen-year-old granddaughter. When Respondent 3B spoke with her older sister, she used English. She later explained that English is her usual language in the city with her older sister, whereas with her other sister, she tends to codeswitch or uses both English and Spanish. Although this linguistic interaction took place in the community, the respondents accommodated to the speech styles of their visitors.

Finally, two interactions involved Spanish with some English. In the first interaction Respondent 3B was observed talking to her forty-year-old cousin, with whom she used mostly Spanish. Occasionally, however, she used some English, when discussing topics that were English-related, such as her living in the city. The final example, Respondent 3C's linguistic behavior with her friends (ages three and five), was reported by her mother. According to Respondent 2C, her daughter uses primarily Spanish with her friends as well as in other situations. However, she does attempt to use English now and then.

In all of the above examples, although the respondents were in their usual environment they did not adhere to the norms of their speech community by using only Spanish. To understand this linguistic behavior, it is important and relevant to make some broader distinctions related to the notion of speech community. I use the Hymesian definition, "a community sharing rules for the conduct and interpretation of speech, and rules for the interpretation of at least one linguistic variety" (Hymes 1972:54). These rules permit speakers to associate particular modes of speaking, topics, or message forms with particular settings and activities. Second and more important is the question, Who are the members of a speech community? Members are individuals who have knowledge of those varieties and speaking rules that potentially enable them to move communicatively within the speech community.

In this study three speech communities are distinguished: the local village, the larger *Hispano* community of northern New Mexico, and the larger population of New Mexico. Some women participate only in the local community or treat it and the *Hispano* community as the same speech community. But for some, the *Hispano* community is developing as distinct from the other groups. And although Spanish is *de rigueur* in the local community and English in the larger New Mexican community, it appears that codeswitching is developing as the appropriate code for the *Hispano* community. This became apparent after visiting various communities with Respondents 3B and 2C during my stay in Córdova as well as taking care of business matters, such as paying utilities, banking, or buying groceries in Española. Codeswitching seemed to be the preferred variety and was quite evident in all the linguistic interactions that I observed.

Recognizing the existence of these three speech communities, then, it follows that one of the most salient criteria in deciding which code to use is what speech community an interlocutor belongs to. Furthermore, a major constraint on actual language behavior of an individual is her network of communication: with which members of which speech communities does this individual interact?

The data presented above also suggest that the respondent's language choice—English, Spanish, or codeswitching—in intergroup interaction in Córdova was principally motivated by accommodation. Convergence in code selection may be attributed to various factors. On one hand, it is possible that a speech community, consciously or unconsciously, perceives its variety as less prestigious. Thus, when speakers interact with outgroup members, this attitude may influence their choice of the more prestigious code, English. However, many of the noncommunity women with whom the respondents interacted used codeswitching, a variety that is also perceived, at least within the dominant society, as less prestigious. This would lead us to believe that convergence to English did not result because of a need for approval or for the potential rewards of adopting English but because of the speaker's verbal repertoire as well as her capacity to innovate.

The capacity to innovate can be influenced by other communities' attitudes toward the Spanish spoken by Cordovans. Respondent 3B mentioned that during her first year in junior high school her classmates would comment, "The people from Córdova speak very fast and you can't understand them," or "I can tell you are from Córdova because your Spanish is different." In addition to becoming aware of the linguistic differences between Córdova and the Española Valley and the attitudes toward Cordovan speech style, it was apparent to Respondent 3B that the children from Córdova had a higher level of proficiency in Spanish than did the children from the other communities. Thus, every time Cordovan women leave their community, it is as if they are crossing borders, which requires innovative behavior; in this situation innovation means changing speech styles to meet their objectives.

Interaction with Noncommunity Members away from Córdova

Of the thirty-four interactions observed between the respondents and noncommunity members in the public domain (that is, all interactions occurring away from the community with outgroup members), twenty-four included the use of English: thirteen were English only; nine involved equal use of Spanish and English; one used all three codes (Spanish, English, and codeswitching); one was primarily in Spanish with some English; and one was primarily in English with some Spanish. Seven interactions were conducted entirely in Spanish and three involved codeswitching exclusively. The dominance of English in these interactions was expected because they occurred in the public domain. Most of these interactions were between the respondents and monolingual English speakers or with third-generation women who were dominant in English. Respondents 1A and 1B used only Spanish in all of their interactions, and the women from the second and third generations used Spanish when interacting with the older generation. Codeswitching was used by Respondents 2B and 2C primarily when interacting with friends who codeswitched.

The most salient variable influencing language choice in the public domain is age, which results in accommodation due to respect for the elderly. Culturally within the Chicano society, courtesy and respect for members of the older generation are often demonstrated by accommodating to their language preferences, that is, convergence to Spanish. Individuals belonging to the younger generations are expected to adhere to this social norm. An example of this kind of accommodation was commented on by a female community member (age forty-seven) who was interviewed but did not participate as one of the respondents in this study:

Los viejitos, pues, *they don't know how to talk English*. Los pobres quieren saber qué está hablando uno, como hay veces que viene mi mom para acá y nos juntamos todas, pues, se ponen a hablar en inglés y les dice mamá, "Hablen en mexicano, que no sé lo que están dicien-do," y las muchachas hablan español con su abuela.

('The elderly, well, they don't know how to talk English. Poor things, they want to know what one is talking about, there are times when my mother comes to visit and we all get together, well, they [the daughters] start to speak English, and my mother tells them, "Speak in Mexicano [Spanish], I don't know what you are saying," and the girls speak Spanish with their grandmother'.)

Respondent 2C also commented on the importance of the social norm of using Spanish with the older generation.

El español se me hace importante por los viejitos si uno va a platicar con ellos. Pues, si tú les dices algo en inglés ellos no te van a enten-der qué les estás diciendo. Como cuando va uno a misa, primero teníamos un padre, la primera vez que vino, les dio misa en inglés, y allí estaban los viejitos; nomás se miraban uno al otro, no sabían qué estaba pasando.

('I think Spanish is important for the elderly if one is going to speak with them. Well, if you tell them something in English they are not going to understand. For example, when one goes to Mass, first we used to have a priest, the first time he came, he gave Mass in English, and there sat the elderly looking at each other, they didn't know what was happening'.)

A final and more detailed example of cross-generational linguistic interac-tion that leads to accommodation is the bridal shower given in honor of Respondent 2B's daughter. It was held at a public hall in a nearby community (population 45,000). Approximately seventy-five women attended and of those attending the majority were aunts, cousins, in-laws, friends, and neigh-bors. Most came from the surrounding smaller villages, and a few were from the city. There were approximately twenty-five first-generation women (ages 55–96), thirty second-generation women (ages 30–54), and twenty of the third generation (ages 2–29). The linguistic interaction among the guests varied. Members of the first generation spoke to one another in Spanish. The second generation spoke Spanish with the first generation, either codeswitched or used Spanish or English among themselves, and used English with some of the third generation. The third generation tended to speak only English among themselves, English with some Spanish to the second generation, and Spanish with the first generation.

Prior to the beginning of the activities of this event, Respondent 2B, her daughter the bride-to-be (twenty-seven years old), and the matron of honor (thirty-five years old) greeted the guests as they arrived. Both mother and daughter greeted those belonging to the first generation in Spanish. The women of the second and third generations were typically greeted in English with some codeswitching, although the guests from Córdova were invariably greeted in Spanish. After the guests had gone through the receiving line, Respondent 2B introduced the bride-to-be and the matron of honor, who were both from the city. English was used by the matron of honor and Spanish and English were used by the bride-to-be. Although the bride-to-be has lived in Albuquerque for ten years, she still follows the rules of discourse of her native speech community. The matron of honor, who is an urban Chicana, did not speak Spanish at the event, although she understands it; when spoken to by Spanish speakers she responded in English. The language behavior of the bride-to-be and the matron of honor reveals how language use during the childhood years will influence language choice in the adult years. An important factor is where a person spent her childhood rather than where she currently lives (Peñalosa 1980). The bride-to-be was reared in Córdova; to deviate from the norm would mark her as an outsider or one who did not respect communal norms. There is obviously a need for the bride-to-be to continue to identify with the community, and she does so by adhering to the community norms, although she has been gone for several years.

The shower took place one week after my arrival in Córdova, prior to any interviews, and I wondered why so much English was spoken. I had anticipated more Spanish because so many women in attendance were Spanish speakers. However, by the end of the shower I concluded that English was primarily used so as to accommodate the out-of-town guests from the city, and furthermore, the setting was in the public domain, which determined the language choice of the majority of the women. I observed the mother of the bride-to-be, Respondent 2B, accommodating to the English spoken by her *comadres* from Albuquerque (who, incidentally, also spoke Spanish). To have spoken Spanish with these women, who were not members of the Cordovan ingroup, might have denied the importance of Spanish as a marker of intragroup solidarity. It is interesting to speculate whether these same women would have used Spanish with their city *comadres* had the shower been held in Córdova. On one hand, I believe they would have, for setting is an exceedingly important variable in language choice for

Cordovans. However, on the other hand, if the city *comadres* initiated the use of English, then the Cordovan women most likely would have accommodated them linguistically.

Once the introductions and acknowledgments were completed, Respondent 2B announced in English that the first game was about to begin. She then switched to Spanish and said, "Voy a usar inglés y español porque sé que hay algunas mujeres aquí que no entienden inglés o prefieren español, incluyendo yo misma! Entonces usaré las dos idiomas. Quiero dar la bienvenida y vamos a jugar un *game*." ('I am going to use English and Spanish because I know there are some women here who do not understand English or prefer Spanish, myself included. So I will use both languages. I want to welcome you and let's play a game.') She proceeded to give the instructions, codeswitching intrasententially. This received a warm response, some applause, and comments in Spanish such as "Ah, que bien" and "No entiendo el inglés muy bien" ('Oh, good'. 'I don't understand English very well'.)

The first game was *Consejos para la Novia* (advice for the bride). This advice was to be given at random, on a volunteer basis. Here are a few examples of the *consejos* given:

1st woman:	Always be ready to go with him.
2nd woman:	Hazle frijoles todos los días, que es la mejor comida. ('Make him beans every day; it's the best food'.)
Mother:	(Repeats the *consejo* in Spanish in case it was not heard the first time. There is applause from the guests.)
Bride:	He likes frijoles. Le gustan los frijoles y las tortillas. ('He likes beans and tortillas'.) We're on our way.
4th woman:	Give him three hugs and three kisses a day.
Bride:	That's a good one. I like that one.
5th woman:	Que no deje su marido ir solo para dondequiera; que se esté junto de ella. ('Don't let your husband go anywhere by himself; he should stay by her'.) (laughter, cheers, and loud applause)
Bride:	I already ... Ese sí me acuerdo. ('That one I'll remember'.)
Mother:	Ese sí te gustó. ('You liked that one'.)
Bride:	Ese me gusta mucho. ('That one I like a lot'.)
5th woman:	You better believe it.

As we can see, these *consejos* were given in Spanish, English, or codeswitching. Other *consejos* given in Spanish and English by the first and second generations were religious and traditional. The advice given in English by the third generation focused on themes of equality. The use of religious and traditional themes by certain women can imply that these women are conserving the mother tongue more than the younger generation. Although the themes of younger women's *consejos* seem to indicate that they are innovative in their views of female-male relationships, the form of the *consejos*, with greater use of English, suggests that the women are innovative in their linguistic behavior as well.

The interaction at this women-only event bears out that the networks within this speech community established throughout the generations are not only dense and multiplex but stable. This stability influences Cordovan women to enter into expanded networks that have been responsible for innovation in language behavior. For example, Respondent 1C, as a *santera*, must interact with a variety of individuals: international tourists, museum curators, and business associates. When she does so, she uses English without hesitation. I attribute this innovative behavior to the strong sense of ingroup cohesiveness and security that has permitted respondents to venture out of the community and enter new social networks. In the process they alter their communal language behavior without feeling a threat to their sense of identity.

Conclusion

The results of this study indicate that a variety of social changes since the 1940s—change from agricultural subsistence to wage labor, greater educational opportunities, decrease in family size, and increasing linguistic and cultural contact with the dominant society—have influenced the language choice of Cordovan women. More important, these changes have affected their role as both innovators and conservators in language use as well as their economic empowerment and educational and social mobility. It is apparent that they have not relinquished their use of Spanish in favor of English but have devised linguistic strategies that allow them to participate effectively in the larger dominant society. These strategies have not only assisted in the maintenance of their mother tongue but possibly have decelerated language shift toward English. Furthermore, there are indications that the Cordovan women have not resisted the innovations that have impinged on their personal and social networks, but have instead used them as strategies in order to adapt to their new environments. In other words, I believe that the Cordovan women have been exceedingly successful as "cultural brokers" as they mediate between two separate realities, the native speech community and the English-speaking community. Rather than succumb to "linguistic terrorism," the deprivation of our mother tongue (Anzaldúa 1987) that accompanies crossing cultural and linguistic borders, Cordovan women have developed strategies in order to resist absolute linguistic assimilation.

Notes

1. The terms *Chicana, Chicano, Hispano,* and *Mexicano,* are used interchangeably in this chapter.
2. According to Rosaura Sánchez (1983), codeswitching is an indicator of social change due to intercultural contact between a subordinate and a dominant group.
3. The speech style/strategy framework provides a valuable approach for studying and explaining linguistic behavior of women and men as members of subordinate and dominant groups. The social identity of group members is enhanced by the knowledge of their own membership in particular groups and the value that the individual gives to this membership. It is not uncommon for people to emphasize in certain situations their ingroup identity and psychological distinctiveness from others by accentuating certain linguistic features. In other situations, group members may desire acceptance and will thus accentuate their shared modes of expression.
4. *Comadrazgo* is a social structure in which people assume symbolic positions of kinship through religious rituals. The godparents of a baptized child become the *compadres* (literally, 'co-parents') of the parents. The godfather is the *compadre* and the godmother is the *comadre.* This linkage can also occur through marriage and confirmation.

References

Adams, David Wallace (1988). Fundamental considerations: The deep meaning of Native American schooling, 1880–1900. *Harvard Educational Review* 58(1): 1–28.

Anzaldúa, Gloria (1987). *Borderlands/La frontera: The new mestiza.* San Francisco: Spinsters/Aunt Lute.

Briggs, Charles (1986). *Learning how to ask.* Cambridge: Cambridge University Press.

Cameron, Deborah, and Jennifer Coates (1989). Some problems in the sociolinguistic explanation of sex differences. In Deborah Cameron and Jennifer Coates (eds.), *Women in their speech communities: New perspectives on language and sex.* London: Longman. 13–26.

Castro, Rafaela (1982). Mexican women's sexual jokes. *Aztlán* 13: 275–93.

Deutsch, Sara J. (1985). Culture, class, and gender: Chicanas in Colorado and New Mexico 1900–1940. Ph.D. diss., Yale University.

Fishman, Joshua A. (1966). *Language loyalty in the United States.* The Hague: Mouton.

—— (1972). *Language in sociocultural change*. Stanford: Stanford University Press.

Foster, Michèle (this volume). "Are you with me?": Power and solidarity in the discourse of African American women.

Galindo, D. Letticia (1992). Dispelling the male-only myth: Chicanas and caló. *Bilingual Review/Revista Bilingüe* 17(1): 3–35.

Galindo, D. Letticia, & María Dolores Gonzales Velásquez (1992). A sociolinguistic description of linguistic self-expression, innovation, and power among Chicanas in Texas and New Mexico. In Kira Hall, Mary Bucholtz, and Birch Moonwomon (eds.), *Locating power: Proceedings of the Second Berkeley Women and Language Conference*. Berkeley: Berkeley Women and Language Group. 162–70.

Giles, Howard (1978). Linguistic difference in ethnic groups. In Henri Tajfel (ed.) *Differentiation between social groups*. London: Academic Press. 361–93.

Gonzales Velásquez, María Dolores (1992). The role of women in linguistic tradition and innovation in a Chicano community in New Mexico. Ph.D. diss., University of New Mexico.

Hymes, Dell (1972). Models of interaction of language and social life. In John J. Gumperz and Dell Hymes (eds.), *Directions in sociolinguistics*. New York: Holt, Rinehart & Winston. 35–71.

Kramarae, Cheris (1981). *Women and men speaking*. Rowley, MA: Newbury House.

Lakoff, Robin (1975). *Language and woman's place*. New York: Harper & Row.

Lewis, Glyn E. (1971). Migration and language in the USSR. *International Migration Review* 5(2): 147–79.

Medicine, Bea (1987). The role of American Indian women in cultural continuity and transition. In Joyce Penfield (ed.), *Women and language in transition*. Albany: SUNY Press. 159–65.

Milk, Robert (1980). The issue of language in education in territorial New Mexico. *Bilingual Review/Revista Bilingüe* 7(3): 212–22.

Milroy, Lesley (1992). *Language and social networks*. 2d ed. Oxford: Basil Blackwell.

Myers, Sara K. (1973). *Language shift among migrants to Lima, Perú*. Chicago: University of Chicago Press.

Nichols, Patricia (1983). Linguistic options for Black women in the rural South. In Barrie Thorne, Cheris Kramarae, and Nancy Henley (eds.), *Language, gender, and society*. Rowley, MA: Newbury House. 54–68.

Peñalosa, Fernando (1980). *Chicano sociolinguistics: A brief introduction*. Rowley, MA: Newbury House.

Sánchez, Rosaura (1983). *Chicano discourse: Socio-historic perspectives*. Rowley, MA: Newbury House.

Sherif, Muzafer (1966). *Group conflict and cooperation: Their social psychology*. London: Routledge & Kegan Paul.

Spender, Dale (1980). *Man made language*. London: Routledge & Kegan Paul.

Spolsky, Bernard (1969). Attitudinal aspects of second language learning. *Language Learning* 19: 271–85.

Stevens, Gillian (1986). Sex differences in language shift in the United States. *Sociology and Social Research* 71(1): 31–34.

Tajfel, Henri (1974). Social identity and intergroup behavior. *Social Science Information* 13(2): 65–93.

Thompson, Roger M. (1974). Mexican American language loyalty and the validity of the 1970 census. *Linguistics* 128: 7–18.

Thorne, Barrie, Cheris Kramarae, and Nancy Henley (eds.) (1983). *Language, gender, and society.* Rowley, MA: Newbury House.

Whiteford, Linda (1980). Mexican American women as innovators. In Margarita B. Melville (ed.), *Twice a minority: Mexican American women.* London: C. V. Mosby.

Yañez, Rosa H. (1990). The complimenting speech act among Chicano women. In John Bergen (ed.), *Spanish in the United States: Sociolinguistic issues.* Washington, DC: Georgetown University Press. 79–85.

Zentella, Ana Celia (1987). Language and the female identity in the Puerto Rican community. In Joyce Penfield (ed.), *Women and language in transition.* Albany: SUNY Press. 167–79.

18

The Writing on the Wall

A Border Case of Race and Gender

Birch Moonwomon

This chapter presents a discourse analysis of a graffiti text concerning an alleged rape. The text is taken from the wall of a women's bathroom stall at the University of California at Berkeley. Because the accused rapists were African American male students who were members of the university's football team and the raped woman was a Chinese American student, the incident associates the politics of gender with the politics of race. The first goal of the examination presented here is to trace the development and import of the graffiti discourse, specifying how textual coherence makes use of out-of-text knowledge. Writers of the graffiti remarks employ implicature (Grice 1975); that is, they make assertions with their statements indirectly, counting on readers to understand the suggested meanings behind the explicit ones. The use of implicature reveals that the writers assume other discourse participants—those who have already written on the wall and the unknown women who may write—share certain cultural knowledge. These assumptions of shared knowledge themselves evoke specifiable societal discourses. A second goal of the analysis of this text is to associate situated, linguistic discourse within societal discourses. The textual debate about male-to-female sexual violence is clearly politicized, involving issues of both gender and race identities and oppressions. I assert that analysis is needed in the study of the intersection of gender and language that associates the content and structure of texts—the products of linguistic discourse—with cultural knowledge that is differently known from different vantage points of social identity saliences.

The term *discourse* is used in two main ways by discourse analysts and social theorists. By *a discourse* sociolinguists and others who study text linguistically mean a collection of sequential linguistic structures above the clause level, in a linguistic performance (Brown & Yule 1983; Gumperz 1982; Levinson 1983; Stubbs 1988), but for some social theorists this term designates a body of knowledge informing language use (de Certeau 1984; Foucault 1977, 1980, 1981; Macdonell 1986; Pêcheux 1982). I will refer to the first usage as *linguistic discourse* and the second as *societal discourse.* A linguistic discourse, of which text is the product, is always situated. A societal discourse, having to do with knowledge that is not privatized, transcends situation. Societal discourses may span many communities or belong to a small group. The text of the linguistic discourse examined here evidences evocation both of societal discourses shared among many communities, such as the discourse on rape, and of at least one discourse that is mainly confined to the campus community, namely, the discourse on the football team's culpability for the rape.

The term *border case* refers to the coincidental coming together of two or more societal tensions in an event or situation, such that aspects of both tensions are salient. Societal tensions are meaningful in terms of social identities, like race, gender, or social-sexual orientation, and dominance-subordination relationships defined in terms of these identities. A border case is the situated co-salience of differently delimited oppressions such as gender oppression and racial oppression.[1] Because social identities are multiple for an individual and dominance-subordination relationships are complex in society, conflicting assertions about the political meaning of an event often vie with one another. The term *border case* was coined by Mary Poovey (1988:12), who notes that because such cases are situated at the "border between two defining alternatives," such as race and gender, they "mark the limits of ideological certainty." She characterizes border cases as sites of debate because they "challenge the opposition upon which all other oppositions are claimed to be based." For instance, within feminist ideology, gender is regarded as the primary basis for opposition; within antiracist ideology, race is regarded as the primary basis for opposition. The term is also used in an article about interracial rape by Valerie Smith (1990:272), who points out that border cases are "precisely those issues that problematize easy assumptions about racial and/or sexual difference."

Linguistic discourses concerning border cases evoke societal discourses that reveal the conflict of priorities. Association of one kind of discourse with the other locates the contradiction of the border case. Discourse about interracial rape is one example of this contradiction.

Feminist and antiracist writers have exposed and countered sexist and racist claims concerning women (white and nonwhite), African American men, and rape (Beck 1982; Brownmiller 1975; Davis 1981; Faludi 1991; French 1992; Russell 1975; Smith 1990). Scholars note that women's accusations of rape have not been believed or, if believed, have not been regarded as important enough for prosecution, and women have been blamed for provoking attack, not putting up enough resistance, and not reporting assaults promptly enough. In our white-dominant, Christian-dominant society, nonwhite and non-Christian women have been characterized as sexually promiscuous and therefore nonvirgin. For this reason, many people believe that such women are not really harmed by sexual violence. At the same time, nonwhite men, and in particular African American men, have been characterized as sexual predators (see Beck 1982; Brownmiller 1975; Davis 1981; Russell 1975; Smith 1990). Against this societal discourse on rape, feminists have insisted that acquaintance rape is more common than stranger rape: men rape the women to whom they have easiest access, or those whom they believe they have a right to control. This makes intraracial rape more common than interracial rape, but because of white dominance, it also makes interracial rape of nonwhite women by white men more common than interracial rape of white women by nonwhite men. Antiracists argue that the false accusation of rape against African American men has been part of the systematic racist injury to the African American community over generations and is therefore significant for its practical and symbolic effect.

The border-case contradiction revealed in the discourse considered in this chapter is due to such issues of racist and sexist terrorism. The contradiction is not in itself resolvable in the isolation of any one instance of linguistic discourse—and, notably, it is not even directly addressed in the data under analysis here. Antiracist societal discourse has resolved that accusations of rape made against African American men serve racism, and feminist discourse has resolved that the dismissal of women's accusations of rape serve misogyny. When an African American man is accused of rape, however, it cannot be the case that the accusation is both false (under sexism) and true (under racism). In the situated, linguistic discourse examined here, this border-case conflict backgrounds the graffiti text and has reality precisely because of out-of-text discourses on rape and race.

In analyzing the graffiti text, I am interested in specifying how a text is shaped by out-of-text knowledge and, conversely, how a situated, linguistic discourse has potential for modifying societal discourses. Both public and private linguistic discourses maintain and change societal discourses. A bathroom graffiti text is a unique site for the association of linguistic with societal discourse because it brings together aspects of public and private language use. It is public in that the audience is impersonal and potentially large, and the message sender, the writer, is distanced from the recipients. It is private in that its content is not liable to wide reportage and in that it seems conversational rather than monologic: a number of writers participate, there is turn-taking, the style is informal, and very personal matters can be discussed.

Women's public-restroom graffiti are *located* (Hymes 1972) in a way akin to that of electronic mail text (see Herring, Johnson, & DiBenedetto, this volume). Both in a public women's restroom and in the cyberspace of electronic mail discourse participants write to potentially numerous, mainly unknown recipients. Contributions are sequenced, but it is common for a contributor to make just one remark and then withdraw. In spite of the turnover of message senders, development of the discussion's subject goes on; coherence is maintained. Furthermore, several different lines of conversational topic development may become elaborated, either from the initial comment or from any comment thereafter.

In several respects women's-restroom graffiti are different from electronic mail discourse and other public-forum discourses that are not face-to-face. Access to the graffiti discourse, which in this case took place in a women's restroom, is limited by sex. Furthermore, the graffiti discourse is located in real rather than electronic space. This means that the traffic through the text location is predictable by the characteristics of persons in the larger locale; in the present case these are mainly university students, faculty, and staff. Sex is important to the location, the setting type; knowledge of Berkeley affairs is important to the discourse in the particular setting.

Another difference is that the location of the graffiti discourse guarantees anonymity while other public-forum discourses do not. The sender of the message on the wall is not identified by even so much as an electronic mail address or a name signed to a letter to the editor. Related to this fact is the possibility that the same writer may contribute several times to the same graffiti discourse, but unless her handwriting or pen style is unusual, the multiple message-sending will go unnoticed. Indeed, it is not important to the graffiti discussion's development whether one person has contributed more than one remark. Each contribution is taken by readers to be the only remark by that individual, unless a contribution indicates otherwise; that is, a developed graffiti discussion is generally read as a text constructed by as many writers as there are separable remarks.

An additional matter related to anonymity, the roles of participants, marks a third difference between graffiti and other discourse locations. Writers are the message senders, those they are formally responding to are the addressees, and other readers are the recipients. More accurately, however, the readers are both message recipients and addressees. In graffiti discourse it is not expected that contributors will read responses to their remarks; they may very well not return to the location. Conversely, in electronic mail discourse senders are likely to read subsequent postings in a discussion.

A final difference between women's-restroom graffiti and other discourses that develop in a public forum is related to the political confrontation genre that is characteristic of this discourse (Nwoye 1993; Moonwomon 1986). Although the advice-giving genre of women's-bathroom graffiti is more widely known (Cole 1991; Davies 1986), political confrontation, characterized by open conflict, is also very common.[2] And contrary to the tendency for confrontation to lead to the silencing of women in other discourses (Herring, Johnson, & DiBenedetto, this volume; Lakoff, this volume), women with opinions unacceptable to other writers do not let themselves be silenced, at least on that account. The debate forum is characterized by the expression of radically conflicting views.

The Incident and its Aftermath

In September 1986 four University of California football players were accused of raping an eighteen-year-old undergraduate in a housing co-op, Dwight Derby. The woman did not press charges against them at the time but decided to do so about a month later. It was known on campus that some or all of the four football players were African Americans and that they were not being legally prosecuted. In the end, they were required to apologize to the woman and to perform community service, although they had not been tried for rape. In the same fall semester, against expectations, the Berkeley football team won the "Big Game," the Thanksgiving game against Stanford University. A photograph of a game rally on campus, printed on the front page of the widely read student newspaper, the *Daily Californian* (November 29, 1986), showed a line of leaping female cheerleaders in juxtaposition to other women who solemnly held signs that protested the university's inaction about the rape.

During the fall a graffiti discourse about the rape began on a stall wall of the women's bathroom in the first floor of a large, central, busy building of classrooms and offices. The discourse continued through the spring semester of 1987. This situated, linguistic discourse is associated with a campus-centered societal discourse about the incident and its aftermath.

Methodology

In May 1987 I traced onto a large gridded sheet the text as it then stood on the wall of a bathroom stall. It was then necessary to establish the number of routes of development and the sequencing of remarks for each route within the whole text. The physical site of the text grows outward from a center, widening with the addition of levels as responses are constructed. A single remark may be responded to by several comments that modify the focus of discussion in different ways. The discussion takes off in different directions, each line of discourse marking its own physical-site levels.

Because the text was a collection of artifacts at a physical site, I was able to use archaeological method, imposing stratigraphy on the site—actually, on the tracing of its contents—to aid the search for sequencing. I subjected the pattern of remarks to horizontal stratigraphical analysis (Thomas 1979). Through examination of physical cues, such as arrows, and content cues, such as responses to nearby remarks, it was possible to discern five routes of sequential remarks and to separate sets of remarks made at different times. Figure 18.1 maps the graffiti patterns, showing each graffito's place in the sequenced levels of the text.

There are thirty-six separate contributions to the discourse. The main text is composed of three series of comments, **a**, **b**, and **c**, each of which begins with the first graffito, *The Big Game = The Big Scam. Boo U.C. Rapists!* There are two other series, **d** and **e**, which begin with metacomments on the main text. Each series contributes to the building of a textual discourse that reflects and shapes conflicting societal discourses about rape.

One device that marks the discourse as confrontation is the use of graphic paralanguage, that is, markers that indicate intonation and expressive force. Graphic paralanguage includes word-circling, multiple underlining, multiple punctuation marks, and the use of capital letters, e.g., **e1** *OBSESSED W/RAPE OR WHAT!* Fifteen remarks use this device to emphasize conflict. In addition, there is recurrent use of phrasal flags that I will call *disagreement flags*, e.g., **c4.1** *Oh fuck you,* and *agreement flags,* e.g., **b6.1** *Good!* Thirteen disagreement flags occur within ten comments; only four agreement flags are found, in four different remarks.

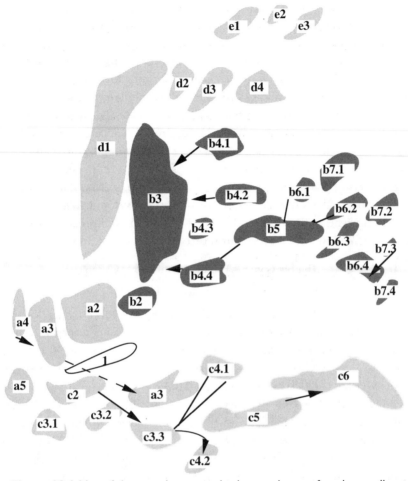

Figure 18.1 Map of the text. Arrows and other markers as found on wall; broken-line arrow connects the two parts of graffito **a.3**.

Despite the confrontational nature of the discourse, writers often mitigate their expressions of disagreement. Two forms of mitigation are found: mitigating remarks that appear at the end of a writer's graffito (e.g., **a2** *And I'm not saying this problem made it acceptable*), which anticipate and attempt to correct misinterpretation; and *yes, but* statements, which appear at the beginning of a writer's comment (e.g., **d4** *No one's saying she deserved to be raped—but . . .*) and introduce the writer's disagreement with a previous writer's statement.

Whereas graphic paralanguage and disagreement flags mark the discourse as a debate, other devices are used to link the linguistic discourse to larger societal discourses in a way intended to determine the outcome of the debate. Rhetorical questions are one such strategy, because the answer is assumed to be known to the writer, the addressee, and the readers as shared knowledge (Levinson 1983). There are twenty-six rhetorical questions, of direct and indirect interrogative forms, appearing in sixteen of the thirty-six graffiti, e.g., **c2** *Isn't the law innocent until proven guilty, or does that apply only to non-violent suspects?* and **a3** *I just wonder why the people responsible for bringing those guys here didn't make sure that they understand* <u>*ours*</u> [i.e., 'our culture']. By contrast, the entire text contains no real queries for information.

Discussion of Series b

This chapter will focus on an examination of the development of one discussion within the graffiti text, the discourse of series **b**, as reproduced in Figure 18.2 (see the Appendix for the graffiti texts of series **a**, **c**, **d**, and **e**):

1.	The Big Game = The Big Scam. Boo U.C. Rapists!
b2.	She enjoyed having sex with 4 football players.
b3.	Amen to you. I don't know whether you're a sister or not. but Amen. I heard she made herself a scapegoat. It was 1 girl with 4 football players in a room getting drunk. What was she doing in there with them by herself and EVERYbody's drunk. get <u>ReaL</u>!
	They say she was down for what she got and then when word got out that she was a superfreak she dreamed it was rape. A MONTH LATER??? BE REAL !!!! Anyway, if it was rape, why didn't anyone hear her scream? Dwight Derby is very quiet. Once again I say Get REAL !!!!
b4.1.	did it occur to you 1) her mouth could have been stuffed or covered 2) she was too terrified 3) she was too outraged/shamed (it's possible)
b4.2.	What an attitude. If you're mugged and you didn't scream does that make it any less a crime?
b4.3.	They say? Male they say?
b4.4.	There is a connection between alcohol and sexual violence—Carrie Nation knew this!
b5. (b4.4)	You fucking bitch! Does that mean if I want to have a drink—share a few laughs w/some friends that I can't complain if they rape me?

b6.1.	good.
b6.2.	What it means is Don't get so drunk you're an easy tar-get.
b6.3.	No. It means y
b6.4.	of course not! It means we women should be aware of how drugs and alchohol bring out violence, and be smart. rape is never the victim's fault.
b7.1. (b6.2)	Getting drunk should be safe. There should be NO DAN-GER.
b7.2. (b6.2)	That's <u>one</u> means of prevention. Another's <u>conviction</u> and <u>punishment</u> of those who RAPE!
b7.3. (b6.4)	We should be aware, but <u>so</u> <u>should</u> <u>they</u>!
b7.4. (b6.4)	So why are we dropping the issue?

Figure 18.2 Text of series **b**. Parenthesized labels for comments indicate responses to former comments, e.g., **b5. (b4.4)** is a comment in stratum 5 responding to the comment b4.4 in stratum 4.

The remarks in series **b**, like those in series **a** and series **c** (see Appendix), develop in response to comment **1** (*The Big Game = The Big Scam. Boo U.C. Rapists!*), which introduces the topic of the rape and associates it with the team and the university. By associating the rape with the team's big win, the writer suggests that the team's victory allows backgrounding of what should remain foregrounded in campus talk about the team: that four team members raped a woman. The writer evokes several out-of-text discourses. One that is confined mainly to the campus community is the discourse about who is accountable for the rape. Linked to this local societal discourse is the less situated discourse concerning general institutional responsibility for sexual violence. Yet another discourse concerns punishment and reward for rape victim and rapist after the crime. The team players who were the rapists shared the reward of the team's glory for winning the "Big Game" and suffered no deprivation; the raped woman, on the other hand, was not compensated in any way for what happened to her.

Series **b** opens with a confrontational response to **1**: *She enjoyed having sex with 4 football players.* The heart of the challenge lies in the writer's refusal to accept the terms of the discourse, the basic claim that the incident was a rape. As a victim of rape, the woman is the object of action; in comment **b2**, however, the writer makes the victim the subject, placing *she* in the subject position in the clause. By focusing on the woman's role as an experiencer in the event, or more specifically as an enjoyer of the action that ensued, the writer makes an explicit counterclaim to the implicit claim of comment **1** that the football players raped the woman. The remark implies that the woman is the wrongdoer, in that she falsely accused men of rape when the acts were really consensual sex. Further implications are that football players are naturally a sexual treat and that the accusing woman has a large sexual appetite because she had sex with four of them at one party. With this comment, then, the text becomes redefined as a debate about whether the incident was rape and who is responsible for wrongdoing—an assertion that is debated for two more strata of text.

The writer of graffito **b2** assumes shared knowledge not only of the alleged rape events but also of the fact that the assertion of rape has not been officially validated. She also relies on readers' cultural knowledge of the model for dismissal of rape charges: the accuser is always liable to be accused of lying and of having enjoyed the act. The societal discourse evoked by her comment is thus the dichotomized discourse on the credibility of rape accusations. A longstanding position within this debate is that charges are, in the unmarked case, not believable because they can too easily be made, and are least believable if the woman and the accused man have been socializing. A newer, feminist position is that charges are, in the unmarked case, believable because sexual violence is a common expression of male domination and because they are not easy to make at all but costly in relived trauma and public exposure.

Comment **1**, then, focuses accusingly on the team, comment **b2** on the woman. The writer of graffito **b3** aligns herself with the second writer and spins out a three-point argument in favor of viewing the incident as sex and false accusation rather than as rape. Using an agreement flag (*Amen to you*) and graphic paralanguage (e.g., *get ReaL!*; *BE REAL!!!!*; *Get REAL!!!!*), she furthers the confrontational tone of the discourse and indicates her own position within the debate by calling upon a new societal discourse, that of race:

(1)   Amen to you. I don't know whether you're a sister or not. but Amen. I heard she made herself a scapegoat. It was 1 girl with 4 football players in a room getting drunk. What was she doing in there with them by herself and EVERYbody's drunk. get ReaL!

They say she was down for what she got and then when word got out that she was a superfreak she dreamed it was rape. A MONTH LATER??? BE REAL !!!! Anyway, if it was rape, why didn't anyone hear her scream? Dwight Derby is very quiet. Once again I say Get REAL !!!!

With her first two sentences this writer evokes both a discourse on Black solidarity and one on race in relation to rape. The remarks *Amen to you, sister,* and *Amen* signal more than agreement with the previous writer; the writer is identifying herself as African American (see Major 1994 and Smitherman 1994), or at least as a woman of color, and assumes shared knowledge that allows correct interpretation of these cues. Aligning herself with the writer of **2b** as a *sister,* she implies they have the same perspective on the incident discussed because similar social realities, racially defined, give these women the same perspective on rape accusations targeting African American men.

By asserting that the woman *made herself a scapegoat,* the writer evokes a campus debate about who (i.e., the raped woman or the accused players) has been mistreated, and in some way sacrificed, in the aftermath of the incident. She asserts that the woman herself is responsible (i.e., *she was down for what she got*) and dismisses the rape accusation as revisionist historicizing: *when word got out that she was a superfreak she dreamed it was rape.* Following each of her rhetorical questions (*What was she doing in there with them by herself and EVERYbody's drunk; A MONTH LATER!!!; Anyway, if it was rape, why didn't anyone hear her scream?*), the writer displays a disagreement flag accompanied by graphic paralanguage: *get ReaL!; BE REAL !!!!; Get REAL !!!!.* With this graphic vehemence, the author asserts that a realistic, nongullible frame of mind requires one to come to certain conclusions: the accusing woman asked for it, wanted it, and later lied about it. The term *REAL* makes its own implicit claim: what is real is that a woman allowed herself to be gang-banged; what is not real is that the four African American football players raped her.

The fourth stratum of series **b** is composed of four remarks, all expressing disagreement with the stance of the **b3** writer. The stratum **4** writers represent feminist voices speaking from anti-rape consciousness. Three of these four remarks use arrows, graphically putting the finger on questionable points in the previous writer's argument. Collectively, the comments deflect responsibility and blame away from the accusing woman, and in doing so they bring about a change of topic. The writer of **b4.1**, for instance, chooses to answer one of the previous writer's questions with another: opposing one question to another carries an implicature in itself, making the point that the first question's answer is not necessarily that the accusing woman did not scream because she was not being raped. By structuring her response as a question, the writer implies that the previous writer is not being *REAL;* it should have occurred to her that there are real impediments to resistance:

(2)

> did it occur to you
> 1) her mouth could have been stuffed or covered
> 2) she was too terrified
> 3) she was too outraged/shamed (it's possible)

On the whole, however, the writer of comment (2) does not make claims by implicature. She appears to assume little shared knowledge, expressing herself with great clarity and explicitness: she lists—using numbers with single parentheses—three possible reasons for not screaming. Projecting her opponent's incredulity, she appends to her comment the assertion that even shame can inhibit loud resistance. Similarly, the writer of **b4.2** also answers the previous writer's final question with another question: *If you're mugged and you didn't scream does that make it any less a crime?* In this way both writers undercut the rhetorical force of the previous writer's demand: *why didn't anyone hear her scream?* Finally, the writer of **b4.3** draws on shared assumptions that are constructed by a feminist discourse: that common knowledge is often male opinion and needs to be examined in light of that fact. Her query *They say? Male they say?* implies that male authority represents male interests and that these contradict female interests, suggesting that the writer of **b3** trusts the wrong sources of information.

The writer of **b4.4** critiques **b3** from a different perspective: *There is a connection between alcohol and sexual violence—Carrie Nation knew this!* Drawing an arrow to the word *drunk* in stratum **3**, the writer implies a connection between men's drinking and male sexual violence, suggesting that the drunken offenders, not the offended woman, are culpable. The writer is indirect in making this point and assumes shared knowledge, perhaps wrongly, when she evokes the figure of Carrie Nation, a radical force in the American temperance movement. She apparently intends readers to construct Nation as a woman who was savvy about violence against women. A premodern feminist image of Nation, however, is a different construction: the hatchet-bearing crazy woman who, in her intemperate protemperance, went too far.

The initial graffito and remarks **b2** and **b3** have already evoked a number of societal discourses concerning institutional responsibility; the different treatment of rapist and rape victim; the credibility of rape accusations; race in relation to accusations of rape; drinking and sexual violence; difficulties and special burdens for the rape victim in pressing charges. Each of these discourses also includes a feminist position or set of positions. The writers in stratum **4** do not call up new out-of-text discourses (except a feminist discourse on revisionist history through the reference to Nation) but align their remarks with feminist stances within several discourses that have already been evoked—those concerning credibility, difficulties for the victim, and alcohol. The remarks in stratum **4** bring about an important shift in conversational focus. The discourse is no longer about a rape or gang sex in the student dorm; it is about who is responsible for sexual violence in general.

In the subsequent remarks I hear voices of young, heterosexual women under pressure. The writer of **b5** begins with a hostile disagreement flag, *You fucking bitch!*, which seems to assume erroneously that the writer of **b4.4** holds women responsible for sexual violence if it occurs in a situation of social drinking. In response to **b4.4** the stratum **5** writer poses a rhetorical question that implies that social drinking is innocent behavior, sharing *a few laughs with some friends*. The topic has become responsibility for sexual violence within drinking situations. Are individual women, on the one hand, or a group of men, on the other, responsible for the prevention and punishment of sexual violence? Backgrounding this issue is the social reality of female undergraduate life. Girls may want their freedom, but they are liable, as women and as young adults, to be harangued with cautionary tales by elders and to be blamed for any trouble that occurs. The development of the graffiti argument is partly based on the tension between two social realities: on one hand, female vulnerability is increased by the emphasis placed on alcohol in campus socializing; on the other, temperance is associated with parental and institutional restraint that undermines the personal liberation of young adults. This social knowledge underlies the logic of the propositions in **b6.2** and **b6.4**: given x, that *drugs and alcohol bring out violence* (**b6.4**), then y, *be smart* (**b6.4**), *Don't get so drunk you're an easy target* (**b6.2**). Writers of **b6.2** and **b6.4** assume shared knowledge of women's special vulnerability in social drinking situations. Their remarks, while voicing a difference with the writer of **b5**, are not in conflict with her in the same way the writer of **b2** opposes **1**, for instance; their stance is educational, not belligerent. The **b6.4** writer ends with a mitigating statement showing comprehension of the point of view of the **b5** writer and claiming it as her own: *of course not! It means we women should be aware of how drugs and alcohol bring out violence, and be smart. rape is never the victim's fault.* Stratum **6** therefore demonstrates a more or less shared perspective on the societal discourses of alcohol, sexual violence, and responsibility for rape prevention.

Perhaps because of the unity of perspective, Level **6** has no graphic paralanguage. Stratum **7**, by contrast, echoes the confrontational stance of the fourth stratum, exhibiting graphic vehemence in the use of capital letters (*There should be NO DANGER*) and underlining (*That's one means of prevention. Another's <u>conviction</u> and <u>punishment</u> of those who RAPE!*;

We should be aware, <u>but so should they</u>!). The writers of **b7.1** and **b7.2** both imply that the writer of **b6.2** wrongly focuses on the drinking behavior of individual women. The comment of the latter author, that conviction and punishment of rapists is a means of rape prevention, implies that action against rapists is better action than women's modification of their own social drinking. Likewise, the writer of comment **b7.3**, *We should be aware, but <u>so</u> <u>should</u> <u>they</u>!* imposes a discursive solidarity among readers in the bathroom stall, asserting that *they,* men, as opposed to *we,* women, are responsible for consciousness about the violence men commit under the influence of drugs and alcohol. All of the comments work together to change the focus of the discussion; three of the remarks in this stratum deflect responsibility from women, just as the comments in **b4** deflected blame from the particular woman raped in the housing co-op.

The excavation of the graffiti site ends with the question of **b7.4**: *So why are we dropping the issue?* Addressed to the writer of **b6.4**, it abruptly returns the discourse to the first topic, the rape of the undergraduate woman by four football players. With this final graffito in series **b** the general question of responsibility for rape and the specific question of the accusing woman's claim are joined. If rape is never the victim's fault, then it is not this victim's fault; why was the case not pursued? The phrase *dropping the issue* refers to the fact that the football players were not criminally charged and were minimally sanctioned by the university. This last remark is in the voice of an impersonal collective, a suitable voice for a discourse that has been considering group responsibility for violence in a general way; yet it focuses attention on the specific incident that has inspired the whole thirty-six–remark discussion on the wall.

Conclusion

The peculiarities of the graffiti discourse location encourage the debate-forum genre, which, in turn, works against the silencing of women. The text I have examined here is a construction by women in communication with other women. They do not have to concern themselves about the intrusion of male presence, male voice; men will not be sending or receiving the messages. Furthermore, the writers confront one another anonymously and in absentia. Altogether, there is a high degree of safety for vehement expression, whether or not a writer's claim is in disagreement with a previous claim in the discourse. What develops is a community discussion of rape and responsibility. Discussion concerning responsibility for sexual violence in general grows from and is linked to argument about responsibility for the particular incident at the University of California.

By calling the discourse a *community discussion,* I mean to suggest that the women's community of the University of California is represented by the graffiti writers. Although the writers in this bathroom stall do not themselves, of course, constitute a community, they are engaging in a practice that has meaning because they are participants in other local communities of practice. The concept of a community of practice (Eckert & McConnell-Ginet 1992, this volume; Lave & Wenger 1991; Wenger 1993) facilitates a consideration of the construction of gender, social-sexual orientation, and other social identities that acknowledges the interdependence of various identities and the importance of ideology. The concept reifies an affiliation of persons mutually engaged in an endeavor; ways of doing, talking, and believing are created out of the practices of a community. The writers of the graffiti text participate in various local and global communities of practice, involving their multiple social identities. Topic development depends on an underlying thematic unity, which itself depends on knowledge of local and global societal discourses. When knowledge is not shared, evocation of a particular societal discourse is not successful and the import of a remark is lost, as happens between remarks **b4.4** and **b5**. Topic development in this text proceeds by changes of topic focus and topic scope, with the focus shifting from local to more global societal discourses.

The discourses evoked here can be reified as territories within which one finds various political vantages, both feminist and nonfeminist, both racist and antiracist. I have specified a number of societal discourses that emerge from the graffiti text, and the list is certainly not exhaustive. Several real conflicts, resting on social identities within different communities of practice, find implicit or explicit expression. One contradiction, finding expression in strata **1** through **4**, lies between racist and sexist terror: rape accusations made against African American men have often been false, but most rape accusations made by women are true. Another contradiction, finding expression in strata **5** through **7**, is that between individual freedom and responsibility: women have the right to behave as if they were free without fear of harassment but when women socialize like men they put themselves at special risk. A third contradiction is that individuals rape and are raped, and so the crime is dealt with as if transcendent of membership in social category or association with institution; but social identities like gender and race are clearly relevant, and it is the institution (in this case, the university) and its apparatus (the football team, the housing co-op party) that provide opportunity, means, and even rationale for sexual violence.

Clause by clause, comment by comment, the changes are effected though the use of graphic paralanguage, through phrasal flags and other lexical choices in particular syntactic positions, and through implicature in rhetorical questions. The structure of the discourse as a debate rests on shared knowledge of the out-of-text discourses; implicature works because of knowledge of these discourses; focus and even topic can change within the graffiti text while coherence is maintained because opposing stances in the societal discourses are known (e.g., within the discourse on credibility of rape accusations) and links among the out-of-text discourses are understood (e.g., between the discourse on responsibility for resistance to assault and the discourse on alcohol and sexual violence).

How might this situated, linguistic discourse modify specific societal discourses? As a public debate in a forum that allows a great range of expression of disagreement, the discourse gives rise to implicatures that other writers are not being realistic or are misassigning blame. As a result of the force of feminist stances concerning credibility and responsibility for staying safe, resisting attack, and reporting attack promptly, societal discourses on rape have changed. The writer of **b3**, however, makes use of nonfeminist stances in other out-of-text discourses in order to construct an argument from an antiracist stance within the discourse on rape and race, and a pro-solidarity stance within the discourse on African American solidarity. Graffito **b3** is informed by the issue of racism, specifically by a body of knowledge associated with the political discourse on racism: the history of accusations of rape made against Black men, resulting in unfair trials or no trials at all, long incarceration, or murder. This contribution can be compared to graffito **a3** (see Appendix), whose writer asks why university football recruiters don't take responsibility for resocializing *those guys* [i.e., football players], whom she goes on to compare to jungle cats turned loose to kill:

(3)   It's very true that there were cultural differences at work in this incident, but I just wonder why the people responsible for bringing those guys here didn't make sure that they understand <u>ours</u>. If they are going to live in our culture, they have to live by our customs— If someone let a Bengal Tiger lose [i.e., loose] on Telegraph and he killed someone, it would be easy to say that the tiger was only reacting as he would have in the jungle, and therefore he couldn't be blamed for murder—
—(cont.) But does that excuse the moron who opened the cage? (If those "imported" football players can't act civilized, send them back where they came from!)

The racism informing this comment allows the writer to make the football players entirely Other, first culturally alien, then, as she develops her theme, wild and nonhuman. The writer is protesting the behavior of the players, the rapists; she is resisting the sexist terror of rape; but her resistance is itself racist. The writer of **b3**, in contrast, makes the raped woman Other, the drunken, sexual *superfreak*. Although she denies the assertion of rape in order to defend against an accusation that is evocative of racist history, her resistance to racism is in this guise sexist.

Finally, although the writer of **b3** uses nonfeminist stances in societal discourses to argue against the rape accusation from what is evidently, given her introductory sentences, a racial solidarity position, her comments are not informed by the discourses concerning the construction of nonwhite women as provocative and promiscuous. Yet this racist and sexist construction of women is another aspect of the border case of race and rape. The utter silence about it in this text is notable. The writers of the text are not silenced themselves—through direct confrontation, they do not let themselves be silenced—but at least three silencings are attempted, two successfully. The first is the unsuccessful attempt by the writers of **b2** and **b3** to silence the accusation that four men raped a woman. The remarks in stratum **4** thwart this attempt. The second attempted silencing, which is effective, is of the antiracist voice evoked through the remarks of the writer of **b3**. The relevance of the race of the accused is simply ignored by subsequent writers. The third silencing is not really an attempt because it is not an act; it is an omission. Nowhere is the raped woman spoken for as a woman of color whose accusation against her attackers has not been officially credited.

Appendix

The following is the remaining text of the graffiti discourse. Like the remarks in series **b**, the remarks in **a** and **c** develop in response to the first graffito: *The Big Game = The Big Scam. Boo U.C. Rapists!* Series **d** and **e** are positioned about **a**, **b**, **c** on the graffiti site. Brackets (] [) indicate that text has been lost from the site, that is, some of the writing on the wall had been removed before the text was copied for analysis.

Series **a**

I.   The Big Game = The Big Scam. Boo U.C. Rapists!

a2.   That rape involved 2 clashing cultures. We need to know more about each other culturally in order to understand each other's actions. (And I'm not saying this problem made it acceptable.)

a3.   It's very true that there were cultural differences at work in this incident, but I just wonder why the people responsible for bringing those guys here didn't make sure that they understand ours. If they are going to live in our culture, they have to live by our customs—If someone let a Bengal Tiger lose on Telegraph and he killed someone, it would be easy to say that the tiger was only reacting as he would have in the jungle, and therefore he couldn't be blamed for murder—

—(cont.) But does that excuse the moron who opened the cage? (If those "imported" football players can't act civilized, send them back where they came from!)

a4.1.   They did. And took advantage of it.

a4.2.   What is our culture? I don't want to be part of a culture/society that says Rape is OK.

Series c

1.   The Big Game = The Big Scam. Boo U.C. Rapists!

c2.   Excuse me, but there was no trial. Isn't the law innocent until proven guilty, or does that apply only to non-violent suspects? I'm a feminist, but not a vigilante—

c3.1.   Excuse me, but they "apologized". If they didn't do it, what did they apologize for?

c3.2.   You're no feminist.

c3.3.   Wake up! 4 guys raped a woman and got away with it. and you're worried about the football team's reputation. Believe me, they have the one they deserve.

c4.1. (c3.3) Oh fuck you—four guys are not the whole team! Don't make the team scapegoats.

c4.2. (c3.3) How could the team have stopped the rape?

c5.1. (c4.1) I agree. People generalize too much.

c5.2. (c4.1) Don't make an innocent girl a scapegoat—next time it'll be you, or your best friend, or your sister, or your daughter! *¼ of all women will have sex forced upon them at some point in their life. . . .

c6. (c5.2)   Bitch! Perhaps that's true, but will it be by a Cal Football Player? Get Real! Any Man can rape!

Series d

d1.   You women all talk as if the only thing a woman has of value in the world is her virginity/sexuality Is sex so sacred for ♀ and not for ♂ ? Is the stigma associated with screwing 4 guys at once equivalent to rape? Maybe she did wake up the next day and couldn't live with last night's decision. I believe it was her choice to be drunk as hell w/4 macho jerks. (And I mean choice not fault.)

d2.   ]women[

]other[
]and not the[
no one Deserves
to be raped

d3.   right on. why is everyone so quick to blame the victim?

d4.   No one's saying she deserved to be raped—but noone deservs to
be wrongly accused of a crime even rape—either! Especially when
they are presumed guilty by the community without even a trial.
(since there wasn't enough evidence to have one)—who deserves
that ?? Read your constitution lately?

d5.   Who decided that there wasn't enough evidence. And was he
right? I don't think so!

Series **e**

e1.   OBSESSED W/RAPE OR WHAT?

e2.   your not? why writing?

Notes

1. See Tara Goldstein (this volume) for an example of the interworkings of gender,
class, and linguistic oppression.

2. The existence of this genre counters the frequent claims that women avoid
direct confrontation and men are conversationally combative, that women are
interactionally cooperative and men competitive (Maltz & Borker 1982;
Tannen 1990). A great deal of evidence has been amassed against this position
(Eder 1990; Goodwin 1988, 1990; Heath 1983; Schofield 1982).

References

Beck, Evelyn Torton (ed.) (1982). *Nice Jewish girls: A lesbian anthology.* Watertown,
MA: Persephone Press.

Brown, Gillian, and George Yule (1983). *Discourse analysis.* Cambridge: Cambridge
University Press.

Brownmiller, Susan (1975). *Against our will: Men, women, and rape.* New York:
Bantam.

Cole, Caroline (1991). Oh wise women of the stalls. *Discourse and Society* 2(4):
401–11.

Davies, Catherine (1986). The anonymous collective conversations of women's graffiti: An analysis of supportive advice-giving. In Sue Bremner, Noelle Caskey,
and Birch Moonwomon (eds.), *Proceedings of the First Berkeley Women and
Language Conference, 1985.* Berkeley: Berkeley Women and Language Group.
108–34.

Davis, Angela (1981). *Women, race and class.* New York: Random House.

de Certeau, Michel (1984). *The practice of everyday life.* Translated by Steven Rendall. Berkeley: University of California Press.

Eckert, Penelope, and Sally McConnell-Ginet (1992). Think practically and look locally: Language and gender as community-based practice. *Annual Review of Anthropology* 21: 461–90.

——— (this volume). Constructing meaning, constructing selves: Snapshots of language, gender, and class from Belten High.

Eder, Donna (1990). Serious and playful disputes: Variation in conflict talk among female adolescents. In Allen Grimshaw (ed.), *Conflict talk: Sociolinguistic investigations of arguments in conversations.* Cambridge: Cambridge University Press. 67–84.

Faludi, Susan (1991). *Backlash: The undeclared war against American women.* New York: Crown.

Foucault, Michel (1977). *Language, counter-memory, practice.* Translated by Donald Bouchard and Sherry Simon. Oxford: Basil Blackwell.

——— (1980). *Power/knowledge: Selected interviews and other writings, 1972–1977.* Translated by Colin Gordon. Brighton: Harvester.

——— (1981). The order of discourse. In Robert Young (ed.), *Untying the text: A post-structuralist reader.* Translated by Ian McLeod. London: Routledge & Kegan Paul.

French, Marilyn (1992). *The war against women.* New York: Summit.

Goldstein, Tara (this volume). "Nobody is talking bad": Creating community and claiming power on the production lines.

Goodwin, Marjorie (1988). Cooperation and competition across girls' play activities. In Alexandra Todd and Sue Fisher (eds.), *Gender and discourse: The power of talk.* Norwood, NJ: Ablex. 55–94.

——— (1990). *He-said-she-said: Talk as social organization among black children.* Bloomington: Indiana University Press.

Grice, H. Paul (1975). Logic and conversation. In Peter Cole and Jerry Morgan (eds.), *Syntax and semantics 3: Speech acts.* New York: Academic Press. 41–58.

Gumperz, John J. (1982). *Discourse strategies.* Cambridge: Cambridge University Press.

Heath, Shirley Brice (1983). *Ways with words.* Cambridge: Cambridge University Press.

Herring, Susan, Deborah A. Johnson, and Tamra DiBenedetto (this volume). "This discussion is going too far!": Male resistance to female participation on the Internet.

Hymes, Dell (1972). Models of the interaction of language and social life. In John Gumperz and Dell Hymes (eds.), *Directions in sociolinguistics: The ethnography of communication.* New York: Holt, Rinehart & Winston. 35–71.

Lakoff, Robin (this volume). Cries and whispers: The shattering of the silence.

Lave, Jean, and Etienne Wenger (1991). *Situated learning: Legitimate peripheral participation.* New York: Cambridge University Press.

Levinson, Stephen (1983). *Pragmatics.* New York: Cambridge University Press.

Macdonell, Diane (1986). *Theories of discourse: An introduction.* New York: Basil Blackwell.

Major, Clarence (1994). *Juba to jive: A dictionary of African American slang.* Harmondsworth: Penguin.

Maltz, Daniel, and Ruth Borker (1982). A cultural approach to male-female miscommunication. In John Gumperz (ed.), *Language and social identity.* Cambridge: Cambridge University Press. 196–216.

Moonwomon, Birch (1986). Toward a study of lesbian speech. In Sue Bremner, Noelle Caskey, and Birch Moonwomon (eds.), *Proceedings of the First Berkeley Women and Language Conference, 1985.* Berkeley: Berkeley Women and Language Group. 96–107.

—— (1992). Rape, race, and responsibility: A graffiti text political discourse. In Kira Hall, Mary Bucholtz, and Birch Moonwomon (eds.), *Locating power: Proceedings of the Second Berkeley Women and Language Conference.* Berkeley: Berkeley Women and Language Group. 420–29.

Nwoye, Onuigbo (1993). Social issues on walls: Graffiti in university lavatories. *Discourse and Society* 4(4): 419–42.

Pêcheux, Michel (1982). *Language, semantics and ideology: Stating the obvious.* Translated by Harbans Nagpal. London: Macmillan.

Poovey, Mary (1988). *Uneven developments: The ideological work of gender in mid-Victorian England.* Chicago: University of Chicago Press. 1–26.

Russell, Diana (1975). *The politics of rape: The victim's perspective.* New York: Stein & Day.

Schofield, Janet (1982). *Black and white in school: Trust, tension, or tolerance.* New York: Praeger.

Sheldon, Amy (1990). Pickle fights: Gendered talk in preschool disputes. *Discourse Processes* 13: 5–31.

—— (1992). Conflict talk: Sociolinguistic challenges to self-assertion and how young girls meet them. *Merrill Palmer Quarterly* 38: 95–117.

Smith, Valerie (1990). Split affinities: The case of interracial rape. In Marianne Hirsch and Evelyn Fox Keller (eds.), *Conflicts in feminism.* New York: Routledge. 271–87.

Smitherman, Geneva (1994). *Black talk: Words and phrases from the hood to the amen corner.* Boston: Houghton Mifflin.

Stubbs, Michael (1988). *Discourse analysis: The sociolinguistic analysis of natural language.* Chicago: University of Chicago Press.

Tannen, Deborah (1990). *You just don't understand: Women and men in conversation.* New York: Ballantine.

Thomas, David (1979). *Archaeology.* New York: Holt, Rinehart & Winston.

Wenger, Etienne (1993). *Communities of practice.* Cambridge: Cambridge University Press.

Constructing Meaning, Constructing Selves

Snapshots of Language, Gender, and Class from Belten High

Penelope Eckert and Sally McConnell-Ginet

During the course of their lives, people move into, out of, and through communities of practice, continually transforming identities, understandings, and worldviews.[1] Progressing through the life span brings ever-changing kinds of participation and nonparticipation, contexts for "belonging" and "not belonging" in communities. A single individual participates in a variety of communities of practice at any given time, and over time: the family, a friendship group, an athletic team, a church group. These communities may be all-female or all-male; they may be dominated by women or men; they may offer different forms of participation to women or men; they may be organized on the presumption that all members want (or will want) heterosexual love relations. Whatever the nature of one's participation in communities of practice, one's experience of gender emerges in participation as a gendered community member with others in a variety of communities of practice.

It is for this reason that we (Eckert and McConnell-Ginet 1992a, b) argued for grounding the study of gender and language in detailed investigations of the social and linguistic activities of specific communities of practice. Following the lead of a number of feminist social theorists (see, e.g., Bem 1993; Butler 1993; Connell 1987; Thorne 1993; di Leonardo 1991), we warned against taking gender as given, as natural. A major moral we drew is that the study of sex differences in language use does not automatically give insight into how gender and language interact in particular communities of practice. Rather, we proposed, the social and linguistic practices through which people construct themselves as different and as similar must be carefully examined. Many of the chapters in this volume, especially those in Part 3, aim to do exactly that.

Gender constructs are embedded in other aspects of social life and in the construction of other socially significant categories such as those involving class, race, or ethnicity. This implies that gender is not a matter of two homogeneous social categories, one associated with being female and the other with being male. Just as important, it also implies that no simple attributes of a person, however complex a combination is considered, can completely determine how that person is socially categorized by herself or by others, and how she engages in social practice. Suppose, for example, we categorize someone as a heterosexual middle-class African American professional woman. The attributes that make up this particular characterization—*heterosexual, middle-class, African American, professional,* and *woman*—all draw on reifications that emerge from and constitute conventional maps of social reality. These reifications structure perceptions and constrain (but do not completely determine) practice, and each is produced (often reproduced in much the same form) through the experience of those perceptions and constraints in day-to-day life.

Language is a primary tool people use in constituting themselves and others as "kinds" of people in terms of which attributes, activities, and participation in social practice can be regulated. Social categories and characterizations are human creations; the concepts associated with them are not preformed, waiting for labels to be attached, but are created, sustained, and transformed by social processes that importantly include labeling itself. And labeling is only part of a more complex sociolinguistic activity that contributes to constituting social categories and power relations among members of a community. How people use language—matters of "style" that include grammar, word choice, and pronunciation—is a very important component of self-constitution. How people talk expresses their affiliations with some and their distancing from others, their embrace of certain social practices and their rejection of others—their claim to membership (and to particular forms of membership) in certain communities of practice and not others. And within communities of practice, the continual modification of common ways of speaking provides a touchstone for the process of construction of forms of group identity—of the meaning of belonging to a group (as a certain kind of member). It is a resource for the orientation of the community and its participants to other nearby communities and to the larger society, a resource for constructing community members' relation to power structures, locally and more globally.

To give concrete substance to these abstract musings, we will examine some social and linguistic practices within several communities of practice related to one another and to a particular institution, a public high school in suburban Detroit. Our data come from Penny's sociolinguistic study[2] of a speech community as defined by that high school, which we shall call Belten High. For this study, Penny did three years of participant-observation in the early 1980s, following one graduating class of six hundred students through their sophomore, junior, and senior years. (More detailed reports on various aspects of this project appear in, e.g., Eckert 1988, 1989, 1990b). Her research yielded a taped corpus of about three hundred hours of speech, including one-on-one interviews, group discussions, and a variety of public events. The original study did not focus on gender issues, and the fact that so much material relevant for thinking about gender construction emerged anyway is testimony to its pervasiveness in this community's practices. In this chapter, we draw on eighty of the one-on-one interviews, emphasizing phonological variation (in particular, pronunciation of certain vowel sounds) and sample stretches of students' talk with Penny about social categories and socially relevant attributes. We use a combination of linguistic and ethnographic data to give a partial picture of how gender, class, and power relations are being mutually constructed in this particular setting. What kinds of identities and relations are the students making for themselves and for others? How does this construction of their social landscape happen? How do different communities of practice get constituted and what is their relation to one another and to the institution of the school? Being female or male, athletic, studious, popular, a cigarette smoker, a beer drinker; staying out all night; wearing certain kinds of clothes and makeup; owning a car; using a certain vocabulary and style of speech; engaging in heterosexual activities such as cross-sex dating; wearing a constant smile; using illicit drugs—constellations of such attributes and activities constitute the raw materials from which the social categories of the school are constructed. It is the significance attached to these constellations and their constituents—their socially recognized meaning—that turns them into socially relevant categories mediating power, affiliation, desire, and other social relations.

Who lunches with whom? Who talks to whom about what? Who touches whom and how (and where)? Who controls which resources? Who is admired or despised by whom? When the answers to such questions depend systematically on people's being classified as belonging to one category rather than another, the social categories involved can interact with communities of practice in two ways: (1) they often form the basis for the formation of category-exclusive communities of practice, defined by their mutual orientation to the school and engaged in finding a mutual life in the school based in this orientation; and (2) the categories themselves and the opposition between them can become the object of practice, defining a larger but more loosely connected community of practice focused on conflict over the practices of everyday life in the shared space community members inhabit. Thus, communities of practice can overlap in significant ways. What makes them all communities of practice is not any shared attributes of their members but the orientation of those members to joint participation in some endeavor, and in a set of social practices that grow around that endeavor.

Schooling in Corporate Practice

The U.S. public high school is designed to dominate and structure the lives of the adolescent age group—not just to provide academic and vocational instruction but to provide a comprehensive social environment. The school organizes sports, musical and dramatic groups, social occasions such as dances and fairs, some social service such as canned-food drives, and governing activities in the form of such things as class offices and student government. These activities are not simply organized by the school for the students. Rather, the school provides the resources and authority for the students themselves to organize these activities, and institutional status and privilege for those who do the organizing. Although an organizational framework with adult supervisors is provided—for example, athletic teams have coaches, bands and choirs have directors, clubs have faculty sponsors—students themselves play substantial organizing roles (e.g., as team captains or club officers).

It is important to emphasize that although participation in this extracurricular sphere is optional, it is also expected. Extracurricular activities are viewed as integral to one's participation in school, and indeed, one's extracurricular career constitutes an important part of an entrance dossier for colleges and universities. The school is the community in which adolescents are expected to participate—a community extracted from the larger adult-dominated community that it serves. It is seen as a community designed especially for—and in the interests of—adolescents, and adolescents are expected to base not only their academic lives but their informal social lives in that institution. Adolescents who do not embrace this community are, therefore, seen as deviant, as "not caring."

Students are expected to compete for control of roles and resources in the production of extracurricular activities, and to base their identities and alliances in this production. This leads to a tight student hierarchy based on institutional roles and on relations with others (both student and adult) in institutional roles—in short, a hierarchy based on control of aspects of the institutional environment, and on the freedoms and privileges associated with this control. Those who participate in this hierarchy are not simply participating in individual interesting activities; they are building extracurricular careers and engaging in a corporate practice that has as much to do with visibility in and control over the school environment as with the content of the individual activities that constitute their careers.

For students participating fully in the extracurricular sphere, then, social status is constructed as a function of institutional status, personal identities are intertwined with institutional identities, and social networks are intertwined with institutional networks. Embedded as they are in a mobile hierarchy, social relations are competitive, and they change with institutional responsibilities, alliances, and status. Students are constrained to monitor their behavior carefully in order to maintain a "responsible" public persona, and to focus their interactions on the network of people in the same school and even the same graduating class who are engaged in this endeavor. In this way, the school offers an introduction into corporate practice. Of course, corporate status and its concomitant freedoms and privileges come at a price. Participating in this hierarchy requires a certain acceptance of the institution's rules and values as articulated by the ultimate institutional authorities, the adults who occupy official positions in the school.

In schools across the United States, communities of practice develop around participation in parts of the extracurricular sphere (a cheerleading squad, a "popular" crowd, a class cabinet), and a broader overarching community of practice develops around engagement in the extracurricular sphere and the mutual building of extracurricular careers. Participants build careers in the extracurricular sphere and achieve a merging of their personal and school networks, their personal and school-based identities. This is a community based on an adolescent version of corporate, middle-class social practice. Although this specific community of practice arises in response to the school institution, it is based to some extent in communities that have been emerging since childhood. Indeed, across the country, the students involved in the school's corporate affairs tend to be college-bound and to come from the upper part of the local socioeconomic range. Many of them have already learned aspects of corporate practice at home, both through exposure to their own parents' participation in such practice and through the middle-class family practices and values that support corporate practices. (For example, middle-class parents generally do not encourage their children to "hang out" in the neighborhood but to cultivate friendships through school; and they commonly discourage their children from having a best friend in favor of having a more fluid network.)

At the same time that these students base their activities, networks, and identities in the corporate sphere of the school, others reject the school as the basis of social life. Indeed, in polar opposition to the corporate community of practice, there is a community of practice based on autonomy from the school. These students base their social lives not in the school but in the local neighborhoods and in the urban–suburban area more generally. Their friendships are not limited to the school or to their own age group, and their activities tend to arise from their alliances rather than vice versa. These students are largely from the lower end of the local socioeconomic hierarchy and embrace, strongly and consciously, working-class norms of egalitarianism and solidarity. They consciously oppose the norm of corporate practice in the school, and they reject the institution as a locus of identity and social life. Because they are bound for the work force immediately after high school, furthermore, the extracurricular sphere has no hold on them as qualification for future success; rather, it appears to them as a form of infantilization and as a hierarchy existing only for its own sake. Their focus is more on the local area and its resources for entertainment, excitement, and employment; they reject environments developed especially for their own age group and seek to participate in what they see as the real world. Furthermore, in this rejection of the school's adolescent environment, they seek independence from adult control over everyday life, their bodies, activities, and consumption practices. This latter oppositional category always has a name: *hoods, greasers, stompers, stoners, grits* (depending on the region and the era) and, in the school in question, *burnouts* (or *burns*) or *jellies* (or *jells*, from *jellybrain*). The two main local names reflect the symbolic status of controlled-substance use for the oppositional category in this particular school at this particular time. These names are used by all in the school, and embraced by those to whom they apply as well as to those who choose to apply it to others. On the other hand, the activities-oriented category in schools is not always given a name, a point we will discuss in the next section. The group may, however, be called something like *collegiates, preppies, soshes* (from *socialite*), or, as in the school in question and other schools around the region, *jocks*, drawing on the symbolic status of athletic achievement for this social group.

In general usage, *jock* designates a committed athlete, and the prototypical jock is male. Except for the jocks themselves, students in Belten High use *jock* to designate a network of girls and boys who achieve visibility through their committed engagement in school-sponsored activities. (As we explain in the next section, this labeling dispute connects to the absence of a name for the activities-oriented category in some schools.) Although sports do provide the surest route to jockdom, especially for boys, other activities also confer that status.

The name *jock* points, then, to one important way in which school corporate culture constructs male dominance. The male varsity athlete is seen by the school institution as representing the school's interests, and this gives him institutional status and privilege. Interscholastic competition affords boys' varsity athletics the most direct way of establishing and defending the school's status and honor. Thus, the status that a boy gains in varsity sports is connected directly to the luster he brings to the school— not to himself personally. This is a useful lesson to learn. Achieving individual status through one's efforts on behalf of an institution—being able to identify one's own interests with institutional interests— is a hallmark of much successful competition in adult corporate practice.

Athletics is also the route that boys are expected to take to prominence. In a conversation with Penny, a group of male athletes extolled the skill, "coolness," and hard work of a male student-government officer. But they pointed out that he had had no choice but to seek a key student office because he wasn't athletic. In general, male athletes see nonathletic activities as an aside: as something one can do casually—because they require no special skill—but possibly as one's civic duty. And the status associated with varsity athletics can be a tremendous advantage for a star athlete who chooses to seek student office, an advantage that can overturn the candidacy of a nonathlete with a long history of experience and service.

Although male varsity athletes can count on their accomplishments to establish their value to the community, their status, there are no parallel accomplishments in school that lend the same kind of status for girls. Because sports still do not yield the same payoff for girls as for boys (in the section "Sports and Toughness" we discuss some of the reasons for this, and also note some changes in progress), the domain in which girls are expected to achieve prominence is already designated as second-best. Girls may receive recognition through prominence in student government, through cheerleading, or through participation in musical or dramatic activities. But for both girls and boys, achieving recognition through these activities seldom if ever evokes the kind of vicarious pride of schoolmates that gives good athletes their special distinction. The female supportive role is formalized in high school in the pairing of such activities as girls' cheerleading and boys' varsity athletics, and in the feminization of organizational activities such as holding bake sales, organizing dances, and the like. Girls tend to do the majority of the behind-the-scenes work for school activities; boys predominate in top managerial roles (class president, student-body president, and so on).

Thus, in a number of ways school corporate culture continues students' education in the male dominance that is characteristic of most American institutions and American society at many levels. It also continues and indeed intensifies education in what Rich (1980) dubbed "compulsory heterosexuality." High school brings an institutionalization of traditional gender arrangements, heterosexuality, and romance. The institutionalization of the heterosexual couple is embodied formally in the king and queen of the high school homecoming and prom. Heterosexuality and romance are also publicly constructed in high school through formal activities like dances and informally in the status of dating and in each class's "famous couple." When the yearbook depicts a "cutest couple," the relation between social status and success in the heterosexual marketplace is made visible.

Although adult corporate practice does not recognize the "cutest couple" in an institution, socializing outside the workplace is still largely driven by business and professional alliances and organized around heterosexual marriage partners. The support role of female cheerleaders for male athletes is succeeded by wifely hosting and presumptive willingness to follow wherever a husband's career trajectory leads. But there are signs of rupture in this conflation of the personal and the institutional in both adolescent and adult practice, and it is driven by ongoing larger-scale changes in gender relations. Just as girls are beginning to reject cheerleading at boys' sports events in favor of playing on their own teams, corporate wives' own careers are making them unavailable to host dinner parties. Gender transformations have begun to challenge the all-encompassing character of corporate practice, albeit on only a small scale. And in a few places, openly gay or lesbian high schoolers are beginning to resist the heterosexual imperative of traditional mixed-sex schools. For example, a group of Los Angeles high schoolers recently organized an alternative "gay prom," which was reported nationally. Fifteen years ago gay and lesbian students were not "out" at Belten High. We don't know to what extent this may have changed, but it is a safe bet that when the yearbook depicts a "cutest couple," they still won't be of the same sex.

The names of the categories that correspond to *jock* and *burnout* at Belten High, and the specific styles and activities that signal their opposition (use of controlled substances, leisure activities, clothing, musical tastes, territorial specialization, and the like), vary regionally and locally and change through time. But it is close to universal in U.S. public high schools for two opposed social categories to arise that represent some kind of class split and that constitute class cultures within the school. And so far as we know, the construction of these cultural groups always interacts in interesting ways with the construction of gender identities and relations (although of course the nature of that interaction may vary significantly). In most U.S. schools, race and ethnicity also enter into the interaction, but in this particular virtually all-white school such social dimensions are salient only inasmuch as they provide the overarching discourse within which whiteness is constructed and differentiated. Indeed, everything that we have discussed and will discuss is at the same time part of the construction of white hegemony.

The jocks and the burnouts arise as class-based communities of practice in response to the school institution. Each is based in the endeavor to build a way of life in and out of school that makes sense and that provides the means to construct valued identities. The jocks emerge out of many students' shared desire to build lives within the school institution and to develop identities and careers based in the extracurricular sphere. The burnouts emerge out of many students' need to find ways to exist in the school that neither implicate them in corporate practice nor cost them their participation in the institution, ways that at the same time allow them to foster a strong sense of identity and participation in their own broader community.

The jocks' and burnouts' opposed orientations to the school, to institutions, and to life are the terrain for daily struggle over the right to define school, adolescence, values. Both categories seek autonomy, but in different places. Jocks seek autonomy in the occupation of adultlike roles within the institution, in building individual identities through school-based careers, and in benefiting from the kinds of institutional freedoms and perks that are the rewards for participation in these careers. Burnouts seek autonomy in the avoidance of adult-run institutions, in laying claim to adult prerogatives, and in the development of networks and activities in the local community, which will be the site of their adult lives. The jocks work the center of the school institution; the burnouts work its margins.

Because it is so basic to life in school, the jock–burnout opposition comes to define the landscape of identities at Belten. Those who are neither jocks nor burnouts commonly refer to themselves as *in-betweens*, and nuances of identity throughout the school are described in the same terms that construct these two categories. Thus, the jock–burnout opposition constitutes the dominant discourse of identity in the school, and one could say that orientation to that opposition engages almost every student in the school in an overarching community of practice. But although both communities emerge from strongly held and positive values, they do not emerge as equal within the school. The jocks embody the institution—their personal relations are inseparable from formal institutional relations and their activities are inseparable from school activities. This bestows an institutional legitimacy and function on their activities and their alliances, including their heterosexual alliances, that stand in stark contrast to the illegitimate status accorded to burnouts' activities and alliances. The coconstruction of social category and gender is indeed intimately connected to the construction of institutional power, a power in which girls and boys do not share equally.

Labeling, Conflict, and Hegemony

Gender and social category are not constructed independently of each other, nor do they exist independently of practice; rather, they are continually coconstructed in the course of day-to-day practice. In the same way, labels do not exist independently of the social practice in which categories are constructed; the use of labels is not simply a matter of fitting a word to a pre-existing category. Rather, labels arise in use in relation to real people in real situations: people label as they chat, make observations and judgments about people, point people out to others, challenge people, and so on. It is through such activities that labels are endowed with meaning. We have already referred to some students as *jocks*, others as *burnouts*. But this is misleading inasmuch as it obscures the very important fact that labeling is a socially significant and contested practice within the school and is part of the continual construction of the categories it designates. The use of the term *jock* or *burnout*, and of terms related to the salient issues around which these categories are constructed (e.g., *slutty, cool, snobby*), is part of the process of constituting categories and identities.

Students coming into the school see the institution as unchanging—they see institutional roles waiting to be filled. But they see their participation or nonparticipation in the school as a creative endeavor. Even though there have "always been" jocks and burnouts, girls and boys, students coming into high school are actively and mutually engaged in constituting selves within the constraints of what has, in their view, always been—and engaging with those constraints in the process.

The jocks and the burnouts seek to define right and appropriate practices, given their relation to the institution of school. Each sees the other community of practice as embodying wrong and inappropriate practices.

For the burnouts, the jocks are "about" competition, hierarchy, advantage, elitism, ambition, image-building. Girl jocks especially are seen as phony, as obsessed with popularity. For the jocks, the burnouts are "about" drugs, trouble, hedonism, lack of ambition. And girl burnouts are often seen by jocks as sleazy, if not slutty. This conflict about category "content" can present itself as a dispute over what category labels "really" mean, but of course words as such are never the real issue. The real issue is the normativity of particular practices and the deviance of others. In the following sections, we will examine labeling practices as part of the construction of social category and gender (along with other aspects of identity such as class, age, and so on). We begin with the issue of what it means to have a label at all.

Because of the deep ideological nature of the split between jocks and burnouts, it is not surprising that the terms *jock* and *burnout* are used differently by people in different places in the school. As we have noted, jocks resist accepting this label—or indeed any label—as a name for a social category defined by extracurricular orientation. Jocks, and particularly male athletic jocks, promote exclusive use of the term *jock* to refer to someone as an athlete. This is illustrated by the following response by a male varsity athlete to Penny's question, which calls the very term into question (*I don't know really ... what that means*):[3]

(1)   DO YOU CONSIDER YOURSELF A JOCK? Somewhat I guess, yeah.
       Just—I don't know really what, you know, what that means. Just, I
       play sports and stuff I guess, you know.

In accepting a self-designation *jock* purely on the basis of athletics, jocks reject any "derivative" meanings. This has more than one effect. Although "playing sports and stuff" might in principle be socially no more consequential than preferring apples to oranges, the status of *jock* is not a socially neutral one. The jock (male) athletes' use of the term *jock* to refer to someone as "simply" being involved in sports suppresses the connection of that involvement to social status, membership, and opportunities. At the same time, given that within the school this term is used to refer to a more generally powerful group in the institution, laying claim to it for athletes alone can have the effect of emphasizing the centrality of athletes to the institution. This latter effect depends, of course, on others' use of the term as a label for the socially dominant activities-oriented group.

The relation between corporate participation and athletics is brought home particularly in the following quotation from one of the outstanding athletes in the school. He had been participating in an independent soccer league, in which the level of play was far above that in the school; here he explains why he gave up the league to play for the school:

(2) WHEN YOU HAVE A TEAM LIKE THAT WHY DO YOU GO INTO HIGH SCHOOL SOCCER? I don't, well, because—because that's—it's—you know, you want to play—recognition, I don't know. We should have stayed but what you do is, when- you—there's high school sports, more people are apt to play that than play in another league, you know, because you have the recognition, scholarships, like that.

In spite of the male athletes' insistence on the narrow meaning, most people in Belten do not use the term *jock* to refer to a person in school simply as an athlete. Rather, they use it to talk about a community of practice: all the people, female and male, who build their lives around school activities. In example (3), a burnout boy directly challenges the equation of jockdom and participation in sports proposed by the (athletic) jock:

(3) I—well—some kids uh who went out for football in seventh grade turned into jocks. Pretty much. But it doesn't—you can—it does-n't make you a jock if you go out and play a sport. Because I played in football in junior high and I wasn't considered a jock. I used to get high before the games.

Being an athlete doesn't make you a jock if you don't adhere to jock values. Here we see that jocks ought not to get high—or at least not be so overt in their defiance of school regulations (the ambivalence of jocks in relation to substance use is discussed in the section "Sports and Toughness.")

Only one male jock in the corpus explicitly admitted that the label could legitimately cover more than athletes. He was a former class president and a talented musician but not an athlete. Note that he does not call himself a *jock* but does acknowledge that athleticism is not all there is to jockdom:

(4) You get your super jocks that—hell they play track and basketball and baseball, and I'm sure those people are going to—"Hey, jock!" That's their middle name practically. But, um, I think you don't have to play sports to be a jock.

In fact, this boy, a leading singer in the school, recognizes that he is frequently referred to as a *choir jock*. The choir, which travels internation-ally, is a prestigious activity in the school and is similar to sports in bring-ing recognition to the school through competition with representatives of other schools. As described by two different choir members, students have specified a difference between a member of the choir and a choir jock: a choir jock is a choir member who gets involved in more than just the singing:

(5)   ... that's that clique. That's what everybody knows about, the concert choir jocks ... I guess it's the officers, you know, the people that are involved, like Dan Smart, our president. I don't know, he's, you know, he's always involved in choir. Then there's Cheryl Smith. Herbie Jackson, he's always, you know, that's his highlight of our school.

(6)   IS THERE A CROWD OF PEOPLE THAT ARE CHOIR JOCKS? Oh, yeah. Definitely. We always talk about them, Kim and I.... We're not involved in choir that much. Yeah I mean we go to a few activities once in a while, but we don't make sure we attend all of them.

But why do so many jocks protest being labeled as members of a social category? Why do they keep trying to explain their being called *jocks* as just a matter of describing athleticism, a socially neutral attribute? A plausible explanation lies in the near-hegemony jocks achieve during the course of the transition from junior high to the senior year of high school. That ascendancy is threatened by being seen as such; jocks' interests require obscuring the social processes that subordinate nonjocks generally and burnouts in particular. It is important for jocks not to see themselves as denying others access to valuable resources by exclusionary processes. It is also important for them to constitute as normative the activities on which their community of practice centers and from which they reap advantage, with those not so engaged defined as socially deviant and thus directly responsible for any disadvantages they may suffer in the school. If the dominant category is not even labeled (and, as we noted earlier, in many schools it is not), then its distinctive interests are somewhat easier to ignore, its hegemonic control over social values and institutional norms more readily established. Two category labels in direct opposition reflect a live ongoing social struggle.

The jocks' status became unmarked in the course of junior high school. The jock and burnout categories reportedly emerged in seventh grade as apparently equal rivals, with core people in them pursuing different activities and espousing different values. In the following quotation, one burnout girl describes the original split in junior high as just such a matter of competing values and choices; she notes explicitly that category labels were used by each group to "put down" the other:

(7)   Yeah, OK, there was, you know, kids that got high and smoked and thought they were really cool like us ((laughter)) and then the

other ones that didn't party or anything, were always getting into
sports and being goody-goodies and, you know, all that stuff so we
just started putting down those people, calling them *jocks* and
everything, and they call us *burns*, and that was just going on for a
while, while we were all at [junior high].

A self-designated "in-between"—a girl with primary burnout connections
and interests but also with many jock ties and interests—describes quite
poignantly the regulative power of the polarized labeling and the conflicts,
internal and public, that those labeling practices helped produce:

(8)   That's—that's where all the—the jock/burn or the jock/jelly thing
       started. Because I didn't hear anything about it in elementary
       school. But once I hit [junior high], you know, that's all you heard
       was, "She's a jock," "She's a jell," you know. And that's all it was. You
       were either one. You weren't an in-between, which I was. I was an
       in-between ((laughter)) because here I was, I played volleyball, now
       what, three years. Baseball, I'll be going on my eighth year, OK? So,
       I get along really good with, quote, jocks, OK, and I get along real-
       ly good with jellies, because I'm right—I'm stuck right in the mid-
       dle. And in my ninth-grade and tenth-grade year, that kind of tore
       me apart a little bit too. Because I didn't—my parents wanted me
       to make a decision. "Now which way are you going to go?"

Near-hegemony had, however, been achieved by the beginning of high
school. Early on in her fieldwork, one of the burnout boys asked Penny
whether she'd yet talked to any "normal" people, reflecting his (perhaps
wry) admission of being relegated to deviant status. With apparently less
ironic distance, a girl who is a star athlete and a popular jock denies hearing
people insult one another by labeling. Rather, according to her, the categories keep enough distance that there is no call for such activity:

(9)   The jocks sort of stayed to themselves, and the burnouts stayed to
       themselves and everybody else kind of stayed to themselves too.
       So you really—if you didn't have to you didn't mix.

She then responds to Penny's query as to whether she thinks of jocks and
burnouts as separate groups:

(10)   The burns, yes. Well, not so much in high school. Like jocks—you're
       not really aware of it.

Though jock hegemony is not total, there is every indication that jocks often manage to present themselves and be taken as the "unmarked" or "default" category, of which "you're not really aware." Only the opponents of the institution are seen as taking a stand with respect to the institution. Although jocks are highly visible, many no longer see themselves as actively orienting toward institutional values in opposing burnouts. Rather, their own attitudes and choices seem "normal" or inevitable in the absence of some kind of social pathology. They no longer see burnouts as in serious conflict with them, presumably at least in part because they now are more or less sure that burnouts will never "lead" them, will not be in controlling positions. In the following example, a jock girl from a burnout neighborhood talks about being the only jock at the bus stop:

(11) But, you know, it doesn't really bother me, I just figure ((laughter)) who cares what they think of me, you know, they're not—they're no uh, you know, president, that they can cut me down.

Early on in the process of constructing institutional affiliation and opposition and the other aspects of class and gender practice found in the school, jock ascendancy was being asserted more directly, according to this jock boy:

(12) There was like—at least once a week it was, "Jocks are going to fight jells after school," you know. DID THEY REALLY? DID YOU GET IN FIGHTS OR WAS IT JUST A LOT OF TALK? Never. Talk. They started it every time. We'd about kill them. Because we had the whole football team, and they wanted to fight the football team. You know. DO YOU REMEMBER WHICH GUYS WANTED TO GET IN FIGHTS? None of the guys on the football team, really, you know—they didn't care.

The quotation reveals an awareness of *jock* as a category label used in conflict. It also indicates the speaker's bravado and (retrospective) claim of fearlessness. We now turn to the matter of this focus on physical prowess in constructing class-based male social relations.

Sports and Toughness: Category Meanings and Male Power

Although the jock boy quoted in example (12) asserts that physical strength was concentrated in jock hands, the jock–burnout split really became visible and contentious when some excellent athletes among the burnouts refused to play on school teams (cf. example (3)). Both jock and burnout boys staunchly asserted that their group could beat the other in any physical contest, whether a game or a fight.

As a number of writers have observed (see, for example, Connell 1987 and Segal 1990), practices aimed at developing and displaying confidence and superior physical strength and skill play a central role in constituting a hegemonic masculinity in the United States and many other Western nations. *Hegemonic* here implies not pervasiveness in fact but power as a (partly fantasy) ideal of manliness. The body aimed at is muscular and tough, able successfully to withstand physical attacks and to defend others against them, able to win in attacks on others. Competitive sports are a primary arena in which such a masculinity is constituted, at least as an ideal.

Organized sports continue to enter into the practices constituting adult masculinities. Even relatively inactive men watch and talk about football games every week of the season. A number of writers have noted the prominence of sports metaphors in business talk, politics, and other areas of corporate life. That "level playing fields" have generally not been thought of as having females running down them is clear. The "locker-room talk" that prototypically occurs among teammates before and after games constructs women as men's sexual prey. Male camaraderie excludes women and includes other men as fellow "tough guys," to be slapped on the back, playfully punched around in certain contexts.

Such kinds of talk and bodily demeanor are, of course, not confined to the corporate world but are part of many male-dominated workplaces. The form in corporate lunchrooms is different from that in factory cafeterias, but a "macho" style of masculinity and male-male interaction rooted in sports and, more generally, physical toughness is common. Indeed, working-class men are often taken as exemplary of this ideal. Jobs that institutionalize force, strength, and even violence—such as building trades, police and prison work, military combat—are low on the class hierarchy but high on the scale of hegemonic masculinity.[4]

Although the burnouts in this school are certainly not the super-tough gang members that are so frequently studied in the city, they are urban-oriented and pride themselves on their relation to the streets: to fights, encounters with the police, the criminal justice system. Much of the early oppositional behavior between jocks and burnouts in elementary school involved contests of physical prowess, both athletic and combative challenges. The burnouts were viewed as "tough," and the jocks were hard-pressed to maintain their own prowess in the face of the burnout challenge.

Hegemonic masculinity emphasizes the possibility of physical force. It has been a central symbolic component in constructing heterosexual men as different from both women and homosexual men—in principle able to beat up either. Of course, both women and gay men have begun to challenge this view of straight men's superiority in physical strength, as attested by the enormous increase, in recent years, in female participation in organized sports and such activities as body-building and by the emergence of the "clone" style among gay men since the gay liberation movement began. But a focus on physical strength remains prominent in constituting heterosexual masculinity and, albeit in different ways, in constructing the picture of a prototypical jock and a prototypical burnout.

For the jocks, then, this physical prowess centers on participation in school-sponsored sports, violence that is tamed and put into service for the institution. The notion that jocks have tamed their violence is a crucial aspect of a more general emphasis on the control of one's urges that is an important component of corporate practice. This control is seen as requiring additional strength and autonomy. (In the section "Snobs and Sluts" we discuss how this control translates into control of sexual urges for jock girls.)

Although girls' varsity athletics is increasing in importance at Belten High as elsewhere, it still has not achieved the same institutional importance as boys'. This is only partly because girls' sports are less well attended and thus girls are less able to bring glory to the school and vicariously to those who identify with it. It is also important that the association of the athlete with physical prowess conflicts with feminine norms, with notions of how a (heterosexual) girl "should" look and behave. Heterosexual femininity is constructed as directly contrasting with the superiority in physical strength embodied in hegemonic masculinity. Too much athleticism and physicality in a girl suggests a "butch" style of femaleness. Thus, it is problematic for an athletic girl to refer to herself as a *jock* because of the "unfeminine" image that the label implies. In example (13) an accomplished female athlete who is part of the popular crowd denies being a jock:

(13)   ... like there's some girls that play baseball and basketball and track, and they're just always—they play football and they just do everything, you know, the real, you know, girl—you can tell, they walk down the halls pushing each other, and, you know. That kind of jock. Yeah, yeah, those kind you know? I wouldn't call my- myself a jock, I'd say. I can be athletic or something like that, but, like people don't call me *jock*, you know.

The disassociation of femininity and athletic prowess presents a powerful double bind for girls, for varsity sports are seen as the ultimate demonstration of accomplishment (and as a kind of accomplishment with greater institutional status than a superb artistic performance). The association of sports with accomplishment is commonly contrasted to other visible school activities, particularly those that are associated with female status, which are seen as relying on popularity. This emerges in the conversation of both female and male jocks, as in the following female athlete's observation, when discussing whether it is necessary to know the right people in order to participate in many activities in high school:

(14) You can't say that for the team sports and stuff—you have to be
      good. But it is nice to know those people, and to be in the com-
      mittees and stuff you still have to be interviewed, but if you're
      interviewed by kids and they like you, you're probably in. The uh
      student council, that's—if you know a lot of people, that's just like
      popularity, sort of. Yeah. I don't know if it is all popularity, but—

Being the girlfriend of a star male athlete is at least as sure a route to female achievement in the jock network as being a star athlete oneself (and perhaps less risky, given the possibility of jeopardizing success in the heterosexual marketplace through being too athletic). We discuss jock girls' pursuit of popularity in the next section. Popularity draws not on the athleticism and physicality associated with prototypical male jockdom but on its visibility.

For burnouts, the labels at Belten focus on substance use rather than physicality. But being a burnout invokes an orientation away from school and toward urban streets and the toughness to walk them freely, to be able to protect oneself in a fight. The image is decidedly not feminine. Although burnout girls can fight, they do not gain the same status as burnout boys for doing so. On the contrary, being tough in a fight is seen as somewhat admirable for boys and men, but girls' (and women's) fighting is quite generally looked down upon and viewed in terms of kicking and scratching rather than "real punchouts." Further, and more important, although girls can fight among themselves, and a few do, they cannot and do not fight boys. Thus, they cannot walk the urban streets with the same sense of personal autonomy that boys can. Burnout girls remain vulnerable to male violence. They cannot really establish their anti-institutional burnout status through being skilled fighters who need not fear others' attacks on their persons. They can, however, draw on other components of burnout toughness to constitute themselves as true "burns." In the next section, we discuss the important place of "coolness" in burnout girls' construction of themselves.

Popularity and Coolness: Category Meaning and Female Agency
The fundamental meaning of being a jock is orientation toward the institution and the possible rewards for ascending its hierarchical structures. The fundamental meaning of being a burnout is resisting the institution and

its regulative constraints. These fundamental category meanings are, as we have already seen, overlaid with many other issues. In particular, girls are effectively barred from the practices most central to establishing category membership: the pursuit of athletic achievement, on the one hand, and of urban toughness on the other. They must therefore engage in other practices to construct their identities as jocks or as burnouts. The pursuit of popularity for jock girls and of coolness for burnout girls allows them to constitute themselves actively as embodying the same basic meanings as the prototypical category members, their male peers. Going out with a jock boy helps the jock girl achieve popularity; going out with a burnout boy or, even better, someone already out of school, reinforces the burnout girl's claim to coolness. Jock girls are not the only ones pursuing popularity; burnout girls do not monopolize coolness. But popularity and coolness do play central roles in constructing class-based ways of being female. We will start with popularity, but coolness enters in almost immediately as connected to burnout popularity in junior high.

Popularity is a complex that combines some kind of likability and good personhood with visibility, community status, and a large number of contacts. The pursuit of the latter three are integral parts of corporate practice, necessary for gaining control of (and strategically dispensing) resources. Inasmuch as the jocks embody the school institution, their networks in some sense define the school community. Thus, their institutional positions not only lend them opportunities for visibility, contacts, and status but center them in a community circumscribed by the school. A burnout or in-between may well have as many social contacts as a jock, but to the extent that these contacts extend outside the school, they remain "unfocused" and do not contribute to a communally constructed visibility. Furthermore, even if one's many ties are in the school, to the extent that they do not include those in power in the school, they cannot provide the opportunities for visibility that contribute to school popularity.

Burnout girls do sometimes talk of themselves or others in their network as "popular." The rubric, however, is always applied in the past tense when the girls are reminiscing about early junior high and the days when burnouts were still in active competition for school-based prominence. Although this prominence was being constructed within the school population, its focus was not on access to school resources but on access to activities outside and "around" school. A girl whom all the burnouts point to as having been popular in junior high, for example, explains why her crowd was the "big shit crowd":

(15) I just think that we used to have a lot of fun, you know, and a lot of—you know, I mean things going outside of school, you know, and a lot of people, you know, looked up at us, you know—"it's really, cool," you know, "I wish I could."

Another burnout girl tells Penny why she wanted to hang out with this same crowd during junior high school:

(16) HOW DID YOU GET TO BE FRIENDS WITH THOSE PARTICULAR PEO-
PLE? Um, popularity. They—they were the popular ones.... By ninth grade, they were the popular ones and, you know, I wanted to be known, I wanted to be known by the guys, and I wanted to be known by this—and I started, you know, hanging around them.

Popular burnouts were highly visible in school as people to hang around if one wanted to join in their fun and "cool" activities outside school. Coolness, as we will see later, is quite overtly aspired to, and the early burnout popularity was as well. In response to Penny's query about how she started hanging around the popular burnouts in junior high, the speaker we just heard above explains:

(17) Um, well, if I'd hear about, "Well, we're all going over to so-and-so's house tonight," you know, I'd say, "You think you guys'd mind if I came along?" you know, and, you know, just slowly, you know, I started to get to know them. I was—I'm not shy but I'm not out-going either. I'm in-between. So I could really, in a way, ask them, and in a way, try to be accepted. That's why I think I started smoking cig-arettes. That's when I started drinking beer, and all of that stuff.

In the following quotation, a burnout girl talks about two other burnout girls who set out intentionally to become popular in junior high. The speaker is an admirer of Joan, the second girl she mentions, and considers her attempts to become popular to be funny but not reprehensible:

(18) I know that one girl, Sally Stella, she's a—I don't know, she was just trying to make friends with everybody so she could be really popu-lar, you know? And she thought she was so beautiful, and she had so many friends, and—I don't know—and Joan Border, like—you know, she can talk to anybody, and she was making a lot of friends too, like—it was like they were competing or something, her and Sally ... trying to see who could get the most friends and ((laughter)) I don't know.

In junior high school, when the jocks had not yet come to dominate status in the school, they and the burnouts were two separate visible popular crowds competing to define "the good life" in school. Both participated in school activities—burnout girls were cheerleaders, burnout boys played on school teams, and both burnouts and jocks attended school dances and athletic events. However, the two categories engaged in these activities on very different terms. The burnouts viewed school activities as opportunities to "party," and their mixing of school activities with "illicit" activities eventually disqualified them from participation. At the same time, the school's insistence on monitoring these activities as a condition of participation led those who had not been sent away to back away. One might say that the issue of popularity—prominence within the school as someone to hang out with— was closed for the burnouts when they left junior high. This analysis is articulated by two burnout girls:

(19) Girl 1:   Well, nobody's really popular
      Girl 2:   anymore
      Girl 1:   Yeah, but like they were popular then.
      Girl 2:   Then they were, yeah.
      Penny: WHAT DID THAT MEAN?
      Girl 1:   To have them be popular?
      Girl 2:   They were the coolest.
      Girl 1:   Yeah. They were the ones that had girlfriends and
                 boyfriends first. They were the ones to try everything
                 new out first. They hung around all the junior high kids
                 first. And uh, that's-
      Penny :   THEY WERE THE ONES EVERYBODY WANTED TO BE WITH?
      Girl 1:   Yeah, yeah, every time I tried to be with them.

But by high school, the burnouts are firmly oriented outside the school and many refer to jocks in general as *the popular crowd*. Just as jockdom is denied as a social category by those in it, so is the pursuit of popularity by jock girls. In example (20) a girl on the outskirts of the central jock crowd talks about an upwardly mobile friend who left her group to try to get in with the right people:

(20) WHO DO YOU SUPPOSE SHE THOUGHT WERE THE RIGHT PEOPLE?
      Um, the popular, the jock people, I think. That's what I think.

Yet, the pressure to deny an interest in popularity for girls aspiring to jock success is so strong that some will use the term *jock* to mask a concern

with popularity, as shown by this extract in which the girl spoken of in
example (20) is (on a different occasion) talking with Penny:

(21) My girlfriends, we kind of tend towards the—I don't know, I—and
      none of my girlfriends are going out with, um,—I don't, I don't like
      to label people, but, burnouts. We, I guess we, we mainly go ((laugh-
      ter)) out with, I guess, the, the athletes, the jocks and stuff. And, um,
      or the, um, the— I wouldn't say popular crowd, but, you know.

As we discuss further below, jock girls need to be circumspect about their
interest in popularity, but jock boys have a different orientation. For jock
boys, popularity is overwhelmingly viewed in terms of contacts, visibility,
and community status. For them, it is clearly tied up with institutional influence, as shown in one class president's discussion of the inevitability of wanting to be popular. He articulates the separation between popularity and
likability:

(22) It starts in sixth grade, I think. You—you want to be popular because
      you're the oldest in the school. You want people to know you. And
      then once you get into junior high, you just have to be. I mean
      just—not because—see, you want to because you—you feel it's the
      right thing to do. You want to—you know, it's a big thing to be pop-
      ular, but a lot of people want to be popular for the wrong reasons.
      They want to be popular because they think it's going to get them
      friends, or, uh, they think things will be easier if they're popular. But
      it's not like that. In fact, it could backfire. You—you create a lot of
      resentment if you become popular for the wrong reasons.

This boy has a clear sense of the connections among popularity, contacts,
and institutional effectiveness. He displays the sense of institutional
responsibility that won him his position and that indeed made him an
unusually effective student-government officer. One should become popular because "it's the right thing to do"; it doesn't bring one friends or make
life generally "easier." The following jock boy told Penny that although
there is no formula for becoming popular, the sine qua non is getting to
know people:

(23) I think—be really outgoing you know, and don't just stay with one
      group of friends, you know—if you just stay really—if you don't
      ever go out and talk to anybody else, then, you know, nobody's
      never going to know who you are or anything if you're just real-
      ly—stay home all the time, so—be outgoing, I think.

Jock boys will admit to the pursuit of prominence—high visibility—as a means to the end of playing a leadership role in the school, winning in the competitive governance game. Still, prominence achieved through selection to the all-state football team takes much less social effort; achieving for the school is all that is necessary for people to "know who you are" and is much less risky than having to take active steps to get to know people. (We discuss some of these risks in the next section.) Above all, this prominence is clearly based on skill and achievement, not on looks, charm, or some doubtful social "manipulation."

For girls, institutional success derives less from individual achievement than from the kinds of relations they can maintain with others. In the adult corporate world, wives still frequently derive status from their husbands' occupations, secretaries from the institutional positions of their bosses. School-based prominence for girls depends very heavily on ties of friendship or romance with other visible people. The pursuit of popularity for girls involves a careful construction of personhood, although this is not generally acknowledged (Eckert 1990a). Hence the cultivation of attractiveness, both beauty and a pleasing personality, becomes a major enterprise, to which cultivation of individual accomplishment typically takes a back seat. This enterprise, we might point out, is supported by a multibillion-dollar teen magazine industry aimed specifically at adolescent girls, providing them with the technology of beauty and personality (see Talbot, this volume). The adult successors are women's magazines and self-help books (including those to help with communication; see Cameron, forthcoming). Thus trained, women are far more likely than men to be obsessed with being the perfect spouse, the perfect parent, the perfect friend—the perfect person, the most loved and liked. They are far less likely to be obsessed with being the highest-paid CEO or the winningest lawyer or the world's top theoretical linguist—the top star in an openly competitive "game." Personal ambition is not, of course, completely out of the question for girls and women. Feminist challenges over the past 150 years to give middle-class women access to educational and occupational equity have opened some alternative routes for women's success. For adolescent girls, as for women in later stages of life (Holland & Eisenhart 1990), however, such ambition has an uphill battle to wage against the "attractive-person" obsession.

The following description by a "second-tier" jock girl of what constitutes popularity and her account of her fear of really popular people foreground the importance (and fragility) of a carefully constructed persona and especially one that the "right" boys will find appealing:

(24)   I think personality has got to be the number one, you know—
       personality is probably the most important. If you've got a really
       good personality, you know, make people laugh all the time, then
       you're pretty much popular. Good looks is probably second run-
       ner up, real close up there! BUT WHEN YOU'RE TALKING ABOUT
       PERSONALITY ... YOU SAY YOU GOT TO MAKE PEOPLE LAUGH AND
       SO ON, BUT WHAT ELSE IS- Well, just so that when you're around
       them you feel comfortable and not, you know, really tense or any-
       thing—That's probably the best. ARE THERE PEOPLE THAT MAKE
       YOU REALLY TENSE? Yes ((laughter)) LIKE WHO? Um, boys in par-
       ticular. Really popular ones. I get really tense around them. I'm
       not—I don't know. The boy atmosphere is just kind of ((laughter))
       I've really been close to girls all my life. I've really had really close
       friends, so it's kind of hard for me—I get really tense around peo-
       ple like that. But—even still—really popular people, I'm still really
       tense around. Maybe I'll say something wrong, maybe, you know,
       I'll do something wrong, and then they'll hate me, and then
       ((laughter)) you know.

What is essential for jock girls is approval from those already prominent,
especially but not only boys. To be seen by those able to grant entry to the
inner circle as desiring such entry is to jeopardize the chances of getting it.

Coolness, we have already seen, is central to burnout girls' popularity
when being the center of a visible crowd in the school is still an issue. But
even after concern with such popularity is left behind, coolness persists as
the core of burnout status for girls. Coolness is a kind of toughness without
the added implication of physical power associated with male burnouts.
Coolness is a viable alternative to institutional popularity: it asserts independence of institutionally imposed norms, willingness to flaunt the
injunctions of authorities and claim all the privileges of adulthood if and
when one so desires. Treating conservative or conventional (especially, in
this case, school-centered institutional) norms with disdain is one way to
constitute oneself as cool, to stake out the territory of burnout status. Just
as institutional status is essential to social status for a jock, female or male,
coolness is essential to social status for a burnout, female or male. And
although a burnout girl may not have access to full burnout status through
fighting or other displays of physical toughness, she can be cool, verbally
and emotionally tough. In example (25) a burnout girl describes how she
and another friend gained status during junior high as the "biggest
burnouts":

(25) But like we got along with everybody and uh we partied every day
      and that was the cool thing. And uh we'd smoke in school and that
      was cool. We used to get E's in classes [a failing grade], that was cool.
      You know? So, I don't know. I guess that's how.

Coolness stands in stark opposition to the jock girls' squeaky-clean image
and their concern with being liked by the appropriate people and respected
as "responsible" school citizens. But of course jock girls are not cowering
goody-goodies, and this opposition poses a threat to their own sense of
autonomy. Thus, just as burnout girls view the quest for popularity as part
of their childish past, jock girls relegate the pursuit of coolness to childhood.
The only time a jock girl mentioned coolness in the entire corpus of interviews was in accounting for burnouts' behavior in junior high school:

(26) Most of the people that were in junior high doing these kind of
      things ended up in high school ((laughter)) doing them even worse,
      so ((laughter)). WHEN DO KIDS START DOING THAT? Probably fifth
      and sixth grade when you think you're really cool—that's your cool
      age. Seventh—sixth, seventh, and eighth grade is your cool age, and
      everybody thinks, "Hey, I'm really cool, man! I'm gonna smoke! I'm
      gonna be real cool!" So that's what—where it starts probably.

Here, disparagingly, smoking is seen as putatively "cool" because it represents defiant assertion of adult privilege. Notice, however, that the speaker
in example (26) stresses the immaturity of those vigorously pursuing coolness, implying that their claims to adult-style autonomy are sham. She is
implicitly defending herself against charges of sheeplike obedience by
constituting herself as having been able to uphold norms when "everybody"
was urging defiance.

Jock girls are the only ones who do not embrace the notion of coolness.
Burnout boys, and the more-partying in-between boys, talk occasionally
about coolness as something to be cultivated, as in example (27), when an
in-between boy told Penny why he could give up cigarettes at any time:

(27) Because I don't need them. I only do them for, you know, the coolness.

And burnout girls talk with humor, but not with shame, about coolness's
affecting their decisions, as shown in example (28):

(28) I would have liked to done cheerleading or volleyball or something.
      AND WHY DIDN'T YOU? Some of it was uncool, you know, it was kind
      of uncool for—because I was considered a big burnout. ((laughter))

Just as jock boys want to insist on their physical toughness, a fair number find coolness appealing. For American boys, there are tensions in jock status connected with the need to assert a certain independence of institutionally imposed strictures on activities while at the same time using the institutional resources for enhancing their personal status. It is important for them to be seen as independent actors who are not institutionally ruled. Being labeled *squeaky-clean* can suggest a meek deference to school (or parental) regulations, whereas there can be a positive value attached to coolness—a stance of disregard for others' assessments, a willingness to engage in practices adults have forbidden, an assertion of disregard for possible negative judgments from others, a kind of social courage. So, although jock boys do not speak of actively pursuing coolness, apparently because they don't want to appear to be "trying," they do sometimes speak of it as a desirable quality and one that influenced their choice of friends in junior high. At the time of this study in Belten High, smoking, alcohol consumption, and (other) drug use were of great importance for defining burnout status. As we have already noted, the name *burnout* and the more local name *jell* or *jelly* (from *jellybrain*) refer directly to drug use. And burnouts, both girls and boys, freely define themselves in these terms. After all, drug use is a powerful symbol of their rejection of adult authority and their assertion of adult autonomy. Thus, although drug use in itself does not establish someone as a burnout any more than athletic skills confirm jock status, it is important for the burnouts to try to hold the jocks to squeaky-cleanness and to reserve drug use for themselves. If one can violate institutional norms and still reap all the institutional privileges, it becomes hard to see what is gained by eschewing institutionally endorsed roads to success. Thus, the well-known fact that many jocks drink and that a number of jock boys do some drugs leads some to assert that such people are not actually jocks, or that the category itself no longer exists (again suggesting its becoming unmarked as discussed earlier). This is illustrated by another quotation from the girl who described herself as "in-between" in example (8):

(29) I've come to believe that there isn't such a thing in Belten, or anybody that I've met, that is a jock. Because I know for a fact that my volleyball ((laughter)) team, after games and after tournaments, we'd have parties, and we'd be drinking. And some of us, you know, I—I play volleyball, and I smoke, and there's a few others that do. And I thought back, and I said, "You guys are supposed to be jocks, what's the problem here?" ((laughter)) you know. And they said, "Hey, you know, we have a good time too," you know.

The opposition that locks jocks and burnouts into these quite divergent identity practices extends its terms into both communities of practice as well. Within the broader jock network, there is a good deal of diversity in behavior: there are clusters of girls who are truly squeaky-clean, and there are clusters of girls who party. The salience of partying in the jock–burnout split leads many jocks to refer to this latter partying cluster as *kind-of burnout*. Similarly, among the burnout girls, there are degrees of "burnout-ness."

The main cluster of burnouts is an extensive neighborhood-based network that goes back to early childhood. The girls and boys in this cluster originally engaged in school activities in junior high school, until, as discussed earlier, their noncorporate orientation came into obvious conflict with school norms. Quite distinct from this large cluster is another, smaller, cluster that is not neighborhood-based but consists of a group of girls who got together in junior high school. These girls were never interested in school activities in junior high except for attending dances, from which they were quickly excluded for drinking and getting high, and they pride themselves on being quite "wild" in comparison with the rest of the burnout girls. They stand out from other burnout girls as extreme in dress, demeanor, substance use, illegal behavior, and so on. One of these girls, in describing the social organization of space in the school courtyard, which constitutes the smoking section and the burnout territory, demonstrates the strategic nature of labeling. (The speech in parentheses in this quotation is directed to passersby.)

(30)   OK, us, you know like the burnout (yeah, 'bye—wait, bum me one) the burnout chicks, they sit over here, you know, and like jocky chicks stand right here.... And then there's like um the guys, you know, you know, like weirdos that think they're cool. They just stand like on the steps and hang out at that little heater. (Say, hey!) And then the poins are inside in the cafeteria, because they're probably afraid to come out in the courtyard.

In this quotation, by referring to a group of burnout and in-between girls who smoke as *jocks*, the main group of burnout boys as *weirdos*, and other in-betweens and all the jocks as *poins* (from *poindexters*), the speaker positions herself and her friends in relation to the rest of the school population. She is defining her group as normative burnouts, and it is not surprising that others have referred to them, in turn, as *burned-out burnouts*.

There are many fault lines in the neat divisions we have made between jocks and burnouts, and many in the school find identification with either group deeply problematic. Some of the strongest disapproval of jocks by nonjocks and of burnouts by nonburnouts is reserved for what are seen as typically female modes of seeking popularity and asserting coolness.

Snobs and Sluts

A major character flaw that many in the school associate with jocks is being stuck-up or snobby. Boys can, of course, be snobs. But it is far easier for boys than for girls to achieve institutional prominence without drawing the charge of being stuck-up. The easiest way is simply to shine on the football field. But not all boys have this option. The successful class president quoted in example (22) clearly saw the potential for others' resentment when one cultivates prominence. He recommends inclusiveness and tolerance of others as the best strategy for not raising others' hackles:

> (31) ... if you're not snobby about it, the people tend to—you t- you tend to overcome, and win a lot more people if you become popular but still at the same time not too snobby. I try to talk to a lot of people now, and like right now, you know, because—because I'm president of the class, there's a lot of people that, sort of like, may know me by name or something, but there's not like really a—a group of people I won't talk to. Because a lot of people, they'll say, "Well, I don't like to talk to people in the courtyard" ((burnouts)), you know. YEAH. RIGHT. That's just the way it is. But I don't see what's wrong with it. It's not like you're s- you're- you're becoming one. Which is not, you know—what they do, it doesn't bother me. If they want to do what they do with their life, it's fine. And you shouldn't distinguish between certain types of t- people. You should just want to relate to as many people as possible.

But for jock girls, pursuit of a wide range of contacts carries with it a threat to the persona they struggle so hard to develop. To talk to a burnout girl "in the courtyard" is indeed to run the risk of "becoming one." Why? Because, as we have said in many different ways, jock girls are judged primarily by their associates and only secondarily by their achievements. For boys, in contrast, the achievements come first. It is overwhelmingly girls who describe other girls as excluding people, as pursuing recognition by the school's stars at the expense of those who are outside the star circle. This is how one burnout girl accounts for not trying out for cheerleading in ninth grade (note that this is not the same girl quoted in (28)):

(32) DID YOU GET INVOLVED IN ACTIVITIES AND STUFF LIKE THAT? Um,
      ninth grade, I was involved in volleyball, because that's when it
      started. Um, dances, here and there. I just went to talk to people.
      I wasn't dancing or nothing. I went to listen to the band and that.
      Um, uh, I can't say I really went to any basketball games or anything
      like that. DID YOU GO OUT FOR CHEERLEADING OR ANYTHING LIKE
      THAT? Now that started in the ninth grade. And that's when I—
      well, how—[I don't] really know how to explain how I felt. I felt
      that at that time, I didn't have to do that to be popular. And I
      thought, "Hmm, cheerleaders—everybody's going to look up at
      them, and they're going to, you know ((laughter)) they're going to
      be stuck-up, and I don't want to be known as a stuck-up cheer-
      leader," and—so I steered away from that. I wanted to be one
      though. YOU WANTED TO BE ONE- That's—that's what was, that—I
      did, you know, because I knew I'd enjoy it. And I thought, "Well, look
      at the ones that were last year. All the girls look down on them.
      'She's a stuck-up cheerleader,'" you know. So—

Here a quintessentially jock activity for girls—cheerleading—is equated
with being seen as stuck-up (and thus to be avoided whatever its other
attractions might be). In example (33), a burnout girl describes how she
assumes jocks view people like her:

(33) I think of like jocks as like sort of higher up, you know, so you think
      that you know, they'd be saying, "Hey," you know, "let's get rid of
      these like diddly little people," you know?

The management of social visibility, as we have seen, preoccupies girls
seeking status as jocks. It does not, however, endear a jock girl to those
who are not welcomed to her orbit, or to her old friends whom she has no
time for because she is so busy networking. Even for a girl who cares only
about her status among the activities-oriented crowd, the twin projects of
cultivating a pleasing personality and pursuing prominence are hard to
balance successfully. If the pursuit of prominence is too evident, even other
institutionally minded people may well reject as stuck-up and snobby the
personality thereby produced. Likability within the jock crowd cannot be
sacrificed, because one needs social ties of friendship or romance for
success as a jock girl: one must be someone others want as a friend or
sweetheart. Good personhood ought to make others feel welcome, not
excluded.

Girl jocks, then, face considerable difficulty. They must regulate their
social alliances with care in order to attain the social visibility they need.

But this regulation tends to involve excluding many, which leads naturally to charges of being a snob. Being a stuck-up snob, however, is inconsistent with the pleasing personality the successful jock girl needs. And of course the good personhood the jock girl constructs is itself seen as laudable, a special kind of achievement compared implicitly to the not-so-good personhood of others who have not made the same effort to seek such goodness. Such invidious comparisons, however silent they may be, also tend to lead those put down by them to view jock girls' pride in their personae as more evidence of their being stuck-up. Thus, part of burnout girls' explicit rejection of popularity by the time they reach high school derives from their despising what they see as the snobbery and sense of superiority of jock girls. But that is not the only reason for their rejection of popularity.

Part of the presentation of a corporate being is as a person who is "in control" of both her professional and her personal affairs. In the interests of presenting an image of corporate competence, jocks uniformly hide personal and family problems from their peers (see Eckert 1989). In addition, they strive to maintain an image of control over their "urges," and for jock girls, this involves importantly a control over their images as heterosexual beings. Burnouts, on the other hand, emphasize "being yourself" and value the sharing of problems. And while burnout girls do not necessarily flaunt heterosexual engagement, they certainly are not concerned with presenting an abstemious image, a concern that would be decidedly "uncool."

It is important to emphasize that it is above all the heterosexual image that is at issue in this opposition rather than sexual behavior itself. Although a jock girl's unpublicized engagement in sexual relations with a boyfriend may be considered her own business, any appearance of promiscuity is not. Indeed, anything that contributes to such an appearance, including styles of hair, dress, and makeup, as well as demeanor, will be seen as "slutty" and can seriously threaten a jock girl's status, costing her female friends as well as the possibility of being judged an appropriate public partner for a jock boy. One jock girl even considered dating too many boys to be dangerous for one's reputation:

(34) Well, maybe there's some, I don't really know, that go out with a different guy every week. Because I—I don't—I don't think that's so much true, because you can—that—that would kind of give you a bad reputation ((laughter)) I think. I don't know. I'd leave a little space in between.

To be labeled a *slut* is to fail in the school's corporate culture. It is not surprising, then, that jocks view the prototypical burnout girl as slutty, and that burnouts view the prototypical jock girl as phony and uptight. The crucial difference is not so much in sexual behavior but in the fact that burnouts, in opposition to jocks, are not concerned with sluttiness—either in image or in behavior. Burnout girls view so-called slutty patterns of dress and demeanor as simply personal characteristics, which they may or may not think problematic, but certainly not as making someone an unsuitable friend. *Slut* is a category label that fuses gender and class.

Both burnout and jock girls actively construct their social statuses and they do so in ways that allow them to cooperate with their male peers in constituting the basic social orientation of their respective categories: resistance to institutional norms in the one case and participation in the hierarchical institutionally sanctioned practice in the other. In both cases, however, the girls lack access to the full repertoire of practices that can constitute category status for boys. And the practices open to girls in each category are highly likely to evoke great hostility from girls in the other category. Burnout girls vigorously reject the relation-cultivating popularity so important to jock girls; they hate the snobbiness and "holier-than-thou" attitudes that they associate with it. Jock girls in turn are contemptuous of the lack of "self-control" associated with coolness. They see coolness as all too easily leading to sluttiness, which they roundly condemn—and work hard to keep at bay.

Burnout girls and jock girls construct strikingly different solutions to the dilemma created for them by the overarching gender structures they all experience, structures characterized by male dominance and heterosexist preoccupation with sexual differentiation. And each group judges the other's strategic moves in response to these constraints very harshly. One result is that the overall differences in normative patterns of practice between burnout and jock girls are far greater than those between burnout and jock boys. After junior high, opposition—and conflict—between burnouts and jocks centers on opposition—and (primarily) symbolic conflict—between burnout and jock girls. This is reflected with startling clarity in patterns of phonological variation, to which we now turn.

Pronouncing Selves

The depth of the jock–burnout opposition in Belten High is borne out by differences in speech between the members of the two categories: differences in vocabulary, in grammar, in pronunciation. But more important, these speech differences are not simply markers of category affiliation. They carry in themselves complex social meanings, like tough, cool, slutty, casual, or mean, and these meanings are part of the construction of categories like those labeled by *female, male, jock, burnout.* Finding these meanings through correlations between the use of linguistic variables and indicators of social practice is a major challenge for sociolinguists. In this section, we focus on several phonological variables that enter into the construction of social identities in Belten High, and that simultaneously are part of what constitutes a "Midwest," or Detroit, or Michigan accent. The production of linguistic styles is part of the production of identities, and local and regional pronunciations provide some of the resources that can be put to stylistic use.

The following discussion focuses on two vowels that have symbolic significance in this community. The symbolic significance is associated with recent innovations in pronunciation, innovations that reflect sound changes in progress:

- (uh) as in *fun, cuff, but* (phonetically [ ]), is moving back so that it comes to sound like the vowel in *fawn, cough, bought* [ ].
- The nucleus [a] of the diphthong (ay) as in *file, line, heist* raises to [ʌ] or [ɔ], so that the diphthong may sound more like the diphthong in *foil, loin, hoist.*

For each of these vowels, pronunciations in the stream of speech will vary from the conservative to the innovative with several stages in between. Most speakers in the community use the full range of pronunciations, generally within the same conversation. However, speakers will vary in the frequency with which they use the more conservative and more innovative pronunciations. It is in the speaker's average pronunciation or in the strategic use of one or the other pronunciation that this variability comes to have social meaning.

The changes described for the vowels above represent linguistic changes in progress, and certain social principles about such changes have emerged over the years (see Chambers 1995; Labov 1972, 1994). In general, sound change originates in locally based, working-class communities and spreads gradually upward through the socioeconomic hierarchy. In this way, new sound changes tend to carry local meaning and to serve as part of the local social-symbolic repertoire. This means that the speech of locally based working-class groups will generally show more of the innovative variants discussed above than that of middle-class groups in the same community. Middle-class speakers, on the contrary, are more likely to avoid clearly local pronunciations inasmuch as they are engaged in corporate institutions that strive to transcend local resources and loyalties. It is to be expected, then, that burnouts, with their heightened locally based identities and loyalties, might use more of the advanced variants for these vowels than do the institutionally identified jocks.

Gender, on the other hand, does not correlate quite as consistently with linguistic variables as class does. Female speakers quite regularly lead in sound change, but there are cases in which they do not.[5] More interesting, gender commonly crosscuts class, so that although working-class women may lead working-class men in a particular sound change, middle-class women may lag behind middle-class men in the same change. Such patterns can emerge only from a co-construction of gender and class, and this co-construction emerges quite clearly in the speech of the students of Belten High.

In across-the-board correlations of (uh) and (ay) with sex and social-category membership, we find that although the backing of (uh) as in *fun*, *cuff*, and *but* correlates only with social category, with the burnouts leading, the raising of the nucleus in (ay) (*file*, *line*, *heist*) correlates only with sex, with the girls leading. Are we to stop with these correlations, and declare that the backing of (uh) "means" burnout and the raising of the nucleus in (ay) "means" female? Are they markers of gender and category membership or are they symbolic of some aspects of social practice and identity that are part of what jocks and burnouts, and females and males, are about? In fact, when we dig deeper, we will see that these data reflect a great complexity of social practice.

Tables 19.1 and 19.2 show figures for correlations of speakers' sex and social-category affiliation (as assigned on the basis of network positions and descriptions by self and others) with the backing of (uh) and the raising of (ay).[6] The correlations in these and subsequent tables are significant at the .001 level, indicating the minimum likelihood that the correlations could be the result of chance. In each table, a probability value is shown for each group of speakers. The absolute numbers are not important, only their relative values; innovative pronunciation is most frequent among the group of speakers for whom the number is highest, least frequent among those for whom it is lowest. When we tease apart sex and social-category membership in the data for (uh), as shown in Table 19.1, we find that within each social category, the girls lead the boys, although particularly among the jocks this lead is not large enough to be significant in itself. We also find that the burnouts' lead over the jocks is somewhat greater among the girls than among the boys. Correlations for extreme raising in (ay) show a pattern similar to those for the backing of (uh), as shown in Table 19.2.

Table 19.1 Correlation of Backing of (uh) with Combined Sex and Social Category

Female jocks	Male jocks	Female burnouts	Male burnouts
.43	.40	.62	.54

Table 19.2 Extreme Raising of the Nucleus of (ay) with Combined Sex and Social Category

Female jocks	Male jocks	Female burnouts	Male burnouts
.38	.28	.79	.50

What can be drawn from the tables is that whatever distinguishes jocks and burnouts also distinguishes boys and girls within those categories; or whatever distinguishes boys and girls also distinguishes jocks and burnouts within those sex groups. One would be hard pressed to establish whether the backing of (uh) or the raising of the nucleus in (ay) is associated with female-ness or burnout-ness. And indeed, what distinguishes gender from sex is that femaleness and maleness cannot be imagined independently of other aspects of identity, such as jock- and burnout-hood.

If these vowels serve to construct meaning in the high school, and if category and gender interact in as complex a way as shown in the earlier sections, we might expect to find some of this complexity reflected in the vowels as well as in labeling practices. Let us turn to the division among the burnout girls discussed earlier, in which burned-out burnout girls distinguish themselves from the "jocky" burnouts. It turns out that these girls are overwhelmingly in the lead in the use of innovative variants of both (uh) and (ay).

Table 19.3 separates the burned-out burnout girls from the "regular" burnout girls. Although the "regular" burnout girls still back (uh) more than the jock girls, the burned-out burnout girls are far more extreme. A similar pattern shows up for the raising of the nucleus in (ay), in which the burned-out burnouts are overwhelmingly in the lead (see Table 19.4).

Table 19.3 Correlation of Backing of (uh) with Combined Sex and Social Category, Separating Two Clusters of Burnout Girls

Female jocks	Male jocks	Main female burnouts	Burned-out female burnouts	Male burnouts
.41	.38	.53	.65	.52

Table 19.4 Extreme Raising of (ay), Combining Sex and Social Category, Separating Two Clusters of Burnout Girls

Female jocks	Male jocks	Main female burnouts	Burned-out female burnouts	Male burnouts
.42	.32	.47	.93	.54

Vowels such as these do not simply fall into a neutral linguistic space. Consider the following segment of conversation with a burned-out burnout:

(35)   ... we used to tell our moms that we'd—uh—she'd be sleeping at my house, I'd be sleeping at hers. We'd go out and pull a all-nighter, you know ((laughter)) I'd come home the next day, "Where were you?" "Jane's." "No you weren't." Because her mom and my mom are like really close—since we got in so much trouble they know each other really good.

Interactions are situations in which social meaning is made. When this girl says to Penny, for example, "We'd go out and pull a all-nighter," raising the nucleus of (ay) in *all-nighter* so that it clearly sounds like *all-noiter*, Penny associates what she perceives about this girl in general, and what the girl is saying in particular, with this element of linguistic style. Presumably, in speaking to Penny in this way, the speaker presents herself as a burned-out burnout—as someone who gets around, does pretty much what she wants, gets in trouble, has fun, doesn't clean up her act too much for an adult like Penny, and so on. In the course of this mutual construction, the variable (ay) takes on meaning—perhaps not in isolation, but at least as a component of a broader style. In their extreme speech, then, the burned-out burnout girls are not simply using phonetic variants with a meaning already set and waiting to be recycled. Rather, their very use of those variants produces a social meaning. They are simultaneously creating meaning for (ay) and for being burned-out burnouts. Thus, as in the labeling discussed in the earlier sections, the use of phonetic variation and the construction of identities are inseparable.

Conclusion

Belten High provides some glimpses of communities of practice at work. Their members are engaging in a wide range of activities through which they constitute themselves and their social relations and project their future life histories. Language, gender, and class are all produced through such social practices. These practices have locally distinctive features, but they show patterns reflecting the influence of a larger society and its institutions. They also reflect a historical location with its particular pasts and prospective futures.

Readers may wonder just which communities of practice exist. Do girls and boys form separate communities of practice? Do jocks and burnouts? What about in-betweens? Jocky jocks? Burned-out burnouts? Does the student body of the whole high school constitute a community of practice?

Questions like this miss a critical point about communities of practice: they are not determined by their membership but by the endeavors that bring those members (and others who have preceded or will succeed them) into relations with one another (which may or may not be face-to-face), and by the practices that develop around, and transform, these endeavors. So certainly most—perhaps all—of the student-body members belong to a community focused on the issues of school-sponsored curricular and extracurricular activities or other practices involving students that occur at school or are relevant to what is going on there. The practices toward which community members are oriented focus on the issues we have briefly discussed, some high-level and others more mundane: how and whether to compete in the school-based hierarchy; how and whether to participate in the heterosexual marketplace; relation to school and family authority; post–high school prospects; who to hang out with during school; what to do directly after school (and with whom); what to do in the evenings and on weekends; where to eat lunch; whether to use drugs; what to wear; how to talk; and so on. Athletic boy jocks and burned-out burnout girls, for example, have different forms of membership in this large community of practice. And in the process of pursuing these different forms of membership, they attend to communities of practice of their own, based on and constituting specific places and points of view within the larger community.

We do not actually have to worry about delimiting communities of practice in advance. Rather, we look at people and the practices mediating their relations to one another in order to understand better the raw materials through which they constitute their own and others' identities and relations. There is no community focused on linguistic practice, no community focused on gender practice, no community focused on class practice. As we have seen, seeking popularity (or refusing to), aspiring to coolness (or refusing to), and similar practices of various kinds are saturated with implications, at one and the same time, for language, gender, and class. And the constitution of socially significant communities—both their membership and the actual content of the practices that make them into a community—has an ongoing history.

We have explored two aspects of language use at Belten: labeling and other kinds of talk about social categories and relations; and variation in the pronunciation of certain vowels. The first gives us a perspective from linguistic content on how gender and class practices and the struggles centered on them proceed. Social labeling discriminates among people and is used as a weapon to divide and to deride. Attempts to define and delimit what labels mean are really attempts to delimit what people and the social structures they build can or should be like. Unequal power in general social processes translates into unequal power in succeeding in definitional projects.[7] The prize, of course, is not controlling what this or that word means; but controlling the immediate direction of this or that aspect of social life, perhaps continuing existing social structures and relations or perhaps transforming them in some way. Social talk helps in the process of institutionalizing power and gender relations, and it helps give local force and bite to larger-scale social constructions.

Investigations of phonological variation offer a way to view similar phenomena but at a different level. Actual uses of language always have a formal aspect as well as content, and form always enriches (and sometimes contradicts) what is conveyed in social talk. Formal properties of utterances in many cases are the only source of social meaning. Of course, how one pronounces a particular vowel on a particular occasion seldom receives the same conscious attention that shapes the content of answers to questions about popularity and coolness. Nor are ordinary people as well able to say what someone else's vowels sounded like as they are to report the content of what she said. But as shown above, the low-level details of pronunciation can give a great deal of information about how people are actively constituting their own social identities and relations. And it is such subtle variations and the social meanings they express that are the stuff of which long-term and large-scale changes in conventions of linguistic practice are made.

Social talk at Belten made it clear to us that there were no separable processes constructing gender and class. Male dominance and class relations are both involved in issues of physical prowess; forms of female agency and class practices link critically to popularity and coolness; and heterosexism informs the content of class-linked femininities and masculinities. General patterns emerge only when we stop trying to partition off matters of class from matters of gender. Similarly, patterns of vowel pronunciation are clarified when we try thinking about class-gender complexes rather than class and gender as independent. Our extracts from interviews also suggest, however, the messiness of practice, its failure to fit perfectly with neat structural analyses, the social ambiguities and contradictions it embodies. Only by continuing to examine different communities of practice and the complexities within them can we really begin to come to grips with the historicity of language, gender, class, and their interactions.

Notes

1. This chapter descends directly from an invited talk we gave on July 20, 1993, at the Linguistic Society of America's Summer Institute, Ohio State University, Columbus. We thank that audience and the many others who have been interested in our ideas for their comments and questions. We thank the editors of this volume, Kira Hall and Mary Bucholtz, for their excellent advice and for their patience. Finally, we thank each other for finishing this project. As before, our names appear alphabetically.
2. This study was funded by the National Science Foundation (BNS 8023291), the Spencer Foundation, and the Horace Rackham School of Graduate Studies at the University of Michigan.
3. All quoted speech is taken from tape-recorded interviews. Penny's speech is printed in upper case. Hesitations, false starts, and so on are not edited out of these materials.
4. See McElhinny (this volume) for discussion of ways women now being hired as police officers are finding to share in normative conceptions of what it means to be a good police officer without jeopardizing their sense of themselves as "feminine."
5. See Eckert (1990a) and Labov (1991) for a piece of the debate about gender and variation.
6. The statistics in this and all following tables were calculated using Goldvarb 2, a Macintosh-based version of the variable-rule program, which is a statistical package designed specifically for the analysis of sociolinguistic variation. For information about the analysis of variation, see Sankoff (1978).
7. See, for example, McConnell-Ginet (1989) for a discussion, albeit more narrowly linguistic, of how social contexts affect definitional success.

References

Bem, Sandra L. (1993). *The lenses of gender: Transforming the debate on sexual inequality.* New Haven: Yale University Press.

Butler, Judith (1993). *Bodies that matter.* New York: Routledge.

Cameron, Deborah (forthcoming). The language-gender interface: Challenging co-optation. In Victoria Bergvall, Janet Bing, and Alice F. Freed (eds.) *Language and gender research: Theory and method.* New York: Longman.

Chambers, J. K. (1995). *Sociolinguistic theory.* Oxford: Basil Blackwell.

Connell, R. W. (1987). *Gender and power: Society, the person and sexual politics.* Stanford: Stanford University Press.

di Leonardo, Micaela (ed.) (1991). *Gender at the crossroads of knowledge: Feminist anthropology in the postmodern era.* Berkeley: University of California Press.

Eckert, Penelope (1988). Sound change and adolescent social structure. *Language in Society* 17: 183–207.

——— (1989). *Jocks and burnouts: Social categories and identity in the high school.* New York: Teachers College Press.

——— (1990a). The whole woman: Sex and gender differences in variation. *Language Variation and Change* 1: 245–67.

——— (1990b). Cooperative competition in adolescent girl talk. *Discourse Processes* 13: 92–122.

Eckert, Penelope, and Sally McConnell-Ginet (1992a). Communities of practice: Where language, gender, and power all live. In Kira Hall, Mary Bucholtz and Birch Moonwomon (eds.), *Locating power: Proceedings of the Second Berkeley Women and Language Conference.* Berkeley: Berkeley Women and Language Group. 89–99.

——— (1992b). Think practically and look locally: Language and gender as community-based practice. *Annual Review of Anthropology* 21: 461–90.

Holland, Dorothy C., and Margaret A. Eisenhart (1990). *Educated in romance.* Chicago: University of Chicago Press.

Labov, William (1972). On the mechanism of linguistic change. In *Sociolinguistic patterns.* Philadelphia: University of Pennsylvania Press. 160–82.

——— (1991). The intersection of sex and social class in the course of linguistic change. *Language Variation and Change* 2(2): 205–51.

——— (1994). *Principles of linguistic change: Internal factors.* Oxford: Basil Blackwell.

McConnell-Ginet, Sally (1989). The sexual (re)production of meaning: A discourse-based theory. In Francine W. Frank and Paula A. Treichler (eds.), *Language, gender, and professional writing: Theoretical approaches and guidelines for nonsexist usage.* New York: Modern Language Association. 35–50.

McElhinny, Bonnie S. (this volume). Challenging hegemonic masculinities: Female and male police officers handling domestic violence.

Rich, Adrienne (1980). Compulsory heterosexuality and lesbian existence. *Signs* (5): 631–60.

Sankoff, David (ed.) (1978). *Linguistic variation: Models and methods.* New York: Academic Press.

Segal, Lynne (1990). *Slow motion: Changing masculinities, changing men.* New Brunswick: Rutgers University Press.

Talbot, Mary (this volume). A synthetic sisterhood: False friends in a teenage magazine.

Thorne, Barrie (1993). *Gender play.* New Brunswick: Rutgers University Press.

About the Authors

MARY BUCHOLTZ is a Ph.D. candidate in the Department of Linguistics at the University of California at Berkeley. She is writing her dissertation on language use at the boundaries of ethnic categories. Her primary research interest is in the interrelationship of language, social identity, and power.

JENNY COOK-GUMPERZ is Professor in the Graduate School of Education at the University of California, Santa Barbara. She has a long-term interest in children's language socialization and has numerous publications relating to the topic. She has recently begun to investigate the role of gender in language socialization.

TAMRA DIBENEDETTO teaches English literature and composition at Riverside Community College. She has co-authored articles with Susan Herring and Deborah A. Johnson on gender and computer-mediated communication.

PENELOPE ECKERT is Professor of Linguistics at Stanford University and Senior Research Scientist at the Institute for Research on Learning. Her research focuses on sociolinguistic variation, with an emphasis on the social-symbolic value of variation and the role of variation in social practice.

MICHÈLE FOSTER is Professor in the Center for Educational Studies at the Claremont Graduate School. Her research and teaching interests include the social and cultural context of education, anthropology of education, educational linguistics, and sociolinguistics, particularly the language of African American women.

SUSAN GAL is Professor of Anthropology at the University of Chicago. Her current research deals with the uses of gender in the construction of political discourses. At present she is working on a collaborative project about the politics of reproduction in Eastern Europe.

TARA GOLDSTEIN teaches in the University of Toronto's Faculty of Education, developing initiatives and practices for the promotion of equity in schools and teacher-education programs. Her current linguistic research examines bilingual life and language choice in multiracial, multicultural, and multilingual high school settings.

MARÍA DOLORES GONZALES VELÁSQUEZ is a research associate with the Linguistic Atlas and Archive Project at the New Mexico/Colorado Spanish Survey, University of New Mexico. She is currently co-editing an interdisciplinary collection of articles on Chicana language use. In addition to her academic research, she is also a published poet and essayist.

KIRA HALL is Assistant Professor of Linguistics in the Department of English at Rutgers University, Camden. Her recent research has focused on the language and culture of Hindi-speaking *hijras* (eunuchs) in North India. She has also worked on the gendered nature of electronic communication. With Anna Livia, she is co-editor of a forthcoming anthology on language, gender, and sexuality.

SUSAN HERRING is Associate Professor in the Linguistics Program at the University of Texas at Arlington. She has recently been investigating gender and politeness on the Internet and is the editor of a forthcoming anthology on computer-mediated communication.

CATHRYN HOUGHTON is a doctoral student in anthropology at Yale University, studying the role of language and the use of representational practices in the production of power, knowledge, and the modern state. Her research, which involves both Indonesia and the United States, focuses on the public discourses of private, subjective, and individual experience, examining the relationship between these discourses and the structures of producer-consumer society.

DEBORAH A. JOHNSON is currently pursuing a Ph.D. in humanities with specializations in linguistics, political science, and women's studies. She has studied self-presentation in political discourse, collaborating with Susan Herring on a sociolinguistic analysis of the 1992 presidential debates.

ROBIN TOLMACH LAKOFF is Professor of Linguistics at the University of California at Berkeley. She has published on topics ranging from the semantic and pragmatic analysis of English modal auxiliaries to speech act theory, language and gender, language and politics, the language of courtrooms, and psychotherapy.

ANNA LIVIA is Assistant Professor in the Department of French at the University of Illinois, Urbana-Champaign. Her most recent research addresses the application of linguistics to literary texts. She is also a novelist and translator and is co-editor, with Kira Hall, of a forthcoming collection of articles on language, gender, and sexuality.

SALLY MCCONNELL-GINET is Professor of Linguistics and Director of Women's Studies at Cornell University. She co-edited a groundbreaking anthology on language and gender, together with Ruth Borker and Nelly Furman. In addition, she has published a number of critical essays on language and gender scholarship.

BONNIE S. MCELHINNY is Assistant Professor in the Department of Anthropology at the University of Toronto. Her research concerns language and political economy, focusing on the uses of postmodernism in feminism and linguistic anthropology. She is particularly interested in the integration of research, teaching, and social action.

NORMA MENDOZA-DENTON is a Ph.D. candidate in linguistics at Stanford University. Her research, which focuses on the role of language in the construction of group identity, explores the variety of ways that identities are defined and manipulated in the sociopolitical arena. Her dissertation focuses on the language behavior and social networks of adolescent Latinas, with an emphasis on urban street gangs.

BIRCH MOONWOMON is Assistant Professor in the Department of English at Ohio State University. She has recently begun work on an ethnographic project with Lindsay Welcome on lesbian life stories. She has published a number of articles on language in the lesbian community.

ELINOR OCHS is Professor of TESL and Applied Linguistics at the University of California at Los Angeles. Her earliest fieldwork involved a ground-breaking study of gender differentiation in Madagascar. Recently, she has turned her attention to issues of language socialization in the United States, where she is involved in an ongoing study of gender and narrative in the American family.

SHIGEKO OKAMOTO is Associate Professor in the Department of Linguistics at California State University, Fresno. In addition to her innovative research on Japanese women's speech, she has published a number of articles on the relation between structure and meaning in Japanese grammatical constructions.

LAUREL A. SUTTON is pursuing a doctoral degree in linguistics at the University of California at Berkeley. Her graduate research is concerned with the intersection of phonetics and sociolinguistics. She has also conducted research on gender issues in electronic discourse.

MARY TALBOT is Lecturer in Linguistics and English at the Institute of Language and Communication, Odense University, Denmark. Her main research and teaching interests are in critical linguistics, with a focus on feminist perspectives in language theory.

CAROLYN TAYLOR is Assistant Professor of Speech Communication at the University of Illinois at Urbana-Champaign. Her research concerns first-language acquisition, incorporating perspectives from ethnography, conversation analysis, and postmodernism into an ongoing study of language socialization.